PLYMOUTH DISTRICT LIBRARY

3 3387 00425 0108

D0848011

422.03 D

Adonis to Zorro :
Oxford dictionary of
reference and allusion /

3330700-250108

Plymouth District Library
223 S. Main St.
Plymouth, MI 48170

Apr 2011

422, 03
D

Adonis to Zorro
OXFORD DICTIONARY OF REFERENCE AND ALLUSION

Adonis to Zorro

OXFORD DICTIONARY OF REFERENCE AND ALLUSION

Third Edition

Edited by ANDREW DELAHUNTY
and SHEILA DIGNEN

First and Second Editions
Edited by Andrew Delahunty, Sheila Dignen,
and Penny Stock

OXFORD

UNIVERSITY PRESS

OXFORD
UNIVERSITY PRESS

Great Clarendon Street, Oxford OX2 6DP

Oxford University Press is a department of the University of Oxford.
It furthers the University's objective of excellence in research, scholarship,
and education by publishing worldwide in

Oxford New York

Auckland Cape Town Dar es Salaam Hong Kong Karachi
Kuala Lumpur Madrid Melbourne Mexico City Nairobi
New Delhi Shanghai Taipei Toronto

With offices in

Argentina Austria Brazil Chile Czech Republic France Greece
Guatemala Hungary Italy Japan Poland Portugal Singapore
South Korea Switzerland Thailand Turkey Ukraine Vietnam

Oxford is a registered trade mark of Oxford University Press
in the UK and in certain other countries

Published in the United States
by Oxford University Press Inc., New York

© Andrew Delahunty, Sheila Dignen, and Penny Stock 2001, 2005, 2010

The moral rights of the authors have been asserted
Database right Oxford University Press (maker)

First published 2001
First published as an Oxford University Press paperback 2003
Second Edition 2005
Third Edition 2010

All rights reserved. No part of this publication may be reproduced,
stored in a retrieval system, or transmitted, in any form or by any means,
without the prior permission in writing of Oxford University Press,
or as expressly permitted by law, or under terms agreed with the appropriate
reprographics rights organization. Enquiries concerning reproduction
outside the scope of the above should be sent to the Rights Department,
Oxford University Press, at the address above

You must not circulate this book in any other binding or cover
and you must impose this same condition on any acquirer

British Library Cataloguing in Publication Data

Data available

Library of Congress Cataloging in Publication Data

Data available

Typeset by SPI Publisher Services, Pondicherry, India
Printed in Great Britain
on acid-free paper by
Clays Ltd, St Ives Plc

ISBN 978-0-19-956745-4

1 3 5 7 9 10 8 6 4 2

This book is dedicated to the memory of Penny Stock

Contents

Introduction to the Third Edition

This third edition bears a different title from its predecessors: the revised title aims to reflect the expanded coverage of this new edition. The first two editions dealt primarily with what might be termed direct allusions, typically names of real people, historical events, or literary characters, mentioned not simply in a factual way (as in 'Hercules was an ancient Greek hero') but in order to conjure up some extra meaning, embodying some quality or characteristic for which the word has come to stand. In broadening the scope of the book we have added many less direct allusions, where a phrase or reference can be traced back to an original story or work. Examples of such indirect allusions are *dog that did not bark, Rosebud, sulk in one's tent,* and *tilt at windmills.* We have also included more historical references (*Bay of Pigs, Charge of the Light Brigade, Checkpoint Charlie, Gettysburg address, peace in our time*), titles of works (*Arsenic and Old Lace, Blade Runner, Lord of the Flies, Rashomon*) and names of writers (*Cheever, Pinter, Wodehouse*) that evoke a particular situation, mood, or genre. Also new to this edition are many phrases and quotations drawn from literature and popular culture (*Beam me up, Scotty, dark night of the soul, little grey cells, the road less travelled, we're not in Kansas anymore*). Finally, we have trimmed back some of the more encyclopedic background material and presented the allusive or connotational force of a name or phrase in a more explicit and focused form.

Clear definitions identify precisely the contexts in which a particular allusion or reference is used. Within an entry, the presence of an asterisk indicates that a particular term has its own entry elsewhere in the text. Italics has been used for the titles of novels, plays, and other full-length works; roman in quotation marks for individual short stories, songs, and poems.

The authors would like to thank Ben Harris, who gave us enthusiastic support and encouragement during his time at Oxford University Press, and Vicki Donald and Rebecca Lane who subsequently took up the reins. We are also grateful to Jackie Pritchard for copyediting the text and to Sheila Ferguson for proofreading it.

Penny Stock, our co-author on the first two editions of this book, died suddenly in 2005. She was a gifted and inspirational lexicographer and a great friend, and we miss her. We hope Penny would approve of this latest incarnation of our book, which we dedicate to her.

A.D.
S.D.

2010

Introduction to the Second Edition

What is an allusion? When we make an allusion we mention the name of a real person, historical event, or literary character, not simply as a straightforward reference (as in 'Hercules was an ancient Greek hero') but in order to conjure up some extra meaning, embodying some quality or characteristic for which the word has come to stand. *The Oxford Dictionary of Allusions* aims to identify and explain such allusions used in English and to illustrate their use by quotations from a variety of texts.

Writers use allusions in a variety of ways. They can be used as a kind of shorthand, evoking instantly a complex human experience embedded with a story or dramatic event. For example, in this passage from *Jude the Obscure*,

> Arabella ascended the stairs, softly opened the door of the first bedroom, and peeped in. Finding that her shorn Samson was asleep she entered to the bedside and started regarding him.

Thomas Hardy's phrase 'shorn Samson' succinctly expresses Arabella's quiet triumph at finally having Jude in her power. Allusions can convey powerful visual images, as Robertson Davies does in his reference to the tangled limbs and snakes of the classical statue of Laocoön in *Leaven of Malice*:

> 'And seeing it's you, I'll give you a hint: the way the string's tied you can get loose at once if he lies down flat and you crawl right up over his head; then the string drops off without untying the knots. Bye now.' And she was off to encourage other strugglers, who lay in Laocoön groups about the floor.

It is often possible to pack more meaning into a well-chosen allusion than into a roughly equivalent descriptive term from the general language either because an allusion can carry some of the connotations of the whole story from which it is drawn, or because an individual's name can be associated with more than one characteristic. Some authors can even use a multiplicity of allusive terms to entertaining effect, as in this quotation from *The Scold's Bridle* by Minnette Walters:

> I watched Duncan clipping his hedge this afternoon and could barely remember the handsome man he was. If I had been a charitable woman, I would have married him forty years ago and saved him from himself and Violet. She has turned my Romeo into a sad-eyed Billy Bunter who blinks his passions quietly when no one's looking. Oh that his too, too solid flesh should melt. At twenty, he had the body of Michelangelo's David, now he resembles an entire family group by Henry Moore.

The majority of allusions in English derive from classical mythology and the Bible, particularly the Old Testament. These ancient stories — the Wooden Horse of Troy, the protracted return home of Odysseus, David and Goliath, the banishment of Adam and Eve from the Garden of Eden — remain very much alive in our collective consciousness. Other fertile sources include folklore and legend (for example, Robin Hood, Lancelot, and Faust); Shakespeare (Romeo, Othello, and Lady Macbeth); Dickens (Micawber, Scrooge, and Pecksniff); the visual style of great artists (Rembrandt and Modigliani); and children's stories (Cinderella, Pinocchio, and Eeyore). Some individual works, such as *Gulliver's Travels*, *Alice's Adventures in Wonderland*, and *The Pilgrim's Progress*, are particularly rich sources. Modern allusions often derive from the visual media of cinema and television (Terminator, Norma Desmond, Del Boy, Archie Bunker), and from the worlds of the comic strip and the animated film (Bambi, Linus blanket, Mr Magoo, Roadrunner). And now we are starting to derive allusions from computer games (Lara Croft).

This second edition of *The Oxford Dictionary of Allusions*, like the first, is largely based on the evidence of the quotations collected as its source material. Unlike the first, it is fully alphabetical. The original edition had a thematic structure with entries grouped under themes such as 'Anger', 'Cunning', and 'Hypocrisy'. In the new edition this structure is preserved in the form of a thematic index, enabling readers to discover different allusions that can be used in similar contexts. The thematic index can be used in the same way as a thesaurus for finding different entries with a similar meaning or theme. For example, Judas is by far the most frequently cited exponent of betrayal, but the thematic index yields other allusions in the same semantic area such as Benedict Arnold, Delilah, and the 'lady in red'. It also reveals other juxtapositions such as changes in allusions over time. For example, in the nineteenth century Jack Sheppard represented the archetype of the person who successfully escaped. In the twentieth century he was replaced by Houdini.

We have added some 300 new entries for this new edition. A number of contemporary allusions have become well-established since the publication of the previous edition and take their place within these pages. These include Princess Diana, Frodo, Bill Gates, Guantanamo Bay, Jerry Springer, Teletubbies, and the X-Files.

The authors would like to thank Ruth Langley and Laurien Berkeley from Oxford University Press. We also thank again those who worked with us on the first edition of the dictionary, particularly Elizabeth Knowles, and the contributors to the reading programme which provided us with the basis of our original database of quotations: Kendall Clarke, Ian Clarke, Robert Grout, Mark Grout, Ruth Loshak, Jane McArthur, Duncan Marshall, Camilla Sherwood, Peggy Tout, and Brigit Viney.

A.D.
S.D.
2005   P.S.

List of subjects and their abbreviations

Advertising (Advert.)
Art
Arthurian legend (Arth. Leg.)
Bible
Cartoons & Comics (Cart. & Com.)
Children's literature (Child. Lit.)
Cinema (Cin.)
Classical mythology (Class. Myth.)
Crime
Dance
Egyptian mythology (Egypt. Myth.)
Fairy tales
Greek mythology (Gk Myth.)
History (Hist.)
Legend & Folklore (Leg. & Folk.)
Literature (Lit.)

Music (Mus.)
Mythology (Myth.)
Norse mythology (Norse Myth.)
Nursery rhymes (Nurs. Rhym.)
Opera
People
Philosophy (Philos.)
Places
Radio
Religion (Rel.)
Roman mythology (Rom. Myth.)
Science
Shakespeare (Shakes.)
Sport
Television (TV)
Theatre

Abaddon [Bible] The 'angel of the bottomless pit' described in the book of Revelation, who presides over a swarm of tormenting locusts that 'have tails like scorpions, and stings' (Rev. 9: 10–11). He is sometimes identified with the Devil and also with Hell. His Greek name is Apollyon.

> ➤ The Devil

> And my father preached a whole set of sermons on the occasion; one set in the morning, all about David and Goliath, to spirit up the people to fighting with spades or bricks, if need were; and the other set in the afternoons, proving that Napoleon (that was another name for Bony, as we used to call him) was all the same as an Apollyon and Abaddon.
> ELIZABETH GASKELL *Cranford* 1851–3

Abdera [Places] An ancient Greek city on the coast of Thrace whose inhabitants, known as Abderites, were proverbial for their stupidity.

> ➤ An abderite, or inhabitant of Abdera, is someone who seems very stupid

> But let me make this perfectly clear, [she] is an abderite, a light-weight and nothing more than a distraction.
> *The Latest on Air America* 2009

Abednego *See* SHADRACH, MESHACH, AND ABEDNEGO.

Abelard and Héloïse [People] **Peter Abelard** (1079–1142), French theologian and philosopher, became tutor to the young **Héloïse** (1098–1164) at the request of her uncle. They fell in love, and when the affair was discovered, the couple fled. Héloïse bore a son and they were secretly married in Paris. However, Héloïse's enraged relatives caught and castrated Abelard, who then became a monk, and required Héloïse to become a nun. Abelard and Héloïse are buried together in Paris, and a book of their correspondence was published in 1616.

> ➤ Devoted but tragic lovers

> She loved him more than ever. She loved him in the way that Héloïse loved Abelard.
> *Hudson Review* 2005

Abraham [Bible] A biblical leader, considered to be the father of the Hebrews. All Jews claim descent from him.

> ➤ A father of a nation; a great leader of a nation or dynasty

> Wendell went on carefully, considerately, 'Let me propose this. Has she ever smoked pot?' 'Not with me around. I'm an old-fashioned father figure. Two parts Abraham to one part Fagin.'
> JOHN UPDIKE *Bech: A Book* 1970

Abraham's bosom [Bible] According to the parable of the rich man and *Lazarus, when Lazarus dies he is 'carried by the angels into Abraham's bosom', whereas the rich man goes to Hell (Luke 16: 23).

> A place where the good rest in peace when they die

Rocka' my soul in the bosom of Abraham.
Traditional Gospel Song

Absalom [Bible] The favourite son of King *David, who led a rebellion against his father. In the subsequent battle, David ordered his men to 'deal gently for my sake with the young man' (2 Sam. 18: 5), but his commander Joab ignored this command and slew Absalom. On hearing of the death of his son, David wept, 'O my son, Absalom, my son, my son Absalom! Would God I had died for thee, O Absalom, my son, my son!' (2 Sam. 18: 33).

> A rebellious son; a favourite son; a son who is much loved despite his wrongdoings

Sometimes, the worthy gentleman would reprove my mother for being over-indulgent to her sons, with a reference to old Eli, or David and Absalom, which was particularly galling to her feelings.
ANNE BRONTË *The Tenant of Wildfell Hall* 1848

Academe, Groves of [Lit.] A quotation from the *Epistles* of the 1st-century AD Roman poet Horace, 'Atque inter silvas Academi quaerere verum' (And seek for truth in the groves of Academe).

> A way of referring to the academic world, especially when seen as isolated from the reality of everyday life

From the serene groves of academe he was hurled into the national and international media spotlight as Archbishop of Dublin.
Sunday Business Post 2002

acceptable face of…[People] A phrase derived from a comment made by the British prime minister Edward Heath in 1973, when he said that the activities of the Lonrho company showed 'the unpleasant and unacceptable face of capitalism'.

> The acceptable aspect of something

David Begg was, for years, the acceptable face of trade unionism, a forward thinker who knew the union movement would have to adapt itself to the modern age.
Irish Examiner 2001

Achates [Class. Myth.] The companion of *Aeneas in Virgil's *Aeneid*, whose fidelity to his friend is exemplary, hence the term *fidus Achates* ('faithful Achates').

> A faithful or loyal companion

For the next three years the captaincy switched between Dexter and Smith, and, for the third time, Cowdrey went to Australia as faithful Achates, this time to Smith.
JOHN THICKNESSE *Obituary of Colin Cowdrey* 2000

Acheron [Gk Myth.] One of the rivers in *Hades, over which the souls of the dead were ferried by *Charon.

> A gloomy or mournful river

[They] then made their way across the river, which under the grey and growing light looked as desolate as Acheron.
G. K. CHESTERTON *The Man Who Was Thursday* 1908

Achilles [Gk Myth.] One of the greatest Greek heroes of the *Trojan War. During his infancy his mother dipped him in the waters of the river *Styx, thus making his body invulnerable except for the heel by which she held him. This vulnerable spot would later prove fatal. The *Iliad* relates how, during the Trojan War, Achilles quarrelled with his commander, *Agamemnon, and retired in anger to his tent, refusing to fight any longer. Later, after the death of his beloved friend *Patroclus at the hand of the Trojan hero *Hector, he did emerge, filled with grief and rage. In revenge, Achilles killed Hector and dragged his body behind the wheels of his chariot round the walls of Troy. Achilles himself was wounded in the heel by a poisoned arrow shot by *Paris, Hector's brother, and died of this wound.

> Someone who displays great anger; someone who avenges the death of a friend; a person's 'Achilles' heel' is their only weak or vulnerable point; Achilles and Patroclus are mentioned as examples of very close male friends

I won't divulge who wins the game, but at a climactic moment, Jack does indulge an Achillean wrath against his brother.
BRUCE WEBER New York Times 2002

Then he went out like Achilles after the death of Patroclus and took some of his feelings out on the opposition.
The Times—Tim de Lisle column (2004)

Close as Achilles and Patroclus, the two of us.
JULIAN BARNES Talking It Over 1991

Africa is the Achilles' heel in our war against terrorism.
DEWAYNE WICKHAM USA Today 2008

Acres, Bob [Lit.] A ridiculous but mild character in Sheridan's The Rivals (1775) who believes himself to be a rival for the hand of Lydia Languish. He is persuaded to fight a duel with her preferred suitor, but on his arrival at the location for the fight he feels his courage 'oozing out at the palms of his hands'.

> Someone whose courage disappears rapidly

'If you are busy, another time will do as well', continued the bishop, whose courage like Bob Acres' had oozed out, now that he found himself on the ground of battle.
ANTHONY TROLLOPE Barchester Towers 1857

Actaeon [Gk Myth.] A hunter who, because he accidentally saw *Artemis (the virgin goddess of the hunt) bathing naked, was changed into a stag and torn to pieces by his own hounds.

> Someone who sees a forbidden sight, especially a naked woman; someone who is punished for a rash or foolish act; someone who is torn apart by hounds

'Rash man!' she said; 'like Actaeon, thou hast had thy will; be careful lest, like Actaeon, thou too perish miserably, torn to pieces by the ban-hounds of thine own passions.'
H. RIDER HAGGARD She 1887

The glimpse Barthes refers to is essentially a glimpse of the forbidden, a sight of what you were not supposed to see, like Actaeon coming upon the goddess Diana naked.
Scotland on Sunday 2002

Action Man* The name of a doll in the form of a well-muscled soldier, launched in Britain in 1966 by Palitoy as a licensed copy of Hasbro's doll GI Joe. The toy came with a variety of military clothes and accessories such as jeeps, guns, climbing ropes, and parachutes.

> A tough hero who engages in difficult physical exploits

Noakes' reputation as the original 'Action Man', parachuting, bobsleighing or climbing Nelson's column, would be taken up by many subsequent presenters.
Screen Online: British television series 2003

Actium [Hist.] A promontory in ancient Greece. In 31 BC it was the scene of a sea and land battle in which the forces of Mark *Antony and *Cleopatra were decisively defeated by the fleet of Octavian (the future Emperor Augustus).

> A decisive defeat

Soon he would be overtaken; but warm in the circle of Leila's arms, as if he were Antony at Actium, he could hardly bring himself to feel fear.
LAWRENCE DURRELL *Mountolive* 1958

Adam and Eve [Bible] According to the book of Genesis, Adam was the first man, created by God from the dust of the ground and God's breath, and Eve the first woman, formed from one of Adam's ribs. They lived together in innocence in the Garden of *Eden, knowing nothing of good and evil and unashamed of their own nakedness. Eve was tempted by the Serpent to eat the forbidden fruit on the tree of the knowledge of good and evil, and in turn she persuaded Adam to do the same. As a punishment for disobeying God's command, they were banished from Eden.

> People in a state of complete innocence and contentment; people whose happiness is destroyed or lost; people who are naked without feeling ashamed

So there they were, naked as Adam and Eve.
PHILIP ROTH *Epstein* 1959

'I feel somehow that it's too beautiful for us to be here—that our being here will bring nothing but evil and harm.' Thomas smiled, wistfully. 'Kind of like Adam and Eve revisiting the Garden of Eden, eh?'
G. S. MONKS *One Last Summer* 2005

Addams Family, The [TV; Cart. & Com.] A spoof horror sitcom derived from a cartoon strip by Charles Addams about a group of bizarre people living in a decaying Gothic mansion. It was shown in the United States from 1964 to 1966 and in the United Kingdom from 1966 to 1968. Gomez and black-haired Morticia Addams and their daughter Wednesday and son Pugsley, with Uncle Fester, Grandmama, and butler Lurch, were the 'creepy, kooky, mysterious and spooky' family, along with cousin Itt.

> Used to suggest that something is weird or grotesque

In fact, Marsha's office was filled with other souvenirs: a human skull, a large specimen bottle with a human fetus preserved in formaldehyde, framed color pictures of gruesome murder scenes. 'Who does your decorating?' I asked. 'The Addams family?'
STEVEN WOMACK *Dead Folk Blues* 1992

He's like something out of Charles Addams.
MARCIA MULLER *Ask the Cards a Question* 1982

Admah and Zeboiim [Bible] According to the book of Deuteronomy (29: 23), the cities of Admah and Zeboiim suffered the same fate as *Sodom and Gomorrah, namely destruction by God as a punishment for their citizens' sinfulness.

> Wicked places

Admirable Crichton *See* CRICHTON.

Adonis [Gk Myth.] An extremely beautiful youth who was loved by both *Aphrodite and *Persephone.

> A handsome young man with a perfectly formed body

If it fits and is well cut, the tailcoat can turn any man—short or gangly, fat or lanky—into an Adonis.
City Journal (New York) 2003

Adullam [Bible] A cave where *David took refuge from Saul because Saul wanted to kill him. When others heard that he was there, they went to join him: 'And every one that was in distress, and every one that was in debt, and every one that was discontented, gathered themselves unto him' (1 Sam. 22: 2).

> ➤ A place where those in trouble can seek refuge

Mixen Lane was the Adullam of all the surrounding villages. It was the hiding-place of those in distress, and in debt, and trouble of every kind.
THOMAS HARDY *The Mayor of Casterbridge* 1886

Aegeus [Gk Myth.] The father of *Theseus. The latter had promised his father that if he successfully destroyed the *Minotaur he would signal this on his return to Athens by hoisting white sails, rather than the customary black ones. This he forgot to do and Aegeus, believing his son to be dead, threw himself to his death from a cliff.

> ➤ Someone who waits on a cliff top, or plunges from it

Nowadays, you're unlikely to see people like Aegeus, waiting on Sounion for a relative to return from the sea.
DIMANA TRANKOVA *Vagabond Magazine* 2009

Aeneas [Class. Myth.] A Trojan leader, son of Anchises and *Aphrodite, and legendary ancestor of the Romans. At the end of the *Trojan War, when Troy was in flames, he carried his ageing father away upon his shoulders. The story of his subsequent wanderings is told in Virgil's *Aeneid*.

> ➤ Someone who goes on a long journey; someone who carries another person

She shook her head, and he lifted her up; then, at a slow pace, went onward with his load....Thus he proceeded, like Aeneas with his father.
THOMAS HARDY *The Return of the Native* 1880

Aeolian [Gk Myth.] **Aeolus** was a mortal who lived on the floating island of Aeolia. He was a friend of the gods, and *Zeus gave him control of the winds. He has given his name to the Aeolian harp, a musical instrument that produces sounds when the wind passes through it.

> ➤ Used to describe music produced by the effect of the wind

Time to drink in life's sunshine—time to listen to the Aeolian music that the wind of God draws from the human heart-strings around us.
JEROME K. JEROME *Three Men in a Boat* 1889

Aesculapius (Asclepius) [Gk Myth.] The son of *Apollo and Coronis, who was instructed in the art of medicine by the centaur Chiron. He was said to have been killed by *Zeus after *Hades had complained that Aesculapius' skills were keeping mortals from the underworld. After his death, he was honoured as the god of medicine and healing.

> ➤ Mentioned in the context of medicine, doctors, or healing

Carl Moss might be willing to protect Merle with the mantle of Aesculapius, up to a point.
RAYMOND CHANDLER *The High Window* 1943

Aesop's fable [Lit.] **Aesop** (6th century BC), who lived as a slave on the island of Samos, traditionally has all Greek fables ascribed to his authorship. The fable, a popular literary form in ancient Greece, is a morality tale in which the characters are animals, a typical example being the story of the hare and the tortoise. *See* HARE AND THE TORTOISE.

> ➤ A story with a moral

I told you that capital thing I heard her say about Craig—that he was like a cock, who thought the sun had risen to hear him crow. Now that's an Aesop's fable in a sentence.
GEORGE ELIOT *Adam Bede* 1859

Agag [Bible] The king of the *Amalekites, whom Saul defeated in battle. Although Saul wanted to spare Agag's life, the prophet *Samuel ordered Agag to be brought to him: 'Then said Samuel, Bring ye hither to me Agag the king of the Amalekites. And Agag came unto him delicately' (1 Sam. 15: 32). Samuel then killed Agag.

➢ Someone who walks gently, or 'delicately'

So as I lay on the ground with my ear glued close against the wall, who should march round the church but John Trenchard, Esquire, not treading delicately like King Agag, or spying, but just come on a voyage of discovery for himself.
J. M. FAULKNER *Moonfleet* 1898

Agamemnon [Gk Myth.] The king of Mycenae and brother of Menelaus. The *Iliad* refers to the wrath of Agamemnon on being told that he must return a captive Trojan girl to her father to appease the god *Apollo: 'Then there stood up in the assembly the hero son of Atreus, wide-ruling Agamemnon, in deep anger: fury filled his dark heart full, and his eyes were like blazing fire.' Agamemnon agreed to return the girl, but demanded that *Achilles hand over to him his concubine Briseis to take her place, which led to the furious quarrel between the two men.

➢ Someone who shows great or terrible anger

The frogs and the mice would be nothing to them, nor the angers of Agamemnon and Achilles.
ANTHONY TROLLOPE *Barchester Towers* 1857

Aganippe [Gk Myth.] A spring sacred to the *Muses on Mount *Helicon, whose waters were believed to give inspiration to those who drank from them.

➢ Mentioned in the context of poetic inspiration

I never dranke of Aganippe well.
PHILIP SIDNEY *Astrophel and Stella* 1586

Age of Enlightenment [Hist.] A European intellectual movement of the late 17th and 18th centuries, emphasizing reason and individualism rather than tradition. It was heavily influenced by 17th-century philosophers such as Descartes, Locke, and *Newton, and its prominent exponents include Kant, Goethe, *Voltaire, *Rousseau, and Adam Smith.

➢ A period of reason and liberalism

The brutalities are of such a nature that one feels Gujarat has not entered an age of enlightenment or if it ever entered it has exited from it and has entered an era of darkness.
Milli Gazette (New Delhi) 2004

Agincourt (Azincourt) [Hist.] A village in France, close to the site of a battle between the French and the English in 1415 during the Hundred Years War. Although the English were heavily outnumbered, the terrain, a muddy valley, suited the English archers. The English lost only about 200 men to French losses of over 5000. The battle is remembered chiefly because of its prominence in *Shakespeare's *Henry V* (1600).

➢ A great battle or heroic victory; also used to invoke a large numbers of things raining down from above

While City racked up corner after corner and the crosses rained in like arrows at Agincourt, genuine sightings of goal were few and far between.
The Press, York 2001

Agnes, St [People] (d. *c.*304) A Roman martyr and the patron saint of virgins. Said to have been a Christian virgin who refused to marry, she was martyred during the reign of Diocletian. Her emblem is a lamb.

> ➤ A pure or innocent virgin

Agonistes [Lit.] A word taken from the title of a 1671 poem by John *Milton, *Samson Agonistes*, about the struggle of the blinded *Samson to maintain his faith. The word was used by T. S. Eliot in the title of his poem *Sweeney Agonistes* (1932) and also by Gary Wills in his *Nixon Agonistes* (1970).

> ➤ Used to suggest that someone is engaged in a struggle or contest
>
>   The Corsair finally understands why foxy Challabi Agonistes, Judith Miller, had to go to jail for a story she didn't write.
>   EUGENE VOLOKH et al. *The Volokh Conspiracy* (Weblog) 2004

Ahab 1. [Bible] (*c.*875–854 BC) The idolatrous king of Israel who married *Jezebel and introduced into Israel the worship of the Phoenician god *Baal. His name became associated with wickedness, especially the offence of honouring pagan gods: 'There was none who sold himself to do what was evil in the sight of the Lord like Ahab, whom Jezebel his wife incited' (1 Kgs. 21: 25).

> ➤ Someone who is full of wicked pride and turns away from God
>
>   'Does Judith or either of the boys ever come down to hear you preach?'…'Nay, they struts like Ahab in their pride, and their eyes drip fatness, nor do they see the pit digged beneath their feet by the Lord.'
>   STELLA GIBBONS *Cold Comfort Farm* 1932

2. [Lit.] The captain of the whaling ship *Pequod* in Herman Melville's *Moby Dick* (1851). The monomaniacal Ahab obsessively pursues Moby Dick, the huge white whale that on a previous voyage had cost him his leg.

> ➤ Someone obsessed with something almost to the point of madness; someone who obsessively pursues a person or an idea
>
>   I could feel the road some twenty inches beneath me, unfurling and flying and hissing at incredible speeds across the groaning continent with that mad Ahab at the wheel.
>   JACK KEROUAC *On the Road* 1957

Ahasuerus 1. [Bible] A Persian king who appears in the Old Testament book of Esther, and is usually identified with *Xerxes (reigned 486–465 BC). In his anger against the Jew Mordecai, who refused to bow down before him, Ahasuerus ordered the extermination of all the Jews. His wife, *Esther, went to him to plead for the life of Mordecai and all the Jews: 'And Esther spake yet again before the king, and fell down at his feet, and besought him with tears to put away the mischief of Haman the Agagite, and his device that he had devised against the Jews' (Esther 8: 3).

> ➤ A man whose wrath is to be feared or appeased; a man who should be approached with trepidation
>
>   Presently my mother went to my father. I know I thought of Queen Esther and King Ahasuerus; for my mother was very pretty and delicate-looking, and my father looked as terrible as King Ahasuerus.
>   ELIZABETH GASKELL *Cranford* 1851–3

2. [Leg. & Folk.] Another name for the *Wandering Jew.

Ahriman [Myth.] The supreme evil spirit who is perpetually in conflict with the supreme good spirit Ahura Mazda (or Ormazd), according to the dualistic cosmology of Zoroastrianism.

This is Bunyan's description of him in The *Pilgrim's Progress*: 'He was clothed with scales like a fish (and they are his pride), he had wings like a dragon, and out of his belly came fire and smoke, and his mouth was as the mouth of a lion.'

> The epitome of evil

Let us help ahura mazda keep on fighting ahriman!
In These Times 2003

Ajax [Gk Myth.] A Greek hero of the *Trojan War, proverbial for his great size and strength. When Agamemnon awarded the armour of the dead *Achilles to *Odysseus and not to him, Ajax went mad with rage, slaughtered a flock of sheep, and then committed suicide in shame.

> A strong, fierce fighter; someone who lays siege to a place; someone who destroys something in a rage, and then feels remorse

She sat as helpless and despairing among her black locks as Ajax among the slaughtered sheep.
GEORGE ELIOT *The Mill on the Floss* 1860

It was like the siege of Troy the next morning. The rain had gone and left dark concrete patches under the drying sun. Arrayed in all their panoply along Hardens Lane, the gentlemen of the press stood in little knots, like so many Ajaxes and Achilles, probing the weak spots of the citadel that was Leighford High.
M. J. TROW *Maxwell's House* 1995

Aladdin's cave [Fairy tales] A cave filled with treasure in a story in *The *Arabian Nights*. Aladdin is born the son of a poor tailor, and a magician tricks him into the cave, in order to retrieve a magic lamp. The magician shuts him into the cave, whereupon Aladdin discovers the secret of the lamp, a jinnee who must do his bidding. He is able to escape the cave, and the 'slave of the lamp' makes him and his mother rich.

> A place full of rare or beautiful treasures

Ever since then the place has remained in my memory the Mecca of fashion, an Aladdin's cave of incomparable splendour.
ANDRÉ BRINK *Imaginings of Sand* 1996

Alamo [Hist.] A fort in San Antonio, Texas, which in 1836 was besieged by the Mexican army during the war between Texas and Mexico. It was defended by a small group of soldiers and civilians, all of whom (including the frontiersman and politician Davy *Crockett) died. The phrase 'Remember the Alamo' was later used as a rallying cry by the Texan army.

> Mentioned in the context of a heroic last stand that ultimately fails

He still had what Donald once described as that 'last Texican at the Alamo look': ready, willing, and able to go down fighting.
TOM CLANCY and STEVE PIECZENIK *Op-Center* 1995

alarums and excursions [Theatre] A stage direction indicating confused noise and bustle, which occurs in slightly varying forms in a number of *Shakespeare's history plays.

> A state of noisy confusion

Alas poor... [Shakes.] A quotation from *Hamlet* (1604), spoken by *Hamlet in a graveyard as he looks at the skull of Yorick, a court jester he had known as a child, and grieves for him: 'Alas, poor Yorick! I knew him, Horatio.' The phrase is often misquoted as: 'Alas, poor Yorick! I knew him well.'

> Used to indicate that someone or something is dead
>
> Alas poor Ford, we knew it well.
> *Sunday Herald* 2001

Alastor [Gk Myth.] A supernatural figure, 'the Avenger', in ancient Greece who sought vengeance after a crime had been committed.

> Someone who seeks vengeance
>
> Their impulse was well-nigh to prostrate themselves in lamentation before untimely rains and tempests, which came as the Alastor of those households whose crime it was to be poor.
> THOMAS HARDY *The Mayor of Casterbridge* 1886

albatross [Lit.] In Samuel Coleridge's poem *The Rime of the Ancient Mariner* the mariner relates how he shot an albatross at sea and as a result of this 'hellish thing', killing a bird of good omen, a curse fell on his ship. As a penance, he was forced to wear the albatross hung round his neck.

> A burden or curse that someone has to bear
>
> Borrowing has become an albatross around the government's neck.
> *Financial Sense Online: 2004 editorials* 2004

Alberich's cloak [Myth.] A cloak of invisibility which is guarded by the dwarf Alberich in the German epic poem the *Nibelungenlied*. Alberich is robbed of the cloak by *Siegfried.

> A means of hiding or remaining invisible
>
> No Alberich's Cloak for Churchill, please.
> *ZNet* 2009

Albion [Places] A name (traditionally from Latin *albus* ('white'), in reference to Dover's chalk cliffs) which is sometimes used to denote Britain or England.

> A way of referring to Britain or England, especially when it is conceived of as a green paradise
>
> When their keepers departed, the 400-odd rodents escaped and set up home under the green trees of Albion.
> *Independent on Sunday* 1993

Alcatraz [Places] A notorious American prison on the island of Alcatraz in San Francisco Bay. Built in 1868, it was originally a prison for military offenders, but was later used for civilian prisoners. From 1934 it held the most dangerous criminals, including the gangster Al *Capone. Alcatraz was closed in 1963.

> A prison with harsh conditions, from which escape is impossible
>
> Others called it [Portsmouth Naval Prison] the Alcatraz of the East because no inmate ever successfully escaped.
> *www.wikipedia.com* 2009

Alcibiades [People] (*c.*450–404 BC) An Athenian general and statesman who had a reputation for debauchery. He had been a student and perhaps a lover of *Socrates.

> Alluded to in the context of drunken debauchery or the pursuit of pleasure
>
> 'You prefer Pecksniff to Alcibiades,' Willie Weaver concluded.
> ALDOUS HUXLEY *Point Counter Point* 1928

Alexander [People] (356–323 BC) The son of Philip II of Macedon, who became king at 19 when his father was assassinated. He defeated the Persians in three major battles, freeing the Greek city states and Egypt from Persian rule, while in Egypt he founded Alexandria. He extended his empire eastwards as far as India before dying young of a fever.

➤ A conqueror; a great leader; a great general

Monday dawned, the sun rising into the inevitable blue sky with the radiant serenity of Alexander entering a conquered province.
REGINALD HILL *On Beulah Height* 1998

Alfred [People] (849–99) The king of Wessex 871–99, generally known as Alfred the Great, who led the Saxons to victory over Danish invaders. The most famous story associated with Alfred is the legend that, when in hiding in Somerset, he forgot to watch a peasant woman's cakes, as he had been asked to do, with the result that they burnt.

➤ Mentioned in the context of burned food

My word, Miriam! You're in for it this time....You'd better be gone when his mother comes in. I know why King Alfred burned the cakes.
D. H. LAWRENCE *Sons and Lovers* 1913

Alger, Horatio [Child. Lit.] (1832–99) An American clergyman and writer of adventure stories for boys. The stories were on the theme of rags to riches, with the hero's initial struggles with poverty eventually leading to fame and wealth. His most popular story was *Ragged Dick* (1867).

➤ Mentioned in the context of a rags-to-riches story

Schliemann was the original Horatio Alger hero. He began his career as a stock boy, sleeping under the counter of the store at night, and ended up a millionaire merchant.
ELIZABETH PETERS *Trojan Gold* 1987

Ali, Muhammad [Sport] An American boxer, born Cassius Clay in 1942, who won the world heavyweight title for the first time in 1964 and regained it in 1974 and 1978, becoming the first boxer to be world champion three times. He retired in 1981. Ali frequently boasted, 'I am the greatest.'

➤ A strong man; someone with unlimited self-confidence

'Scream, damn it!' He grabbed a handful of my nightie and tried to tear it. I defy Mohammad Ali to rend a wad of Dacron; it just stretches, interminably.
ELIZABETH PETERS *Silhouette in Scarlet* 1983

You've seen the loosey-goosey Packers, confident as Muhammad Ali before a fight as they strut around their hotel with not a care in the world.
Los Angeles Times 1998

Ali Baba [Fairy tales] A character in the story of 'Ali Baba and the Forty Thieves' (one of the stories in *The *Arabian Nights*). Ali Baba discovers a secret cave in which the thieves keep their stolen treasures, which can only be accessed by a magic door which opens to the command, 'Open sesame'.

➤ Ali Baba's cave is mentioned in the context of a place full of beautiful or rare treasures

The town is nothing special, but there's a place on the outskirts that beckons like Ali Baba's fashion cave—piles of shoes, endless rows of suits and dresses, great meadows of handbags that multiply before one's eyes, and all of it marked way down.
Time Europe Magazine 2004

Alice in Wonderland [Lit.] Lewis Carroll's children's story *Alice's Adventures in Wonderland* (1865) is an account of a young girl's experiences in a surreal, illogical, dreamlike world. At the beginning of the story Alice follows a white rabbit down a rabbit-hole and finds herself apparently tumbling down a very deep well, eventually landing with a thump in Wonderland. Alice finds a little door that is too small for her to fit through until she drinks from a bottle labelled 'Drink me' and immediately starts to shrink. Not long after this she is required to eat a cake labelled 'Eat me', to make her grow taller. Further strange incidents occur as Alice encounters a succession of outlandish creatures. At the end of the story Alice wakes from what has apparently been a dream. Alice is depicted in John Tenniel's illustrations with long blonde hair. In Carroll's sequel, *Through the Looking-Glass* (1871), the illustrations show Alice's hair held back with a wide hairband, now known as an Alice band.

➢ Used in the following contexts: a puzzling, illogical or surreal situation; falling steeply; a girl with long blonde hair tied or held back; the feeling of being too big or too small

The plane was unmistakably going down, down, down, like Alice in the rabbit hole.
F. SCOTT FITZGERALD *The Last Tycoon* 1941

What would they make of the wedding photos stuck in the back of his bureau drawer? Of Vic, with her Alice-in-Wonderland hair and pale, innocent face.
DEBORAH CROMBIE *All Shall Be Well* 1995

'Yes,' I admitted, feeling enormous, like Alice after she'd OD'd on Eat Me mushrooms. Size 2 women have that effect on me.
LINDA BARNES *Cold Case* 1997

I felt like Alice in Wonderland, in a mirror image of the world I'd always inhabited.
CAROL ANN HARRIS *Storms* 2007

alien corn [Bible] A phrase taken from the poem 'Ode to a Nightingale' by John Keats. The poem alludes to the biblical story of Ruth, who followed her mother-in-law to Bethlehem and became a gleaner in the fields. Keats muses on the song of the nightingale and wonders if it is:

> Perhaps the self-same song that found a path
> Through the sad heart of Ruth, when sick for home,
> She stood in tears among the alien corn.

➢ A faraway or unfamiliar landscape; also used to suggest that someone feels homesick in an unfamiliar place

all for one and one for all [Lit.] The rallying-cry of the group of friends (Athos, Porthos, Aramis, and D'Artagnan) whose adventures are celebrated in Alexandre Dumas's novel *The *Three Musketeers* (1844).

➢ Used to suggest a strong feeling of solidarity among a group

It was, without doubt, a case of 'all for one and one for all' at the Kilmead Road Action Group Meeting, held at Scoil Ide Naofa on Thursday, May 30. The atmosphere was one of total solidarity with the issue of making the Kilmead Junction safe.
Kildare Nationalist 2002

all-singing all-dancing [Theatre] A phrase derived from a series of posters produced in 1929 to promote the new sound cinema such as the one advertising the Hollywood musical *Broadway Melody*, which proclaimed the words *All talking All singing All dancing*.

➢ With every possible modern attribute, or able to perform any function

They want the latest, all singing all dancing equipment that tests every part of their anatomy while cycling or running.
This Is Wiltshire news stories 2003

All's Well that Ends Well [Shakes.] The title of one of Shakespeare's comedies (1623); a proverbial saying dating from the late 14th century.

➤ Used in the context of a difficult situation which has a satisfactory outcome

And thankfully, all's well that ends well, when the lovers are united and the complications untangled.
Fresh Lime Soda: Movie reviews 2005

all the king's horses and all the king's men [Nurs. Rhym.] A quotation from the nursery rhyme about *Humpty Dumpty:

> Humpty Dumpty sat on a wall,
> Humpty Dumpty had a great fall.
> All the king's horses and all the king's men
> Couldn't put Humpty together again.

➤ Used to suggest that something cannot be repaired or put right

If it [the computer system] goes down, all the king's horses and all the king's men can't get it up and running again.
DeveloperDotStar 2005

all the world's a stage [Shakes.] The opening sentence of a monologue from *As You Like It* (1623) (II. vii. 139–66), which develops into a description of the Seven Ages of Man.

> All the world's a stage,
> And all the men and women merely players;
> They have their exits and their entrances,
> And one man in his time plays many parts.

➤ Used to convey the idea that people perform different roles during their lives

Demonstrating that all the world is a stage, Thurman places his protagonist in a context of masks, theatres, duplicities, and lies in order to consider the problematics of racial and sexual identity.
MELUS 2004

Alsatia [Places] An area around Whitefriars, London, in the seventeenth century, which became a sanctuary for criminals and debtors. The name is taken from Alsace, the much disputed territory between France and Germany.

➤ A sanctuary from the law

But Maggie always appeared in the most amiable light at her aunt Moss's: it was her Alsatia, where she was out of reach of law—if she upset anything, dirtied her shoes, or tore her frock, these things were matters of course at her aunt Moss's.
GEORGE ELIOT *The Mill on the Floss* 1860

Amalekite [Bible] A member of the Amalekites, a nomadic tribe of *Canaan and the Sinai peninsula, reputedly descended from *Esau's grandson Amalek. They waged war against the *Israelites, for whom the Amalekites represented perpetual treachery and hostility: 'The Lord will have war with Amalek from generation to generation' (Exod. 17: 16).

➤ Someone treacherous or evil

But he, sly fox, son of Satan, seed of the Amalekite, he saw me looking at him in the church.
OLIVE SCHREINER *The Story of an African Farm* 1883

Amazon [Gk Myth.] A member of a race of female warriors alleged to exist on the borders of the known world.

> A tall, strong, athletic woman; a fierce or aggressive woman (adjective *Amazonian*)

The image I lingered on the longest was, unsurprisingly, of Francoise. Francoise as an Amazon, frozen, with a spear poised above her head, concentrating fiercely on the shapes beneath the water.
ALEX GARLAND *The Beach* 1996

Simultaneously the communists (secretly in cahoots with the dictator's amazonian wife) plan their own insurgency.
Time Magazine 2004

Ambridge [Radio] The fictional village in the radio soap opera *The *Archers*, which was first broadcast in 1950 by the BBC and described as 'an everyday story of country folk'.

> An idyllic rural village

The very term 'farm subsidies' conjures up images of sweet, ruddy-cheeked residents of Ambridge.
JohannHari.com 2005

ambrosia [Gk Myth.] The food of the Greek gods and the source of their immortality.

> Delicious or reviving food

The rolls didn't taste quite as good as they had done in the cool of the morning, but as I ate I began to feel better. The tepid water was a benison, and the fruit was ambrosia itself.
MARY STEWART *My Brother Michael* 1960

American dream [Hist.] The traditional social ideals of the United States, such as equality, democracy, and material prosperity. The term is first recorded from the 1930s.

> Used when referring to the success or aspirations of ordinary Americans

Hirshhorn left Latvia at the age of 6 and fulfilled the rags-to-riches American dream, his enormous fortune being made mainly from uranium mining.
IAN CHILVERS *A Dictionary of Twentieth-Century Art* 2000

Amin, Idi [Hist.] (1925–2003) A Ugandan soldier and head of state from 1971 to 1979. In 1971 he overthrew President Milton Obote and seized power, subsequently presiding over a regime characterized by brutality and repression.

> A cruel or ruthless leader

Don't forget what I told you in the motel room. About the world getting crazier and crazier. Besides, maybe the cultists were camera shy when your professor friend studied them but not anymore. Weirdos change, like anyone else. Jim Jones was everyone's hero until he turned into Idi Amin.
JONATHAN KELLERMAN *Blood Test* 1986

Amos and Andy [TV] An American radio show, which was first broadcast in 1928 and in 1951 became the first television sitcom with an all-black cast. The show came to an end in the mid-1960s after pressure from black groups, who accused it of promoting stereotypes of black people.

> Mentioned in the context of a racial stereotype, especially a stereotypical accent

The danger of using dialect is, of course, the risk of writing unintentional comedy and the greater peril of re-creating the queasy horror occasioned by racist classics of the

past: it's a real problem when characters in a naturalistic novel sound like Amos and Andy, Tonto or Fu Manchu.
FRANCINE PROSE *New York Times* 1996

Anak [Bible] A man of great stature who founded a race of giants known as the Anakim. 'And there we saw the giants, the sons of Anak, which come of the giants: and we were in our own sight as grasshoppers, and so we were in their sight' (Num. 13: 33).

> ➤ A very large person or creature

Even without the backing of rational argument, Mirabelle was a fearsome disputant. With it, she towered like the sons of Anak, and Ursell became as a grasshopper in her sight.
REGINALD HILL *Singing the Sadness* 1999

Ananias [Bible] The husband of Sapphira, who sold a possession to give money to the apostles, but lied about the price, in order to keep some money for himself. On being found out and accused of lying to God as well as to men, he 'fell down, and gave up the ghost' (Acts 5: 5).

> ➤ Someone who lies in order to keep something for themselves; someone who is punished or struck dead for lying

We must not, like Ananias and Sapphira, reserve behind some darling lust, some favourite sin, while we pretend to make sacrifice of our worldly affections.
SIR WALTER SCOTT *Peveril of the Peak* 1823

Children at school said that anyone who told a lie might be struck dead like Ananias.
ALISON UTTLEY *The Country Child* 1931

Anansi [Leg. & Folk.] The trickster spider in West African folk tradition. In some stories he tricks the supreme god into allowing disease to enter the world.

> ➤ Someone who uses clever trickery to achieve their aims

Cautioning members about the 'Brer Anansi' arithmetic, Leacock asked them not to reduce the usefulness of the Federation because 'trade unions are becoming weaker in these parts'.
News (St Vincent) 1994

Ancien Régime [Hist.] The political and social system in France before the revolution of 1789.

> ➤ An old system of government, especially when characterized by corruption and nepotism

Within a historical context, devolution is in its infancy and if Scottish people want to return to the ancien regime then their political immaturity is worse than even Gerald Warner believes.
Scotland on Sunday 2006

Ancient Mariner [Lit.] The central character and narrator in Samuel Coleridge's poem *The Rime of the Ancient Mariner* (1798). He stops a wedding guest at the door of the church where a wedding is about to take place, and insists on recounting his tale to the guest. The mariner relates how he shot an albatross at sea, thus bringing a curse upon the ship. The ship was becalmed near the Equator and everyone except the mariner perished.

> ➤ A compulsive speaker irresistible to his audience; someone boring a reluctant listener; someone who insists on telling their tale of woe; someone who seems to have invited a curse upon their head

Like the Ancient Mariner, they cannot resist buttonholing strangers in order to inform them of the facts.
LOUIS DE BERNIÈRES *Captain Corelli's Mandolin* 1994

I am becoming like the Ancient Mariner, stopping one in three to rant about our boundary survey.
New Zealand Listener 2005

Andersen, Hans Christian [Fairy tales] (1805–75) A Danish author and poet who is most famous for his fairy tales, which first appeared in 1835 and include 'The Emperor's New Clothes', 'The Snow Queen', 'The Red Shoes', 'The Ugly Duckling', and 'The Little Mermaid'.

> ➤ A great storyteller

    'He says that according to the grapevine—alias his mates at Kensington—nobody's very anxious for the job. With the last two supers dying in harness, they reckon Shepherd's Bush is a poisoned chalice. That's why we've had the night watchman so long.'
    'They're a right bunch of Hans Andersens down at Kensington,' said Slider.
    CYNTHIA HARROD-EAGLES *Blood Lines* 1996

Andersonville [Places] A village in south-west Georgia in the United States. It was the site of a notorious Confederate prison, where dreadful conditions led to the death of over 12 000 Union soldiers.

> ➤ A prison with very harsh conditions

Androcles [Lit.] A runaway slave in a story by Aulus Gellius (2nd century), who extracted a thorn from the paw of a lion. The lion later recognized him and refrained from attacking him when he faced it in the arena.

> ➤ Someone who befriends an animal

    I freed it [the turtle] and, like Androcles, found that I had a new best friend.
    DiverNet.com: Travel 2004

Andromeda [Gk Myth.] The daughter of Cepheus and Cassiopeia, king and queen of Ethiopia. Cassiopeia boasted that her daughter was more beautiful even than the *Nereids, or sea-nymphs, which angered *Poseidon. As a punishment, Poseidon sent a sea-monster to destroy the land and agreed to end the punishment only if Andromeda was sacrificed to the sea-monster. Andromeda was therefore chained to a rock and left to her fate. She was saved by Perseus, who flew to her rescue on the winged horse and slew the sea-monster.

> ➤ Someone who is chained or tied to something

    I mean, it's bad enough being forced to appear on a television programme in the first place, let alone chained to a series like Andromeda to a rock.
    JOHN MALCOLM *Into the Vortex* 1996

Andy Capp *See* CAPP.

Angel of Death [Rel.] Death is sometimes personified as a winged messenger, often cloaked and in the form of a skeleton, called the Angel of Death.

> ➤ Someone with a thin, gaunt appearance; also mentioned in the context of death

    Every so often I thought: What if the engine dies on us—what then? And saw a skinny man, like the Angel of Death, watching us from the rag of a cactus's shade.
    PAUL THEROUX *The Old Patagonian Express* 1978

    Some day soon the Angel of Death will sound his trumpet for me.
    BRAM STOKER *Dracula* 1897

angry young man [Lit.] A member of a group of socially conscious British writers of the 1950s, including the playwright John Osborne. The phrase, the title of a book (1951) by Leslie Paul, was used by Osborne in the publicity material for his play *Look Back in Anger* (1956), in which the characteristic views were articulated by the anti-hero Jimmy Porter.

> ➤ A young man who is dissatisfied with and speaks out against existing social and political structures
>
> Eminem is an angry young man with a violent edge.
> *CineScene film reviews* 2002

Animal Farm [Lit.] A fable by George *Orwell (1945) which satirizes Russian Communism as it developed under Stalin. The animals on the farm, led by the pigs, revolt against the farmer and achieve a life of apparent freedom and equality. However, power gradually corrupts their rulers until the ideal of all animals being equal is replaced by the slogan 'all animals are equal but some animals are more equal than others'. By the end of the book the ruling elite have become ruthless dictators and the animals are again living in fear.

> ➤ Mentioned in the context of a lack of equality or a ruthless dictatorship
>
> It's strange that the Animal Farm brand of equality is always unacceptable when players' rights and money matters are concerned, but when it comes to other issues it's fine for blame to be dished out on a 'some are more equal than others' basis.
> *Western People (Co. Mayo)* 2003
>
> Labour conferences now resemble the last chapter of Animal Farm. No one dares speak.
> *The Sunday Times* 2005

Annie *See* ORPHAN ANNIE.

annus horribilis [People] A phrase (literally 'dreadful year' in Latin) used by Queen Elizabeth II in 1992 when she was looking back on a year in which there had been marital difficulties for her children and a fire at Windsor Castle. The phrase was modelled on the phrase *annus mirabilis.

> ➤ A year characterized by many problems
>
> In January, America was facing an annus horribilis mired in a weak, jobless recovery and worry over a war in the Middle East.
> *BusinessWeek Magazine* 2003

annus mirabilis [Lit.] A phrase (literally 'wonderful year' in Latin) used in the title of a 1667 poem by Dryden: *Annus Mirabilis: the year of wonders, 1666*. *See also* ANNUS HORRIBILIS.

> ➤ A year characterized by much success
>
> It is right that the magnificent form of Vijay Singh, who has been enjoying his own annus mirabilis in 2004, should be unstintingly celebrated.
> *The Sunday Times* 2004

another fine mess [Cin.] A catchphrase used by the film comedy duo *Laurel and Hardy. The phrase was typically used by the blustering Ollie as he surveyed the devastation caused by the accident-prone Stan: 'Well, this is another fine mess you've gotten us into.'

> ➤ Used to blame someone for a problem or difficult situation
>
> This is another fine mess the Labour government have gotten us into.
> *Barbelith Underground Forums: Switchboard* 2005

Antaeus [Gk Myth.] A giant, son of the sea-god *Poseidon and the earth-goddess Gaia. He forced all-comers to wrestle with him, and overcame and killed them until he was defeated by Hercules. Antaeus was invincible as long as he touched the earth (enabling him to draw new strength from his mother), but was lifted into the air by *Hercules and crushed to death in his arms.

> ➤ Someone who needs to return home or 'touch base' in order to feel revitalized; someone who is very strong or good at fighting (adjective *Antaean*)

Still I knew I hadn't come out to Westport just to escape the phone and the doorbell. It was more that I needed to touch base, so to speak. Antaeus coming to earth so he might renew his strength.
ROBERT A. CARTER *Written in Blood* 1992

Holding on at Blue Corner doesn't require Antaean strength.
Asian Diver Magazine 2003

Antichrist [Bible] An evil opponent of *Jesus Christ who, according to the New Testament, will ultimately be defeated by Christ at his second coming.

> ➤ An opponent of Christ; an opponent of an accepted doctrine or belief

Every religion, it seems, has its heretics who must be stoned—and as a Sunday Telegraph article put it, Lomborg is the 'anti-Christ of the green religion'.
Spiked Online (2004)

Antigone [Gk Myth.] The daughter of *Oedipus and his mother Jocasta. According to Sophocles' play *Antigone* (441 BC), when blind Oedipus left Thebes, Antigone accompanied him and they travelled eventually to Colonus, near Athens. In their absence, Antigone's brothers Polyneices and Eteocles killed each other in their fight over who would rule Thebes. Jocasta's brother Creon decreed that Polyneices started the fight and ruled that he was not to be buried. Antigone defied his ruling and was herself ordered to be walled up alive in a tomb, whereupon she hanged herself.

> ➤ A beautiful woman; a woman who defies authority

Is she pretty? More—beautiful. A subject for the pen of Nonnus, or the pencil of Zeuxis. Features of all loveliness, radiant with all virtue and intelligence. A face for Antigone. A form at once plump and symmetrical, that...would have been a model for Venus of Cnidos.
THOMAS LOVE PEACOCK *Crotchet Castle* 1831

Who is this Antigone who would stand before the walls of the city and risk public censure?
BARBARA PARKER *Suspicion of Guilt* 1995

Antiphates' wife [Gk Myth.] Antiphates was the chief of the Laestrygonians, a tribe of flesh-eating giants encountered by *Odysseus and his companions on their journey back to Ithaca. According to *Homer's account, his wife was repulsive-looking.

> ➤ An ugly woman

Mandras' mother was one of those perplexing creatures as ugly as the mythical wife of Antiphates, of whom the poet wrote that she was 'a monstrous woman whose ill-aspect struck men with horror'.
LOUIS DE BERNIÈRES *Captain Corelli's Mandolin* 1994

Antisthenes [Philos.] (*c.*445–*c.*365 BC) The founder of the Cynic school of philosophy, whose pupils included *Diogenes. Antisthenes despised art and learning, and the luxuries and comforts of life, and taught that virtue consists in self-control and independence of worldly needs.

> ➤ Someone who extols the virtues of abstinence and self-control

Antony and Cleopatra [Hist.] **Mark Antony** (*c.*83–30 BC), a Roman general and triumvir, met *Cleopatra, the queen of Egypt, and followed her to Egypt, where he stayed with her during the winter of 41–40 BC. After their defeat at the Battle of *Actium in 31 BC, the couple fled back to Egypt. Antony, after being erroneously informed of Cleopatra's suicide, fell on his sword. Cleopatra is said to have committed suicide by being bitten by an asp. Their love affair forms the basis of *Shakespeare's play *Antony and Cleopatra* (1623).

➤ Passionate or tragic lovers

Passion is destructive. It destroyed Antony and Cleopatra, Tristan and Isolde.
W. SOMERSET MAUGHAM *The Razor's Edge* 1944

Anubis [Egypt. Myth.] The Egyptian god of the dead and the protector of tombs, who conducted the souls of the dead to their judgement. Anubis was the son of Osiris and is often represented with the head of a jackal.

➤ Mentioned in the context of death

Aphrodite [Gk Myth.] The goddess of beauty, fertility, and sexual love, identified by the Romans with *Venus. She is supposed to have been born from the sea-foam on the shores of the island of Cythera, and references to Aphrodite sometimes exploit this feature of the myth.

➤ A beautiful woman; a person emerging from the sea

Eighteen he remembered her, and not too tall, with almost masculine features below short chestnut hair: brown eyes, full cheeks and proportionate lips, like Aphrodite his inward eye had commented time and time again, only a little sweeter.
ALAN SILLITOE *The Loneliness of the Long Distance Runner* 1959

Apocalypse [Bible] A name given to the book of Revelation, the last book of the New Testament. The book recounts a divine revelation of the future to St John, including the total destruction of the world: 'And, lo, there was a great earthquake; and the sun became black as sackcloth of hair, and the moon became as blood' (Rev. 6: 12). Following this comes the last battle between the forces of good and evil, the final defeat of *Satan, and the creation of a new heaven and earth. The four agents of destruction, personified in the Four Horsemen of the Apocalypse, are Pestilence, Famine, War, and Death.

➤ An event of great or total destruction; a nuclear holocaust (adjective *Apocalyptic*)

The land about them was laid to waste in a small but extravagant apocalypse; bushes were uprooted and leafless, the ground was littered with little pieces of bridge.
LOUIS DE BERNIÈRES *The War of Don Emmanuel's Nether Parts* 1990

For a year I had lived with the possibility of Liam Brady's transfer to another club in the same way that, in the late fifties and early sixties, American teenagers had lived with the possibility of the impending Apocalypse.
NICK HORNBY *Fever Pitch* 1993

Apollo [Gk Myth.] One of the sons of *Zeus. He came to be associated with the sun and was sometimes given the epithet *Phoebus (the Bright One). Apollo later usurped *Helios' place as the god of the sun who drove the sun's chariot across the sky each day. He had a wide range of other attributes such as music (his instrument was a seven-stringed lyre), medicine, poetic inspiration, archery, prophecy, and pastoral life. Apollo, representing order, reason, and self-discipline, is often contrasted with *Dionysus, representing creativity, sensuality, and lack of inhibition. In art Apollo is represented as an ideal type of male beauty.

➤ A handsome and graceful young man; also mentioned in the context of beautiful music or healing

I do not admire the tones of the concertina, as a rule; but oh! how beautiful the music seemed to us both then—far, far more beautiful than the voice of Orpheus or the lute of Apollo.
JEROME K. JEROME *Three Men in a Boat* 1889

The little priest was not an interesting man to look at, having stubbly brown hair and a round and stolid face. But if he had been as splendid as Apollo no one would have looked at him at that moment.
G. K. CHESTERTON 'The Hammer of God' in *The Innocence of Father Brown* 1911

He had only a nodding acquaintance with the Hippocratic oath, but was somehow aware that he was committed to Apollo the Healer to look upon his teacher in the art of medicine as one of his parents.
JOHN MORTIMER *Paradise Postponed* 1985

Apollyon [Bible] The 'angel of the bottomless pit' described in the book of Revelation (9: 11). In Christian thought he is often identified with the *Devil. In Bunyan's *The *Pilgrim's Progress*, Apollyon is the foul fiend, the personification of evil, who bars Christian's way but is ultimately defeated by the latter's virtue.

> ➢ A devil or evil fiend

  Feeling stronger than ever to meet and subdue her Apollyon, she pinned the note inside her frock, as a shield and a reminder.
  LOUISA M. ALCOTT *Little Women* 1868

Apple of Discord [Gk Myth.] A golden apple marked with the words 'for the fairest' that *Eris, the Greek goddess of discord, threw among the guests at the wedding of Peleus and Thetis, causing disagreement between three goddesses, *Hera, *Athene, and *Aphrodite. The goddesses asked *Paris to judge which of them was the fairest; Aphrodite won the contest by offering him *Helen of Troy as a bribe. His choice of Aphrodite led ultimately to the Trojan War.

> ➢ A cause of disagreement or conflict

  Macedonia…became the apple of discord between the newly forming nation-states that were destined to replace the Ottoman Empire.
  New York Review of Books 1995

Appleseed, Johnny [People] (1774–1847) The nickname of John Chapman, who planted orchards for settlers in Pennsylvania, Ohio, Indiana, and Illinois.

> ➢ Someone who sows, plants or distributes things

  What about the doctor down in Hillsborough? The one with the runaway daughter and the fistful of amphetamines he's scattering around like Johnny goddam Appleseed?
  MAX BYRD *Finders Weepers* 1983

Apples of Sodom *See* DEAD SEA FRUIT.

après moi le déluge [Hist.] A phrase meaning 'After me, the deluge', attributed to Louis XV of France (1710–74).

> ➢ Used in the context of someone leaving a place or job and predicting disaster or chaos after their departure

  If Brown loses the next election, history will judge Blair and his shrinking court as the only true magicians of middle England. Après moi le déluge has a powerful pull: it's only human to need to be missed.
  Guardian Unlimited: Comment is Free column 2006

Arabian Nights, The [Lit.] A collection of exotic and fantastic stories written in Arabic, also called *Arabian Nights' Entertainments* or *The Thousand and One Nights*. The stories are set in the following framework: Shahriyar, the king of Samarkand, has executed all his wives following the wedding night until he marries *Scheherazade, who saves her life by entertaining him with a story each night for 1001 nights. The tales include the stories of *Aladdin, *Ali Baba, and *Sinbad the Sailor.

> ➤ Mentioned in the context of exotic or fabulous stories

> As I talked I was aware that it sounded like some horrible Arabian Nights fairy tale, and yet it was actually happening to us.
> ZANA MUHSEN *Sold* 1991

Arachne [Gk Myth.] A weaver who challenged the goddess *Athene to a weaving contest and wove a piece of cloth representing the loves of the gods. When Athene could find no flaw in the cloth, she refused to admit that Arachne had won the contest, destroying the cloth and changing Arachne into a spider.

> ➤ Mentioned in the context of weaving, or beautiful cloth

Aramis *See* THREE MUSKETEERS.

Arcadia [Places] A mountainous district in the Peloponnese of southern Greece. Arcadia (or Arcady) represents in classical poetic fantasy an idealized region of rural contentment and simplicity. The association of Arcadia with beautiful music may derive from the fact that Arcadia was the home of *Pan, the god who frequented mountains, caves, and lonely places, and invented the pan pipes.

> ➤ A paradise; a place with beautiful music (adjective *Arcadian*)

> It was as though the wood and the strings of the orchestra played Arcadian melodies and in the bass the drums, softly but with foreboding, beat a grim tattoo.
> W. SOMERSET MAUGHAM *The Painted Veil* 1925

> Their little valley in the mountains was densely wooded and well watered, and the guerrillas lived a life of Arcadian simplicity and leisure, only venturing forth when one of them had a good idea about what to blow up next.
> LOUIS DE BERNIÈRES *The War of Don Emmanuel's Nether Parts* 1990

Archers, The [Radio] A radio soap opera described as 'an everyday story of country folk', first broadcast in 1950 by the BBC. The programme portrays the inhabitants of a fictional Midlands village, *Ambridge, and in particular a farming family, the Archers. *The Archers*, now broadcast on Radio 4, is the longest-running radio serial in the world.

> ➤ Used to invoke idyllic rural life

> Soon Davenport described the layout of the village. He spoke of Stonebury in almost reverential terms, characterising it as the epitome of a rural world that was vanishing. The sort of place where you'd half expect the Mayor of Casterbridge to bump into the cast of the Archers and have a chummy discussion about the price of turnips.
> DEXTER DIAS *False Witness* 1995

Archimago [Lit.] The evil enchanter in Edmund Spenser's *The Faerie Queene* (1590, 1596), who symbolizes hypocrisy and can change his appearance to trick and deceive people.

> ➤ Someone who can change their own appearance, or the appearance of objects

> Fiction is like Archimago in *The Faerie Queene*—he can control material reality to disadvantage his opponents.
> GAY CLIFFORD *The transformations of allegory* 1974

Archimedes [Science] (*c.*287–212 BC) A Greek mathematician and inventor. He supposedly made the discovery of the principle of fluid displacement when taking a bath and seeing the water overflow. Archimedes ran naked through the streets shouting 'Eureka! Eureka!' ('I have found it! I have found it!').

> ➤ Someone who experiences a moment of sudden inspiration (adjective *Archimedean*)
>
> Charlie looks at a water sprinkler and has an Archimedes moment: he realizes that the same mathematical principle that allows him to track the path of drops to determine their point of origin could be applied to the distribution of crime scenes on a map. *Clive Thompson, Weblog* 2005
>
> [He] leapt out of bed in high Archimedean excitement when the name entered his head. *London Review of Books* 2004

Arden [Places] The Forest of Arden is the name of a former forest region of north Warwickshire in the English Midlands, the setting of most of *Shakespeare's *As You Like It* (1623).

> ➤ A paradise; a rural idyll
>
> Sheila's home was called the Rectory, and it was in the country, but nowhere like the Forest of Arden. It was in a bleak, poor village in East Anglia, where the red brick rectory was the grandest building after the church. TESSA HADLEY *A Mouthful of Cut Glass* 2005

Arden, Enoch [Lit.] In Tennyson's poem of the same name (1864), Enoch Arden is shipwrecked with two companions. When his fellow survivors die, Enoch patiently waits to be rescued and after ten years a ship finally does appear.

> ➤ Someone who waits patiently for a long time
>
> I knew I could outwait them. I could outwait Enoch Arden if I had to. But it would be nice if, when they finally got sick of waiting, I knew which way they'd exit. ROBERT B. PARKER *Walking Shadow* 1994

are you now or have you ever been … ? [Hist.] A question used by US government officials working for the Permanent Subcommittee of Investigations under Senator Joseph *McCarthy. The committee carried out a campaign against supposed communists, and questioned citizens on their suspected membership of the Communist Party: 'Are you now, or have you ever been, a member of the Communist Party?'

> ➤ Used when suggesting there may be a witch hunt against certain political views
>
> I'm tempted to ask you are you now or have you ever been a liberal? *CNN transcripts: Reliable Sources* 2005

are you sitting comfortably? Then we'll begin [Radio] A phrase used as the introduction to stories on *Listen with Mother*, a BBC radio programme for pre-school children broadcast from 1950 to 1982.

> ➤ Used as a light-hearted introduction to a story or explanation
>
> That's right people, it's a revolution out there of the beer kind, and here's the low-down. So are you sitting comfortably? Good, then we'll begin. *Salient Magazine* 2005

Ares [Gk Myth.] The son of *Zeus and *Hera and the god of war, corresponding to the Roman god *Mars.

> ➤ Mentioned in the context of war

Argonauts [Gk Myth.] The group of heroes who accompanied *Jason on board the ship *Argo* in the quest for the Golden Fleece. The Argonauts included *Hercules, *Orpheus, *Theseus, *Nestor, and *Castor and Pollux.

> ➤ People who embark on a long sea voyage; people who meet adventures at sea

> 'Come along, Captain Robinson,' he shouted, with a sort of bullying deference under the rim of the old man's hat; the Holy Terror gave a submissive little jump. The ghost of a steamer was waiting for them. Fortune on that fair isle! They made a curious pair of Argonauts.
> JOSEPH CONRAD *Lord Jim* 1900

Argus **1.** [Gk Myth.] A giant with 100 eyes, who never slept with more than one pair of eyes at a time, so he was able to keep watch constantly. After *Hermes had killed Argus on behalf of *Zeus, *Hera took the eyes to deck the peacock's tail.

> ➤ Someone who is acutely vigilant or observant

> Woe betide the six-foot hero who escorts Mrs Proudie to her pew in red plush breeches, if he slips away to the neighbouring beer shop, instead of falling into the back seat appropriated to his use. Mrs Proudie has the eyes of Argus for such offenders.
> ANTHONY TROLLOPE *Barchester Towers* 1857

2. [Gk Myth.] The craftsman who built the ship *Argo*, on which *Jason and the Argonauts voyaged to recover the Golden Fleece.

> ➤ A skilled craftsman or woodworker

Ariadne [Gk Myth.] The daughter of King *Minos of Crete and Pasiphae. She fell in love with *Theseus and helped him escape from the labyrinth of the *Minotaur by giving him a ball of thread, which he unravelled as he went in and followed back to find his way out again after killing the Minotaur.

> ➤ Ariadne's string is mentioned in the context of guiding someone back the way they have come

> You can head off and explore guided by intuition, then hit the 'home' button, which, like Ariadne's ball of string, guides you back to your start point.
> *icon magazine online* 2005

Ariel [Shakes.] A fairy or spirit in Shakespeare's play *The Tempest* (1623), who has no physical form or substance and is therefore divorced from human emotions.

> ➤ Something that has no clear shape or form

> She had never shown any repugnance to his tenderness, but such response as it evoked was remote and Ariel-like.
> EDITH WHARTON *The Custom of the Country* 1913

Aristeides the Just (Aristides, Aristedes) [Hist.] (d. *c.*468 BC) A Greek military commander and politician who became one of the rulers of Athens. After disagreements with another prominent politician, a vote was taken and he was banished temporarily from Athens. One citizen supposedly remarked that he was voting against Aristeides even though he did not know who he was, because he was sick of always hearing him called 'the Just'.

> ➤ Someone who people turn against because they are praised too much

> She's too good, too kind, too clever, too learned, too accomplished, too everything. She's too complete, in a word. I confess to you that she acts on my nerves and that I feel about her a good deal as that intensely human Athenian felt about Aristedes the Just.
> HENRY JAMES *Portrait of a Lady* 1881

Aristophanes [Lit.] (*c.*448–380 BC) An Athenian comic playwright whose plays include *The Clouds, The Wasps,* and *Lysistrata.*

> A great comedian or comic writer

> What might be tragedy if Sophocles got hold of it, is funny in the four or five daily frames of the funnies. While the funnies live, Aristophanes is never quite dead.
> ROBERTSON DAVIES *The Cunning Man* 1994

Aristotle [Philos.] (384–322 BC) A Greek philospher and scientist, who established the inductive method of reasoning, maintaining that systematic logic, based upon syllogism, was the essential method of all rational enquiry and hence the foundation of all knowledge.

> A philosopher; someone who thinks in a rational and logical way (adjective *Aristotelian*)

> 'I don't understand why you denigrate yourself so much,' Charlotte said in mock desperation. 'You're a combination of Getty and Aristotle, compared to most of the management this lot will have encountered.'
> REBECCA TINSLEY *Settlement Day* 1994

> [It is] a scandal so shameful that it makes the justification for invading Iraq sound like an exercise in Aristotelian logic.
> *Spiked Online* 2006

Ark [Bible] The book of Genesis relates how God warned *Noah that he was going to send a great flood to destroy the world and instructed him to build the Ark, a huge ship, to save his family and a pair of every species of animal and bird.

> Something 'out of the Ark' is very antiquated or out of date

> Then he sat down near his brief-case on the far side of a scarred oak table that came out of the Ark. Noah bought it second-hand.
> RAYMOND CHANDLER *The Long Goodbye* 1953

Ark of the Covenant [Bible] A box containing tablets giving the law as revealed to *Moses by God. It was considered sacred by the *Israelites, and was carried by them on their wanderings.

> An extremely sacred object

> They took the big pot round with them from job to job, it was their Ark of the Covenant almost.
> GWENDOLINE BUTLER *A Dark Coffin* 1995

Armada [Hist.] A Spanish naval invasion force sent against England in 1588 by Philip II of Spain. It was defeated by the English fleet and almost completely destroyed by storms off the Hebrides.

> A large fleet of warships or other vehicles; a large group of angry or bellicose people

> A massive armada of Federation and Klingon ships goes to retake DS9.
> *DVD Verdict* 2003

Armageddon [Bible] The site of the last battle between the forces of good and evil before the Day of *Judgement, according to the book of Revelation.

> A destructive conflict on a huge scale

> He has read somewhere that eighty per cent of all aircraft accidents occur at either take-off or landing....By taking the non-stop polar flight to London, in preference to the two stage journey via New York, Zapp reckons that he has reduced his chances of being caught in such an Armageddon by fifty per cent.
> DAVID LODGE *Changing Places* 1975

Armstrong, Neil [Hist.] (b. 1930) The American astronaut who was the first to walk on the lunar surface in July 1969 as part of the Apollo 11 mission. As he set foot on the surface, he spoke the famous words, 'That's one small step for (a) man, one giant leap for mankind.'

➤ Someone who takes a step forward into the unknown; someone wearing a spacesuit

Hazel felt herself standing at the precipice of a whole new way of thinking. She felt like Neil Armstrong just about to take that one small step.
GABRIEL HARTNELL *The Compendium* 2004

I felt like a cross between Neil Armstrong and the Michelin Man.
Fast Company Magazine 2004

Arnold, Benedict [Hist.] (1741–1801) An American general in the American Revolution, chiefly remembered as a traitor who in 1780 plotted, with the British army major John André, to betray the American post at West Point to the British. When the plot was discovered, Arnold escaped and later fought on the side of the British.

➤ A traitor who changes sides during a war or conflict; someone who betrays their friends or countrymen

He had carried Mark O'Meara's clubs in the 1997 matches before switching to the young Spaniard. On an alcoholic high after his country's win, a burly American fan no doubt saw him as a golfing Benedict Arnold.
The Guardian 1999

Around the World in Eighty Days [Lit.] The title of a novel (1873) by Jules Verne. The novel tells the story of a trip around the world by Phileas *Fogg and his valet Passepartout, in which they use many different forms of transport, including train, boat, sledge, and elephant.

➤ Mentioned in the context of a round-the-world trip

A team of adventurers led by Irish woman Caroline Casey, who are going Around The World in Eighty Ways to raise funds for the Jack and Jill Children's Foundation, will be in Carlow on Thursday.
Carlow Nationalist 2002

Arsenic and Old Lace [Theatre; Cin.] A play by the American playwright Joseph Kesselring, written in 1939. It is perhaps better known through the 1944 film adaptation starring Cary Grant. The plot, a black comedy, centres around two elderly spinsters who have taken to murdering lonely old men by poisoning them with a glass of home-made elderberry wine laced with arsenic, strychnine, and 'just a pinch of cyanide'.

➤ Mentioned in the context of a genteel elderly lady with a slightly sinister air

Aunt Lil's house was filled with antiques, and there is a touch of the air of Arsenic and Old Lace about Volk's portrait of her.
Sunday Business Post 2002

Artemis [Gk Myth.] The virgin goddess of chastity, the hunt, and the moon. She was believed to protect virgins and women in childbirth. A huntress, she was often depicted with a bow and arrows, and noted for her strength and speed. The Romans called her *Diana.

➤ A beautiful and innocent young woman

The purity of his nature, his freedom from the grosser passions, his scrupulous delicacy, had never been fully understood by Grace till this strange self-sacrifice in lonely juxtaposition to her own person was revealed. The perception of it added something that was little short of reverence to the deep affection for him of a woman who, herself, had more of Artemis than of Aphrodite in her constitution.
THOMAS HARDY *The Woodlanders* 1887

Artful Dodger [Lit.] The nickname of Jack Dawkins, a clever young pickpocket and a member of *Fagin's gang of thieves in Dickens's *Oliver Twist* (1837–8). He is known for quick-wittedness and his ability to get himself out of trouble without ever being caught.

> ➤ A pickpocket; a clever criminal who avoids getting caught

Dozens of little Artful Dodgers hustling the white men who invaded their parents' country.
ARMISTEAD MAUPIN *Babycakes* 1984

In these supposedly rational times, the spectacle of someone repeatedly engaging in sexual behaviour which is dangerously risky, and, potentially, exceedingly self-destructive, provokes many people to resort to some psychopathological explanation. Many see President Clinton as an Artful Dodger who just got caught.
The Independent 1998

Arthur, King [Arth. Leg.] Historically perhaps a 5th- or 6th-century Romano-British chieftain or general, in legend the king of Britain who presided over the knights of the *Round Table at *Camelot. According to legends, after being fatally wounded by his nephew Mordred, the dying king was borne away to the island of *Avalon, where he was buried. In some versions of the legend it is said that Arthur is not dead but sleeping, ready to awaken and return in the hour of Britain's need. Arthurian legend is associated with the romantic notion of chivalry and courtly love.

> ➤ Mentioned in the context of heroic and chivalrous deeds; someone who is sleeping and will wake to help or rescue others (adjective *Arthurian*)

They are drunk with the knightly love one reads about in the Arthurian legends—knight and rescued lady.
LAWRENCE DURRELL *Clea* 1960

Like King Arthur, see, she wasn't really dead; just sleeping (around) till her people felt in need of her once more. And now she's back.
JULIE BURCHILL 'The Phantom Nympho Rides Again' in *Sex and Sensibility* 1989

ashes to ashes, dust to dust [Rel.] A phrase from the burial service in the *Book of Common Prayer*: 'we therefore commit this body to the ground, earth to earth, ashes to ashes, dust to dust; in sure and certain hope of the Resurrection to eternal life.'

> ➤ Used in the context of the inevitability of death, or the transience of life

All set for an ecologically friendly burial in the shallow grave of your choice. Back garden? No problem, you'll be compost in a year. Ashes to ashes, dust to dust: something from which no amount of plastic surgery, boob lifts, lipo and Botox is going to save any of us.
Scotland on Sunday 2004

Ashtoreth (Ashtaroth) [Bible] The name used in the Bible for the Phoenician goddess *Astarte, the goddess of sexuality and sexual love. Worship of her is condemned in the Bible, and in Christianity she was associated with sexual promiscuity.

> ➤ A loose woman

The bailiff was pointed out to Gabriel, who, checking the palpitation with his breast at discovering that this Ashtoreth of strange report was only a modification of Venus, the well-known and admired, retired with him to talk over the necessary preliminaries of hiring.
THOMAS HARDY *Far from the Madding Crowd* 1874

Aspasia [People] A famous Greek courtesan, daughter of Axiochus of Miletus. She came to Athens, where she acquired fame by her beauty, culture, and wit. She so captivated *Pericles that he made her his lifelong companion.

> A courtesan; a loose woman

  The Athenian virgins…grew up into wives who stayed at home…and looked after the husband's dinner. And what was the consequence of that, sir? that they were such very insipid persons that the husband would not go home to eat his dinner, but preferred the company of some Aspasia or Lais.
  THOMAS LOVE PEACOCK *Crotchet Castle* 1831

Asphodel [Gk Myth.] The Plain of Asphodel is described in *Homer's *Odyssey as the part of *Hades where the ghosts of the dead lead a vague, unsubstantial life, a shadowy continuation of their former life where 'the soul hovers to and fro'.

> A lonely and mournful place

  It was dreadful to be thus dissevered from his dryad, and sent howling back to a Barchester pandemonium just as the nectar and ambrosia were about to descend on the fields of asphodel.
  ANTHONY TROLLOPE *Barchester Towers* 1857

Assisi *See* FRANCIS OF ASSISI.

Astaire, Fred [Dance] (1899–1987) An American actor, singer, and dancer. His long-standing dance partner was Ginger *Rogers, and together they made many successful film musicals including *Top Hat* (1935) and *Shall We Dance?* (1937).

> An elegant dancer

  He was taller than me and more graceful by far—had a Fred Astaire kind of elegance that my brother and I had totally missed out on.
  ANNE TYLER *A Patchwork Planet* 1998

Astarte [Bible] A Phoenician goddess of fertility and sexual love, corresponding to the Babylonian *Ishtar, the Egyptian *Isis, the Greek *Aphrodite, and others. She is referred to in the Bible as *Ashtoreth or Ashtaroth, and worship of her is linked with worship of *Baal and similarly condemned: 'And the children of Israel did evil again in the sight of the Lord, and served Baalim, and Ashtaroth' (Judg. 10: 6). In Christianity, she became associated with sexual promiscuity.

> A loose woman

Atalanta [Gk Myth.] A huntress who was extremely fleet-footed. She had been warned against marriage by the Delphic oracle (*see* DELPHI) and so refused to marry any man unless he first defeated her in a race. If the runner lost, he was put to death.

> A woman who is a fast runner; a woman who races against men

  Even in the early days when she had lived with her parents in a ragged outskirt of Apex, and hung on the fence with Indiana Frusk, the freckled daughter of the plumber 'across the way', she had cared little for dolls or skipping ropes, and still less for the riotous games in which the loud Indiana played Atalanta to all the boyhood of the quarter.
  EDITH WHARTON *The Custom of the Country* 1913

Athene (Pallas Athene) [Gk Myth.] The Greek goddess of wisdom, of war, and of handicrafts. She corresponds to the Roman goddess *Minerva. Athene is said to have sprung fully grown and fully armed from the brain of her father Zeus. She is usually represented in sculpture and paintings in armour.

➤ Mentioned in the context of something that appears fully formed

Darwin was a passionate anti-saltationist, and this led him to stress, over and over again, the extreme gradualness of the evolutionary changes that he was proposing. The reason is that saltation, to him, meant what I have called the Boeing 747 macromutation. It meant the sudden calling into existence, like Pallas Athene from the head of Zeus, of brand-new complex organs at a single stroke of the genetic wand.
RICHARD DAWKINS *The Blind Watchmaker* 1986

Athos *See* THREE MUSKETEERS.

Atlantis [Gk Myth.] A legendary island continent in the ocean west of the *Pillars of Hercules. According to *Plato in the *Timaeus*, Atlantis was beautiful and prosperous and ruled part of Europe and Africa, but following volcanic eruptions it was swallowed up by the sea.

➤ A place that has disappeared

Under the clouds out there it's as still, and lost, as Atlantis.
THOMAS PYNCHON *Gravity's Rainbow* 1973

Atlas [Gk Myth.] One of the Titans, punished for rebelling against *Zeus by being made to support the heavens on his shoulders. The image of Atlas holding up the sky, or sometimes the earth itself, is a common one in art and literature.

➤ Someone who is forced to bear a heavy burden

I am like a spy who has signed a covenant of perpetual secrecy, I am like someone who is the only person in the world that knows the truth and yet is forbidden to utter it. And this truth weighs more than the universe, so that I am like Atlas bowed down forever beneath a burden that cracks the bones and solidifies the blood.
LOUIS DE BERNIÈRES *Captain Corelli's Mandolin* 1994

Atlas, Charles [People] (1894–1974) The name adopted by the body-builder Angelo Siciliano, a '98-pound weakling' who became 'the world's strongest man'. The advertisements for his body-building course carried the famous slogan 'You too can have a body like mine'.

➤ A strong, muscular man

In one photograph a man stands on a beach, holding in his stomach, puffing his chest out, and rippling his biceps à la Charles Atlas.
Journal of the Australian Association of Writing Programs 2004

Atreus [Gk Myth.] The progenitor of a family known as the House of Atreus. His brother *Thyestes laid a curse on the family after Atreus had tricked him into eating the flesh of Thyestes' own sons at a feast. The family was subsequently involved in mutual murder and betrayal for several generations.

➤ Mentioned in the context of a family that seems cursed with misfortune

It is also possible to view Williams as a tragic figure, cursed like the house of Atreus or Kennedy.
Observer sport monthly 2004

Attila the Hun [Hist.] (406–53) The king of the Huns who, having attacked and devastated much of the Eastern Roman Empire in 445–50, invaded the Western Empire but was defeated by the Romans and the Visigoths in 451. He and his army, noted for its savagery, were the terror of Europe during his lifetime, and Attila later came to be called the Scourge of God.

➤ A cruel or ruthless leader; a ruthless empire-builder; someone who causes destruction or devastation

Colonel Gadaffi's metamorphosis from dictator to sensitive writer is as incongruous as Attila the Hun revealing a passion for Buddhist theology.
The Observer 1996

To some, Bill Gates is the Attila the Hun of computer software; if he can't buy it, he takes it by force of research and development.
Chief Executive 2002

Aucassin and Nicolette [Lit.] The subjects of a popular late 13th-century French romance. Aucassin, son of the count of Beaucaire, falls in love with Nicolette, a Saracen captive. They endure a number of misfortunes and adventures but are eventually reunited and married.

> Devoted and faithful lovers

'I repeat, madame, something has occurred.' 'Peter is away,' said Harriet. 'Is that what your gimlet eyes have discovered?' 'But you trust him, non? You expect him back, like the faithful Aucassin?' 'Well, yes,' said Harriet, 'I do.'
DOROTHY L. SAYERS and JILL PATON *Thrones, Dominations* 1998

Augean stables [Gk Myth.] The stables of the king of Augeas, which housed a very large herd of oxen and had never been cleaned out. Hercules undertook the task of cleaning them as one of his twelve labours. He achieved this task by diverting two rivers, the Alpheus and the Peneus, through the stables.

> Mentioned in the context of cleaning up a mess or putting right a corrupt or morally unacceptable situation

I am convinced we need fundamental constitutional reform at all levels. We must cleanse the Augean stables at Westminster of the mess of patronage and special interests which do so much to discredit democracy.
EMMA NICHOLSON *The Observer* 1995

Augustine, St [People] (354–430) One of the early Christian leaders and writers known as the Fathers of the Church. He is often remembered for praying in his *Confessions* (*c.*400): 'Give me chastity and continency, but not yet.'

> Mentioned in the context of something good that is promised in the future, but not yet delivered

The computers, we were told, would be able to swiftly and easily examine all ballots, rather than just a sample, and give a full and fair distribution of votes. However, this is true only in theory. Like St Augustine and virtue it is a case of 'yes but not yet'.
Limerick Leader 2004

Aunt Chloe [Lit.] In Harriet Beecher Stowe's *Uncle Tom's Cabin* (1851), *Uncle Tom, a Negro slave, is about to be sold to a slave trader and separated from his family. When his wife Chloe protests at how unfair this is, Uncle Tom urges her to look on the bright side: 'Let's think on our marcies!' Aunt Chloe then repeats this advice to their children.

> Someone who urges others to look on the bright side

We needed that lesson, and we won't forget it. If we do, you just say to us, as old Chloe did in Uncle Tom, 'Tink ob yer marcies, chillen! Tink ob yer marcies!'
LOUISA M. ALCOTT *Little Women* 1868

Aurora [Rom. Myth.] The goddess of the dawn. From the early 18th century, the word has been used to designate a natural electrical phenomenon which gives rise to streamers of reddish or greenish light in the sky, known as 'aurora borealis' or 'northern lights', and 'aurora australis' or 'southern lights'.

> A way of referring to the dawn

Auschwitz [Hist.] A concentration camp established by the Nazis in 1940 near the town of Oświęcim (Auschwitz) in German-occupied Poland in the Second World War. Initially, Poles were sent there, then gypsies and prisoners of war, and finally European Jews, many of whom were sent to the gas chambers.

> ➤ A place of unimaginable horror

His round face stayed angry, even after he restored the smile. 'But I understand. The cognitive dissonance must be painful for you. Coming here expecting Pleasure Island and getting Auschwitz.'
JONATHAN KELLERMAN *The Web* 1995

Austerlitz [Hist.] A battle which took place in 1805 near the village of Austerlitz (now Slavkov in the Czech Republic). It was a victory for Napoleon *Bonaparte but a serious defeat for the allied Austrians and Russians.

> ➤ A decisive defeat

If Stansted was O'Leary 's Austerlitz, Charleroi could be, by his own admission, his Waterloo.
Sunday Business Post 2003

Autolycus [Gk Myth.] A cunning thief who stole animals from the herds of *Sisyphus. He had the power to change the appearance of whatever beasts he stole and so, although Sisyphus noticed that his own herds were growing smaller and those of Autolycus were growing larger, he was unable to make any accusations. Autolycus is also the name of a character in *Shakespeare's *Winter's Tale* (1623), a light-fingered rogue, 'a snapper-up of unconsidered trifles'.

> ➤ Someone who steals things without others noticing

At home with his partner, Marianne, in the Fife village of Kingskettle, he is a sort of Autolycus of the accent, a snapper-up of unconsidered trifles—words used by the locals like, say, 'scart' for scratch.
Scotland on Sunday 2002

Avalon [Arth. Leg.] The place to which *Arthur was conveyed after his death.

> ➤ A paradise; a place of peace and contentment

When Melanie just can't stand the insanity of her everyday life, she goes to her Avalon—a place of peace and reflection.
FFWD Weekly 2001

Avenger of Blood (Revenger of Blood) [Bible] A man in ancient Israel who had the right to avenge the death of one of his kinsmen. The practice is mentioned several times in the Bible, for example in Numbers (35: 19): 'The revenger of blood himself shall slay the murderer; when he meeteth him, he shall slay him.'

> ➤ Someone who kills a person to avenge another death

[They] footed it as if the Avenger of Blood had been behind them.
SIR WALTER SCOTT *The Bride of Lammermoor* 1819

Avenging Angel [Bible] The Angels of Vengeance, or Avenging Angels, were the first angels created by God. Traditionally there are twelve Avenging Angels, and they are sometimes associated with the role of punishing wrongdoers.

> ➤ Someone who kills another person in vengeance, or for a righteous cause

He thought of himself as an heroic avenging angel of death, not as a wandering boy with a rifle that would bruise his shoulder every time he fired it.
LOUIS DE BERNIÈRES *The War of Don Emmanuel's Nether Parts* 1990

Avernus [Gk Myth.] A lake near Cumae and Naples. Close to the lake was the cave through which *Aeneas descended to the underworld. The name means literally 'Without Birds', from the belief that its poisonous waters would cause any bird that attempted to fly over it to fall into the water.

➤ A lonely or desolate place

Now London has become her Avernus, and she herself has become like Eliot's Sybil of Cumae, suspended in a cage, longing to die.
Hudson Review 2003

Aveyron *See* WILD BOY OF AVEYRON.

Azrael [Rel.] The angel who, in Jewish and Islamic mythology, severed the soul from the body at death.

➤ Mentioned in the context of death

Baal [Bible] The most important god in the pantheon of the Canaanites. He was the god of storms, associated with the rain that alleviated drought and brought agricultural fertility. There is considerable opposition to the worship of Baal in some books of the Old Testament, particularly from the prophets, such as *Elijah and *Jehu. In Christianity, Baal has been seen as a demon and a ruler in Hell.

> ➤ A devil
>
> There, down tubes which fed into the cellar, it was dropped into the sighing vent of an incinerator which sat like evil Baal in a dark corner.
> RAY BRADBURY *There Will Come Soft Rains* 1950

Baba Yaga [Leg. & Folk.] A witch in Russian folklore who lives in a house that stands on chicken legs, flies about in a mortar using a pestle for an oar, and eats children.

> ➤ An ugly woman
>
> My friends weren't lying, my date really did look like Baba Yaga.
> *City Pages: The Online News and Arts Weekly of the Twin Cities* 2004

Babbitt [Lit.] The main character in a 1922 novel of the same name by the American author Sinclair Lewis. George Follansbee Babbitt is a prosperous real-estate agent who lives a dull, routine life in a fictional small town and supports traditional American small-town values.

> ➤ Someone who is unimaginative and conforms to traditional values (noun *Babbittry*)
>
> It was President Woodrow Wilson, she shows, who first advocated 'a global traffic in values as well as commodities,' with little regard for sovereignty, and the Rotary Club that boasted the virtues of 'Babbittry' to its European members.
> *Foreign Affairs magazine* 2005

Babel [Bible] According to the book of Genesis, there was a time near the beginning of the world when all men lived in one place and all spoke the same language. They built a tall tower, the Tower of Babel, in an attempt to reach up to Heaven. On seeing the tower, God was concerned that man was becoming too powerful and so decided to thwart him by introducing different languages. He therefore went down to 'confound their language, that they may not understand one another's speech' (Gen. 11: 7). Once different languages were introduced and men no longer understood one another, the building of the tower stopped.

> ➤ Used in the context of a noisy confusion of voices or a chaotic mixture of languages
>
> The crew's mess on board the *Kronos* is a Tower of Babel of English, French, Filipino, Danish, and German.
> PETER HØEG *Miss Smilla's Feeling for Snow* 1992
>
> Then the bedlam of Ellis Island—a maelstrom of people and bundles and a babel of tongues.
> *DVD Verdict* 2003

'Babes in the Wood' [Fairy tales] The title of a story about two infants, brother and sister, who are abandoned in a wood by their uncle, who wants their property. The children die and a robin covers them with leaves. The wicked uncle loses his own sons and his property, and dies in jail.

> Abandoned children; young, unsophisticated innocents who are likely to be taken advantage of; people who are lost and unable to find their way

Everything looked strange and different in the darkness. We began to understand the sufferings of the Babes in the Wood.
JEROME K. JEROME *Three Men in a Boat* 1889

He could not get away from the fact that if he had been brought up as she had they would have been no more fit to find their way about than the Babes in the Wood.
EDITH WHARTON *The Age of Innocence* 1920

These individuals may be babes in the woods, but their sincerity and eagerness to please makes them so lovable that people rarely take too much advantage of them.
Pattaya Mail 2002

Babylon [Hist.] An ancient city in Mesopotamia which lay on the Euphrates and was first settled around 3000 BC. Hammurabi made Babylon the capital of the Babylonian Empire and it became renowned for its grandeur and decadence.

> A place or group that is considered to be materialistic, corrupt, and associated with the pursuit of sensual pleasure (adjective *Babylonian*)

One subset of the disaffected youth of '68, disillusioned with the reimposition of Gaullist order, simply fled the modern Babylon of Paris and set up communes in the hidden valleys of the Cevennes.
Environmental History 2000

Bacchanalia [Gk Myth.] The annual feast and celebrations in honour of the Greek god *Dionysus, also called *Bacchus. The celebrations were characterized by wild orgies and drunkenness.

> Used to refer to drunkenness, or wild or drunken partying (adjective *Bacchanalian*)

Jagger runs and cycles; Aerosmith singer Steve Tylor has banned sugar, salt, wheat, yeast, fat, red meat and alcohol from his band's menus. Even the Grateful Dead while publicly burning the Bacchanalian flame at both ends, were secretly calorie watching.
The Independent 1997

Wine slopped from the urns he held in each hand as he shouted from the bottom of his lungs, 'Let the Bacchanalia begin!'
Modern Drunkard Magazine Online 2005

Bacchante (Maenad) [Gk Myth.] A female devotee of the cult of *Dionysus, also known as *Bacchus. The Bacchantes took part in frenzied, orgiastic, and ecstatic celebrations at the festivals of Dionysus.

> A wild, drunken woman

The wonderfully lush Carrie Ahern has a mysterious role—echoing Latsky, being manipulated like a doll, dancing like a bacchante.
The Village Voice 2003

Bacchus [Gk Myth.] Another name for the Greek god *Dionysus, the son of *Zeus and Semele. Originally a god of the fertility of nature, associated with wild and ecstatic religious rites, in later traditions he is a god of wine who loosens inhibitions and inspires creativity in music and poetry.

> Used to invoke orgiastic or drunken revelry (adjective *Bacchic*)

> She was shaken by a Bacchic and bawdy mood.
> GRAHAM GREENE *Brighton Rock* 1938

> Why not snack at Snack Taverna? Put a little Bacchus back into your life.
> *Amateur Gourmet* 2005

Bach, Johann Sebastian [Mus.] (1685–1750) A German composer and organist, the outstanding representative of German baroque music. Bach was a master of counterpoint and developed the fugue form (in which a succession of parts or voices are interwoven) to a high art.

> ➤ Mentioned in the context of complex musical patterns

> The music of our Lord's skin sliding over His flesh!—more exact than the fugues of Bach.
> NATHANAEL WEST *The Dream Life of Balso Snell* 1931

Bacon, Francis [Philos.] (1561–1626) A philosopher and essayist, best known as the author of *The Advancement of Learning* (1605) and many essays.

> ➤ Mentioned as an exemplar of a beautiful, often epigrammatic, English writing style

> For his orations convulsed his hearers and his contributions were excellent, being patriotic, classical, comical, or dramatic, but never sentimental. Jo regarded them as worthy of Bacon, Milton, or Shakespeare.
> LOUISA M. ALCOTT *Little Women* 1868

Baggins, Bilbo [Lit.] The main character in *The Hobbit* (1937) by J. R. R. *Tolkien. He is a hobbit, a member of an imaginary race of small, hairy-footed, burrow-dwelling people. Accompanied by a party of dwarves and the wizard Gandalf, Bilbo travels a great distance and experiences many adventures before finally winning his share of the dwarves' lost treasure. He is a somewhat reluctant adventurer, often wishing himself back in his nice, warm hobbit-hole. During his adventures he acquires a magic ring that confers invisibility on the wearer.

> ➤ Someone who avoids adventure and prefers a quiet life; someone who has the power to become invisible

> 'I'll call myself Mary,' Alison said, loudly enough to be sure of his hearing. 'That sounds nice and innocuous.' 'No one would suspect a meek, mild Mary of any skullduggery,'... It would be like wearing a cloak of invisibility or Bilbo Baggins' stolen magic ring.
> SUSAN KELLY *Hope Will Answer* 1992

> Like Bilbo Baggins the [Conservative] party has preferred to settle among the hobbits and dream of times past, rather than take the field against Labour's orcs.
> *The Sunday Times* 2005

Baggins, Frodo [Lit.] One of the central characters of *The Lord of the Rings* (1954–5) by J. R. R. *Tolkien. He is a hobbit, a small hairy-footed creature who lives in a burrow. Frodo ultimately succeeds in his quest to destroy the One Ring.

> ➤ Someone on a difficult or dangerous quest

> The England captain could lead his players there to stare at the empty space. Youngsters could be taken there and be inspired by the Frodo-like challenge of bringing them [the Ashes] home.
> *The Guardian* 1997

Baiae [Places] A small town on the Bay of Naples with warm springs containing minerals which became a fashionable resort for the ancient Romans.

> ➤ Mentioned in the context of healthy-looking people (adjective *Baian*)

That Royal port and watering-place, if truly mirrored in the minds of the health-folk, must have combined, in a charming and indescribable manner, a Carthaginian bustle of building with Tarentine luxuriousness and a Baian health and beauty.
THOMAS HARDY *The Return of the Native* 1880

Balaam's ass [Bible] Balaam, the prophet, was travelling with his donkey when an angel appeared and stood in the path of the donkey. The donkey, on seeing the angel, moved aside from the path, whereupon Balaam beat the donkey and forced it back onto the path. The angel again stood in the donkey's path, and the donkey again turned aside and was beaten. The third time the angel stood in front of the donkey it lay down and Balaam again beat it. 'And the Lord opened the mouth of the ass, and she said unto Balaam, What have I done unto thee, that thou hast smitten me these three times?' (Num. 22: 28). Balaam replied that the donkey had mocked him, whereupon the donkey pleaded that it had never done anything like this before. 'Then the Lord opened the eyes of Balaam, and he saw the angel of the Lord standing in the way, and his sword drawn in his hand: and he bowed down his head, and fell flat on his face' (Num. 22: 31).

➢ Mentioned in the context of a very surprising event

With one accord, aghast, they turned and stared at her. They felt as Balaam must have felt when his ass broke into speech.
SOMERSET MAUGHAM *The World Over* 1951

Balboa, Vasco Núñez de [People] (1475–1519) A Spanish explorer who became the first European to sight the Pacific Ocean, in 1513.

➢ Mentioned in the context of someone who feels awestruck by the sight of the sea or a landscape

At last he reached the summit, and a wide and novel prospect burst upon him with an effect almost like that of the Pacific upon Balboa's gaze.
THOMAS HARDY *Far from the Madding Crowd* 1874

Balder [Norse Myth.] The son of *Odin. Beautiful and popular, he was the god of light. When Balder had a dream that he would die, his mother Frigga exacted a promise from all things that they would not harm him, but she overlooked the mistletoe. *Loki tricked the blind god Hodur into throwing a branch of mistletoe at Balder, and this killed him.

➢ Someone who has one point of weakness

Bambi [Cin.] The title of a Walt *Disney animated film, first released in 1942 and rereleased in 1947, about a young deer growing up in the forest whose mother is shot by a hunter. In a memorable scene, Bambi, the young deer, learns how to stand on the ice of a pond in wintertime.

➢ Someone struggling to remain upright on a slippery surface; someone naive and gentle; someone who looks lost and alone

Looking a little like Bambi on roller skates, she is not the same player who ambushed Serena Williams in SW19 last summer.
Scotland on Sunday 2005

Banquo's ghost [Shakes.] In *Macbeth* (1623), the victorious Scottish generals *Macbeth and Banquo meet three witches who prophesy that Macbeth will be king and that Banquo's heirs will sit on the throne. Macbeth murders the king and takes his crown and then, in an attempt to defeat the prophecy, hires three murderers to kill Banquo and his son. At a banquet held by the Macbeths, Macbeth sees the ghost of Banquo in his own place None of the guests present can see the ghost, but Macbeth is so distressed that Lady *Macbeth brings the banquet to a hasty close.

> Someone from the past who is present at an event and reminds a person of their past crimes

Hovering like Banquo's ghost around the conference will be the former Chancellor Kenneth Clarke.
The Observer 1997

Barbie° The name of a doll made by Mattell Inc. in the form of a conventionally attractive American young woman. A companion male doll is called Ken.

> A young woman who is attractive but lacks intelligence or individuality

'It's very nice to see you…again,' she replied feebly in her honeyed drawl. With her smooth, peachy makeup, she looked remarkably like a Barbie doll.
SPARKLE HAYTER *What's a Girl Gotta Do?* 1994

Opposite him, across the sweeping curve of the presentation console, were two Ken-and-Barbie-style presenters of indeterminate age.
BEN ELTON *Popcorn* 1996

Bardolph [Shakes.] One of *Falstaff's companions in *Henry IV* and *Henry V*. His bright red nose inspires Falstaff to say to him: 'Thou art our admiral, thou bearest the lantern in the poop, but 'tis in the nose of thee; thou art the Knight of the Burning Lamp' (*1 Henry IV*).

> Someone with a large red nose

If beauty is a matter of fashion, how is it that wrinkled skin, grey hair, hairy backs and Bardolph-like noses have never been 'in fashion'?
Frontiers: Penguin Popular Science 1994

Bardot, Brigitte [Cin.] (b. Camille Javal, 1934) A French actress whose appearance in the film *And God Created Woman* (1956) established her reputation as an international sex symbol. After retiring from acting she became an active supporter of animal welfare and of the cause of endangered animal species.

> A beautiful woman; someone who loves animals, especially cats

France and style go hand in hand, like Brigitte Bardot and cats.
Sunday Herald 2001

Barmecide's Feast [Lit.] In *The *Arabian Nights*, a prince of Baghdad named Barmecide invites Schacabac, a poor beggar, to dine with him. The table is set with ornate plates and dishes, but all are empty. When, to test Schacabac's humour, Barmecide asks his guest how he finds the food, and offers him illusory wine, Schacabac declines, pretending to be already drunk, and knocks Barmecide down. Relenting, Barmecide gives Schacabac a proper meal.

> Something, especially food or hospitality, that is in fact illusory or unreal

For if all these experiences relieved the boredom of a well-brought-up young lady's life in Mayfair, they nonetheless proved a Barmecide feast. Bell hungered for a more substantial life.
Hudson Review 2001

Barnum, Phineas Taylor [People] (1810–91) An American showman, businessman and entertainer, who billed his circus, opened in 1871, as 'The Greatest Show on Earth'. Ten years later he founded the Barnum and Bailey circus with his former rival **Anthony Bailey** (1847–1906). Barnum is widely credited with coining the phrase 'There's a sucker born every minute'.

> A great showman; someone with great entrepreneurial and marketing abilities; also mentioned in the context of an overly-glitzy show or extravagant publicity stunt, or someone who is easily taken in

Spielberg is the grand master of want see. Like some latterday PT Barnum, he has turned cinema-going into a circus experience.
Sunday Herald 2002

If it is a hype, I have been as suckered as ever one of Barnum's dupes was.
Scotland on Sunday 2002

To celebrate the 10th anniversary of their 'Got Milk?' advertising campaign, they've come up with an advertising stunt so tacky it'd make P. T. Barnum puke.
AlterNet: Jim Hightower columns 2002

Bartholomew, St [People] An apostle who is said to have been martyred in Armenia by being flayed alive, and is hence regarded as the patron saint of tanners.

➢ Someone who is flayed

If they knew how old I am they would flay me with their terrible brushes—flay me like St Bartholomew.
ROBERTSON DAVIES *Fifth Business* 1970

Bartleby [Lit.] 'Bartleby the Scrivener' (1856) is a short story by Herman Melville. The story is narrated by a New York lawyer who tells of Bartleby, one of his scriveners, or copyists, who when asked to do more than simply copying says 'I would prefer not to'. Eventually, he even stops copying and eating, and gradually wastes away.

➢ Someone who declines to do something

'I'll buy you dinner.' 'I don't wanna.' 'And give you some cash for your time.' 'I don't wanna,' repeated this modern-day Bartleby.
LAURA LIPPMAN *The Last Place* 2002

Barton, Dick [Radio] The hero of the radio series *Dick Barton Special Agent*, broadcast between 1946 and 1951, who courageously pursued and defeated arch-criminals.

➢ Someone who pursues wrongdoers

Sky Captain is the personification of these, with a dash of Bulldog Drummond and a hint of Dick Barton Special Agent.
Film Inside Out 2004

Bash Street Kids [Cart. & Com.] A set of characters featuring in the British comic *The Beano* since the 1950s. The 'kids' are scruffily dressed and irreverent, with a knack for creating mayhem through their various exploits. The characters include Danny, 'Erbert, Fatty, Plug, Smiffy, and Spotty.

➢ Naughty children; young people who rebel against authority; scruffily dressed children

Steve Marriott, Ronnie Lane, Ian 'Mac' McLagan and Kenney Jones were pop's Bash Street Kids: naughty boys climbing the school railings and thumbing their noses at the establishment.
BBC Popular Music Reviews 2004

basilisk [Leg. & Folk.] A legendary monster, the king of serpents, which could reputedly strike someone dead with its stare.

➢ Used to describe a cold stare

Without softening very much the basilisk nature of his stare, he said, impassively: 'We are coming to that part of my investigation, sir.'
JOSEPH CONRAD *The Secret Agent* 1907

Bastille, The [Places] A fortress in Paris, built as a royal castle by Charles V, and completed in 1383. Used as a prison in the 17th and 18th centuries, it became a symbol of repression. It was stormed and sacked by the Parisian mob in 1789 on 14 July, now commemorated as Bastille Day, marking the beginning of the French Revolution.

> ➤ A prison from which escape is almost impossible

> Harry and I have different names for the nursing home in which we live. Some days we call it the Bastille or the Château d'If…On very bad days, Harry calls it the Gulag.
> *Strange Horizons stories* 2004

Bates, Norman [Cin.] The murderous knife-wielding psychopath in the Alfred *Hitchcock thriller *Psycho* (1960).

> ➤ A psychopathic killer

> Changing my grip on the tool, I hold it like Norman Bates and stab at the rock.
> *Outside Online Magazine* 2004

Bates motel [Cin.] The motel owned by Norman Bates, the psychopathic killer in the Alfred *Hitchcock thriller *Psycho* (1960). The film is remembered especially for its shocking murder scene in which a woman is repeatedly stabbed in a shower.

> ➤ A hotel with a sinister appearance or atmosphere; also mentioned when describing unpleasant showers

> What followed was about as much fun as a night at the Bates Motel.
> *Inc. Magazine* 2002

> Those old structures were classics. Sure, a lot of them were dusty and damp, offering uncomfortable wooden seats, claustrophobic locker rooms, and the scariest showers this side of the Bates Motel. But they had character and quirks.
> *Basketball Digest* 2004

Bathsheba [Bible] The beautiful wife of *Uriah the Hittite (2 Sam. 11) whom King *David took as his mistress after he had seen her bathing from the roof of the palace. David sent for her, slept with her, and she became pregnant. David then arranged for Uriah to be sent into the front line of the battle in which the *Israelites were besieging Rabbah, and he was killed. After Bathsheba's period of mourning, David married her (2 Sam. 11).

> ➤ A beautiful married woman

Batman and Robin [Cin.; Cart. & Com.] The crime-fighting superheroes Batman and Robin made their first appearance in 1939 in an American comic strip, and have since appeared both on television and in films. In normal life the two are the wealthy Bruce Wayne and his young ward Dick Grayson, but as Batman and Robin, with the aid of clever gadgets and their speedy *Batmobile, they fight against cunning super-criminals such as the Joker and the Penguin in order to protect Gotham City.

> ➤ Two people who battle against evil; two people who work together as partners

> Eliot Spitzer, New York State's attorney general, is at it again. Like Batman out to save a sordid Gotham City, he continues to pursue and torment the professional investment community, vowing to end everything from fraud to conflicts of interest that affect investors.
> *Business Week Magazine* 2003

> And when we look at history we can see that there is no schism between church and state or between art and science. The two are as intertwined as Batman and Robin.
> *American Atheist Magazine* 2003

Batmobile [TV] The fast and futuristic car driven by *Batman and Robin.

> A futuristic-looking car

I mean, he's married, which is a scary thing, and he's got the sort of car keys that you jangle confidently, so he's obviously got, like, a BMW or a Batmobile or something flash.
NICK HORNBY *High Fidelity* 1995

Battle of Britain [Hist.] A series of air battles fought over Britain from August to October 1940, in which the RAF successfully resisted raids by the numerically superior German air force. The phrase was coined by Winston *Churchill in a speech to the House of Commons on 18 June 1940: 'What General Weygand called the "Battle of France" is over. I expect that the Battle of Britain is about to begin.'

> Used to describe a contest between two British competitors or teams

The Manchester United v Rangers duels will command the most attention, and what will inevitably be dubbed 'the Battle of Britain' has added interest in that United boss Alex Ferguson once played for the Glasgow club.
Irish Examiner 2003

Battle of the Bulge [Hist.] An unofficial name for the military campaign in the Ardennes in 1944–5, when German forces attempted to break through Allied lines and almost succeeded in doing so.

> Used humorously to describe an attempt to lose weight

It should come as no surprise the number one New Year's resolution in North America is losing weight. However, while most of us put up a good fight, we eventually lose the battle of the bulge.
Richmond News (BC) 2004

Battus [Gk Myth.] A shepherd of *Arcadia, who saw the god *Hermes steal the flocks of Admetus. He was bribed by the god not to tell, and pointing to a stone declared: 'Sooner will that stone tell of your theft than I.' When he was tricked into breaking his promise, Hermes turned him into a stone.

> Someone who reveals a secret; someone who is punished for revealing a secret; someone who is turned to stone

Bay of Pigs [Hist.] A bay on the south-west coast of Cuba. In 1961 it was the scene of an unsuccessful attempt by US-backed Cuban exiles to invade the country and overthrow the regime of Fidel Castro. The incident was seen as a complete failure and source of great embarrassment to the US government.

> A humiliating military failure

Basically, the combination we used in Afghanistan is highly unlikely to work in Iraq and would lead to probably another Bay of Pigs.
CNN transcripts: Late Edition 2002

Beam me up, Scotty [TV] A phrase attributed to Captain Kirk in the American television series *Star Trek*, asking to be transported instantly back to the spaceship. In fact, the phrase was never used, the nearest equivalent found in the series being 'Beam us up, Mr Scott'.

> Used to indicate a wish to be immediately removed from a place or situation, especially because there seems to be a lack of 'intelligent life' there

When the court heard how PC Marchant found the helmet when he returned to Southampton Central police station, the judge said: 'Somehow it got back to the station all by itself? Beam me up Scotty!'
This is Hampshire news stories 2004

Bean, Mr [TV; Cin.] The main character in a British comedy television series of the same name, which was first broadcast in 1990. Mr Bean, created and played by Rowan Atkinson, is described by his creator as 'a child in a grown man's body', and the series followed the exploits of the character as he attempted to deal with the problems of everyday life, often causing mayhem in the process. The series has inspired two feature films and an animated cartoon spin-off.

➤ Someone who inadvertently causes disruption or mayhem

Waving his arms wildly above his head like a flustered Mr. Bean, he inadvertently knocked the microphone stand over before eventually becoming tangled in the cable.
X-Press Online 2004

Beardsley, Aubrey [Art] (1872–98) An English artist and illustrator who worked in the art nouveau style. Beardsley's work, often dealing with grotesque or erotic subjects, epitomized the 'decadence' of the 1890s.

➤ Used when describing someone of grotesque appearance (adjective *Beardsleyan*)

He kept a bevy of boys himself, over whom he ruled with great severity, jealous and terrible as a Beardsleyan queen.
JOHN BANVILLE *The Book of Evidence* 1989

beast with two backs [Shakes.] A quotation from *Othello* (1602–4), referring to a man and woman in the act of sexual intercourse. A similar phrase had been used by Rabelais earlier.

➤ A way of referring to sexual intercourse

What's so bad about a bunch of hot young women who want to make the beast with two backs?
DVD Verdict 2005

Beatrice [Lit.] The young woman, Beatrice Portinari, to whom the Italian poet *Dante was platonically devoted all his life.

➤ A woman who is an idealized object of love

...you were always my Beatrice. My Laura. I thought, who wants second best?
LOUIS DE BERNIÈRES *Captain Corelli's Mandolin* 1994

Beatrice and Benedick [Shakes.] The two chief characters in the romantic comedy *Much Ado about Nothing* (1600). At the start of the play Benedick is determined to remain a bachelor, and the characters engage in mutual barbed teasing. When their friends and relatives trick each of them into believing that the other is in love, each does, in fact, fall for the other. At the end of the play, still teasing each other, they agree to marry.

➤ Mentioned in the context of a couple who spar with each other in order to hide their mutual attraction

beat swords into ploughshares [Bible] A quotation from the Old Testament: 'They shall beat their swords into ploughshares, and their spears into pruning-hooks: nation shall not lift up sword against nation, neither shall they learn war any more' (Isa. 2: 4).

➤ To make peace

Hezbollah is in the process of trying to beat some of their swords into ploughshares.
CNN transcripts: Anderson Cooper 360 Degrees 2003

Beau Geste [Lit.] The title of a 1924 adventure story by P. C. Wren, dealing with the exploits of the French Foreign Legion. It contains a famous scene in which, with hardly any soldiers left alive to defend a fort, the corpses of the dead are arranged on the fort's battlements to give the illusion of a strongly armed presence.

> ➤ Mentioned in the context of a battle in the desert, a last-ditch defence, or a place that is almost empty

> Caz got back to John Street for half past two. There were a couple of voices in the back office behind the front desk, but other than that, the place was still a cheap version of Beau Geste meets the Marie Celeste.
> ALEX KEEGAN *Kingfisher* 1995

Beauty and the Beast [Fairy tales] The title of a tale in which a beautiful young woman, Beauty, is forced to live with the Beast, an ugly monster, in order to save her father's life. Having come to pity and love the Beast, she finally consents to marry him. Her love frees the Beast from the enchantment he is under and he is restored to the form of a handsome prince.

> ➤ A couple of widely contrasting physical attractiveness

> Attorney Callender handed the writ of habeas corpus to the Lieutenant and Fats said, 'Come on, Katy,' and took the tall mini-skirted, naked-looking, hot-skinned, cold sex-pot by the elbow and marched her toward the door. They looked like Beauty and the Beast.
> CHESTER HIMES *Blind Man with a Pistol* 1969

Beavis and Butthead [Cart. & Com.] Two dim-witted, dirty-minded cartoon teenagers who torture animals, snigger at words they think rude or suggestive, and like extremely loud rock music. They were created by Mike Judge, and the television series of the same name in which they featured was broadcast on MTV from 1993 to 1997.

> ➤ Rude or uncouth teenagers

> So while you're snickering like Beavis and Butthead—or simply staring at the screen… you can feel safe in the knowledge that it comes rubber-stamped by the guy that directed *Being John Malkovich*.
> *Sunday Herald* 2002

Becher's Brook [Sport] A notoriously difficult fence jumped during the annual Grand National horse race at Aintree Racecourse. It is renowned for the number of horses who fall while negotiating it.

> ➤ Someone's downfall

> On a day when the National threw up another fantastic race, the Oval turned into Killyleagh's Becher's Brook.
> *Down Democrat* 2002

Beckett, Samuel [Lit.] The plays of the Irish writer and playwright Samuel Beckett (1906–89), such as *Waiting for Godot* (1955), *Krapp's Last Tape* (1958, pub 1959), and *Play* (1964), express the author's bleak view of the vanity and futility of human endeavour in the face of man's inevitable death and oblivion.

> ➤ Mentioned in the context of a bleak or hopeless outlook on life (adjective *Beckettian*)

> It is a joy sufficiently muted to accord with prevailing moods that range from Chekhovian-autumnal to Beckettian-wintry.
> *New York Review of Books* 1997

Bedlam [Places] The popular name of the Hospital of St Mary of Bethlehem, founded as a priory in 1247 at Bishopsgate, London, and by the 14th century a mental hospital.

> ➤ A state of wild disorder or noisy uproar

After a few more minutes of finding their way through the former hotel the main staircase was in sight, the calm silhouette of Mack standing in the middle of a picture of pure bedlam.
HAPPY VOLTAIRE *Memorable* 2004

Bedonebyasyoudid, Mrs [Child. Lit.] A character encountered by Tom after he becomes a water-baby in Charles Kingsley's children's story *The Water-Babies* (1863). She rewards good behaviour and punishes bad, illustrating the moral lesson that you reap what you sow.

> ➤ Someone who is morally judgemental and punishes others for past deeds

> Any qualms I might have had about deceiving Anita, disappeared completely on her wedding day. She had turned into Mrs Be-Done-By-As-You-Did.
> FAY WELDON *Life Force* 1992

Beeching, Lord Richard (1913–85) An English engineer who became chairman of the British Railways Board in 1963. Known as 'Dr Beeching', he is remembered chiefly for the 'Beeching Plan', a scheme which led to the substantial contraction of the rail network in the UK and the closure of many small stations.

> ➤ Someone who is responsible for cutting important government services or funding

> If this goes ahead, Falconer will be like Dr Beeching: synonymous with environmental disaster.
> *Guardian Unlimited columnists* 2005

Beelzebub [Bible] The god of the Philistine city Ekron (2 Kgs. 1). He is mentioned in several of the Gospels, where he is called 'the prince of demons'.

> ➤ The Devil

> Winterborne was standing in front of the brick oven in his shirt-sleeves, tossing in thorn-sprays, and stirring about the blazing mass with a long-handled, three-pronged Beelzebub kind of fork.
> THOMAS HARDY *The Woodlanders* 1887

Beersheba *See* DAN TO BEERSHEBA.

Beethoven, Ludwig van [Mus.] (1770–1827) A German composer, born in Bonn. Although he began to be afflicted with deafness in 1802, an affliction which became total by 1817, his musical output was prodigious.

> ➤ Someone who is deaf

> I soon found out why Old Chong had retired from teaching piano. He was deaf. 'Like Beethoven!' he shouted to me. 'We're both listening only in our head!'
> AMY TAN *Two Kinds* 1989

Belch, Sir Toby [Shakes.] The uncle of Olivia in *Twelfth Night*, known for his love of good food and drink, for 'cakes and ale'.

> ➤ Someone who eats and drinks to excess

> At present I share Balliol with one…man…who rather repels me at meals by his…habit of showing satisfaction with the food: Sir Toby Belch was not in it.
> ALDOUS HUXLEY *The Letters of Aldous Huxley* 1915

Belle Dame Sans Merci, La [Lit.] The title of a ballad by John Keats, published in 1820. It tells the story of a knight who becomes enthralled by the charms of a fairy woman who pretends to love him and care for him, as a result of which his strength fails him and he is seen 'alone and palely loitering'.

➢ An unattainable woman of perfect beauty; a woman who inspires a self-destructive love

I imagine she was one of the few women who ever turned you down....If she'd remained here in Pine Grove, married, turned into an ordinary aging housewife, you'd have forgotten her. But the mystery and the romance of her life, added to her rejection, transformed her into the unattainable ideal woman. La Belle Dame sans Merci.
ELIZABETH PETERS *Naked Once More* 1989

belle époque [Hist.] A phrase (meaning 'beautiful era' in French) used to refer to the period in European history from the late 19th century until the First World War. The era was considered to be a golden age for the upper classes.

➢ A golden age, or era of great success

McSweeney's has entered its belle époque on the Web and in print.
Flak Magazine: Web articles 2004

Bellerophon [Gk Myth.] The son of Glaucus and the grandson of *Sisyphus. Riding the winged horse *Pegasus, Bellerophon completed many difficult tasks, but at the end of his life he was alone and an outcast.

➢ A hero or rescuer; an outcast

Henchard was stung into bitterness; like Bellerophon, he wandered away from the crowd, cankered in soul.
THOMAS HARDY *The Mayor of Casterbridge* 1886

Jeremy Rifkin is a modern-day Bellerophon, fighting to stop pharming—and any other research involving chimeras, for that matter.
Spiked Online 2004

Belphoebe [Lit.] A daughter of the nymph Chrysogone and a chaste huntress in Edmund Spenser's *Faerie Queene* (1590, 1596).

➢ A beautiful young woman; a huntress

She had a look, he thought fancifully, of a modern Belphoebe in those garments, sunny hair and the accoutrements of a huntress.
A. S. BYATT *The Virgin in the Garden* 1978

Belsen [Hist.] Bergen-Belsen was a Nazi concentration camp near the city of Celle in north-west Germany. Many thousands of prisoners died there from starvation or disease while others were shot.

➢ A place of horrific suffering; also mentioned when describing someone who is painfully thin

Or else take the contemporarily untenable position that evil, undiluted by any hint of childhood trauma, does exist in the world, exists for its own precise sake, the pustular bequest from the beast, as inexplicable as Belsen.
JOHN D. MACDONALD *The Deep Blue Goodbye* 1964

Posh can't seem to gain weight, no matter how many photos the press publishes of her that make her look like an escapee from Belsen.
Rum and Monkey 2004

Belshazzar [Bible] A king of *Babylon who, according to the Bible, gave a great banquet for 1000 of his lords (Dan. 5: 1–28). During the banquet they drank from goblets taken from the temple and praised the gods of gold, silver, bronze, iron, wood, and stone. Suddenly the fingers of a human hand appeared and wrote on the wall the words 'Mene, Mene, Tekel, Upharsin'. Daniel translated the words, explaining to Belshazzar that his reign was over, that he had been weighed in the balance and found wanting, and that his kingdom would be divided and given to the *Medes and the Persians. *See also* WRITING ON THE WALL.

> Belshazzar's feast can be mentioned in the context of a magnificent meal; Belshazzar's name can also denote someone whose doom is certain

'I always like this room,' said Spandrell as they entered. 'It's like a scene for Belshazzar's feast.'
ALDOUS HUXLEY *Point Counter Point* 1928

And there at the centre of his desk was a large buff envelope with his name printed on it in a hand which was unmistakably Dalziel's. Why did the name Belshazzar suddenly flit into his mind?
REGINALD HILL *Child's Play* 1987

Benedick *See* BEATRICE AND BENEDICK.

Ben Hur [Cin.] The hero of Lew Wallace's novel *Ben-Hur, a Tale of the Christ* (1880). Set in Rome at the time of *Jesus, the novel tells the story of Ben Hur, a Jew who converts to Christianity. The story was popularized by two Hollywood epics, a 1925 silent film and a 1959 remake starring Charlton Heston. Both films featured memorably exciting scenes of a chariot race.

> The chariots in Ben Hur are used to invoke the image of a fast race, or things hurtling along at top speed

Leslie Beck's Life Force is the energy not so much of sexual desire as of sexual discontent: the urge to find someone better out there, and thereby something better in the self, the one energy working against the other, creating a fine and animating friction: or else racing along side by side, like the Chariots in Ben Hur, wheels colliding, touching, hell-bent, sparking off happiness and unhappiness.
FAY WELDON *Life Force* 1992

Bennet, Mrs [Lit.] A character in Jane Austen's *Pride and Prejudice* (1813). The vulgar, gossipy Mrs Bennet is preoccupied with finding wealthy husbands for her five unmarried daughters.

> A mother who schemes to gain advantage for her children

So, by some mysterious transference, the children's birthday party has turned into a battleground of social ambitions, ripe for the attention of a contemporary Jane Austen. No one considers the embarrassment of the mother who can't afford to keep up, or the danger of turning our children into spoilt little brats. Or is it merely a harmless indulgence in parental pride? After all, today's Mrs Bennets aren't trying to marry off their five-year-olds, they just want the fun of dressing them up and clucking over them.
The Independent 1996

Beowulf [Leg. & Folk.] A legendary Scandinavian hero celebrated in the Old English epic poem *Beowulf*. The poem describes Beowulf's killing first of the monster *Grendel in King Hrothgar's hall, then of Grendel's mother in an underwater cave, and finally Beowulf's own death in combat with a dragon.

> Used to evoke a very distant past

We were on a beach, and someone…suggested we engrave our names in big letters upon the sand, then one of us would mount the promenade and photograph inscription plus inscriber. A cliché in Beowulf's time, I know, but you can't keep coming up with new games.
JULIAN BARNES *Talking It Over* 1991

Bergerac, Cyrano de [People] (1619–55) A French soldier, duellist, and writer of comedies and satires. He is supposed to have had a prodigiously long nose. He is celebrated in the play by Edmond Rostand that bears his name (1897).

> ➤ Someone with an extremely large nose

> Derek Griffiths is a young coloured comedian with a face like crushed rubber…and a hooter to rival Cyrano de Bergerac.
> *The Times* 1972

Berlin Wall [Hist.] A wall was built in 1961 between East and West Berlin in order to curb the numbers of East Germans fleeing to the West. Originally, it was a low barbed-wire barricade but it was rebuilt several times, each time bigger and stronger until eventually it was a heavily guarded concrete barrier with an average height of 3.6 metres (11.8 feet) with fortifications. For many years, anyone caught escaping over the wall was shot. On 9 November 1989, following the collapse of the communist regime in East Germany, the wall was opened up. It was subsequently dismantled.

> ➤ A barrier that is almost impossible to cross

> After three days of his model performance, Judy had given up the daybed in the dressing room and come back to the bedroom. True, the Berlin Wall now ran down the center of the bed, and she wouldn't give him an inch of small talk. But she was always civil to him when Campbell was around.
> TOM WOLFE *The Bonfire of the Vanities* 1987

> The aim is to break down the 'Berlin walls' which separate health and community care, in Secretary of State for Health Frank Dobson's phrase.
> *The Independent* 1997

Bermuda Triangle [Places] An area of the western Atlantic bounded by Bermuda, Florida, and Puerto Rico which is supposedly associated with an unusually high number of unexplained disappearances of ships and aircraft.

> ➤ A place or situation in which things disappear inexplicably

> Sometimes the cash arrived; other times it wound up in the accounting equivalent of the Bermuda Triangle.
> *The Register* 2003

best-laid plans (of mice and men) [Lit.] A phrase originally from Robert Burns's poem 'To a Mouse' (1786): 'the best-laid schemes of mice and men gang aft agley' (the best prepared of plans often go wrong).

> ➤ Used when saying that things rarely go according to plan

> 'War is one of the great tests that separates planning from execution,' writes Erik Durschmied in his latest book. But then there is always the 'chance factor' that can put paid to the best-laid plans of mice and military men.
> *Northern Rivers Echo News* 2003

best of all possible worlds [Lit.] In *Voltaire's satire *Candide* (1759), Candide's tutor, Dr *Pangloss, a philosophical optimist, repeatedly assures Candide that 'all is for the best in the best of all possible worlds'.

> ➤ Used when describing an ideal situation

> Investors are moving out of a period when they enjoyed the best of all possible worlds.
> *Sunday Business Post* 2004

Bethesda [Bible] A pool in Jerusalem that was supposed to have healing powers. It was there that *Jesus healed a paralytic 'who had been ill for thirty-eight years'.

> ➤ A place where someone is healed

> She has sent her here to be healed, even as the Jews of old sent their diseased to the troubled pool of Bethesda.
> CHARLOTTE BRONTË *Jane Eyre* 1847

better to reign in Hell than serve in Heaven [Lit.] A quotation taken from John *Milton's poem *Paradise Lost* (1667), in which *Satan, cast out of Heaven, decides that in some ways he is better off because he at least has his freedom, and it is 'Better to reign in Hell than serve in Heaven'.

> ➤ Used when discussing someone's choice between enjoying freedom and power in a situation that is not ideal, or life without these things in a more ideal situation

> Another complication is Paisley's declining health...Of course he would love to end his career as first minister, but sharing the top job with Beelzebub McGuinness may not quite look like the divine intervention he has been threatening us with for years. Like many before him, he has come down 30 long years to finally face John Milton's exquisite dilemma, that of Satan in Paradise Lost whether to reign in hell or serve in heaven.
> *Sunday Business Post* 2004

Beulah [Bible] A name for the land of Israel (Hebrew, literally 'Married Woman'). In Bunyan's The *Pilgrim's Progress, Beulah lies beyond the *Valley of the Shadow of Death and also out of the reach of *Giant Despair: 'Yea, here they heard continually the singing of birds, and saw every day the flowers appear in the earth...in this country the sun shineth night and day.'

> ➤ A paradise

> I thought sometimes I saw beyond its wild waters a shore, sweet as the hills of Beulah.
> CHARLOTTE BRONTË *Jane Eyre* 1847

Beverly Hillbillies, The [TV] A popular US television series (1962–71) about a hillbilly family transported to Beverly Hills, California, after finding oil on their land. The series presented the family as stereotypical country folk unfamiliar with the ways of modern city life.

> ➤ Used to evoke a traditional rustic way of life

> Gore has undergone a bizarre makeover and now sounds like he's auditioning for the Beverly Hillbillies. His enthusiasm for the information superhighway has been replaced with nostalgic references to the dirt-track leading to his daddy's farm.
> *Sunday Herald* 2000

Big Bad Wolf [Child. Lit.] A wolf in the folk tale 'The Three Little Pigs', who tries to kill and eat the three pigs, repeating his refrain that 'I'll huff and I'll puff and I'll blow the house down'.

> ➤ An archetypal or stereotypical villain

> 'Organized labor groups are often seen as the big bad wolf,' says Gunderson, a former Dow Jones employee.
> *Inc. Magazine* 2004

Big Brother [Lit.] A character in George *Orwell's novel *Nineteen Eighty-Four* (1949). Big Brother is the head of the totalitarian Party and dictator of the state in which Winston Smith lives. His portrait, with the caption 'Big Brother is watching you', is ubiquitous.

> A person or government that is ever present and watches people at all times

He censored our reading, selected our playmates—we weren't allowed many—and watched us like Big Brother.
BARBARA MICHAELS *Search the Shadows* 1988

Under new Big Brother legislation, Whitehall departments, local councils, the Food Standards Agency and many other bodies were to be allowed to request details of communications made by any British telephone and internet user.
Sunday Herald 2002

Big Daddy [Sport] The stage name of the British wrestler Shirley Crabtree (1930–97), famous for his 64-inch chest. The name has also been applied to other well-known figures, including Idi Amin. It is also the name of the wealthy patriarch of the Pollitt family in Tennessee Williams' play *Cat on a Hot Tin Roof* (1955).

> Anyone or anything that is the largest or most important of its kind; also used when describing a man with a large waistline

Kelkoo is the big daddy of price-comparison websites.
MotleyFool.co.uk: Comment 2003

The way I figure it, all I have to do is get my big daddy gut down to a manageable size, and I'll be the best exotic dancer ever to grace a gas station.
Philadelphia Weekly (2004)

Big Ears [Child. Lit.] A character in children's stories by Enid *Blyton, an elderly man with a white beard and large ears who is a friend to *Noddy.

> Someone with large ears; someone who is good at listening

PC Wayne Holland is hoping his new Chief Constable is known as Big Ears. 'I hope he is prepared to listen carefully to the troops,' said the 29-year-old constable based at Moss Side.
Manchester Online: Manchester Evening News 2002

Big-Endians and Little-Endians [Lit.] In Jonathan Swift's *Gulliver's Travels* (1726) the Big-Endians are a group of people in Lilliput who believe that boiled eggs should be broken at the big end rather than at the little end, as commanded by the Emperor of Lilliput. As a result of this disagreement Lilliput and the neighbouring land of Blefuscu have 'been engaged in a most obstinate war for six and thirty moons past'.

> Mentioned in the context of a prolonged dispute over a seemingly trivial matter

Biggles [Lit.] A fictional British pilot who was the hero of many adventures in two world wars in books by Captain W. E. Johns.

> Someone who demonstrates old-fashioned British stiff-upper-lip courage and patriotism; someone who has many narrow escapes; also used to invoke stereotypical Second World War flying gear

Brown, it should be said, has shown an ability to take evasive action on this issue in a way that would have done Biggles proud.
The Sunday Times 2006

The Bandits utilise everything from Biggles helmets to colanders in their costumes.
www.RobotFist.com 2003

Bighorn *See* LITTLE BIGHORN.

'Big Rock Candy Mountain' [Mus.] The title of a US song about a hobo's idea of Paradise, where there are cigarette trees, and 'the hens lay soft-boiled eggs'. The song was first recorded in 1928 by Harry McClintock.

> ➤ A paradise
>
> It is hard to think of a challenge that is not ducked or a dilemma that is not dodged in Kennedy's big rock candy mountain.
> *The Sunday Times* 2004

Bilko, Sergeant [TV] The main character in the US television series *Bilko*, which was shown from 1955 to 1959. Played by Phil Silvers, Sergeant Bilko, who is in charge of a small US army base in Kansas, spends the majority of his time trying to earn money through various get-rich-quick scams.

> ➤ An easy-going wide boy; a soldier with no interest in performing his duties well
>
> Putting Richie Dixon in charge of coaching is like putting Sergeant Bilko in charge of the Normandy landings.
> *Scotland on Sunday* 2002

Bill and Ben [TV] The two puppet 'Flowerpot Men' of the British television series *The Flowerpot Men*, that was broadcast in the 1950s and 1960s and then revived in an animated version in 2001. Bill and Ben were two little men made of flower pots, who lived at the bottom of a garden and spoke to each other in their own childlike language that included words such as 'flobberpop' for 'flowerpot'.

> ➤ Two people or animals that look very similar to each other

Billy Liar [Lit.] Keith Waterhouse's 1959 novel, which tells the story of Billy Fisher, a compulsive daydreamer who dreams of a better and more glamorous life.

> ➤ A daydreamer who lives in a fantasy world
>
> It's as much of a fantasy as any Billy Liar daydreamed.
> *Sunday Herald* 2001

Billy the Kid [Crime] The nickname of an American bandit and bank robber, whose real name was William H. Bonney (1859–81). He allegedly committed his first murder at the age of 12. He was finally shot by sheriff Pat Garrett.

> ➤ A cowboy or outlaw who looks very young
>
> He did not look like a jailbird. Billy the Kid and Crippen did not look like Murderers.
> FRANK PARRISH *Voices from the Dark* 1993

Birnam Wood [Shakes.] In *Macbeth* (1623) the witches assure *Macbeth that he will not be defeated until Birnam Wood comes to Dunsinane Castle. Later, when the army of Malcolm and Macduff passes through Birnam Wood, Malcolm instructs every man to cut a branch, and under the camouflage of this 'leafy screen' the army marches on Dunsinane, giving the impression that the wood is indeed moving.

> ➤ 'Birnam wood moving to Dunsinane' is used in the context of vegetation that seems to move, or something that is very unlikely to happen
>
> When the curtain call came, some of the girls who had been serving as ushers rushed to the footlights like Birnam Wood moving to Dunsinane, loaded with bouquets.
> ROBERTSON DAVIES *The Manticore* 1972

Bismarck, Karl Otto Eduard Leopold von [Hist.] (1815–98) A Prussian-German politician and statesman. He became chancellor of Germany in 1871, and later became known as the Iron Chancellor. He presided over the reorganization and unification of Germany.

> ➤ A leader who is responsible for unifying a group or country

Clark…called Kaishu the 'Bismarck of Japan' for his role in unifying the Japanese nation in the dangerous aftermath of the fall of the Tokugawa.
JADE DRAGON *Online* 2003

Black Death [Hist.] The name commonly given to the great epidemic of bubonic plague that killed between a third and a half of the population of Europe in the mid-14th century. The plague originated in central Asia and China and spread rapidly through Europe, transmitted by the fleas of black rats.

➢ A disease that causes devastation or large numbers of deaths

Foot-and-mouth has been widely discussed and treated as if it were the Black Death in drag.
www.spiked-online.com 2004

Black Friday [Hist.] A day of financial panic on the New York stock exchange in September 1869, brought about by an attempt by two wealthy businessmen to corner the market in gold. They failed, and the price of gold crashed, leaving many investors out of pocket. The phrase has been used to describe other particularly bad days on stock markets in New York and London, such as Black Tuesday, in October 1929, which signalled the beginning of the Great Depression, and Black Monday, in October 1987, when the market plunged by over 20 per cent in one day.

➢ A day of severe financial losses

Procter & Gamble's earnings bombshell on Wall Street two weeks ago could prove to be a shock on the magnitude of Marlboro's Black Friday of 1993.
Brandweek 2000

Black Hander [Hist.] A member of a group called the Black Hand. The name Black Hand has been used by a number of secret societies, most notably a group of terrorists and blackmailers composed mainly of Sicilians active in the United States in the late 19th and early 20th centuries. The name was also used for a secret society which aimed at the unification of the southern Slavs at the beginning of the 20th century.

➢ Someone who behaves in a secretive, suspicious manner

He became the Black Hander once more. He looked this way and he looked that. He peeped hither and peered thither. Then he lowered his voice to such a whisper that I couldn't hear a damn word.
P. G. WODEHOUSE *Laughing Gas* 1936

Black Hole of Calcutta [Places] A dungeon in Fort William, Calcutta. Following the capture of Calcutta by Siraj-ud-Dawlah, nawab of Bengal, 146 English prisoners were said to have been confined there in a narrow cell, 20 feet square, for the night of 20 June 1756. Only 23 people survived to the morning, all the others suffocating.

➢ A severely overcrowded place

Mr Galloway described one address in Brick Lane as a 'black hole of Calcutta', claiming that 14 people who did not live there had been registered to vote.
The Observer 2004

Blade Runner [Cin.] The title of a 1982 US science fiction film starring Harrison Ford which depicts a dystopian Los Angeles in 2019, in which police assassins known as blade runners hunt down genetically engineered beings called 'replicants'.

➢ Used to evoke a society divided into warring factions; also used when describing a futuristic city landscape

But today, the collapse of civil society (and the civic fabric) into adversely opposed factions seems almost as immanent in most developed countries. Blade Runner is just over the horizon.
Architectural Review 2005

On clear days you can see Mount Fujiyama and as night falls the neon lights up Shinjuku like something out of Blade Runner.
World's Best Bars 2004

Blaise, Modesty [Cart. & Com.] The heroine of a strip cartoon created by Peter O'Donnell and first published in the London *Evening Standard* in 1963. A retired gangster, she fights against crime and wrongdoing showing great courage and resourcefulness.

➤ A woman who fights against crime or injustice

Blake, William [Art] (1757–1827) An English artist and poet. His intensely imaginative and visionary watercolours and engravings include illustrations for *The Book of Job* (1826), for works by *Dante and *Shakespeare, and for his own *Prophetic Books* (1783–1804). His figures are usually heavily muscled.

➤ Mentioned when describing someone with a muscular body; also used in the context of something that looks imagined rather than real

And the people in the streets, it seemed to him, whether milling along Oxford Street or sauntering from lion to lion in Trafalgar Square, formed another golden host, beautiful in the antique cold-faced way of Blake's pastel throngs.
JOHN UPDIKE *Bech: A Book* 1970

Blefuscudian navy [Lit.] In Jonathan Swift's *Gullivers Travels* (1726), Gulliver finds himself in the land of Lilliput, where the people are only 6 inches tall. They have a continuing historic war with the people of the neighbouring land of Blefuscu. During Gulliver's stay, Blefuscu has amassed a navy and is preparing to launch it over the sea between the islands, a channel 800 yards wide and at its deepest, 6 feet. Gulliver conceives a plan to assist the Lilliputians in which he wades and swims over to Blefuscu, terrifying the sailors, who flee back to land. He ties the Blefuscudian boats together and then pulls them back across the channel.

➤ Something that looks tiny or seems very insignificant

'Pete, honey!' cried Chung, heading towards him with lesser beings bobbing in her wake like the Blefuscudian navy behind Gulliver.
REGINALD HILL *Child's Play* 1987

Bligh, Captain [People] (1754–1817) A British naval officer who was the captain of HMS *Bounty* on a voyage to Tahiti and the West Indies in 1787. In 1789 part of the crew, under the first mate, Fletcher Christian, mutinied, setting Bligh and eighteen crew adrift in an open boat with few supplies and no charts. They succeeded in sailing to Timor, a journey of nearly 4000 miles. Two films about this event, both entitled *The Mutiny on the Bounty* (1935, 1962), have depicted Bligh as domineering and authoritarian.

➤ A tyrant; a leader who suffers a mutiny

According to Peasemarch, his butler, with whom I correspond, his manner towards her is still reminiscent of that of Captain Bligh of the Bounty displeased with the behaviour of one of the personnel.
P. G. WODEHOUSE *Cocktail Time* 1958

As Captain Bligh discovered, where there's mutiny there is no bounty.
www.inc.com/magazine 2003

Blimp, Colonel [Cart. & Com.] A pompous, irascible, elderly character invented by the
cartoonist David Low during the Second World War.

> Someone with reactionary Establishment opinions, who is opposed to anything new

It is sad to find the editor of one of the few outlets in favour of radical change adopting
the attitude, and language, of a Colonel Blimp.
The Ecologist 2000

Blind Pew [Lit.] The sinister blind pirate in R. L. Stevenson's *Treasure Island* (1883), a
'horrible, soft-spoken, eyeless creature', whose approach is signalled by the tapping of his
stick along the road. It is Pew who delivers the dreaded 'Black Spot' to the old captain at the
Admiral Benbow inn, and who leads the pirates' attack on the inn.

> Someone who is blind, especially someone with a sinister air; also mentioned in the
> context of a repeated tapping sound

[He] has all the visual sophistication of Blind Pew.
MICHAEL BILLINGTON *Guardian Unlimited* 2004

And in his loft there was a tap-tapping, like Blind Pew's stick.
HUGH NOBLE *Sword Dance* 2000

Blitz [Hist.] A name given to the German air raids on Britain in 1940. Londoners were
renowned for carrying on with their everyday lives despite the difficulties and hardships they
faced, an attitude encapsulated in the slogans of the time: 'London can take it' and 'Business
as usual'.

> Used to invoke a spirit of close cooperation, in which people work together for the
> common good despite individual hardships

Blair can't just conjure up a new Blitz spirit to suit his newfound focus on homeland
security.
Spiked Online 2004

Blitzkrieg [Hist.] The tactic of intense and swift military attack used by German forces during
the Second World War. The word literally means 'lightning war'.

> A swift and intense battle

It's a blitzkrieg of the media kind, in which one gold-heavy company slugs it out with
another.
Bright Lights Film Journal 2003

Blondel [Leg. & Folk.] According to tradition, Blondel de Nesle, a French poet, was the friend
of Richard I of England, known as Richard Cœur de Lion. Blondel set out to find the king after
Richard, returning from the Holy Land in 1192, was imprisoned by the duke of Austria. Sitting
under the castle window, Blondel sang a song in French that he and the king had composed
together. Half-way through, Richard took the song up himself to reveal his whereabouts.

> Someone who sings beneath another person's window

Two ground-floor windows, three upstairs, all shuttered....I felt like Blondel beneath
Richard Cœur-de-Lion's window; but not even able to pass messages by song.
JOHN FOWLES *The Magus* 1977

blood, sweat, and tears [Hist.] A phrase based on a speech by Winston *Churchill in
May 1940, in which he spoke about what he could offer the country for its immediate future:
'I have nothing to offer but blood, toil, tears and sweat.'

> Hard work and suffering

A media plan is a lot of things—part innovation, part resourcefulness, part luck. But maybe the biggest part is good, old-fashioned blood, sweat and tears.
Brandweek 2001

Bloody Tower [Places] A nickname for a part of the *Tower of London, built in 1377–99. It derived its name from the belief that it was the place where the *Princes in the Tower were murdered.

➤ A place where people have been held captive and killed

Bloom, Leopold [Lit.] A Jewish advertisement canvasser in James Joyce's novel *Ulysses* (1922). The novel charts the wanderings of Bloom and Stephen Dedalus, a young poet, around Dublin on 16 June 1904. The various chapters roughly correspond to the episodes of *Homer's *Odyssey*, with Bloom representing *Odysseus and Stephen Telemachus. In the course of the story, a public bath, a cemetery, a newspaper office, a library, public houses, a maternity hospital, and a brothel are visited.

➤ Someone who travels to all parts of a city

As a youth, he worked variously as a bricklayer, coffin-polisher and artist's model at the local college of art. The milk round, however, was special; it offered him a daily, Bloom-like odyssey of Edinburgh and he grew to know its streets so well that even when he had left it far behind, he would be able to trace its contours in his head.
The Guardian 1998

Bluebeard [Fairy tales] A character in a tale by Charles Perrault. In the story, Bluebeard has a reputation for marrying women who subsequently disappear. He leaves his most recent wife, Fatima, in charge of their house while he is away, instructing her not to open a locked room in the house, although he leaves her the key. Overcome with curiosity, she opens the room, only to discover the bodies of his previous wives.

➤ A cruel or murderous husband; Bluebeard's Castle is mentioned as a place of danger, where grisly deeds are performed

This is one of the strangest cases this court may ever have heard. The case of a Bluebeard who kept his wife a virtual prisoner in their flat in Muswell Hill.
JOHN MORTIMER *Rumpole of the Bailey* 1978

It occupied an entire Chicago block, a veritable Bluebeard's Castle (the neighbors actually called it the castle) with airtight, soundproof rooms and a chute for transporting bodies to the basement and a special kiln.
New York Metro: Books 2004

Bluebottle [Radio] A character in *The Goon Show*, an extremely popular BBC radio comedy series which ran from 1952 to 1960. Bluebottle, played by Peter Sellers, spoke in a comical high-pitched, whiny voice.

➤ Used when describing a very high-pitched voice

Wilson did his Bluebottle voice. 'Whatever it is, do not drop it my Kap-i-ten.'
HUGH NOBLE *Sword Dance* 2000

Blyton, Enid [Child. Lit.] (1897–1968) A prolific author of children's books, including the *Noddy books, series such as the *Famous Five and the Secret Seven, and school stories such as the Malory Towers series. The majority of her books were published in the 1940s and 1950s, and in the stories children have many exciting adventures but always manage to remain safe and well fed.

➤ Mentioned in the context of a fictional era of idealized childhood innocence, or people setting off on a fun but safe adventure

Deciding that my student life was becoming far too boring, I gathered together two other like-minded souls, and in finest Enid Blyton style we began our search for adventure.
Cherwell Magazine Online 2004

Boadicea *See* BOUDICCA.

Boeotia [Places] A district of ancient Greece known for the stupidity of its inhabitants.

> Mentioned when describing someone as a very stupid person (adjective and noun *Boeotian*)

An opportunity…which I should have been a Bœotian indeed had I neglected.
JOHN GIBSON LOCKHART *Valerius* 1821

Bohemia [Places] An area that was formerly a central European kingdom, but now forms the western part of the Czech Republic. It was thought to be a place where gypsies came from, and became associated with an unconventional way of life.

> A district frequented by artists, writers, and other socially unconventional people; also used to describe a person with an unconventional appearance or lifestyle (adjective *Bohemian*)

She had an air of upper-middle class bohemia about her.
JOHANN HARI *www.johannhari.com* 2003

boldly go where no man has gone before [TV] A quotation from the American television science fiction series **Star Trek*. The mission of the **Starship Enterprise*, with its famously split infinitive, was 'to boldly go where no man has gone before'.

> To do something new and innovative

And with more regulation around the corner, other IT firms are now likely to focus on putting their books in order, rather than boldly going where no man has been before.
Spiked Online 2004

Bonaparte, Napoleon [Hist.] (1769–1821) A French military leader who became Emperor of France in 1804. He conquered and ruled much of Europe until his final defeat at the Battle of *Waterloo in 1815.

> An autocratic ruler; someone who wields great power; someone with expansionist or empire-building desires (adjectives *Bonapartist, Napoleonic*)

With his expertise, energy and international contacts, he could really put Rummidge on the map, and that would be kind of fun. Morris began to project a Napoleonic future for himself at Rummidge.
DAVID LODGE *Changing Places* 1975

Conditions are ripe for the emergence of a Bonapartist dictatorship in the USA.
Capital and Class 2001

Blair's support for the NATO policy on Kosovo was a mad act of Bonapartist adventurism.
London Review of Books 2003

Bond, James [Cin.] The secret agent 007 in the novels by Ian Fleming and a series of highly successful films. His 'double-0' code number indicates that he is licensed to kill. Bond is a suave and resourceful hero, with a taste for fast cars and beautiful women, who likes his vodka dry martini to be 'shaken and not stirred'. Many of the films based on Fleming's novels feature sophisticated gadgets and include a scene in the villain's vast, often subterranean, high-tech headquarters or control room.

> A suave hero; also mentioned in the context of a far-fetched plot, high-tech or futuristic gadgetry, or a dramatic rescue

He was still lightheaded, and grew more so as he sipped his Bintang. Then he realised, he said, that she had managed to put something in his beer: some drug. I laughed at this. Too much James Bond, I suggested.
CHRISTOPHER J. KOCH *The Year of Living Dangerously* 1978

But forget flashy cars with ejector seats, or fountain pens packed with explosives. The real-life 007s in Robin Cook's 'refocused' SIS may find a bottle of mosquito repellent more useful in their new mission: to combat Asia's ruthless drug traffickers.
The Independent 1997

This is particularly true following the manager's decision to make a playing comeback at the age of 40. There are already signs it could produce a Coventry rescue act of which any James Bond would be proud.
The Observer 1997

Bones, Brom [Lit.] In Washington Irving's story 'The Legend of Sleepy Hollow' (1820), Brom Bones impersonates a ghostly headless horseman, using a pumpkin and a hat for the head that he is supposedly carrying, to scare off his rival suitor, Ichabod *Crane.

> Someone who scares people with fake supernatural effects

Bonnie and Clyde [Crime] Two criminals, **Bonnie Parker** (1911–34) and **Clyde Barrow** (1909–34), who led a gang in the United States that conducted a series of robberies and murders. They were shot dead in their car by police in Louisiana in 1934. A film presenting a rather glamorized version of their lives, *Bonnie and Clyde* (1967), ends with a memorable slow-motion sequence depicting their bodies jerking and falling in a barrage of gunfire.

> A young criminal couple who go on a crime spree; a young couple on the run from the law

Determined to defend her honour, the couple are soon on the run pursued by all and sundry—a modern day Bonnie and Clyde.
Film Focus 1994

Together this Bonnie and Clyde of the Valley held up gas stations and liquor stores.
Observer Music Monthly Magazine 2004

Bonnie Prince Charlie (Charles Edward Stuart) [Hist.] (1720–88) Also known as the Young Pretender, the son of James Stuart and pretender to the British throne. After spending time in exile in France, he returned to Scotland and led the Jacobite uprising of 1745-6, invading England and advancing as far as Derby. However, he was driven back to Scotland and defeated at the Battle of Culloden. He again escaped to France and died later in exile in Rome. Bonnie Prince Charlie became the subject of much romantic literature, and his supporters always hoped that he would one day return and defeat the English.

> An exiled leader who returns to save his people

But they would never find a leader. If there was some exiled prince of Chaka's blood, who came back like Prince Charlie to free his people, there might be danger; but their royalties are fat men with top hats and old frock coats, who live in dirty locations.
JOHN BUCHAN *Prester John* 1910

Book of Kells [Rel.] An illuminated manuscript of the Gospels kept at Trinity College, Dublin. It is thought to have been made on the island of Iona by Irish monks in the 8th or 9th century. Lavishly decorated with full-page illustrations, it is considered the most distinguished of the manuscripts of its type still extant.

> A beautifully decorated manuscript or old book

The scrolls were quite bitty. I know they're ancient and mysterious and I wasn't
expecting them to resemble the Book of Kells but, either Israel withheld the best
samples or I'm too hard to impress.
Sunday Business Post 2000

Boone, Daniel [People] (1735–1820) An American explorer, hunter, and frontiersman, who
travelled west from North Carolina to Kentucky, and later moved to Missouri, claiming
that Kentucky was 'too crowded'. The publication of *The Adventures of Daniel Boone* in 1784
established him as an American folk hero.

> Someone with a pioneering spirit and love of adventure; a skilled marksman

It is Harvey who strives hardest to live up to his father's expectations to fulfil
the role of an American hero in the frontier spirit, like Davy Crockett and
Daniel Boone.
KENNETH MILLARD *Contemporary American Fiction: An Introduction to American Fiction
Since 1970* 2000

No matter how many guns you own or how much firearms enthusiasm is in your soul,
you can't achieve Daniel Boone status without shooting—a lot.
American Handgunner 2005

Boop, Betty [Cart. & Com.] A glamorous, sexy, animated cartoon figure featuring in
movies produced by Fleischer Studios in the 1930s. She has enormous eyes, long eyelashes,
a rosebud mouth, and a short curly bob of hair. Dressed in a short, backless dress, she has
adventures and sings musical numbers in a high-pitched voice.

> A woman whose excessive make-up and false eyelashes give her the appearance of
> the cartoon character; a woman with a childlike, high-pitched voice

Her bangs are arranged in tiny spit curls around her face; an aging Betty Boop, down
to the spidery eyelashes.
LISA SCOTTOLINE *Final Appeal* 1994

Her voice embodied a Betty Boop sweetness, but had the power to hold out through
the band's more than hour long set without losing a trace of its strength.
ChartAttack Live Reviews 2000

Borden, Lizzie [Crime] (1860–1927) An American woman acquitted in 1893 of the charge of
murdering her father and stepmother the previous year. Nevertheless, many believed that she
had killed them, giving rise to a popular rhyme:

<blockquote>
Lizzie Borden took an axe
And gave her mother forty whacks;
When she saw what she had done
She gave her father forty-one!
</blockquote>

> A female murderer, especially one who uses a knife or axe

Nor, if Becky actually does kill Jos, is the deed done with a knife. Whatever else, Becky
is no Lizzie Borden.
JOHN SUTHERLAND *The Literary Detective: 100 Puzzles in Classic Fiction* 2000

Boreas [Gk Myth.] A Greek god, the personification of the north wind.

> A way of referring to the north wind

The dusty drops of the Widow's chandelier were laced with gossamer cobwebs and
chimed and tinkled in the fierce draughts that gusted through Arden, as if Boreas and

Eurus were holding a competition somewhere in the vicinity of the front hall or the great eagle Hraesvelg was flying up and down just to annoy them.
KATE ATKINSON *Human Croquet* 1997

Borgias [Hist.] A Neapolitan family, whose members included **Cesare Borgia** (1476–1507) and **Lucrezia (Lucretia) Borgia** (1480–1519). Cesare was a ruthless political and military leader, and was said to be the model for the ruler in Machiavelli's *The Prince*. Lucrezia, for her part, is alleged to have committed incest with both her father and her brother.

➢ Mentioned in the context of ruthless plotting and the use of poison to dispatch enemies

All cabinets are riddled with frictions, but this lot seem to be consumed with more feuds than the Borgias, and to have a similar penchant for poisoning as the preferred method of bumping off rivals.
The Observer 1997

Borodino [Hist.] The site of a bloody battle between French and Russian troops in 1812, in which the French eventually won through and continued their march to Moscow but took 33 000 casualties. The Russians withdrew with 44 000 casualties.

➢ A site of much bloodshed

Lisa carries in her spirit matters she knows not of. I find that interesting. I find that enthralling, indeed. I look at Lisa and wolves howl across the steppe, the blood flows at Borodino, Irina sighs for Moscow.
PENELOPE LIVELY *Moon Tiger* 1988

Borrow, George [Lit.] (1803–81) An English writer and traveller. His travels in England, Europe, Russia, and the Far East provided material for his narrative of gypsy life, *Lavengro* (1851), and its sequel, *The Romany Rye* (1857). These works present a partly factual, partly fictional account of his travels.

➢ A traveller, especially one who travels on foot

Their perambulations put George Borrow's tours into the Sunday stroll bracket.
www.thisispembrokeshire.net 2004

Borrower [Child. Lit.] *The Borrowers* (1952) by Mary Norton is the story of Pod, Homily, and Arrietty, a family of tiny people living beneath the floors of an old country mansion. They 'borrow' everything they need from the household of the 'human beans' above them.

➢ A tiny person; someone who takes things that belong to others, but does not regard it as stealing

She felt like a borrower in the land of giants.
BATHBURN *Sex Drugs and Rock n Roll* 2002

Bosch, Hieronymus [Art] (*c.*1450–1516) A Flemish painter whose allegorical works are filled with grotesque creatures, horribly ugly people, and macabre images, often set in strange Hell-like landscapes. Bosch's caricature-like faces are typically deformed, bloated, cadaverous, or disease-ridden.

➢ Used to describe people or animals whose appearance is grotesque

He still wasn't entirely happy about Goodenough's sexual inclinations. 'If you'd seen that gay bar,' he told Vera. 'I mean I don't care what people do but it was like a vision of Hell by Hieronymus Bosch.'
TOM SHARPE *Grantchester Grind* 1995

Boston Tea Party [Hist.] The name given to a violent demonstration by American colonists in 1773, prior to the War of American Independence. As a protest against the imposition of a tax on tea by the British parliament, in which they had no representation, the colonists dressed as native Americans, boarded three British ships moored in the harbour of Boston, Massachusetts, and threw overboard their cargo of tea.

> A rebellion

Even Montgomery County, Md., home of the FDA, is plotting to join the mini-rebellion. 'We've got a Boston Tea Party here,' laments one agency official.
Business Week Magazine 2004

Botticelli, Sandro [Art] (1445–1510) A Florentine painter of religious and mythological subjects, whose work includes such paintings as *Primavera* ('Springtime') and *Birth of Venus*. Botticelli is known for the delicate beauty of his *Madonnas and goddesses and for his gracefulness of line. His women usually have pale skin and long, wavy, fair hair.

> Used when describing a beautiful and graceful young woman

She had, yes, I suppose a Botticelli beauty, long fair hair, grey violet eyes.
JOHN FOWLES *The Magus* 1966

Boudicca (Boadicea) [Hist.] (d. AD 62) A queen of the Iceni tribe of Britons living in East Anglia. She led a revolt against the Romans, succeeding in sacking Colchester (Camulodonum) and London (Londinium), and razing St Albans (Verulamium) to the ground. The Iceni were finally defeated by the Roman governor of Britain, Suetonius Paulinus. An enduring popular image of Boudicca is that of her standing, in armour, driving a chariot.

> A female rebel; a female warrior; a woman wearing 'warpaint'; a woman driving a chariot

Riding high, and cognisant of the popularity of bellicosity, the Boudicca of Finchley turned on an enemy closer to home.
Scotland on Sunday 2004

Keira's got some funky woad face paint like a Glastonbury Boudicca.
Guardian Friday Review 2004

Bountiful, Lady [Lit.] A wealthy character in George Farquhar's comedy *The Beaux' Stratagem* (1707).

> A woman whose generosity is coupled with a certain degree of condescension

This is not simply a case of a wealthy woman doing her Lady Bountiful bit, but rather a full-time commitment to improving the world in which we live.
Scotland on Sunday 2004

Bounty [Hist.] A British navy ship which, in 1789, was bound from Tahiti to the Cape of Good Hope and the West Indies under the command of Captain *Bligh. Some members of the crew, led by Fletcher Christian, mutinied and set the captain and eighteen companions adrift in an open boat. The episode was popularized by two films, made in 1935 and 1962, both called *The Mutiny on the Bounty*.

> Mentioned in the context of a rebellion

'He's gone too far, it's too late.' Another put it more bluntly: 'Mutiny on the Bounty wouldn't be too far away.'
Sunday Business Post 2003

Bovary, Emma [Lit.] The main character in Flaubert's novel *Madame Bovary* (1857). Emma is married to a country doctor in provincial Normandy but, aspiring to a more romantic and sophisticated life, she is drawn into first one affair and then a second. When the second affair ends, she kills herself with arsenic.

➤ Someone who is dissatisfied with their life, and aspires to a more romantic or glamorous lifestyle

Your team may contain a want-away striker. For all his brilliance, beauty and flair, the want-away striker, like Emma Bovary or Nicola Six, has become restlessly aware that his destiny is elsewhere.
The Independent 1999

Bowery Boys [Cin.] A group of layabouts from Brooklyn who featured in a series of comic B movies produced between 1946 and 1958. The earlier films, in the 1940s, were gangster melodramas. Later, they descended into slapstick.

➤ Mentioned in the context of sleazy inner-city gang life

'Oh, brother,' Casey muttered as they got out of the cab. 'I've never seen a news stand that beat up.' 'Relax, will you?' R.J. told her. 'It looks like a Bowery Boys set.'
STEPHEN BOGART *Play it Again* 1994

Boy's Own [Cart. & Com.] The *Boy's Own Paper* was a popular boys' magazine sold in the late 19th and early 20th century. Founded by W. H. G. Kingston and published from 1879 until 1967, the magazine contained exciting adventure stories with titles such as 'From Powder Monkey to Admiral' and 'How I Swam the Channel'.

➤ Used to describe an exciting adventure

Pointless his journey may have been, but it is still an exhilarating *Boys' Own* adventure story.
SEBASTIAN SHAKESPEARE *Literary Review* 1994

'Boy who Cried Wolf, The' [Lit.] The title of a fable attributed to *Aesop about a shepherd boy who entertains himself by repeatedly crying, 'Wolf!' whereupon villagers rush to his rescue. Later, when his flock really is attacked by a wolf, the villagers ignore his cries for help, believing them to be false again. In some versions of the story the flock is eaten, and in other versions the boy himself is devoured by the wolf.

➤ Someone who falsely warns of impending misfortune and is not believed when real disaster strikes

When oil prices receded after the 1980–81 recession, America returned to its love affair with gas-guzzling cars. Conservationists seemed like the boy who cried wolf. Now, however, we face a real wolf.
BusinessWeek Magazine 2001

Boy Wonder [TV; Cart. & Com.] Another name for Robin, the young crime-fighting partner of the superhero *Batman in the American comic strip and films. Robin's real-life persona is Dick Grayson, a young ward of Bruce Wayne, Batman's alter ego.

➤ A young superhero; a young person with a lot of talent

A clinical finish from Everton's boy wonder Wayne Rooney earned Everton a point against Charlton at the Valley last night in an entertaining 2-2 draw.
Croydon Guardian 2003

Bracknell, Lady [Lit.] Gwendolen Fairfax's mother in Oscar *Wilde's comedy *The Importance of Being Earnest* (1895). In a famous scene Gwendolen's suitor, Jack Worthing, explains that he was discovered as a baby in a handbag, to which Lady Bracknell responds 'A handbag?' The incredulous, withering delivery of this line by Edith Evans in the 1952 film of Wilde's play is well known and often imitated.

> Used when mentioning handbags, or in the context of someone asking a question in a very emphatic and condescending way

'Why are you walking around with it in your handbag?' he demanded, giving Lady Bracknell a run for her money.
VAL MCDERMID *Clean Break* 1995

'The reason I came to tell you about it tonight was to warn you that you will almost certainly be woken at dawn by drumming.' 'Drumming?' bellowed the dean, giving the word an emphasis and inflexion reminiscent of Lady Bracknell and the handbag.
RUTH DUDLEY EDWARDS *Murder in a Cathedral* 1996

Brady Bunch, The [TV] An American television series about the family of a second marriage between a widow and widower. The wife, Carol, had three daughters while the husband, Mike, had three sons. The family lived in suburbia, where the parents presided over good-natured tussles between the children, all accompanied by cheerful shiny-white-toothed smiles. The series was shown between 1969 and 1974 in the United States and on ITV from 1970 to 1973.

> A large family, or a large crowd of people doing something together; also mentioned in the context of a happy family that seems too good to be true

Hawai'i called to the US mainland via music, image, hula skirt, and resort hotel, and the paradise-seekers came in droves like the Brady Bunch.
Jacket Magazine 2000

And when his mother moved him to Canada and into a north Toronto neighbourhood, 'it wasn't quite the wholesome Brady Bunch thing I expected,' he says. 'More guns and drugs than I expected.'
Eye Weekly (Toronto) 2005

Brando, Marlon [Cin.] (1924–2004) An American actor whose films include *A Streetcar Named Desire* (1951), *On the Waterfront* (1954), and *The *Godfather* (1972). He often played tough men from harsh backgrounds, and was particularly associated with the mumbling delivery of his lines.

> A tough guy who does not speak very much

Colin the Englishman is distrusted because he talks not too much but too well. Real painters grunt, like Marlon Brando.
MARGARET ATWOOD *Cat's Eye* 1988

Brave New World [Lit.] The title of a satirical novel by Aldous Huxley (1932) which portrays a futuristic world in which human emotion has been eradicated, babies are bred in laboratories, and citizens are conditioned to accept their social destiny willingly. The phrase comes originally from the words of *Miranda in *Shakespeare's *The Tempest* (1623):

> How beauteous mankind is! O brave new world,
> That has such people in't!

> A future world that seems to offer hope and new opportunities; also mentioned in the context of a world dominated by science, especially genetic engineering or cloning

So I spent the next quarter-century ignoring my father's advice to jump into the brave new world of computer programming, thus missing my chance to found Microsoft.
Florida Times-Union: Charlie Patton column 2003

Yet again, the spectre of a Brave New World is conjured up, in which designer babies are cloned to order, and we sacrifice our humanity on the altar of science.
Spiked Online 2004

Bray *See* VICAR OF BRAY.

bread and circuses [Hist.] A translation of the Latin phrase *panem et circenses*, used by the Roman satirist Juvenal (AD *c*.60–*c*.130). Writing about the needs of the modern citizen, Juvenal said: 'Only two things does he anxiously wish for—bread and circuses.'

➤ Entertainment or political policies that are offered by a government to its people in a cynical attempt to keep the people happy

George Bush is offering bread and circuses, declaring that the US will put a space station on the moon and a man on Mars.
Northern Rivers Echo News 2004

Brendan, St [People] (484–577) An Irish abbot. The *Navigatio Brendani* (The Navigation of St Brendan, *c*.1050) recounts the story of a voyage made by St Brendan and a band of monks to a land of saints far to the north and west of Ireland, possibly Orkney or the Hebrides.

➤ A traveller by sea

Brer Rabbit [Leg. & Folk.] The trickster rabbit hero of many of the tales told by Uncle Remus in Joel Chandler Harris's various volumes of folklore tales published between 1881 and 1910.

➤ Someone who is used to enduring hardships and deprivation; someone who uses their wits to survive

Dusty ride, isn't it? I don't mind it myself; I'm used to it. Born and bred in de briar patch, like Br'er Rabbit.
WILLA CATHER *A Death in the Desert* 1905

It seems to me that when Bill Gates tells the judge (and the public on TV), 'Do anything you want to Microsoft, but please don't break it into two separate companies,' he's saying it like Br'er Rabbit.
Computer Technology Review 2000

Brief Encounter [Cin.] The title of a 1945 British film about a short love affair between a married suburban housewife and a doctor that she meets at a railway station. The affair, although characterized by intense emotions, is not physically consummated and ends when both realize the impossibility of the situation.

➤ A brief romantic meeting or affair characterized by strong emotions

With elegance and charm to spare, Emily Hurson and Ryan McVittie play two strangers whose brief encounter in a library one rainy afternoon unleashes emotional torrents.
Eye Weekly (Toronto): Arts section 2003

Brigadoon [Theatre] A Broadway musical by Lerner and Loewe set in Scotland, where a village, Brigadoon, lies under an enchantment that makes it invisible to the rest of the world except for one day every hundred years. Two American visitors, Tommy Albright and Jeff Douglas, arrive on the appropriate day and discover the village. Tommy falls in love with local girl Fiona, but if she leaves with him, Brigadoon will be lost for ever; if he stays, he will be cut off for ever from his family, friends, and normal life.

➤ A place shrouded in fog or mist, that slowly becomes visible; a place that appears and disappears, or comes to life and then becomes quiet again

Ferus Gallery emerged like Brigadoon out of the foggy hills of West Hollywood.
Art in America 2003

Like an Arctic Brigadoon, the Icehotel appears each year in mid-December and vanishes at the end of April.
Business Week Magazine 2001

Britannia [Places] The personification of Britain, usually depicted as a helmeted woman with a shield and trident. The patriotic song 'Rule, Britannia' is from *Alfred: A Masque* (1740), attributed to the Scottish poet James Thomson (1700–48).

➢ A way of referring to Britain, especially as an expression of strong patriotism

There's something deliciously ironic about the fact that two Australians are at the helm of a film in which Britannia rules, the French are soundly thrashed and Englishmen have hearts and ships of oak.
Eye Weekly (Toronto): Film section 2003

Britomart [Lit.] In the third book of Edmund Spenser's *The Faerie Queene* (1590, 1596) Britomart searches the world for Artegall, the knight of Justice. She is disguised as a knight wearing a helmet and armour.

➢ A young woman in armour

If she was Belphoebe, Frederica, in a kind of brief knitted corselet of dark grey wool with a glitter in it, and boots with a metallic sheen, was Britomart, her hair itself cut into a kind of bronze helmet, more space-age, maybe, than Renaissance.
A. S. BYATT *The Virgin in the Garden* 1978

Brobdingnagian [Lit.] Brobdingnag is the land inhabited by giants in book II of Swift's *Gulliver's Travels* (1726).

➢ Used to describe anything that is gigantic in size or scale

Eight football pitches could be accommodated in its Brobdingnagian interior.
Architectural Review 2002

Brodie, Miss Jean [Lit.] An Edinburgh schoolmistress during the 1930s, in Muriel Spark's novel *The Prime of Miss Jean Brodie,* first published in 1961. She is a spinster with firm views on the education of young women, remembered for saying: 'I am putting old heads on your young shoulders...all my pupils are the crème de la crème.'

➢ A prim schoolmistress; someone who speaks in a polite, precise, and authoritative voice

Kevin would exclaim, 'Yoghurt! Steamed vegetables! Lots of fruit!—this is Miss Jean Brodie warning you!' Gabe would just smile feebly, sleep sand in his eyes.
EDMUND WHITE *Farewell Symphony* 1997

Brontë [Lit.] The Brontë sisters, **Charlotte** (1816–55), **Emily** (1818–48), and **Anne** (1820–49), together with their brother **Branwell** (1817–48), grew up in Haworth, Yorkshire. The novels written by the sisters (*Jane Eyre,* 1847, *Shirley,* 1849, and *Villette,* 1853, by Charlotte; *Agnes Gray,* 1847, and *The Tenant of Wildfell Hall,* 1848, by Anne; and *Wuthering Heights,* 1847, by Emily) address the emotional lives of their characters, who are capable of strong passions. They combine romance with realism. Emily's work in particular, evokes the landscape of the moors to which she was deeply attached.

➢ Used in the context of strong feelings of love or passion; also used to invoke wild moorland countryside

I raised the back of one hand to my brow, and affected a Bronté-esque tone. 'Oh Stephanie, my beloved. Why do you have to torture me this way?'
ROGER FREDERICK *The Shrewdness of Apes* 2005

'Brother, can you spare a dime?' [Mus.] The title of a song with lyrics by Edgar Harburg, composed in the 1930s during the Great Depression in the USA. The song has become iconic of the thousands of people reduced from comfortable circumstances to begging during the period. A British film made in 1975 about the Great Depression used the same title.

> Used to invoke a heartless attitude by authorities towards those experiencing financial difficulties

And for consumers this will mean that the days of free Internet access are effectively over because in the world of economics there are never any free lunches and you certainly don't get 'Something For Nothing'. Brother, Can You Spare A Dime?
MotleyFool.co.uk: Comment 2002

brother's keeper, my [Bible] A phrase taken from *Cain's response to God in the book of Genesis when asked the whereabouts of his murdered brother. Saying that he did not know where his brother was, Cain asked, 'Am I my brother's keeper?' (Gen. 4: 9).

> Used when discussing how much responsibility people have or should have for the welfare of others

It's that fundamental belief—I am my brother's keeper, I am my sister's keeper—that makes this country work.
Black Enterprise 2004

Brown, Buster [Cart. & Com.] A US comic strip created by R. F. Outcault and published in the Sunday newspapers from 1902 until the 1920s. Buster Brown was a mischievous but likeable boy. His clothes inspired the 'Buster suit', which became a popular garment for young boys in the early years of the 20th century. This was a smock-like suit with a broad white collar. The character was also taken up by the Brown Shoe Company, so 'Buster Brown shoes' were also popular.

> A mischievous boy; also used to invoke the smock-like suit and broad white collar typically worn by the cartoon character

Except for his Buster Brown collar, he was dressed like a man, in long trousers, vest and jacket.
NATHANIEL WEST *The Day of the Locust* 1939

Brown, Capability (Lancelot Brown) [People] (1716–83) An English landscape gardener who evolved an English style of natural-looking landscape parks.

> Someone skilled in garden design

We now have a lovely house with a small garden and I am looking forward to next year when we can get the garden sorted. Capability Brown I am not, Incapability Lao Wai I am.
Shanghai Star 2002

Brown, John [Hist.] (1800–59) An American abolitionist who sought to free slaves by force. He was captured in 1859 after raiding a government arsenal at Harpers Ferry in Virginia in an attempt to arm runaway slaves and start an uprising. Brown was tried and executed, and became a martyr for abolitionists. He is remembered in the song 'John Brown's Body', which was popular in the North during the American Civil War.

> Someone who fights against injustice; someone prepared to die for their beliefs

'Lincoln,' Booth told his sister, 'is walking in the footsteps of old John Brown.'
Houston Chronicle: Book Reviews 2005

Bruegel, Pieter (Pieter Brueghel, Breughel) [Art] (c.1525–69) A Flemish artist, known as Pieter Bruegel the Elder and nicknamed Peasant Bruegel. Bruegel produced landscapes, religious allegories, and satirical paintings of peasant life, such as *Peasant Wedding Feast* (1566). His work displays a real interest in village customs combined with a satirical view of folly, vice, and the sins of the flesh.

> Used to invoke rustic or peasant life

The conference at Durban was but the formal core of a giant carnival, something like a medieval ice fair in a Bruegel painting.
Time Magazine—Michael Elliott column 2004

Brummell, Beau (George Poryan Brummell) [People] (1778–1840) A well-known dandy and friend of the Prince Regent, later George IV. He was known for his elegant dress sense.

➤ An elegantly dressed man

Here's some tips for aspiring buskers: look the part, don't dress like Beau Brummel, make eye-contact and be seen to be having a rare time.
Scotland on Sunday 2003

Brutus, Marcus Junius [Hist.] (85–42 BC) A Roman senator who, with *Cassius, was a leader of the conspirators who assassinated Julius Caesar in AD 44. Caesar's dying words as he was stabbed by his friend Brutus are supposed to have been 'Et tu, Brute?' ('You too, Brutus?'). Brutus subsequently committed suicide after being defeated by *Antony and Octavian at Philippi.

➤ Someone who betrays a friend or leader

But his naked ambition has long raised fears among his colleagues and superiors—the fear that he is a Brutus waiting to attack his Caesar.
Taipei Times 2001

Brynhild [Myth.] A *Valkyrie whom Sigurd won by penetrating the wall of fire behind which she lay in an enchanted sleep, from which he revived her. She corresponds to Brunhild in the *Nibelungenlied*, the wife of Gunther, who instigated the murder of *Siegfried. As Brunnhilde, she is one of the main characters in Wagner's operatic cycle *The Ring of the Nibelungs*.

➤ A strong woman; a female warrior

Brynner, Yul [Cin.] (1915–85) A US film star whose films include *The King and I* (1956) and *The Magnificent Seven* (1960), but is probably remembered chiefly for his shaved head.

➤ Someone with a completely bald head

...tall, cheerful man with a Yul Brynner hairstyle (he jokes of being 'follicly challenged'), a keen intellect and a penchant for icon-smashing.
Globe & Mail 1994

Buchan, John [Lit.] (1875–1940) A Scottish novelist chiefly remembered for his adventure stories, often featuring elaborate cross-country chases. Of these, the five thrillers featuring his hero Richard Hannay are perhaps the most popular, particularly *The Thirty-Nine Steps* (1915).

➤ Mentioned in the context of an exciting adventure story

In the old days it was Salt Lake Flats, Utah, now it's the Nevada desert. If you are British, and in the John Buchan tradition, you have to go abroad to enjoy the true spirit of speedy adventure.
The Observer 1997

Buckingham Palace [Places] The official residence of the British sovereign in Westminster, London. It has 19 state rooms, 52 principal bedrooms, 188 staff bedrooms, 92 offices, and 78 bathrooms.

➤ A very large or luxurious residence

She had been enchanted by her night in the hotel: when you're young and poor and the best thing you've ever slept in was a $20 room by the railroad tracks, the Hilton must seem like Buckingham Palace.
JOHN DUNNING *The Bookman's Wake* 1995

Buddha, the [Rel.] (*c*.563–*c*.480 BC) An Indian religious teacher (b. Siddhartha Gautama) and the founder of Buddhism. Statues or pictures represent him in a state of tranquil meditation.

> ➤ Someone sitting cross-legged on the ground; someone in a state of serene calm

The gorilla…sat like a hairy mystified Buddha on the shallow ledge.
ALICE WALKER *Entertaining God* 1994

Now his face was as serene as a Buddha.
BARBARA PARKER *Suspicion of Guilt* 1995

Bugs Bunny [Cart. & Com.] A cartoon rabbit who first appeared in 1938 in a Warner Brothers animated cartoon. He has two prominent front teeth, wide white cheeks, and tall vertical ears. He successfully resolves his feuds with other characters using wit and resourcefulness and his trademark line is 'Eh. What's up, Doc?'

> ➤ Someone with very large front teeth

Sporting Bugs Bunny teeth and straggly sun-bleached hair, Ledger gives one of his most impressive performances as dippy, easily distracted hippie Skip.
Scotland on Sunday 2005

Bull, John [Art] The personification of England or of an Englishman, first appearing in the satire *Life is a Bottomless Pit; or, The History of John Bull* by John Arbuthnot (1712). He has often appeared in cartoons in the 19th and 20th centuries and is usually depicted as a stout country squire in tailcoat, breeches, a top hat, and boots.

> ➤ The typical Englishman; English people collectively

'Don't you think the English nation perfect in every respect?' asked Sallie. 'I should be ashamed of myself if I didn't.' 'He's a true John Bull.'
LOUISA M. ALCOTT *Little Women* 1868

In 1799, when Napoleon was still vying for power, General Hoche, a schoolboys' hero and onetime lover of Madame Bonaparte, had landed in Ireland and almost succeeded in defeating John Bull outright.
JEANETTE WINTERSON *The Passion* 1987

Bulldog Drummond *See* DRUMMOND.

Bull Run [Hist.] The site of two battles fought between the Union and Confederate armies during the American Civil War. In the first battle in 1861 General Jackson's Confederate Army held off Union troops until relieved by reinforcements, in the process earning for Jackson the nickname Stonewall. In the second battle, General Robert E. Lee defeated the Union army, driving them from the battleground and forcing them to retreat to Washington, DC.

> ➤ A battle

Bumble, Mr [Lit.] The beadle of the parish in Dickens's *Oliver *Twist* (1837–8) who makes the orphan Oliver's life a misery. He is a fat, pompous, petty tyrant.

> ➤ A pompous or inflexible official (noun *Bumbledom*)

He had fought in the open, like a man, against stupidity, and Bumbledom, and mediocrity, and he knew the world well enough to expect a bitter return.
ROBERTSON DAVIES *Leaven of Malice* 1954

Bunbury [Lit.] The fictitious character invented by Algy Moncrieff in *Wilde's *The Importance of Being Earnest* (1895), whose sickly disposition requiring visits from Algy provides a refuge for him when he wishes to avoid engagements in town, in particular to avoid his aunt, Lady *Bracknell.

> An excuse one can use to leave home and avoid commitments

'Your sister phoned. One or the other of them—they hardly ever say—I told her you were in Norfolk. Norfolk's getting to be your Bunbury, isn't it?' Troy had need of a Bunbury. If there was one thing his life lacked it was a good, irrefutable Bunbury.
JOHN LAWTON *Black Out* 1995

Bunker, Archie [TV] The main character in the US television sitcom *All in the Family* shown on CBS from 1971 to 1991. The series derived from the British series *Till Death Us Do Part* and has approximately the same situation, that of a bigoted working-class man fighting with his daughter and son-in-law. Like Alf *Garnett, Archie, a dock foreman, also rails at his downtrodden wife and his ethnic neighbours.

> An intolerant or racist bigot

This asswipe is as racist as Archie Bunker, only more dangerous.
In These Times 2004

Bunker Hill [Hist.] A hill near Boston which was the site of the first pitched battle of the American Revolution in 1775, where the American colonists were forced to retreat by superior British weaponry. Although the victory was British, the colonists' tenacity and the losses they inflicted on the British boosted the Americans' morale.

> A battle fought with great courage

Bunter, Billy [Child. Lit.] The rotund schoolboy hero of a series of stories by Frank Richards set in a boys' public school called Greyfriars. The stories first appeared in the *Magnet* comic in 1908. Known as 'the Fat Owl of the Remove' on account of his large, round spectacles, Bunter has an obsessive love of 'tuck' and is willing to do anything, even steal from his friends, in order to obtain it.

> An overweight boy; someone who eats to excess

In 1953, the Tory government of Mr Churchill lifted the wartime rationing on sweets. That day I was violently sick. But not before consuming a quantity of toffee, chocolate, sherbet and gobstoppers with a Bunter-like passion.
TRISTAN GAREL-JONES *The Observer* 1996

Every second kid coming up the road is a Billy Bunter lookalike with their fists stuck in crisp bags.
The Kingdom (Killarney, Co. Kerry) 2003

Bunyan, Paul [Leg. & Folk.] An American folk hero, a giant lumberjack of tremendous strength, who was accompanied on his travels by Babe, a gigantic blue ox.

> A very tall, strong man

A huge Paul Bunyan type man in the hellish glow of an iron foundry is using gigantic iron pliers and tongs to manipulate small metal objects.
American Journal of Clinical Hypnosis 2004

Buridan's ass [Philos.] Buridan, a French scholastic philosopher at the end of the 12th century, is credited with the following sophism: if a hungry ass were placed exactly between two haystacks in every respect equal, it would starve to death, because there would be no motive why it should go to one rather than to the other.

> A person who cannot decide between two courses of action and who adopts neither

So she continued to brood and suffer, standing flat as Buridan's Ass between equal bundles of hay...
ALEXANDER THEROUX *Adultery* 1987

Burke and Hare [Crime] Two bodysnatchers, **William Burke** (1792–1829) and his accomplice **William Hare**, who operated in Edinburgh in the early 19th century. Burke was convicted of murdering those whose bodies he subsequently sold for dissection.

> ➤ Murderers; bodysnatchers

> Muir describes the story, resurrecting Welsh's most antisocial creations, the Doyle crime family, as a 'latter-day Burke and Hare'.
> *Sunday Herald* 2001

Burne-Jones, Edward [Art] (1833–98) An English painter and designer whose work was largely inspired by medieval legends and other literary themes. His paintings, in subdued tones and peopled by pale knights and damsels, evoke a romantic mythical dreamworld.

> ➤ Used to invoke romantic good looks

> A silly woman would say he looked romantic. He reminded you of one of the knights of Burne-Jones though he was on a larger scale and there was no suggestion that he suffered from the chronic colitis that afflicted those unfortunate creatures.
> W. SOMERSET MAUGHAM 'The Human Element' in *The World Over* 1951

burning bush [Bible] According to the story in the Bible, God appeared to *Moses in the form of a burning bush: 'And the angel of the Lord appeared to him in a flame of fire out of the midst of a bush; and he looked, and lo, the bush was burning, yet it was not consumed' (Exod. 3: 2).

> ➤ A sign or means of communication from God

> The mushroom cloud was the twentieth century equivalent of the burning bush.
> CHARLES HOSFORD *One Night in Ghadames* 2002

Butch Cassidy *See* CASSIDY.

Butler, Rhett [Lit. Cin.] The dashing and charming hero of Margaret Mitchell's novel *Gone with the Wind* (1936). The book was made into an immensely popular Hollywood film in 1939, with the role of Butler played by Clark Gable. Set at the time of the American Civil War, the book tells the story of Butler's romance with southern belle Scarlett *O'Hara.

> ➤ An attractive romantic hero

> He looked at himself in the floor length mirror. 'My, my Miss Scarlet,' he said, 'your Rhett Butler's ready for you tonight. Not bad.
> E. C. PATTERSON *dancaster.com* 2003

butterfly effect [Lit.] A phrase derived from the title of a paper (1979) by the American mathematician and meteorologist Edward Lorenz (1917–2008): 'Predictability: Does the flap of a butterfly's wings in Brazil set off a tornado in Texas?'

> ➤ Used when talking about small changes that have significant knock-on effects

> There is a sense that progress and understanding will require something new—an economics of virtuous circles, thresholds and butterfly effects, in which small changes have very large effects.
> *Taipei Times* 2005

Byron, Lord [Lit.] (1788–1824) An English Romantic poet, famous for his passionate love affairs as much as for his poetry. His major works include *Childe Harold's Pilgrimage* (1812–18) and *Don Juan* (1819–24). He travelled widely in Europe, and left England permanently following a series of scandals, most notably the suggestion of incest with his sister, and problems with debts.

> ➤ A passionate romantic hero who leads an unconventional, adventurous life (adjective *Byronic,* noun *Byronism*)

He's got a streak of his father's Byronism. Why, look at the way he threw up his chances when he left my office; going off like that for six months with a knapsack, and all for what?—to study foreign architecture—foreign!
JOHN GALSWORTHY *The Man of Property* 1906

Anyway, there I am on my own and who should turn up but, yes! Carl Phipps, all brooding and Byronic looking in a big coat.
BEN ELTON *Inconceivable* 1999

Byzantine [Hist.] The Byzantine Empire between the 4th and 15th centuries was characterized by highly ritualized politics and complex bureaucratic structures.

> ➤ Used to describe something extremely convoluted and devious

[They are] trying to cut 'bureaucracy' and claw power away from the Byzantine layers of local education administration.
The Observer 1997

Caesar [Hist.] The title given to Roman emperors from **Augustus** (63 BC–AD 14) to **Hadrian** (AD 76–138). The title is usually taken to refer to **Julius Caesar** (100–44 BC), who established the First Triumvirate in ancient Rome with Pompey and Crassus and became consul in 59 BC. He commanded large parts of Gaul, extending Roman rule to the west, and invaded Britain in 55–54 BC. He later became emperor of Rome, and was assassinated by conspirators in 44 BC.

> ➢ A powerful leader
>
> Some commentators even began to see Bill Gates as a sympathetic figure, like Caesar in his last days.
> *Linux Journal* 2000

Caesar's wife [Hist.] Pompeia, the wife of Julius Caesar. When it was suggested that she was having an extramarital affair, Caesar divorced her saying that, although he knew nothing of the affair, 'Caesar's wife must be above suspicion.'

> ➢ A person who is required to behave in such a way that no suspicion of guilt can ever fall on them
>
> If you are running a trading operation, you have to be like Caesar's wife, beyond reproach.
> *Business Week Magazine* 2001

Cagliostro, Count Alessandro [People] (1743–95) A charlatan and adventurer born in Palermo, whose real name was Giuseppe Balsamo. He claimed to be able to grant everlasting youth to anyone who would pay him for his secret. Cagliostro was imprisoned for life by the Inquisition on the grounds of his association with freemasonry.

> ➢ Someone who does not seem to age
>
> Odd, really, I never thought of Marat having a beginning. I thought he was thousands and thousands of years old, like Cagliostro.
> HILARY MANTEL *A Place of Greater Safety* 1992

Cagney, James [Cin.] (1899–1986) An American film star. He was a talented and versatile actor although he is usually remembered chiefly for his roles as a tough gangster in films such as *The Public Enemy* (1931) and *White Heat* (1949). He won an academy award for his role as the vaudeville dancer George M. Cohan in *Yankee Doodle Dandy* (1942).

> ➢ A tough gangster or macho man
>
> 'O.K. Where the hell do you think you're going babe?' 'That is pure Cagney.'
> REGINALD HILL *On Beulah Height* 1998

Cain [Bible] The first-born son of *Adam and Eve, according to the book of Genesis, who murdered his younger brother Abel. Cain was a tiller of the ground and Abel a keeper of sheep. When they brought their offerings to God, Abel's lamb was accepted but Cain's offering from his harvest was not. In jealous anger Cain killed his brother. Once his crime was revealed, Cain was cursed by God for ever. He was cast out from his homeland and forced to live a life of vagrancy as an outcast for the rest of his life. God branded him with a mark, to indicate that no one should kill him and shorten his nomadic punishment. The phrase 'mark of Cain' has come to stand for the sign of a murderer.

➤ An outcast; a murderer; a man jealous of his brother; someone who bears an external mark which shows their inner corruption

'If I had only got her with me—if I only had!' he said. 'Hard work would be nothing to me then! But that was not to be. I—Cain—go alone as I deserve—an outcast and a vagabond.'
THOMAS HARDY *The Mayor of Casterbridge* 1886

Like Cain in Genesis, Lum Choy's scar on his forehead marks him, symbolizing the kind of man he is: deceitful, repulsive, externally as well as internally.
MELUS 2001

cakes and ale [Shakes.] A quotation from *Twelfth Night* (1601): 'Dost thou think because thou art virtuous there shall be no more cakes and ale?' The phrase was used as the title of a 1930 novel by W. Somerset Maugham.

➤ Merrymaking

This is the worst kind of destructive Puritanism—denying other people cakes and ale because you've never enjoyed them yourself.
The Sunday Times 2004

Calamity Jane [People] (*c.*1852–1903) A nickname given to Martha Jane Burke, the famous American frontierswoman, because she is said to have warned that 'calamity' would come to any man who tried to court her. Often dressing in men's clothes, she was renowned for her skill at riding and shooting.

➤ A prophet of disaster

Savvy tourists are beginning to realize that the inaccurate media reports, plus exaggerated 'Calamity Jane' government travel advisories about alleged disease, pestilence, and plague in Phuket, are 'just a crock of BS,' as Siam Palm and Jungle Boyz nightclub owner Khun Allen puts it.
The Advocate 2005

Calchas [Gk Myth.] The wisest of the Greek soothsayers at the time of the Trojan War. He is supposed to have died of grief and disappointment after another soothsayer, Mopsus, was shown to be better than him at prophecy.

➤ A prophet

Caliban [Shakes.] A character in *The Tempest* (1623). A brutish and misshapen monster, Caliban is the son of the witch Sycorax, and was the sole inhabitant of the island before Prospero's arrival.

➤ A man of savage and bestial nature

We see he has the flickering eyes of a Caliban.
DAVID DEE *Prince of Midnight* 2003

Caligula, Gaius Caesar Germanicus [Hist.] (AD 12–41) A Roman emperor, whose nickname, Caligula, came from the miniature military boots (*caligulae*) that he wore as a small child. His brief reign was notorious for its cruelty and tyrannical excesses. Caligula was famously supposed to have given a consulship to his horse Incitatus.

➤ A cruel tyrant; someone who gives a special honour to an animal

I just want him to go on making films that expose our rat's nest of world leaders as charlatans and warmongers whose greed for power and obscene stacks of money makes Caligula look like Gandhi.
The Observer 2004

To my mind, his most serious competition [for BBC Sports Personality of the Year] comes from a couple of horses—Best Mate and Persian Punch—and keen as the British are on animals, I don't think they are ready to go the full Caligula and promote a nag to such a prestigious position.
The Observer 2003

Calvary [Bible] The hill, also known as *Golgotha, just outside Jerusalem where *Jesus Christ was crucified.

➤ An experience of intense mental suffering

Of course, the FA Cup could still prove United's Calvary this season, as it nearly did in the third round against Sunderland, who led at Old Trafford and Roker Park.
The Guardian 1996

Calvin, John [People] (1509-64) A French Protestant theologian and reformer, a leader of the Protestant Reformation in France and Switzerland.

➤ Used in the context of strict puritanism and a rigid moral code (adjective *Calvinist*; noun *Calvinist*)

'I never agreed with all that entertainment for the tourists,' the old man added. 'At least the gambling and whoring. I'm no Calvinist, but to me that's just dirty money.'
PAUL JOHNSTON *Body Politic* 1997

Calydonian boar hunt [Gk Myth.] When *Artemis sent a huge boar to devastate the land of Calydon, its ruler, Meleager, assembled a band of heroes, including *Castor and Pollux, *Theseus, and *Jason, to hunt the boar in what became known as the Calydonian boar hunt. Meleager himself killed the boar and gave the head to *Atalanta, who had first wounded it.

➤ A great hunt

Calypso [Gk Myth.] A nymph who lived on the island of Ogygia. When *Odysseus was shipwrecked on the island, Calypso took him for her lover, offering him immortality if he would become her husband. She kept him on her island for seven years until Zeus intervened and ordered her to release him.

➤ A woman who is dangerously attractive to men

Perhaps he had too fixed an idea of what a siren looked like and the circumstances in which she appeared—long tresses, a chaste alabaster nudity, a mermaid's tail, matched by an Odysseus with a face acceptable in the best clubs. There were no Doric temples in the Undercliff; but here was a Calypso.
JOHN FOWLES *The French Lieutenant's Woman* 1969

Camelot [Arth. Leg.] The court of the legendary King *Arthur and his Knights of the *Round Table. The name was applied to the White House of John F. Kennedy's presidency (1961-3) on account of Kennedy's youth and glamorous image, which inspired hopes of a new golden age in the USA.

➤ An idealized place of government

Beazley lurked on the sidelines of Conference mourning his lost imperium, his Camelot that was not to be.
Northern Rivers Echo News 2003

Camilla [Gk Myth.] A Volscian princess, dedicated when young to the service of *Diana. A huntress and warrior, Camilla was so fast a runner she could run over a field of corn without crushing it, and over the surface of the sea without her feet getting wet.

> ➤ A woman who can run very swiftly
>
> Margaret ran, swift as Camilla, down to the window.
> ELIZABETH GASKELL *North and South* 1854–5

Camille [Cin.] The title of several films based on the novel and play by Alexandre Dumas (*fils*) *La Dame aux camélias* (1852). The version starring Greta *Garbo in 1936 followed six previous silent films. The story is that of the beautiful tubercular courtesan Marguerite Gautier, who has a doomed love affair with the innocent young Armand Duval. Their romance cannot be sanctioned by society and his father persuades Marguerite to give up Armand for his own benefit. She dies of her disease (in the Garbo film, dying in Armand's arms). The story is also the basis for Verdi's *La Traviata*.

> ➤ A tragic young woman of delicate health
>
> As she started to speak she coughed slightly, then, laughing, said, in a low, rich voice, a trifle husky: 'You see I make the traditional Camille entrance—with the cough.'
> WILLA CATHER *A Death in the Desert* 1905

Camp David [Places] The country retreat of the US president, in the Appalachian Mountains in Maryland. President Carter hosted talks there between the leaders of Israel and Egypt, which led to the Camp David agreements of 1978 and the peace treaty between Israel and Egypt of 1979.

> ➤ Mentioned in the context of peace negotiations
>
> Let us pledge to make this spirit of Camp David a new chapter in the history of our nations.
> *CNN transcripts: Larry King Live* 2003

Canaan [Bible] The land, later known as Ancient Palestine, which the *Israelites gradually conquered and occupied during the latter part of the second millennium BC. In the Bible, it was the land promised by God to *Abraham and his descendants (Gen. 12: 7).

> ➤ A promised land or heaven
>
> Yet from those origins was born a spiritual and social narrative that posited Canada as Canaan for generations of American slaves.
> *Eye Weekly (Toronto): Film section* 2005

Candaules [People] (d. *c.*685 BC) A king of Lydia who continually praised his wife's beauty to his favourite officer, Gyges. Eventually, he insisted that Gyges should see the queen naked, in order to prove how beautiful she was. Though Gyges was to remain hidden, the queen realized what had happened and sent for Gyges, offering him the alternatives of killing the king and ruling with her as his wife or dying immediately. He opted for life and killed the king.

> ➤ A man who is betrayed by a woman
>
> 'My observation has been that we get the women we deserve, King Candaules,' I said.
> ROBERTSON DAVIES *The Deptford Trilogy* 1970

Candide [Lit.] The naive young hero of *Voltaire's satire of the same name, published in 1759. Accompanied by his tutor, *Pangloss, who assures him repeatedly that 'all is for the best in the best of all possible worlds', Candide has many adventures and suffers many mishaps, often as a result of his ingenuous and trusting nature.

> Someone who is young, innocent, and naive; someone who always sees the best in a situation

Δ modern Candide recently arrived from the rural South, he needs knowledge as much as therapy.
Hudson Review 2005

I'll just focus on the positive, like Candide.
Sofia Echo 2004

cannot tell a lie [Hist.] A phrase attributed to the American President George *Washington, when he reputedly admitted to chopping down his father's prized cherry tree.

> Used when admitting to wrongdoing or admitting an unpalatable truth

Like any good father I want my daughter to be happy. I wish her nothing but healthy and loving relationships, filled with joy and laughter and intimacy. Just not yet. I cannot tell a lie: I'm eased by the postponement of her entrance to the thorny world of dating.
Sofia Echo 2004

Canute [Hist.] (d. 1035) A Danish-born king of England, Denmark, and Norway. According to the famous story, Canute reproved his flattering courtiers by demonstrating that, although he was king, he did not have the power to stop the incoming tide. He is traditionally remembered, however, as foolishly and obstinately attempting to command the advancing waves to stay back and failing.

> Someone who attempts to prevent an inevitable change, particularly when their attempt is futile

'Globalisation was a fact of life that wasn't going away and we couldn't stand on the shore like King Canute,' says an M&S spokeswoman.
BBC News: Business 2004

Cape Horn [Places] The extreme tip of South America, notorious for its bad weather and dangerous sea currents which make it very difficult to navigate around safely.

> Any point or cape that is difficult to navigate around; a problem that is difficult to overcome

'There is a Cape Horn of the mind, too, which is as difficult to double as the real. Monstrous? Yes, I would allow that its waves are monstrous.
TIMOTHY MO *An Insular Possession* 1986

On July 14 they launched into a soupy fog from Surf Beach, heading south toward Point Conception—known as 'the Cape Horn of the Pacific' for its rocky headlands and northwesterly gales.
Outside Online Magazine 2003

Capone, Al [Crime] (1899–1947) A gangster who was notorious for his involvement in organized crime in Chicago in the 1920s. Though it was never possible to find sufficient evidence to convict him of his crimes, he was eventually imprisoned in 1931 for tax evasion. Capone died in prison.

> A gangster

If you 're feeling like Al Capone with a fat bank roll and a baseball bat, the Brothers [with their album] are achieving the desired effect.
Pitchfork.com record reviews 2002

Capp, Andy [Cart. & Com.] A British comic strip character created by Reg Smythe, which has appeared in the *Daily Mirror* and *Sunday Mirror* newspapers since 1957. Andy Capp is a stereotypical working-class British man, who wears a trademark cloth cap and indulges in traditional working-class pursuits such as pigeon racing, darts, and snooker.

> ➤ A stereotypical working class man; a man wearing a cloth cap
>
> The kind of people going into allotments is changing. There is a definite trend with more women and more younger people. There is more organic gardening. The Andy Capp image is fading.
> *Sunday Herald* 2000

Capra, Frank [Cin.] (1897–1991) An Italian-born US film director. Many of his films, such as *Mr Smith Goes to Washington* (1939) and *It's a Wonderful Life* (1946), celebrate the idea of the humble common man whose idealism, honesty, and goodness always triumph over materialism, deceit, and selfishness.

> ➤ Used when describing a rose-tinted view of the world in which honesty and goodness triumph (adjective *Capraesque*)
>
> Spielberg has gone for a Capra-esque tale of human spirit triumphing against the odds.
> *IndieLondon film reviews* 2004

Capulet [Shakes.] Juliet's quick-tempered father in *Romeo and Juliet* (1599). He flies into a rage when his daughter refuses to marry Count Paris, violently berating her for her disobedience and threatening to drag her to the church if necessary.

> ➤ A domineering father

Caravaggio, Michelangelo Merisi da [Art] (*c.*1571–1610) An Italian painter whose paintings are distinctive in their dramatic use of light and shade (chiaroscuro), often showing figures against a very dark background with light shining from one side or from below onto their faces.

> ➤ Mentioned when describing a scene in which there is contrasting light and shade
>
> [The table] was lit by one tall lamp with a dark shade; the light flowed downwards, concentrated on the white cloth, and was then reflected up, lighting our faces strangely, Caravaggio fashion, against the surrounding darkness.
> JOHN FOWLES *The Magus* 1966

Carnaby Street [Places] A street in the West End of London which became famous in the 1960s as a centre of the popular fashion industry.

> ➤ Mentioned in the context of 1960s fashion and popular culture
>
> The autumn range will include…a punk-style orange and black jumper dress for £19.99 based on a '60s Carnaby Street feel.
> *Yorkshire Post Today* 2003

Carry On films [Cin.] A series of British comedy films, the first of which, *Carry On Sergeant*, was made in 1958 and the last in 1974. Starring comedians such as Sid James, Kenneth Williams, Barbara Windsor, and Hattie Jacques, the films were characterized by a combination of bawdy humour, bad puns, and slapstick comedy.

> ➤ Used when describing a situation of complete chaos or confusion
>
> All of our tours have been like something out of a Carry On film. We've never had one go to plan yet.
> *Punk and Oi in the UK: band interviews* 2002

Cartland, Barbara [Lit.] (1901–2000) An English writer of light romantic fiction, which she produced prolifically over many years. Her popular romances include *Bride to a Brigand* (1983) and *A Secret Passage to Love* (1992).

> Used when talking about a clichéd or saccharine love story

You would think a man capable of imagining a universe full of such fantastic characters could draw on some real-life inspiration that would make love between Anakin Skywalker and Padme seem less like a cheesy Barbara Cartland romance or a douche commercial. *Trinidad Guardian* 2005

Carton, Sidney [Lit.] The lazy English barrister in Dickens's *A Tale of Two Cities* (1859) who loves Lucie Manette and strongly resembles Charles Darnay, whom she falls in love with and marries. When Darnay is imprisoned in Paris, about to face the guillotine, Carton sacrifices himself by taking Darnay's place in prison. On the scaffold, he utters the famous last words of the novel: 'It is a far, far better thing I do, than I have ever done; it is a far, far better rest that I go to, than I have ever known.'

> Someone who sacrifices their own life to save another; someone who faces death bravely

When the clerk of the court asked his name he gave it with the air of Sidney Carton at the guillotine, only gloomier.
GILLIAN LINSCOTT *Stage Fright* 1994

Casanova, Giovanni Jacopo Casanova de Seingalt [People] (1725–98) An Italian adventurer, spy, gambler, and librarian who, according to his *Memoirs*, engaged in a prodigious number of promiscuous love affairs.

> A man who has a lot of success with women; a philanderer

It seemed the young prince was already a Casanova in the making, an expert at coaxing and cajoling girls.
GALE GREEN *The Kids* 2005

Casey [Lit.] The eponymous hero of the late 19th-century ballad 'Casey at the Bat' by Ernest L. Thayer. Casey was confidently expected to save the day in a baseball game but, having not even tried to hit the first two balls, he struck out on the third: 'There is no joy in Mudville—Mighty Casey has struck out.' *See also* NO JOY IN MUDVILLE.

> Mentioned in the context of something that fails when success was confidently expected

Cassandra [Gk Myth.] A daughter of Priam, king of Troy. *Apollo loved her and gave her the gift of prophecy. When she resisted his advances, he turned the gift into a curse by ensuring that, although her prophecies were true, they would not be believed.

> Someone who gives dire warnings of impending disaster; someone whose warnings go unheeded

One doesn't have to be a shrieking Cassandra to say that the oil and gas age is coming to a close.
AlterNet.org: EnviroHealth 2004

Stiglitz paints himself as an economic Cassandra whose constant (and constantly correct) predictions of the harm brought on by IMF policies are always ignored.
Reason Magazine 2003

Cassidy, Butch [Crime] (1866–1937?) An American outlaw whose real name was Robert Leroy Parker. He formed a gang called the Wild Bunch, which was responsible for numerous train and bank robberies and murders in the United States. Cassidy and his partner, the Sundance Kid, went to South America and it is not known what then happened to them or how they died. The film *Butch Cassidy and the Sundance Kid* (1969), starring Paul Newman and Robert Redford, romanticized their lives and showed them dying by running from a hiding place into a hail of bullets.

> A young outlaw or criminal who attracts a certain admiration

Police found their investigations were hampered by many people treating the two
criminals like a modern-day Butch Cassidy and the Sundance Kid
Yorkshire Post Today 2003

Cassius [Hist.] Gaius Cassius Longinus (d. 42 BC) was a praetor in ancient Rome who allied
himself with the aristocrats who opposed Julius Caesar. He managed to enlist Marcus *Brutus to be a
part of a conspiracy, of which they were joint leaders, to assassinate Caesar in AD 44.
In *Shakespeare's play *Julius Caesar* (1623), Cassius is described as having a 'lean and hungry look'.

> A conspirator or plotter; someone hungry for political power

Maxwell could be as conspiratorial as Cassius when he had a mind.
M. J. TROW *Maxwell's Movie* 1998

Castalia [Gk Myth.] The Castalian spring was a spring on Mount *Parnassus that was
sacred to *Apollo and to the *Muses, and its waters were said to have the power of inspiring
the gift of poetry in those who drank of them.

> Mentioned as a source of poetic inspiration (adjective *Castalian*)

A stream of prophecy, which rivalled the truth and reputation of the Delphic oracle,
flowed from the Castalian fountain of Daphne.
EDWARD GIBBON *History of the Decline and Fall of the Roman Empire* 1781

Castor and Pollux [Gk and Rom. Myth.] The twin sons born to Leda, wife of Tyndareus,
after her seduction by *Zeus. They were believed to have hatched from a single egg. Castor was
the son of Tyndareus and was mortal; Pollux was the son of Zeus and was immortal. When
Castor was killed, Pollux offered to share his immortality between them, spending half their
time below the earth with *Hades and the other half on *Olympus. They were eventually
transformed by Zeus into the constellation Gemini so that they would not be separated.

> Two people who are inseparable

They operated in perfect, entwined counterpoint—a diplomatic Castor and Pollux.
ED VULLIAMY *The Observer* 1997

Catch-22 [Lit.] The title of a novel by Joseph Heller (1961), which deals with the dilemma of
an American airforce bombardier who wishes to avoid combat duty. In order to do so, he has
to be adjudged insane, but since anyone wishing to avoid combat duty is obviously sane, he
must therefore be fit for duty.

> A situation or dilemma to which there is no solution because each possible solution
> will bring more problems

It was a Catch 22. The more we took from the land, the less the land had to give, so the
more stuff we had to put on the land to get the same results.
The New Farm: Feature articles 2004

Cato (Marcus Porcius Cato) [People] (234–149 BC) Known as Cato the Elder or Cato the
Censor, a Roman statesman, orator, and writer. As censor in 184 BC he was vigorously opposed
to luxury and decadence and tried to restore simplicity to Roman life. He became convinced
that Rome would never be safe until Carthage was destroyed, ending all his speeches in the
Senate with the words 'Delenda est Carthago' ('Carthage must be destroyed').

> Someone who advocates severity and austerity in matters of morality; someone who
> believes passionately that something should be destroyed

Other editors, who were disguised neither as preachers nor as farmers, donned newsprint
togas and appeared as modern Catos, ready to shed the last drop of their ink in defence of
those virtues which they believed to be the exclusive property of the party not in power.
ROBERTSON DAVIES *Leaven of Malice* 1954

I feel about email as Cato felt about Carthage, but with much better reason.
STOWE BOYD *Corante.com: Get Real* 2004

Caulfield, Holden [Lit.] The adolescent hero of J. D. Salinger's novel *The Catcher in the Rye*, published in 1951. He is an archetypal adolescent rebel, full of angst and disaffection and rebelling against all that is 'phoney', 'corny', and 'old bull'. After being expelled from an expensive private school, Caulfield goes to New York, but after a series of unsuccessful adventures, including an encounter with a prostitute and an abortive reunion with an old girlfriend, he is forced to go back home and is sent by his parents for psychiatric treatment.

> ➤ A teenage rebel who criticizes the shallowness of the world

> Like an overgrown Holden Caulfield, he always seems to come back around to proclaiming the phoniness and vanity and emptiness of everyone around him.
> *AlterNet.org: Movie Mix* 2004

Cecilia, St [People] (2nd or 3rd century) A Roman martyr. According to legend, she took a vow of celibacy but was forced to marry a Roman. She converted her husband to Christianity, and both were martyred. She is frequently pictured playing the organ and is the patron saint of church music.

> ➤ Mentioned in the context of music

> They have combined their voices, such as they are, even if they could be supposed to be 'parlor voices', 'thin voices', 'poor voices' or any other kind of voice than St. Cecilia's own.
> *Harper's Monthly* 1880

Celestial City [Lit.] The destination of Christian's pilgrimage in John Bunyan's religious allegory *The *Pilgrim's Progress*. After encountering on the way such adversaries as *Giant Despair and *Apollyon, the foul fiend, *Christian finally arrives at the Celestial City, set on a hill. The gates are opened and Christian sees that 'it was builded of pearls and precious stones, also the street thereof was paved with gold'.

> ➤ A paradise; an ideal place that one aspires to reach

> In the far distance, he implied, it might even be able to see the end of its journey: the celestial city Gartner calls the 'Plateau of Productivity'.
> *The Register* 2005

centaur [Gk Myth.] One of a race of creatures who has the upper body, arms, and head of a man and the body and legs of a horse.

> ➤ Something that is a fusion of two very different things

> This Polish-Thai gastronomic centaur signals either overinventiveness or a commendable resistance to good cooking's greatest foe, perfunctoriness.
> *New York Metro: The Underground Gourmet* 2004

centre cannot hold, the [Lit.] A phrase taken from the 1919 poem 'The Second Coming' by W. B. Yeats, evoking social disintigration:

> Things fall apart, the centre cannot hold;
> Mere anarchy is loosed upon the world

> ➤ Used to evoke a real or feared disintegration of the social order

> In days darker than these the poet W. B. Yeats had a sense that 'Things fall apart; the centre cannot hold'. I think Irish Catholics know now how that feels.
> *Western People (Co. Mayo)* 2002

Cerberus [Gk Myth.] The three-headed dog that guarded the entrance to *Hades. Cerberus could be appeased with a cake, as by *Aeneas, or lulled to sleep, as by *Orpheus, with lyre music. One of the twelve labours of *Hercules was to bring him up from the underworld.

➤ A person or animal that guards the entrance to a place

Their attempts to escape are constantly frustrated by Sid's pit bull that, as a modern Cerberus, guards the door.
Journal of Popular Film and Television 2005

Cesare Borgia *See* BORGIAS.

Chagall, Marc [Art] (1887–1985) A 20th-century painter and stained-glass artist, who was born a Russian Jew but in 1922 moved to France, where he lived for most of the rest of his life. His paintings mix reality with surrealistic fantasy in rich colours, often depicting scenes from Russian Jewish village life, Jewish and biblical themes, and Russian folklore. He also created twelve stained-glass windows for the Hadassah University Hospital in Jerusalem.

➤ Used to invoke a combination of bright or lurid colours

Mrs Coppett's make-up was so lurid, particularly the green eyelids, and so clumsily applied that in the half-light she looked like something Chagall had painted in a particularly inspired mood.
TOM SHARPE *Ancestral Vices* 1980

Challenger, Professor [Lit.] The distinguished zoologist and anthropologist who leads the expedition to the land of dinosaurs in Arthur Conan *Doyle's *The Lost World* (1912). He also appears in other books by Conan Doyle and is a somewhat irascible and unconventional scientist, given to developing his own individual and rather unlikely theories.

➤ A mad scientist

If you took a living body and cut it up into ever smaller pieces, you would eventually come down to specks of pure protoplasm. At one time in the last century, a real-life counterpart of Arthur Conan Doyle's Professor Challenger thought that the 'globigerina ooze' at the bottom of the sea was pure protoplasm.
RICHARD DAWKINS *The Blind Watchmaker* 1986

Chamberlain, Neville [Hist.] (1869–1940) A British Conservative statesman and prime minister in 1937–40. In 1938 he signed the *Munich agreement ceding the Sudetenland (then in Czechoslovakia) to Germany, and returned to Britain triumphantly waving a copy of the agreement, which he claimed would bring 'peace in our time'.

➤ A peacemaker; someone carrying a piece of paper with an important message; someone who makes a promise that is impossible to keep

I feel like Chamberlain, because I have in my hand a piece of paper that signifies why this is a very bad idea.
New Zealand Parliamentary Debates 2003

Never mind that these are impossible promises—much like Neville Chamberlain's 'peace in our time'.
BETSY NEWMARK *Betsy's Page* 2004

Chamber of Horrors [Places] A section of the Madame *Tussaud's waxworks in London that contains a macabre series of tableaux of notorious murderers at their work and of scenes of torture.

➤ A horrific place

...Abu Ghraib, Guantanamo and other US chambers of horrors tucked away in desolate corners of the world.
World Socialist Website 2005

Chandler, Raymond [Lit.] (1888–1959) A US crime novelist remembered as the creator of the hard-boiled private detective Philip Marlowe. The novels are noted for their tough realistic style and their portrayal of corruption at the heart of big business.

> ➤ Mentioned in the context of an exciting crime thriller, a hard-boiled private detective, or corrupt businessmen (adjective *Chandleresque*)

A style of business writing has emerged that transforms single-mindedly avaricious real estate developers into characters from a Raymond Chandler novel.
Bad Subjects Magazine 2000

His first novel, Squeeze Play, was a Chandleresque thriller published under the pseudonym 'Paul Benjamin'.
MARGARET DRABBLE *The Oxford Companion to English Literature* 2000

Chan, Charlie [Cin.] The ace Chinese detective who appeared in over 40 films from 1925 to 1945. The films are loosely based on six novels by Earl Derr Biggers. Charlie Chan is witty and has an endless supply of aphorisms. He is a family man with fourteen children and usually has assistance from his impulsive number one son or number two son in solving murder mysteries. The films are often criticized now for portraying Oriental stereotypes.

> ➤ A detective, especially a Chinese one

I cruised on autopilot, my thoughts sliding from Uncle Fred to Joe Morelli to Charlie Chan. Life was good for Charlie Chan. He knew freaking everything.
JANET EVANOVICH *High Five* 1999

Chaney, Lon [Cin.] (1883–1930) An American film actor (b. Leonidas Frank Chaney) who starred in mainly silent films. He was known as 'the man of a thousand faces' because of his talents at make-up and miming. In *The *Phantom of the Opera* (1925), a horror film based on a novel by Gaston Leroux, he played the phantom, a disfigured genius who lives in the cellars of the Paris Opera.

> ➤ Someone with a hideous appearance; a wild or destructive madman

Two white doves coo in a cage hanging from the ceiling. Their soft song is totally wrong. This scene begs for Lon Chaney, the mad 'Phantom of the Opera', wildly attacking the organ.
SUSAN SUSSMAN with SARAJANE AVIDON *Cruising for Murder* 2000

Chang and Eng [People] (1811–74) The original Siamese twins, born in Siam and joined by a fleshy band in the region of the waist. They married sisters and each fathered several children.

> ➤ Two people or things that are always together or very closely associated

Now envy and antipathy, passions irreconcilable in reason, nevertheless in fact may spring conjoined like Chang and Eng in one birth.
HERMAN MELVILLE *Billy Budd* 1924

Chaplin, Charlie [Cin.] (1889–1977) An English film actor and director. In many of his silent comedies, such as *The Kid* (1921) and *The Gold Rush* (1925), he portrayed a little tramp who wore a bowler hat and baggy trousers, twirled a cane, and had a characteristic wide-legged walk.

> ➤ Used when describing a wide-legged or tottering walk

Maxwell hobbled around Southern Hills on a peg leg, wobbling like Charlie Chaplin.
Golf Digest 2001

Chappaquiddick [Hist.] A place in Massachusetts where, on 8 July 1968, Edward Kennedy, at that time a likely US presidential candidate, drove off a bridge. His passenger, Mary Jo Kopechne, drowned, and Kennedy himself was found guilty of leaving the scene of an accident. It is widely thought that this event blighted his chance of becoming president.

➤ A serious error of judgement that subsequently dogs someone's career

The most notorious case, that of the 14-year-old resistance hero, Stompie Mocketsi Seipei, became Mrs Mandela's Chappaquiddick.
The Independent 1995

Charge of the Light Brigade [Hist.] A charge by the British cavalry in 1854 during the Battle of Balaclava in the Crimean War. A misunderstanding between the commander of the Light Brigade and his superiors led to the charge being ordered, with the soldiers riding straight into cannon fire and being slaughtered. The charge was immortalized in the 1854 poem 'The Charge of the Light Brigade' by Alfred, Lord Tennyson.

➤ Mentioned in the context of a situation in which victory or success is impossible, or a battle in which soldiers face a much more heavily armed enemy

For a company losing £600,000 a week such a strategy would be regarded by most business people in the private sector as comparable to the Charge of the Light Brigade.
Sunday Business Post 2004

It's looking like a charge of the light brigade situation until Aragorn (Viggo Mortensen) rushes off into the mountains and persuades the ghosts who live there to come and fight on their side.
Film Inside Out 2003

Charlemagne [Hist.] (742–814) The king of the Franks in 768–814. He defeated and Christianized the Lombards, Saxons, and Avars and created the Holy Roman Empire, which he ruled from 800 to 814. As well as encouraging commerce and agriculture, he promoted the arts and education.

➤ A leader or ruler of a large empire

You can conquer the world like Charlemagne. But you better be prepared to kill everyone and you better start with me.
TOM COATES *Plastic Bag* 2003

Charles, Nick and Nora [Lit.] Nick Charles is the retired detective hero of Dashiell Hammett's *The Thin Man* (1932). Nora Charles is his wealthy wife. Together the pair investigate and solve the murder of an eccentric inventor. A film starring William Powell and Myrna Loy was released in 1934.

➤ A pair of amateur detectives

'Pull him in,' was Superintendent Malcolm's order over the car phone. 'Pull both of them in. If they're going to play Nick and Nora Charles all over the place, they must expect to have their collars felt.'
M. J. TROW *Maxwell's Flame* 1995

Charlie *See* BONNIE PRINCE CHARLIE.

Charon [Gk Myth.] The ferryman who ferried the souls of the dead across the rivers *Styx and *Acheron to *Hades. He was described as an old but vigorous man, with a hideous countenance, long white beard, and piercing eyes. His clothes were tattered and filthy.

> A sinister-looking old man; a boatman; someone whose presence heralds death

The central void of the doorway, guarded by the ghostly Fanny, an exotic Charon, suggests the proximity of death.
Magazine Antiques 2004

A battered leaking boat, paddled by a bearded Charon look-alike, materialised from nowhere.
VITALI VITALIEV *Travel Intelligence: Vitali Vitaliev articles* 2005

Charybdis *See* SCYLLA AND CHARYBDIS.

Château d'If [Places] A castle on a small rocky island named If off the coast of Marseille in the Mediterranean Sea. It was built in 1524 and was later used as a state prison. The castle features in Alexandre Dumas's novel *The Count of Monte Cristo* (1844), being the site of incarceration for Dumas's hero, Edmund Dantès, for a period of fourteen years until he escapes.

> A prison where conditions are harsh, and from which escape is impossible

Harry and I have different names for the nursing home in which we live. Some days we call it the Bastille or the Château d'If, other days Bedlam.
Strange Horizons Stories 2004

Chatterley, Lady [Lit.] The main character in D. H. Lawrence's *Lady Chatterley's Lover*, first published privately in Florence in 1928, published in full by Grove Press in the United States in 1959 and by Penguin in 1960. Constance Chatterley is married to Sir Clifford Chatterley, who after being injured in the First World War is confined to a wheelchair. After an unsuccessful affair, she falls in love with Oliver Mellors, a gamekeeper and ex-Indian army officer and they have a passionate affair.

> A married woman who has a lover, particularly an upper class woman who falls in love with a working class man

Adamson has always maintained he was having a Lady Chatterley style relationship with solicitor's wife, Lady Rosalthe, after she turned him down for a cleaning job at her Cotswold home.
Cotswold Journal news stories 2004

Chaucer, Geoffrey [Lit.] (*c.*1343–1400) A poet who is best known for his *Canterbury Tales* (*c.*1387), in which 29 pilgrims who have met at the Tabard Inn in Southwark agree to each tell a story to pass the time. The collection's reputation for coarse or ribald humour is based on some of the better-known stories, such as 'The Miller's Tale'.

> Mentioned in the context of ribald humour

He could also break wind at will, with a prolonged whining note of complaint, and when he did so in class and then looked around with an angry face, whispering, 'Who done that?' our mirth was Chaucerian, and the teacher was reduced to making a refined face, as if she were too good for a world in which such things were possible.
ROBERTSON DAVIES *Fifth Business* 1970

Checkers speech [Hist.] The name given to a speech made by US President Richard Nixon in 1952. Nixon had been accused of surreptitiously accepting money for his vice-presidential campaign, and in a high-profile speech on television he asserted his family's modest means and financial independence, but admitted accepting a Spaniel (named Checkers) as a gift.

> A political speech in which a politician speaks in a very personal way in order to win support from the public

Whether her confession was a calculated commercial move, or something more like a Checkers speech, it's true that she writes about Bill Clinton in this book with an affection that one imagines would be hard—though not impossible—to fake.
New York Metro: Books 2004

Checkpoint Charlie [Hist.] A nickname given to a checkpoint on the border between East and West Berlin, before the demolition of the *Berlin Wall in 1989.

➤ A border crossing, especially one that people cannot cross freely

Space faring nations are more interested in satellites, asteroids and getting to the moon or Mars these days...not political checkpoint charlies in space.
The Register 2005

Clearing customs in Europe is always a pleasure compared to the new Checkpoint Charlie ordeal that flying to the US has become.
Eye Weekly (Toronto): News and City sections 2003

Cheeryble brothers [Lit.] The elderly wealthy twins, Charles and Edwin Cheeryble, who employ Nicholas Nickleby in Dickens's novel of the same name (1838–9). They are cheerful and benevolent and help Nicholas, his mother and sister, and Madeleine Bray, with whom Nicholas has fallen in love.

➤ Philanthropists or generous people who help others

The notion of the Inland Revenue as the Cheeryble brothers of our day, dispensing £1.9bn of excess benefits to the undeserving, will boggle most people's minds.
Scotland on Sunday 2005

Cheever, John [Lit.] (1912–82) A US novelist and short story writer. His works are set in the suburbs of American cities and typically portray a lack of real communication between people, or the emotional emptiness and lack of community of suburban life.

➤ Mentioned in the context of superficial relationships or suburban life which is superficially pleasant but empty or sinister beneath the surface (adjective *Cheeveresque*)

The Body Artist begins with a set piece worth of John Cheever, with a married couple having breakfast, two people living in the same place but not quite together.
Sunday Herald 2001

Chernobyl [Hist.] A town near Kiev in Ukraine, site of a 1986 accident at a nuclear power station which resulted in a serious escape of radioactive material.

➤ A disaster of huge proportions

Is SARS China's Chernobyl?
New Perspectives Quarterly 2003

Cheshire Cat [Child. Lit.] A large cat grinning from ear to ear, encountered by *Alice in Lewis Carroll's *Alice's Adventures in Wonderland* (1865). When Alice asks the Duchess the reason for the cat's grin, the Duchess replies, 'It's a Cheshire Cat, and that's why.' Later Alice watches the Cheshire Cat vanish, 'beginning with the end of the tail, and ending with the grin, which remained some time after the rest of it had gone'. The expression 'to grin like a Cheshire cat', meaning to grin fixedly and broadly, pre-dates Carroll's story.

➤ Someone who smiles broadly; someone or something that disappears or melts away; something that lingers after other parts have disappeared

Dave and Chapman came stumbling back to our tent at Leeds Festival shouting 'Bo!' and snapping their fingers together Ali G style, grinning like Cheshire cats.
RobotFist.com 2004

In the course of this appeal some reference was made to the fact that assets, like the Cheshire cat, may disappear unexpectedly.
Decisions of the Ontario Superior Court of Justice 2002

Labour policies are like the Cheshire cat: look twice and they have disappeared, leaving only Mr Blair's enduring smile.
Independent on Sunday 1996

Chewbacca [Cin.] The large Wookiee, covered with long fur, who accompanies Hans Solo in the original *Star Wars* trilogy of films (*Star Wars*, 1977; *The Empire Strikes Back*, 1980; and *Return of the Jedi*, 1983). Played by Peter Mayhew, Chewbacca is an expert starship pilot and frequently tinkers with the pair's beloved starship freighter, the *Millennium Falcon*, in efforts to improve its performance.

> Someone who has a scruffy but endearing appearance

Dog is both cool and corny wrapped up in one big scruffy package, kind of like Chewbacca.
DVD Verdict 2005

Chicken-Licken [Fairy tales] A chicken in a traditional fairy story who feels an acorn fall onto his head from a tree and believes that the sky is falling. She proceeds to warn each of her friends Hen-Len, Cock-Lock, Duck-Luck, Goose-Loose, Gander-Lander, and Turkey-Lurkey that the sky is falling, until they fall prey to Fox-Lox, who takes them back to his foxhole and eats them.

> Someone who warns of impending disaster in a way that is not believable

Despite what chicken licken thought in the children's tale, the sky did not fall in and we have to hope that it doesn't on this occasion either.
Irish Examiner 2001

Chillon *See* PRISONER OF CHILLON.

Chimera [Gk Myth.] A fire-breathing monster with a lion's head, a goat's body, and a serpent's tail.

> A creature made up of parts taken from different animals; something unrealistic that one hopes for but can never achieve

This idea of a clear species identity is what makes the idea of hybrids or chimeras so disturbing.
Scotland on Sunday 2005

Some in America, in spite of Iraq, still pursue the chimera of total safety through total dominance.
Guardian Unlimited columnists 2005

Chinese Wall [Places] Another name for the *Great Wall of China, a fortified wall in northern China which extends for 2400 kilometres (1500 miles) from Kansu province to the Yellow Sea north of Beijing. It was first built in the 3rd century BC, as a protection against Turkish and Mongol invaders. In finance, the term is applied to a prohibition against the passing of confidential information from one department of a financial institution to another.

> A literal or figurative barrier that keeps people or things separate

As the company's artistic director Matthew Lenton points out, there is no cultural Chinese Wall between theatre for the young and stage productions for adults.
Scotland on Sunday 2003

Chingachgook [Lit.] The old Indian chief in *The Last of the Mohicans* (1826) and other novels by James Fenimore Cooper. Chingachgook, with his son Uncas, the last of the Mohican aristocracy, accompanies the scout Hawkeye (or Natty Bumppo) in his adventures.

> A faithful friend and companion; someone skilled in tracking people or animals

She scanned the ground at the edge of the hardstanding in hope of seeing something to show that someone had headed down the slope. Rapidly she realized it was not a very profitable way of spending her time. She was no Chingachgook to read in bent and heather who had passed this way and when.
REGINALD HILL *On Beulah Height* 1998

Chips, Mr [Lit.] A nickname given by pupils to the classics teacher Mr Chipping in James Hilton's novel *Goodbye, Mr Chips* (1935). Mr Chips devotes himself to teaching generations of boys at the school until his retirement.

> A dedicated schoolmaster

While clearly not every teacher sets out on their career path with aspirations of becoming Mr Chips, one has to wonder exactly why so many fall by the wayside.
Scotland on Sunday 2005

Chiron [Gk Myth.] A learned *centaur who acted as tutor to many heroes in their youth, including *Jason, *Hercules, and *Achilles.

> A wise person; a teacher

Something less unpleasingly oracular he tried to extract; but the old sea Chiron, thinking perhaps that for the nonce he had sufficiently instructed his young Achilles, pursed his lips, gathered all his wrinkles together, and would commit himself to nothing further.
HERMAN MELVILLE *Billy Budd* 1924

Chitty Chitty Bang Bang [Lit.; Cin.] The title of a series of stories for children (subtitle *The Magical Car*) written by Ian Fleming, the author of the James *Bond spy novels. The magical car can fly and turn itself into a hovercraft. A highly successful musical film based on the stories was made in 1971.

> An old-fashioned car with no roof

'It is a real Chitty Chitty Bang Bang motor and it is in impressive condition,' said auctioneer Robert Horner.
Yorkshire Post Today 2003

Chloe *See* AUNT CHLOE; DAPHNIS AND CHLOE.

Christ *See* JESUS.

Christian [Lit.] The central character of John Bunyan's religious allegory The *Pilgrim's Progress* (1678, 1684) who undertakes a pilgrimage to the *Celestial City, encountering on the way such adversaries as *Giant Despair and *Apollyon, the foul fiend.

> Someone who is on a long and difficult journey; someone who carries a burden or encounters many problems

It is her way of talking, and like Christian in Pilgrim's Progress, she carries a burden physically represented by a bed—the child's bed, the place where she had sex, the beginning of her troubles.
OnlineReviewLondon.com: theatre reviews 2004

Christie, Agatha [Lit.] (1890–1976) An English writer of detective fiction, in particular 'whodunnits'. Many of her novels feature one or other of her two most famous detective creations, the Belgian Hercule *Poirot and Miss Jane *Marple.

> ➤ Mentioned in the context of a murder mystery, especially one with a complicated plot
>
> With more bizarre twists and turns than an Agatha Christie mystery, the Yorkshire corpse in a suitcase inquiry now stretches half way across the globe.
> *Yorkshire Post Today* 2002

Christie, John Reginald Halliday [Crime] (1898–1953) An English murderer who killed his wife, for which he was hanged, and confessed to strangling five other women. It is also possible that he killed the wife and daughter of Timothy Evans, who were living in his house, for which Evans was hanged in 1950.

> ➤ A murderer
>
> He's guilty and he still gets me to find him an out. Nothing is ever totally certain in this business. Sow a seed of doubt and you might end up believing Crippen was innocent. Or Christie.
> PETER LOVESEY *The Summons* 1995

Churchill, Winston [Hist.] (1874–1965) A British politician and prime minister who led the coalition government during the Second World War. He was a gifted orator whose wartime speeches, broadcast over the radio in his deep, slightly rasping voice, included many famous passages such as 'We shall fight on the beaches, we shall fight on the landing grounds, we shall fight in the fields and in the streets, we shall fight in the hills; we shall never surrender.' He is also remembered for his large, slightly jowly face.

> ➤ Mentioned in the context of a determination never to surrender; also used when describing a skilled orator, or a slow, powerful speaking style; used humorously to describe someone with a heavy-jowled face (adjective *Churchillian*)
>
> There's no Churchillian sense of collective defiance, a city united in a desire for justice or revenge.
> *Irish Examiner* 2005
>
> In a remarkable speech, almost Churchillian, on October 2, 2001 Tony Blair said, 'We need, above all, justice and prosperity for the poor and dispossessed.'
> *Whole Earth* 2002
>
> He's a squishy little baby, he looks exactly like Winston Churchill, he cries, burps and farts.
> *Scotland on Sunday* 2005

Cicero, Marcus Tullius [People] (106–43 BC) A Roman orator, statesman, and writer.

> ➤ Someone with great eloquence or skills in oratory (adjective *Ciceronian*)
>
> Heroes numbered many Native Americans—notably Winnetou, who speaks with Ciceronian eloquence.
> *Sunset Magazine* 2002

Cimmerian [Gk Myth.] A member of a tribe of people who lived in a land on the edge of the world that was perpetually covered with mist and cloud and where the sun never shone. In *Homer's *Odyssey* the land of the Cimmerians is the place nearest to *Hades, the land of the dead.

> ➤ Used when describing a dark or gloomy place
>
> A kind of landscape and weather which leads travellers from the South to describe our island as Homer's Cimmerian land, was not, on the face of it, friendly to women.
> THOMAS HARDY *The Return of the Native* 1880

Cinderella [Fairy tales] A character in a traditional fairy story. Cinderella is treated harshly by her stepmother and stepsisters, kept in poverty, dressed in rags, and forced to do menial tasks. When her stepsisters go off to a royal ball leaving Cinderella behind, she is found weeping by her *fairy godmother, who waves her wand, turning a pumpkin into a coach, six mice into horses to pull it, and a rat into a coachman. Cinderella's rags are turned into beautiful clothes and glass slippers appear on her feet. She is instructed by her fairy godmother to leave the ball by midnight, before her beautiful clothes and coach and horses revert to their normal forms. At the ball she meets the prince and then, rushing away at the stroke of midnight, she leaves behind a glass slipper. The prince announces that he will marry whoever can wear the slipper, and he eventually discovers that it fits only Cinderella.

> ➤ Someone or something kept in a state of poverty and not allowed to enjoy the benefits that others enjoy; someone whose life is transformed from poverty to riches; also mentioned in the context of a complete or magical transformation, or a late-night deadline that must be adhered to

Mental health has long been considered the Cinderella of the health service.
The Hindu: Literary Review 2002

The Dave Matthews Band is a Cinderella story of a band that started from scratch and became one of the biggest rock and roll bands of the last decade.
DVD Verdict 2000

Unless a deal was struck that night, the offer would vanish like Cinderella at midnight.
Business Week Magazine 2004

Circe [Gk Myth.] A sorceress who lived on the island of Aeaea. She detained *Odysseus on Aeaea for a year on his return from the *Trojan War. Although she turned his men into swine, Odysseus managed to protect himself from this fate using the mythical herb moly, and he was able to make her restore his men to their human form.

> ➤ A bewitching, dangerously attractive woman

Like Circe or a siren, she employs pleasure to lure men into her control.
Criticism 2003

Citizen Kane [Cin.] A US film made in 1941, directed by and starring Orson Welles, often said to be the best film ever made. The film relates the life story of Charles Foster Kane, who, coming from a poor background, rises to become a wealthy newspaper magnate, only to see his personal life and relationships disintegrate. He spends his final years living alone and isolated in his mansion Xanadu.

> ➤ The best film of a particular type; a cinematic masterpiece

Titchmarsh's old-school tuition tape covers pretty much everything you need to know about looking after your acres. In fact, it's the Citizen Kane of Gardening videos.
Sunday Herald 2000

Clapham Junction [Places] A railway station in the London borough of Wandsworth. Many trains from London's Waterloo and Victoria stations pass through Clapham Junction and so the station is one of the busiest in Europe by number of trains using it.

> ➤ A very busy place

It's like Clapham Junction in here.
www.Londonnet.co.uk 2009

Claude [Art] (1600–82) A French landscape painter (full name Claude Lorraine) who was celebrated for his subtle and poetic treatment of light. His paintings lead the eye into the expansive panoramas through variations of colour: dark greenish-brown in the foreground, light green in the middle distance, and blue in the far distance.

> Used to invoke a landscape of subtle tones and gentle curves

The sea and the mountains floated in the steady evening sunshine. It was all peace, elements and void, golden air and mute blue distances, like a Claude.
JOHN FOWLES *The Magus* 1977

Clay, Cassius *See* MUHAMMAD ALI.

Cleaver, June and Ward [TV] The parents of Beaver in the television series *Leave it to Beaver*, which was broadcast in the United States by CBS between 1957 and 1963. June (played by Barbara Billingsley) was a quintessential American 1950s-style Mom, a homemaker who kept her house spotless and brought up her two children, Beaver and Wally. Ward, who was played by Hugh Beaumont, was her responsible businessman husband.

> A stereotypical 'perfect' married couple of the 1950s

There's no denying that few families today resemble Ward and June Cleaver's on Leave it to Beaver.
American Demographics 2000

Despite her liberal upbringing, she's a regular June Cleaver housewife.
MELIKA ELENA *Second Place* 2005

Cleopatra [Hist.] (69–30 BC) The queen of Egypt in 47–30 BC. She is usually remembered for her beauty, for her affairs with Julius *Caesar and Mark *Antony, and for committing suicide by allowing herself to be bitten by an asp. Her relationship with Antony is the subject of *Shakespeare's *Antony and Cleopatra* (1623) and John Dryden's *All for Love* (1678), while her relationship with Caesar is the subject of George Bernard Shaw's *Caesar and Cleopatra* (1907).

> A woman of exotic beauty and allure; also used when describing a straight, shoulder-length bob, or heavy eye make-up, both of which are associated with Cleopatra

In a word, all Cleopatra—fierce, voluptuous, passionate, tender…and full of…rapturous enchantment.
NATHANIEL HAWTHORNE *The Marble Faun* 1860

Her dark hair was cut in a Cleopatra bob.
JOAN BEECH *Follow the Red Dirt Road* 2004

Close Encounter [Cin.] A phrase taken from the title of a science fiction film *Close Encounters of the Third Kind* (1977) about encounters with aliens.

> A situation in which you come into close contact with something, especially something potentially dangerous

But a close encounter of the whale kind was enough to leave even this seasoned professional in awe.
ABC regional—Gold Coast 2004

Cloud Cuckoo Land [Lit.] The imaginary city built in the air by birds in *Aristophanes' play *The Birds*.

> Any fanciful realm; a world or state of mind that exists only in a person's imagination, distanced from reality

The government is in cloud-cuckoo-land if it thinks privatising prisons will solve the mess.
The Observer 2004

Clouseau, Inspector [Cin.] A character played by Peter Sellers in the comedy film *The Pink Panther* (1963) and its sequels. He was a stupid, bungling, accident-prone police detective. In the 2006 *Pink Panther* revival and its 2009 sequel, Clouseau is played by Steve Martin.

> ➤ A bungling detective

Even the most amateur Inspector Clouseau would conclude that this is the work of one gang.
Bradford and District news stories 2004

Clytemnestra [Gk Myth.] The wife of *Agamemnon, king of Mycenae. During her husband's absence at the *Trojan War she took a lover, Aegisthus. On Agamemnon's triumphant return from the war, she and Aegisthus laid a trap for him, murdering him in his bath.

> ➤ An evil woman; a woman who murders her husband

To me, she seemed like a figure in a Greek tragedy—all parts played, all oracles read, all actions come full circle. Clytemnestra, having dealt the inevitable blow, waiting, waiting.
LINDA BARNES *Cold Case* 1997

coat of many colours [Bible] The coat given to *Joseph by his father. The coat was seen by Joseph's brothers as confirming that Joseph was their father's favourite son, and they 'hated him, and could not speak peaceably unto him' (Gen. 37: 4).

> ➤ Mentioned in the context of someone's position as a favourite

Blair's coat of many colours unravels as Tories claim chic Generation Blair politics has always been about looks.
Sunday Business Post 2002

Cobley, Uncle Tom (Uncle Tom Cobbleigh) [Mus.] A phrase from a traditional British folk song 'Widecombe Fair' which lists all the people who are going to the fair, including, finally, 'Old Uncle Tom Cobley and all'.

> ➤ Used when suggesting that a list contains a very large number of people

There are few people who deliberately set themselves up for the public mauling he received at the hands of politicians, business leaders, broadcasters, journalists, Uncle Tom Cobley and all.
Scotland on Sunday 2002

Cockaigne (Cockayne) [Leg. & Folk.] In medieval legend, an imaginary land of luxury and idleness, where good food and drink were plentiful.

> ➤ An imaginary place of great happiness

She watched the car drive away. It was going to Cloud Cuckoo Land; it was going to the Kingdom of Cockaigne; it was going to Hollywood.
STELLA GIBBONS *Cold Comfort Farm* 1932

Colditz [Places] A medieval castle near Leipzig in eastern Germany. It was used as a top-security prison camp during the Second World War, particularly for prisoners who were known as likely escapees, and became famous as a camp from which escape was considered almost impossible.

> ➤ A prison from which escape is impossible

Former residents described Bryn Estyn as the 'Colditz of residential care'.
The Observer 1996

Cold War [Hist.] A state of political hostility which existed between the Soviet bloc countries and the Western powers after the Second World War.

> A long-lasting state of hostility between countries, organizations, or people

Already, there are signs of a new Cold War emerging as the US and China seek to curry favour with poor African countries that are seen to have potential as oil suppliers.
Guardian Unlimited columnists 2005

The strong showings of the ANC and the DA in Wednesday's general election may sharpen the cold war between the two parties.
Daily Dispatch Online 2004

Collins, Wilkie [Lit.] (1824–89) An English novelist chiefly remembered as the writer of the first full-length detective stories in English, notably *The Woman in White* (1860) and *The Moonstone* (1868).

> Mentioned in the context of an exciting mystery or adventure story

To be at Headingley yesterday was to be a part of a drama as gripping as anything the fertile mind of Wilkie Collins could have dreamed of.
The Guardian: Ashes 2005

Colossus (Colossus of Rhodes) [Hist.] A huge bronze statue of the sun-god *Helios standing beside the harbour entrance at Rhodes, one of the seven ancient wonders of the world. According to Pliny the Elder it stood 30.5 metres (100 feet) high. The Colossus was built *c.*292–280 BC and was destroyed in an earthquake in 224 BC. The familiar image of a statue so vast that its legs were either side of the harbour, used by *Cassius in *Julius Caesar*, is not historically accurate.

> A very tall, strong, or influential person or organization

Why, man, he doth bestride the narrow world
Like a Colossus; and we petty men
Walk under his huge legs, and peep about
To find ourselves dishonourable graves.
WILLIAM SHAKESPEARE *Julius Caesar* 1623

Young Shane Guthrie was a colossus at centre back giving a towering performance all through.
The Kingdom (Killarney, Co. Kerry) 2002

For years, Fannie Mae has stood like a colossus astride global financial markets.
Business Week Magazine 2004

Columbo [TV] A police detective from the Los Angeles Police Department, memorably played by Peter Falk in the TV series *Columbo*. Working alone to solve his murder cases, he wears a shabby raincoat and affects an air of naive puzzlement as he questions his suspects, often catching them off guard with one last question just as he is apparently taking his leave. The viewers know who the murderer is from the start, and wall-eyed, cigar-smoking Columbo guesses who he or she is early on and then tries to puzzle out how the crime was committed and obtain the necessary evidence to prove it.

> A detective; someone who asks one final question before they leave

He was like Columbo. He always had 'just' that one more thing to ask.
Ron Miller film noir columns (2004)

Columbus, Christopher [Hist.] (1451–1506) An Italian explorer who, sponsored by the rulers of Spain, Ferdinand and Isabella, set out across the Atlantic Ocean in 1492 with the intention of reaching Asia and proving that the world was round. In fact, he discovered the New World, reaching the Bahamas, Cuba, and Hispaniola (now the Dominican Republic and Haiti). He made three further journeys, during which he also discovered the South American mainland.

> ➤ An explorer
>
> I feel a little bit like Columbus—set down in a strange, new land full of new wonders, new discoveries.
> *Bright Lights Film Journal* 2003

come in from the cold [Lit.] A phrase taken from the title of a 1931 spy novel by John Le Carré about a British agent in the former East Germany who wanted to return to the west.

> ➤ To 'come in from the cold' is to return from a position of isolation to one of acceptance or safety
>
> There aren't many people like Nasir Abas, a terrorist leader who came in from the cold and chose to speak out.
> *CNN transcripts: Insight* 2005

come up and see me some time [Cin.] A phrase used by the actress Mae West (1892–1980) in more than one of her films, as an invitation with a sexual innuendo.

> ➤ Mentioned in the context of a sexual invitation
>
> She fixed me with a 'come up and see me' look.
> *Ron Miller film noir columns* 2004

Comstock, Anthony [People] (1844–1915) A US crusader against pornography, obscenity, birth control, and gambling.

> ➤ Mentioned in the context of censorship on the grounds of obscenity (noun *comstockery*)
>
> Obscenity cases feel faintly anachronistic, the comfort crimes of the legal system. Indeed, given the incredible freedom of expression we enjoy today, it's tempting to laugh off this latest instance of Comstockery.
> *Reason Magazine* 2004

Comus [Lit.] The title of a masque, or pastoral drama, written by *Milton and presented to the earl of Bridgewater at Ludlow Castle in 1634. Comus is an imaginary Greek god who has the power to turn the faces of travellers into those of wild animals. Into his clutches comes the Lady, who has become separated from her brothers. She finds herself in 'a stately Palace', in an enchanted chair, with Comus and his crew of enchanted travellers. Her brothers, who have had the assistance of a spirit, Thyrsis, in the form of a protective herb root, arrive and disperse Comus and the crew of travellers and eventually the Lady is freed from her chair.

> ➤ Mentioned in the context of someone trapped in a place, or a group of people who disappear
>
> Effigies, donkey, lanterns, band all had disappeared like the crew of Comus.
> THOMAS HARDY *The Mayor of Casterbridge* 1886

Conan the Barbarian [Cin.] A 1981 film starring Arnold *Schwarzenegger as Conan. The film was based on the sword-and-sorcery adventure stories by Robert E. Howard about Conan of Cimmeria which appeared in *Weird Tales* in the 1930s. Conan, a Dark Ages barbarian warrior (garbed in rather sketchy leather armour and boots), freed from slavery, seeks to avenge the murder of his parents by a warlord.

> ➤ An aggressive or tyranical leader
>
> Those who put him in power say he's already proved a supreme no-nonsense leader, a veritable Conan the Barbarian of politics.
> *Scotland on Sunday* 2003

Concordia [Rom. Myth.] The Roman goddess of peace and harmony.

➤ A way of referring to peace

Confucius [Philos.] (551–479 BC) A Chinese philosopher and teacher of ethics. He spent much of his life as the moral teacher of a group of disciples, expounding his ideas about the importance of practical codes of personal morality, etiquette, and statesmanship which formed the basis of the philosophy of Confucianism. His teachings and sayings were collected by his pupils after his death.

➤ A very wise person, or someone whose sayings have deep meaning (adjective *Confucian*)

'The smaller red peppers,' she says like Confucius, 'are the spicier ones.'
Golf Digest 2004

Connecticut Yankee [Lit.] The hero of Mark Twain's satirical fantasy *A Connecticut Yankee in King Arthur's Court* (1889). The 'yankee', Hank Morgan, is a Connecticut mechanic who is knocked unconscious in a fight and awakens to find himself transported back to 6th-century *Camelot. Using his 19th-century knowledge of technology and history, he determines to introduce to Arthur's kingdom the supposed benefits of advanced civilization.

➤ Someone who feels as if they have been transported back to an earlier time

Constance [Shakes.] The mother of Arthur, the king's nephew and a claimant to the throne, in *King John* (1623). Her son's death draws from her a passionate expression of grief:

> Grief fills the room up of my absent child,
> Lies in his bed, walks up and down with me,
> Puts on his pretty looks, repeats his words.

➤ A woman who feels great grief over the loss of a child

Few of us wish to disturb the mother of a litter of puppies when mouthing a bone in the midst of her young family. Medea and her children are familiar to us, and so is the grief of Constance.
ANTHONY TROLLOPE *Barchester Towers* 1857

Cook, Captain James [People] (1728–79) An English navigator and explorer, who led expeditions to the Pacific in the *Endeavour*, to the Antarctic in the *Resolution*, and finally to try to discover a passage round the north coast of America from the Pacific. He was forced to turn back from his last voyage and, reaching Hawaii, was killed by the islanders.

➤ An explorer

You wave an airy adieu to the boys on shore, light your biggest pipe, and swagger about the deck as if you were Captain Cook, Sir Francis Drake, and Christopher Columbus all rolled into one.
JEROME K. JEROME *Three Men in a Boat* 1889

Cookie Monster [TV] One of the puppet creations of Jim Henson that has appeared in the television series *The Muppet Show* and *Sesame Street*. The Cookie Monster is a large blue creature with a sweet tooth and voracious appetite.

➤ Someone who finds it difficult to resist sweet foods

I know I shouldn't eat cookies—but I just can't help myself. I'm a cookie monster!
American Fitness 2004

Cook's tour [People] A guided tour organized by the travel agent Thomas Cook (1808–92), who founded the travel firm named after him in 1841 and originated the guided tour.

> A journey in which many places are visited briefly, or a discussion in which many things are touched on briefly

For perspective, Brown gives the reader a Cook's tour of the major modern schools of thought in the philosophy of science.
First Things Magazine 2004

Cooper, Gary [Cin.] (1901–61) An American film actor who is often associated with his role as the small-town marshal Will Kane in the film *High Noon* (1952). In an iconic scene at the climax of the film, Cooper walks alone down the street to confront several outlaws single-handedly.

> A strong, determined hero

If something looks retro and masculine, if it makes men feel like Gary Cooper, they'll buy it.
FocusOnStyle.com 2004

Cophetua, King [Leg. & Folk.] A legendary African king who was unmarried and had come to disdain women. One day when he was out riding he saw a beggar-maid 'clad all in gray', fell in love with her and proposed marriage. Their marriage was happy and successful. The story is told in the ballad 'King Cophetua and the Beggar-Maid' in Thomas Percy's *Reliques of Ancient English Poetry* (1765).

> A man who falls in love with a woman instantly and proposes marriage immediately

'He'll come and see you,' said Sylvia. 'No, he won't,' said Eiluned. 'Why not?' said Harriet. 'I like that young man,' said Eiluned. 'You needn't grin. I do like him. He's not going to do the King Cophetua stunt, and I take off my hat to him. If you want him, you'll have to send for him.'
DOROTHY SAYERS *Strong Poison* 1930

Corcoran, Captain [Opera] The captain of HMS *Pinafore* in Gilbert and Sullivan's opera of the same name. He sings a song in which he proudly tells his crew of the things that he 'never, never' does. When challenged, he concedes that this is not quite true:

> 'What, never?'
> 'No, never.'
> 'What, never?'
> 'Well—hardly ever.'

> Used when conceding that 'never' is too strong a word, and 'hardly ever' is more realistic

Nature is so wondrously complex and varied that almost anything possible does happen. Captain Corcoran's 'hardly ever' is the strongest statement that a natural historian can make.
STEPHEN JAY GOULD *Ever Since Darwin* 1978

Cordelia [Shakes.] One of the daughters of *Lear in *King Lear*. When the king asks his three daughters which of them loves him the best, the two older sisters, Goneril and Regan, flatter their father with extravagant declarations of their love. The youngest daughter, Cordelia, is the only one to speak truthfully, acknowledging that she loves her father according to her duty, but refusing to say that she will always love only him, for when she marries she must also love her husband. Lear furiously denounces what he believes to be her lack of love for him: 'So young and so untender?' Cordelia replies: 'So young, my lord, and true.' Later, however, when the king has lost his sanity, it is Cordelia, rather than either of her sisters, who takes him in and cares for him.

> A daughter with a strong and devoted love for her father

Mrs. Whittaker was Cordelia-like to her father during his declining years.
DOROTHY PARKER *The Wonderful Old Gentleman* 1944

Coriolanus [Shakes.] The main character in the play of the same name. He is a proud, courageous soldier who shows in an arrogant outburst in the forum his contempt for the Roman rabble and resentment at having to solicit their votes.

> ➤ An arrogant politician or leader

There was just a hint of Coriolanus going before the plebs as Lord Irvine defended his choice of wallpaper to the select committee.
BBC Radio 4 1998

Cornucopia [Gk Myth.] The horn of Amalthea, a she-goat or goat-nymph, whose milk *Zeus drank when he was first born. In gratitude, Zeus placed Amalthea's image among the stars as the constellation Capricorn. Zeus also took one of Amalthea's horns and endowed it with the magical property of refilling itself endlessly with whatever food or drink was desired. The horn of plenty was later stylized as the Cornucopia (from the Latin *cornu copiae*, literally 'horn of plenty'), pictured as a goat's horn spilling over with fruit, flowers, and stalks of corn.

> ➤ Mentioned in the context of an unending and bountiful supply of food, or other things

There was a cornucopia of food and drink almost forbidding in its plentitude.
FRED CHAPPELL *Farewell, I'm Bound to Leave You* 1997

They require a cornucopia of drugs to maintain their health.
The New Farm: Columns 2004

Coronation Street [TV] The title of a long-running British television series which deals with the lives of people living in a terraced street in an industrial city in the north of England.

> ➤ Mentioned in the context of stereotypical northern British working-class life

Correggio, Antonio Allegri da [Art] (*c.*1494–1534) An Italian painter of the High Renaissance. His best-known works are a series of frescos in the Camera di San Paolo and other Parma churches, painted in a sensual style, with a soft play of light and colour and striking use of foreshortening. These frescos often depict frolicking cherubs with an exuberance that captures the vitality and joyfulness of children.

> ➤ Used when describing happy young children

The rush of conflicting feelings was too great for Maggie to say much when Lucy, with a face breathing playful joy, like one of Correggio's cherubs, poured forth her triumphant revelation.
GEORGE ELIOT *The Mill on the Floss* 1860

Corridors of Power [Lit.] The title of a 1964 novel by C. P. Snow about the workings of government.

> ➤ A way of referring to the senior levels of government or administration

No Aboriginal voice is heard in the corridors of power.
AMMSA Windspeaker 2004

Cortés, Hernando (Hernán Cortez) [Hist.] (1485–1547) A Spanish adventurer who conquered Mexico, then known as New Spain. In 1519 he scuttled his own ships at Veracruz, to make retreat impossible.

> ➤ An explorer in a foreign land; someone who has 'burned his boats' and is committed to a course of action

This was the first sign of humanity she had encountered among the Starkadders, and she was moved by it. She felt like stout Cortez or Sir James Jeans on spotting yet another white dwarf.
STELLA GIBBONS *Cold Comfort Farm* 1932

Like Cortez, Shrub has burned his boats.
Whiskey Bar 2003

country mouse *See* TOWN MOUSE AND COUNTRY MOUSE.

course of true love never did run smooth [Shakes.] A quotation from *A Midsummer Night's Dream* (1595):

> Ay me! for aught that I could ever read,
> Could ever hear by tale or history,
> The course of true love never did run smooth.

➤ Used to highlight difficulties in romantic or other relationships

He falls in love with Polly Baker, the daughter of the theatre owner, but the course of true love never runs smoothly in musical theatre.
Bradford and District news stories 2004

Cousteau, Jacques [People] (1910–97) A French underwater explorer. He invented the Aqualung and a process for filming underwater. Several of his films of underwater life, including *The Silent World* (1956), won Academy Awards.

➤ A deep-sea diver or explorer

You may have to queue for the final treat: a trip back upstairs to a half-decent café via the glass lift, inside the tank. For a few upwardly mobile seconds you feel like Jacques Cousteau.
The Press, York (Newsquest) 2005

Cowardly Lion [Child. Lit.] One of the companions of *Dorothy in her journey to find Oz in the children's story *The *Wizard of Oz* by L. Frank Baum (1900). The lion roars very loudly to frighten other creatures away and to disguise the fact that he is scared of them himself. He hopes that the Wizard of Oz will give him courage, although, in fact, he acts bravely to protect his companions throughout their travels.

➤ Someone who acts with bravado but is a coward underneath

This small-minded appeal to jingoism not only batters facts, it also makes the U.S. look like the Cowardly Lion of world politics.
New York Times 1993

Cox and Box [Opera] The title of an operetta by Burnand and Sullivan (1867). Cox and Box are two lodgers whose occupations allow their landlady to let the same room out to each of them, one using it by day and one using it by night. They discover their landlady's duplicity when Cox, who sleeps in the room at night, is given a holiday. The operetta was based on a play entitled *Box and Cox* by J. M. Morton, published in 1847.

➤ Mentioned in the context of an arrangement in which people share something or take turns to use it

Yongue and Donald lived like Cox and Box, with Yongue getting up as Donald prepared for bed and going to bed when Donald was getting up.
BRIAN SWEET *Steely Dan: Reelin' in the Years* 2000

Crane, Hart [People] (1899–1932) An American poet born in Ohio. In 1932, after a period in Mexico, where he failed to write an epic poem on Montezuma, and believing he had betrayed the woman he loved, he committed suicide by leaping from the deck of SS *Orizaba* in the Caribbean off the coast of Florida.

➤ Someone who commits suicide by jumping off a ship

I was considering an exit in the style patented by Hart Crane when finally, at long last, the boat mercifully pulled into harbor.
Dead Drunk Dublin 2004

Crane, Ichabod [Lit.] A village schoolmaster in Washington Irving's short story 'The Legend of *Sleepy Hollow' (1820). Ichabod, who is skinny and gangly and has a nose 'like a snipe', is a suitor to a local girl, Katrina Van Tass. His rival suitor, Brom Bones, disguises himself as a ghostly headless horseman and scares the timid Ichabod out of the village.

➤ A thin, lanky man

He had an Ichabod Crane body and a wild thatch of Einstein-like white hair.
DEANNIE MILLS FRANCIS *Trap Door* 1995

Cratchit, Bob [Lit.] Ebenezer *Scrooge's clerk in Dickens's *A Christmas Carol* (1843). He is poorly paid (15 shillings a week), and the father of five living in a small four-roomed house in Camden Town. His youngest son, Tiny Tim, is weak and crippled. Despite his poverty, Cratchit is a devoted husband and father.

➤ Someone who is honest, open, and cheerful in spite of their difficult circumstances

Suffice it to say he's no Bob Cratchit. So pervasive is this depressing, hostile atmosphere that when the inevitable uplifting, 'happy' ending comes, it rings completely hollow.
DVD Verdict 2001

Creation [Bible] The name given to the account in the book of Genesis of God's creating of the universe and the first people, *Adam and Eve.

➤ The very distant past

This has been a key principle of taxation since the Creation.
The Observer 1997

Creature from the Black Lagoon, The [Cin.] A 1954 film in which a party of scientists in the Amazon in search of fossils discover a mysterious fanged creature which is half-man and half-fish. He is a prehistoric 'Gill man' who comes from the legendary Black Lagoon.

➤ A monster; someone with a dirty and hideous appearance

She looked like the Creature From the Black Lagoon. 'Yuck...' Twilli mumbled, disgusted with her filthy appearance.
CRYSTAL OF PSYCHE *Remember the Past* (2003)

Crichton, Admirable (James Crichton) [People] (1560–85) A Scottish scholar, poet, and linguist who travelled in France and Italy, served in the French army, and died in a brawl in Mantua. His career was described by Sir Thomas Urquhart in his writings in praise of the Scots nation *The Discoverie of a Most Exquisite Jewel* (1652) and the Admirable Crichton developed a reputation as a perfect man with many varied talents. J. M. Barrie adopted the phrase as the title of his play *The Admirable Crichton* about a perfect butler cast on a desert island with his employers.

➤ A perfect servant

In The Butler, an engaging Andrew Jones serves up a wicked servant that would have the Admirable Crichton turning in his grave.
IndieLondon theatre reviews 2004

Crippen, Dr (Hawley Harvey Crippen) [Crime] (1862–1910) An American-born British murderer. Crippen poisoned his wife, burying her remains in the cellar of their London home, for which crime he was later hanged. He nearly escaped, boarding an Atlantic liner with his secretary, but the suspicious captain of the ship contacted the police by radiotelegraphy, the first use of this medium in a criminal investigation, and he was apprehended.

➤ A murderer or evil person

Gary's client, the Dr Crippen of fund management, was delirious with joy.
REBECCA TINSLEY *Settlement Day* 1994

Crocker, Betty° [Advert.] The name given to a range of American food products such as cake and other food mixes. The name was invented by the milling company the Washburn Crosby Company of Minneapolis (later part of General Mills), which received many requests for information about baking in the 1910s and early 1920s and wished to make the replies sound more personal. In 1924 a radio cookery show was broadcast with actresses playing the part. In 1936 an official portrait was made of Betty Crocker (which changes periodically) and many Americans believed that Betty Crocker was a real woman.

➤ A woman who is skilled at baking

'Selina made a chocolate pie, which I'm shocked to say tasted pretty good.' 'Oh yeah, she's a regular Miss Betty Crocker.'
STARSPRINKLES 9604 *Games of the Heart* 2003

Crockett, Davy [People] (1786–1836) An American frontiersman who fought in military campaigns and was elected to the US Congress in 1826. He died fighting for Texas at the *Alamo. He is typically portrayed in films wearing clothes made of animal skins and a characteristic hat with a racoon tail hanging down at the back.

➤ A rugged outdoors hero; someone who dresses in animal skins, or wears a hat decorated with a racoon tail

Belt-buckles the size of Texas are de rigueur and one gentleman is wearing an eight-gallon hat topped with a raccoon tail for that essential Davy Crockett look.
Scotland on Sunday 2004

Croesus [People] (6th century BC) The last king of Lydia, a country on the east coast of the Aegean Sea in what is now Turkey. He was famed for his great wealth. The phrase 'as rich as Croesus' has become proverbial.

➤ A very rich man

The stakes will be very high (the winners rich as Croesus, the losers dead).
Boston Review 2003

In 1999, Agro and his wife, Camille, examined his 401 (k) retirement plan and felt like Croesus.
CFO: Magazine for Senior Financial Executives 2001

Croft, Lara [Computer games] The heroine of the video game *Tomb Raider°*. She is an animated archaeologist who hunts down artefacts from ancient ruins often in circumstances of extreme danger. She is well armed and combat-trained while wearing skin-tight clothing and high heels, and she has a bust of considerable dimensions. Two films have been made of her adventures starring Angelina Jolie as Croft: *Lara Croft Tomb Raider* (2001) and *Lara Croft Tomb Raider: The Cradle of Life* (2003).

➤ A female adventurer; a woman with a large bust

Vega is a chic cross between Lara Croft and Nancy Drew, legislating her way through the difficult issue of water rights and the setting of Europe-wide water pollution standards.
Reason Magazine 2003

The rare female characters are usually blatently sex objects: as well-endowed as Lara Croft circa Tomb Raider 3.
The F Word: Reviews (2002)

Cromwell, Oliver [Hist.] (1599–1658) The English general who led the parliamentary forces, or Roundheads, against Charles I in the English Civil War. After the Roundhead victory, Cromwell helped to arrange the trial and execution of Charles I and set up a republican government, becoming in 1653, as lord protector, the ruler of Scotland, Ireland, and England and Wales.

> ➤ An anti-royalist revolutionary

> The pity of it is, I hear such stuff from my peers. Elegant ideas for a social re-ordering. Pleasing plans for a community of reason. And Louis is weak. Let him give an inch, and some Cromwell will appear. It'll end in revolution.
> HILARY MANTEL *A Place of Greater Safety* 1992

Cronus (Cronos) [Gk Myth.] One of the *Titans and the father of *Zeus. Cronus married his sister Rhea, and because he knew that he would one day be supplanted by one of the new gods, he swallowed all his children at birth. Rhea hid Zeus and gave Cronus a stone to swallow instead. As an adult, Zeus forced Cronus to bring up the stone and all the other children. Cronus and the Titans fought the new Olympian gods but lost to them.

> ➤ A father who eats or destroys his own children

> 'He's an impulsive young lad,' said Dalziel. 'But good-hearted. I'll have a fatherly word with him.' He gave her a savage smile suggesting the father he had in mind was Cronos.
> REGINALD HILL *On Beulah Height* 1998

Cruella de Vil *See* DE VIL.

Crusoe, Robinson [Lit.] The eponymous hero of Daniel Defoe's novel *Robinson Crusoe*, who survives a shipwreck and lives on an uninhabited island for 24 years, at first alone and later joined by *Man Friday. One of the most memorable episodes in the novel is Crusoe's horrified discovery of a footprint on the beach.

> ➤ A castaway; someone who is alone in an uninhabited place

> They just made it to an island and were stranded on a beach like Robinson Crusoe, not knowing what to expect.
> *Daily Dispatch Online* July 2004

cry wolf [Lit.] An allusion to the fable of the *Boy who Cried Wolf.

> ➤ To falsely warn of impending misfortune, with the result that you are not believed when real disaster strikes

> What we have to do is not go into scaremongering for fear that we 'cry wolf' just once too often.
> *Bradford and District news stories* 2005

Cumaean Sibyl [Rom. Myth.] The prophetess (or Sibyl) of the Temple of *Apollo at Cumae in south Italy who guided *Aeneas through the underworld in the *Aeneid*. It was said that in her youth Apollo had been enamoured of her and had offered to give her whatever she wished. She took a handful of sand and asked to live as many years as there were grains of sand in her hand, but she forgot to ask for health and youth as well. So she grew old and decrepit and had already lived 700 years by the time Aeneas encountered her.

> ➤ A woman who looks extremely old

cupboard was bare [Nurs. Rhym.] A quotation from the nursery rhyme 'Old Mother *Hubbard':

> Old Mother Hubbard
> Went to the cupboard
> To fetch her poor dog a bone.
> But when she got there
> The cupboard was bare,
> And so the poor dog had none.

➤ Used when suggesting that there is no food or no money available

We were barely breaking even, and the cupboard was bare.
BusinessWeek Magazine 2004

Cupid [Rom. Myth.] The Roman god of love, corresponding to the Greek god *Eros. He is often pictured as a beautiful naked boy with wings, carrying a bow and arrows, with which he wounds his victims and makes them fall in love. According to the story, Cupid fell in love with the beautiful Psyche. He visited her only at night in the dark, insisting that she did not see what he looked like. When Psyche succumbed to curiosity and lit a lamp while he slept, a few drops of hot oil fell on him and woke him. He left her, and she wandered across the earth looking for him. Eventually Psyche was reunited with Cupid and married him in heaven.

➤ A way of referring to love; a matchmaker; someone who brings lovers together or causes them to fall in love

Struck by cupid's arrow, the princess decided to go against her family's wishes and start a new life with the mysterious man.
ZIZZER *The Sword of Sorrow* 2003

Under the guise of modern-day cupids, sites like Match.com, Matchmaker.com, XSeeksY. com and Swoon.com have taken aim at Lonely Hearts in cyberspace, with the hope of hooking up couples and turning a buck or two in the process.
Brandweek 2000

curiouser and curiouser [Child. Lit.] A phrase used repeatedly by *Alice in Lewis Carroll's children's story *Alice's Adventures in Wonderland*, as she encounters ever stranger characters and adventures.

➤ Used to suggest that something is strange or inexplicable

Pyper has had the opportunity to amend his entry every year for the past 10 years but has neglected to do so, even though Who's Who diligently sends him his entry for correction and amendment each year. Curiouser and curiouser.
Sunday Herald 2002

Currier and Ives [Art] A New York City lithography shop run by **Nathaniel Currier** and **Jim Ives** that sold coloured prints between 1834 and 1907. They described themselves as 'publishers of cheap and popular pictures', and their prints depicted the history of America in the second half of the 19th century in pictorial form.

➤ Used to invoke a stereotypical or idealized picture of American rural or small-town life

As soon as the ice is safely solid, Evergreen Lake…presents a scene reminiscent of a Currier & Ives lithograph. Skaters circle a section of ice set against a backdrop of pine-covered rolling hills.
Sunset Magazine 2002

Custer's last stand [Hist.] The name given to the Battle of *Little Bighorn in which the American cavalry general **George Armstrong Custer** (1839–76) was killed. Custer was sent to Dakota to protect goldminers and railway surveyors against the Sioux after gold had been found in what had been Sioux tribal lands. In 1876, while scouting, his regiment, the 7th Cavalry, came upon a large encampment of Sioux and Cheyenne in the Little Bighorn valley in southern Montana. Custer and his men were surrounded and killed by the Sioux under their leader, Sitting Bull.

➤ A desperate battle against a more powerful adversary; a final defeat, which leads to someone's death or downfall

'It was a bit like Custer's last stand in the second half for them,' said McGeough. 'We had ten attacking players near the end and threw everything at them.'
Irish Examiner 2003

Cyclops [Gk Myth.] One of a race of savage one-eyed giants (the Cyclops or Cyclopes) who were said to have lived as shepherds or to have made thunderbolts for *Zeus. The building of massive prehistoric structures was supposed to have been the work of the Cyclops.

➤ A monster with one large eye; a giant (adjective *Cyclopean*)

He leered, winking like a Cyclops as he handed over a couple bucks' worth, flipping through the money roll as though it was his own.
Strange Horizons stories 2003

The aqueducts...were lofted on arcaded structures of Cyclopean proportions.
Apollo Magazine 2003

Dachau [Hist.] A Nazi concentration camp just outside the town of Dachau in Bavaria from 1933 to 1945. Hundreds of prisoners died in medical experiments to find a cure for malaria, and a gas chamber was built in 1942. Pictures of the skeletal survivors of the camp shocked the world when the camp was liberated at the end of the war.

> ➤ A horrific place of great suffering
>
> They looked like people coming out of Dachau at the end of World War II.
> *CNN transcripts: Larry King Live* 2004

Dad's Army [TV] The title of a popular British television series about the Home Guard, the British citizen army organized in 1940 to defend the UK against invasion. In the television series, the Home Guard of Warmington-on-Sea is led by the pompous bank manager Captain Mainwaring and features a range of men from the elderly butcher Corporal Jones to the young and naive Private Pike.

> ➤ An amateur and incompetent army, especially one made up of elderly men
>
> There is only one thing that the public wants and that is more properly trained police officers, not a Dad's Army of cooks, bottle-washers and gardeners.
> *Yorkshire Post Today* 2001

Dada [Art] An early 20th-century artistic and literary movement which rejected traditional moral and aesthetic values and emphasized the illogical and absurd. The movement was started in Zurich in 1916 by the poet Tristan Tzara and others, and soon spread to New York, Paris, and Cologne. One of the most famous works produced was Duchamp's version of the *Mona Lisa* decorated with a moustache and an obscene caption.

> ➤ Used when describing something unconventional, illogical, or absurd (adjectives *Dadaist, Dadaesque*)
>
> We're not sure if anything we say can make the ludicrous HP-Compaq Sircam Merger any more ridiculous, but subversive Dadaist elements inside Hewlett Packard's Cupertino headquarters are hell bent on trumping us
> *The Register* 2002

Daddy Warbucks *See* WARBUCKS.

Daedalus [Gk Myth.] An Athenian craftsman who fled from Athens to Crete after jealously killing his pupil Talos, whose skills threatened to outdo his own. In the service of King *Minos of Crete, Daedalus designed and built the Labyrinth in which the *Minotaur was kept. When Minos later refused to allow him to leave Crete, he escaped by making wings for himself and his son *Icarus. Although Daedalus escaped and flew to safety, Icarus flew too high and the sun melted the wax holding his wings together, so that he plunged to his death.

> ➤ A builder of labyrinths; a clever craftsman or maker of clever or complicated devices; a maker of a flying machine

With its exterior like the giant Bakelite 'Box-brownie' of the 1930s, inside its design could well be attributed to a latter day Daedalus because it is a labyrinth that almost outdoes the one of Crete.
Sofia Echo 2002

If they provide an aerodrome in which the hopeful Daedalus may try his wings, and find them wanting, they will have served their purpose.
Jacket Magazine 2002

Dalek [TV] An imaginary alien creature in the long-running BBC television science fiction series *Doctor Who* (from 1963). The ferocious Daleks are the Doctor's most persistent enemy. Round with domed tops, they are approximately 5 feet high, and have various sink-plunger-style appendages. They are inclined to utter the syllables 'Ex-ter-min-ate' or, in response to such an instruction, 'I o-bey', in robotic voices.

➤ A ruthless person with no compassion; someone who obeys orders in an unquestioning way; someone who repeats the same phrase over and over again; also used to describe a robotic voice

Harrison went about his business with all the ruthlessness of a dalek.
Scotland on Sunday 2004

'May I have your attention please,' says a voice that sounds like a Dalek with a Spanish accent.
Saga Magazine 2004

Daley, Arthur [TV] A character in the ITV series *Minder* (1979–94), a shady wheeler-dealer always full of schemes to make money quickly, usually involving selling goods of dubious origin. Daley always managed to avoid being arrested, but never actually made any money from his schemes.

➤ A shady businessman who is willing to operate outside the law

Most people are put off by Arthur Daley types who give you the hard sell and expect you to sign on the dotted line there and then.
Sligo Weekender 2002

Dalí, Salvador [Art] (1904–89) A Spanish painter and prominent member of the Surrealist movement, who was greatly influenced by Sigmund *Freud's writings on dreams and the unconscious. Many of his paintings depict fantastic dream images painted with almost photographically realist detail and set in arid Catalan landscapes.

➤ Used when describing something that looks unnatural or surrealistic

Many of its grotesque characters behave as if they have leapt straight from the canvas of a Salvador Dali painting.
Sunday Herald 2000

Damascus, road to [Bible] The site of the sudden and dramatic conversion to Christianity undergone by *Saul of Tarsus. With a reputation as a committed persecutor of Christians, he had set out planning to take prisoner any Christians he found in Damascus. On the way he suddenly found himself the centre of a blinding light and, falling to the ground, heard God's voice crying 'Saul, Saul, why persecutest thou me?' (Acts 9: 4). Saul, later known as *Paul, became a powerful and influential Christian.

➤ Mentioned in the context of a sudden realization, particularly a sudden conversion to a belief, opinion, or cause

Aer Rianta has apparently undergone a 'Road to Damascus' conversion and is offering comfort, space, new bars and restaurants, and a dazzling array of food from across the globe before passengers fly off to their holiday destination.
The Sunday Business Post 2001

Damocles *See* SWORD OF DAMOCLES.

Damon and Pythias (Damon and Phintias) [Leg. & Folk.] Legendary friends of the 4th century BC. The tyrant Dionysius I of Syracuse had sentenced Pythias to death. When Pythias went home to settle his affairs, Damon stood surety with his life for Pythias' return to certain execution. Pythias did return in time to redeem his pledge and was then reprieved.

➤ Firm and faithful friends

Of course she thinks, since I'm Fontclair's groomsman, he and I must have been Damon and Pythias for years.
KATE ROSS *Cut to the Quick* 1993

Dan Dare *See* DARE.

Daniel [Bible] A devout Jew who spent his life as one of those taken into exile in *Babylon. He had a gift for interpreting visions and dreams. He was able to explain the meaning of a strange dream that *Nebuchadnezzar, the king of Babylon, had had, for which he was made the king's chief adviser. Later, Daniel interpreted a second dream of Nebuchadnezzar to foretell his insanity, which immediately came to pass.

When, after a successful career, he was appointed sole administrator over all the other officials and princes, they plotted to bring about Daniel's downfall. They asked King Darius to establish a decree saying that for 30 days no one should pray to any God or man except the king. Daniel ignored this command. As a result of this disobedience, he was cast into the *lions' den and left for the night. In the morning he was discovered by the king, unscathed. Daniel explained, 'My God hath sent his angel, and hath shut the lions' mouths, that they have not hurt me' (Dan. 6: 22).

In the apocryphal book of *Susanna, Daniel is portrayed as a wise judge, proving the falsely accused Susanna to be innocent. In *Shakespeare's *The Merchant of Venice* (1600), *Shylock praises Portia, who is disguised as a lawyer, with the words:

> A Daniel come to judgment! Yea, a Daniel!
> O wise young judge, how I do honour thee!

➤ Someone showing courage when facing great danger alone without any material protection; a wise judge

I was quite overcome with astonishment, Major Scobie, to sit in a police court and hear true facts from the mouths of policemen....I said to myself, Yusef, a Daniel has come to the Colonial Police.
GRAHAM GREENE *The Heart of the Matter* 1948

Don't you feel like Daniel setting off for the lion's den, going back there? If you really think one of the Fontclairs is a murderer, how can you sit down to dinner with them, sleep under their roof?
KATE ROSS *Cut to the Quick* 1993

Dante (Dante Alighieri) [Lit.] (1265–1321) An Italian poet whose epic *The Divine Comedy* (*c.*1309–20) relates the poet's imagined visit to Hell (in the part of the poem titled *Inferno*), Purgatory, and Paradise. Dante's first book, *La vita nuova* (*c.*1290–4), details, in poetry and prose, his adoration for *Beatrice Portinari. He was platonically devoted to her all his life, although she did not apparently return his love and both were married to others.

➤ Mentioned in the context of a hideous or horrific sight, suggestive of the horrors of Hell; any hell-like vision or scene can be described as being like 'Dante's Inferno' (adjective Dantean)

Bored, she stepped outside, on to a steel gallery overlooking the factory floor. She surveyed the scene, feeling more than ever like Dante in the Inferno. All was noise, smoke, fumes and flames.
DAVID LODGE *Nice Work* 1988

Beijing became a Dantean pit of underworld activity in the years following the country's economic expansion.
PAUL JOHNSTON *Body Politic* 1997

Dan to Beersheba [Bible] According to the book of Judges, the people of Israel were 'gathered together as one man, from Dan even to Beersheba' (Judg. 20: 1). Dan was a town in the north of *Canaan, the Promised Land to which *Moses led the people of Israel in the Bible. It marked the northern limit of the ancient kingdom of Israel. Beersheba, which still exists, was the town which marked the southern limit of the kingdom.

➤ Something that happens 'from Dan to Beersheba' happens everywhere

What profits it to have a covenanted State and a purified Kirk if a mailed Amalekite can hunt our sodgers from Dan to Beersheba?
JOHN BUCHAN *Witch Woods* 1927

Daphne [Gk Myth.] A nymph, daughter of Peneus, with whom the god *Apollo fell in love. In attempting to escape his pursuit, Daphne called upon the gods for help and was turned into a laurel tree. Daphne is often depicted in art literally rooted to the spot as she undergoes her transformation, for example in Bernini's marble sculpture *Apollo and Daphne* (1622–5).

➤ Someone becoming immobile or transfixed to the spot

Alexander slid into the seat beside her, Alexander's Old Spice smell brushed her nostrils, Alexander's soft-modulated voice murmured no, surely not muscle-bound, but with her nerves chained up in alabaster and she a statue, or as Daphne was, root-bound, that fled Apollo.
A. S. BYATT *The Virgin in the Garden* 1978

Daphnis and Chloe [Lit.] The subjects of an ancient Greek pastoral romance, *Daphnis and Chloe*, by Longus (AD 2–3). The story relates how the two young people meet, fall in love, and discover sexual desire, eventually marrying.

➤ Young lovers

Darby and Joan [Lit.] A devoted old married couple, living in domestic harmony, originally described in a poem in the *Gentleman's Magazine* (1735):

> Old Darby, with Joan by his side,
> You've often regarded with wonder:
> He's dropsical, she is sore-eyed,
> Yet they're never happy asunder.

➤ An old happily married couple

I can assure you I don't want any procession at all. I should be quite contented to go down with Alexandrina, arm in arm, like Darby and Joan, and let the clerk give her away.
ANTHONY TROLLOPE *The Small House at Allington* 1862

Darcy, Mr (Fitzwilliam Darcy) [Lit.] The hero of Jane Austen's novel *Pride and Prejudice* (1796), who courts and finally wins Elizabeth Bennet. He is wealthy and extremely handsome, with a proud and rather aloof manner.

➤ A dashing romantic hero

She was busy running her tresses through her manicured fingers and flapping her blue-mascaraed eyelashes at James Rattray-Potter, who was propped against the desk in a suave, man-of-the-world pose, ankles crossed. He was a generic Mills and Boon hero to Dominic Planchet's Mr Darcy, but I could see that his brand of florid good looks would appeal to secretaries and girls who lacked confidence.
LAUREN HENDERSON *The Black Rubber Dress* 1997

Dare, Dan [Cart. & Com.] A comic-strip cartoon hero who appeared in the *Eagle* comic between 1950 and 1967. A commander of the Space Fleet, Dan Dare battled against his arch-enemy from Venus, the *Mekon.

➤ A space-age hero

The Middle East, with all its complexities and dangers and religious tension—yes, and its evils—is being turned into a comic strip in which Dan Dare will launch his space-age high-tech at the Mekon of Baghdad.
The Independent 1998

Dark Ages [Hist.] A term designating the period in the West between the fall of the Roman Empire and the high Middle Ages (that is, from about the 5th to the 11th century), so called because it used to be regarded as a time of relative unenlightenment and obscurity.

➤ Suggesting any unenlightened or ignorant period or, when used humorously, any little-regarded period before the present; to 'live in the Dark Ages' is to be old-fashioned or prejudiced in one's behaviour and attitudes

Jim's brow darkened. 'Look, old son. The law's no place for Luddites. We're in business, remember? We need to compete, to provide a decent service.' 'I haven't heard Kevin or Jeannie Walters complaining.' 'You've done a superb job, I'm the first to say so. But we must move with the times. We can't keep living in the Dark Ages.'
MARTIN EDWARDS *Yesterday's Papers* 1994

Darkest Africa [Places] Before Africa had been fully explored by Europeans it was known to them as the Dark Continent. Darkest Africa was therefore an unexplored land far away from modern European life and full of potential dangers. The term may have originated from titles of works by the explorer Henry Morton *Stanley, *Through the Dark Continent* (1878) and *Through Darkest Africa* (1890).

➤ An unknown region

dark night of the soul [Lit.] A phrase from David Lewis's 1864 translation of the *Complete Works* of St John of the Cross (1542–91), and later popularized by F. Scott Fitzgerald in the form 'In a real dark night of the soul it is always three o'clock in the morning.'

➤ A period of utter despair or mental suffering, often during a personal crisis or preceding a difficult decision someone has to make

You still get the occasional dark night of the soul, when you see yourself alone on your deathbed, childless and abandoned. But more often you get these glimmers of a peaceful and exciting life with no responsibilities to anyone but yourself.
Montreal Mirror 2001

dark Satanic mills [Lit.] A phrase from the preface to William *Blake's poem *Milton* (1804–10), later set to music as the hymn 'Jerusalem'.

➤ Referring to the harsh working conditions in the factories of the Industrial Revolution; industrialization generally

The transformation of the town and its environment since then have been dramatic and it's one more reason why I get so irritated by people in London who still believe Lancashire towns are full of dark, Satanic mills with shuffling figures in clogs.
Bolton Evening News 2005

Darling, Grace [People] (1815–42) The daughter of a lighthouse keeper on the Farne Islands off the coast of Northumberland who became a national heroine when in September 1838 she and her father rowed through a storm to rescue the survivors of the wrecked *Forfarshire*.

➤ A young woman or girl who shows great courage

When she was seventeen, she had been somewhere between Queen Elizabeth I and Grace Darling, with a will of tungsten and the biddability of a mobile howitzer.
SAM LLEWELLYN *Maelstrom* 1995

D'Artagnan *See* THREE MUSKETEERS.

Darth Vader *See* VADER.

Dartmoor [Crime] A high-security prison on Dartmoor, a moorland district in Devon, originally built to hold French prisoners of war during the Napoleonic Wars.

➤ A prison

Darwin, Charles [Science] (1809–82) An English naturalist and geologist who formulated the theory of evolution by natural selection to explain the origin of animal and plant species. His work *On the Origin of Species* was published in 1859 and *The Descent of Man* in 1871.

➤ Mentioned in the context of evolution and the 'the survival of the fittest', the idea that those that best adapt to a changing environment are those that thrive (adjective *Darwinian*)

The great thing about the business is how Darwinian it is. We have to swim or die—if you are found wanting over a period of time, you've either got to change what you're doing or find something else to do.
Film Comment 2001

David [Bible] The youngest son of Jesse, David was noted as a musician and is traditionally regarded as the author of the Psalms. When still a shepherd boy, David accepted the challenge from the Philistine champion *Goliath to single combat. Although Goliath was over 9 feet tall and wore full armour including a brass helmet, David went to fight him armed only with a sling and five pebbles. Using the sling, he struck Goliath on the forehead and killed him.

On Saul's death David was made king of Judah and later he was chosen as ruler of the whole of Israel. He made Jerusalem his capital and reigned there for 33 years. David's later years were darkened by the rebellion and death of his favourite son, *Absalom.

➤ Allusions to David and Goliath are often in the context of an individual or small, relatively powerless, group defeating a powerful or global organization

Every day we hear of more Italian armies driven back or defeated, and we feel the jubilation of David with Goliath dead at his feet.
LOUIS DE BERNIÈRES *Captain Corelli's Mandolin* 1994

On this public relations battlefront the odds against a Greenpeace victory shorten dramatically. A master of global communications, the environmental group recently played David against Shell's Goliath over the Brent Spar and won.
The Observer 1995

David and Jonathan [Bible] In the Old Testament (1 Sam. 18: 1–3, 20: 17), Jonathan, the son of Saul, and *David, Saul's appointed successor as king of Israel, swore a compact of love and mutual protection: 'the love of Jonathan was knit with the soul of David, and Jonathan loved him as his own soul.' When Saul grew jealous of David's popularity and sought to bring about his death, Jonathan repeatedly tried to intercede on David's behalf with his father.

> Mentioned in the context of male friendship

Why should you not make friends with your neighbour at the theatre or in the train, when you know and he knows that feminine criticism and feminine insight and feminine prejudice will never come between you! Though you become as David and Jonathan, you need never enter his home, nor he yours.
E. M. FORSTER *Where Angels Fear to Tread* 1905

da Vinci, Leonardo [Art] (1452–1519) An Italian painter, sculptor, scientist, and engineer, generally celebrated as the supreme example of the Renaissance genius. Some of his well-known paintings, such as the *Mona Lisa* and *The Virgin of the Rocks*, demonstrate his careful use of *sfumato*, the technique of achieving a transition from light to shadow by gradually shading one into the other.

> Used when describing a person set against a landscape, with subtle contrasts of light and shadow

She reminded him of a Leonardo more than ever; her sunburnt features were shadowed by fantastic rocks; at his words she had turned and stood between him and the light with immeasurable plains behind her.
E. M. FORSTER *A Room with a View* 1908

Day, Doris [Cin.] (b. Doris Kappelhoff, 1922) US actress and singer who played the cheerful, freckle-faced girl-next-door in numerous musicals and comedies in the late 1940s and early 1950s. In the late 1950s and early 1960s she appeared in a series of innocent sex comedies such as *Pillow Talk* (1959), in which she habitually played the virginal heroine. Groucho *Marx claimed to have 'been around so long I can remember Doris Day before she was a virgin'.

> A wholesome girl-next-door; used to suggest virginity

Maybe because I wanted to lend the moment that sort of corny Doris Day romance, make it more memorable than it otherwise would have been.
NICK HORNBY *High Fidelity* 1995

There was a rap on the door and my sister bounced in, looking Doris Day–Meg Ryan perky. Probably perfect for California, but we don't do perky in Jersey.
JANET EVANOVICH *Seven Up* 2001

day of infamy [Hist.] Following the surprise attack by Japanese war planes on US ships and aircraft based at *Pearl Harbor, Hawaii, Franklin D. Roosevelt, in an address to Congress, described 7 December 1941 as 'a date which will live in infamy'.

> Referring to a shameful or treacherous act

Inside the capitol, history in the making, a sweeping intelligence bill. Supporters say it will help prevent America from experiencing another day of infamy.
CNN transcripts: Lou Dobbs Tonight 2004

Dead Sea Fruit Fruits reputed to grow at *Sodom, near the Dead Sea. Also known as Apples of Sodom, they were beautiful to look at but bitter to the taste or full of ashes.

> Something that promises pleasure but brings only disappointment

He had looked for rapturous joy in loving this lovely creature, and he already found that he met with little but disappointment and self-rebuke. He had come across the fruit of the Dead Sea, so sweet and delicious to the eye, so bitter and nauseous to the taste.
ANTHONY TROLLOPE *Barchester Towers* 1857

Dean, James [Cin.] (1931–55) An American actor best remembered for his role in the 1955 film *Rebel without a Cause*. The film opened just weeks after Dean's death in a car crash, and he became strongly associated with the character he played in the film, a confused, rebellious, and self-destructive adolescent.

> ➤ Mentioned in the context of youthful rebelliousness
>
> Over her shoulder, the trailer door opened. Lonnie stood there in a pair of worn jeans and a white T-shirt. He could do James Dean with the best of them, I thought.
> STEVEN WOMACK *Dead Folks' Blues* 1992

Death [Bible] One of the Four Horsemen of the Apocalypse: 'And I looked, and behold, a pale horse, and his name that sat on him was Death' (Rev. 6: 8). The other horsemen were Pestilence, War, and Famine.

> Not knowing whether to expect friend or foe, prudence suggested that he should cease his whistling and retreat among the trees till the horse and his rider had gone by, a course to which he was still more inclined when he found how noiselessly they approached, and saw that the horse looked pale, and remembered what he had read about Death in the Revelation.
> THOMAS HARDY *The Woodlanders* 1887

Degas, Edgar [Art] (1834–1917) A French painter and sculptor associated with Impressionism. He is best known for his drawings, paintings, and pastels of ballet dancers, cabaret artistes, and women dressing and bathing.

> ➤ Used to suggest scenes reminiscent of Degas's paintings
>
> She was a big, sexy brunette—as Garcia said, 'Something straight out of Degas.'
> JACK KEROUAC *On the Road* 1957

Deimos [Gk Myth.] One of the sons of *Aphrodite and *Ares. He is sometimes seen as a personification of fear.

Deirdre [Leg. & Folk.] In Irish legend, the beautiful daughter of the harper to King Conchobar of Ulster. According to a prophecy her beauty would bring death and ruin to the men of Ulster. Although she was the intended bride of Conchobar, she fell in love and eloped with Naoise. When Naoise was treacherously slain by Conchobar, Deirdre took her own life, ending her misery.

> ➤ A tragic or grieving woman

Del Boy (Derek Trotter) [TV] The lead character in the television sitcom *Only Fools and Horses* (1981–96). In pursuit of easy wealth, and with the assistance of his naive younger brother Rodney, he runs Trotter's Independent Trading Company, selling dodgy products, which he stores in their council flat. Memorably played by David Jason, Del Boy is a classic wide boy.

> ➤ A lovable rogue; someone involved in black-market dealing
>
> That is, the businessmen, financiers, entrepreneurs and Del Boys who have been happy to skirt the limelight so sought after by our elected representatives and provided by our starstruck media.
> SHEENA MCDONALD *The Guardian* 1988

Delectable Mountains [Lit.] In Bunyan's *Pilgrim's Progress*, the summit of the Delectable Mountains, Emmanuel's Land, is within sight of the *Celestial City.

> ➤ An ideal place or paradise
>
> We call this hill the Delectable Mountain, for we can look far away and see the country where we hope to live some time.
> LOUISA M. ALCOTT *Little Women* 1868

Delilah [Bible] According to the Old Testament book of Judges, Delilah used her guile to extract from *Samson the secret of his prodigious strength so that she could betray him to the Philistines in return for money. Samson told her that his great strength lay in his long hair and that if it were cut short he would 'become weak, and be like any other man'. Delilah had his hair shaved while he slept, after which she delivered him up to the Philistines.

➤ A treacherous woman; a temptress

Ay, and I fancy I've baited the hook right. Our little Delilah will bring our Samson.
ANTHONY HOPE *The Prisoner of Zenda* 1894

Delphi [Places] The site of the Delphic oracle on the slopes of Mount *Parnassus in ancient Greece, which was consulted on a wide range of religious, political, and moral questions. The pronouncements of the Oracle were made by the priestess of *Apollo, Pythia. They were often ambiguous and riddle-like and had to be interpreted.

➤ A Delphic prediction or warning is one that is enigmatic or difficult to interpret

This really is very pleasant—to escape. I'm not sure why it is, but I find that a roomful of 'scholars' tends to bring on an attack of mental indigestion. That Delphic tone they love to take. And something chilly and unhelpful about them too.
CAROL SHIELDS *Mary Swann* 1990

Demeter [Gk Myth.] The goddess of cornfields and fecundity, whose symbol is an ear of corn. She was the mother of *Persephone, and when Persephone was abducted by *Hades and taken to the underworld, Demeter wandered around looking for her daughter and swore that the earth would remain barren until Persephone was restored to her. A compromise was finally reached whereby Persephone would spend six months of each year with her mother, the time when plants grow and produce fruit, and six months of each year with Hades in the underworld, the time when the earth is cold and barren.

➤ A mother searching for her daughter

So, every Saturday night, which is morning in Budapest, my mother waits by the phone, like Demeter at the entrance to the realm of Hades, where, Persephone, her abducted daughter is getting ready to surface from the vortex of the dark.
www.ashladle.org 2004

Demodocus [Gk Myth.] A blind bard at the Phaeacian court of Alcinous who, according to *Homer's *Odyssey*, entertained *Odysseus with his songs telling of the adulterous love of *Ares and *Aphrodite and of the famous story of the *Wooden Horse of Troy.

➤ A storyteller

It was quite impossible—recounting tales in the presence of people who knew them already. She wondered how Taliesin, Demodocus and all the other storytellers had coped.
ALICE THOMAS ELLIS *The 27th Kingdom* 1982

Demosthenes [People] (384–322 BC) An Athenian orator and statesman famous for a series of orations attacking the rising power of Philip of Macedon.

➤ An eloquent or persuasive speaker

The explorer waxes eloquent as Antony, Demosthenes and the Speaker of the House all rolled into one.
T. CORAGHESSAN BOYLE *Water Music* 1981

Dennis the Menace [Cart. & Com.] A trouble-making boy who first appeared in the British comic *The Beano* in 1951. Dennis has a shock of thick black hair, wears a red and black striped jumper, and has a dog called Gnasher. A character of the same name has appeared in US comic strips also since 1951, though he is blond and younger than the British Dennis.

> A naughty or mischievous boy

But the most toxic aspect of the film is little Pete himself, a patient who would make the young Francis of Assisi look like Dennis the Menace.
Eye Weekly (Toronto) 2004

Depression *See* GREAT DEPRESSION.

Desdemona [Shakes.] In *Othello* (1622), Desdemona is the daughter of a Venetian senator who falls in love with and marries the Moorish general *Othello. The treacherous *Iago, Othello's ensign, convinces Othello that Desdemona is being unfaithful to him and, although she is completely innocent, Othello murders her in jealous rage.

> A woman falsely accused of adultery

Desmond, Norma [Cin.] The ageing retired silent-screen star in the film *Sunset Boulevard* (1950), played by Gloria Swanson. An impecunious Hollywood scriptwriter, Joe Gillis, stumbles upon her mansion when on the run from men who are trying to repossess his car. She persuades him to stay to write a script for her 'comeback movie'. Sublimely narcissistic, she is delusional about her current celebrity status and becomes increasingly possessive of Joe, whom she eventually shoots dead. By the time the cameras finally come for her, she is sufficiently deluded to believe they are celebrating her, rather than filming the news story of Joe's murder.

> An ageing, fading film star; a performer past their prime; often referred to along with the line 'I *am* big. It's the *pictures* that got small' or 'All right, Mr. DeMille, I'm ready for my close-up'

Many people believe he has become the Norma Desmond of pop, retreating into his mansions, tentatively offering a new single every few years, and refusing to be ready for his close-up.
JohannHari.com 2005

As Norma Desmond might have remarked, classical music didn't get small—the media world that it's trying to be part of got real, real big.
GirlHacker's Random Log 2002

Deucalion [Gk Myth.] The son of *Prometheus. When *Zeus, angered by the crimes of men, decided to destroy them by a great flood, Prometheus warned Deucalion, who built a boat for himself and his wife, Pyrrha, in which they floated until the waters subsided and they safely came to land on Mount *Parnassus. *See also* FLOOD.

> Someone who survives a great flood

Devil [Rel.] In Christian and Jewish belief, the supreme spirit of evil, the enemy of God, and the tempter of humankind. Popularly, the Devil is often represented as a man with horns, a forked tail, and cloven hooves, an image derived from figures of Greek and Roman mythology such as *Pan and the satyrs. The Devil is known by numerous names, especially *Satan *and* *Lucifer. Other names include 'the Evil One', 'Old Harry', 'Old Nick', and 'the Prince of Darkness'.

> A way of referring to utter evil or wickedness, or temptation

But it was only a thought, put into my head by the Devil, no doubt.
MARGARET ATWOOD *Alias Grace* 1996

de Vil, Cruella [Child. Lit.; Cin.] The rich, evil, screeching villainess in Dodie Smith's *One Hundred and One Dalmatians* (1956), who steals 99 Dalmatian puppies in order to make a spotted fur coat from their skins. Two Disney film versions have been made, an animated one in 1961 and a live-action remake in 1996.

➢ A cruel or evil woman; a woman who is cruel to animals; a woman who loves fur coats

'Yes, I do,' she agrees, giving a dry Cruella De Vil laugh.
Sunday Herald 2001

How smart they all look in suits, with sumptuous Cruella de Vil furs slung around their elegant shoulders.
Scotland on Sunday 2003

Devil's Island [Places] A small island off the coast of French Guiana. It was used as a convict settlement, initially for prisoners with contagious diseases but later for political prisoners. Its most famous prisoner was Alfred *Dreyfus. His trial, imprisonment, and eventual release caused a major political crisis in France.

➢ A rough or isolated prison; a remote place to which someone is banished

Spurrier hopes to make South Carolina his Elba, the beachhead from which he'll once again conquer the college rankings. If history is any guide, though, it's more likely to be his Devil's Island.
www.slate.com 2005

Diana [Rom. Myth.] Identified with the Greek goddess *Artemis and associated with hunting, virginity, and, in later literature and art, with the moon. She was the personification of feminine grace and vigour.

➢ A beautiful young woman, especially one associated with hunting or athleticism

In her dress of white and silver, with a wreath of silver blossoms in her hair, the tall girl looked like a Diana just alighting from the chase.
EDITH WHARTON *The Age of Innocence* 1920

Diana, Princess [People] (1961–97) Princess of Wales (b. Lady Diana Frances Spencer). In 1981 she married Charles, the prince of Wales, with whom she had two sons, William and Harry. She and Prince Charles later divorced. Diana died on 31 August 1997, following a car crash in Paris, which led to a prolonged and widespread display of public mourning. Diana devoted much time to charitable work, concentrating particularly on helping children, homeless people, and AIDS sufferers, and at the time of her death she had also become known for her work for a campaign to ban landmines. She is also remembered for a candid television interview in 1995.

➢ Someone whose death causes a mass expression of public mourning; a celebrity involved in high-profile charitable work; someone giving a confessional TV interview; a glamorous female public figure

It is really a caring multinational in a special post-Diana way.
The Observer 1998

They expected the violent murder of Anna Lindh, the Swedish foreign minister campaigning for a yes vote, to create a Princess Diana-like wave of sympathy.
The Guardian 2005

Diaspora [Hist.] The dispersion of the Jews beyond Israel, following the *Babylonian and Roman conquests of Palestine.

➢ The scattering of people from their original home

The company says that the size of the jewellery market related only to the Irish diaspora worldwide is approximately £2 billion annually.
The Sunday Business Post 2001

Dickensian [Lit.] The novels of **Charles Dickens** (1812–70) are notable for their satirical humour and treatment of contemporary social problems, including the plight of the urban poor. Characteristics of the novels that can be alluded to include: the vivid portrayal of some of the novelist's more eccentric or physically grotesque characters; the depiction of social deprivation in such settings as slums, workhouses, and debtors' prisons; the description of brutal educational establishments such as Dotheboys Hall in Dickens's *Nicholas Nickleby*.

> ➤ Used in the context of: a person's almost caricature-like oddness in behaviour, mannerisms, or appearance; conditions of poverty, squalor, and hardship; a corrupt and brutal educational regime

> I can't help describing him as if he were some sort of Dickensian freak.
> ROBERTSON DAVIES *The Manticore* 1972

> So Eddie and his older brother, Mark, were suddenly dispatched to boarding school when they were six and eight respectively—unfortunately, a Dickensian school which rang to the thwack of the cane.
> *The Observer* 1997

Dido and Aeneas [Lit.] Dido was the queen of Carthage, and the story of her love affair with *Aeneas is recounted in Virgil's *Aeneid* (29–19 BC). Aeneas, on his way home from Troy, is shipwrecked off the coast of Carthage, where Dido falls in love with him. The affair is consummated when, during a storm while out hunting, they take shelter in the same cave. Aeneas, however, is commanded by Jupiter to sail to Italy. Seeing the ships preparing to leave, Dido pleads with Aeneas, begging him to stay. When he has departed, she kills herself by building a pyre and throwing herself on it.

> ➤ Tragic lovers; mentioned in the context of a woman who is abandoned by her lover and kills herself

> In such a night
> Stood Dido with a willow in her hand
> Upon the wild sea-banks, and waft her love
> To come again to Carthage.
> WILLIAM SHAKESPEARE *The Merchant of Venice* 1600

> Peter, on the other hand, though not blind to its flaws, felt himself duty driven to work from within. A right pious little Aeneas, *Italiam non sponte sequor* and all that crap. Which made her...Odysseus? Fat, earthy, cunning old Odysseus? Hardly! That was much more Andy Dalziel. Then Dido? Come on! See her chucking herself on a pyre 'cos she'd been jilted. Helen? Ellie looked at herself in the mirror. Not today.
> REGINALD HILL *On Beulah Height* 1998

die is cast, the [Hist.] A saying originally translated from Julius Caesar's words (in Latin, 'iacta alea est') at the crossing of the Rubicon with his army in 49 BC. This act meant that he was irrevocably committing himself to war, hence his reference to dice being thrown, with no chance of the result being changed.

> ➤ Used when a decisive step or decision has been taken that cannot be changed

> The nation's 14 million smokers braced Friday for a new law which comes into force Monday banning them from smoking in public places including bars, restaurants, discotheques and offices. There have been two delays in applying the regulation, but now the die is cast.
> *Taipei Times* 2005

Dillinger, John [Crime] (1903–34) An armed bank robber based in Indiana, named the FBI's 'public enemy number one' in 1933. He was shot dead by FBI agents in Chicago acting on information given by his girlfriend, now popularly known as the Lady in Red.

> ➤ A criminal or bank robber
>
> 'You always wanted it that way, Jess. You changing your mind?' 'No. It's just...' He sighed. 'Spring'. 'Don't feel bad. It turns even the best of us to mush.' 'Leave it to Tark—more Diogenes than Dillinger these days—to understand that.'
> MEG O'BRIEN *Eagles Die Too* 1993

Dimmesdale, Arthur [Lit.] A character in Nathaniel Hawthorne's *The Scarlet Letter* (1850). A young and much-respected church minister, he keeps secret the fact that he is the father of Hester *Prynne's illegitimate baby while she is ostracized by the community and condemned to wear a scarlet 'A', for 'adulteress', on her bosom. Hester's husband, under the assumed name of Roger Chillingworth, discovers his secret and tortures him mentally with it until he finally confesses publicly and dies in Hester's arms.

> ➤ A man with a secret
>
> In all, the doctor he reminded me of most was Dr. Roger Chillingworth in Hawthorne's *Scarlet Letter*. Appropriate enough, because I sat facing him as full of shameful secrets as the Reverend Arthur Dimmesdale.
> PHILIP ROTH *My Life as a Man* 1970

Diogenes [Philos.] A Greek philosopher (*c*.400–*c*.325 BC), the most famous of the Cynics. He promoted self-sufficiency and the denial of physical pleasure and rejected social conventions. According to legend he lived in a barrel, to demonstrate his belief that the virtuous life was the simple life. One story told of him is that he carried a lantern out in daylight, saying that he was seeking an honest man.

> ➤ Someone who chooses to live a solitary life without physical comforts; a cynical observer of the world; someone who exposes the truth or tries to find honest people
>
> He immediately built himself a grass hut, Indian style, thatched it with palm, and to the wonder of the locals began to live like Diogenes and labour like Sisyphus, except with better results.
> LOUIS DE BERNIÈRES *The War of Don Emmanuel's Nether Parts* 1990
>
> Nassau needs its Diogenes, patrolling the streets with a lamp, looking for that honest bold parliamentarian who is not afraid to act.
> *Bahamas Blog* 2005

Dionysus [Gk Myth.] The son of *Zeus and the mortal Semele; also called *Bacchus. Originally a god of the fertility of nature, in later traditions Dionysus is a god of wine who loosens inhibitions and inspires creativity in music and poetry. His cult was celebrated at various festivals throughout the year, some of which included orgies and ecstatic rites. His female devotees were called the *Bacchantes, or maenads. Dionysus, representing creativity, sensuality, and lack of inhibition, is often contrasted with *Apollo, representing order, reason, and self-discipline. Dionysus was said to have made an expedition to eastern lands including India, spreading his cult and teaching mankind the elements of civilization and the use of wine. On his travels Dionysus is frequently represented drawn in a chariot by tigers and accompanied by *Pan, *Silenus, and a rowdy retinue of satyrs and maenads.

> ➤ Used in the context of frenzied and unrestrained abandon or ecstasy, or uninhibited or rowdy revelry (adjectives *Dionysian* and *Dionysiac*)

Someone dimmed the lights and turned up the sitar music. They swayed and pressed and wriggled against each other in the twanging, orange, smoky twilight, it was a kind of dance, they were all dancing, he was dancing—at last: the free, improvised, Dionysian dancing he'd hankered after.
DAVID LODGE *Changing Places* 1975

Oh, how Sir Gerald…would love to be able to wallow in that filth with such Dionysian abandon!
TOM WOLFE *The Bonfire of the Vanities* 1987

Dirty Harry [Cin.] The nickname of Harry Callaghan, a tough San Francisco police inspector played by Clint Eastwood in several films including *Dirty Harry* (1971) and *Magnum Force* (1973). When violent criminals escape justice through lack of evidence, Callaghan resorts to his own brutal vigilante methods of law enforcement.

> A police officer who uncompromisingly takes the law into his own hands

The 2,000 or so people who earn their living chasing bail jumpers are essentially unscreened, untrained, unlicensed and unregulated. They operate outside the laws that apply to everyone else, even laws that impose restrictions on the police, and it's a line of work that tends to appeal to those who have Dirty Harry fantasies and macho, self-dramatising visions of hunting down 'skippers' and returning them to justice in the boots of their cars.
The Observer 1997

Disney, Walt [Cin.] (1901–66) The creator of *Donald Duck and *Mickey Mouse, sometimes associated with the 'cute' portrayal of animals, both in such full-length animated cartoons as *Snow White* and *Bambi* and in his nature documentaries.

> Mentioned in the context of the sentimental portrayal of animals

There are a lot of animals slaughtered in his books. He isn't Walt Disney, no. He was interested in cruelty, I agree.
JULIAN BARNES *Flaubert's Parrot* 1984

Dives [Bible] The name (from the Latin for 'rich') traditionally given to the rich man in the parable of the rich man and *Lazarus (Luke 16: 19–31). The rich man lived in great luxury while Lazarus was a beggar at his gate, covered with sores and longing even for the crumbs from the rich man's table. When both died, Dives found himself in Hell and, looking up, saw Lazarus being taken up to Heaven by Abraham. Abraham explained to him that he had already had good things in his lifetime whereas Lazarus had not. Consequently, Lazarus received comfort in the afterlife while the rich man endured agony.

> A rich man who shows no charity to the poor in life and is punished in the afterlife

Remember, we are bid to work while it is day—warned that 'the night cometh when no man shall work'. Remember the fate of Dives, who had his good things in this life. God give you strength to choose that better part which shall not be taken from you!
CHARLOTTE BRONTË *Jane Eyre* 1847

Dixon of Dock Green [TV] A long-running BBC TV series (1955–76) set in a London police station. Jack Warner played George Dixon, a kindly old-style British 'bobby' or police officer. Episodes tended to deal with fairly low-level crime in the local community and always ended with Dixon summing up with a homily to the effect that 'crime does not pay'.

> Mentioned in the context of nostalgia for the days of the 'bobby on the beat'

In reality, police officers cost money and the halcyon days of Dixon of Dock Green, when the beat bobby was a lynchpin of the community, have gone.
Yorkshire Post Today 2001

Doasyouwouldbedoneby, Mrs [Child. Lit.] In Charles Kingsley's children's story
The Water-Babies (1863), a benevolent character encountered by Tom after he became a
water-baby. She teaches that you should behave towards others in the way that you would
want them to behave to you.

> ➤ Mentioned in the context of advice to someone to act well towards others

Dr Dolittle *See* DOLITTLE.

Dr Foster *See* FOSTER.

Doctor Who [TV] A long-running science-fiction BBC television series in which the
eponymous Doctor, a 720- (or 900-) year-old Time Lord from the planet Gallifrey, travels
through space-time in his time machine, the *Tardis. The periodic need for Time Lords to
'regenerate' has allowed several different actors to play the part of the Doctor, all with different
personalities and styles.

> ➤ Mentioned in the context of high-tech gadgetry
>
> Using a phase-locked loop—which sounds like something out of Doctor Who...the
> technology gives RDRAM an effective clock frequency of 3.2GHz.
> *The Register* 2001

Dodge City [Places] A frontier town in Kansas with a reputation for rowdiness until Wyatt
Earp became chief deputy marshal in 1876 and introduced order.

> ➤ A place characterized by lawless or unregulated conflict, particularly involving gunfights
>
> Sally handed me the translation of the coded message and looked around. 'I thought
> there'd be wanted posters on the walls and gun racks filled with shotguns.' 'This isn't
> Dodge City,' Lula said. 'We got some class here. We keep the guns in the back room with
> the pervert.'
> JANET EVANOVICH *Four to Score* 1998

dogs of war [Shakes.] A phrase from *Julius Caesar* (1599), when Mark *Antony prophesies
war in Rome following Caesar's assassination:

> Cry, 'Havoc!' and let slip the dogs of war,
> That this foul deed shall smell above the earth
> With carrion men, groaning for burial.

> ➤ The chaos accompanying military conflict; also sometimes applied to mercenary soldiers
>
> The dogs of war, once unleashed, cannot easily be controlled.
> *New Zealand Listener* 2004

dog that did not bark, the [Lit.] A phrase from Arthur Conan *Doyle's Sherlock
*Holmes story 'Silver Blaze' (1892). Holmes refers to 'the curious incident of the dog in the
night-time', namely that a watchdog did not bark during the theft of a racehorse from a stable,
suggesting that the dog probably knew the thief.

> ➤ Used when there is significance in the very fact that a particular event did not happen
>
> The absence of European slaves, like the dog that did not bark, is perhaps the clue to
> understanding the slave trade and the system it supported.
> STANLEY ENGERMAN, SEYMOUR DRESCHER, AND ROBERT PAQUETTE (eds) *Slavery* 2001

Dolittle, Dr [Child. Lit.] In Hugh Lofting's books (1920–52), Dr John Dolittle is an
animal-loving doctor whose human patients desert his practice because his house
resembles a menagerie. Dolittle decides that he would much prefer to treat animals

instead, and his parrot Polynesia helps him to learn all the animal languages, starting with the ABC of birds.

> Mentioned in the context of love for animals or the ability to talk to animals

For some reason, syntax has remained beyond the reach of nonhuman animals, even beyond those clever dogs and apes that, of late, have become icons for those who want to believe, as Anderson puts it, that Doctor Dolittle was right.
Natural History 2004

Donald Duck [Cart. & Com.] A cartoon character created by Walt *Disney who has a distinctive high-pitched, quacking voice.

> Used to describe a quack-like voice

Besides, he was kind of a sweet kid and had a voice like Donald Duck.
JOSEPH WAMBAUGH *The Glitter Dome* 1981

Don Juan (Don Juan Tenorio) [Leg. & Folk.] A legendary Spanish nobleman famous for his seductions. The character appears in various works of literature and music, such as Mozart's opera *Don Giovanni*, Byron's poem *Don Juan*, and the 'Don Juan in Hell' section of Shaw's play *Man and Superman*.

> A man with a reputation for seducing women

It was a highly original, rather overwritten piece of sustained description concerned with a Don Juan of the New York slums.
F. SCOTT FITZGERALD *The Beautiful and the Damned* 1922

'Marigold's taken up choral singing. They're doing the Saint Matthew Passion.' 'Oh yes. And what passion are you doing, Featherstone?' Miss Trant looked at her host with some suspicion. Featherstone, thinking he was being treated like a dangerous Don Juan, was flattered.
JOHN MORTIMER *Rumpole's return* 1980

Do not go gentle into that good night [Lit.] The title of a 1952 poem by the Welsh poet Dylan Thomas. It is addressed to his dying father, whom he implores to 'rage, rage against the dying of the light'.

> Used when urging someone not to give up without a struggle

Today's middle-aged, today's seniors, will not go gentle into that good night. Nor should they.
A Voyage to Arcturus (weblog) 2004

Don Quixote [Lit.] The ageing hero of a romance, *Don Quixote de la Mancha* (1605–15) by Miguel de Cervantes. He determines to become a knight and sets out on his scrawny old horse, *Rosinante, with his squire Sancho *Panza, to win the love of the village girl *Dulcinea, who is elevated in Don Quixote's mind to the ideal of womanly beauty.

> A tall, lean, thin-faced man; a hopeless or mistaken dreamer; a fanciful or naïve idealist; a person obsessive to the point of insanity; a person engaged on an illusory or impossible quest ('tilting at windmills')

We are most of us like Don Quixote, to whom a windmill was a giant, and Dulcinea a magnificent princess: all more or less the dupes of our own imagination.
THOMAS LOVE PEACOCK *Nightmare Abbey* 1818

A tall, thin, Don Quixote-looking old man came into the shop for some woollen gloves.
ELIZABETH GASKELL *Cranford* 1851–3

Doolittle, Eliza [Theatre; Cin.] In Bernard Shaw's play *Pygmalion* (1913), the cockney flower-seller who is coached by the phonetician Professor Henry *Higgins to acquire a standard accent and to fit into upper-class society.

> A woman with a male mentor; a woman taught or coached how to speak or behave in a more genteel way; someone who undergoes a transformation
>
> If they've succeeded Radio 1 will have pulled off the biggest makeover since Higgins' remodelling of Eliza Doolittle.
> *Sunday Herald* 2000

Do-Right, Dudley [TV] A character in a segment of Jay Ward's animated television series *The Rocky and Bullwinkle Show* (1961–4). He is a dedicated but not very bright Canadian Mountie who is always trying to catch his deadly foe Snidely Whiplash.

> Someone dedicated and conscientious in what they do, though (sometimes) inept
>
> 'Seems like any other place. Scotty showed me around last night.' 'Dudley, you mean.' He laughed. 'Dudley Do-right. Goes to church every Sunday, coaches the hockey team. Wouldn't say shit if he had a mouthful.'
> TED WOODS *On the Inside* 1990

Dormouse [Child. Lit.] One of the characters that *Alice meets at the Mad Hatter's tea party in Lewis Carroll's *Alice's Adventures in Wonderland* (1865). The Dormouse snoozes all through the tea party, despite attempts to wake it by pinching it.

> Mentioned in the context of sleepiness

Dorothy [Child. Lit.] The heroine of L. Frank Baum's story *The Wizard of Oz* (1900), who is carried away from her home in Kansas to a magical land by a cyclone. She journeys to meet the *Wizard of Oz in the hope that he will help her return home. Though he initially appears to be intimidatingly powerful, the wizard, when challenged by Dorothy, turns out to be a fraud, not a wizard at all but an old man who was blown to Oz from Omaha in a balloon.

> Someone who finds themselves in a strange land, far from home; someone who returns home after a long journey or many adventures; someone who stands up to a person in authority
>
> We can only hope our American friends return to Kansas like Dorothy, all the wiser for having found the courage to stare down authority rather than cower before it.
> *The Republic—Vancouver's Opinionated Newspaper* 2004

Dotheboys Hall *See* SQUEERS.

> A harsh school where the pupils are mistreated
>
> Mr Le Feuvre was obviously traumatised by his schoolboy experiences. Did he attend Dotheboys Hall?
> *Saga Magazine* 2005

Doubting Thomas [Bible] One of the twelve apostles in the New Testament, known also as Thomas Didymus, meaning 'twin' in Aramaic. After the Crucifixion, when *Jesus appeared before the disciples to show them that he had risen from the dead, Thomas was not present. When the other disciples told Thomas that they had seen Jesus, he said he would not believe that it was true 'except I shall see in his hands the print of the nails, and put my finger into the print of the nails, and thrust my hand into his side' (John 20: 25).

> An incredulous or sceptical person

Since he became news, he's been at pains to let the figures speak for themselves. 'The lab data's there in black and white.' It's also in the Vanderbilt computer system which means others can review it. When doubting Thomases from the press or the medical world come to speak to him, 'I print out the lab sheets, boom, boom, boom.'
The Observer 1997

dove *See* NOAH.

down the rabbit-hole *See* RABBIT-HOLE.

Doyle, Arthur Conan [Lit.] (1859–1930) A Scottish novelist remembered for his exciting adventure stories such as *The Lost World*, and for his creation of the character of Sherlock *Holmes.

> ➤ Mentioned in the context of adventure or detective stories

I told the story well…I described an attack on my life on the voyage home, and I made a really horrid affair of the Portland Place murder. 'You're looking for adventure,' I cried; 'well, you've found it here. The devils are after me, and the police are after them. It's a race that I mean to win.' 'By God!' he whispered, drawing his breath in sharply, 'it is all pure Rider Haggard and Conan Doyle.'
JOHN BUCHAN *The Thirty-Nine Steps* 1915

Its beaches are as white as washing powder and softer than caster sugar, its mountainous interior as dramatic and primeval as any Conan Doyle Lost World, and its people as warm and friendly and attractive as any on earth.
www.travelintelligence.net 2005

Draco [People] (7th century BC) An Athenian legislator, remembered for the notorious severity of his codification of Athenian law.

> ➤ Used to describe a harsh or severe law or punishment (adjective *Draconian*)

The CBI has condemned the measures as 'Draconian'. But Beckett is convinced that tough action is needed.
The Observer 1997

Dracula [Lit.; Cin.] The famous Count Dracula, created by Bram Stoker in his 1879 novel *Dracula*, is a vampire, one of the Undead, who lies in his coffin by day and comes out at night to suck blood from the necks of his victims. He can only be destroyed by having a stake driven through his heart while he is resting.

> ➤ Mentioned in the context of drinking blood

I knew I'd gone as white as a piece of chalk since coming in as if I'd been got at by a Dracula-vampire.
ALAN SILLITOE *The Loneliness of the Long Distance Runner* 1959

'I know some people believed that, coming from a family as old as ours, he should have chosen a British girl. I've never been of that narrow way of thinking. We should always be ready to welcome new blood of the right kind.' I just stopped myself saying Count Dracula would agree with her.
GILLIAN LINSCOTT *Stage Fright* 1994

Drake, Sir Francis [Hist.] (c.1540–1596) An English explorer and privateer, the first Englishman to see the Pacific and the first to sail round the globe. He harried the Spanish, both in Spain and in South America, and took a leading part in foiling the Spanish *Armada in 1588. Despite Spanish protests, he was knighted in 1581 by Queen Elizabeth I.

> ➤ A seafaring adventurer or explorer

Galleon is an action/adventure title set in a world that is like Sinbad meets Sir Francis Drake, high fantasy on the high seas.
www.armchairempire.com 2003

Dresden [Places] A city in eastern Germany, on the river Elbe. It was one of Germany's most beautiful cities until it was almost totally destroyed by heavy Allied bombing on the night of 13 February 1945. Dresden has been extensively rebuilt since 1945.

➤ A city or area laid waste by aerial bombing

It would be a firestorm, a Dresden or Tokyo with 60 years of new technology.
eatthestate.org 2003

Drew, Nancy [Child. Lit.] The name of an American teenage detective created in the 1930s by Edward Stratemeyer and the heroine of a series of novels for children written by a variety of writers under the name Carolyn Greene.

➤ Someone, especially a girl or young woman, trying to solve a mystery

He shook his head. 'What happened?' 'I fell into a yucca plant.' 'Ouch!' He flinched in sympathy. 'Just jumped up and bit you, huh?' 'What I get for playing Nancy Drew,' I said, and told him about chasing the burglar who'd broken into Andy Bynum's house.
MARGARET MARON *Shooting at Loons* 1994

Dreyfus, Alfred [Hist.] (1859–1935) A French army officer of Jewish descent who in 1894 was falsely accused of passing military secrets to the Germans. His trial, imprisonment on *Devil's Island, and eventual release caused a major political crisis in France.

➤ An innocent person falsely accused or punished

He may become something of the Dreyfus of the Internet business.
New York Metro 2004

Drummond, Bulldog [Lit.] The hero of a series of stories by 'Sapper', published from 1920 onwards. Drummond is an ex-army officer who fights against the master criminal Carl Peterson.

➤ A determined hero, with a stiff-upper lip resilience to adversity

Sky Captain is the personification of these, with a dash of Bulldog Drummond and a hint of Dick Barton Special Agent.
Film Inside Out 2004

Dufy, Raoul [Art] (1877–1953) A French painter and textile designer, whose chief subjects were racecourses, boating scenes, and society life. Dufy's style is characterized by bright colours and lively calligraphic draughtsmanship.

➤ Used to evoke a colourful outdoor scene reminiscent of a Dufy painting

There was a bright wind, it was a Dufy day, all bustle, movement, animated colour.
JOHN FOWLES *The Magus* 1977

Dulcinea [Lit.] The name of *Don Quixote's love in Cervantes' picaresque romance *Don Quixote de la Mancha*, published in 1605–15. Her real name is Aldonza Lorenzo, but Don Quixote, who naively idealizes her, gives her the name Dulcinea del Toboso and finds in her inspirations for his many deeds of misplaced heroism.

➤ An idealized woman; a female object of devotion

No one in his senses would dream of following her. To idealize so repulsive a Dulcinea one would have to be madder than Don Quixote himself.
ALDOUS HUXLEY *Point Counter Point* 1928

Duncan, Isadora [Dance] (1878–1927) An American dancer who developed a new style of fluid barefoot dancing derived from classical Greek art. She travelled widely in Europe, and founded several dancing schools there. She was strangled accidentally when her trailing scarf became entangled in the wheel of a car.

> A female dancer; someone strangled in a way reminiscent of Isadora Duncan's death

The girl, on her knees, arms thrown back, was a dancer. She was effecting some kind of Isadora Duncan, swan-raped, Noh swoon: demonstrating both her 'inner stillness' and the power she exercised over her body.
IAIN SINCLAIR *Downriver* 1991

Later, in the country, she skips along like a child (before falling like Isadora Duncan, brought down by her own scarf).
www.sensesofcinema.com 2000

Dunkirk (Dunkerque) [Hist.] A port on the north French coast from where over 335 000 Allied soldiers were evacuated under German fire during the Second World War by a mixture of naval and ordinary civilian vessels. Although from a military point of view this represented a defeat, the soldiers having been forced to retreat to the shore, Dunkirk is remembered by the British as something of a triumph.

> The term 'Dunkirk spirit' refers to a stubborn refusal to admit defeat no matter how dangerous or difficult the circumstances

Technical lighting and electronic glitches reduced Glyndebourne's new smash hit to a concert performance, in costume, against plain black drapes, relying on music, text and everybody's Dunkirk spirit.
Oxford Times 1994

The Metro was crowded but a Dunkirk spirit reigned. On personal observation, passengers were unusually polite to one another and almost chatty.
The Independent 1997

Durante, Jimmy [Theatre; Cin.] (1893–1980) A US pianist–comedian who had a long career in vaudeville, nightclubs, and films. He referred to his splendid nose as his 'schnozzola'.

> A person with a large nose

Even Jimmy Durante's famous schnozzola, which Keith had had a chance to see up close…was a peanut compared to Sperry's.
VINCE STANTON *Keith Partridge Master Spy* 1971

Dutch Boy, Little [Child. Lit.] The tale of the Little Dutch Boy is recounted as a story entitled 'The Hero of Haarlem' in Mary Mapes Dodge's children's classic *Hans Brinker; or, The Silver Skates* (1865). The boy is returning from a visit when he hears the sound of trickling water and sees a small hole in the dyke. He climbs up the dyke and plugs the hole with his finger in order to stop it becoming enlarged and leading to flooding. The boy undergoes a terrible ordeal alone all night and unable to move before being rescued and relieved at daybreak the following morning.

> Someone attempting to stem the flow of something or avert a disaster

But now that president sometimes looks rather like the boy with his hand in the dyke, behind which the water is building up pressure.
The Observer 1997

Dying Swan *See* PAVLOVA.

Eagle has landed, the [Hist.] A phrase from the first words heard from the surface of the moon, spoken by the US astronaut Neil *Armstrong on 21 July 1969: 'Houston, Tranquility Base here. The Eagle has landed.' *Eagle* was the name of the lunar module. *The Eagle Has Landed* is also the title of a 1975 novel by Jack Higgins, about a fictional Nazi plot to kill Winston *Churchill.

> ➤ Used to announce the arrival of someone or something

> When Badger arrived there he got in easily, notwithstanding his laptop, notebooks and a copy of New Journalism with two articles by, of course, the recently late Hunter S Thompson. (The in-flight magazine was really very poor.) So he SMS-ed me: 'The eagle has landed.'
> *Sunday Independent (S. Africa)* 2005

Ealing comedy [Cin.] One of a series of film comedies made in the post-war decade at the Ealing Studios in west London. These include *Whisky Galore!* (1948), *Passport to Pimlico* (1948), and *The Lavender Hill Mob* (1951), and are characterized by gentle humour, colourful characters, and slightly surreal storylines often featuring communities or individuals rebelling against authority.

> ➤ Used to suggest whimsical humour

> It was always going to be a high-risk venture. Led by mutton-chopped part-time farmer and astronomer Colin Pillinger on the kind of budget that would scarcely cover Nasa's coffee bill, Beagle 2 bore all the hallmarks of an Ealing comedy.
> *Scotland on Sunday* 2004

Earhart, Amelia [People] (1898–1937) An American aviator, the first woman to fly the Atlantic in 1928, and the first woman to do so solo in 1932, completing the journey from Newfoundland to Londonderry in a time of 13¼ hours. The aircraft carrying Earhart and her navigator, Frederick J. Noonan, disappeared over the Pacific Ocean during a subsequent round-the-world flight in 1937.

> ➤ Mentioned in the context of mysterious disappearance

> While not exactly ecstatic about it, Judge Patrick Naugle doesn't quite relegate this movie to the place where you'll find your missing socks, pens, and Amelia Earhart.
> *www.dvdverdict.com* 2004

East Lynne [Lit.] The title of a best-selling Victorian novel (1861) by Ellen Wood, in which a young woman abandons her children but later returns in the guise of a governess to care for them. One of the stage versions of the novel features the famous line 'Dead! Dead! And never called me mother!'

> ➤ Used to invoke a highly melodramatic or sentimental situation

Easy Rider [Cin.] A 1969 film starring Peter Fonda and Denis Hopper, in which two drug-dealing bikers travel across the American south on stretched Harley-Davidson choppers.

> ➤ Mentioned in the context of someone travelling by motorbike

But Ben Roethlisberger sure could have used a little of that innate wisdom and vision away from the field this offseason, to see that the rewards didn't justify the risks he was taking in playing the role of Easy Rider in Pittsburgh. As it turns out, in defending both his ownership of his beloved motorcycle and his refusal to don a helmet when he rode it, the Steelers' franchise quarterback, for once, was acting his age.
Sports Illustrated 2006

Eccles [Radio] A character in *The Goon Show*, an extremely popular BBC radio comedy series which ran from 1952 to 1960. Eccles, played by Spike Milligan, spoke in a slow, foolish-sounding voice.

> Someone speaking in a ponderous, stupid-sounding voice

Echo [Gk myth.] A nymph who kept *Hera talking when she wanted to spy on the infidelities of *Zeus, her husband, with the other nymphs. Hera punished Echo by depriving her of speech except for a repetition of the last words spoken to her. Echo fell in love with *Narcissus but was rejected by him and gradually wasted away until there was nothing left but her voice.

> Someone who disappears with only their voice remaining

What a sheer waste of herself to be dressed thus while another was shining to advantage!...The power of her face all lost, the charm of her emotions all disguised, the fascinations of her coquetry denied existence, nothing but a voice left to her: she had a sense of the doom of Echo.
THOMAS HARDY *The Return of the Native* 1880

Eden (Garden of Eden) [Bible] The home of *Adam and Eve in the biblical account of the Creation, from which they were banished by God for their disobedience in eating the forbidden fruit of the Tree of Knowledge. It is imagined as a place of lush beauty ('Eden' means 'Delight').

> A place or state of supreme happiness, innocence, and concord

Yet this was—the way she relayed it—a redeemed forest and an Eden.
THOMAS KENEALLY *The Playmaker* 1987

For the first seven thousand feet it is the Garden of Eden, a luxuriance of orchids, humming-birds, and tiny streams of delicious water that run by miracle alongside every path.
LOUIS DE BERNIÈRES *The War of Don Emmanuel's Nether Parts* 1990

Edsel [Hist.] A car launched by the Ford Motor Company in 1957 as part of a $250 million investment in an attempt to compete with General Motors and in particular with their Oldsmobile. The car was a complete flop.

> Mentioned in the context of a total failure or commercial disaster

Apple had a lousy 2000 after its G4 Cube became the company's Edsel.
Brandweek 2001

Eeyore [Child. Lit.] The gloomy old grey donkey in A. A. Milne's books about *Winnie the Pooh.

> Someone who is deeply pessimistic or gloomy

Eeyore of the Year was, as usual, a toss-up between Peter Owen ('If anything, it is getting worse') and Tom Rosenthal ('Among those books which sold less badly').
The Bookseller 1995

Einstein, Albert [Science] (1879–1955) A German-born American mathematician and theoretical physicist who formulated the theory of relativity. He was awarded the Nobel Prize for physics in 1921. Einstein is often regarded as the greatest scientist of the 20th century.

> An extremely intelligent person; the phrase 'no Einstein' is commonly used to mean 'unintelligent'

You didn't have to be Einstein to get the number, but it would have taken more than one step, because Roz had herself listed in the phone book as Rosie O'Grady, having tired of the hate calls that her father's last name sometimes attracted.
MARGARET ATWOOD *The Robber Bride* 1993

El Dorado [Leg. & Folk.] The fabled city or country of gold (literally 'the Gilded One') sought in the 16th century by the Spanish conquistadores, who believed it existed somewhere in the area of the Orinoco and Amazon rivers.

> A place of fabulous wealth

One should have thought a transfer to a continental club would have made more sense, even though Italian football is no longer the El Dorado it used to be.
Sunday Telegraph 1995

Electra [Gk myth.] The daughter of *Agamemnon and *Clytemnestra. She persuaded her brother *Orestes to kill Clytemnestra and her lover, Aegisthus, in revenge for the murder of Agamemnon. In psychoanalytical theory, an Electra complex is a daughter's subconscious sexual attraction to her father and hostility towards her mother, corresponding to the *Oedipus complex in a son.

> Mentioned in the context of a daughter's unconscious sexual desire for her father

Lara Croft is a dominatrix with an acute Electra complex who craves love from her dead father and, having found a time machine, is given the chance to resurrect him.
Flak Magazine 2004

Elementary, my dear Watson [Lit.] A phrase supposedly said by Sherlock *Holmes to Dr Watson. Although these precise words are not found in any of Conan *Doyle's writings, the phrase is familiar from subsequent film adaptations of the Sherlock Holmes stories.

> Used to say that something is simple

If you want to sell someone something, what you are selling has to solve a problem the buyer is having. It can't be about them helping you, it has to be about you helping them. If you do that, you have a sale. Elementary, my dear Watson? You bet, but a good reminder nonetheless.
USA Today 2004

Elephant Man (Joseph Merrick) [People] (1862–90) A man born with severe facial deformities caused by a rare disease, now thought to be Proteus syndrome. As an adult he was exhibited as a fairground freak, the Elephant Man, until he was rescued by the surgeon Sir Frederick Treves and given sanctuary in the London Hospital.

> An extremely ugly person

If either party...does not wish to continue the relationship, they must clearly and considerately state this in a manner that reassures the other party that they are not the Elephant Man/Woman without being patronising.
HELEN FIELDING *Bridget Jones's Diary* 1999

Elephant's Child, The [Child. Lit.] One of *Kipling's *Just-So Stories* (1902), relates how the elephant got his trunk. The Elephant's Child is full of 'satiable curiosity' and constantly asks questions of his animal relatives. When he asks the crocodile what he eats for dinner, the crocodile catches hold of the Elephant's Child's short snout and tries to pull him into the water so he can eat him. In the tug-of-war that follows, the Elephant's Child's nose is elongated into a trunk.

> ➤ Mentioned in the context of curiosity

I was torn between calling Caroline to tell her the deal was off and the elephant child's 'satiable curiosity' to find out what had rattled Chigwell so badly.
SARA PARETSKY *Toxic Shock* 1990

Eleusinian mysteries [Hist.] The most famous of the 'mysteries', or religious ceremonies, of ancient Greece, held at the city of Eleusis near Athens. They were dedicated to the corn goddess *Demeter and her daughter *Persephone, and were thought to celebrate the annual cycle of death and rebirth in nature. Such mysteries or mystery religions were secret forms of worship, and were available only to people who had been specially initiated.

> ➤ Mentioned in the context of an obscure or mysterious area of knowledge

Been playing golf? I thought so. Wonderful game, so fascinating, such a challenge, as much intellectual as physical, I understand. I wish I had time for it myself. One feels so much at sea when talk turns to mashie-niblicks, cleeks, and mid-irons. Quite an Eleusinian mystery.
LOUIS DE BERNIÈRES *Captain Corelli's Mandolin* 1994

He knew that some of us would grasp the Eleusinian mysteries of abstract math, reach the top drawer, as he liked to say, and make it to the floor above.
Commonweal 2002

El Greco [Art] (1541–1614) A Spanish painter born in Crete as Domenikos Theotokopoulos. His portraits and religious works are characterized by elongated and distorted figures, solemn facial expressions, and vibrant use of colour (blues, lemons, livid pinks). Among his famous works are the altarpiece *The Assumption of the Virgin* (1577–9) and the painting *The Burial of Count Orgaz* (1586).

> ➤ Used to describe a thin person; also used to suggest colours reminiscent of an El Greco painting

Mrs Overend had recently got rid of her black-and-orange striped divans, cushions and sofas. In their place were curiously cut slabs, polygons, and three-legged manifestations of Daisy Overend's personality, done in El Greco's colours.
MURIEL SPARK *The Collected Stories* 1958

Senor Aguirre joined his El Greco hands and looked at me over the spire of his fingertips.
JOHN BANVILLE *The Book of Evidence* 1989

Elijah [Bible] (9th century BC) A Hebrew prophet who maintained the worship of *Jehovah against that of *Baal and other pagan gods. According to the Bible, he was carried to heaven in a chariot of fire: 'And as they still went on and talked, behold, a chariot of fire and horses of fire separated the two of them. And Elijah went up by a whirlwind into heaven' (2 Kgs. 2: 11–13).

> ➤ Someone ascending or carried upwards into the sky

Elisha [Bible] (9th century BC) A Hebrew prophet, disciple and successor of *Elijah, whose mantle he received: 'And [Elisha] took up the mantle of Elijah that had fallen from him, and went back and stood on the bank of the Jordan' (2 Kgs. 2: 13).

> ➤ Mentioned in the context of the passing of a mantle from one person to another

But like the prophet in the chariot disappearing in heaven and dropping his mantle to Elisha, the withdrawing night transferred its pale robe to the breaking day.
HERMAN MELVILLE *Billy Budd* 1924

Elli [Norse Myth.] The personification of old age who in the form of Utgard, *Loki's foster-mother, a toothless old crone, wrestles the mighty *Thor to the ground.

> ➤ Used to illustrate the point that no one, not even the strongest, can withstand old age

Ellis Island [Hist.] An island in the bay of New York that from 1892 until 1943 served as an entry point for immigrants to the USA, and later (until 1954) as a detention centre for people awaiting deportation. More than twelve million immigrants passed through Ellis Island.

> Used to symbolize immigration to the USA; also suggesting any point of arrival used by people as a gateway to a place

The real Roswell, New Mexico, has been so eager to capitalize on its reputation as the Ellis Island of the alien hordes that two years ago it actually sponsored an 'Encounter 97' celebration of the fiftieth anniversary of the first visitation.
New York Metro 2004

Elm Street *See* NIGHTMARE ON ELM STREET.

Elysium (Elysian Fields) [Gk myth.] The name of the fields at the end of the earth to which certain favoured heroes were conveyed by the gods to enjoy a life after death.

> A place of perfect happiness or bliss

Antoine and Françoise with their children, but without ever knowing why, joined the refugees for the sake of their vision of elysium and because of Don Emmanuel's enthusiasm.
LOUIS DE BERNIÈRES *The War of Don Emmanuel's Nether Parts* 1990

emperor's new clothes [Child. Lit.] Hans Christian Andersen's story *The Emperor's New Clothes*, first published in 1836, tells the story of an emperor obsessed with beautiful clothes. He is visited by two swindlers who promise to make him the most beautiful clothes ever seen. Using an empty loom, they pretend to weave the cloth and stitch the clothes, telling the Emperor that the cloth they are using is invisible to anyone who is unfit for his office or stupid. Although no one, including the Emperor, can see the clothes, all collude in the deception for fear of appearing foolish or incompetent. The Emperor parades naked through the streets of the town, with all the people cheering except for one small boy who cries, 'But the Emperor has nothing on at all!'

> Used to describe something that is promised or believed in but does not in fact exist

Common sense is a very poor guide to scientific insight for it represents cultural prejudice more often than it reflects the native honesty of a small boy before the naked emperor.
STEPHEN JAY GOULD *Ever Since Darwin* 1978

end of the rainbow [Leg. & Folk.] According to legend, there is a pot of gold buried at the spot where a rainbow comes down and touches the earth. The end of the rainbow is therefore a distant place where dreams come true. The idea was popularized by the song 'Over the Rainbow' which features in the 1939 film *The *Wizard of Oz*, and begins with the words:

> Somewhere over the rainbow
> Way up high,
> There's a land that I heard of
> Once in a lullaby.

> The end of a quest or fulfilment of a dream

The Japanese stock market was the last-but-one in a long line of Wall Street Loreleis. Like Xerox, conglomerates, and convertible debentures, it had been the legendary pot of gold at the end of some local rainbows. Those happy few blessed with foresight got more than sordid, material gain. They got brief immortality.
EMMA LATHEN *Sweet and Low* 1978

Endor, Witch of [Bible] In the book of Samuel, the woman consulted by Saul when he was
threatened by the Philistine army. At his request she summoned up the ghost of the prophet
Samuel, who prophesied the death of Saul and the destruction of his army by the Philistines.
Rudyard *Kipling associates Endor with spiritualism in his poem 'The Road to Endor':

> Oh, the road to Endor is the oldest road
> And the craziest road of all!
> Straight it runs to the Witch's abode
> As it did in the days of Saul.

> ➤ Someone who raises the spirits from the dead; alluded to in the context of prophecy,
> witchcraft, or spiritualism

> I merely lit that fire because I was dull, and thought I would get a little excitement
> by calling you up and triumphing over you as the Witch of Endor called up Samuel.
> I determined you should come; and you have come!
> THOMAS HARDY *The Return of the Native* 1880

Endymion [Gk myth.] A beautiful young man who was loved by the moon goddess *Selene.
According to one version of his story, *Zeus caused him to sleep for ever so that he would
remain eternally young and handsome. This story is the basis of Keats's poem *Endymion*
(1818).

> ➤ Used to suggest sleepiness, youthfulness, or male beauty

> But your Endymion, your smooth, Smock-fac'd Boy...shall a Beauteous Dame enjoy.
> JOHN DRYDEN *Juvenal Satires X* 1693

England expects [Hist.] A phrase from Lord *Nelson's famous signal to the English
fleet before the Battle of *Trafalgar in 1805: 'England expects that every man will do his duty.'

> ➤ Used, especially in sport, before a contest involving England

> The setbacks have reduced the pressure on Eriksson to succeed, but only on the
> understanding that this tournament has come too early and that he will deliver a
> World Cup victory in 2006. England expects.
> *Sunday Herald* 2002

Enterprise *See* STARSHIP ENTERPRISE.

Epeius [Gk myth.] A skilled craftsman who built the *Trojan Horse with the help of *Athene.

> ➤ A craftsman

Epicurus [Philos.] (341–271 BC) A Greek philosopher who founded a school of philosophy
that espoused hedonism, described by Epicurus in one of his letters thus: 'We say that pleasure
is the beginning and end of living happily.' In his philosophy, happiness is achieved by
becoming free from pain and anxiety by, among other things, freeing oneself from fear of the
supernatural and death.

> ➤ Used to describe someone devoted to the pursuit of pleasure, in particular to refined
> and tasteful sensuous enjoyment (adjective *Epicurean*)

> Ten o'clock was the hour fixed for this meeting, and Wimsey was lingering lovingly
> over his bacon and eggs, so as to leave no restless and unfilled moment in his morning.
> By which it may be seen that his lordship had reached that time of life when a man
> can extract an Epicurean enjoyment even from his own passions—the halcyon period
> between the self-tormenting exuberance of youth and the fretful *carpe diem* of
> approaching senility.
> DOROTHY SAYERS *Have his Carcass* 1932

Erato [Gk myth.] One of the nine *Muses, associated especially with the lyre and lyric love.

> Mentioned in the context of lyric poetry

Now, Erato, thy poet's mind inspire,
And fill his soul with thy celestial fire.
VIRGIL *Aeneid VII* trans. John Dryden 1697

Erebus [Gk myth.] The primeval god of darkness, born from Chaos right at the beginning of the world. The name was later identified with *Hades, and is used with this meaning in the *Iliad* and the *Odyssey*.

> Used to suggest darkness

The motions of his spirit are dull as night,
And his affections dark as Erebus:
Let no such man be trusted.
WILLIAM SHAKESPEARE *The Merchant of Venice* 1600

Erinyes [Gk myth.] The avenging spirits of punishment, better known as the *Furies.

> A group of people pursuing someone in order to torment or punish them for a wrongdoing they have committed

European culture has reached this breaking point...The rebellion does not come from the head, but from the gut, and in all countries of Europe. It is a rebellion of the Erinyes—ugly, brutal.
Senses of Cinema 2004

Eris [Gk myth.] The Greek goddess of discord.

> Someone who causes disagreement or conflict between people

Eros [Gk myth.] The god of love, usually represented as a winged boy with a bow and arrows; called *Cupid by the Romans.

> A way of referring to sexual love or the libido

The dark tides of Eros, which demand full secrecy if they are to overflow the human soul, burst out during carnival like something long dammed up.
LAWRENCE DURRELL *Balthazar* 1958

She had loved Private Dukes and spawned a false oath to save him—affronting solider deities for the sake of honeyed, treacherous Eros.
THOMAS KENEALLY *The Playmaker* 1987

Esau [Bible] Along with *Jacob, one of the twin sons of *Isaac and Rebecca, Esau being the first-born. He is described as a red, hairy man (Gen. 25: 25). When faint with hunger one day, Esau begged his brother for some of the food he was preparing, a '*mess of pottage' (lentil stew). Jacob would only give Esau the food if he swore to sell Jacob his birthright as the elder of the twins. The book of Genesis also relates how Jacob, with his mother, Rebecca's, help, dressed as his elder brother Esau in order to obtain the blessing of their father, Isaac. When Esau found out what Jacob had done, he hated him and swore to kill him.

> Someone who chooses to accept material comfort in exchange for something more valuable; someone filled with anger and hatred

He's of a rash, warm-hearted nature, like Esau, for whom I have always felt great pity.
GEORGE ELIOT *Adam Bede* 1859

As for those benighted creatures who are disgracefully happy with their chains, they must be prevented from bartering their birthrights, like female Esaus, for a mess of pottage in the guise of a bribe to stay at home.
Glasgow Herald 1998

Escher, M. C. [Art] (1902–72) A Dutch graphic artist, whose prints often exploit puzzling visual paradoxes and illusions. Many of his works play with perspective to create examples of impossible architecture. One of his most famous images is the lithograph *Ascending and Descending* (1960), in which hooded figures endlessly walk up (or down) a staircase.

> Used to describe scenes or pictures that involve curious perspectives and optical illusions

The house was taking on the appearance of an Escher drawing—lots of steps leading nowhere.
FAYE KELLERMAN *Sanctuary* 1994

Like an Escher print, this is music that seems to ascend infinitely over a nearly twelve-minute span.
www.classical.net 2003

Esther [Bible] In the Old Testament book that bears her name, a woman who was chosen on account of her beauty by King *Ahasuerus of Persia to be his queen in place of the deposed queen *Vashti. Esther used her influence with him to save the *Israelites in captivity from persecution. She is one of the most popular Jewish heroines.

> A beautiful woman; a woman whose intervention saves someone from punishment

Presently my mother went to my father. I know I thought of Queen Esther and King Ahasuerus; for my mother was very pretty and delicate-looking, and my father looked as terrible as King Ahasuerus.
ELIZABETH GASKELL *Cranford* 1851–3

Estragon [Theatre] In Samuel *Beckett's play *Waiting for Godot* (1952), one of the two tramps who discuss philosophical issues while they await the arrival of the mysterious character Godot.

> Someone who waits patiently

I approached the Audi and passed it. Fielding was reading a paper and seemed to be waiting. They were great lads for waiting. They could have out-waited Estragon.
RICHARD HALEY *Thoroughfare of Stones* 1995

ET [Cin.] In the 1982 Steven Spielberg film *E.T.—The Extraterrestrial*, an alien being accidentally left behind by a mission to earth befriends a lonely suburban boy. The boy helps him to build a makeshift radio transmitter after ET has expressed his desire to make contact with his home planet with the phrase 'ET phone home'. At the end of the film a spaceship comes to take ET back home.

> Used to refer to extraterrestrial life

If ET ever phones home, chances are Earthlings wouldn't recognize the call as anything other than random noise or a star.
www.physorg.com 2005

Et tu, Brute? [Hist.; Shakes.] Julius Caesar's supposed dying words (Latin for 'You too, Brutus?') as he realized that his friend *Brutus was one of his assassins. The phrase is best known from *Shakespeare's play *Julius Caesar* (1623).

> Used to reproach a friend, colleague, or ally for an act of betrayal

I have always respected The Nation as one of the few remaining sources of responsible journalism, so it was with a sinking Et tu Brute? feeling that I read David Hawkes's 'review' of Stephen Jay Gould's last book, The Structure of Evolutionary Theory.
The Nation 2002

Etty, William [Art] (1787–1849) An English artist best known for his sensual paintings of the nude.

➤ Used to describe a female nude

She was his passive victim, her head resting on his shoulder, marble made warmth, an Etty nude, the Pygmalion myth brought to a happy end.
JOHN FOWLES *The French Lieutenant's Woman* 1969

Eumenides [Gk myth.] An alternative name for the *Furies.

Euphrosyne [Gk myth.] One of the three *Graces.

Eureka [Science] According to the famous story, the Greek mathematician and inventor *Archimedes is supposed to have leapt out of his bath and run naked through the streets shouting 'Eureka! Eureka!' ('I have found it! I have found it!). He had just hit upon the principle of fluid displacement after seeing his bath water overflow.

➤ Used when someone makes a discovery or breakthrough

There was a Eureka! moment when we realized we had a partial skeleton of an undiscovered species.
National Geographic 2003

Euterpe [Gk myth.] One of the nine *Muses, associated especially with lyric poetry and flute-playing.

➤ A way of referring to music

He offended her by refusing to go into a dance-hall on the grounds that the music was so bad that it was a sacrilege against St Cecilia and Euterpe and Terpsichore, when she just wanted to go in and lose her unhappiness in dancing.
LOUIS DE BERNIÈRES *Señor Vivo and the Coca Lord* 1991

Eve [Bible] According to the book of Genesis, the first woman, wife of *Adam, who lived in innocence with Adam in the Garden of *Eden. Tempted by the *Serpent, Eve ate the forbidden fruit from the *Tree of Knowledge. Having eaten, and committed the first sin, she then persuaded Adam to do the same: 'And the eyes of them both were opened, and they knew that they were naked.' As a punishment for disobeying God's command, they were banished from Eden. Because Eve had eaten first and then tempted Adam, God told her that as a punishment women would henceforth always suffer in childbirth: 'I will greatly multiply thy sorrow and thy conception; in sorrow thou shalt bring forth children.'

➤ A temptress; a naked woman; a woman alone in a place; a woman banished from a place

There she stood before us as Eve might have stood before Adam, clad in nothing but her abundant locks.
H. RIDER HAGGARD *She* 1887

I was firm as a man could be till I saw those eyes and that mouth again—surely there never was such a maddening mouth since Eve's!
THOMAS HARDY *Tess of the D'Urbervilles* 1891

Everything you always wanted to know [Lit.; Cin.] A phrase popularized by
David Reuben's 1970 best-seller *Everything You Always Wanted to Know About Sex
(But Were Afraid to Ask)*, and subsequently used as the title of a comedy film (1972) directed
by Woody Allen.

> ➤ Describing a comprehensive source of information about a subject

> The website is in English and French and has an enormous news section about everything
> you always wanted to know about the Olympics, but forgot to ask.
> *Sofia Echo* 2004

Evil One [Bible] Another name for the *Devil or *Satan, the arch-tempter in the Bible.

> ➤ The Devil; used in the context of temptation

> Where, to what distance apart, had her father wandered, led by doubts which were to
> her temptations of the Evil One?
> ELIZABETH GASKELL *North and South* 1854–5

> Sophia wandered about, a prey ripe for the Evil One.
> ARNOLD BENNETT *The Old Wives' Tale* 1908

Excalibur [Arth. Leg.] King *Arthur's sword. It had been embedded in a stone and Arthur
was able to draw it out when no one else could move it, thus proving himself the rightful
king of England.

> ➤ Mentioned in the context of something that is difficult to remove

> The wall had a surprising grip on it. It was like the whole structure of that wall had settled
> down around this useless, forgotten piece of iron. I said to Valentina: 'This is like trying
> to extract the sword Excalibur from the stone!'
> ROSE TREMAIN *The Way I Found Her* 1998

Exodus [Bible] The second book of the Bible, relating the departure of the *Israelites
under the leadership of *Moses from their slavery in Egypt and their journey towards the
promised land of *Canaan. This journey is ascribed by scholars to various dates within
the limits *c.*1580–*c.*1200 BC.

> ➤ A mass departure of people, especially emigrants

> The English Department had changed its quarters since his arrival at Rummidge....The
> changeover had taken place in the Easter vacation amid much wailing and gnashing
> of teeth. Oy, oy, Exodus was nothing in comparison.
> DAVID LODGE *Changing Places* 1975

Exorcist, The [Cin.] The title of a disturbing 1973 horror film about a 12-year-old
girl called Regan (played by Linda Blair) who is possessed by the *Devil. In two of
the film's many shocking scenes, Regan's head rotates all the way round and she projectile
vomits.

> ➤ Mentioned as an example of an extremely frightening film; also alluded to in the
> context of someone's head spinning round or copious vomiting

> In fact, can I just add that the British penal system in general makes me spit fire and
> makes my head revolve around just like Regan off The Exorcist.
> *dooyoo.co.uk* 2005

Eyre, Jane (and Mr Rochester) [Lit.] Jane Eyre is the heroine of Charlotte *Brontë's
novel of the same name (1847). Jane, an orphan, grows up to be an independent woman
who earns her living first as a teacher then as a governess. In the latter occupation she meets
Mr Rochester, father to her illegitimate pupil Adèle. The couple fall in love and, although

Jane is initially resistant to the idea, they eventually agree to marry. The ceremony is disrupted, however, and it is revealed that Mr Rochester is already married to an insane Creole woman, Bertha, who has been kept in an upstairs room in Mr Rochester's house. Jane flees and nearly marries another man, but is eventually reunited with Mr Rochester after his house has burned down, his wife has been killed in the fire, and he himself has been badly burned and injured.

➤ Devoted lovers

face that launched a thousand ships, the [Lit.; Gk Myth.] A description of *Helen of Troy, the most beautiful woman in the world whose abduction by the Trojan prince Paris led to the *Trojan War. Doctor Faustus, in Marlowe's play of that title (1604), calls up her spirit and addresses her with these well-known lines:

> Was this the face that launch'd a thousand ships
> And burnt the topless towers of Ilium?

The thousand ships were those of the Greek fleet that sailed to Troy.

> ➤ A beautiful woman; quoted (often with a variation of the word 'ships') in the context of a person or image from which a large number of a particular type of thing ultimately derive
>
> Prize pic has to be Alberto Korda's iconic image of Che Guevara, the face that launched a thousand T-shirts.
> *Sunday Herald* 2001

Facing-Both-Ways, Mr [Lit.] One of several characters who are relatives of Mr By-Ends in the first part of John Bunyan's *The *Pilgrim's Progress* (1678).

> ➤ Someone who changes their behaviour or opinions to please different people
>
> There is a serious danger that Britain's national interests will be betrayed if the Government try to assure the United States that we are four-square behind NATO and, at the same time, seek to assure our EU partners that we are at the heart of Europe. However, that is the typical stance of Mr. Facing Both Ways, our Prime Minister.
> GERALD HOWARTH (in the House of Commons) 2003

Fagin [Lit.] In Charles Dickens's novel *Oliver *Twist* (1838), the leader of the gang of child pickpockets into whose hands the runaway Oliver falls.

> ➤ A pickpocket or thief; an adult leading a group of children in some illegal activity
>
> Of course this is true. All good writers, if they are honest, will acknowledge that when they come across a good thing in someone else's work, either consciously or unconsciously they store it away for the day when inspiration fails. And if writers are pickpockets, then Shakespeare is our Fagin, always on the look out for a shiny new phrase.
> *The Observer* 1999
>
> In their search for company they may be lucky enough to find a kindly outreach worker from a charity, or join a gang of other street children, but too often the overtly friendly offer of help turns out to come from a modern Fagin, or drug dealer, or pimp or paedophile.
> *Amnesty International Magazine* 1999

fairest of them all [Fairy tales] A quotation from the traditional tale *Snow White and the Seven Dwarfs*. In the story, *Snow White's stepmother is proud and vain and regularly demands of her magic mirror:

> Mirror, mirror on the wall,
> Who is the fairest of them all?

➤ The most beautiful person or thing

What value is a Rose unless she has a crown that marks her out to be the most beautiful and fairest of them all?
The Sligo Weekender 2005

fairy godmother [Fairy tales] In the story of *Cinderella, the fairy godmother finds Cinderella weeping because she cannot go to the royal ball. The fairy godmother transforms a pumpkin into a coach, mice into horses, and Cinderella's rags into beautiful clothes so that she is able to attend the ball.

➤ Someone who can magically grant someone's wishes

Perhaps everyone's assuming that a fairy godmother is going to surface at retirement time to wave a magic wand to ward off the impending poverty.
www.fool.co.uk 2002

Fall, the (the fall of Man) [Bible; Rel.] The time in Jewish and Christian theology when humankind fell from a state of innocence into a state of sin. This is taken to be the act of disobedience by *Adam and Eve in the Garden of *Eden in eating from the Tree of Knowledge of good and evil.

➤ Used to refer to a loss of innocence or a lapse into a sinful state

But as in Regensburg DP camp, between Eden and the Fall lay only the briefest interval.
THOMAS KENEALLY *A Family Madness* 1985

Falstaff, Sir John [Shakes.] The fat, witty, good-humoured old knight in *Henry IV* and *The Merry Wives of Windsor*. Falstaff's enormous paunch prompts the young Prince Hal to ask: 'How long is't ago, Jack, since thou sawest thine own knee?' Observing Falstaff fleeing an ambush, Hal remarks:

> Falstaff sweats to death
> And lards the lean earth as he walks along.

➤ A large, fat, jovial man, especially one fond of food and drink (adjective *Falstaffian*)

It was all so fine, so precise, and it was a wonder that this miracle was wrought by a whiskered Falstaff with a fat belly and a grubby singlet showing through the layers of wet, sour hessian.
PETER CAREY *Oscar and Lucinda* 1988

The professor was a big, jovial man of Falstaffian appearance.
MARJORIE ECCLES *A Species of Revenge* 1996

Famous Five [Child. Lit.] A group of four children (Julian, Dick, Anne, and George) and their dog (Timmy) who have adventures together in children's stories (1942-63) by Enid *Blyton.

➤ Used when describing an unlikely adventure, or an era of idealized childhood innocence

In a scene straight from the pages of a Famous Five novel, Millthorpe School pupils Bee Boon, and Rachael Waite, both aged 15, dug up more than a dozen pieces of gold and silver jewellery while larking around in West Bank Park, off Acomb Road.
The Press, York 2004

far, far better thing [Lit.] A phrase from the words at the end of Charles Dickens's *A Tale of Two Cities* (1859): 'It is a far, far better thing that I do than I have ever done; it is a far, far better rest that I go to, than I have ever known.' They are Sydney Carton's last thoughts as he ascends the scaffold to face the guillotine, taking the place of Charles Darnay.

➤ Used to refer to an act of self-sacrifice, often in a noble cause

Of course animal rights activists are free to disagree. For example, I can imagine a PETA activist explaining that PETA's video of half-naked women wrestling in tofu is a far, far better thing than feeding the hungry.
AnimalRights.net 2004

far from the madding crowd [Lit.] A phrase used in Thomas Gray's 'Elegy Written in a Country Churchyard' (1751), and later also taken as the title of a novel by Thomas Hardy (1874). 'Madding' here means 'acting madly, frenzied'.

➤ In a peaceful or secluded place, far away from the noise and bustle of people

For a long weekend in winter, far from the madding crowd, I can't think of anywhere better.
The Sunday Times 2004

Fatal Attraction [Cin.] The title of a film (1987) starring Glenn Close and Michael Douglas, about a rejected lover vengefully terrorizing the man who has spurned her and his family. In one memorable scene, she boils the family's pet rabbit. At the climax to the film, she resists a number of attempts to kill her, at one point emerging from the bath after it has appeared that she has been drowned.

➤ Mentioned in the context of a woman acting vengefully after having been spurned by her lover; used to refer to someone who survives repeated attempts to kill or defeat them

Breaking back the real battle came in the ninth game of the set, when both players had countless chances to win, but neither could kill off the other. Like a scene from Fatal Attraction, every time you thought the mortal blow had been dealt, the wounded rose from the metaphoric bathtub.
Scotland on Sunday 2004

As with Rasputin or Glenn Close's Fatal Attraction bunny-boiler, it seems as if it will take more than one crack to kill off the England team.
Guardian 2010

Fat Controller [Child. Lit.] In the Revd W. Awdry's series of books about Thomas the Tank Engine (first appearing in 1946), the accurately named Fat Controller presides over the Big Station with self-important and bureaucratic officiousness.

➤ Used to describe a rotund man who controls or is in charge of something

The edict has gone out from Michael Grade, the Fat Controller of ITV: this channel will spit in the face of plagiarism and fly the flag for innovation.
Guardian 2009

Fate [Myth.] The name given to a goddess who controls people's destinies, especially one of the *Fates or one of the *Norns.

➤ A way of referring to a person's destiny or fate

Not only is the hand of Fate discernible in this affair; Fate has been leaving fingerprints all around the place ever since Higgins got his bright idea.
ROBERTSON DAVIES *Leaven of Malice* 1954

Fates [Class. Myth.] Three sisters, daughters of Night, who presided over the birth, life, and death of every mortal individual. They were represented as three women spinning: Clotho, who held the distaff and spun the thread of a person's life, Lachesis, who drew off the thread and determined the luck that a person would have, and Atropos, who cut short the thread and so determined when a person's life would end. They were also called, by the Greeks, the Moirae and, by the Romans, the Parcae.

> A way of referring to a person's destiny or fate

The Fates had unexpectedly (and perhaps just a little officiously) removed an obstacle from his path.
SAKI 'Cross-Currents' in *Reginald in Russia* 1910

Father Christmas *See* SANTA CLAUS.

Father Time [Leg. & Folk.] The personification of time, usually depicted as an old bearded man with a scythe and hourglass.

> A way of referring to time; an old man with a white beard

The American portion of our community 'saw in' the greatest day of their national calendar in a fittingly splendid style and circumstances today a fortnight previous. As our issue of that very date proceeded to the press some days earlier, not possessing mastery of Old Father Time and his scythe, we were unavoidably prevented from commenting on those happy rites.
TIMOTHY MO *An Insular Possession* 1986

Father William [Child. Lit.] In Lewis Carroll's *Alice's Adventures in Wonderland* (1865), the Caterpillar instructs Alice to recite the poem 'You are old, Father William'. She begins:

> 'You are old, Father William,' the young man said,
> 'And your hair has become very white;
> And yet you incessantly stand on your head—
> Do you think, at your age, it is right?'

Father William is also sprightly enough to turn back-somersaults and balance an eel on the end of his nose.

> Someone who has an aged appearance, especially when they also act in a lively way

He had gone partly bald, which made him look like a youthful Father William.
SARA PARETSKY *Toxic Shock* 1990

fatted calf [Bible] In the parable of the *Prodigal Son told by *Jesus in the Bible (Luke 15: 11–32), the father welcomed his spendthrift son home and ordered the servants to 'bring hither the fatted calf, and kill it; and let us eat and be merry'.

> To 'kill the fatted calf' is to produce one's best food to celebrate something, especially a prodigal's return

Earle wasn't the first country star to abuse drugs, nor was he the first to land behind bars. Nevertheless, when he returned to civilian life, Nashville didn't exactly kill the fatted calf for him.
New York Metro 2004

Faust [Leg. & Folk.; Theatre] The subject of a medieval legend and subsequently of dramas by Marlowe (*Dr Faustus*, 1604) and Goethe (*Faust*, 1808, 1832). In the Marlowe version, Faustus, greedy for earthly power, sells his soul to *Mephistopheles in exchange for 24 years during which Mephistopheles will provide anything he wants. For much of the time, however, he is despondent and dissatisfied, and he experiences the agony of utter despair as his contract with Mephistopheles ends and his life and soul are forfeit.

> Someone ambitious for earthly power and riches; to enter 'a Faustian pact' is to sacrifice one's spiritual or moral values for material gains

The thought gave him deep satisfaction. In Faustian moments he dreamed of going on, after fixing Jane Austen, to do the same job on the other major English novelists, then the poets and dramatists.
DAVID LODGE *Changing Places* 1975

[If] I had been offered the chance to play for Liverpool as a child...on condition that I agreed to die on my 30th birthday. I would have signed this Faustian contract in a twinkling.
Radio Times 1997

Fawkes, Guy [Hist.] (1570–1606) A Catholic extremist who, with a small group of colleagues, was involved in the *Gunpowder Plot, a conspiracy to blow up James I and his parliament on 5 November 1605. After being discovered in the cellar of the House of Lords with barrels of gunpowder, Fawkes, together with seven of his co-conspirators, was tried and executed.

➤ A clever schemer or secret conspirator; a person who attempts (especially unsuccessfully) to remove someone from power

Missis was, she dared say, glad enough to get rid of such a tiresome, ill-conditioned child, who always looked as if she were watching everybody, and scheming plots underhand. Abbot, I think, gave me credit for being a sort of infantile Guy Fawkes.
CHARLOTTE BRONTE *Jane Eyre* 1847

He'd have called in the Dean, the Treasurer, the Seneschal and these other fellows in the Cathedral, and they'd have put the Box in the Cathedral treasure vaults. And you know what kind of vaults those are: Guy Fawkes and his powder wouldn't get through those, as we know from bitter experience.
JOHN MASEFIELD *The Box of Delights* 1935

Fawlty, Basil [TV] The highly irascible hotelier played by John Cleese in the BBC television comedy series *Fawlty Towers*, which ran from 1975 until 1979. He is temperamental, rude to the guests, and loses his temper uncontrollably with the slightest provocation.

➤ A man who is bad-tempered, rude, or snobbish

How Not to Become a Basil Fawlty. Resist the temptation to explode at work—it might feel better out than in, but invariably you will end up directing your anger at the innocent, either at home or in the office.
The Independent 1998

Feeding of the five thousand [Bible] The miracle by which Jesus fed the five thousand who had gathered to hear him on the only food which they had, five loaves and two fishes. When everyone had eaten, the fragments filled twelve baskets.

➤ Mentioned in the context of providing food for a large number of people

Marsey heard the mewing the moment Ree put her key in the lock. 'It's going to be a bit like the feeding of the five thousand for a few minutes,' Ree said with a slightly tense smile.
www.fictionpress.com

Fell, Dr John [People] (1625–86) An Anglican divine and Dean of Christ Church, Oxford. One of his students was Thomas Brown, who later became a well-known satirist. Dr Fell asked Brown to translate one of the epigrams of Martial:

> Non amo te, Sabidi, nec possum dicere quare;
> Hoc tantum possum dicere, non amo te.
> (I do not love you, Sabidius, and I cannot say why;

All I can say is this, that I do not love you.)

Thomas Brown's famous translation read:

> I do not love thee, Dr Fell,
> The reason why I cannot tell;
> But this I know, and know full well,
> I do not love thee, Dr Fell.

➤ A person whom one dislikes for no particular reason

Look, I don't really care for Franklin much more than you do, John, but it's a perfectly irrational dislike. He's done nothing to me at all—or to you, for that matter. It's a pure case of Dr Fell.

SUSAN HILL *Strange Meeting* 1971

Fellini, Federico [Cin.] (1920–93) An Italian film director whose films include *La strada* (1954), *La dolce vita* (1960), and *8½* (1963). His most characteristic works are surreal dream-like fantasies, full of circus-like imagery and grotesque characters.

➤ Used to suggest a fantastical or surreal situation

I once fantasized that I would celebrate my retirement with a large party out of Fellini, where all the colleagues and students who were important to me would reappear and would do one last circle dance.

Academe 2002

Fenris-wolf [Norse Myth.] The offspring of *Loki, god of mischief, and a giantess; also known as Fenrir. The gods brought him to Asgard, where he grew huge, powerful, and fierce. Eventually, only the god *Tyr, who had played with him as a cub, would go near the wolf. The gods feared him, so they tricked him into being fettered. He broke the fetters. So they had a light soft fetter made which would be impossible to break. With this he was securely held until *Ragnarok, the destruction of the world, but he bit off Tyr's hand by way of revenge.

➤ A destructive force, especially one restrained or held in check by something

The telegraph is a limp band that will hold the Fenris-wolf of war. For now, that a telegraph line runs through France and Europe, from London, every message it transmits makes stronger by one thread, the band which war will have to cut.

RALPH WALDO EMERSON *English Traits* 1856

Fermat's last theorem [Science] **Pierre de Fermat** (1601–65) was a French mathematician, a founder of probability theory and number theory. In 1640 he formulated the proposition 'There do not exist positive integers x, y, z, n such that $xn + yn = zn$ when n is greater than 2.' Intriguingly, Fermat noted that he had 'a truly wonderful proof of this proposition but it does not fit into the margin of this page'. For the next 350 years mathematicians tried to furnish a proof for what became known as Fermat's last theorem (or Fermat's theorem), until Andrew Wiles finally succeeded in 1995.

➤ A long-standing quest to find the solution to a problem

You know this infallible system I have for becoming very rich by judicially investing in the velocity and stamina of horses with legal names? Ascot was going to provide the ultimate proof of its validity, a sort of Fermat's Last Theorem for racing.

MARCEL BERLINS *The Guardian* 1997

fiddle while Rome burns *See* NERO.

fifteen minutes of fame [Art] A reference to the American artist Andy Warhol's prediction in 1968 that 'In the future everybody will be famous for fifteen minutes.'

> Used to refer to someone enjoying a brief period of fame or celebrity before fading back into obscurity

There have been a lot of winners of reality TV shows who never went anywhere, of course, and it remains to be seen whether Parks can parlay her fifteen minutes of fame into a lasting career as a performer.
After Ellen 2004

final frontier [TV] A quotation from the American television science fiction series *Star Trek*. The mission of the *Starship *Enterprise* was to explore space, the 'final frontier'.

> A final challenge that must be overcome

It held him in good stead when India toured Pakistan, the country that has for long been the final frontier for Indian cricket.
Kashmir Times 2004

Final Solution [Hist.] The euphemistic term coined by the Nazis for their policy of exterminating European Jews. Introduced by Heinrich Himmler and administered by Adolf Eichmann, the policy resulted in the murder of 6 million Jews in concentration camps between 1941 and 1945.

> Genocide; any scheme to ultimately solve or eliminate a problem

And so to the Balkans; and here the book tends to become a disheartening parade of one massacre or mass-impaling hard on the heels of another. All too frequently, a 'final solution' was suggested.
Scotland on Sunday 2003

finest hour, one's [Hist.] A phrase associated with a speech by Winston *Churchill on 18 June 1940 during the Battle of Britain: 'If the British Empire and its Commonwealth lasts for a thousand years, men will say, "This was their finest hour."'

> The time of one's greatest achievement

President Bush showed up with 35 minutes worth of material for a 90-minute debate. It was not his finest hour.
CNN transcripts: In the Money 2004

finger in the dyke [Child. Lit.] A reference to the Little *Dutch Boy in Mary Mapes Dodge's children's classic *Hans Brinker; or, The Silver Skates* (1865). The story describes how the boy, returning home from a visit, hears the sound of trickling water and sees a small hole in a dyke. He climbs up the dyke and plugs the hole with his finger in order to stop it becoming enlarged and leading to flooding.

> An action which is taken to solve a small problem quickly, to prevent it from becoming more serious

Flanagan is adopting a finger in the dyke approach to running his media group.
Scotland on Sunday 2005

Finn, Huckleberry [Lit.] The main character in *The Adventures of Huckleberry Finn* (1884) by Mark Twain. He is a spirited, self-reliant, and unconventional boy who fakes his own death in order to escape from his drunken, brutal father and he has many adventures.

> Mentioned in the context of childhood adventures, especially on a river

So off we went, at 1am, down to the Black Warrior at Lock 5, took off our clothes and slipped into the water. It was real Huckleberry Finn stuff. Not an electric light to be seen, just the faint blue glow of the sky and the shadows of the trees on the water.
HANA LOFTUS *Bottom Drawer* 2005

fire and brimstone [Bible] A biblical description of the torments of Hell, as in 'a lake which burns with fire and brimstone' (Book of Revelation) and 'upon the ungodly he shall rain snares, fire and brimstone, storm and tempest' (Psalm 11). A fire-and-brimstone sermon is one in which the preacher threatens the congregation with damnation in hell for their sins.

➤ A way of referring to torment in Hell

The fire and brimstone of Hell may have been extinguished long ago, at least from our belief-system, but angels and their place in the heavenly scheme of things are as secure as ever.
Carlow Nationalist 2002

Flash Gordon *See* GORDON.

Flintstones [TV] An animated TV series (1960–66) about a Stone Age couple, Fred and Wilma Flintstone. The vehicles and devices they use are based on their modern-day counterparts, but are made of stone, wood, and animals skins, and often powered by animals.

➤ Used to describe something outmoded or unsophisticated

It is more reminiscent of the Flintstones school of reception and documentation than a modern-day health service.
Irish Examiner 2002

float like a butterfly, sting like a bee [Sport] The phrase used by the US boxer Muhammad *Ali to describe his style of fighting, in which he moved nimbly on his feet and landed stinging punches on his opponents

➤ To move nimbly and attack swiftly and with force when fighting

A former gymnastic champion has proved he can not only float like a butterfly but sting like a bee after landing an army boxing title in his first-ever championship.
Croydon Guardian 2003

Flood [Bible] In the biblical story related in Genesis, God brought a great flood upon the earth in the time of *Noah because of the wickedness of the human race. Apart from Noah, his family, and the animals he was instructed to shelter on the ark, all inhabitants of the earth perished in the Flood, which lasted for 40 days and 40 nights. There are similar flood myths in other traditions, such as in the epic of Gilgamesh and in the Greek legend of *Deucalion.

➤ Mentioned in the context of flooding; references to a time before the Flood are intended to suggest the very distant past

Putting an arm around his sopping half-sleeve shirt, I say, 'I bet if you set your mind to it you could go back before the Flood.'
PHILIP ROTH *The Professor of Desire* 1978

But at last we came upon the shore, and were tumbled out upon the dry land. What a restoration that was; I felt like a giant who had survived the Flood.
PETER ACKROYD *The House of Dr Dee* 1993

Flora [Rom. Myth.] The goddess of flowers and spring, depicted in Sandro *Botticelli's celebrated painting *Primavera*.

➤ A person carrying flowers

I rang the door-bell, holding my flowers spread across both outstretched forearms. I did not want to appear like a delivery man. Rather I was a simple, a frangible petitioner, assisted only by the goddess Flora.
JULIAN BARNES *Talking It Over* 1991

Flowerpot Men *See* BILL AND BEN

Flying Dutchman [Leg. & Folk.] A legendary ghost ship supposed to be seen in the region of the Cape of Good Hope and presaging disaster. It was said to haunt the seas eternally as a result of a murder that had been committed on board. The term is sometimes applied to the ship's captain. In Wagner's opera of the same name (1843), Captain Vanderdecken is freed from a curse when he finds a woman willing to sacrifice herself for him.

➢ Someone cursed to wander forever

   She didn't sleep until I put her in the car seat and drove around for an hour, looking like the Flying Dutchman—a haggard soul lashed to the wheel.
   www.lileks.com 2001

Flynn, Errol [Cin.] (1909–59) An Australian-born American actor who became famous for his swashbuckling roles in such costume adventure films as *Captain Blood* (1935) and *The Adventures of Robin Hood* (1938).

➢ A dashing hero; mentioned in the context of swashbuckling sword-fighting

   I gave him a smile. *Dawn Patrol*. Errol Flynn courageous in the face of certain doom.
   ROBERT CRAIS *Lullaby Town* 1992

fly too close to the sun [Gk Myth.] A reference to *Icarus who, according to Greek mythology, attempted to fly to freedom from Crete on wings constructed by *Daedalus. However, the wings were attached by wax, and when Icarus flew too close to the sun, the wax melted and he fell to his death.

➢ To fail or be in danger of failing, because of excessive ambition

   I'm a software engineer flying too close to the sun.
   Linux Journal 2001

Fogg, Phileas [Lit.] In Jules Verne's novel *Around the World in Eighty Days* (1873), the Englishman Phileas Fogg wagers other members of his London club that he can travel around the world in 80 days. He just manages it, travelling with his French valet Passepartout by many forms of transport including train, boat, sledge, and elephant.

➢ Someone who travels to many different countries or around the world

   Decker thumbed through Yalom's passport—pages of stamped entries back into the States, Yalom's residing country. Then there were many other pages of foreign ink—Canada, Mexico, countries of Western and Eastern Europe including Russia, entries from the Far East, Latin America, and Africa. Lots from Africa—Egypt, South Africa, Kenya, Namibia, Liberia, Angola, Sudan, Ethiopia, Zaire, plus a host of other countries Decker didn't know existed....Marge said, 'Yalom was quite the Phileas Fogg.'
   FAYE KELLERMAN *Sanctuary* 1994

Fonteyn, Margot [Dance] (1919–91) The stage name of the English classical ballet dancer Margaret Hookham. She danced for the company that became the Royal Ballet and was trained by Ninette de Valois. She started her partnership with Rudolph *Nureyev in 1962 and created many roles with notable choreographers such as Frederick Ashton and Kenneth MacMillan. Fonteyn was named 'prima ballerina assoluta' in 1979, a title that has only been awarded three times.

> A female dancer, especially a ballet dancer

'That's Bella on the terrace of our hotel.' Featherstone had produced his wallet, from which he proudly drew a number of creased and faded snaps from the space between his credit cards and his cheque book. 'What's she doing?' said Miss Trant, giving a cursory look, 'The Dying Swan?' 'Oh, yes,' said Featherstone proudly. 'Quite a little Margot Fonteyn, isn't she?'
JOHN MORTIMER *Rumpole's Return* 1980

forbidden fruit [Bible] According to the account in the book of Genesis, God commanded *Adam and Eve not to eat the fruit of the Tree of Knowledge but, tempted by the Serpent, Eve disobeyed him and then persuaded Adam to do the same: 'So when the woman saw that the tree was good for food, and that it was a delight to the eyes, and that the tree was to be desired to make one wise, she took of its fruit and ate; and she also gave some to her husband, and he ate' (Gen. 3: 6).

> Something that is desired or enjoyed all the more because it is not allowed, especially illicit sexual pleasure

Later, we had to sneak. I'd hired on at Rent-a-Back by then, and she would ride along on my jobs—spend the day with me while her parents thought she was swimming at their club. 'Oh forbidden fruit! No wonder you two were attracted,' Sophia said.
ANNE TYLER *A Patchwork Planet* 1998

Force, the [Cin.] The energy field created by all living things that gives the Jedi their power in the *Star Wars films. According to Obi-Wan Kenobi, 'It surrounds us and penetrates us. It binds the galaxy together'. Villainous characters, such as Darth *Vader, embrace the 'Dark Side' of the Force.

> A power that seemingly enables someone to achieve something or affects a person's behaviour

...Burton's most recent efforts, though clearly capable of such beauty, have all been undermined by the shiny, mood-killing kitsch that his Ed Wood gloried in so effectively. Come back to the Dark Side, Tim, the Force is stronger here.
Reverse Shot 2005

Forth Bridge [Places] A cantilevered railway bridge built in 1890 across the Firth of Forth, linking Fife and Lothian on the east coast of Scotland. The bridge requires constant maintenance, notably regarding its painted surfaces: as soon as workers have finished painting the bridge, they immediately have to start repainting it.

> Mentioned (especially in the phrase 'like painting the Forth Bridge') when describing a never-ending or arduous task

So a treaty that took ten years to negotiate is out of date before it even comes into force. What you might call the Forth Bridge theory of arms control.
BBC Radio 4 1995

Fort Knox [Places] A building in north Kentucky, part of a military reservation, which houses the US gold reserves in the form of bullion.

> A place that is extremely secure and well guarded

It's important to chip away at Ford's defences here because they seem to be protecting the Fort Knox of his imagination.
The Observer 1997

Fortuna [Rom. Myth.] The goddess of fortune, often represented turning a wheel.

> A way of referring to random luck or change

Fortuna's wheel had turned on humanity, crushing its collarbone, smashing its skull, twisting its torso, puncturing its pelvis, sorrowing its soul.
JOHN KENNEDY TOOLE *A Confederacy of Dunces* 1980

Fortunate Isles [Class. Myth.] The place to which people in classical times believed the souls of heroes and the good were conveyed to a life of bliss. They were also known as the *Islands of the Blest or the *Happy Islands.

> ➤ A heaven or paradise

forty acres and a mule [Hist.] The settlement that was promised in 1865 to freed slaves at the end of the American Civil War. Following emancipation, General Sherman promised every African-American family a plot of 40 acres of arable land, and a mule for ploughing, but the bill to ratify this was later vetoed by President Andrew Johnson.

> ➤ An unfulfilled promise
>
> If, though, the goal is parity for gay partnerships on more complete, societal terms, I think the proposal as it is now will come up very short. But hey, it may be the start of something, I suppose, a bit of incrementalism. I hope you get your forty acres and a mule.
> *www.barbelith.com* 2003

for whom the bell tolls [Lit.] A phrase from John Donne's 'Meditation XVII' (1624): 'And therefore never send to know for whom the bell tolls; it tolls for thee.' The phrase was later used by Ernest *Hemingway as the title of his 1940 novel set during the Spanish Civil War.

> ➤ Used to convey the idea that human beings are mutually dependent
>
> The public's got to realise this case is about them. You know, it's 'for whom the bell tolls; it tolls for all of us' because everyone of us is going to need a drug sometime in our life.
> *The Health Report* (programme transcripts) 2001

Foster, Dr [Nurs. Rhym.] According to the nursery rhyme,

> Doctor Foster went to Gloucester
> In a shower of rain.
> He stepped in a puddle right up to his middle,
> And never went there again.

> ➤ Used in the context of refusing or being reluctant to return to a place

Fountain of Youth [Leg. & Folk.] A legendary spring which was supposed to have the power of renewing youth and in which *Alexander the Great and his army were said to have bathed and been restored to the prime of life. In the early 16th century it was sought by the Spanish explorer Juan Ponce de León.

> ➤ Used to suggest that someone has had their youth restored
>
> The ride invigorated Waltrip, then 51, like a bath in the Fountain of Youth.
> *Sporting News* 2002

Four Horsemen of the Apocalypse *See* APOCALYPSE.

four legs good, two legs bad [Lit.] A phrase from the fable *Animal Farm* (1945) by George *Orwell which satirizes Russian Communism as it developed under Stalin. When the animals on the farm, led by the pigs, revolt against the farmer and take control, one of their slogans affirming the supremacy of animals over humans is 'four legs good, two legs bad'.

> ➤ Used to suggest a simplistic interpretation of what is acceptable and what is not

Sweeney adopts the 'four legs good, two legs bad' approach to all questions of state ownership.
The Sunday Times 2004

Francis of Assisi, St [Rel.] (*c*.1181–1226) An Italian monk (b. Giovanni di Bernardone) who founded the Franciscan order of friars, an order devoted to chastity, poverty, and obedience. St Francis exemplifies humility, simple faith, and in particular a great love for, and empathy with, birds and animals. He is often depicted in art preaching to birds or holding wild animals.

➤ Someone who loves, or talks to, animals or birds

You can always tell that the crash is coming when I start getting tender about Our Dumb Friends. Three highballs, and I think I'm St. Francis of Assisi.
DOROTHY PARKER *Just a Little One* 1944

Sure he could get under your skin but so would St Francis of Assisi on a job like this. He'd have spent all his time looking at the bloody birds in the Jungle instead of reading his cue-cards.
JULIAN BARNES *A History of the World in 10½ Chapters* 1989

Frank, Anne [People] (1929–45) A German Jewish girl who was born in Frankfurt am Main and fled with her family from the Nazis in 1933. After the Nazi occupation of the Netherlands, where they were living, she hid with her own family and four others in a sealed-off upper room (usually referred to as an attic) in Amsterdam. During this period of incarceration, she wrote a diary, which was published in 1947. The fugitives were betrayed in 1944 and Anne died in *Belsen concentration camp.

➤ Someone hiding in a secret room, especially in dangerous circumstances; someone keeping a diary

At least I now knew how to get round client confidentiality. Forget the thumbscrews and the cigarette burns. Give her a cup of Horlicks and a new pair of tights and she'd tell you Anne Frank was in the attic.
MIKE RIPLEY *Angel Confidential* 1995

Frankenstein [Lit.] Mary Shelley's gothic novel (1818) relates the exploits of Victor Frankenstein, a Genevan student of natural philosophy, who builds a grotesque manlike creature out of corpses and brings it to life. The creature, or monster, superhuman in size and strength and terrible in appearance, inspires horror in all who see it, but is miserably lonely and longs to be loved. When Frankenstein refuses to create a mate for his creature, it turns on him and murders both his bride and his brother. Frankenstein decides that he must destroy his own creation, but is himself killed by his monster, which then goes away to end its own life, distraught at the death of its creator.

➤ A monstrous creation that turns on or destroys its originator; something assembled from disparate or ill-matching parts to form a whole

There are some things they don't share, however. Charles, for instance, is human (despite what he likes to think to the contrary) but Richard is possibly not. Possibly an extra-terrestrial experiment gone wrong in fact—an alien's idea of what a human is like, put together from spare parts, the creation of a Martian Frankenstein.
KATE ATKINSON *Human Croquet* 1997

Frankly, my dear...[Cin.] A quotation from the 1939 film *Gone with the Wind*, based on Margaret Mitchell's novel. The dashing Rhett *Butler (played by Clark Gable) famously dismisses Scarlett *O'Hara (Vivien Leigh) and her fears for her future with the words, 'Frankly, my dear, I don't give a damn.'

➤ Used when expressing complete indifference to someone's plight

Even if world champions England had been on tour these last few weeks, it would still have been a case of, frankly my dear no-one gives a damn.
Scotland on Sunday 2004

French Connection, The [Cin.] A 1971 film about the drug trade in New York starring Gene Hackman as a police detective. The film features a memorable and exciting car chase.

➤ Mentioned to suggest an exciting car chase

We won't soon forget the story of New York City's fastest bicycle messenger, whose daily death-defying rounds make the chase in 'The French Connection' look tame...
powerlineblog.com 2004

Freud, Sigmund [People] (1856–1939) An Austrian neurologist and psychotherapist who was the first to draw particular attention to the role of the subconscious mind in human behaviour. He also emphasized the importance of sex as a prime motive force in human behaviour. A Freudian slip or accident is a remark, gesture, or action, apparently accidental, that in fact reveals subconscious desires or fears, especially sexual ones.

➤ Mentioned in the context of subconscious desires or feelings being revealed (adjective *Freudian*)

The loss of the manuscript, I thought, was a Freudian accident.
I. B. SINGER *The Lecture* 1968

'I learnt a whole lot from my mother,' he says. 'About music, relationships, being a good person, loving people, the whole of life. I learnt about everything from her. Every single day I think about her. All through the day.' Dr Freud would probably have had a field day with him.
The Observer 2004

Friday *See* MAN FRIDAY.

Frodo *See* BAGGINS.

frog prince [Fairy tales] In the story *The Frog Prince*, a princess, playing with a golden ball, inadvertently drops it into a fountain. A frog, who is really a handsome prince placed under an enchantment, offers to retrieve the ball if she will, in return, love him and let him be her companion. The princess agrees, but when the frog demands to sleep in her bed, she throws it against the wall. As the frog falls, he turns back into a handsome prince. In some versions, the frog is transformed back into a prince after being kissed by a princess.

➤ Used to suggest transformation from an unattractive to an attractive state, particularly in the context of a woman seeking a suitable male partner

I don't mean I've done a sudden transformation. I'm not a frog that's been kissed by a princess or whatever the fairy tale is.
JULIAN BARNES *Talking It Over* 1991

Fudd, Elmer [Cart. & Com.] An animated cartoon character in a series of Warner Brothers films. He is a short, dim-witted hunter who goes after, but is generally outwitted by, *Bugs Bunny. He is known for saying 'Be vewy, vewy quiet. I'm hunting wabbits.' Underneath his tall, red stovepipe hat he is bald.

➤ Someone who looks or sounds like Elmer Fudd; an inept hunter or marksman

Truth is, when Tiger and Vijay are in the same field, Singh is about as efficient a marksman as Elmer Fudd.
Sports Illustrated: Inside Golf 2004

full monty [Cin.] A phrase from *The Full Monty*, a 1997 British comedy film about a group of unemployed workers in Sheffield who decide to form a male striptease act in order to earn some money. The phrase *full monty* (meaning 'the full amount') is used in the film to mean 'a complete strip'.

> A full strip, with the removal of all clothes

There were shrieks from some of the potential students on the delegation, many of whom would have come from backgrounds where the exposure of any body parts is frowned upon, let alone a Full Monty display.
Carlow Nationalist 2000

Fu Manchu [Lit., Cin.] A moustached Chinese master-criminal created by the British writer Sax Rohmer (1883?-1959), first appearing in the novel *Dr Fu Manchu* (1913) and subsequently in several films.

> Used to describe an archetypal 'oriental' villain

Maxwell looked at the Chief Inspector. If he read the man aright, here was one who gave nothing away, let nothing slip; whose face was a mask of inscrutability for the world. Miles Warren made Fu Manchu look like an *ingénue*.
M. J. TROW *Maxwell's Flame* 1995

Furies [Gk Myth.] The avenging spirits of punishment, often represented as three winged goddesses with snakes twisted in their hair; also known as the *Erinyes. Their names were Alecto, Megaera, and Tisiphone, and they relentlessly pursued and punished wrongdoers who had otherwise escaped punishment, often when there was no human avenger left alive. Among the crimes they were particularly concerned with were the killing by one member of a family of another, blasphemy against the gods, and treachery to a host or guest. They were sometimes called the Eumenides, 'the kindly ones', a euphemism intended to placate them.

> A group of people pursuing someone in order to torment or punish them for a wrongdoing they have committed

The Vengeance, uttering terrific shrieks, and flinging her arms about her head like all the forty Furies at once, was tearing from house to house, rousing the women.
CHARLES DICKENS *A Tale of Two Cities* 1859

He eyed them with distaste, resenting this universal calm at a time when he himself was feeling like a character in a Greek tragedy pursued by the Furies.
P. G. WODEHOUSE *Cocktail Time* 1958

Gabriel [Bible] An archangel, used by God to deliver revelations to people on earth. It was Gabriel who foretold the birth of *Jesus to the Virgin Mary. In Christian tradition, Gabriel will blow the trumpet to announce the Resurrection. In Islam, Gabriel was the archangel who appeared to the Prophet *Muhammad and revealed the Koran to him.

> Used to refer to an unexpected revelation; 'Gabriel's trumpet' is used in the context of a loud noise or blowing hard

Blowing harder than Gabriel's trumpet, it is, and enough snow already down to bury a whale.
JOAN AIKEN *The Whispering Mountain* 1968

Treading in the hallowed footsteps of Mrs Beeton we must somehow convince ourselves that our civilisation is not based on a technique developed by an ignorant, dirty, illiterate low life who wouldn't understand a recipe if it was delivered by the Archangel Gabriel.
Combat-Online 2004

Gadarene swine [Bible] The herd of pigs into which *Jesus, preaching in the territory of the Gadarenes, cast the demons that had possessed a madman. As a result the pigs ran down a steep cliff into the Sea of Galilee and were drowned.

> Used in the context of a headlong or potentially disastrous rush to do something

As we report today, and as we have consistently argued throughout this Gadarene rush towards war, there has to be a justification for any attack.
Sunday Herald 2002

Witnessing hi-tech firms dive into China is like watching the Gadarene swine.
First Monday Journal 2005

Galahad, Sir [Arth. Leg.] One of the knights of the Round Table, the son of Sir *Lancelot. His purity, nobility, and virtue were such that he was destined to succeed in the quest for the *Holy Grail.

> A man of great nobility, integrity, or courtesy; a chivalrously heroic person; a man who comes to a woman's rescue

The usher called her again. I dropped the remnants of the small cigar on the marble floor of the Shire Hall and ground it underfoot. The lance was in the rest, Sir Galahad Rumpole was about to do battle for the damsel in distress, or words to that effect.
JOHN MORTIMER *Rumpole of the Bailey* 1978

If the Stanley Cup is hockey's Holy Grail, the goalie is Sir Galahad. So, aside from the sure bets, which goalie has a chance to ride through his hometown on a white horse, carrying Lord Stanley's Cup?
Sporting News 2003

Galatea [Gk Myth.] The name of an ivory statue of a woman carved by the sculptor *Pygmalion, who fell in love with his own creation. *Aphrodite brought the beautiful statue to life and Pygmalion married her.

> Used in the context of a creator falling in love with his creation or of something inanimate being brought to life; also used (with *Pygmalion*) in the context of the social or educational transformation of a protégé

With delightful humor, tinged with equally delightful seriousness, Adam teaches Jacie, and she, in turn, teaches him. It is a twist on the Pygmalion story, with Galatea giving back as much as she receives—or more.
New York Metro: Theater 2004

Galileo (Galileo Galilei) [Science] (1564–1642) An Italian astronomer and physicist. Under threat of torture from the Inquisition he publicly recanted his heretical view that the sun was the centre of the universe and the earth moved around the sun, but is later reported as declaring 'Eppur si muove' ('But it does move').

> Someone who defiantly upholds scientific truth and integrity

Remember Galilyo. Always stick up for yourself!
v. s. NAIPAUL *A House for Mr Biswas* 1969

Gamp, Mrs [Lit.] In Dickens's *Martin Chuzzlewit* (1844), Sarah Gamp is a gin-drinking and somewhat disreputable nurse who carries a large cotton umbrella. She continually refers to an imaginary Mrs Harris to validate her opinions.

> A nurse of a disreputable class; *gamp* is a dated British term for an umbrella, especially a large, unwieldy one

In her teens she [Florence Nightingale] announced she wanted to be a nurse. Her parents were horrified as nurses of the day were regarded as a lewd, lecherous, grasping and drunken lot, the disreputable Sairey Gamp, so delightfully portrayed in Dickens' 'Martin Chuzzlewit', being regarded as the prototype.
Ockham's Razor (programme transcripts) 2004

Gandalf [Lit.] The white wizard in J. R. R. *Tolkien's fantasy adventures *The Hobbit* (1937) and *The Lord of the Rings* (1954–5).

> A wizard

Gandhi, Mahatma [Hist.] (1869–1948) An Indian nationalist and spiritual leader who pursued a policy of passive resistance and non-violent civil disobedience in opposition to British rule in India. Regarded as the principal force in achieving India's independence, he was assassinated in 1948.

> A pacifist or one who engages in non-violent struggle

I remained almost transcendentally calm, Christ-like in my turning of the other cheek and Gandhi-like in my restraint from smacking him in the mouth.
Musings from Middle England (blog) 2005

Ganesh (Ganesha) [Rel.] The Hindu elephant-headed god of wisdom and prudence. He is usually depicted coloured red, with a pot belly and one broken tusk, riding a rat. Ganesh is worshipped as the remover of obstacles and the patron of learning.

> Mentioned in the context of wisdom and learning

Gang of Four [Hist.] In China, the leaders of a radical group who attempted to take power on Mao Zedong's death in 1976, but who were arrested and imprisoned. In the UK, the term was applied to a group of four prominent Labour MPs who broke away from the Labour Party in 1981 to form the Social Democratic Party.

> Any group of four people who act collectively

[Olazabal] was one of a Gang of Four—the others were Seve Ballesteros, Bernhard Langer and Nick Faldo—who last year demanded an independent audit of the European Tour's finances.
Sunday Herald 2001

Ganymede [Gk Myth.] A Trojan youth who was so beautiful that he was carried off by an eagle to be *Zeus's cup-bearer.

> A youth of extraordinary beauty and desirability; a man's young male lover; a young man serving drinks

Now listen: were it by any chance the case that Oliver's radiant sexuality occasionally put aside the workaday, and were his heliotropic gaze to turn towards Stoke Newington's unlikely Ganymede, then, to enlist a vernacular which my accuser herself will be able to grasp, *I wouldn't have any trouble there, mate.*
JULIAN BARNES *Talking It Over* 1991

Garbo, Greta [Cin.] (1905–90) A Swedish-born US actress, known for her haunting beauty, her husky, accented voice, and her aloof, mysterious screen presence. She retired from films in 1941 and remained a recluse from then until her death. The phrase 'I want to be alone', used by Garbo in the 1932 film *Grand Hotel*, became closely identified with her.

> Used to refer to an individual who desires privacy, is aloof, or lives as a recluse

In the days that followed, Schwarzenegger seemed to pull a Greta Garbo, perhaps not wanting to be alone, but not exactly running a high-profile event.
CNN transcripts: Live From… 2003

A cultural icon of the twentieth century who wrote some of its most memorable songs, Dylan is almost equally famous for a reticence that makes Garbo seem like a socialite.
Contemporary Review February 2005

Garden of Eden *See* EDEN.

Gargantua [Lit.] A large-mouthed giant with a huge and insatiable appetite in François *Rabelais's satire *Gargantua* (1534). It is from his name that we derive the word *gargantuan*, meaning 'enormous or gigantic'.

> An enormous or voracious person or institution (adjective *Gargantuan*)

The nature of the IRS and its role dictate that it will always be what it is. It must be intrusive, tyrannical, and ruthless in order to perform its job of feeding the tax-devouring Gargantua that the Federal Government has become.
Financial Sense Online: 2005 editorials 2005

Garibaldi, Giuseppe [Hist.] (1807–82) The hero of the movement for Italian independence and unification. He led a volunteer force, the Red Shirts, to victory in Sicily and southern Italy, thereby playing a key role in the establishment of a kingdom of Italy.

> A patriotic hero and leader of a country's movement for independence

Slowly Russo began to shake his head from side to side: this was no Capone, this was a Garibaldi!
PHILIP ROTH *You Can't Tell a Man by the Song He Sings* 1959

Garnett, Alf [TV] The central character of the BBC TV series *Till Death Us Do Part* (1964–74), played by Warren Mitchell. A working-class bigot from the East End of London, he is best remembered for haranguing his family every week with his right-wing, xenophobic, and racist views.

> A racist bigot; a person expressing forthright views in a furious, foul-mouthed rant

I guess the thing that bugs me the most is the inherent racism that I see in much of the commentary and debate. I don't mean the blatant Alf Garnett type of bigotry. I mean a more subtle form which is displayed by even the most well meaning and sincere people.
Sydney Morning Herald Webdiary 2001

Garrick, David [Theatre] The foremost *Shakespearian actor of 18th-century England and manager of Drury Lane Theatre for nearly 30 years (1747–76).

> ➤ A great actor

'Is the play up to viewing, Mr Garrick?' one or other of the gentlemen would periodically ask Ralph, and Ralph was ecstatic for this merely whimsical comparison of himself to the great actor–manager.
THOMAS KENEALLY *The Playmaker* 1987

Gates, Bill [People] (b. 1955) The US computer entrepreneur who co-founded the computer software company Microsoft. He became the youngest multi-billionaire in American history.

> ➤ A person of enormous wealth; a successful entrepreneur; a computer expert

He was the least computer-literate person I had ever met and compared to him I was Bill Gates in person.
GERALD HAMMOND *Illegal Tender* 2000

Those accused of crimes are entitled to certain constitutional protection, which we must cherish, and the victims of a crime—whether a Bill Gates or the poorest street-sweeper in a slum—are entitled to the same respect.
Indie Gay Forum 2004

Gatsby, Jay [Lit.] The title character of F. Scott Fitzgerald's 1925 novel *The Great Gatsby*. Gatsby is a self-made millionaire with a mysterious past—his fortune has been amassed from bootlegging and shady business dealings—who seeks to enhance his social status by joining Long Island's high society and flaunting his wealth with lavish parties.

> ➤ Used to refer to someone's attempt to reinvent themselves; an example of the *nouveau riche*; a wealthy person with a mysterious past

Unfailingly well-mannered, dressed and disciplined, Kees strove to rise Gatsby-like from sturdy but obscure origins in the middle of the country to greater East Coast prominence.
The Nation 2002

GCHQ [Places] The Government Communications Headquarters (or GCHQ) is the UK government department responsible for monitoring communications intelligence, which since 1953 has been based in Cheltenham, Gloucestershire.

> ➤ Mentioned in the context of electronic surveillance

'Yet he hasn't been out for the last twenty-four hours. I would have known.' Harry did not doubt it. Living next door to GCHQ would have carried less risk of surveillance.
MARTIN EDWARDS *Yesterday's Papers* 1994

Gehenna [Bible] Hebrew name for the Valley of *Hinnom, a valley to the south of Jerusalem. Hinnom was known as the Valley of Slaughter, and was used for idolatrous worship, with children being burnt alive as sacrifices to *Baal and *Moloch.

> ➤ Used to refer to the fires of Hell; a place of torment

Gekko, Gordon [Cin.] The predatory and ruthless company trader played by Michael Douglas in the 1987 film *Wall Street*. He is particularly associated with the philosophy 'Greed is good', a phrase the character uses in the film.

> A ruthless, avaricious businessman

We live in a society where even Gordon Gekko might be taken aback, where greed runs rampant and people only pay lip service to the basic ethical considerations that many of us take for granted.
CHUD.com film reviews 2005

Genghis Khan [Hist.] (1162–1227) A military leader and founder of the Mongol Empire, which at his death stretched from the Pacific to the Black Sea. Though a brilliant military leader and administrator, he acquired a reputation for horrific cruelty. Modern-day right-wing views are sometimes humorously described as being 'to the right of Genghis Khan'.

> A ruthless conqueror or tyrannical ruler; used to refer to someone who holds right-wing or reactionary political views of the most extreme kind

What he is and what he says he is—two different things. I think the guy's a hard-nosed reactionary. To the right of Genghis Khan.
JANE STANTON HITCHCOCK *The Witches' Hammer* 1995

George III [Hist.] (1738–1820) King of Great Britain and Ireland from 1760 to 1820. He suffered from repeated bouts of mental illness, and in 1811 it became clear that the king's mental health made him unfit to rule, as a result of which his son was made regent. It is now believed that the king suffered from porphyria, a rare hereditary disease. This episode in British history was popularized by the 1994 film *The Madness of King George*, based on Alan Bennett's play.

> Someone who is mentally ill or insane

Even we hacks live with the unspoken dread that, quite suddenly, we could become as cuckoo as King George III and be offered jobs as *Daily Mail* leader writers.
The Guardian 1997

George, St [Rel.] Patron saint of England. He is reputed in legend to have slain a dragon, and may have been martyred near Lydda in Palestine some time before the reign of Constantine.

> The archetypal dragon-slayer and rescuer of fair maidens

If Davis wins, he's St. George against the Republican dragon. If he loses, what Republican wants to claim credit for the next few years anyway?
Betsy's Page (blog) 2003

Geppetto [Child. Lit.] The carpenter who makes *Pinocchio, the wooden puppet that comes to life in the story *Le avventure di Pinocchio* (1883) by G. Lorenzini, who wrote under the name of Carlo Collodi.

> A puppet-maker or carpenter

Next to the shoe store was the jewelry store that had always had a clever clockwork display that fascinated me as a child. The display changed every few months and it was like something out of Gepetto's workshop, with little human and animal figures going in and out of miniature buildings, dancing, playing instruments.
JOHN MADDOX ROBERTS *A Typical American Town* 1995

Gestapo [Hist.] The German secret police under the Nazis. It was founded by Hermann Goering in 1933 and was feared for the ruthlessness of its suppression of opposition to the Nazis, especially in its methods of interrogation.

> Used to refer to brutal oppression, interrogation, or torture

There would have been a place in the Gestapo for the lady; she had a way of interrogation that could reduce the sturdiest girls to tears in the first five minutes.

JOHN FOWLES *The French Lieutenant's Woman* 1981

Naturally, civil libertarians come out of the woodwork claiming that Gestapo tactics are being used to stifle freedom of expression.
Interested Participant (blog) 2004

Gethsemane [Bible] A garden lying in the valley between Jerusalem and the Mount of Olives, where Jesus went with his disciples to pray on the night before his Crucifixion and where he was betrayed by Judas.

> ➤ A place of mental or spiritual suffering and endurance

Terrified by the poor girl's suffering—or, better, unable to bear her horror of him—and at the end of his patience, Zampano abandons Gelsomina asleep in the snow, in her own private Gethsemane.
Hudson Review 2004

Getty, Jean Paul [People] (1892–1976) An American industrialist who made a large fortune in the oil industry. Widely described as the world's richest man, Getty was a noted art collector and was also renowned for his miserliness, allegedly keeping a public payphone for the use of his guests.

> ➤ An extremely wealthy man; a miser

Wotan gave off a Getty-like air of miserly, gnawing coldness, his 'black dwarf' counterpart Alberich (the snakishly convincing Peter Sidhom) a warmer than usual humanity.
The Guardian 2000

Gettysburg address [Hist.] A speech delivered on 19 November 1863 by President Abraham *Lincoln at the dedication of the national cemetery on the site of the Battle of Gettysburg, a decisive battle of the American Civil War. It has come to be regarded as a masterpiece of oratory.

> ➤ A great speech or piece of oratory

Bush's call that day was no Gettysburg address, but it served its purpose, and in an era of carefully scripted phrases and considered rhetoric, it was both intensely powerful and moving.
Perspective (ABC Radio National) transcripts 2003

Ghost of Christmas Past [Lit.] The first of the three ghosts to visit *Scrooge in Dickens's *A Christmas Carol* (1843). The ghost allows Scrooge to revisit his childhood in order to shock him into changing his ways.

> ➤ Something that returns after a long absence and reminds a person of their forgotten past

Fergie will recall the amount of matches in which the talismanic Eric Cantona—who returned to Old Trafford like the ghost of Christmas past last week—scored decisive lone goals.
Scotland on Sunday 2004

Giacometti, Alberto [Art] (1901–66) A Swiss sculptor and painter noted for his emaciated and extremely elongated human figures.

> ➤ Used to describe an exaggeratedly tall and thin person or human form

Their Giacometti-like thinness is a withering by pitiless experience.
CAMILLE PAGLIA *Sexual Personae 1990*

Giant Despair [Lit.] A character in *The *Pilgrim's Progress* by John Bunyan (1678, 1684). The giant finds *Christian and his companion Hopeful sleeping in the grounds of his castle, Doubting Castle, and imprisons them in the castle dungeon.

> Used to refer to utter despair or hopelessness

Gibbon, Edward [Lit.] (1737–94) An English historian and author of *The History of the Decline and Fall of the Roman Empire* (1776–88), generally regarded as a monumental work of literature as well as historical analysis. The famous remark 'Another damned, thick, square book! Always scribble, scribble, scribble! Eh! Mr Gibbon?' is usually attributed to the duke of Gloucester.

> Used to describe a wordy or pompous style of writing (adjective *Gibbonian*)

He has swapped Orwellian clarity for Gibbonian fustian.
Backword (blog) 2004

Gibson Girl [Art] **Charles Dana Gibson** (1867–1944) was an American artist and illustrator whose drawings popularized the fashionable ideal of American womanhood in the late 1890s and early 1900s: full-bosomed, wasp-waisted, and dressed in tailored Edwardian style.

> A type of wholesome femininity characteristic of a fashionable young American woman of the late 19th and early 20th centuries

The young girl in the picture had a massed pile of light hair, and a sharp waist, and that plump-softness of skin and slightly heavy Gibson-girl handsomeness of feature that the age so much admired.
JOHN FOWLES *The Magus* 1966

Gilderoy's kite [Hist.] Gilderoy was a famous Scottish highwayman said to have been hanged in 1638, higher than other criminals because of the wickedness of his crimes. To be hanged higher than Gilderoy's kite is to be punished more severely than the very worst criminal.

> 'Higher than Gilderoy's kite' can be used to mean extremely high or out of sight

gild the lily [Shakes.] A phrase drawn from a quotation from *King John*: 'To gild refined gold, to paint the lily'.

> To embellish something excessively, to add unnecessary ornamentation to something

I like his playing, and he is a fine musician, but sometimes it feels like he is gilding the lily in these performances. A simpler approach would have been more characteristic of the composer.
Classical Net reviews 2005

Gilead [Bible] In the book of *Jeremiah, the prophet laments the fact that there is no remedy for the Jews' distress with the words 'Is there no balm in Gilead? Is there no physician there?' The phrase 'balm in Gilead' has come to mean 'comfort in distress, succour'.

> Used when asking whether there is any remedy or consolation

There was a long pause and Junior stood sucking on an eyetooth and studying deep on something, and then he said, What you about to learn is they ain't no balm in Gilead.
CHARLES FRAZIER *Cold Mountain* 1997

Gin Lane [Art] The title of William *Hogarth's famous 1751 print depicting a scene of drunkenness and squalor in 18th-century London. Gin-drinking was widespread at the time, and regarded by many as a cause of crime and other social problems.

> Used to describe a scene of drunkenness and squalor

In his intrepid trip down the stairs he encountered every sort of vice: fornication, crack smoking, heroin injecting, dice games and three-card monte, and more fornication…. 'It's bloody Hogarth,' said Steiner. 'Gin Lane. Except that it's vertical.'
TOM WOLFE *The Bonfire of the Vanities* 1987

Ginnungagap [Norse Myth.] The Great Void, the dark space between *Niflheim, the land of the dead, and Muspelheim, the region of intense heat. It had no beginning or end and no night and day. Also spelt Ginnung-Gap.

> ➢ A complete void; a dark or empty chasm

> The night in all its fulness met her flatly on the threshold, like the very brink of an absolute void, or the antemundane Ginnung-Gap believed in by her Teuton forefathers. For her eyes were fresh from the blaze, and here there was no street lamp or lantern to form a kindly transition between the inner glare and the outer dark.
> THOMAS HARDY *The Woodlanders* 1887

Gioconda, La [Art] An alternative title for the *Mona Lisa*.

> ➢ Used to describe an enigmatic smile

Giotto (Giotto di Bondone) [Art] (*c.*1267–1337) An Italian painter generally recognized as the founder of Florentine painting and the initiator of a more naturalistic and dramatic style in contrast to the rather stiff, two-dimensional design of Byzantine art. According to the story in Vasari's *Lives of the Artists* (1550), when the Pope sent for an example of Giotto's work before commissioning him to paint in St Peter's, he drew a perfect circle with one turn of his hand.

> ➢ Mentioned in the context of someone drawing a perfect circle

> Coincidentally, or perhaps by design—like Giotto drawing a perfect freehand O—Norman Lewis from his first to his last book came full circle, beginning and ending in the Spain of 1934.
> *Saga Magazine* 2004

glasnost [Hist.] The policy of more political openness which was initiated in the Soviet Union by the leader Mikhail Gorbachev from 1985.

> ➢ Any policy of increased political openness

> The way the Chinese handled the 1990 Asian Games does not augur well for those who believe the Olympics could mean a Soviet-style glasnost and openness in China.
> *Sunday Herald* 2001

Gloucester [Shakes.] In *King Lear*, the earl of Gloucester has his eyes put out by the duke of Cornwall. The blinding of Gloucester is one of the most gruesome scenes in Shakespeare.

> ➢ Mentioned in the context of someone being blinded

Godfather [Cin.] The common term for the head of an American Mafia family, popularized by the 1972 film *The Godfather* (based on Mario Puzo's novel), together with its two sequels. The original Godfather, Don Corleone (played by Marlon Brando in the film), is succeeded by his son Michael (played by Al Pacino). The films document the power struggles and vendettas between the Corleones and other Mafia families.

> ➢ A ruthless and powerful head of a criminal dynasty or organization

> Set in Rock Island, Illinois in 1929, it tells the story of Michael O'Sullivan, the chief hitman for John Looney, the town's Irish Godfather of crime.
> *Special Circumstances (blog)* 2005

Godiva, Lady [Hist.] (d. 1080) An English noblewoman, wife of Leofric, earl of Mercia. According to a 13th-century legend, she rode naked through the marketplace of Coventry, clothed only in her long, golden hair, to persuade her husband to reduce the heavy taxes he had imposed on the people. All the townspeople stayed indoors and refrained from watching, except for *Peeping Tom.

> A naked woman among other people who are clothed; a woman with extremely long hair

To say I was cold would be like saying Lady Godiva was underdressed.
KATHY REICHS *Death du Jour* 1999

There have always been hair fashions and most women have run the gamut from gamine to Lady Godiva before settling for something serviceable in between.
Sunday Herald 2000

Godot [Theatre] In Samuel *Beckett's play *Waiting for Godot* (1952), two tramps, *Estragon and Vladimir, discuss philosophical issues while they await the arrival of the mysterious character Godot. Godot never does arrive.

> A long, seemingly endless, wait for someone or something can be described as like 'waiting for Godot'

But waiting for a political scene that won't inspire loathing is probably like waiting for Godot.
Taipei Times 2003

They are all fleeing from the Machiavellian clutches of a divide-and-rule movie producer, cryptically referred to as KL, who has a Godotesque capacity for haunting the conversation without ever appearing.
Guardian 2004

Godzilla [Cin.] A huge fictitious dinosaur-like monster who was aroused from the seabed by an atomic explosion and threatened to destroy Tokyo. He first appeared in a 1955 film, and later in several sequels.

> A gigantic, rampaging, destructive monster

Team Bush now stomps down the halls of power like Godzilla trampling the streets of Tokyo.
AlterNet: Arianna Huffington columns 2002

Goebbels, Joseph [Hist.] (1897–1945) Hitler's minister of propaganda. He had control of the press and radio, and used these in order to control the flow of information to the German public and thus further the Nazi cause.

> A propagandist

I mean, let's face it, the propaganda that the car industry puts out would give Goebbels and Stalin a run for their money in terms of pure Utopian disinformation.
BEN ELTON *Inconceivable* 1999

Goldberg, Rube (Reuben) [Art] (1883–1970) A US comic-strip artist known for his drawings of ludicrously complex machinery designed to perform simple everyday tasks.

> Used to describe any unnecessarily complicated and inefficient machine, structure, or system

The thing [space shuttle] was then, and is now, a Rube Goldberg contraption of breathtaking audacity. It's an airplane clamped onto the side of a highly explosive booster rocket, as if with a rubber band.
Whole Earth 2002

What a Rube Goldberg monstrosity: layer upon layer of weird safeguards and limitations just to make sure that the new system can do what the current system already does, namely provide a guaranteed, stable retirement income for old people.
KEVIN DRUM *Political Animal* 2005

Golden Fleece [Gk Myth.] The fleece of pure gold taken from the ram that carried Phrixus through the air to Colchis on the Black Sea. Phrixus sacrificed the ram to *Zeus and offered its fleece to Aeetes, king of Colchis, who hung it from an oak tree guarded by a dragon that never slept. *Jason set out with the Argonauts to find and recover the Golden Fleece, which he did with the help of *Medea.

> Something of great value, especially something that is difficult to obtain

Everyone is looking for it. It's like the search for the Golden Fleece or the fountain of youth—a better way to burn fat and show off that chiseled six-pack.
Men's Fitness Magazine 2002

golden goose [Fairy tales] In a traditional tale, a goose which laid golden eggs. It was killed in an attempt to possess the source of this wealth, which as a result was lost.

> A continuing source of wealth or profit that may be exhausted if it is misused

TV broadcasting companies should remember that it is viewership ratings that fetch them advertisement revenue. Let them not kill the golden goose, in this case the viewers, by making it too expensive for them to watch TV.
The Hindu 2004

Goldilocks [Fairy tales] A little blonde-haired girl in the traditional story 'Goldilocks and the Three Bears'. She visits the bears' house, eats the little bear's porridge (which is neither too hot nor too cold, but 'just right'), and is eventually found by the bears asleep in his bed.

> A person with light blonde or golden hair; also used to refer to a choice or preference that is 'just right', balanced between two extremes

'Fish,' he said to the beard, 'this is Goldilocks.' I smiled rigidly. I am not a blonde.
MARGARET ATWOOD *The Edible Woman* 1969

What do your competitors charge? That is a good place to start. Like Goldilocks, you do not want to be too hot or too cold. You want to be just right.
USA Today 2005

Golgotha [Bible] A hill, just outside Jerusalem, where *Jesus was crucified. Golgotha is also known as *Calvary—both names come from words, in Aramaic and Latin respectively, meaning 'the Place of the Skull'.

> An experience of intense mental suffering or sacrifice

For Russia, these four years from Barbarossa to Berlin are the Golgotha, the national crucifixion, the sacrifice that would redeem the country in the eyes of the world.
chrenkoff.blogspot.com 2005

Goliath [Bible] The Philistine giant who issued a challenge to single combat to any opponent from the *Israelite army. The challenge was accepted by the young *David, who slew the over nine-foot tall Goliath with a stone from a sling.

> A large or powerful person or organization, especially one being challenged by someone small and weak

Fischer was a maximalist, a killer, and he slew the Goliath of Soviet chess.
The Independent 1992

Gollum [Lit.] In J. R. R. *Tolkien's *The Hobbit* (1937) and *The Lord of the Rings* (1954–5), Gollum is a former hobbit named Smeagol who has been transformed by the power of the One Ring (his 'precious') he once possessed into a repulsive but pitiful creature. Gollum accompanies Frodo *Baggins on part of his quest to destroy the ring but, consumed by a desire to regain possession of it, is a furtive and untrustworthy guide.

> Someone who is unwilling to share a prized possession

Upon giving the disc an inaugural whirl, my feelings morphed from mere family pride into Gollum-like covetousness, and I've guarded our copy ever since.
Pitchfork.com record reviews 2004

Worse than that, the grasping, indolent toad made absolutely no effort to clear the rest of the table so that once he was back in his lair, nursing his precious bottle like Gollum, the dirty glasses and stained napkins remained for half an hour, mocking us, until I myself stacked them up and took them to the kitchen.
GILES COREN *The Times* 2005

Gomorrah *See* SODOM AND GOMORRAH.

Gone with the Wind [Cin.] The title of a novel by Margaret Mitchell, set during the American Civil War and made into a film in 1939 starring Clark Gable and Vivien Leigh. At the centre of the plot is the romance between Scarlett *O'Hara and the dangerously dashing Rhett *Butler.

➤ Mentioned as an example of glamorous or overblown romanticism

That Gore kiss: Rodin it was not, far less Gone with the Wind, but it sure as heck did wonders for the vice-president's ratings. A minute or two of mingled body fluids and suddenly the wooden man in the suit becomes the all-American lover-boy.
Sunday Herald 2000

good cop, bad cop [Cin.] An expression referring to scenes in police films in which a suspect is interrogated by two police officers. In some such scenes, in a deliberate strategy, one officer is aggressive and hostile, while the other is apparently gentle and sympathetic.

➤ Referring to a situation in which someone is dealt with (especially by a pair of people) alternately in a sympathetic and a hostile manner

Appropriate for a song that often has the feel of an interrogation, there's a kind of good cop/bad cop dynamic at work here, as though the reasonable side of Wright's personality holds sway over the verses while the easily agitated half routinely wades in to throw a temper tantrum.
Eye Weekly 2004

Goodfellow, Robin *See* PUCK.

Good Samaritan [Bible] One of *Jesus's parables tells of a Samaritan who stopped to help a victim of thieves left wounded by the roadside and already ignored by a priest and a *Levite, both of whom passed by on the other side. The Samaritan, by contrast, 'had compassion, and went to him and bound up his wounds, pouring on oil and wine; then he set him on his own beast and brought him to an inn, and took care of him'. Inhabitants of Samaria would have been regarded by the Jews as enemies and outcasts, having split from mainstream Judaism.

➤ Used to describe a person who is helpful and compassionate, especially to a stranger in adversity

That Brian Cassidy from the hotel, he was going to let her die right there, but a Good Samaritan in the garage, he sometimes feeds her on the sly when Mr Cassidy isn't watching, he called for an ambulance.
SARA PARETSKY *Ghost Country* 1998

Goody Two-Shoes [Child. Lit.] The heroine of a 1765 children's book by John Newbery, published under the full title *The History of Little Goody Two-Shoes; Otherwise called, Mrs Margery Two-Shoes. With the Means by which she acquired her Learning and Wisdom, and in consequence thereof her Estate.* An orphan who is delighted with a pair of new shoes (from which she gets her nickname), Margery becomes educated and ultimately wealthy through her own virtue and industry.

> ➤ A smugly virtuous person; someone who is 'too good to be true'

I shouldn't gloat and I don't smoke, but there was something strangely magnificent about John Reid's straight-sets victory over Miss Goody Two Shoes, aka Patricia Hewitt, in the Cabinet battle over smoking in English pubs last week.
Scotland on Sunday 2005

Goons [Radio] *The Goon Show* was an extremely popular BBC radio comedy series which ran from 1952 to 1960. The Goons were originally Peter Sellers, Harry Secombe, Spike Milligan, and Michael Bentine, and the off-beat humour was expressed through a set of regular characters, including *Eccles and *Bluebottle, who spoke in silly voices and were involved in absurd plots.

> ➤ Mentioned in the context of absurd humour

It sounds like the scenario for a Goon Show, but in the 1930s New Zealand did, in fact, experience an epidemic of exploding trousers.
The Science Show (programme transcripts) 2004

Gordian knot [Leg. & Folk.] Gordius was a peasant who was chosen king of Phrygia, whereupon he tied the pole of his wagon to the yoke with an intricate knot. An oracle prophesied that whoever undid it would become the ruler of all Asia. *Alexander the Great is said to have simply cut through the knot with his sword.

> ➤ A complex problem or task; 'to cut the Gordian knot' is to solve a seemingly inextricable problem by force or by evading the conditions that caused the problem in the first place

Prime Minister Junichiro Koizumi on Tuesday cut the Gordian knot by sacking his foreign minister of nine months, Makiko Tanaka. With one stroke Koizumi not only solved his legislative problems but gave some relief to many of Japan's diplomatic allies.
Asian Political News 2002

Gordon, Flash [Cart. & Com., Cin.] The spaceman hero created by the American cartoonist Alex Raymond in 1934 and featuring in various radio, television, and film serials. He has many adventures in space, notably on the planet Mongo, where he combats the evil emperor Ming the Merciless.

> ➤ A space-age adventurer; someone in a dangerous predicament (reminiscent of the cliff-hanging scenes with which episodes of *Flash Gordon* would habitually end)

Over the past few weeks it has been obvious that GM is in more trouble than Flash Gordon, with Automotive News showing the drastic cuts that CEO Rick Wagoner has had to announce for the ailing automaker.
Pattaya Mail 2005

Gorgon [Gk Myth.] The Gorgons were three sisters, Stheno, Euryale, and *Medusa (the only mortal one), who had snakes for hair and the power to turn anyone who looked at them to stone.

> ➤ A frightening or repulsive woman

She was wearing something very like a man's evening suit, made in dark velvet, and looked remarkably elegant. I was beginning not to notice her Gorgon face.
ROBERTSON DAVIES *The Manticore* 1972

Goshen [Bible] The fertile region in Egypt allotted to *Jacob and the *Israelites, where there was light during the plague of darkness: 'there was thick darkness in all the land of Egypt three days…but all the people of Israel had light where they dwelt'.

> ➤ A place of plenty and comfort; a place of light

It's a bleak and barren country there, not like this land of Goshen you've been used to.
GEORGE ELIOT *Adam Bede* 1859

Gotham *See* WISE MEN OF GOTHAM.

Goths [Hist.] A Germanic people who, along with the *Vandals, Visigoths, *Huns, etc.,
overran part of Roman Europe in the 4th and 5th centuries AD.

> ➤ Used to suggest the idea of ravaging invasion

Lord's is still here, the sun can still shine, England can still win a Test match, God is still,
after all, in his heaven and, contrary to initial impressions, all is right with the world. The
Goths and the Vandals are farther from the gate than we feared, those things we hold
dear are yet undestroyed and mere anarchy is not loosed upon the earth after all.
SIMON BARNES *The Times* 2004

Götterdämmerung [Myth.] In Germanic mythology, the Twilight of the Gods, their
destruction and that of the world in a final battle with the forces of evil. This is the title of the
last opera in Wagner's *Ring Cycle*.

> ➤ Used to refer to the cataclysmic downfall of a powerful organization or regime

That same night at the national stadium, England faced their gotterdammerung against
the All Blacks.
Scottish Rugby 1991

Gould, Jay [People] (1836–92) A US railroad financier and speculator. His efforts to corner
the gold market are said to have caused the financial panic of *Black Friday, on 24 September
1869.

> ➤ Mentioned in the context of financial predatoriness

But you can't make Milton K. Rogers rich, any more than you can fat a hide-bound colt. It
ain't *in* him. He'd run through Vanderbilt, Jay Gould, and Tom Scott rolled into one, in less
than six months, give him a chance, and come out and want to borrow money of you.
W. D. HOWELLS *The Rise of Silas Lapham* 1885

Goya (Francisco José de Goya y Lucientes) [Art] (1746–1828) A Spanish painter and etcher.
He became official portrait-painter to the Spanish court, producing portraits of extraordinary,
sometimes brutally frank, realism. Goya also painted society portraits, many of women dressed
in the style of a *maja*, in traditional black Spanish dress with black lace mantilla. His set of 65
etchings *The Disasters of War* (1810–14) depict the French occupation of Spain and express the
cruelty and horror of war through scenes of death, execution, pillage, and famine. One such
engraving, called *Great Exploits with Dead Men*, depicts mutilated corpses hanging from a tree.

> ➤ Used to evoke a picture of death, mutilation, and the horror of war

Three bodies hung from the branches, pale in the shadow, as monstrous as Goya etchings.
JOHN FOWLES *The Magus* 1966

It is collective memory that Spielberg relies on in the film's first twenty-five Goyaesque
minutes of war horrors rather than the actual mind and experience of the aged veteran
we see in the cemetery.
Journal of Popular Film and Television 2002

Grable, Betty [Cin.] (1916–73) A US film actress and dancer whose 'million-dollar legs'
made her the most popular pin-up of the Second World War. She was a curly-haired blonde
with a peaches-and-cream appeal.

> ➤ A woman with attractive legs

[Muhammad Ali's] legs were long and beautifully formed. Framed by the bottom seam of his white trunks and the tops of his white socks and boxing slippers, they were the equivalent of Betty Grable's legendary gams.
Observer Sport Monthly 2003

Graces [Gk Myth.] Three beautiful goddesses, Aglaia, Thalia, and Euphrosyne, daughters of *Zeus, who personified charm, grace, and beauty, which they bestowed upon the world as physical, intellectual, artistic, and moral qualities. Artistic depictions of the goddesses, such as Antonio Canova's sculpture *The Three Graces* (1813–16), often show them embracing in a tight huddle.

➤ A group of three beautiful women

The girls from the pop group Liberty X [are] doing their best to present themselves as the best of friends by huddling together and looking like a contemporary, clothed version of the Three Graces. By standing so close together, they create the impression that you couldn't slip a piece of paper, let alone a disagreement, between them.
Scotland on Sunday 2005

Gradgrind, Thomas [Lit.] The chief character in Dickens's *Hard Times* (1854). He believes in 'facts and calculations', thinking he is following the precepts of utilitarianism. He brings these principles to the task of raising his five children, ruling out their imagination and creativity and starving them of affection.

➤ A person who adheres too strictly to a set of rules or principles; one who believes only in cold, hard facts

Obviously the ideal of education for its own sake, which is at the heart of every civilised society, will suffer as businesses demand a utilitarian curriculum. No business believes poets are more important than accountants. The loss would matter less if the new Gradgrinds were providing Britain with coherent and demanding vocational education to replace the widely ridiculed NVQs.
The Observer 1997

Grandison, Sir Charles [Lit.] The hero of Samuel Richardson's novel *The History of Sir Charles Grandison* (1753–4). He was intended to represent the author's ideal of a perfect English gentleman, a model of formal courtesy and chivalric magnanimity.

➤ A courteous English gentleman; used to refer to a manner or deportment thought to reflect such qualities (adjective *Grandisonian*)

Maggie actually forgot that she had any special cause of sadness this morning, as she stood on a chair to look at a remarkable series of pictures representing the Prodigal Son, in the costume of Sir Charles Grandison, except that, as might have been expected from his defective moral character, he had not, like that accomplished hero, the taste and strength of mind to dispense with a wig.
GEORGE ELIOT *Mill on the Floss* 1860

Grandma Moses *See* MOSES, GRANDMA.

Grand Old Duke of York [Nurs. Rhym.] According to the rhyme,

The Grand Old Duke of York,
He had ten thousand men,
He marched 'em up to the top of the hill
And he marched 'em down again.

The historical duke referred to was Frederick Augustus, Duke of York and Albany (1763–1827), second son of George III. He commanded the English army in Flanders.

> Used to refer to something rising to a certain point and then immediately falling again

With long-term interest rates, it has been like the Grand Old Duke of York. Having been marched back up to the top of the hill, they've been marched right back down again over the past three months.
The Independent 2004

grassy knoll [Hist.] A reference to conspiracy theories surrounding the assassination of President John F. Kennedy in 1963. According to those who do not accept that Lee Harvey Oswald acted alone, the real assassin was an unidentified gunman on a 'grassy knoll' overlooking the route of the motorcade in Dallas.

> A way of referring to any suspected conspiracy

If this problem is to be properly answered we need to determine where the 'second' memory card is or whether it even exists. Heh. Second shooter theory. All we need now is a grassy knoll.
Scoop 2004

Gray, Dorian [Lit.] In Oscar *Wilde's novel *The Picture of Dorian Gray* (1890), an extraordinarily handsome young man who remains youthful-looking while the portrait he has had painted ages on his behalf and reflects the ravages of his inner moral corruption.

> A person who looks unnaturally young, especially if they are also suspected of having a somewhat degenerate lifestyle; sometimes the reference is to 'the portrait in the attic'

'My old hero Tony Benn says Churchill would be kicked out of the Labour party now for being too left wing,' says Bremner. 'The entire point of Blair was that he was going to restore our faith in politics. I think there must be a Dorian Gray painting of Blair somewhere in the attic.'
The Sunday Times 2004

Hopkins is the Dorian Gray of boxing; he never seems to get old.
Boxing Insider 2004

Great Depression [Hist.] A prolonged period of economic depression in the United States, Europe, and elsewhere during the 1930s following the Wall Street stock market crash in 1929.

> Mentioned in the context of an economic slump or widespread unemployment and poverty

Great Divide (Continental Divide) [Places] Another name for the Rocky Mountains, a range of mountains in North America that extends from the US–Mexico border to the Yukon territory in northern Canada.

> A boundary marking a fundamental division between two groups or states

For the ever-growing masses of English speakers, basic communication is now a breeze. The Babel of old hardly interfere, and instead adds richness and texture to life in Europe. But for those on the other side of the Great Divide, Europe's unification—its opportunities and pitfalls alike—is still shrouded in mystery.
Business Week Magazine 2001

Great Escape, The [Cin.] The title of a 1963 film about a mass escape by Allied prisoners of war from a German prisoner-of-war camp during the Second World War. The film was based on a book of the same title by Paul Brickhill.

> A mass escape from a prison; a sporting victory achieved after defeat had seemed inevitable

To their credit they kept fighting to the end and despite trailing 77–61 with 3:55 left, Gillespie almost pulled off another great escape with a succession of baskets and when he drained two threes in 18 seconds.
The Kingdom (Killarney, Co. Kerry 2003

Greatheart [Lit.] A character in Part 2 of *The *Pilgrim's Progress* by John Bunyan (1684), who escorts and guards Christiana and her children on their pilgrimage. He slays *Giant Despair and overcomes various other monsters.

> A courageous hero or warrior

> He may be stern; he may be exacting; he may be ambitious yet; but his is the sternness of the warrior Greatheart, who guards his pilgrim convoy from the onslaught of Apollyon.
> CHARLOTTE BRONTË *Jane Eyre* 1847

Great Leap Forward [Hist.] An unsuccessful attempt made under Mao Zedong in China 1958–60 to speed up the process of industrialization and improve agricultural production by reorganizing the population into large rural collectives and adopting labour-intensive industrial methods.

> A dramatic change or advance, often an unsuccessful one

> For Mr Blair, a Prime Minister on his last lap, a third term is his final chance to make his Great Leap Forward.
> *Guardian* 2005

Great Wall of China [Places] A fortified wall in northern China, extending 2400 kilometres (1500 miles) from Kansu province to the Yellow Sea north of Beijing. It was first built in the 3rd century BC, as a protection against Turkish and Mongol invaders. Most of the present wall dates from the Ming dynasty.

> A protective barrier; a massive construction

> For all the French talk of erecting a cultural Great Wall of China against Americanism, the closest you can come in Europe to New Jersey or northern Virginia is the sprawl of dormer-bungalows, malls, fast-food joints and broken marriages that surrounds large French cities—just the kind of background from which both girls came.
> *The Independent* 1998

> We're like a brick manufacturer at the start of the construction of the Great Wall of China. Intel delivers the basic building blocks that will be used in a massive worldwide infrastructure construction project for years to come.
> *Canadian Shareowner* 2001

Great White Hope [Sport] The term coined for a white boxer who might beat Jack Johnson, the first black boxer to be world heavyweight champion (1908–15). There were a succession of unsuccessful white challengers until Jess Willard beat Johnson in 1915.

> A person who is expected to achieve great things or bring success; someone on whom people's hopes are centred

> Michael Howard may be a changed man—in a week he has gone from the grim reminder of failed Tory governments to the Great White Hope of his party and from shadow chancellor to expectant leader of the opposition—but some things will always remain the same.
> *Scotland on Sunday* 2003

Greek chorus [Theatre] In ancient Greek tragedy, a group of performers who comment on the main action, typically speaking and moving together.

> A group of people offering comments on a situation as it unfolds

The interviews form a kind of Greek chorus, a child's version of the half-comprehended adult action that takes place around them.
Scotland on Sunday 2002

Greeks bearing gifts [Gk Myth.] The phrase 'Beware Greeks bearing gifts' alludes to *Laocoön's words of warning to the Trojans not to admit the large wooden horse, supposedly an offering to *Athene, into the walls of Troy: 'Timeo Danaos et dona ferentes' ('I fear the Greeks even when they bring gifts').

➤ Mentioned in the context of a gift or peace offering given with a suspected intention of doing harm

Beware of Greeks bearing gifts—unless of course they're in the tourist business. The industry is expecting an Olympic-sized exodus following the end of the games and there are some appealing prices around.
The Sunday Times 2004

Grendel [Lit.] The ferocious monster who terrorizes the court of the Danish king Hrothgar in the Old English poem *Beowulf*. Grendel is fought and slain by the Geatish hero Beowulf, after which Grendel's mother comes after Beowulf to avenge her son's death, only to be herself killed.

➤ A monstrous beast

It therefore goes without saying that back in my own playing days not only were people better mannered but the ball was a real beast of a thing, a globular Grendel fashioned from bloody hides stitched together with gristle and pumped full of pain and rage.
HARRY PEARSON *Guardian* 2008

Gretchen [Lit.] The simple, innocent girl seduced and then abandoned by *Faust in Goethe's *Faust* (1808).

➤ A girl thought to resemble Gretchen; a typically German girl or woman

She is, and will most likely remain, the last woman I made love to. Love? Can I call it that? What else can I call it. She trusted me. She smelled the blood and the horror and did not recoil, but opened herself like a flower and let me rest in her for a moment, my heart shaking, as we exchanged our wordless secret. Yes, I remember her. I was falling, and she caught me, my Gretchen.
JOHN BANVILLE *The Book of Evidence* 1989

Gretna (Gretna Green) [Places] A village in the Dumfries and Galloway region of Scotland just north of the English border. It was formerly a popular place for couples eloping from England to be married according to Scots law, without the parental consent required in England for those who were under age.

➤ Used to refer to elopement

'Do not ask me, sir,' Remington says coldly. 'I am not here to give you the directions to Gretna. You will not from this moment see my niece nor are you to attempt to open any communication with her, open or clandestine.'
TIMOTHY MO *An Insular Possession* 1986

Grimm [Child. Lit.] The brothers **Jacob** (1785–1863) and **Wilhelm** (1786–1859) Grimm published their collection of traditional fairy tales between 1812 and 1822. Many of the tales, such as 'Hansel and Gretel', deal with such primitive childlike fears as being deserted by parents or being attacked by wild animals.

➤ Mentioned in the context of a situation that resembles a fairy tale, especially a frightening or gruesome one

You want to be careful with weights though—don't overdo it or you'll end up looking like something that lives under a bridge in a Grimm fairy tale. If you catch yourself telling anyone you'll grind their bones to make your bread, it's time to take a few weeks off.
Imprint Online 2005

Grim Reaper [Leg. & Folk.] A cloaked figure wielding a scythe, the traditional personification of death.

> A way of referring to death

Finally, be sure to buy some term life insurance. For about $100 a month, you can make sure that your family will have $1 million if the Grim Reaper shows up a tad too soon.
USA Today 2003

Grinch [Child. Lit.] In the US children's story *How the Grinch Stole Christmas* (1957) by Dr Seuss, the Grinch is a mean-spirited creature whose heart is 'two sizes too small' and who hates the idea of Christmas. He tries to spoil Christmas for the people of Whoville by stealing their presents, food, decorations, and Christmas trees, but finds on Christmas morning that everyone is singing and celebrating despite his efforts.

> A mean-minded spoilsport, especially at Christmas time

You could call this bill the Grinch tax. If it comes in time for Christmas, it's going to be a tax on toys and shoes and baby clothes and all sorts of things that are important to American families.
CNN transcripts: Lou Dobbs Tonight 2003

Please can you get me his autograph? How many times have I heard that from friends before setting off to interview a player. It's not that I'm a Grinch but the answer tends to be 'no'.
MARK POUGATCH *The Times* 2004

Griselda [Lit.] The heroine of the last tale of Boccaccio's *Decameron* (1353), used by Chaucer for 'The Clerk's Tale' (*c.*1387) in *The Canterbury Tales*. Griselda's husband, the Marquis Walter, subjects her to various cruelties to test her love and patience, including making her believe that her children have been murdered and that he intends to divorce her and remarry. Griselda bears his cruelty to the end, when her children are restored to her and her husband accepts her again as his wife.

> A patient or obedient wife

Clifford didn't look happy but he went. I waited, hands folded in my lap like patient Griselda.
SARAH LACEY *File under: Deceased* 1992

Groundhog Day [Cin.] 2 February in the United States, the day when the groundhog is said to come out of its burrow at the end of hibernation. According to tradition, if the weather is sunny enough for the groundhog to see its own shadow, then this is supposed to portend six more weeks of winter weather. In the 1993 film *Groundhog Day*, a TV weather presenter finds himself reliving the same day over and over again.

> Something is 'like Groundhog Day' when an experience is being repeated again and again

It's starting to feel like Groundhog Day after every Rovers game these days. Another game, another 1–0 defeat and another worried glance over the shoulder at the closing relegation pack.
Bolton Evening News 2005

Grub Street [Lit.] The name of a street in Moorgate in London, inhabited in the 17th and 18th centuries by minor or impoverished writers and journalists.

➤ Used to refer to the world of literary hacks

This is also an envy free zone because I am so far removed from Grub Street with its horrible toxins. In a metropolis as a writer you get clogged up with these. *www.thevacuum.org.uk* 2004

Grundy, Mrs [Lit.] An off-stage character from Thomas Morton's play *Speed the Plough* (1798), whose name is repeatedly invoked with the words 'What will Mrs Grundy say?' In the play she represents conventional propriety and prudery.

➤ A prude; 'Grundyism' is the narrow-minded condemnation of unconventional beliefs or behaviour

Hardy's delicacy of description serves a number of purposes. First, and most simply, he could not be as frank on matters of sexual detail as he might have liked. Mrs Grundy—in the form of his editors and publishers—would not let him. JOHN SUTHERLAND *The Literary Detective* 2000

Grünewald, Mathias [Art] (*c.*1460–1528) A German painter whose most famous work, the nine-panel *Isenheim Altar*, contains scenes of figures suffering, with twisted limbs and contorted postures. The central panel of the altar depicts the crucifixion of Christ, with Christ's body distorted by the torture of the Cross and covered with festering wounds.

➤ Used in the context of grotesque horror

The truly nightmarish element in the flashback sequence is not the death of Tony Gadelo—that is, as the gentle Reverend Mr. Playfair remarks, 'just one of those things,' the sort of accident that might happen in any sport involving strong physical contact—but the press photographers, figures updated from Bosch or Grunewald, who climb through the ropes once the ringside physician has pronounced death. *Eire-Ireland: Journal of Irish Studies* 2001

Guantanamo Bay [Places] The US naval base in Cuba. Since 2002 part of the base has been used as a high-security detention centre for suspected al-Qaida and Taliban prisoners captured in Afghanistan and elsewhere.

➤ Used in the context of detention, especially when without trial and for an indefinite period, and perhaps involving human rights abuses and torture

Asylum seekers and advocates said detention centers like the tan brick former warehouse in Queens are a little like local Guantanamos, in the sense that the asylum detainees have no way to know how long they will be locked up. *OUP Incomings* 2004

Guerre, Martin [People] A 16th-century Gascon peasant who disappeared from his village for nine years. Subsequently a certain Arnaud du Thil, bearing a close resemblance to Guerre, presented himself as the missing man and was accepted by Guerre's wife as her husband. He was later revealed as an impostor by the true Martin Guerre. The story is the subject of the film *Le Retour de Martin Guerre* (1982).

➤ Someone who returns after a long absence

Guinevere [Arth. Leg.] The wife of King *Arthur and the lover of *Lancelot. Her adulterous affair with Lancelot is seen as contributing to the destruction of the *Round Table and ultimately to Arthur's death.

➤ The wife of a leader, especially when involved in an adulterous affair

Before that winter, Jagger had met her once or twice at parties, but after he had occasion to see the dumpy flat where the Dunbars lived, he looked anew at the blonde with the amazing body and smile. Faithfull brought out the Lancelot in him. She was too fair to be stuck in such dismal surroundings. Soon Jagger began sleeping with his Guinevere.
Sunday Herald 2001

Gulag Archipelago [Hist.] The name of the system of forced-labour camps in the Soviet Union, specifically in the period 1930–55, in which hundreds of thousands, perhaps millions, died. The term became widely known in the West in the 1960s and 1970s with the translation of Alexander Solzhenitsyn's works, notably *The Gulag Archipelago*.

➤ An oppressive prison-like environment

It is highly likely that some of these people (genuine refugees as well as illegal immigrants) will be condemned to remain indefinitely in detention behind barbed wire fences on these islands at our expense. I sincerely hope I'm wrong, but it looks to me like we are in the process of building our own little Gulag Archipelago.
Sydney Morning Herald Webdiary 2001

Gulliver, Lemuel [Lit.] The hero of Jonathan Swift's satire *Gulliver's Travels* (1726). In the first part of the book, Gulliver is shipwrecked on the island of Lilliput, a land inhabited by tiny people only 6 inches tall. In a famous episode, Gulliver wakes on the shore of Lilliput and finds himself unable to move, his arms and legs tied down to the ground. In his next adventure, Gulliver visits Brobdingnag, a land inhabited by giants who are as tall as steeples. He visits many other strange lands, encountering a range of curious people and creatures.

➤ A giant dwarfing those around him; a small person among giants; someone who is restricted in some way, especially by petty constraints

Having stabbed one leader in the back, he felt he could not do it again. Besides, he owed Margaret Thatcher no loyalty—and he feels genuine loyalty to Major. Bound by Lilliputian cords, the great Gulliver could do nothing but hope.
The Observer 1995

The smaller university presses such as Edinburgh and Manchester are but Lilliputians to Oxford's Gulliver.
Daily Telegraph 1995

Gummidge, Worzel [Child. Lit.; TV] The talking scarecrow with straw hair who is the central character of a series of children's books by Barbara Euphan Todd, later televised.

➤ A person with a scarecrow-like appearance

Charlie Dimmock is to make-up what Worzel Gummidge was to dress sense!
GINA SNOWDOLL *Eeeeeks It's a Blog* 2001

Gunga Din [Lit.] Rudyard *Kipling's poem 'Gunga Din' (1892) tells of an Indian water-carrier who is killed bringing water to a wounded English soldier in the battlefield. The poem ends with the famous lines:

> Tho' I've belted you an' flayed you,
> By the livin' Gawd that made you,
> You're a better man than I am, Gunga Din!

➤ Mentioned (usually in the phrase 'you're a better man than I am, Gunga Din') when expressing admiration for someone's daring, courage, or selflessness

But to try and keep an airplane upright via needle-ball-airspeed in turbulence and storm penetration? You'd be a better man than I, Gunga Din.
Plane and Pilot Magazine 2001

Gunn, Ben [Lit.] The marooned pirate in Robert Louis Stevenson's adventure story *Treasure Island* (1883). Abandoned on the island by his shipmates, he has spent three years alone, living on 'goats and berries and oysters', and dreaming of toasted cheese.

> ➤ A castaway
>
> It tells how in 1999 she took her three sons to Pigeon Island at the eastern end of the Solomon Islands. She wanted them to share her experience of the Ben Gunn life while she researched the story of Diana Hepworth, a former Vogue model who has lived in the South Seas for the past half century.
> *Sunday Herald* 2000

Gunpowder Plot *See* FAWKES, GUY.

Gurth [Lit.] In the opening chapter of Walter Scott's novel *Ivanhoe* (1819), the swineherd Gurth is described wearing a brass collar welded round his neck and engraved with the words 'Gurth, the son of Beowulph, is the born thrall of Cedric of Rotherwood'.

> ➤ Mentioned when describing something such as a collar or ring that cannot easily be removed
>
> Between them [the bull's nostrils], through the gristle of his nose, was a stout copper ring, welded on, and irremovable as Gurth's collar of brass.
> THOMAS HARDY *The Mayor of Casterbridge* 1886

Gyges [Leg. & Folk.] (*c*.685–*c*.657 BC) A Lydian shepherd who, according to the story told by *Plato, descended into a chasm, where he found a horse made of brass. He opened its side and found inside it the body of a man of great size. Gyges removed from the man's finger a brazen ring which, when he wore it, made him invisible. He subsequently used this ring to make himself known to the queen, marry her, and usurp the crown of Lydia's king *Candaules.

> ➤ Mentioned in the context of invisibility
>
> By their subjugation of the press, the political powers in America have conferred on themselves the greatest of political blessings—Gyges' ring of invisibility.
> *AlterNet: Norman Solomon columns* 2004

Hades [Gk Myth.] Also known as *Pluto, the brother of *Zeus and *Poseidon and the lord of the underworld, the abode of the spirits of the dead. Those who died were said to have gone to the house of Hades. The name later came to refer to the place itself, a place of perpetual darkness and gloom. The lowest region of Hades, called *Tartarus, was reserved for the punishment of the wicked for their misdeeds.

> ➤ A way of referring to Hell or eternal punishment

> He stood motionless, undecided, glaring with his eyes, thinking of the pains and penalties of Hades.
> ANTHONY TROLLOPE *Barchester Towers* 1857

> On we went for many minutes in absolute awed silence, like lost souls in the depths of Hades.
> H. RIDER HAGGARD *She* 1887

Hagar [Bible] The Egyptian maid of *Abraham's wife, *Sarah. Hagar bore Abraham a son, *Ishmael. After Sarah gave birth to *Isaac, Hagar and Ishmael were driven out of Abraham's household by Sarah and took flight into the desert.

> ➤ An outcast

> Beside the milk-bush sat the Kaffir woman still—like Hagar, he thought, thrust out by her mistress in the wilderness to die.
> OLIVE SCHREINER *The Story of an African Farm* 1883

Haggard, Rider [Lit.] (1856–1925) An English writer of thrilling adventure novels. Many of his novels are set in Africa, drawing on the time he spent in South Africa in the 1870s. His best-known novels are *King Solomon's Mines* (1885) and *She* (1889).

> ➤ Mentioned in the context of adventures, expeditions, safaris, etc. in Africa

> 'You're looking for adventure,' I cried; 'Well, you've found it here. The devils are after me, and the police are after them. It's a race that I mean to win.' 'By God,' he whispered, drawing his breath in sharply, 'it is all pure Rider Haggard and Conan Doyle.'
> JOHN BUCHAN *The Thirty-Nine Steps* 1915

> If it all sounds like Cecil B. de Mille's architect on a date with H. Rider Haggard's interior decorator, this may be an injustice.
> JOHN BORTHWICK *Travel Intelligence* 2005

halcyon days [Gk Myth.] Fourteen days of calm weather, believed in ancient times to occur about the winter solstice when the halcyon (a mythical bird usually identified with a species of kingfisher) was brooding. The bird was said to breed in a nest floating at sea, charming the wind and waves into calm.

> ➤ A period of time in the past that was idyllically happy and peaceful

If you're itching to recall the halcyon days of rail travel, there are 100 or so private cars in the U.S. certified to ride on Amtrak or VIA Rail Canada trains, and about half of them are available for hire.
BusinessWeek Magazine 2004

Ham [Bible] One of *Noah's sons. According to the book of Genesis, he disrespectfully mocked his father when he saw him drunk and naked. In return Noah cursed Ham's son *Canaan, prophesying that he would be 'the lowest of slaves' to his brothers. This episode was sometimes used in the 19th century as a biblical justification of African slavery, black people being referred to as 'children of Ham' or 'sons of Ham'.

➤ A way formerly of referring to black people

...he turned his nose full upon a small Kaffir of two years old. That small, naked son of Ham became instantly so terrified that he fled to his mother's blanket for protection...
OLIVE SHREINER *The Story of an African Farm* 1883

He has the heart of a poet and a king, and it is God's curse that he has been born among the children of Ham.
JOHN BUCHAN *Prester John* 1910

Hamadryad [Class. Myth.] A nymph who lived in trees and died when the tree died.

➤ A beautiful young woman

'I shall be sitting for my second portrait then,' she said, smiling. 'Will it be larger than the other?' 'Oh, yes, much larger. It is an oil-painting. You will look like a tall Hamadryad, dark and strong and noble, just issued from one of the fir-trees, when the stems are casting their afternoon shadows on the grass.'
GEORGE ELIOT *The Mill on the Floss* 1860

Hamlet [Shakes.] A legendary prince of Denmark, the hero of the play of the same name (1604). Hamlet is a tormented character, devastated by the death of his father and remarriage of his mother, and uncertain as to what action to take. He is obsessively introspective and delivers long soliloquies expressing his mental anguish, most famously his contemplation of suicide in the speech beginning 'To be, or not to be: that is the question.'

➤ Someone who talks at length, expressing anxieties, doubts, or unhappiness; someone who is fatally indecisive

I said I wanted to be best man, I said I wanted a church wedding. I went on about it. I started shouting. I came the Hamlets a bit. I was drunk at the time, if you must know.
JULIAN BARNES *Talking It Over* 1991

The biggest problems, analysts say, have been his Hamlet-like indecisiveness and his hands-off management style in a tech industry that increasingly demands speed and conviction.
BusinessWeek Magazine 2001

handwriting on the wall *See* WRITING ON THE WALL.

➤ A warning of impending disaster

Microsoft saw the handwriting on the wall regarding the future of travel agency commissions (virtually a thing of the past), and promptly exited the travel agency business by selling their interest in Expedia.
USA Today 2003

Hanging Gardens of Babylon [Hist.] One of the Seven Wonders of the World, said to have been built by *Nebuchadnezzar (*c.*600 BC) for his wife Amytis, who longed to be reminded of the mountains and greenery of her native Media. Built in a series of terraces, the gardens were irrigated by a hydraulic system, using water from the Euphrates.

> ➤ An impressive or elaborate garden

> While it seemed like a really great idea at the time to design your own re-creation of the Hanging Gardens of Babylon, in hindsight it's a little more time consuming than you'd envisioned.
> *The Helpful Gardener* 2003

Hannibal [Hist.] (247–182 BC) A Carthaginian general who in the second Punic War attacked Italy via the Alps, which he crossed in 218 BC with an army of about 30000 and 40 elephants. Hannibal inflicted a series of defeats on the Romans over a period of sixteen years but failed to take Rome itself. After being recalled to Africa to defend Carthage he was defeated at Zama by Scipio Africanus in 202 BC. Hannibal has subsequently enjoyed a reputation as one of history's great military geniuses.

> ➤ A military commander; mentioned (together with elephants) in the context of a journey or operation presenting enormous logistical challenges

> The problem with a representative sample is that it involves the complex sort of long-distance logistics that got Hannibal and a troop of elephants over the Alps, and that is just the quantitative focus groups, never mind the qualitative bits.
> *Namibia Economist* 2003

Hansel and Gretel [Child. Lit.] A brother and sister who appear in a traditional fairy story first published by the Brothers *Grimm. Abandoned in a forest by their parents, the terrified children come across a house made of bread, cakes, and sweets. The house in fact belongs to a witch, who imprisons the children and plans to eat them. Hansel and Gretel succeed in killing the witch by pushing her into her own oven, and escape back to their parents. In some versions of the story, they find their way home by following a trail of breadcrumbs they have left.

> ➤ Children lost or abandoned; mentioned (together with breadcrumbs) in the context of following a trail to safety

> As I watched Scratch, I realized that while I was learning quite a bit about this topic, I was still as lost as Hansel and Gretel in the forest. I had no trail of breadcrumbs to follow as the movie went from point A to B to C.
> *DVD Verdict* 2002

'Happy Days Are Here Again' [Mus.] The title of a song written by Milton Ager and Jack Yellen and first recorded in 1929. It was used as Franklin D. Roosevelt's campaign song in the 1932 presidential campaign.

> ➤ Used to convey optimism

> You hear it all around you. The U.S. economy is in recovery; stimulus efforts are finally paying off. The stock market is ripping and roaring and happy days are here again.
> *Financial Sense Online* 2004

Happy Hooligan *See* HOOLIGAN.

Happy Islands [Class. Myth.] The place to which people in classical times believed the souls of heroes and the good were conveyed to a life of bliss. They were also known as the *Islands of the Blest or the *Fortunate Isles.

> ➤ Heaven or paradise

Hardy, Andy [Cin.] The Hardy family appeared in a series of Hollywood films between 1937 and 1947. They were portrayed as a typical all-American family who embodied homely small-town values. In 1942 the films were accorded a special Academy Award 'for representing the American Way of Life'. The clean-living teenager Andy Hardy was played by Mickey Rooney, often associated with the phrase 'let's do the show right here'.

➤ A wholesome, all-American boy

'It was a bunch of young people not realizing the gravity of what they were doing,' Winans said. It sounded like a strange inversion of an Andy Hardy movie—let's put together an insider-trading ring.
The Black Table 2003

hare and the tortoise [Lit.] 'The Hare and the Tortoise' is the title of one of *Aesop's fables. It tells the story of a hare who is so confident that he can win a race with a tortoise that he takes a nap. When he awakes, he finds that the tortoise has plodded slowly but surely to the finishing line and the hare is unable to sprint fast enough to beat him.

➤ Two people or institutions, one of which moves swiftly while the other makes slow, steady progress

Science and the law are like the hare and the tortoise: as science streaks ahead, the law lumbers after.
Scotland on Sunday 2005

Harpagan [Lit.] The titular miser in Molière's comedy *L'Avare* (The Miser). When forced to choose between the casket containing his treasure and the woman he loves, he chooses the treasure.

➤ A miser

In old-fashioned times, an 'independence' was hardly ever made without a little miserliness as a condition, and you would have found that quality in every provincial district, combined with characters as various as the fruits from which we can extract acid. The true Harpagons were always marked and exceptional characters.
GEORGE ELIOT *The Mill on the Floss* 1860

harpies [Class. Myth.] Fierce, rapacious monsters with the heads and bodies of women and wings and claws of vultures (originally from the Greek *harpuiae*, meaning 'snatchers').

➤ A cruel, grasping, or shrewish woman

And all the time, as we were pitching it in red hot, we were keeping the women off him as best we could, for they were as wild as harpies.
ROBERT LOUIS STEVENSON *The Strange Case of Dr Jekyll and Mr Hyde* 1886

Harvey [Cin.] A six-foot-tall rabbit created by Mary C. Chase in her 1944 comic play *Harvey* and popularized in a 1950 film of the same name. Harvey is invisible to everyone except the drunken Elwood P. Dowd.

➤ An imaginary or invisible companion

Hauser, Kaspar [People] (1812–33) A German foundling who mysteriously appeared in Nuremberg in 1828, aged 16, dressed in peasant clothes, and behaving like an infant. He later claimed to have been reared in isolation, spending most of his life confined in a small underground cell. Speculation about his true origins included the theory that he was the rightful heir to the Grand Duchy of Baden.

➤ A mysterious foundling or feral child

To any stray inheritor of these primitive qualities found, like Caspar Hauser, wandering dazed in any Christian capital of our time, the good-natured poet's famous invocation, near two thousand years ago, of the good rustic out of his latitude in the Rome of the Caesars, still appropriately holds.
HERMAN MELVILLE *Billy Budd* 1924

Havisham, Miss [Lit.] A character in Dickens's *Great Expectations* (1861) who was jilted by her bridegroom on her wedding day and spent years afterwards sitting in her room alone, wearing her wedding dress.

➢ A reclusive woman; a jilted bride

I love Magda and Jeremy. Sometimes I stay at their house, admiring the crisp sheets and many storage jars full of different kinds of pasta, imagining that they are my parents. But when they are together with their married friends I feel as if I have turned into Miss Havisham.
HELEN FIELDING *Bridget Jones's Diary* 1996

If you find yourself standing in your living room approximately half an hour before guests are due to arrive, wondering if anyone is going to show up, congratulations. You are in distinguished company. Everyone who has ever thrown a party has had the Miss Haversham fantasy.
BreakupGirl 2000

Haw-Haw, Lord [People] (1906–46) The nickname given to William Joyce, who made propaganda broadcasts in English from Nazi Germany. The nickname referred to his drawling nasal delivery, thought to mimic the 'haw-haw' quality supposedly typical of upper-class people.

➢ Someone who spreads or broadcasts propaganda

The entire article is scandalous propaganda indeed worthy of Lord Haw-Haw.
dissectleft.blogspot.com 2004

Hawking, Stephen [Science] (b. 1942) An English theoretical physicist whose main work has been on quantum gravity and black holes. Confined to a wheelchair because of a progressive disabling neuromuscular disease, he performs his complex mathematical calculations mentally. He is the author of *A Brief History of Time* (1988).

➢ An extremely intelligent man

In front of an ecstatic but still disbelieving crowd Newcastle out-played, out-fought and, most of all, out-thought their visitors, whose coach is supposed to be the game's Stephen Hawking.
The Guardian 1997

Who would think you'd need Stephen Hawking-like intelligence to assemble some poles and drape canvas over them?
DiverNet.com: Travel 2004

Heart of Darkness [Lit.] The title of a novel (1902) by Joseph Conrad, in which the narrator Marlow journeys by river deep into the jungle of the Belgian Congo in search of the ivory trader Mr Kurtz. He finds that the once civilized and compassionate Kurtz has descended into savagery.

➢ A place of savagery and barbarism; the dark or depraved side of human nature

The train from London to Norfolk is like Heart of Darkness—the further you get towards Norwich, the louder beat the tribal drums, the more fear enters your heart.
www.plasticbag.org (blog) 2001

If you appreciate movies that don't compromise on their comedic journey into the heart of darkness, this is for you.
ReelViews 2003

Heathcliff [Lit.] The passionate gypsy hero of Emily *Brontë's romantic novel *Wuthering Heights* (1847). He has long dark hair and a rugged, wild attractiveness.

> ➤ A passionate, rugged romantic hero

Dominic, as always, had positioned himself slightly back from the family group, his black suit and darkly brooding eyes giving him a touch of Heathcliff.
LAUREN HENDERSON *The Black Rubber Dress* 1997

He seemed much younger than her, had Heathcliff-type hair and wore jeans.
The Independent 1997

Heath Robinson, William [Art] (1872–1944) An English cartoonist who drew humorous cartoons of absurdly ingenious and complicated machines which performed simple everyday tasks. Like that of Rube *Goldberg, his name has become synonymous with any device or system that seems unnecessarily complicated.

> ➤ Used to describe something ingeniously or ridiculously overcomplicated in design or construction

One gets a curious impression of high technology combined with primitive improvisation, of something slightly Heath Robinson about the whole endeavour. On one page the airship is shown attached at its nose to the purpose-built docking mast at Cardington but stabilised along its length with cables attached on the ground to cricket-pitch rollers!
Journal of Transport History 2001

Hebe [Gk Myth.] The goddess of youth, daughter of *Zeus and *Hera. She had the power of restoring the aged to youth and beauty. Hebe attended on Hera and was the cup-bearer of the gods, in which role she was later succeeded by *Ganymede. Her Roman name was Juventus.

> ➤ A woman in her early youth

Girlhood just ripening into womanhood…Upon my word—a very Hebe!'
ANNE BRONTË *The Tenant of Wildfell Hall* 1848

Hecate [Gk Myth.] In some Greek myths, one of the forms of the triple-formed goddess *Artemis: *Selene in the sky, Artemis on the earth, and Hecate in the underworld. Later Hecate was regarded as the goddess of dark places, often associated with ghosts and sorcery and worshipped with offerings at crossroads. In statues Hecate was often represented in triple form, with three heads or three bodies standing back to back. She appears with the three witches in *Shakespeare's *Macbeth* (1623).

> ➤ Mentioned in the context of witchcraft or to refer to something that is composed of three parts

I have a great abomination of this learned friend; as author, lawyer, and politician, he is triformis, like Hecate.
THOMAS LOVE PEACOCK *Crotchet Castle* 1831

Hector [Gk Myth.] The leading Trojan hero in the *Trojan War, eldest son of Priam and *Hecuba. He was killed in single combat by *Achilles, in revenge for the death of Patroclus. Achilles then dragged his body behind the wheels of his chariot three times round the walls of Troy. *Homer's *Iliad* ends with the funeral of Hector.

> ➤ A heroic warrior

Mind you, Olivier and St. Clare were both heroes—the old thing, and no mistake; it was like the fight between Hector and Achilles.
G. K. CHESTERTON *Father Brown Stories* 1931

Hecuba [Gk Myth.] The wife of King Priam of Troy and mother of numerous children, including *Hector, *Paris, *Cassandra, and *Troilus. *Homer's *Iliad* tells of her suffering and grief during the *Trojan War as she witnesses the deaths of many of her sons at the hands of the Greeks, in particular the slaying of her eldest son, Hector, by *Achilles and the desecration of his body.

> A bereft and mourning woman; mentioned in the context of terrible grief, especially as the result of the death of one's children

Heep, Uriah [Lit.] The shrewd, deceitful clerk of the lawyer Mr Wickfield in Dickens's *David Copperfield* (1850). Feigning humility, he describes himself as 'so very 'umble', while repeatedly wringing his hands. He insinuates his way into Mr Wickfield's confidence and becomes one of his partners. Heep uses this position to defraud people of money, until he is exposed, sent to prison, and condemned to transportation for life.

> Mentioned in the context of obsequiousness and exaggerated self-denigration; used to describe a gesture of rubbing hands together as one speaks

He has these annoying mannerisms—he wrings his hands, just like Uriah Heep!
KATE CHARLES *A Dead Man Out of Mind* 1994

Roth deserves special mention for his role as Oliver Cromwell, initially a weasly little character with a kind of Uriah Heep obsequiousness.
Namibia Economist 2004

Hefner, Hugh [People] (b. 1926) The founder of *Playboy*, an erotic magazine for men, in 1953. He later set up the Playboy chain of nightclubs, whose 'bunny girl' hostesses wore skimpy costumes which incorporated a rabbit's ears and tail.

> Used to suggest sexual permissiveness and a hedonistic lifestyle

Digital distribution is about abundance, efficiency, and convenience; it needs middlemen like Hugh Hefner needs more Viagra.
The Guardian Friday Review 2003

Heidi [Child. Lit.] Johanna Spyri's novel *Heidi* (1881) tells the story of an orphaned Swiss girl who from the age of five is brought up in idyllic alpine surroundings. When she is eight, Heidi is taken to a more prosperous city life in Frankfurt but she pines until returned to the mountains.

> Mentioned in the context of Swiss girls and alpine scenery

In a tight Tyrolean tunic and skirt, embroidered with forget-me-nots, she looked a bit like Heidi.
CHRISTOPHER HOPE *Darkest England* 1996

Heisenberg principle [Science] According to the 'uncertainty principle' in quantum physics deduced by the German physicist **Werner Heisenberg** (1901–76), it is impossible for both the momentum and the position of a particle to be precisely determined at the same time. The very act of observation alters what is being observed.

> Mentioned to describe a situation in which the act of observing something affects or alters what is being observed

But no outsider, no matter how well-intentioned, should be allowed to forget Heisenberg's Uncertainty Principle: one cannot study a phenomenon without somehow

affecting it. Like ecotourism, which has much the same effect on an environment as the supposedly more vulgar kind, contact with other cultures affects them.
www.butterfliesandwheels.com 2004

But there's a media equivalent of Heisenberg's uncertainty principle (which holds that the process of observing a scientific experiment can affect the result—or something like that): The more journalists you have hanging around and reporting that Davos is a secret confab of terribly important people, the less true it is.
www.slate.com 2002

Helen [Gk Myth.] The daughter of *Zeus and Leda who grew into the most beautiful woman in the world. She married Menelaus, and her abduction by the Trojan prince *Paris led to the *Trojan War. Doctor Faustus, in Marlowe's play of that title (1604), calls up the spirit of Helen of Troy and addresses her with these well-known lines:

> Was this the face that launch'd a thousand ships
> And burnt the topless towers of Ilium?

➤ Used when describing a beautiful woman

I, whose loveliness is more than the loveliness of that Grecian Helen, of whom they used to sing, and whose wisdom is wider, ay, far more wide and deep than the wisdom of Solomon the Wise.
H. RIDER HAGGARD *She* 1887

Helicon [Gk Myth.] The largest mountain of *Boeotia, associated with the *Muses. The spring of *Aganippe and fountain of *Hippocrene, believed to give inspiration to those who drank of their waters, were on its slopes.

➤ A way of referring to poetic inspiration

Helios [Gk Myth.] The Greek sun god, represented as a charioteer who each day drove the chariot of the sun pulled by four white horses across the sky from east to west. Helios was later supplanted by *Apollo.

➤ A way of referring to the sun

Hell [Rel.] According to Christian, Jewish, and Islamic tradition, the place of punishment where the souls of the damned are condemned after death. It is described in the Bible as 'everlasting fire, prepared for the devil and his angels' (Matt. 26: 41) and 'a lake of fire, burning with brimstone' (Rev. 19: 20).

➤ A place of great heat; a place of punishment or suffering

Héloïse *See* ABELARD AND HÉLOÏSE.

Hemingway, Ernest [Lit.] (1899–1961) A US novelist, short-story writer, and journalist, whose works include *For Whom the Bell Tolls* (1940) and *The Old Man and the Sea* (1952). He had a reputation for machismo and for celebrating such tough masculine pursuits as big-game hunting, bull-fighting, and deep-sea fishing.

➤ A macho writer, artist, film-maker, etc

Cameron is what used to be quaintly called a man's man. For pleasure, he likes to race cars and shoot guns in the desert. But nothing, he'll tell you, is as 'hard, as physically demanding' as making films. Play sceptical and suggest, for mischief, that messing with images is hardly a proper manly pursuit and he'll turn into Hemingway with a lens.
The Observer 1998

Peckinpah's Hemingwayesque machismo reached self-parodistic levels and beyond.
Bright Lights Film Journal 2004

Henry, Patrick [Hist.] (1736–99) An American political leader and patriot. A few weeks before the beginning of the War of American Independence he made a famous speech urging the American colonies to revolt against English rule. The speech contained the famous words 'I know not what course others may take, but as for me, give me liberty or give me death!'

> ➤ Mentioned in the context of American patriotism or oratory

> I'm flying a flag these days. The Stars and Stripes, Old Glory, America's flag—OUR flag! I've strapped it to my '97 made-in-the-USA Ford Escort, and I'm zipping around town as proudly as anyone else in the red, white and blue, like some modern-day Patrick Henry on wheels.
> *AlterNet: Jim Hightower columns* 2001

> Jimmy Spencer, on the other hand, gives speeches. He's the Patrick Henry of NASCAR. Ask him about the weather or the federal budget or the price of kumquats, and 15 minutes later he'll still be rattling on and on and on.
> *Auto Racing Digest* 2002

Hephaestus *See* VULCAN.

Hera [Gk Myth.] The wife and sister of *Zeus. She was worshipped as the queen of heaven and as a marriage goddess, associated with fertility and childbirth. In many stories she is depicted as jealously enraged by the philanderings of her husband, Zeus. Her Roman equivalent is *Juno.

> ➤ A jealous or wrathful wife

Heraclitus [Philos.] (*c*.500 BC) An early Greek philosopher who maintained that all things in the universe are in a state of constant change and that the mind derives a false idea of permanence of the external world from the passing impressions of experience. His gloomy view of the fleeting character of life led to him being called 'the weeping philosopher'.

> ➤ Mentioned in the context of pessimism

> He laments, like Heraclitus the Maudlin Philosopher, at other Men's Mirth.
> SAMUEL BUTLER *Remains* 1759

Hercules [Class. Myth.] A hero of superhuman strength and courage (called Heracles by the Greeks), usually depicted with a lion-skin, club, and bow. He was the son of *Zeus by Alcmene, wife of Amphitryon. He performed twelve immense tasks, or 'labours', imposed on him by Amphitryon, king of Argos. The labours were as follows:

1. The killing of the lion of Nemea, which Hercules strangled with his bare hands, and whose skin he cut off with its own claws and afterwards wore.
2. The killing of the Lernaean *Hydra, a water-serpent with many heads, each of which when cut off gave place to two new ones. With the help of his companion Iolaus, Hercules seared each neck with a burning torch as he cut off the head.
3. The capture of an incredibly swift stag, the Cerynean Hind, sacred to *Artemis. Hercules had to capture it unharmed, which he did by pursuing it for a year and finally ensnaring it.
4. The capture of a destructive wild boar that lived on Mount Erymanthus. Hercules drove the boar from its lair, then chased it through the snow until it became exhausted.
5. The cleansing of the stables of Augeas, which had never been cleaned out. Hercules accomplished the task by diverting the two rivers Alpheus and Peneus so that they flowed through the stables and washed away the piles of dung.
6. The killing of the carnivorous birds near Lake Stymphalus. He drove them out of the trees by clashing bronze castanets and then shot them down with his bow.
7. The capture of the Cretan wild bull, which Hercules succeeded in bringing back alive to Eurystheus.

8. The capture of the mares of Diomedes, which fed on human flesh. In so doing Hercules fed Diomedes to his own mares.
9. The obtaining of the girdle of *Hippolyta, the queen of the *Amazons.
10. The capture of the oxen of the three-bodied monster Geryon.
11. The obtaining of the golden apples from the garden of the nymphs of the Hesperides. Hercules achieved this with the help of *Atlas, the giant who bore the world on his shoulders.
12. The removal from *Hades of the three-headed dog, *Cerberus, which guarded the entrance to the underworld

After his death he was granted immortality among the gods.

➤ An exceptionally strong or muscular man; a 'Herculean task' is one that is formidably difficult

A man entered who could hardly have been less than six feet in height, with the chest and limbs of a Hercules.
ARTHUR CONAN DOYLE *A Scandal in Bohemia* 1892

He had already been at work on it for more than seven years and as yet, he would say to anyone who asked him about the progress of the book…'It's a labour of Hercules.'
ALDOUS HUXLEY *Point Counter Point* 1928

These cases, and thousands more in scores of other countries, are detailed in *Index on Censorship*, the bimonthly magazine which has just celebrated (though that hardly seems an appropriate word) its 25th anniversary. The magazine has a Lilliputian circulation and a Herculean task: winning for the people of the world one of the most basic of human rights, the freedom of expression.
The Guardian 1997

Hermes [Gk Myth.] The messenger of the gods, identified with the Roman god *Mercury.

➤ A messenger

Her letter was delivered to me one morning a world ago in the pleasant town of Arcady by a helmed and goggled Hermes on a bike.
this-space.blogspot.com 2004

Herne the Hunter [Leg. & Folk.] In English legend, a ghostly hunter with stag's antlers who haunted Windsor Forest. Herne was said to have been in medieval times a keeper in the forest who hanged himself from a tree known as Herne's (or later *Falstaff's) oak. According to *Shakespeare's *Merry Wives of Windsor* (IV. iv), he

> doth all the winter-time, at still midnight,
> Walk round about an oak, with great ragg'd horns;
> And there he blasts the tree, and takes the cattle,
> And makes milch-kine yield blood, and shakes the chain
> In a most hideous and dreadful manner.

➤ Mentioned as an example of something frightening in a forest at night

He anxiously descended the ladder, and started homewards at a run, trying not to think of giants, Herne the Hunter, Apollyon lying in wait for Christian.
THOMAS HARDY *Jude the Obscure* 1895

Hero and Leander [Leg. & Folk.] In the ancient Greek legend or folk tale, Hero lived on one side of the Hellespont (now named the Dardanelles) and her lover, Leander, lived on the other. Every night he would swim across to her, guided by a torch that she held for him. One night there was a storm, the torch went out, and Leander drowned. His body was washed up on the shore the next morning and Hero threw herself into the sea. The story was told in a poem by Musaeus (AD 5-6), and provides the subject matter for poems by Marlowe and Hood.

➢ Tragic lovers (similar to Romeo and Juliet)

Herod and Salome [Bible] Salome was the daughter of Herodias, wife of King Herod Antipas. She danced for her stepfather, the king, 'whereupon he promised with an oath to give her whatsoever she would ask'. Salome was instructed by her mother to demand the head of John the Baptist, as a punishment for John's condemning her marriage. 'And the king was sorry: nevertheless for the oath's sake, and them which sat with him at meat, he commanded it to be given her' (Matt. 14: 6–9).

➢ Alluded to in the context of a woman extracting a reward or promise from a powerful man, especially one that involves violence against someone else

I remembered that he considered all this to be pleasure, as Herod thought Salome's dance was fun until he heard what she wanted as a reward.
EDMUND WHITE *A Boy's Own Story* 1982

Herod the Great [Bible] (*c*.74–4 BC) The Roman king of Judaea who, according to Matthew's Gospel, ordered the Massacre of the Innocents, hoping that by killing all male children under two he would ensure the death of the infant *Jesus.

➢ Mentioned in the context of the killing of children on a large scale

All babies start off looking like the last tomato in the fridge, but 'cute', 'gorgeous' and 'adorable', which were the adjectives Lucy was throwing about the place with gay abandon, struck me as the ravings of an insane and blind woman. Quite frankly, I began to see King Herod in a wholly different light.
BEN ELTON *Inconceivable* 1999

As if Putin could have known that people had sunk to such depths of depravity that they would do a Herod and slaughter the innocents. Beslan is impossible to understand.
Western People 2004

Herriot, James [People] (1916–95) The pseudonym of James Alfred Wight, who used his experiences working as a veterinary surgeon in north Yorkshire as the source for a series of short stories, collected in *If Only They Could Talk* (1970), *All Creatures Great and Small* (1972), and *The Lord God Made Them All* (1981). His amusing and extremely popular stories were made into a British television series as well as a number of films.

➢ Mentioned in connection with a love of animals; a vet

How much fun can that be? Driving up hill and down dale, hitting much loved hamsters and guinea pigs over the head. Dealing with a child's hysteria as you kill its dog. Everyone is expecting James Herriot to turn up, but instead they get Dr Mengele. The Angel of Death.
The Sunday Times 2005

Hesperus *See* WRECK OF THE HESPERUS.

Higgins, Henry [Theatre; Cin.] A professor of phonetics in George Bernard Shaw's play *Pygmalion* (1913) and the later musical *My Fair Lady* (filmed in 1964). He embarks on a six-month experiment to teach the cockney flower girl Eliza Doolittle how to speak properly so that he can pass her off in polite society as a duchess. Professor Higgins has an irascible, bullying manner with his pupil.

➢ A male mentor of a woman; a man who teaches or coaches someone how to speak or behave in a more genteel way

Damien Foster is a self-styled Henry Higgins. He coaches AFL footballers in the finer points of etiquette, grooming, and considerate behaviour—that is, how not to get into drunken scuffles in public places.
Sports Factor (programme transcripts) 2001

High Noon [Cin.] The title of a classic 1952 western starring Gary Cooper. He plays a small-town marshal who, deserted by the rest of the townspeople, has to confront alone a gang of four outlaws who are due to arrive in town on the noon train.

➤ Mentioned when someone is facing a potentially fatal confrontation

Farsley Celtic boss Sinnott has his own derby experiences and knows the unique atmosphere that will confront the players for their High Noon showdown.
thisisbradford.co.uk 2004

Hillary, Sir Edmund [People] (1919–2008) A New Zealand mountaineer and explorer. In 1953 Hillary and Tenzing Norgay were the first people to reach the summit of Mount Everest, as members of a British expedition.

➤ Someone thought of as a climber or mountaineer

Footballers enter their pre-season training phase with a high level of trepidation. Hills that would have Edmund Hillary quaking and road runs that Paula Radcliffe wouldn't tackle in a jeep…
Scotland on Sunday 2003

Hindenburg [Hist.] The name of a German airship, the largest ever built, that was intended to provide a luxury passenger service across the Atlantic. On 6 May 1937, while landing in New Jersey from its inaugural flight, the *Hindenburg* burst into flames and was completely destroyed, with 36 of the 97 people aboard being killed.

➤ A terrible disaster, catastrophe, or failure

An actor who phones in this role or who lacks an inherent likeability will provide the spark to ignite a conflagration until the movie crashes to earth in flaming Hindenburg horror.
DVD Verdict 2002

Hindley, Myra [People] (1942–2002) A woman convicted in 1966, together with her lover Ian Brady, of the notorious Moors Murders, in which several children were sadistically killed and their bodies buried on Saddleworth Moor, near Manchester. She was commonly described in the press as 'the most evil woman in Britain'.

➤ An evil or sadistic woman

The people who conduct animal experiments are scientists, not sadists. But even if they had the morals of Myra Hindley, their work would still be worthwhile.
Spiked Online 2004

Hinnom [Bible] The Valley of Hinnom to the south of Jerusalem was known as the Valley of Slaughter (Jer. 7: 31–2). According to the Bible, it was used for idolatrous worship, with children being burnt alive as sacrifices to the idol *Moloch, and there is a strong association between the name and the fires of Hell.

➤ Used to refer to the fires of Hell; a place of torment

The lightning had struck the tree. A sulphurous smell filled the air; then all was silent, and black as a cave in Hinnom.
THOMAS HARDY *Far from the Madding Crowd* 1874

Hippocrates [People] (*c.*460–377 BC) Probably the most famous of all physicians, although almost nothing is known about him. His name was attached to a body of ancient Greek medical writings which contained diverse opinions on the nature of illness and treatment. The Hippocratic oath, named after him, is an oath stating the duties of physicians, formerly taken by those taking up medical practice.

> ➤ A doctor or healer; a way of referring to medicine
>
> The renowned British Hippocrates of the Pestle and Mortar.
> RICHARD STEELE *The Spectator* 1711

Hippocrene [Gk Myth.] A fountain sacred to the *Muses on Mount *Helicon, created for them by the winged horse *Pegasus, who stamped his moon-shaped hoof. It was believed to give the power of poetic inspiration to those who drank of it. It is alluded to in John Keats's poem 'Ode to a Nightingale'.

> ➤ A way of referring to poetic or literary inspiration
>
> O for a beaker full of the warm South,
> Full of the true, the blushful Hippocrene.
> JOHN KEATS *Ode to a Nightingale* 1820

Hippolyta (Antiope) [Gk Myth.] The queen of the *Amazons, a race of fierce fighting women warriors.

> ➤ A strong or fierce woman
>
> No one…could any longer doubt the speaker to be the British Hippolyta of her epoch, and so the earliest progenitress of Parliament's petticoated invaders.
> *Chambers Journal* 1909

Hiroshima [Places] A city and port on the south coast of the island of Honshu, western Japan. It was the first city to be the target of an atomic bomb, dropped by the United States on 6 August 1945, which resulted in the deaths of more than a third of the city's population of 300 000.

> ➤ Mentioned in the context of destruction on a huge scale
>
> There was every likelihood that they would freeze on Friday, or fry, or vanish in pure energy with nothing left of them but shadows like the men of Hiroshima after the lightburst.
> A. S. BYATT *The Virgin in the Garden* 1978

Hitchcock, Alfred [Cin.] (1899–1980) An English film director chiefly associated with suspenseful thrillers such as *Psycho* (1960) and *The Birds* (1963), in which huge flocks of birds turn on people and attack them.

> ➤ Used to suggest suspense or fear
>
> As I bend over to resume my pyrotechnics there is a whirring sound, as if in response to the peacock's shriek, and when I look up I see a great multicoloured cloud descending. It's the birds, even more of them than I have seen before, covering the sky…I hunch down to protect myself. This is pure Hitchcock.
> ANDRÉ BRINK *Imaginings of Sand* 1996

Hitler, Adolf [Hist.] (1889–1945) The Austrian-born founder of the National Socialist German Workers' Party (Nazi Party) and Chancellor of the Third Reich in 1933–45. Following his appointment as Chancellor of Germany in 1933, he established a totalitarian regime, the Third Reich, proclaiming himself Führer ('Leader'). His territorial aggression led to the Second World War, and his anti-Semitic policies to the *Holocaust.

> A tyrannical or despotic person

Little Hitlers, every one, Diamond thought. How does anything ever get decided these days? Maybe on the orders of a bigger Hitler, like me.
PETER LOVESEY *The Summons* 1995

And within a few weeks, Saddam—and yes, he *is* a venal, cruel, wicked, evil man—was being transformed into the Hitler of Iraq, just as the Israelis had called Yasser Arafat the Hitler of Beirut in 1982, and just as Eden had called Nasser the Mussolini of the Nile in 1956.
The Independent 1998

hobbit [Lit.; Cin.] One of an imaginary race similar to humans, of small size and with hairy feet, in the stories of J. R. R. *Tolkien. They live in burrows and their name was said by Tolkien to mean 'hole-dweller'.

> Used to describe something that is small in size or scale

Valerie Jane lived in a Hansel and Gretel storybook cottage on Crescent Heights, complete with a mock thatched roof and a Hobbit-sized red door that she no doubt needed to duck to enter.
LINDSAY MARACOTTA *Playing Dead* 1999

Hoffa, Jimmy [People] (1913–*c*.1975) A US labour leader, president of the Teamsters' Union (transport workers) from 1957. He disappeared mysteriously in 1975 and is believed to have been murdered.

> Someone who has disappeared in mysterious circumstances

Finding first-rate outfield arms today is like searching river bottoms for Jimmy Hoffa.
Show 1990

Hogarth, William [Art] (1697–1764) An English painter, engraver, and satirist. His series of engravings on 'modern moral subjects', such as *A Rake's Progress* (1735) and *Marriage à la Mode* (1743–5), satirized the vices of both high and low life in 18th-century England. *Gin Lane* (1751), depicting a scene of drunkenness and squalor, is one of Hogarth's most famous prints.

> Used when describing scenes of vice, squalor, prostitution, or drunkenness (adjective *Hogarthian*)

You could be forgiven, should you read the newspapers, for thinking that Britain is in the grip of a Hogarthian booze-fuelled nightmare.
Spiked Online 2004

Holmes, Sherlock [Lit.] An extremely perceptive private detective in a series of stories by Arthur Conan *Doyle. Holmes's exceptional powers of observation and deductive reasoning enable him to solve the seemingly impenetrable mysteries that are brought to him by troubled clients. Probably the most famous fictional detective of all, Holmes plays the violin, smokes a pipe, has an opium habit, and wears a deerstalker. He is a master of disguise. Holmes is assisted by his stalwart associate Dr Watson, with whom he shares rooms at 221B Baker Street, London. His arch-enemy is the criminal mastermind Professor *Moriarty.

> A person demonstrating acute powers of observation and deduction; a person who solves a mystery

At once I took up my pipe, violin and deerstalker like a veritable Sherlock. I have always been an X-marks-the-spot man. 'Let us go and revisit it,' I said briskly.
LAWRENCE DURRELL *Clea* 1960

This is the 'inorganic mineral' theory of the Glasgow chemist Graham Cairns-Smith, first proposed 20 years ago and since developed and elaborated in three books, the latest of

which, *Seven Clues to the Origin of Life*, treats the origin of life as a mystery needing a Sherlock Holmes solution.
RICHARD DAWKINS *The Blind Watchmaker* 1986

Holocaust [Hist.] The name given to the mass murder of Jews and other persecuted groups under the German Nazi regime. In the period 1941–5 more than 6 million European Jews were killed in concentration camps such as *Auschwitz, *Dachau, and Treblinka as part of Adolf Eichmann's 'Final Solution', the Nazi policy of exterminating Jews.

➤ Genocide

Baroness Thatcher stepped up the political pressure for a military crackdown on the Serbs last night—with a call for air strikes, a suggestion that Western inaction had 'given comfort' to the aggressor and a warning of a 'second Holocaust'.
The Independent 1992

Holofernes [Bible] In the Apocrypha, the Assyrian general of *Nebuchadnezzar's forces, who was beheaded by *Judith.

➤ A man who has been beheaded

As I passed, Herr Stroh shuffled out to his front door, rather drunk. He did not see me. He was looking at the clock where it hung in the sunset, he looked up at it as did the quaking enemies of the Lord upon the head of Holofernes.
MURIEL SPARK *The Collected Stories* 1958

Holy Grail [Leg. & Folk.] An object of quest in medieval legend, supposed to be the dish or cup used by *Jesus Christ at the Last Supper and in which Joseph of Arimathea had caught some of the blood of the crucified Christ. By the early 13th century it was closely associated with the Arthurian cycle of legends as a symbol of perfection sought by the knights of the *Round Table.

➤ The object of a long and difficult quest

How many months he will be away we don't know yet, but he is setting out with all the air of a knight in search of the holy Grail.
LAWRENCE DURRELL *Mountolive* 1958

I've won the America's Cup. It's considered the Holy Grail of yachting.
STUDS TERKEL *American Dreams: Lost and Found* 1980

Holy of Holies [Rel.] A sacred inner chamber in the temple in Jerusalem in which the *Ark of the Covenant was kept before it was lost.

➤ A place that is considered to be extremely important or sacred

She discerned that Mrs Wilcox, though a loving wife and mother, had only one passion in life—her house—and that the moment was solemn when she invited a friend to share this passion with her. To answer 'another day' was to answer as a fool. 'Another day' will do for brick and mortar, but not for the Holy of Holies into which Howards End had been transfigured.
E. M. FORSTER *Howards End* 1910

Homer [Lit.] (8th century BC) A Greek epic poet to whom the *Odyssey* and the *Iliad* are traditionally attributed, though it is probable that these were based on much older stories which had been passed down orally. Homer is traditionally supposed to have been blind, and is sometimes referred to as the Blind Bard.

➤ Used to describe an epic journey or voyage, especially one that is hazardous; used to denote actions and events that happen on a grand, superhuman scale or people who perform such actions (adjective *Homeric*)

The papers in South Africa eulogised them [the Springboks rugby team] in Homeric terms.
Daily Telegraph 1995

The story of the yachtsman's rescue—with its primal Homeric resonances of shipwreck and mythic rebirth—delighted the world.
The Guardian 1997

Homer sometimes nods [Lit.] A saying (also found in the form 'even Homer nods') recorded in English from the late 14th century, but deriving ultimately from the Roman poet Horace commenting on the Greek epic poet *Homer, 'I'm aggrieved when sometimes even excellent Homer nods.' 'Nods' here means 'becomes drowsy', implying a momentary lack of attention.

➢ Used to say that even the greatest expert can make a mistake

Conversely it is possible for a competent arbitrator to make a mistake which causes substantial injustice and which needs to be put right by the court but in circumstances where, in the general sense, the applicant retains full confidence in the arbitrator. After all, Homer does sometimes nod.
England and Wales High Court (Commercial Court) Decisions 2000

Hood, Robin *See* ROBIN HOOD.

Hooligan, Happy [Cart. & Com.] An American comic-strip character who appeared from 1900 to 1932, an Irish tramp with a red nose and a tin can for a hat. He was an innocent and an unconquerable optimist despite the fact that his attempts to help himself and others often ended with his falling into the hands of the law.

➢ An innocent optimist

Never tol' you 'bout him. Looked like Happy Hooligan. Harmless kinda fella. Always was gonna make a break. Fellas all called him Hooligan.
JOHN STEINBECK *The Grapes of Wrath* 1939

Hooverville [Places] A name given to shanty towns built by impoverished unemployed people in the United States during the Great Depression. The shanty towns were named after the president of the time, Herbert C. Hoover.

➢ A shanty town

And now in my mind I stood upon the walk looking out across the hole past a Hooverville shanty of packing cases and bent tin signs, to a railroad yard that lay beyond.
RALPH ELLISON *Invisible Man* 1952

Hopper, Edward [Art] (1882–1967) An American realist painter. Works such as *Early Sunday Morning* (1930) and *Nighthawks* (1942) depict scenes from everyday American city life in which static figures appear in bleak settings such as motel rooms, gas stations, and diners, conveying an atmosphere of loneliness and isolation.

➢ Used to describe a scene or mood of solitude, loneliness, or boredom in an urban setting (adjective *Hopperesque*)

Childcott's balding head gleamed briefly as he turned his head to stare out of the window at the Edward-Hopper-type starkness of suburban London after the shops have closed.
SUSAN MOODY *Grand Slam* 1994

Sidewalks and park benches are empty, creating a Hopperesque atmosphere of alienation and detachment.
Art in America 2003

Horatius (Horatius Cocles) [Hist.] (530–500 BC) A Roman hero who volunteered to be one of the last three defenders of a bridge over the river Tiber against an Etruscan army under Lars Porsena intent on invading Rome. Initially, he and two others, Herminius and Lartius, fought on the bank while the Roman army crossed back to Rome and prepared to destroy the bridge. His companions darted across to Rome just before the bridge fell, but Horatius swam back across the Tiber in full armour. The story of Horatius' defence of the bridge is retold in the poem 'Horatius at the Bridge' in *Lays of Ancient Rome* (1842) by Macaulay.

> Mentioned in the context of someone single-handedly defending a bridge or other place

   To the abuse in front and the coaxing behind she was equally indifferent. How long she would have stood like a glorified Horatius, keeping the staircase at both ends, was never to be known. For the young lady whose sleep they were disturbing awoke, and opened her bedroom door, and came out onto the landing.
   E. M. FORSTER *Where Angels Fear to Tread* 1905

   Then Border, who has spent the summer like Horatius on the bridge while Lars Porsena Botham scared off everyone else, edged a slanting Ellison delivery to second slip, and England were through.
   The Guardian 2005

Horn of Plenty *See* CORNUCOPIA.

the horror, the horror [Lit.] The dying words of Mr Kurtz in Joseph Conrad's 1902 novel *The *Heart of Darkness*. They express despair at the realization that beneath an exterior of civilized human behaviour lies the potential for savagery.

> Used, especially humorously, to express disgust or horror

   Back in 2003, two successive early spring frosts wiped out a large amount of vines. In Gisborne, they lost about 90% of the Chardonnay. The horror, the horror.
   Auckland Midweek Magazine 2005

Horsemen of the Apocalypse *See* APOCALYPSE.

Hotspur (Harry Hotspur) [Shakes.] A name given to Sir Henry Percy (1364–1403), son of the first earl of Northumberland. He is a character in *1 Henry IV* (1598). Known for his fiery, uncontrolled temper and impetuousness, he is described in the play as a 'wasp-stung and impatient fool'.

> An impetuous or hot-headed person

   I must say anger becomes you; you would make a charming Hotspur.
   THOMAS LOVE PEACOCK *Crotchet Castle* 1831

Houdini, Harry [People] (1874–1926) A Hungarian-born American magician and escape artist (b. Erik Weisz), famous for his escapes from chains, handcuffs, padlocks, straitjackets, and numerous locked containers.

> Someone who is able to escape from any situation, however dangerous or difficult

   Her wrists and ankles had been cuffed to a solid wooden chair that was bolted to the stone-flagged floor. 'How's she going to make a break?' I asked. 'Unless she happens to be related to Houdini, of course.'
   PAUL JOHNSTON *Body Politic* 1997

   'Thankfully, we got our act together to give ourselves this chance and hopefully now with our support behind us we can do a Houdini and retain our AIL status,' said Quinlan.
   Irish Examiner 2001

Hound of the Baskervilles, The [Lit.; Cin.] The title of a novel by Arthur Conan
*Doyle (1902) featuring the detective Sherlock *Holmes. In the story, set mainly on Dartmoor,
a monstrous and supposedly demonic hound is believed to haunt, and hunt to their deaths,
the Baskerville family, in revenge for their ancestor Hugo Baskerville's crimes.

> ➤ A ferocious dog

> But the red-eye did what the red-eye does. Oh, my Jesus, I look like the Hound of the
> Baskervilles.
> MARTIN AMIS *London Fields* 1989

'House of Usher, Fall of the' [Lit.] The title of one of Edgar Allan *Poe's *Tales of
Mystery and Imagination* (1839), set in an eerie mansion in the vault of which Roderick Usher
has buried his sister alive.

> ➤ Used to evoke mystery and supernatural happenings

> She motioned frantically to him not to make a noise....'My dear, why all this
> Fall-of-the-House-of-Usher stuff?'
> STELLA GIBBONS *Cold Comfort Farm* 1932

> My hair is hanging along my cheeks, my skirt is swaddling about me. I can feel the
> cold damp of my brow. I must look like something out of 'The Fall of the House of Usher.'
> DOROTHY PARKER *The Waltz* 1944

Houyhnhnms [Lit.] In Jonathan Swift's *Gulliver's Travels* (1726), a race of intelligent talking
horses, who have 'a general disposition to all virtues', have no conception of evil, and try
always to 'cultivate reason, and to be wholly governed by it'. They live alongside the barbaric
Yahoos, who resemble human beings but have no intelligence or reason and live entirely
according to their animal instincts.

> ➤ A horse thought of as having human characteristics

Hubbard, Mother [Nurs. Rhym.] In the rhyme, Old Mother Hubbard

> went to the cupboard,
> To fetch her poor dog a bone.
> But when she got there
> The cupboard was bare,
> And so the poor dog had none.

> ➤ Mentioned in the context of a place that is completely empty

> He opened the fridge door only to find the bar filled with bottled water. For Reed it might
> as well have been Old Mother Hubbard's cupboard.
> JOHN WESTCOTT *Den of Thieves* 2006

hubris [Lit.] In Greek tragedy, excessive pride or defiance of the gods, which led to total
failure or destruction, brought about by the avenging goddess *Nemesis.

> ➤ Excessive pride or self-confidence

> In both Japan and the West, the fall of the tiger economies has been read as a simple tale
> of hubris and nemesis.
> *The Observer* 1997

huff and puff [Child. Lit.] A quotation from the folk tale of *The Three Little Pigs*, in
which the *Big Bad Wolf comes to the houses built by the three little pigs and threatens: 'I'll huff
and I'll puff and I'll blow the house down.' The wolf does this successfully with two of the
houses, but is unable to blow down the third house, which is made of bricks.

> ➤ To make threats or try to harm someone, but with no success

Not only did deterrence work then, you could argue it's worked for 10 years now against Saddam, ever since the end of the Gulf War. He's huffed and puffed, but he hasn't really done anything.
CNN transcripts: Late Edition 2002

Hughes, Howard [People] (1905–76) An American millionaire businessman and film producer. He is remembered as being a recluse for the last 25 years of his life, during which time he suffered from obsessive-compulsive disorder, germ phobia, and paranoia.

➤ Used to describe an individual who desires privacy or lives as a recluse; someone demonstrating obsessive-compulsive behaviour, especially in relation to hygiene

But as Olazabal was producing his pyrotechnics, David Gilford was slipping surreptitiously around in 67. This excellent Staffordshire player is as determinedly anonymous as Howard Hughes and despite the presence of microphones in the press interview area, it was still difficult to make out what he was saying.
The Guardian 1995

It wasn't the happiest living arrangement of my life, mainly because the Spanish girl had an obsession with cleanliness to rival Howard Hughes, and I was extremely untidy and never remembered to empty the bin.
Sunday Herald 2000

Hulk (the Incredible Hulk) [Cart. & Com.] A US comic-book character. The scientist Bruce Banner is exposed to gamma ray radiation which causes him to be transformed periodically into the Hulk, a huge, green-skinned, manlike monster of extraordinary strength.

➤ A man of seemingly superhuman strength or proportions

Humphrey, Sir (Sir Humphrey Appleby) [TV] The senior civil servant in the television series *Yes, Minister* (1980–2) and *Yes, Prime Minister* (1986–8). While appearing to defer to his minister and later prime minister Jim Hacker, Sir Humphrey in fact aims to run things behind the scenes as Whitehall deems appropriate.

➤ A senior civil servant or bureaucrat

It is good to know that Sir Humphrey survived the fallout on 1 May and that policy is still in the same old safe pair of hands.
The Observer 1997

Humpty Dumpty [Nurs. Rhym.] A character whose name is taken to refer to an egg:

> Humpty Dumpty sat on a wall,
> Humpty Dumpty had a great fall.
> All the king's horses, and all the king's men
> Couldn't put Humpty together again.

➤ Something fragile, especially when, once damaged, it cannot be restored

It is, we would remind our readers…impossible to make an omelette without first breaking eggs. We…cannot wait to see the great Chinese Humpty Dumpty given a forceful shove off his wall of secrecy and deceit and broke all to pieces. Not all the Emperor's men shall put him together again.
TIMOTHY MO *An Insular Possession* 1986

We should not bang on about Gascoigne throwing it away because in our hearts we always knew that this was a footballer as fragile as Humpty Dumpty with a bout of vertigo.
PAUL WEAVER *The Guardian* 1998

Hunchback of Notre Dame [Lit.; Cin.] Another name for *Quasimodo.

> Mentioned in the context of physical ugliness

Extending this metaphor is Saleem's physical appearance, which makes the Hunchback of Notre Dame look positively pin-up.
Scotland on Sunday 2003

Huns [Hist.] A warlike nomadic people who originated in north-central Asia and overran Europe in the 4th–5th centuries. Led by *Attila, they inflicted devastation on the Eastern Roman Empire, invaded Gaul, and threatened Rome.

> Mentioned in the context of a large number of people moving across an area and causing destruction

Various veterans had told him tales. Some talked of gray, bewhiskered hordes who were advancing with relentless curses and chewing tobacco with unspeakable valor; tremendous bodies of fierce soldiery who were sweeping along like the Huns.
STEPHEN CRANE *The Red Badge of Courage* 1895

Hyde, Mr [Lit.] In Robert Louis Stevenson's *The Strange Case of Dr Jekyll and Mr Hyde* (1886), the separate, purely evil, personality that the physician Dr *Jekyll is able to assume by means of a drug he discovers.

> A person who reveals an unsuspected evil side to their character can be said to be 'changing into Mr Hyde'

Now we are getting to know Mr Hyde. Only he isn't Dr Jekyll's gaudy monster, who trampled a child; he is just a proud little boy who hurt some humble people, and knew it and enjoyed it.
ROBERTSON DAVIES *The Manticore* 1972

'Domestic violence,' said Boehlinger. 'More P.C. crap. All we do is rename things. It's wife-beating! I've been married thirty-four years, never laid a finger on my wife! First he woos her like Prince Charming then it all goes to hell in a handbasket and he's Mr Hyde—she was *frightened* of him, Miss Connor. Scared clean out of her mind. That's why she left him.'
JONATHAN KELLERMAN *Billy Straight* 1998

Hydra [Gk Myth.] A many-headed snake of the marshes of Lerna in the Peloponnese, whose heads grew again as they were cut off. As one of his labours, *Hercules had to kill the Hydra. With the help of his companion Iolaus, he did this by searing each neck with a burning torch as he cut off the head.

> Used when talking about something that seems to be never-ending or indestructible because new parts keep developing

The footnotes engulfed and swallowed the text. They were ugly and ungainly, but necessary, Blackadder thought, as they sprang up like the heads of the Hydra, two to solve in the place of one solved.
A. S. BYATT *Possession* 1990

Yet, it had no real effect. The supplies of cocaine from Colombia remained constant, and as one of the Hydra's heads was cut off, another dozen sprang up to replace it.
MEL STEIN *White Lines* 1997

Hygiea [Gk Myth.] The Greek goddess of health, the daughter of *Aesculapius.

> A way of referring to health

Hymen [Gk Myth.] The son of *Dionysus and *Aphrodite, and the Greek god of marriage, usually represented as a handsome young man crowned with flowers and carrying a torch.

> A way of referring to marriage

I myself sincerely hope that Captain Anderson, gloomiest of Hymens, will marry them aboard so that we may have a complete collection of all the ceremonies that accompany the forked creature from the cradle to the grave.
WILLIAM GOLDING *Rites of Passage* 1980

Hypatia [Philos.] (*c*.370–415) A Greek philosopher, astronomer, and mathematician. She was head of the Neoplatonist school at Alexandria and wrote several learned treatises. She was murdered by Christian fanatics opposed to her Neoplatonist philosophy.

> Mentioned as an example of an extremely intelligent or scholarly woman

'A little bit of a bore sometimes,' Molly went on. 'But mind you, a most charming creature. I've known her since we were children together. Charming, but not exactly a Hypatia.'
ALDOUS HUXLEY *Point Counter Point* 1928

Hyperboreans [Gk Myth.] A fabled race worshipping *Apollo and living in a land of perpetual sunshine and happiness in a distant northerly land 'beyond the north wind'.

> Alluded to as people enjoying perpetual happiness; used to refer to cold northern climes (adjective *Hyperborean*)

It's the unnatural combat of the four primal elements.—It's a blasted heath.—It's a Hyperborean winter scene.—It's the breaking-up of the ice-bound stream of Time.
HERMAN MELVILLE *Moby Dick* 1851

Hypnos [Gk Myth.] The Greek god of sleep, son of Nyx (night).

> A way of referring to sleep

I woke up this morning with the panicky feeling that I'd overslept and was either late for work or going to miss my flight...A few deep breaths and some rubbing of the eyes sent Hypnos and Morpheus packing and I realized that it's only Sunday, I'm not in a hotel and I've got another day until I'm back in the trenches.
bobzyeruncle.com (weblog) 2003

Hyrcania [Places] An ancient mountainous region bordering the Caspian Sea noted for its rough wooded terrain full of serpents and wild beasts.

> Used to describe a wild or inhospitable place

Iago [Shakes.] The villainous ensign in *Othello* (1622). Partly out of anger at being passed over for promotion and partly out of a general, bitter envy of *Othello, Iago brings about an end to Othello's success and happiness by tricking him into believing that his wife *Desdemona has been unfaithful to him. As a result of this, Othello kills first Desdemona and later himself. Although Iago is secretly plotting the downfall of Othello, the latter believes Iago to be completely loyal and honest.

> ➤ Used to suggest scheming duplicity

> Antonino Saragusi is wonderfully insidious as Polinesso, really capturing the man's dangerous, Iago-like charm.
> *The Guardian* 2003

Icarus [Gk Myth.] The son of *Daedalus, who constructed wings which he and Icarus used to fly to freedom from Crete. However, the wings were attached by wax, and when Icarus flew too close to the sun, the wax melted and he fell to his death in the Aegean Sea.

> ➤ Someone who fails because of excessive ambition; someone who tries to fly but fails

> To fly into the air on flapping wings is the goal of two North American engineers. They have already flown a radio-controlled model ornithopter on a flight lasting almost three minutes, and they believe that within three years they could create an ornithopter that would carry a person into the skies—hopefully with more success than Icarus.
> *New Scientist* 1992

> The spyglass allowed him to see spindles, feathery bullets, black shudders or other shudders of indistinct hue, who flung themselves from a taller tree aiming at the ground with the insanity of an Icarus eager to hasten his own destruction.
> UMBERTO ECO *The Island of the Day Before* 1994

Ides of March [Hist.; Shakes.] In the ancient Roman calendar, 15 March. According to Plutarch, a soothsayer warned Julius Caesar to 'beware the Ides of March'. Caesar was assassinated on that day.

> ➤ Mentioned to warn of impending danger; mid-March

> In one form or another, the Red Sox have blown up every season since 1918, and they were in full crisis mode this year even before the Ides of March.
> *Sporting News* 2001

Importance of Being Earnest, The [Lit.] The title of a stage comedy by Oscar *Wilde, first produced in 1895. It concerns the attempts of two fashionable young gentlemen, Jack Worthing and Algy Moncrieff, to court two young women, Gwendolen Fairfax and Cecily Cardew. The play is full of witty dialogue and confusions of identity.

> ➤ Used (often with another word or name substituted for 'Earnest') to say that a particular person or thing is important

> A gaggle of A-list celebrities, including Harry Potter author J. K. Rowling and U2's Bono, gushed with praise for Morrissey in last year's UK Channel 4 documentary about the singer, The Importance of Being Morrissey.
> *www.believermag.com* 2005

Incredible Hulk *See* HULK.

Ingres, Jean Auguste Dominique [Art] (1780–1867) A French painter whose elegant portraits and sensuous female nudes, including *La Grande Baigneuse* (1808), demonstrate his brilliant draughtsmanship.

> ➤ Used to describe a female face or nude figure reminiscent of an Ingres painting
>
> But when I see her in dreams…it is not with that terrible aspect she wore the last time I saw her, when her face could hardly be called a face at all, but with the look of a portrait by Ingres or Goya, a full pale face, with dark, lustrous eyes, a fixed, unchanging regard, and two or three black curls, or crescents of curls, stealing down over her forehead.
> L. P. HARTLEY *The Go-Between* 1953
>
> As Simon watches her leaning into the brightly lit tub, a figure lifted out of an Ingres painting, he is seized with something he has not felt in months: inspiration.
> *Journal of Popular Film and Television* 2000

inquisitor [Hist.] An officer of the Inquisition, a court set up by the Catholic Church, originally in the 13th century, to determine whether individuals were heretics. The inquisitors of both the original Inquisition and the later Spanish Inquisition were known for their ruthlessness and use of torture.

> ➤ Used in the context of any intensive or sustained questioning or 'grilling'
>
> 'The wearing of dark glasses,' she said, 'is a modern psychological phenomenon. It signifies the trend towards impersonalization, the weapon of the modern Inquisitor.'
> MURIEL SPARK 'The Dark Glasses' in *The Collected Stories* 1961

Invasion of the Body Snatchers, The [Cin.] The title of a science fiction film released in 1956 and remade in 1978 and 1993. In the film, alien plantlike pods are able to replicate and replace the population of a small town with physical duplicates, emotionless 'pod people'.

> ➤ Used to describe a situation in which someone's behaviour suddenly and radically alters, or in which everyone starts to conform and lose their individuality
>
> In what can best be described as an Invasion of the Body Snatchers scenario (go to bed a hack and wake up without emotion and hellbent on world domination), another business editor has joined the wonderful world of PR.
> *Sunday Herald* 2002

Invisible Man, The [Lit.; Cin.] The title of a novel by H. G. *Wells, published in 1897, in which a scientist by the name of Griffin discovers a means of making himself invisible. Although he himself is completely invisible, his clothes remain visible, as do his footprints. The story was filmed in 1933 with Claude Rains as the scientist, and there have been numerous other film and television versions.

> ➤ Someone who cannot be seen or has disappeared
>
> Between the arrogant, stretched legs of that colossus ran a stringy pattern of grey footprints stamped upon the white snow. 'God!' cried Angus involuntarily; 'the Invisible Man!'
> G. K. CHESTERTON 'The Invisible Man' in *The Innocence of Father Brown* 1911
>
> Hull City's Rui Marques, signed last summer to a modest fanfare, has not been seen since and could audition for The Invisible Man.
> *Guardian* 2006

Isaac [Bible] In the Old Testament, God commanded *Abraham to take his son Isaac and offer him as a burnt offering. Abraham did as he was bidden: he built an altar, laid wood on it, bound his son, and laid him on the altar. Abraham took a knife and was just about to slay Isaac when the angel of the Lord appeared and said 'Lay not thine hand upon the lad, neither do any thing unto him' (Gen. 22: 12). When Abraham looked up, there was a ram caught in a thicket nearby, which Abraham took and used instead of his son for the burnt offering.

> A child whose life is threatened by a parent; someone who escapes death or danger at the last moment

Then he puts that conclusion to an existential test—the parent and the sick child on the moral precipice, which he compares to Abraham and Isaac.
The New Atlantis 2004

Isaiah [Bible] An Old Testament prophet whose prophecies are contained in the book of Isaiah. He warned the *Israelites that they had adopted foreign or unacceptable religious practices and that they should return to their former religious rites. Isaiah predicted the fall of Jerusalem and of Judah.

> A prophet, or a person who predicts or warns about something

Once the lonely hero of the battle against appeasement in the 1930s, an Isaiah crying out in the desert against Hitler and Nazism, Churchill has come under attack for self-promotion as well as exaggerating his opposition to appeasement before the Second World War.
Contemporary Review 2002

Iscariot, Judas [Bible] The disciple who, in return for thirty pieces of silver, betrayed *Jesus to the Jewish authorities with a kiss of identification. When he learned that Jesus had been condemned to death, he realized the enormity of his betrayal and repented, returned the money to the priests who had paid him, and then hanged himself (Matt. 27: 3–5).

> A person who treacherously betrays a friend; a 'Judas kiss' is an act of betrayal; someone who feels guilt and repentance

Are we to watch our words and stick out our necks to the knives of potential traitors here in this place where we meet to put our minds and hearts in the struggle…are we to sit with Judas in our midst?
NADINE GORDIMER *My Son's Story* 1990

Alan Smith has left Leeds United to join Manchester United. This, apparently, is shocking. Disloyal, treacherous, Judas Iscariot reincarnate before our eyes.
The Times 2004

Iseult *See* TRISTRAM AND ISEULT.

Ishmael [Bible; Lit.] The son of *Abraham by *Hagar, the maid of Abraham's wife *Sarah. Ishmael was cast out when Sarah gave birth to *Isaac. The name is used for the narrator of Herman Melville's *Moby Dick*, the opening words of which are 'Call me Ishmael'.

> An outcast

I always did hate those people…and they always have hated and always will hate me. I am an Ishmael by instinct as much as by accident of circumstances, but if I keep out of society I shall be less vulnerable than Ishmaels generally are.
SAMUEL BUTLER *The Way of All Flesh* 1903

Ishtar [Myth.] The Babylonian and Assyrian goddess of sexual love, fertility, and war.

Isis and Osiris [Egypt. Myth.] Isis was an ancient Egyptian goddess married to her brother, the god Osiris, who was king of Egypt. Together with their son Horus, they formed a trinity.

> Incestuous lovers

If we are in a new world now, then this world's Goddesses are Technology and Trade. They are not opposed to each other…They are siblings, twins, even lovers (don't tut-tut, think of Castor and Pollux, Siegmund and Sieglinde, Van and Ada Veen, Isis and Osiris). *jim.blogspot.com* 2002

Islands of the Blest [Class. Myth.] The place to which people in classical times believed the souls of heroes and the good were conveyed to a life of bliss, often located near where the sun sets in the west. They were also known as the *Fortunate Isles or the *Happy Islands.

➤ Heaven or paradise

There were no lands of sunshine, heavy with the perfume of flowers. Such things were only old dreams of paradise. The sunlands of the West and the spicelands of the East, the smiling Arcadias and blissful Islands of the Blest—ha! ha! JACK LONDON *In a Far Country* 1900

Isolde *See* TRISTRAM AND ISEULT.

Israelites [Bible; Hist.] The Hebrew people who were living in slavery in Egypt at some period during the second millennium BC. They were rescued from their plight by *Moses, who led them to the land of *Canaan, the biblical name for an area of ancient Palestine west of the river Jordan, which had been promised to the descendants of *Abraham by God.

➤ People enslaved and in poverty, or liberated from this plight

'If I go furze-cutting we shall be fairly well off.' 'In comparison with slaves, and the Israelites in Egypt, and such people!' THOMAS HARDY *The Return of the Native* 1880

Ithuriel [Lit.] In *Milton's *Paradise Lost* (1667), one of the cherubim, 'a strong and subtle spirit', who is sent by Gabriel to search for Satan in the Garden of *Eden. Touched by Ithuriel's spear, which 'no falsehood can endure', Satan starts up in his own shape and is ejected.

➤ The touch of Ithuriel's spear can be invoked when describing any touch to a person which provokes a strong reaction

Rainbarrow had again become blended with night when Wildeve ascended the long acclivity at its base. On his reaching the top a shape grew up from the earth immediately behind him. It was that of Eustacia's emissary. He slapped Wildeve on the shoulder. The feverish young innkeeper and engineer started like Satan at the touch of Ithuriel's spear. THOMAS HARDY *The Return of the Native* 1880

Ivan the Terrible [Hist.] (1530–84) Ivan IV, born Ivan Vasilyevich, was the grand duke of Muscovy in 1533–47 and proclaimed himself the first tsar of Russia in 1547. As he grew increasingly paranoid and tyrannical, he conducted a reign of terror against the Boyars (the old Russian aristocracy), executing thousands of people. He consequently acquired the nickname 'the Terrible'.

➤ A fearsome, cruel, or tyrannical person

All Black props have traditionally been employed to frighten small boys into finishing their greens and going to bed when the threat of the bogey man fails. History has endowed them with the sort of reputation that only Ivan the Terrible could envy. *Scotland on Sunday* 2005

Ixion [Gk Myth.] A Thessalian king who tried to seduce *Hera, for which he was punished by being bound to a fiery wheel that revolved unceasingly through the underworld.

➢ Used (often in the phrase 'Ixionian wheel') to suggest endless torment

So, floating on the margin of the ensuing scene, and in full sight of it, when the half-spent suction of the sunk ship reached me, I was then, but slowly, drawn towards the closing vortex....Round and round, then, and ever contracting towards the button-like black bubble at the axis of that slowly wheeling circle, like another Ixion I did revolve.

HERMAN MELVILLE *Moby Dick* 1851

J'accuse [Hist.] The title of the open letter written by Émile Zola to the President of the French Republic protesting at the trial and conviction of Alfred *Dreyfus.

> Used in the context of a passionate accusation or denunciation

> She vents a righteous indignation worthy of Zola's J'accuse! when describing, for instance, the living conditions of urban squatters or the conditions of workers in a factory.
> *Context Magazine* 2003

'Jack and the Beanstalk' [Fairy tales] In the children's story of this name, Jack exchanges his mother's cow for some magic beans from which an enormous beanstalk grows up into the clouds. Jack climbs up and steals treasure from the giant's castle, eventually cutting down the beanstalk and killing the giant.

> Mentioned in the context of something growing rapidly

> The mammoth tree, one of the tallest flowering plants alive, shoots up and up and up, disappearing into the sky like Jack's beanstalk.
> *Outside Online Magazine* 2005

> I was 26 and went from having no ties to having two stepchildren for half the week and then two babies as well. It was a bit like Jack and the Beanstalk: you plant the seeds, and, the next day, wow!
> *The Sunday Times* 2006

'Jack the Giant-Killer' [Fairy tales] The title of an old nursery tale about Jack, the son of a Cornish farmer in the time of King *Arthur. After killing his first giant by trapping him in a pit, Jack acquires a coat that makes him invisible, shoes that give him great speed in running, and a magic sword, and with the help of these he rids the land of giants.

> Someone who defeats a much more powerful opponent

> If her father would but come by in the gig and take her up! Or even if Jack the Giantkiller, or Mr. Greatheart, or St. George who slew the dragon on the halfpennies, would happen to pass that way!
> GEORGE ELIOT *Mill on the Floss* 1860

Jack the Ripper [Crime] The name given to an unidentified English 19th-century murderer. From August to November 1888 at least six prostitutes were found brutally murdered, their bodies mutilated. The crimes were never solved, but the authorities received taunting notes from a person calling himself Jack the Ripper, who claimed to be the murderer.

> A brutal murderer of women; someone who savagely attacks someone

> It was his persistently negative, not to say paranoid, ferocity as a reviewer that brought Churton Collins the opprobrium of his peers...He was a sort of Jack the Ripper of the literary journals.
> *Contemporary Review* 2003

Jacob [Bible] In the Old Testament, the son of *Isaac and Rebecca and twin brother of *Esau, Esau being the first-born. The story of the *mess of pottage tells how one day Esau, returning from the countryside, found Jacob cooking 'red pottage of lentils', or lentil stew. He was extremely hungry and asked for some of the stew. Jacob would only give Esau the food if he swore to sell Jacob his birthright as the elder of the twins. Esau sold his birthright to Jacob and had the stew (Gen. 25: 29–34). In another story, Jacob, with his mother Rebecca's help, dressed as his elder brother Esau in order to obtain the blessing of their father Isaac, who was old and unable to see well. He put on Esau's clothes and his mother put the skins of young goats on his hands and neck so that they would feel hairy like Esau's. Despite recognizing Jacob's voice, Isaac was fooled. He therefore gave Jacob the blessing of the first-born, which should have belonged to Esau.

According to another story, one night Jacob wrestled with a man until the break of day, refusing to release him until he blessed Jacob. The man eventually revealed himself to be an angel.

Jacob fell in love with *Rachel, the daughter of his uncle Laban. He offered to work for seven years in return for Rachel's hand in marriage. At the end of the seven years Jacob was tricked into marrying Leah, Rachel's elder sister. He was given Rachel a week later, after promising to work for a further seven years.

> ➤ Jacob and Rachel can be alluded to as patient lovers; Jacob's pottage is something pleasant and immediately satisfying for which one gives up something far more valuable; someone who tricks or deceives others to gain what he wants; someone wrestling or engaged in a struggle

'Croft's going to marry Bell!' exclaimed Eames, thinking almost with dismay of the doctor's luck in thus getting himself accepted all at once, while he had been suing with the constancy almost of a Jacob.
ANTHONY TROLLOPE *The Small House at Allington* 1862

New Deliverance was borderline charismatic and not the sort of church I felt comfortable attending; but at lunch the day before, Nadine had caught me off guard—a fudge delight cookie has the power to cloud minds—and laid on the guilt. 'Isabel says you went to her and Haywood's church last Sunday and to Seth and Minnie's Sunday before last, but you haven't been to ours in almost two years.' With Jacob's pottage rich and chocolaty on my tongue, I had no quick words with which to resist.
MARGARET MARON *Southern Discomfort* 1993

But finally it is impossible to escape those monsters that devour from the inner depths, and the only ways to vanquish them are either to wrestle with them like Jacob with his angel or Hercules with his serpents, or else ignore them until they give up and disappear.
LOUIS DE BERNIÈRES *Captain Corelli's Mandolin* 1994

Jacobean [Theatre] An adjective describing the plays written during the reign of James I of England (1603–25). The revenge tragedies of this period, such as Webster's *The White Devil* (1612) and *The Duchess of Malfi* (1623) and Middleton's *The Changeling* (1622), typically feature scenes of carnage and mutilation.

> ➤ Used to suggest a situation involving murder, plotting, and revenge

The ensuing drama—with more corpses piled up centre stage than a Jacobean revenge tragedy—appeared to reach crisis proportions with the resignation of Scottish Opera's chief executive, the high-profile Ruth Mackenzie...
Sunday Herald 2000

Jacob's ladder [Bible] At a place that he named Bethel, the Hebrew patriarch *Jacob had a dream: 'And he dreamed that there was a ladder set up on the earth, and the top of it reached to heaven; and behold, the angels of God were ascending and descending on it!' (Gen. 28: 12).

> Used in the context of a way up to heaven; a long ladder or staircase

In our dreams we sometimes struggle from the oceans of desire up Jacob's ladder to that orderly place. Then human voices wake us and we drown.
JEANETTE WINTERSON *The Passion* 1987

Jain [Rel.] Jainism is a non-theistic religion founded in India in the 6th century BC by the Jina Vardhamana Mahavira. One of its central doctrines is non-injury to any living creatures.

> Mentioned in the context of non-violence towards humans, animals or plants

The total abstainer from all forms of animal product enjoys a clear, Jain-like conscience to parade before the rest of us. He or she can claim that his presence on earth hurts no other creature.
JEREMY PAXMAN *The Observer* 1995

James, Jesse [Crime] (1847–82) A US bank and train robber who formed a gang of outlaws with his brother Frank. In 1882 a member of the gang shot Jesse in order to claim the reward on his head.

> Used to describe someone as an adventurous and heroic outlaw

But that night he hadn't pitied himself, he had been imbued with all the self-complacency of the man behind the gun. He had thought condescendingly of Jesse James—such a cheap, two-bit chiseler compared with himself.
CHESTER HIMES *Prison Mass* 1933

Janus [Rom. Myth.] One of the earliest Roman gods, generally represented as Janus Bifrons ('With Two Faces') by a head with two faces looking in opposite directions, one facing forwards and the other facing backwards. He was thus a god of wisdom and knowledge, as he had knowledge of the past and was able to see the future. He was also the god of doorways, and of beginnings and endings.

> Someone with two faces; a person or thing able to face in two directions at once

It is, of course, its essentially schizophrenic outlook on society that makes the middle class such a peculiar mixture of yeast and dough....Now this Janus-like quality derives from the class's one saving virtue, which is this: that alone of the three great castes of society it sincerely and habitually despises itself.
JOHN FOWLES *The French Lieutenant's Woman* 1969

All over the world, nationalism is 'Janus-faced'—it can be liberating and inclusive, or chauvinistic and exclusive.
Inside Indonesia 2001

Jared [Bible] According to the book of Genesis, one of the patriarchs. Jared is supposed to have lived to be 962 years old and was the grandfather of *Methuselah (who lived seven years longer).

> Someone who is very old

It was one of those faces which convey less the idea of so many years as its age than of so much experience as its store. The number of their years may have adequately summed up Jared, Mahalaleel, and the rest of the antediluvians, but the age of a modern man is to be measured by the intensity of his history.
THOMAS HARDY *The Return of the Native* 1880

Jason and the Argonauts [Gk Myth.] Jason, the son of the king of Iolcos in Thessaly, was the leader of the Argonauts in the quest for the Golden Fleece. Among the dangers they faced on their perilous voyage were the Symplegades, or clashing cliffs, which clashed together and crushed ships as they passed between them. At Colchis, King Aeetes agreed to give Jason the fleece provided he accomplished various tasks, including yoking a pair of fire-breathing bulls, and sowing a field with dragon's teeth (from which sprang up armed men). The 1963 film *Jason and the Argonauts* is known for its stop-motion animation and special effects.

> Heroes or adventurers

> On press night next Friday, Ken Wagstaff and Chris Chilton will be there in the audience, and for me, as a kid growing up in Hull, they were living legends. It was like having Jason and the Argonauts down the road.
> *The Press, York* 2004

Jeeves [Lit.] The resourceful and unflappable valet of Bertie *Wooster in a series of novels by P. G. Wodehouse. According to Bertie, Jeeves 'shimmers' into a room: 'There was Jeeves, standing behind me, full of zeal. In this matter of shimmering into rooms the chappie is rummy to a degree. You're sitting in the old armchair, thinking of this and that, and then suddenly you look up, and there he is' (*My Man Jeeves*, 1919).

> The perfect servant, especially one who is efficient, diplomatic, and sober in manner; someone who moves inconspicuously

> Knebworth opened the door and was there with champagne and the tall glasses. Grizel had said to Bone before this that Knebworth had Jeeves' trick of shimmering in. One became aware of him manifesting rather than entering.
> STAYNES and STOREY *Bone Idle* 1993

> The man had already made it clear that he was a stickler for protocol and inclined to be pompous, a Jeeves in police uniform.
> PETER LOVESEY *The Vault* 1999

Jeffreys, Judge (George Jeffreys) [People] (*c*.1645–1689) A Welsh judge who took part in the Popish Plot prosecutions and from 1683 was chief justice of the King's Bench. Judge Jeffreys became popularly known as the Hanging Judge because of his brutal sentencing at the Bloody Assizes of 1685, when he condemned to the gallows 300 or so supporters of the duke of Monmouth's rebellion.

> A cruel or severe judge; mentioned in the context of hanging someone

> Frightfully sorry to keep you waiting, Mater, but I had to say a word to Biggy. He's having a rotten time, and that old Jeffreys of a judge looks as though he was getting measured for a black cap.
> DOROTHY L. SAYERS *Strong Poison* 1930

> 'Sir Frederick Foxgrove was known and respected as a wise judge and just sentencer. His behaviour in Court was always a model of dignity.' In other words, old Foxy was Judge Jeffries without the laughs.
> JOHN MORTIMER *Rumpole's Return* 1980

Jehoshabeath [Bible] According to the Old Testament, Ahaziah was a king of Judah who followed *Ahab in his worship of *Baal instead of God. He was killed by *Jehu, and after his death his mother 'arose and destroyed all the seed royal of the house of Judah' (2 Chr. 22: 10). However, her daughter Jehoshabeath took one of the sons, Joash, and hid him in a bedchamber to keep him safe.

> Someone who saves or protects another person

Jehovah [Bible] An Old Testament name for God used by Christians.

> Used in the context of the severity of divine retribution; the 'voice of Jehovah' can be used to describe a loud and booming voice

Standing as she stood in Grammer Oliver's shoes, he was simply a remorseless Jehovah of the sciences, who would not have mercy, and would have sacrifice; a man whom save for this, she would have preferred to avoid knowing.
THOMAS HARDY *The Woodlanders* 1887

The thousand voices burst out with that almost supernatural sound which choral singing always has. Enormous, like the voice of Jehovah.
ALDOUS HUXLEY *Point Counter Point* 1928

Jehu [Bible] (841–815 BC) A king of Israel, known for driving his chariot very fast and recklessly. According to the Old Testament book of Kings: 'he driveth furiously' (2 Kgs. 9: 20).

➤ A fast or furious driver

A drunken postilion…who frightened her by driving like Jehu the son of Nimshi, and shouting hilarious remarks at her.
GEORGE ELIOT *Adam Bede* 1859

Those who only ever saw him behind a desk supposed the Mercedes was a status symbol. But Sale learnt his trade before mobile phones, when the ability to drive like Jehu could mean the difference between hold-the-front and a page-two filler, and when the need arose he could still burn rubber like a Hollywood stuntman.
JO BANNISTER *The Primrose Switchback* 1999

Jekyll and Hyde [Lit.] In Robert Louis Stevenson's *The Strange Case of Dr Jekyll and Mr Hyde* (1886), Dr Jekyll discovers a drug that allows him to create a separate personality, Mr *Hyde, through which he can express the evil side of his character. Periodically, he changes from the worthy physician into the evil Hyde, and eventually Hyde gains the upper hand over Jekyll.

➤ The term 'Jekyll and Hyde' can be used to refer to someone whose personality appears to undergo an abrupt transformation, particularly from gentleness to aggressiveness or violence; a person who reveals an unsuspected evil side to their character can be said to be changing into Mr Hyde

I told her that she had had a lucky escape from my father, but she defended him, saying, 'He is another person when he is on his own with me. He is so sweet and kind.' Yes, and so was Dr Jekyll.
SUE TOWNSEND *The Growing Pains of Adrian Mole Aged 13¾* 1984

Under normal circumstances Bruce was a happy drinker, not one of those sad Jekyll and Hyde characters who turn into social psychopaths with their third glass.
BEN ELTON *Popcorn* 1996

Jephthah's daughter [Bible] Jephthah was a judge of Israel who sacrificed his daughter to fulfil a rash vow he had made that if victorious in battle he would sacrifice the first living thing that he met on his return home.

➤ Used in the context of the sacrifice of one's child

Jeremiah [Bible] An Old Testament prophet whose prophecies are contained in the book of Jeremiah. These concern the unhappy fate that awaits the *Israelites because they have rebelled against God. The book of Lamentations, foretelling the destruction of Jerusalem, is traditionally attributed to him.

➤ Someone who predicts doom or disaster

His was a soft world, fuzzy with private indecisions masked by the utterance of public verities which gave him the appearance of a lenient Jeremiah.
TOM SHARPE *Porterhouse Blue* 1974

Since we have so far emerged comparatively unscathed from all these predicted
plagues and catastrophes, it is hard to take too seriously the latest Jeremiah-like
pronouncements of Lacey and his colleagues about beef.
The Observer 1996

Jericho [Places] A town in Palestine, one of the world's oldest settlements and believed to
have been occupied from at least 9000 BC. According to the Bible, Jericho was a Canaanite city
destroyed by the *Israelites after they crossed the Jordan into the *Promised Land, led by
*Joshua. Its walls were flattened by the shout of the army and the blast of the trumpets.

> ➤ Mentioned in the context of walls falling down or a deafening sound

> As Jenny Long drove to the hospital the next morning she sang softly to herself. She
> was quite confident that it wouldn't be long before Harry gave in and said it was time
> they got married. After all, even Jericho fell in the end.
> MAX MARQUIS *Written in Blood* 1995

> Since when has doing slightly better than average been worthy of praise? When
> you're trying to encourage a kid who struggles at Maths maybe, but when you're
> dealing with bloated multi-millionaire musicians who blow their own horns so loud
> they could fell the Walls of Jericho? Come on.
> *www.londonist.com* 2005

Jeroboam [Bible] One who rebelled against *Solomon and, after Solomon's death,
encouraged the *Israelites to rebel against Solomon's successor, Rehoboam. Jeroboam
incited the Israelites to commit the sin of idolatry, encouraging them to worship two golden
calves as gods. He also established a priesthood and, even though warned against it, continued
to appoint priests. In punishment God decreed that Jeroboam's entire family, 'the house of
Jeroboam', be destroyed.

> ➤ Mentioned in the context of a family that seems cursed with misfortune

> 'How horrid that story was last night! It spoiled my thoughts of today. It makes me feel
> as if a tragic doom overhung our family, as it did the house of Atreus.' 'Or the house
> of Jeroboam,' said the quondam theologian.
> THOMAS HARDY *Jude the Obscure* 1894

Jesuit [Rel.] A member of the Society of Jesus, a Roman Catholic order of priests founded
in 1534 by St Ignatius Loyola, Francis Xavier, and others to do missionary work throughout
the world. The Jesuits have also been noted as educators and theologians.

> ➤ The term 'Jesuitical' has acquired a pejorative use to describe a person who uses
> over-subtle, hair-splitting arguments

> He was as diligent as any Jesuit at arranging the arguments in every case under *Pro*
> and *Contra* and examining them thoroughly.
> ROBERTSON DAVIES *Tempest-Tost* 1951

Jesus Christ [Bible] The central figure of the Christian religion, a Jewish religious leader
worshipped by Christians as the Son of God and the saviour of mankind. The main sources
of his life are the four Gospels of Matthew, Mark, Luke, and John.
   According to these accounts, Jesus was born in Bethlehem to Mary, the wife of Joseph,
a carpenter of Nazareth, having been miraculously conceived. At the age of 30 Jesus was
baptized by *John the Baptist in the river Jordan. He spent 40 days fasting in the wilderness,
where he was challenged by *Satan with a series of temptations. Jesus came out of the
wilderness to begin his ministry and for the next three years taught and preached in Galilee.
He chose a group of twelve disciples to accompany him. Jesus told parables (such as those of
the *Good Samaritan and the *Prodigal Son), healed the sick, and performed miracles,

including turning water into wine and raising *Lazarus from the dead. In his Sermon on the Mount he preached love, humility, and charity. His teachings aroused the hostility of the *Pharisees and the governing Romans.

Jesus was finally betrayed to the authorities in Jerusalem by *Judas Iscariot, one of his disciples. He was arrested and turned over to the Romans as a blasphemer and political agitator. Following a hurried trial and despite the misgivings of the Roman procurator, Pontius *Pilate, Jesus was condemned to be crucified at *Calvary, outside Jerusalem. On the third day after his death his tomb was found to be empty. According to the New Testament, he rose from the dead and ascended into heaven.

> A good or virtuous person; someone who is humble and meek; a person going through a long period of solitude and contemplation; someone who successfully resists temptations

'I been thinkin', he said. 'I been in the hills thinkin', almost you might say like Jesus went into the wilderness to think His way out of a mess of troubles.'
JOHN STEINBECK *The Grapes of Wrath* 1939

Well, he looks awfully nice. Of course you never really know someone till you've been married to them for a while and discover some of their scruffier habits. I remember how upset I was when I realized for the first time that after all Joe wasn't Jesus Christ.
MARGARET ATWOOD *The Edible Woman* 1969

Jezebel [Bible] A Phoenician princess of the 9th century BC, the wife of *Ahab, king of Israel. Jezebel was denounced by *Elijah for promoting the worship of the Phoenician god *Baal, and trying to destroy the prophets of Israel. According to the story, when Jezebel heard that *Jehu had come, she 'painted her face, and tired her head' and looked down from the window at him. At Jehu's order, she was thrown out of a window and killed. Her carcass was eaten by dogs, so that when they went to bury her, 'they found no more of her than the skull, and the feet, and the palms of her hands'.

> Representing female depravity, shamelessness, and wickedness; a woman who uses too much make-up

'Mr Slope,' said Mrs Proudie, catching the delinquent at the door, 'I am surprised that you should leave my company to attend on such a painted Jezebel as that.'
ANTHONY TROLLOPE *Barchester Towers* 1857

Certainly, she had not seduced him; had not vamped him like some wicked Jezebel.
RANDALL KENAN *Let the Dead Bury their Dead* 1992

Jim [Lit.] In Mark Twain's novel *Huckleberry Finn* (1884), a runaway slave who meets up with Huck and travels with him down the Mississippi on a raft. During the course of the book Jim is sold back into slavery and then rescued again by Huck and Tom Sawyer.

> Huck and Jim are alluded to as an example of a racially mixed friendship

I was trying to tell you that I know many things about you—not you personally, but fellows like you…With us it's still Jim and Huck Finn. A number of my friends are jazz musicians, and I've been around. I know the conditions under which you live—why go back, fellow? There is so much you could do here where there is more freedom.
RALPH ELLISON *Invisible Man* 1952

Joan of Arc, St [Hist.] (*c.*1412–1431) A French heroine and martyr also known as the Maid of Orléans. The daughter of peasants, as a teenager she heard voices she believed to be the voices of saints urging her to fight for the Dauphin against the English in the Hundred Years War. She led the French army to relieve the English siege of Orléans and then led the Dauphin through occupied territory to Reims, where he was crowned Charles VII. Unable to persuade the king to support further attacks on the English, Joan was captured by the Burgundians, who sold her to the English in 1430. The English tried her as a heretic and burnt her at the stake. She was canonized in 1920.

> A great heroine or a female martyr

So, slipping and sliding, with Jane now circling helplessly around them and now leading the way, like a big-arsed Joan of Arc, they reached Jane's pad.
JAMES BALDWIN *Another Country* 1963

Her cheeks were flushed, her eyes sparkling, her question a battle cry. She had the simple, single-minded, passionate fervor of a Joan of Arc: This is right. It must be done. I must do it, whatever the cost.
KAREN KIJEWSKI *Wild Kat* 1994

Job [Bible] The Old Testament book of Job tells the story of a prosperous man whose patience and piety God tries, first by taking away his wealth and then by heaping other misfortunes upon him, including 'loathsome sores from the sole of his foot to the crown of his head' (Job 2: 7). In spite of all his suffering, Job remains humble and accepting: 'the Lord gave, and the Lord hath taken away; blessed be the name of the Lord' (Job 1: 21). He does not lose his confidence in the goodness and justice of God, and his patience is finally rewarded with wealth and long life.

> Alluded to as the epitome of forbearance; in the USA, extreme poverty can be described by mention of 'Job's house cat' or 'Job's turkey'

Amiable as the old man was, prolonged exposure to him would test anyone's patience. But Dolly Harris would have made Job seem like a chain-smoking neurotic.
MARTIN EDWARDS *Yesterday's Papers* 1994

'But stop nets do stop fish,' I said, enjoying the novelty of his position enough to play devil's advocate. 'Well, of course they do. But if they stopped *all* the fish, crews on the east would be richer'n Midas and those working the westermost part of Bogue Banks would be poorer'n Job's house cat.'
MARGARET MARON *Shooting at Loons* 1994

Job's comforter [Bible] According to an episode in the story of *Job, his three friends Eliphaz, Bildad, and Zophar come to comfort him but only increase his distress by telling him that his misfortunes are the result of his sinfulness. Job responds to this with the words 'Miserable comforters are ye all' (Job 16: 2).

> Someone whose attempts to give sympathy and comfort have the opposite effect

'Of course,' she added in true Job's-comforter style, 'I needn't take them all today.'
RAYMOND FLYNN *A Public Body* 1996

John Bull *See* BULL.

John O'Groats to Land's End [Places] John O'Groats is a village at the extreme north-eastern point of the Scottish mainland. Land's End is a rocky promontory in south-west Cornwall, which forms the westernmost point of England. John O'Groats and Land's End are considered to be the two extreme ends of the British mainland.

> Used to refer to the entire length of Great Britain

The sexual antics of public figures—Cecil Parkinson, Bill Clinton, Paddy Ashdown, Frank Bough, Alan Clark—never fail to send the same old-maidish frisson reverberating from John O'Groats to Land's End.
The Guardian 1993

John the Baptist [Bible] A Jewish preacher and prophet, who preached at the time of Jesus, demanding that his hearers repent of their sins and be baptized.

> Someone who prophesies or prepares the way for the arrival of another; a forerunner

He was a John the Baptist who took ennoblement rather than repentance for his text.
THOMAS HARDY *The Return of the Native* 1880

Johnson, Dr (Samuel Johnson) [Lit.] (1709–84) An English lexicographer, writer, critic, and celebrated conversationalist. In 1773 he undertook a journey with James Boswell to the Scottish Highlands and Hebrides, recorded in his *A Journey to the Western Islands of Scotland* (1775) and in Boswell's *Journal of a Tour to the Hebrides* (1785).

> A witty conversationalist; a literary polymath

Even Dr Johnson could not have carried on a conversation when he was walking down Fleet Street at the speed of an express train.
W SOMERSET MAUGHAM *Cakes and Ale* 1930

Jolly Green Giant [Advert.] The trademark of the Green Giant food company, producers of sweetcorn and other tinned and frozen vegetables. He is a friendly, cheerful, green-skinned giant who booms, 'Ho, ho, ho!'

> A large, cheerful man; someone with a deep laugh

My father sits at the head of the table, beaming like the Jolly Green Giant.
MARGARET ATWOOD *Cat's Eye* 1988

Jolly Miller [Opera] Isaac Bickerstaffe's comic opera *Love in a Village* (1762) contains a song about the jolly miller, in which the miller declares, 'I care for nobody, not I, If no one cares for me'.

> Used to suggest the idea of being self-sufficient

And then sometimes, very disquietingly for poor Susan, he would suddenly interrupt his emotions with an oddly cynical little laugh and would become for a while somebody entirely different, somebody like the Jolly Miller in the song. 'I care for nobody, no, not I, and nobody cares for me.'
ALDOUS HUXLEY *Point Counter Point* 1928

Jonah [Bible] A Hebrew minor prophet, who was commanded by God to 'go to Nineveh, that great city, and cry against it; for their wickedness is come up before me' (Jonah 1: 2). However, Jonah refused to obey God's command and, instead, embarked on a ship bound for Tarshish. God sent a storm as punishment and, to save the ship, the other sailors cast Jonah into the water as a bringer of bad luck, whereupon the storm abated. Jonah was then swallowed by a huge fish (traditionally a whale), and spent three days and three nights in its belly, in which time he repented and prayed to God to save him. After three days 'the Lord spake unto the fish, and it vomited out Jonah upon the dry land' (Jonah 2: 10).

> A bringer of ill luck; someone who survives a very difficult or dangerous situation

His presence was a perpetual reminder of bad luck, and soon he was suffering the cold shoulder that had been my lot when Happy Hannah first decided I was a Jonah.
ROBERTSON DAVIES *World of Wonders* 1975

I am back: again and again I am back, from the belly of the whale disgorged.
J. M. COETZEE *Age of Iron* 1990

Jonathan *See* DAVID AND JONATHAN.

Jones, Indiana [Cin.] The whip-cracking archaeologist-explorer hero of the film *Raiders of the Lost Ark* (1981) and its sequels. The films are set in the 1930s and all feature hair-raising chase sequences. The first film was promoted with the slogan 'The hero is back'.

> A daring adventurer

Foreign correspondents were a revered, much romanticized group—the Indiana
Joneses of journalism.
New Yorker 1995

'What about you?' I said crossly. 'If you hadn't been behaving like some sexagenarian
Indiana Jones, we wouldn't have got into this mess in the first place.'
MICHÈLE BAILEY *Haycastle's Cricket* 1996

Joseph [Bible] The son of *Jacob and *Rachel. In his boyhood, Joseph was his father's
favourite son, and when his father gave him a coat of many colours his brothers became
jealous. They also resented him for his prophetic dreams. They attacked him, stripped him of
his coat, and threw him into a pit. Then they sold him into slavery to the Ishmaelites, who
brought him to Egypt. Taking his coat, Joseph's brothers dipped it in the blood of a kid they
had killed and took it to their father to convince him that Joseph was dead.

In Egypt, Joseph was bought by Potiphar, an Egyptian officer, in whose house he was soon
made overseer. *Potiphar's wife tried to seduce him but Joseph repeatedly refused her
advances because of his loyalty to his master. Potiphar's wife subsequently made a false
accusation that he had attempted to rape her and as a result Joseph was put in prison. There
he interpreted the dreams of *Pharaoh's butler and baker. Two years later Pharaoh was
troubled by dreams that he could not understand and, hearing of Joseph's gift from his
butler, sent for him. Joseph interpreted Pharaoh's dream as predicting seven years of plenty
followed by seven years of famine, advising Pharaoh to store grain in preparation for the
long famine ahead. Joseph became adviser to Pharaoh and rose to high office, eventually
becoming governor of Egypt.

During the famine years, Jacob sent his sons to Egypt to try to buy corn. When Joseph's
brothers came to him for help, Joseph at first treated them roughly but, when his
brothers revealed how their father had suffered since his disappearance, he eventually
revealed to them who he was. He was reconciled with his family and helped them during a famine
in *Canaan, showing particular compassion for his father and his youngest brother, Benjamin.

> ➢ An interpreter of dreams; a powerful person who acts with kindness and loyalty to his
>   own people; a man who remains chaste

The honour and love you bear him is nothing but meet, for God has given him great
gifts, and he uses them as the patriarch Joseph did, who, when he was exalted to a
place of power and trust, yet yearned with tenderness towards his parent, and his
younger brother.
GEORGE ELIOT *Adam Bede* 1859

I don't believe you ever knew what a sore touch it was with Boy that you were such a
Joseph about women. He felt it put him in the wrong. He always felt that the best
possible favour you could do a woman was to push her into bed.
ROBERTSON DAVIES *The Manticore* 1972

Joshua [Bible] *Moses' successor as leader of Israel, who led the *Israelites in their return
to the land of *Canaan. The book of Joshua includes an account of the Israelites' victory over
the Amorites, during which Joshua prayed to God: ' "Sun, stand thou still at Gibeon, and
thou Moon in the valley of Aijalon." And the sun stood still, and the moon stayed, until the
nation took vengeance on their enemies' (Josh. 10: 12–13).

> ➢ Mentioned in the context of the sun or moon standing still

We were gaining about twenty minutes every day, because we were going east so
fast—we gained just about enough every day to keep along with the moon. It
was becoming an old moon to the friends we had left behind us, but to us Joshuas it
stood still.
MARK TWAIN *The Innocents Abroad* 1869

Jotuns [Norse Myth.] A race of frost giants who fought against the gods for possession of the world. While the gods lived in Asgard, the home of the Jotuns was Jotunheim.

➤ Used to describe something that is gigantic in size or scale

The Amphitheatre was a huge circular enclosure, with a notch at opposite extremities of its diameter north and south. From its sloping internal form it might have been called the spittoon of the Jotuns.
THOMAS HARDY *The Mayor of Casterbridge* 1886

Judas Iscariot *See* ISCARIOT.

Jude, St [Rel.] One of the apostles, also known as Judas and traditionally identified with Thaddaeus. St Jude is regarded as the patron saint of hopeless causes.

➤ Mentioned in the context of a hopeless cause

With an LLB from Baltimore University, he introduced himself as a graduate of Agnew U. and boasted that Spiro had been his professor of Legal Ethics. A fierce defender of hopeless cases, he dubbed himself 'the St. Jude of the judicial system' and startled prosecutors and juries with his audacious courtroom antics.
MATTHEW MEWSHAW *True Crime* 1991

Judgement Day [Rel.] In Christian tradition, the day when God will judge all the living and the dead and reward or punish them accordingly.

➤ The end of the world; a time when people or things are definitively judged

At that there was a great outcry in the courtroom, like the uprush of voices at the Judgement Day; and I knew I was doomed.
MARGARET ATWOOD *Alias Grace* 1996

Competing in the Olympics is like Judgement Day for the athletes.
Guardian 2004

Judith [Bible] In the apocryphal book of Judith, a rich and beautiful Jewish widow who saved the town of Bethulia from a siege by the Babylonian army. She entered the enemy camp and, having promised to sleep with the Babylonian general *Holofernes, was left alone with him in his tent. When Holofernes fell into a drunken sleep, she cut off his head with his own sword.

➤ A woman who cuts off a man's head

For he had thought that if anyone might darkly store up a vengeance it was Nancy. Perhaps she intended, like Judith with Holofernes, to bed down with him and decapitate him in his sleep.
THOMAS KENEALLY *The Playmaker* 1987

Juggernaut (Jagannath) [Rel.] In Hindu mythology, the name (meaning Lord of the World) of an image of Krishna annually carried in procession on an enormous cart. Devotees of the god are said to have thrown themselves under its wheels to be crushed in the hope of going straight to paradise.

➤ Used to denote a huge destructive force that crushes whatever is in its path

That human Juggernaut trod the child down and passed on regardless of her screams.
ROBERT LOUIS STEVENSON *The Strange Case of Dr Jekyll and Mr Hyde* 1886

And now, young Pongo, stand out of my way, or I'll roll over you like a Juggernaut.
P. G. WODEHOUSE *Cocktail Time* 1958

Juliet *See* ROMEO AND JULIET.

Juno [Rom. Myth.] The wife and sister of Jupiter, and queen of Heaven, equivalent to the Greek *Hera. In many stories Juno is depicted as jealously enraged by the philanderings of her husband. She was also angered at being slighted by Paris when he chose *Aphrodite (the Roman *Venus) instead of her as the fairest of three goddesses.

> A jealous or wrathful wife; a woman of stately beauty (adjective *Junoesque*)

Not allowed to dispose of money, or call any thing their own, they learn to turn the market penny; or, should a husband offend, by staying from home, or give rise to some emotions of jealousy—a new gown, or any pretty bawble [sic], smooths Juno's angry brow.
MARY WOLLSTONECRAFT *A Vindication of the Rights of Women* 1792

We know what was the wrath of Juno when her beauty was despised. We know too what storms of passion even celestial minds can yield. As Juno may have looked at Paris on Mount Ida, so did Mrs Proudie look on Ethelbert Stanhope when he pushed the leg of the sofa into her lace train.
ANTHONY TROLLOPE *Barchester Towers* 1857

Jurassic [Science] In geology, the Jurassic period lasted from about 213 to 144 million years ago. Dinosaurs were abundant and attained their maximum size. The term was popularized by Steven Spielberg's blockbuster dinosaur film *Jurassic Park* (1993).

> Used to describe something extremely out of date or antiquated

Call me Jurassic, but I couldn't care less about authenticity and immediacy when I'm engrossed in a good story.
The Observer 1997

Jurassic Park [Cin.] The title of a film (1993) based on a book of the same name by Michael Crichton (1991). The plot features a theme park inhabited by dinosaurs which have been created from DNA taken from ancient mosquitoes preserved in amber. The dinosaurs are not supposed to be able to breed, but it is discovered that one particularly dangerous species, the carnivorous velociraptor, is able to reproduce. At the end of the film the velociraptors are moving out of the confines of the park.

> A type of environment where savagery prevails; a system that descends into chaos because safety controls fail to work

For prison is like Jurassic Park, but infinitely more dangerous: a single-sex society where some specimens, through a freak of genes, can mutate to the opposite sex. And others, through an excess of libido, willingly lose the ability to differentiate.
PAUL BENNETT *False Profits* 1998

Just William [Child. Lit.] **William Brown** is the unruly, usually grubby-faced, schoolboy created by Richmal Crompton and featuring in the *Just William* series of children's books (1922–70). Though well intentioned, William has the knack of unwittingly producing chaos. He is the leader of a gang of friends known as the Outlaws.

> A naughty or unruly boy

Detective Superintendent Honeyman was a small, tidy man with a pale face and a repressed expression, which always made Slider think of Richmal Crompton's William scrubbed clean and pressed into his Eton suit for a party he didn't want to go to.
CYNTHIA HARROD-EAGLES *Blood Lines* 1996

Kafka, Franz [Lit.] (1883–1924) A Czech novelist whose works portray the individual's isolation, bewilderment, and anxiety in a nightmarish, impenetrably oppressive world. In *The Trial* (1925), Joseph K. is arrested and subjected to a baffling ordeal by sinister figures of authority. In *The Metamorphosis* (1915) a man awakes one morning to find himself transformed into a giant cockroach.

> ➤ Used when describing an illogical or sinister situation; also mentioned in the context of a person who is transformed into an insect or animal (adjective *Kafkaesque*)
>
> When she brought them in, he understood her apprehensiveness at once. He could see that they were men of tremendous authority. He had never read Kafka, but if he had he would have recognized them. They wore black suits, and did not smile when they greeted him, or offer to shake hands.
> ALAN PATON *Ah, But Your Land Is Beautiful* 1981
>
> When I asked why, the spokesman, a decent man just trying to earn a crust like the rest of us, tried his best to explain the Government's Kafkaesque logic.
> *The Observer* 1997

Karenina, Anna [Lit.] The heroine of Leo Tolstoy's novel of the same name (1873–7). Anna has a love affair with Count Vronsky, and when she becomes pregnant she confesses her adultery to her husband Karenin, who insists she choose between himself and her lover. She chooses Vronsky but, unable to tolerate the social isolation that this leads to, eventually kills herself by throwing herself under a train.

> ➤ An adulteress
>
> It was one thing reading Tolstoy in class, another playing Anna and Vronsky with the professor.
> PHILIP ROTH *My Life as a Man* 1970

Karloff, Boris [Cin.] (1887–1969) A British-born American actor, who was born William Henry Pratt. His gaunt looks made him particularly well suited to roles in horror films, and his most memorable performance was as the monster in **Frankenstein* (1931).

> ➤ A man with a gaunt or ghoulish appearance
>
> The people protecting you have morticians who could make Boris Karloff look like Marilyn Monroe.
> TOM SHARPE *Grantchester Grind* 1995

karma [Rel.] In Buddhist philosophy, the doctrine that the sum total of a person's actions and experiences in all their incarnations determines the fate of their next incarnation.

> ➤ A good or bad feeling or atmosphere
>
> Linking your gallery with a charitable organization during the holidays helps generate good karma and good P.R.
> *Art Business News* 2001

Karnac [Places] A village in Egypt, on the Nile near Luxor. It is the site of ancient Thebes, whose ruins, including the great temple of Amun, still survive there.

> An empty or deserted place

Half-past ten in the morning was about her hour for seeking this spot—a time when the town avenues were deserted as the avenues of Karnac.
THOMAS HARDY *The Mayor of Casterbridge* 1886

Kelly, Ned [Crime] (1855–80) An Australian outlaw whose father had been transported from Ireland. Kelly headed a four-man gang of bandits, notorious for killing three policemen in 1878. After an attempted train ambush, Kelly tried to escape in a homemade suit of armour, but was apprehended and hanged.

> An outlaw hero

Unfortunately for us these youth believe they are the Robin Hoods and the Ned Kellys of their small world because they have a fan club of equally gullible followers who think bringing down services around the world is cool.
Northern Rivers Echo News 2004

Kent, Clark [Cin.; Cart. & Com.] A US comic-book and film character, who appears to be a shy bespectacled reporter for the *Daily Planet* newspaper. However, when trouble threatens he transforms himself into *Superman, a superhero from the planet Krypton who is able to fly and has superhuman strength. Clark Kent's instant transformation takes place out of sight and typically in a telephone box, from which he emerges fully garbed in cape and tights as Superman.

> A shy or mild-mannered reporter; someone who transforms himself or herself completely in appearance or character; also mentioned when describing large glasses with a thick frame

Using his investigative journalism skills, this mild-mannered Clark Kent type uncovers the terrorist nest and turns into an unstoppable killing machine.
Eye Weekly (Toronto): Film section 2002

One of my nicknames when I played for the Lakers was Superman, not for my ability but for those big, black Clark Kent glasses.
Sporting News 2002

Keystone Kops [Cin.] A troupe of film comedians led by Ford Sterling who, between 1912 and 1920, made a number of silent comedies at the Keystone Studios in Hollywood. Dressed in oversized police uniforms, the bumbling Keystone Kops took part in chaotic chase scenes involving daring comic stunts.

> Bumbling, incompetent police officers

Quinlan refers to the Mexican authorities as 'Keystone Kops'.
Journal of Popular Film and Television 2005

killing fields [Hist.; Cin.] Areas of countryside where large numbers of people were executed in Cambodia under the rule of Pol Pot and the Khmer Rouge in the late 1970s. The phrase passed into the language following the release of a film about the events entitled *The Killing Fields* in 1984.

> A place of large-scale death or suffering

A special issue of The Sunday Times Magazine in 1998, titled 'Who is killing the countryside?', pointed to the 'killing fields' of Cambridgeshire, where intrusive farming methods 'are slowly stripping the landscapes of natural features and wildlife habitat'.
Spiked Online 2004

kindness of strangers [Lit.] The final words spoken by Blanche Dubois as she is taken away to an asylum at the end of Tennessee Williams's 1947 play *A Streetcar Named Desire*. As others taunt her or pin her down, the doctor speaks gently to her and persuades her to come with him. She tells the doctor: 'I have always depended on the kindness of strangers.'

➤ Charity or kindness

Unlike most nonprofit organizations, which live year to year on budgets that depend upon grants and the kindness of strangers, Carstedt's goal is to create a self-sustaining organization.
Fast Company Magazine 2001

King, Martin Luther [Hist.] (1929–68) A US Baptist minister and civil rights leader who opposed discrimination against blacks by organizing non-violent resistance and peaceful mass demonstrations. He was awarded the 1964 Nobel Peace Prize. A brilliant and inspiring orator, his most famous speech repeats the words 'I have a dream'. King was assassinated in Memphis, Tennessee, in 1968.

➤ A champion of oppressed people

'My boyfriend, Ladies and Gentleman,' Joe announced with mock-solemnity...'the Martin Luther King of gay people everywhere.'
ARIADNE ETHEREAL *Choice* 2002

King Kong [Cin.] A gigantic, monstrous ape featured in the film of the same name, originally made in 1933 and remade in 2005. Kong is discovered on a remote Pacific island, captured, and brought to New York to be exhibited. He escapes and runs amok in the city, climbing the Empire State Building with the heroine in his grasp before fighter planes shoot him down.

➤ A large, aggressive monster; someone who sweeps obstacles or opponents out of their path easily; someone or something on top of a skyscraper

He lets a beat pass, then pounds his chest like King Kong and lets loose a gutteral 'ROWRR!'
The Black Table 2003

This trio of rocks towers above the valleys and hills of Nepal like King Kong over a New York skyscraper.
Scotland on Sunday 2006

King over the Water [Hist.] The Jacobite name for the exiled James II, who remained 'over the water' in France. The term was later used for the son and grandson of James II, the Old Pretender and Young Pretender respectively.

➤ A king or leader in exile, either literally or metaphorically

And some in the party still want the 'King over the Water' Alex Salmond, to return to the helm of the party.
Scotland on Sunday 2004

Kipling, Rudyard [Lit.] (1865–1936) An English novelist, short-story writer, and poet, who was born in India. Poems such as 'The White Man's Burden', 'If', and '*Gunga Din' came to be regarded as epitomizing British colonial and imperialistic attitudes. His other works include stories such as *The Jungle Book* (1894) and the *Just So Stories* (1902)

➤ Mentioned in the context of old-fashioned and idealized colonialist attitudes (adjective *Kiplingesque*)

The trumpets had sounded a fanfare and the thousand had sung the four verses of Everard's rather Kiplingesque 'Song of the Freemen'.
ALDOUS HUXLEY *Point Counter Point* 1928

Rather the Kipling type, you know. Very keen on his work. Hearty. Empire-builder and all that sort of thing.
SOMERSET MAUGHAM *The World Over* 1952

Kitchener, Lord (first Earl Kitchener of Khartoum) [Hist.] (1850–1916) The well-known image on a famous recruiting poster during the First World War that carried his large-moustached face and pointing finger above the slogan 'Your country needs you!'

> ➤ Used to invoke the image of someone pointing a finger and demanding action from individuals; also used to describe a large, extravagant moustache

We will only get these [water] filters when the people say enough is enough and like Lord Kitchener said, 'That means You.'
This Is Wiltshire news stories 2003

They stood next to each other, like pieces opposing each other on a chess board, oblivious of the interest of the ageing porter with the Lord Kitchener moustache.
PETER CAREY *Illywhacker* 1985

Klimt, Gustav [Art] (1862–1918) An Austrian painter and designer, the greatest of art nouveau painters. He achieved a jewelled effect in his work similar to mosaics, combining stylized human forms with decorative and ornate clothing or backgrounds in elaborate patterns, often using gold leaf. One of his most famous paintings is *The Kiss* (1909).

> ➤ Used when describing a mosaic-like appearance

She was pale, and looked tired and distracted. I noticed for the first time how she had aged. The woman I knew fifteen years ago was still there, but fixed inside a coarser outline, like one of Klimt's gem-encrusted lovers.
JOHN BANVILLE *The Book of Evidence* 1989

Klondike [Places] The area around the River Klondike in north-west Canada. In 1896, gold was discovered there, leading to the gold rush in 1897–8 during which thousands of people rushed to the area to mine.

> ➤ A rush to make money quickly

Once the green light was given by city planners for big business to cash in their York sites, it has been like a Klondike gold rush to jump on the gravy train.
The Press, York (Newsquest) 2004

Knox, John [People] (*c*.1505–1572) A Scottish Protestant reformer, the founder of the Presbyterian Church of Scotland.

> ➤ Someone who expresses strong views on moral rectitude or shows puritanical disapproval of others

Madeleine Redman described him, with Gallic extravagance, as a mixture of John Knox and Lord Byron—a too-extreme polarity.
Jacket Magazine 2002

Kojak [TV] The bald-headed police detective played by Telly Savalas in the American television series of the same name (1973–7). His catchphrase was 'Who loves ya, baby?'

> ➤ A detective; a bald man

Many of the sallies were aimed at his lack of hair. He was called Kojak at first, but this was a gross slander; Farmer's hair receded at the temples and was less than luxuriant on the crown, that was all.
MAX MARQUIS *Written in Blood* 1995

Kong *See* KING KONG.

Kon-Tiki The name of the raft made of balsa logs in which, in 1947, the Norwegian anthropologist Thor Heyerdahl sailed from Peru to the islands of Polynesia in order to prove that ancient people could have migrated in this way.

> Mentioned in the context of a long, difficult journey

Kosovo [Places] An autonomous province of Serbia, the majority of whose people are of Albanian descent. In 1999, it was subjected to ethnic cleansing by Serbian paramilitary forces, resulting in the bombing of Belgrade by Nato.

> A country where killing of civilians takes place on a large scale

If there were another Kosovo—let's say Montenegro, for example—what lessons were learned from the original that could be put to use here?
CNN transcripts: Insight 2000

Krakatoa [Places] A small volcanic island in Indonesia. An eruption in 1883 destroyed most of the island.

> Mentioned in the context of a loud explosive noise

He took the lectern to a Krakatoa of applause.
MARTIN AMIS *The Information* 1995

Kraken [Leg. & Folk.] An enormous mythical sea-monster said to appear off the coast of Norway and attack ships. It looked like a gigantic squid and, according to the earliest stories dating from the 12th century, was the size of an island. A poem by Tennyson (1830) describes the Kraken waking from 'his ancient, dreamless, uninvaded sleep' and a science fiction novel by John Wyndham has the title *The Kraken Wakes* (1953).

> A monster; something that awakes or revives after a long period of dormancy

What I am talking about are those lapses that first begin to awaken the Kraken of irritation in the reader's mind.
The Observer 2001

Kristallnacht [Hist.] The night of 9 November 1938, when windows of Jewish shops and homes were smashed across Germany and Austria by Nazis. The word literally means 'night of crystal', referring to the broken glass produced by the smashing of shop windows.

> An intense period of vandalism and attacks directed at one particular group of people

With Vajpayye and Advani at the helm, pledged to save Hindutva and sacrifice India, it would be natural for them to expect a seventy-two hour long Kristallnacht in Gujarat, with Modi presiding over the pogrom against Muslims.
Milli Gazette (New Delhi) 2004

Krueger, Freddy [Cin.] The scarred killer with knives for fingernails who brutally murders teenagers in their dreams in the horror film *Nightmare on Elm Street* (1984) and its sequels.

> An evil killer; someone with a lot of scars on their body; someone with very long fingernails

How lucky fate wasn't running a dating agency, I thought bitterly. It would probably pair up Mother Theresa with Freddie Kruger.
LIZ EVANS *Who Killed Marilyn Monroe?* 1997

Kryptonite [Cin.; Cart. & Com.] A fictional green rock, the alien mineral that can weaken the powers of the US comic-book superhero *Superman and would ultimately kill him if he were to be exposed to it for long enough. Individual pieces of kryptonite are fragments of Superman's home planet, Krypton.

> ➤ Something that can bring about a person's downfall

Kids would be like kryptonite to my career.
RICHARD DOOLEY *Brainstorm* 1998

Kublai Khan [Hist.] (1214–94) A Mongol emperor of China and founder of the Yuan dynasty. The grandson of *Genghis Khan, by 1259 he had completed his family's conquest of China and established his capital on the site of the modern Beijing. He had his residence, described in Coleridge's poem 'Kubla Khan' (1816) as 'a stately pleasure-dome', in *Xanadu, an ancient city in south-east Mongolia.

> ➤ Mentioned when describing a luxurious and exotic-looking building

'Turn off and drive round the ring road,' he said suddenly to Abigail as the Kubla Khan glass domes of the new shopping centre at the top of the town came into view.
MARJORIE ECCLES *A Species of Revenge* 1996

Labyrinth [Gk Myth.] A huge maze constructed by *Daedalus at Knossos (also Cnossos or Cnossus) in Crete for King *Minos. It was designed as a home for the *Minotaur, a creature with a man's body and a bull's head. The Labyrinth was such a complex network of passages and chambers that it was thought no one could escape from it.

➤ An intricate or complicated arrangement

His mind was a dark labyrinth, intricate and convoluted, with a Minotaur of some kind crouching at the core. There was something frightening as well as fascinating about him.
JOHN SPENCER HILL *The Last Castrato* 1995

Lady in Red [Crime] The name given to the mysterious mistress of the bank robber and murderer John *Dillinger (named the FBI's 'public enemy number one' in 1933). She betrayed Dillinger's whereabouts to the FBI, whose agents shot him dead in Chicago in 1934.

➤ A woman who betrays a man

'But what about the money?' she asked. China hooted. 'She's makin' like she's the Lady in Red that told on Dillinger.'
TONI MORRISON *The Bluest Eye* 1970

Lady of the Lake [Arth. Leg.] The sorceress who gave the sword *Excalibur to *Arthur and regained it when he died. She stole the infant *Lancelot from his parents, raised him in her lake, and presented him to King Arthur when he had grown to manhood. In many versions of the legend, she is identified with *Nimue (or Vivien), the mistress of *Merlin.

➤ A woman with supernatural powers; a woman who emerges from water

Laelaps [Gk Myth.] A hound so swift that it always caught its quarry.

➤ Something or someone very swift

Lais [People] A celebrated Greek courtesan, a Sicilian, carried to Corinth at the time of the Athenian expedition to Sicily. Popular with philosophers like *Demosthenes, Xenocrates, and *Diogenes, she was killed by the townswomen, who were jealous of her beauty.

➤ A courtesan

The Athenian virgins…grew up into wives who stayed at home…and looked after the husband's dinner. And what was the consequence of that, sir? that they were such very insipid persons that the husband would not go home to eat his dinner, but preferred the company of some Aspasia or Lais.
THOMAS LOVE PEACOCK *Crotchet Castle* 1831

Lake, Veronica [Cin.] (1919–73) A petite US film actress who often played slinky femmes fatales in 1940s thrillers. She had a distinctive peek-a-boo hairstyle, her long blonde hair draped over one eye, a style much imitated by filmgoers of the time.

➤ A femme fatale; also used to describe a woman's hairstyle in which the hair falls over one side of the face

Her hair is wild, one side lifted away from her face by a pretty jeweled thing Clark doesn't recognize, the other falling in cascading curls across the right side of her face. 'Nice Veronica Lake look,' Clark says, reaching out to tug a lock of hair.
KIRA LERNER et al. *About Schuyler Falls* 2001

Lamb of God [Bible] A name sometimes given to *Jesus in the Bible, the lamb being a symbol of innocence and meekness.

➢ The epitome of innocence and goodness

These people are the lambs of God, and I won't have you perverting them.
CHRISTIAN BERTRAND *Dorom* 2000

Lancelot [Arth. Leg.] The most famous of King *Arthur's knights of the *Round Table. Unfortunately, he fell in love with *Guinevere, Arthur's wife. When Arthur was informed about their affair, the lovers fled to Lancelot's castle. Lancelot later returned to fight alongside Arthur in his battle with Mordred but was too late to save the king and, finding that Guinevere had taken the veil, became a priest.

➢ A chivalrous hero; a rescuer

'You must have fainted. You slid forward off the lounger and nearly fell in the pool. *He*,' Kat made up by emphasis for not knowing his name, 'came along just at the right moment and got you out. Sir Lancelot.'
STAYNES and STOREY *Dead Serious* 1995

land of milk and honey [Bible] A quotation from the Old Testament, in which God promised *Moses to deliver the *Israelites from slavery in Egypt to a land of plenty: 'And I am come down to deliver them out of the hand of the Egyptians, and to bring them up out of that land unto a good land and a large, unto a land flowing with milk and honey' (Exod. 3: 8).

➢ An imagined land of plenty and happiness

For many, California may symbolise the land of milk and honey—a type of American El Dorado.
The Sunday Business Post 2001

Land of Nod [Bible] The land east of *Eden to which *Cain was banished after he had slain his brother Abel (Gen. 4: 16).

➢ A mythical land of sleep

I wished that I, too, could close my eyes and drift into the land of nod.
ROZALIA TEREGRIN *The Scarlet Turncoat* 2003

Land of Promise *See* PROMISED LAND.

Laocoön [Gk Myth.] A *Trojan priest who warned the Trojans not to let the *Wooden Horse into Troy: 'Do not trust the horse, Trojans. Whatever it is, I fear the Greeks even when they bring gifts.' As a punishment from the gods for this attempted intervention, he and both his sons were crushed to death by two enormous sea-serpents. A classical marble sculpture (*c.*50 BC) of the death-struggle of Laocoön and his sons, with the serpents coiled around their limbs, was rediscovered in the Renaissance and is now in the Vatican Museum. It is, in fact, this sculpture rather than the story that is often alluded to.

➢ Mentioned in the context of someone wrestling with a snake, or a group of intertwined bodies

Like Laocoon wrestling the snake, Zobernig tangled with a 100-meter, flexible, air-filled blue tube in a choreography both playful and grim.
Art in America 2005

Other strugglers…lay in Laocoon groups about the floor.
ROBERTSON DAVIES *Leaven of Malice* 1954

Laodicean [Bible] A member of a group of Christians who were indifferent to religion, being 'lukewarm, and neither cold nor hot' (Rev. 3: 16).

➤ Someone who is or seems indifferent, showing no strong feeling

He felt himself to occupy morally that vast middle space of Laodicean neutrality which lay between the Communion people of the parish and the drunken section.
THOMAS HARDY *Far from the Madding Crowd* 1874

Laon and Cythna [Lit.] A brother and sister in Shelley's epic poem *The Revolt of Islam* (1818). The pair attempt to organize a revolution along the lines of Shelley's idea of the French Revolution, and consummate their success sexually. However, their success is short-lived.

➤ A couple who are close, but not in a sexual way

'Their supreme desire is to be together—to share each other's emotions, and fancies, and dreams.' 'Platonic!' 'Well no. Shelleyan would be nearer to it. They remind me of—what are their names—Laon and Cythna.'
THOMAS HARDY *Jude the Obscure* 1896

Lassie [Cin.] The name of a loyal and intelligent collie in a series of films, originally created by Eric Knight in the children's story *Lassie Come Home* (1940). Lassie is remembered particularly for saving her owner from dangerous situations.

➤ A dog that helps rescue its owner

After only eight weeks, Orca hit the national headlines following his amazing rescue in which he ran off and managed to get the attention of a nearby jogger. In a scene straight out of Lassie, he led him to his stranded owner in the ditch and the alarm was raised.
The Press, York (Newsquest) 2004

Last Judgement [Rel.] The judgement of people that, according to Christianity and some other religious traditions, will take place at the end of the world.

➤ A time when people or things are definitively judged

last refuge of scoundrels [Lit.] A quotation based on a pronouncement made by Samuel *Johnson (1709–84) that 'Patriotism is the last refuge of a scoundrel.'

➤ Used when saying that a particular action or line of argument has no real justification or validity

He intends, he claims with a straight face, to cut red tape, bureaucracy and civil service numbers. That is always the last refuge of shadow chancellors whose sums make no sense.
Guardian Unlimited columnists 2005

Last Supper [Bible] The supper eaten by *Jesus and his disciples on the night before the Crucifixion, according to the New Testament.

➤ A final meal before one's death

Laughing Cavalier [Art] A popular name for a 1624 portrait by Frans Hals of an unknown man sporting an enigmatic smile.

➤ Someone who smiles or laughs a lot

He is a jolly, easily amused, laughing cavalier of an all-rounder.
Sportstar Magazine 2005

Laura [Lit.] The Italian Renaissance poet *Petrarch's name for the woman in praise of whom his sonnet sequence is written. Her identity is not known.

➤ A woman who is an idealized object of love

...you were always my Beatrice. My Laura. I thought, who wants second best?
LOUIS DE BERNIÈRES *Captain Corelli's Mandolin* 1994

Laurel and Hardy [Cin.] **Arthur Stanley Jefferson** (1890–1965), known as Stan Laurel, and **Norvell Hardy Junior** (1892–1957), known as Oliver Hardy, became one of the most famous comic film duos of all time. The thin Stan, often looking confused, scratching his head, and bursting into tears, and the fat, blustering, bossy Ollie appeared in many films together from the 1920s until the 1940s, and their simple slapstick humour and disaster-prone adventures have enjoyed enduring popularity.

➤ Mentioned in the context of bumbling incompetency or a slapstick routine; also used to describe two people of contrasting girths

For the majority of the film they seem to bumble around their workplace like Laurel and Hardy.
Senses of Cinema 2001

Towering over them were two policemen who reminded me of Laurel and Hardy. The podgy one...was holding the lady's patterned bag, the skinny one was questioning one of the older boys.
ROGER FREDERICK *Fishing for Angels* 2005

Lautrec *See* TOULOUSE-LAUTREC.

Lawrence, St [People] (d. 258) A Roman martyr and deacon of Rome. According to tradition, Lawrence was ordered by the prefect of Rome to hand over the Church's treasure, in response to which he assembled the poor people of the city and presented them to the prefect. For this he was put to death by being roasted on a gridiron.

➤ Someone who dies by being roasted

It is very easy to talk of repentance, but a man has to walk over hot ploughshares before he can complete it; to be skinned alive as was St Bartholomew; to be stuck full of arrows as was St Sebastian; to lie broiling on a gridiron like St Lorenzo!
ANTHONY TROLLOPE *Barchester Towers* 1857

Lawrence of Arabia (T. E. Lawrence) [People] (1888–1935) A British soldier and writer who, from 1916 onwards, helped to organize and lead the Arab revolt against Turkey. His book *The Seven Pillars of Wisdom* (1926) was an account of the events of this period.

➤ A brave, romantic adventurer; also used to invoke a typical desert scene

One minute he thinks he's in Apocalypse Now and heading up the Mekong Delta, the next he thinks he's Lawrence of Arabia riding on a camel through the north African desert.
Scotland on Sunday 2002

Lazarus [Bible] **1.** The name of the ailing beggar who sat at the gate of the rich man (traditionally named *Dives) in the parable of the rich man and Lazarus (Luke 16: 19–31). Lazarus was covered with sores and begged for crumbs from the rich man's table. He was rewarded for his misfortunes in life by being taken to Heaven by *Abraham after death.

➤ A poor man, especially when contrasted with a rich man

How, in the modern world, does Dives help Lazarus?
Guardian Unlimited columnists 2005

2. [Bible] The brother of Mary and *Martha and a friend of *Jesus who was raised from the dead by Jesus in a miracle described in the New Testament. Lazarus had already been dead for four days when Jesus arrived at the tomb: 'He cried with a loud voice, Lazarus, come forth. And he that was dead came forth, bound hand and foot with graveclothes: and his face was bound about with a napkin' (John 11: 43–4).

➤ Someone who appears to come back to life; something that experiences a revival after a period of complete failure

Kevin Bonner went down like a shot duck, only to arise like Lazarus when the red card was produced.
Kildare Nationalist 2003

lean and hungry look [Shakes.] A quotation from *Julius Caesar* (1623), in which Caesar observes:

> Let me have men about me that are fat;
> Sleek-headed men, and such as sleep o' nights.
> Yond Cassius has a lean and hungry look;
> He thinks too much. Such men are dangerous.

➤ Used when describing someone who is ruthlessly ambitious

But each time, the Hyderabad wonder boy would mess it all up in the last couple of rounds. So, when he landed in Kochi with a lean and hungry look, one sensed his time had come.
Sportstar Magazine 2004

leap in the dark [Lit.] A quotation from the attributed last words of the English philosopher Thomas Hobbes (1588–1679), 'I am about to take my last voyage, a great leap in the dark.'

➤ A daring step into the unknown whose consequences are unpredictable

You are asking parents to take a leap in the dark with their children because you have no idea what form this new school will take.
Rochdale Observer 2003

Lear, King [Shakes.] A legendary early king of Britain who is the central figure in *King Lear* (1623). In the play, the foolish and petulant old king divides his kingdom between his two elder daughters, Goneril and Regan, but is subsequently driven mad by his outrage at the grudging hospitality and ill treatment he feels he receives at their hands. His 'mad scenes' take place on a heath in a violent storm. Before his wits leave him, Lear speaks of his fear of becoming deranged:

O let me not be mad, not mad, sweet heaven! Keep me in temper; I would not be mad!

➤ A madman; someone who gives vent to uncontrollable rage

We are all scared of it, be honest. Madness. Don't tell me, as you flick through these pages in that rather airy way of yours, that you have never considered the dark, almost subliminal fear that you might awake one morning as barking as Lear, for I know better.
The Guardian 1997

He is like King Lear raging into the wind.
Sunday Business Post 2004

Lebensraum [Hist.] The word (literally 'living space' in German) which German nationalists in the mid-20th century used for land which they claimed was needed for the survival and healthy development of their nation.

> Land that a country takes from another by force in order to provide living space for its citizens

Can it be that the American mercenary army is creating the 21st Century version of Lebensraum for an increasingly land hungry Israel?
In These Times 2004

Lecter, Hannibal [Lit.; Cin.] The brilliant psychiatrist turned psychopathic serial killer in *The Silence of the Lambs* (1988) and other books by Thomas Harris, later made into films. Dr Lecter eats his victims after killing them, hence his nickname Hannibal the Cannibal. He has maroon eyes and six fingers on his left hand.

> A psychopathic killer; a cannibal

Jason Marion as Munich is cool, charming, elegant and as dangerous as Hannibal Lecter on crack cocaine.
StageLeft.com.au reviews 2003

A real-life Hannibal Lecter who ate the brain of one of his victims was told today that he would remain behind bars for the rest of his life
Manchester Online: Manchester Evening News 2005

Lee, Christopher [Cin.] (b. 1922) A prolific English actor chiefly associated with the roles he played in horror films made by the British film company Hammer, most notably *Dracula* (1958). More recently, he has also played the wizard Saruman in the *Lord of the Rings* films.

> Someone with a commanding physical presence and a rich deep voice

'And the lemon sponge,' Atherton's voice descended to a tomb of horror, 'was made with synthetic flavouring.' 'Dear God!' Hollis responded like a poor man's Christopher Lee. 'I can't believe it!'
CYNTHIA HARROD-EAGLES *Shallow Grave* 1998

Legion, my name is [Bible] A quotation from the New Testament (Mark 5) when *Jesus commands a demon possessing a man to come out, and asks his name. The demon answers: 'My name is Legion, for we are many.'

> Used when saying that there are large numbers of people or things

OK, let's start naming all the songs from the civil rights movement that we remember. And their names are legion.
In These Times 2004

Legree, Simon [Lit.] The cruel cotton plantation owner in Harriet Beecher Stowe's *Uncle Tom's Cabin* (1851–2) to whom Tom is sold and who beats Tom to death.

> A cruel or violent person, especially a white person inflicting violence on a black person

Finally, there is the tragic action of black-on-black violence, so that if a black person is injured or killed, it is not by a Simon Legree but by another black person.
Hudson Review 2005

Leonardo da Vinci *See* DA VINCI.

Leontes [Shakes.] The king of Sicily in *The Winter's Tale* (1623). Leontes mistakenly believes that his wife Hermione has been unfaithful to him with his childhood friend Polixenes. In his jealousy he attempts unsuccessfully to have Polixenes poisoned, throws Hermione into prison, and orders that his own baby daughter Perdita be left on a desert shore to die.

> A jealous husband

Leporello [Opera] The servant of Don Giovanni, the legendary Spanish seducer of
women, in Mozart's opera *Don Giovanni* (1787). In a famous scene, Leporello recites the
catalogue he has compiled of his master's sexual conquests, categorized by nationality
and type.

> ➤ Someone who publicizes the amorous conquests or achievements of another
>
> He has walked away with so many awards that he needs a Leporello to sing the list of
> his triumphs.
> *Psychiatric Times* 2000

Lesbos [Places] A Greek island in the eastern Aegean. Its artistic golden age of the late 7th and
early 6th centuries BC produced the poet *Sappho, whose love poems express her passionate
friendships with women. This explains the association of the island with female homosexuality
and the derivation of the words 'lesbian' and 'Sapphic'.

> ➤ Mentioned in the context of lesbian love
>
> My good friend and mentor Peggy O'Reggis lives in a universe in which men are only
> marginally visible. Ditto my lawyer, Virginia Goodchild, a committed citizen of Lesbos.
> CAROL SHIELDS *Mary Swann* 1990

L'état c'est moi [Hist.] A phrase attributed to *Louis XIV of France, indicating his
complete political power.

> ➤ Used when suggesting that someone behaves as if they have complete political power
>
> From the offset, his White House has been shamelessly partisan. Kyoto Treaty? There's
> the bin. International law? C'est moi. Tax cuts for the rich? Yip, they create wealth.
> *Scotland on Sunday* 2004

Lethe [Gk Myth.] One of the rivers of the underworld *Hades, whose water caused those
who drank it to lose all memory of their past life on earth.

> ➤ Mentioned in the context of oblivion, forgetfulness, or death
>
> In his seven-year voyage on the waters of Lethe (the north island of New Zealand actually),
> Gordon forgot all about Eliza (not to mention us) and came back with a different wife
> altogether.
> KATE ATKINSON *Human Croquet* 1997

let them eat cake [Hist.] A remark attributed to *Marie Antoinette, the wife of Louis XVI
and queen of France. She was known for her extravagant lifestyle and, on being told that the
poor people of Paris were unable to afford bread, reputedly replied: 'Qu'ils mangent de la
brioche' ('let them eat cake').

> ➤ Used to suggest an arrogant indifference to the plight of the poor
>
> 'I half expect his solution to hunger and homelessness in the city will be to let them eat
> cake,' the New York Daily News quoted Rep. Anthony Weiner as saying.
> *HealthTalk.ca: Health News archive* 2005

Leviathan [Bible] A sea-monster mentioned in a number of passages in the Bible (e.g. Job
41; Ps. 74: 14). Biblical scholars have identified the monster as a whale or crocodile. Thomas
Hobbes's title *Leviathan* refers to sovereign power in his treatise on political philosophy,
published in 1651.

> ➤ A whale; anything immense or extremely powerful
>
> How can Britain compete with these new economic leviathans?
> *The Sunday Times* 2004

Levite [Bible] A member of the Hebrew tribe of Levi. In the story of the *Good Samaritan, a Levite passes by on the other side and does not help the traveller who has been robbed and assaulted (Luke 10: 30–7).

➤ Someone who ignores a person who is suffering or fails to help a person in need

I had to pass through what was known at the time as 'Cardboard City', and felt so guilty as I walked by like the Priest or Levite, trying but failing to ignore the many calls for help.
Sligo Weekender 2004

Liar *See* BILLY LIAR.

Lilliputian [Lit.] In book 1 of Jonathan Swift's *Gulliver's Travels* (1726), *Gulliver finds himself shipwrecked on the island of Lilliput. The tiny Lilliputians are only 6 inches tall and, as Gulliver discovers, are as small-minded as they are small-bodied, being petty, pretentious, and factious.

➤ A person or thing that is unusually small (adjective *Lilliputian*)

Gordon House is Lilliputian by today's building standards
Architecture Week 2001

Lincoln, Abraham [Hist.] (1809–65) An American Republican statesman and the sixteenth president of the United States from 1861 to 1865. He is sometimes referred to as Honest Abe or the Great Emancipator on account of his involvement in the abolition of slavery. He was noted for oratory and his eloquent speeches, including his speech of 1863 during the American Civil War at the dedication of the cemetery of those killed in the Battle of Gettysburg, known as the *Gettysburg address. As well as his oratory and political achievements, Lincoln is also remembered for his physical appearance. He was a tall man, standing over 6 feet, and had a gaunt face with sunken, wrinkled cheeks.

➤ An orator; an honest man; a tall, thin man with a gaunt face

If they're as honest as Abe Lincoln, there's still the problem that they're making you trust the security of their servers.
TechDirt news 2004

In high school I weighed 175 to 180. I looked like Abraham Lincoln. I was 6 foot 3, biggest thing in the class.
CNN transcripts: Larry King Live 2003

Linus blanket [Cart. & Com.] A piece of old blanket carried as a comforter by Linus, a character in the *Peanuts* cartoon strip, created in 1950 by Charles M. Schulz. The cartoons feature a group of children, including Charlie Brown with his dog Snoopy.

➤ Anything that provides reassurance and a feeling of security

Roy went to the closet for a jacket. He gave it to his brother who laid his bible down and put on the coat, then picked up the bible again. It was his Linus blanket, I figured. He never went anywhere without it.
TED WOOD *A Clean Kill* 1995

lion in winter [Lit.] A phrase taken from the title of a 1968 play *The Lion in Winter*, by James Goldman, about the life of King Henry II in his later years. The play was also made into a successful Hollywood film starring Peter O'Toole as Henry and Katherine Hepburn as Queen Eleanor.

➤ A powerful man who remains proud and strong even in old age

Look at Arnold Palmer. He's 71. He can't always hear you, he can't always see you, he can't much more than bend at the waist to line up putts. He for sure can't create the 350–yard lightning bolts touched off by today's Masters children. Yet here he is, the lion in winter, silver haired, his face walnut brown.
Sporting News 2001

lions' den [Bible] The book of *Daniel in the Old Testament relates how King Darius established a decree saying that no man should pray to any man or god except the king for 30 days. Daniel, a devout Jew, ignored the command, and as a punishment was cast into the lions' den and left for the night. In the morning he was discovered by the king, unscathed. Daniel explained: 'My God hath sent his angel, and hath shut the lions' mouths, that they have not hurt me' (Dan. 6: 22).

➤ A place of great danger or intimidation

The Manchester club have got a pedigree of going into the Italian lions' den and taking something.
SquareFootball.net (2005)

Little Bighorn [Hist.] The Battle of Little Bighorn, also referred to as *Custer's last stand, was a defeat for George Custer and his troops at the hands of Sioux warriors. The battle took place in the valley of the Little Bighorn river in what is now Montana.

➤ A decisive defeat

Little Engine that Could, The [Child. Lit.] The title of a children's picture-book by Watty Piper (1945), illustrated by Lois Lenski. It tells the story of a small railway engine that pants encouragingly as it struggles up a slope: 'I think I can—I think I can—I think I can.'

➤ Something that succeeds contrary to expectations, by making slow, steady but determined progress

Linux is proving to be the little engine that could.
Baseline 2003

little grey cells [Lit.] A phrase used by the Belgian detective Hercule *Poirot in novels by Agatha *Christie. He states on many occasions that in order to deduce the identity of a murderer one must use the 'little grey cells'.

➤ The brain or the power of intellect

While the satisfying four-course meal added taste to the occasion, the generous indulgence of Rioja wines dulled the 'little grey cells', making it a hard case to crack.
The Press, York (Newsquest) 2001

Little Match Girl [Child. Lit.] The main character in a story of the same name by Hans Christian *Andersen (1848). She is so poor that she tries to warm herself by lighting the matches that she was intending to sell. Her body is found the next morning, frozen to death in the snow.

➤ A poor girl; someone selling something on the streets in cold weather; someone who is very cold

I tripped through the sleet like the little match girl.
The Observer 1996

Little Nell [Lit.] A name given to Nell Trent, the child heroine of Charles Dickens's novel *The Old Curiosity Shop* (1841). Exhausted by her attempts to protect her grandfather from the clutches of the evil moneylender Daniel Quilp, she eventually dies. Her prolonged deathbed scenes, full of pathos, epitomized Victorian sentimentality for later readers but were immensely popular at the time. The novel was originally serialized in instalments and the story goes that crowds of American readers would rush to the New York docks for news of the heroine's fate from ships arriving from England, asking 'Is Little Nell dead?' Oscar *Wilde famously said that 'One would have to have a heart of stone to read the death of little Nell without dissolving into tears...of laughter.'

> A child who suffers through poverty or ill health; also mentioned in the context of excessive sentimentality

He suffered from...a childhood that would have made Little Nell's seem rosy.
Classical Net Reviews 2003

As with the death of Little Nell, one would have to possess a heart of stone not to laugh at the poor-lonesome-me histrionics of Avril Lavigne.
Guardian Unlimited columnists 2005

Little Orphan Annie *See* ORPHAN ANNIE.

Little Red Riding Hood *See* RED RIDING HOOD.

Livingstone, Dr [People] (1813–73) A Scottish missionary and explorer, who began his missionary career in Bechuanaland in 1841. On extensive travels, he discovered the Zambezi river in 1851 and the Victoria Falls in 1855. In 1866 he went in search of the source of the Nile, and was found in poor health by Henry Morton *Stanley in 1871. Stanley is said to have greeted him with the famous words 'Dr Livingstone, I presume?'

> Someone who is eventually found after much searching

The pursuit of Andy, while not really deserving comparison with Stanley's exploits in locating Dr Livingstone, was a pretty awesome experience.
The Press, York (Newsquest) 2001

loaves and fishes [Bible] A reference to the story of the miracle in the New Testament in which *Jesus and his disciples fed a crowd of 5000 with 'five loaves and two fishes'.

> Used in the context of stretching a meal to provide for more people than was planned; also mentioned in the context of something that miraculously multiplies

On Wednesday night, David and I gate-crashed the Hilton-on-Todd. Francoise managed to do the loaves and fishes thing with an exotic Indonesian dish she'd prepared for Ian and his grand-daughter, Sarah, visiting from Queensland.
Alice Springs News 2004

Fossil fuels and forests are like the loaves and fishes, Reconstructionists say, miraculously multiplying for true believers.
AlterNet.org: EnviroHealth 2004

Lochinvar [Lit.] The hero of a ballad that features in Sir Walter *Scott's verse romance *Marmion* (1808). Lochinvar is a young Highlander who goes to the wedding of the woman he loves, abducts her, and rides away with her:

> So faithful in love, and so dauntless in war,
> There never was knight like the young Lochinvar.

> A romantic hero

Mr Radice charts Tony Blair's metamorphosis from Young Lochinvar to The Prince (Machiavelli's kind).
Contemporary Review 2005

Lohengrin [Leg. & Folk.] The son of *Perceval and a knight of the *Holy Grail, according to medieval Germanic legend. He was summoned from the temple of the Holy Grail and taken in a swan-drawn boat to Antwerp, where he rescued Elsa, the princess of Brabant, from a forced marriage. He consented to marry her himself, on condition that she did not ask who he was, because as a knight of the Grail he was obliged not to disclose his identity. Elsa broke this condition on their wedding night and Lohengrin was carried away in the swan-boat back to the Grail castle. The story of Lohengrin, sometimes called the Swan Knight, is the subject of an opera by *Wagner (1850).

➤ Someone carried by boat, or a newly wedded man

'*Wedded*' he shouted again, seizing the towel with a magnificent operatic gesture, and went on singing while he rubbed as though he had been Lohengrin tipped out by an unwary Swan and drying himself in the greatest haste before the tiresome Elsa came along.
KATHERINE MANSFIELD *Mr Reginald Peacock's Day* 1920–4

Loki [Norse Myth.] The god of mischief and discord, who was instrumental in the death of *Balder. Loki discovered that mistletoe was the only substance that had not been asked by Balder's mother Frigga to swear that it would not harm her son and so was the only thing to which Balder was vulnerable. Loki shaped a dart from the wood and tricked the blind god Hod into throwing it at Balder, who immediately fell dead to the ground. For this Loki was punished by the gods by being bound to a rock.

➤ A prankster or mischief maker

On one flank Singer is a trickster, a prankster, a Loki, a Puck.
CYNTHIA OZICK *Art & Ardour* 1984

Lolita [Lit.] The young girl heroine of Vladimir Nabokov's novel of the same name (1958). The novel concerns the obsession of the middle-aged Humbert Humbert with his 12-year-old stepdaughter Lolita, whom Humbert describes as a 'nymphet'.

➤ A sexually precocious young girl

The shot captured a virtual sea of Lolitas dressed in makeup, halter tops and platform shoes.
Brandweek 2000

Loman, Willy [Lit.] The main character in Arthur Miller's play *Death of a Salesman* (1949), a travelling salesman for a lingerie company. He comes to realize that his life has been a complete failure, and finally commits suicide in order to help his son get a new start in life with the insurance money.

➤ Someone who is a complete failure

If he could sympathize with losers like Willy Loman, he was, nevertheless, determined not to share their lot.
CBC.ca: Theatre 2005

loneliness of the long distance runner [Lit.; Cin.] A phrase taken from the title of a 1959 novel by Alan Sillitoe, *The Loneliness of the Long Distance Runner*. The novel tells the story of Colin, a working-class boy spending time in a borstal after being caught robbing a bakery. He finds solace in long-distance running, and is encouraged to compete by the borstal authorities, keen to bring honour upon their establishment. Colin, however, stops short of the finish line in an important race he is winning in order to express his defiance of the authorities who are holding him prisoner. The book was made into a successful film.

➤ Used when suggesting the lonely nature of any difficult solitary activity

The loneliness of the long distance writer is not an option when you have a writing partner.
Ideas Factory 2004

Lone Ranger [TV] A masked law-enforcer in the American west, created in 1933 by George W. Trendle and Fran Striker for a radio series and popularized in a later television series (1956–62). His true identity remains concealed and he is known only as the 'masked man' or 'masked rider'. In the stories he is sometimes accompanied by a Native American called *Tonto.

> An individual who acts alone in undertaking a rescue mission of some kind

We need to realise that we are stronger when we work together not when everyone plays the lone ranger.
Limerick Leader 2004

Long John Silver *See* SILVER.

long march [Hist.] An epic 6000-mile trek from south-east to north-west China undertaken by a group of 100000 embattled Chinese communists under Mao Zedong in 1934–5. Of the 100000 who started the march, only 20000 survived.

> A long and difficult journey; a period of great difficulty

Competent governance and institution building is the long march ahead in post-Saddam Iraq.
New Perspectives Quarterly 2004

Longstocking, Pippi [Child. Lit.] The main character in a series of children's books (1945–59) by the Swedish writer Astrid Lindgren. She is a 9-year-old girl with red hair, long mismatched stockings, and superhuman strength. Pippi lives alone in an old house, with a monkey and a horse but entirely unsupervised by adults.

> A feisty young woman

You zip through the first two thirds of Shutterbabe cheering for the diminutive and… feisty heroine who once resented having to hide her 'inner Pippi Longstocking under a lacquered Barbie mask'.
New York Metro: Books 2004

Look Back in Anger [Lit.] The title of a 1956 play by John Osborne about Jimmy *Porter, an amiable but disaffected young man. Through the character of Porter, Osborne articulated the views of a group of socially conscious writers of the 1950s known as the '*angry young men'.

> To feel angry about a past event

If Leeds fail to qualify for the Champions League today, manager David O'Leary will look back in anger at Manchester United's controversial visit to Elland Road two months ago.
Irish Examiner 2001

looking-glass [Child. Lit.] In Lewis Carroll's children's story *Through the Looking-Glass* (1871), *Alice enters an illogical dreamlike world by walking through a large looking-glass.

> Mentioned in the context of a situation that seems completely illogical or divorced from reality

For now, though, the focus is on whether the Fed will succeed in goosing growth. And in the looking-glass world of cheap credit, that's by no means clear.
BusinessWeek Magazine 2003

Lord of the Flies [Lit.] The title of a 1954 novel by William Golding about how a group of schoolboys descend into savagery and murder when they are stuck on a desert island with no adult supervision following a plane crash.

> Mentioned in the context of children behaving in a wild or lawless way

The streets are littered with children and teenagers who are like something out of the Lord of the Flies, feral youths with no education and no prospects.
Carlow Nationalist 2001

Lorelei [Leg. & Folk.] The name of a rock at the edge of the Rhine, held to be the home of a siren with long blonde hair whose song lures boatmen to destruction. The name can also be applied to the siren herself.

➤ A dangerously fascinating woman; a siren; anything that lures someone to their destruction

Queenstown sits on the shores of Lake Wakatipu like one of the Lorelei waiting to lure hapless English cricketers to their doom.
Manchester Evening News 2002

lost generation [Hist.] The generation that reached maturity during or just after the First World War, and that had lost large numbers of its men during the war years. The term was applied by Gertrude Stein to disillusioned young American writers who moved to Paris in the 1920s and, disillusioned with the values of society, sank into cynicism and hedonism.

➤ A generation that feels isolated from the rest of society because it has suffered in some way

With their futures seemingly secure, many young and mid-career workers took on big debts as they splurged on expensive houses, cars, and vacations. Now, many of them feel like a lost generation, worried that their peak earning years are behind them even as their expenses jump.
BusinessWeek Magazine 2002

We were like a lost generation of kids without a background or history.
Free Williamsburg magazine 2001

Lot [Bible] A nephew of *Abraham in the Bible. According to the book of Genesis (19: 24), Lot, an inhabitant of the town of *Sodom, was seen by God to be a righteous man. He was allowed to escape from the town before God destroyed it by fire and brimstone in order to punish the depravity and wickedness of its inhabitants.

➤ A righteous person; someone who is spared in a cataclysm

We thought a bolt had fallen in the middle of us, and Joseph swung onto his knees, beseeching the Lord to remember the Patriarchs Noah and Lot; and, as in former times, spare the righteous, though he smote the ungodly.
EMILY BRONTË *Wuthering Heights* 1847

What the deuce is the hurry? Just so must Lot have left Sodom, when he expected fire to pour down upon it out of burning brass clouds.
CHARLOTTE BRONTË *The Professor* 1857

Lothario [Lit.] A character from Nicholas Rowe's play *The Fair Penitent* (1703), a womanizer described as 'that haughty, gallant, gay Lothario'.

➤ A womanizer or libertine

All too often men who work in tourist resorts are condemned as lecherous Lotharios interested only in sex.
The Independent 1997

Lot's wife [Bible] According to the book of Genesis (19: 24), God destroyed the towns of *Sodom and Gomorrah by fire and brimstone as a punishment for the depravity and wickedness of their inhabitants. *Lot, the nephew of *Abraham, was allowed to escape from the destruction of Sodom with his family. His wife disobeyed God's order not to look back at the burning city and for this she was turned into a *pillar of salt.

> Someone who suffers as a result of looking behind, or looking back to the past

If she turned to look, she might turn into a pillar of salt, she told herself, like Lot's wife in the bible.
LORD-OF-FOOLS *Unregarded Truths* 2005

Lotus-Eaters [Rom. Myth.] People described in *Homer's *Odyssey* as living in a far-off land and eating the fruit of the lotus. When some of *Odysseus' men taste the fruit they lose their desire to return home and 'their only wish was to linger there with the Lotus-Eaters, to feed on the fruit and put aside all thought of a voyage home'.

> People who are content to do nothing

If everyone sits and rests like lotus eaters, nothing can be achieved.
Milli Gazette (New Delhi) 2004

Louis XIV [Hist.] (1638–1715) A French king, also known as the Sun King. He appointed himself to be his own chief minister, and kept tight control over government and policy. He is said to have coined the phrase *'L'état c'est moi' ('I am the state'). His reign was a period of magnificence in terms of art and literature and represented a time of great power for the French in Europe.

> A wealthy and powerful person

Michael came in soaked to the skin—his taxi had broken down and he'd walked the rest of the way—but still behaving as if he was Louis XIV making a grand entrance at a court ball.
PETER DICKINSON *The Yellow Room Conspiracy* 1995

Lovelace [Lit.] The dashing but unscrupulous womanizer who attempts to seduce the virtuous Clarissa in Samuel Richardson's novel *Clarissa* (1747–8).

> A womanizer

Mr Dagonet's notion of the case was almost as remote from reality. All he asked was that his grandson should 'thrash' somebody, and he could not be made to understand that the modern drama of divorce is sometimes cast without a Lovelace.
EDITH WHARTON *The Custom of the Country* 1913

Lowry, L. S. [Art] (1887–1976) An English painter who spent most of his life in Salford, near Manchester. He is best known for his paintings of northern industrial townscapes peopled by small matchstick figures.

> Used to invoke an industrial landscape with factories or mills in the background; also used to describe a scene with many matchstick-like figures

The second shot, taken two years earlier, shows a classic Rowntree Park snow scene that could come straight out of an LS Lowry painting.
The Press, York (Newsquest) 2004

Lubyanka [Places] A building in Moscow that was used as a prison and as the headquarters of the KGB.

> A prison where people are kept and tortured secretly

Insein is Burma's Lubyanka, a 'Special Jail' outside Rangoon where political prisoners are systematically tortured and broken down by the military junta.
Kashmir Herald 2004

Lucan, Lord [People] (b. 1934) A British aristocrat who mysteriously disappeared in 1974 on the night that his wife was attacked and his children's nanny was murdered. He has never been found.

➤ Someone who disappears and cannot be found

Yet again, he displayed the elusive nature of a Lord Lucan as he succeeded in evading the prying cameras outside Mountjoy.
Irish Examiner 2002

Lucifer [Bible] Another name for the *Devil or *Satan, whose name means literally 'Bearer of Light'. According to the Bible, Lucifer was the leader of the angels who rebelled against God and as a punishment were hurled from Heaven down to Hell: 'How art thou fallen from heaven, O Lucifer, son of the morning! how art thou cut down to the ground, which didst weaken the nations!' (Isa. 14: 12). Lucifer is also another name for the Morning Star, the planet Venus.

➤ A devil; someone who falls from grace; someone whose excessive pride leads to their own destruction

Sam Houston famously described [him] as being 'as ambitious as Lucifer and cold as a lizard'.
Alabama Review 2004

Mandelson fell twice, like Lucifer, not because of what he had done, but because of who he was.
Guardian Unlimited columnists 2005

Lucretia (Lucrece) [Leg. & Folk.] A woman who was raped by Sextus, a son of Tarquinus Superbus, king of Rome, and took her own life. According to tradition, this incident led to the expulsion of the Tarquins from Rome by a rebellion under Brutus, and the introduction of republican government. The story is told in *Shakespeare's poem *The Rape of Lucrece* (1594).

➤ A woman who is raped; a woman who takes her own life following a rape

He then, though I struggled against him, kissed me and said, 'Who ever blamed Lucretia? The shame lay on the ravisher only.'
SAMUEL RICHARDSON *Pamela* 1740

Lucrezia Borgia *See* BORGIAS.

Lucullus [People] (c.110–56 BC) A wealthy Roman general who led a luxurious life and was famed for hosting spectacularly lavish feasts.

➤ Mentioned when describing a large or lavish feast

No one gazing at a Feast of Lucullus could ever have experienced the sensations that overtake the shopper in the produce department of a modern American supermarket in early summer.
Guardian Unlimited columnists 2005

Luddites [Hist.] A group of early 19th-century English textile workers who believed that the introduction of new machinery was threatening their jobs. They responded by breaking up the machines. The name derives from a workman called Ned Ludd, nicknamed King Ludd, who is thought to have destroyed two stocking frames.

➤ Someone who opposes change, especially in the form of new technology

US Trade Representative Robert Zoellick has launched a scathing attack on the EU for what he called its 'Luddite' and 'immoral' moratorium on genetically modified crops.
The New Farm: News stories 2003

Luke, St [People] An evangelist who is traditionally believed to be the author of the third Gospel and the Acts of the Apostles. He was a physician, thought to be the person referred to in Colossians as 'Luke, the beloved physician' (Col. 4: 14).

➤ Mentioned in the context of doctors and medicine

Lysistrata [Lit.] The heroine of a comic play of the same name by Aristophanes, first produced in 411 BC. The play was both written and set during the Peloponnesian War between Athens and its empire and Sparta and the Peloponnesian states. Lysistrata decides that the men are not serious about negotiating for peace, so she assembles women from both sides of the conflict and persuades them to refuse to have sex with their husbands until there is peace. The play ends with Lysistrata and the women triumphant and a banquet for both sides in the Acropolis.

➤ A woman who refuses to have sex with her husband or partner as a form of protest

Men should be taking equal responsibility for contraception as well. I take the Lysistrata approach. No equal responsibility for contraception, no sex.
Shanghai Star 2004

Macavity [Lit.] One of the cats in T. S. Eliot's collection of poems *Old Possum's Book of Practical Cats* (1939). Macavity the Mystery Cat is the criminal mastermind, the 'fiend in feline shape', who always has an alibi and always manages to elude Scotland Yard and the Flying Squad: 'For when they reach the scene of crime—Macavity's not there!'

> ➤ Someone who always manages to elude the forces of the law; someone who is notable by their absence

He's in danger of becoming the Macavity of Scottish politics: a leader who was never really there.
Scotland on Sunday 2004

Macbeth [Shakes.] The main character in the play of the same name (1623). Macbeth, spurred on by his wife Lady *Macbeth, kills King Duncan so that he can assume the throne in Duncan's place. After this murder, and the subsequent murder of *Banquo, which Macbeth and his wife also order, they are both troubled by guilt for what they have done. Macbeth becomes distracted and suffers nightmares and visions as a result of his feelings of guilt.

> ➤ Someone who is haunted by guilt for their past actions

Like Macbeth, he is haunted by the spectre of treacherous acts.
Film Inside Out 2003

Macbeth, Lady [Shakes.] The wife of *Macbeth in *Macbeth* (1623). Lady Macbeth, ambitious for her husband's advancement, spurs him on, despite his hesitation and reluctance, to murder King Duncan so that Macbeth will seize the throne. The first murder is followed by others and eventually Lady Macbeth loses her wits and is observed sleepwalking and rubbing her hands in an attempt to remove the spots of blood that she imagines to be on them. She finally goes mad and commits suicide.

> ➤ An ambitious, cold-blooded, and scheming woman; someone haunted by guilt; someone who washes their hands or rubs them together; someone who sleepwalks

With his wife egging him on like Lady Macbeth, Basha decides that he wants the top job for himself.
LYN GARDNER *Guardian Unlimited Reviews* 2004

But can you IMAGINE the guilt? I feel like Lady Macbeth with the blood on my hands.
BreakupGirl advice column 2000

I begin to feel like Lady Macbeth, endlessly washing, washing, trying to get rid of the stink that clogs my nostrils and permeates the very air.
World Socialist Website 2003

McCarthy, Joseph Raymond [Hist.] (1909–57) An American Republican senator. He became chairman of the Permanent Subcommittee on Investigations in 1953 and carried out a campaign against supposed communists, which resulted in many citizens who were suspected of being members of the Communist Party being blacklisted and facing discrimination.

> ➤ Mentioned in the context of a witch-hunt, especially a political one

You preside over the worst witch hunt in public life since Senator McCarthy.
Guardian Unlimited: The Antiwar Movement 2003

Machiavelli, Niccolò di Bernardo dei [People] (1469–1527) An Italian statesman and political philosopher. His best-known work is *The Prince* (1532), in which he argues that rulers may have to resort to methods that are not in themselves desirable in order to rule effectively.

> Someone who uses deceit and cunning in the pursuit of personal power (adjective *Machiavellian*)

When he was running for the job, they described him as an amiable but uncurious and dimwitted scion. Three years later those same critics are describing him as a Machiavelli bent on a 'radical' agenda at home and abroad.
OpinionJournal (WSJ): Leisure and the Arts 2004

This revelation is most definitely not spin, leaked as part of a Machiavellian plot.
Guardian Unlimited columnists 2005

McLuhan, Marshall [People] (1911–80) A Canadian writer and thinker who was particularly interested in the ways in which different communication media affect societies. He claimed that electronic forms of communication had turned the world into a 'global village'.

> Mentioned in the context of modern electronic forms of communication (adjective *McLuhanite*)

Fusing synthesized music, still and digital video imagery, spoken word, vocals, percussion, lighting and a good deal of attitude, TDP creates a bombardment on the brain that would make Marshall McLuhan proud.
FFWD Weekly (Calgary) 2003

Mad Hatter [Child. Lit.] A character in Lewis Carroll's *Alice's Adventures in Wonderland* (1865). *Alice attends a bizarre tea party in the company of the Hatter, the *March Hare, and the *Dormouse. The Hatter's conversation consists mainly of non sequiturs and strange riddles like 'Why is a raven like a writing-desk?' To be 'as mad as a hatter' is to be wildly eccentric, a phrase that derives from the effects of mercury poisoning that was formerly a common disease suffered by hatters.

> Someone who is completely mad; the Mad Hatter's Tea Party is mentioned when describing something that operates in a chaotic way

Mr Dirwan accused Justice Minister Michael McDowell of engaging in 'Alice in Wonderland' thinking with what he described as a mad hatter proposal.
Irish Examiner 2005

For example, had the yen reversed rapidly…as many expected—AIB treasury would still be operating like a mad hatter's tea party and none of this would have come to light.
Sunday Business Post 2002

Madonna [Rel.] A name for the Virgin Mary, the mother of *Jesus Christ, used especially when she is represented in a painting or sculpture. The word literally means 'My Lady'.

> A woman of serene and saintly beauty, or one of perfect virtue and purity

As she stitches away at her sewing, outwardly calm as a marble Madonna, she is all the while exerting her passive stubborn strength against him.
MARGARET ATWOOD *Alias Grace* 1996

Maecenas, Gaius Cilnius [People] (d. 8 BC) A wealthy Roman statesman and patron of Virgil, Horace, and other poets.

> A wealthy patron of the arts

But let's just say for the moment that Saatchi was a Maecenas to an important generation of British artists, and that even if he never buys another painting, or mounts another show, we should be grateful to him for giving us Sensation.
LYNN BARBER *The Observer* 2000

maenad [Gk Myth.] A female participant in the orgiastic rites of *Dionysus. The maenads were also known as Bacchae.

➤ A woman who behaves in a wildly abandoned way

I do not think I shall ever forget the impression she made on me at the party at which I first saw her. She was like a maenad. She danced with an abandon that made you laugh, so obvious was her intense enjoyment of the music and the movement of her young limbs.
W. SOMERSET MAUGHAM *The Human Element* 1951

Mafeking (Mafikeng) [Hist.] A town in South Africa that was attacked by Boers at the start of the Boer War. It was defended by British troops during a seven-month siege before they were relieved by the British army. The success of the defence was a boost to national morale at a time when the course of the war was turning against the British.

➤ Mentioned in the context of relief from a siege or a difficult situation

It is not surprising that many of his staff view Vodafone's bid like the relief of Mafeking, believing that the cellular phone giant will be a less demanding employer.
Scotland on Sunday 2003

Mafia [Crime] A secret society of organized criminals, which originated in Sicily in the 13th century and now operates internationally, especially in the United States, where it developed among Italian immigrants under the name of Cosa Nostra.

➤ A group of people who have control of an activity; a group who stick together and ruthlessly avenge wrongs done to any of their members

There is the fashion mafia which favours impossibly perfect models, thus driving well-adjusted size 14s to self-doubt and cottage cheese.
Sunday Herald 2000

Lucas bought me a penknife. He is trying to bribe me into liking him again. Hard luck, Lucas! Us Moles never forget. We are just like the Mafia, once you cross us we bear a grudge all our lives.
SUE TOWNSEND *The Secret Diary of Adrian Mole Aged 13 3/4* 1982

Magdalene *See* MARY MAGDALENE.

Magi [Bible] The 'three wise men from the East' (Matt. 2: 1) who travelled to Bethlehem to pay homage to the infant *Jesus and bring him gifts of gold, frankincense, and myrrh. Later tradition identified them as kings and named them Caspar, Melchior, and Balthazar.

➤ People bearing gifts

Like magi who carry bad news, White's characters smuggled tragedy and madness in their luggage.
Big Ideas (ABC Radio National) transcripts 2004

magic beans [Fairy tales] The beans that Jack exchanges for his mother's only cow in the children's fairy story of *'Jack and the Beanstalk'. Although the beans grow into an enormous magic beanstalk and ultimately lead to Jack and his mother becoming rich, Jack's mother is initially furious that he has traded the valuable cow for a handful of apparently worthless beans.

> Something which promises great things but may turn out to be worthless

We weren't the only state duped into selling our regulated utilities for some magic beans.
AlterNet: Will Durst columns 2001

magic bullet [Leg. & Folk.] A bullet with special powers in several legends or folk tales, such as the silver bullets used in stories to kill vampires and werewolves.

> A medicine that can cure a seemingly incurable illness; a remedy with the power to solve a problem instantly

Needless to say, there's no magic bullet to cure the cancer.
Spiked Online 2006

The Government keeps thrashing around for that magic bullet, desperate to eliminate this crisis once and for all.
The Observer 2004

Maginot Line [Hist.] A line of fortifications constructed by the French along their eastern border between 1929 and 1934, which was considered to be impregnable but was outflanked by German forces in 1940.

> Something that is intended to protect or defend, but can be easily circumvented

Corporate governance is a bit like the Maginot Line—it's fine until someone sneaks around it.
Sunday Herald 2002

Magna Carta [Hist.] A charter of liberty and political rights that was obtained from King John of England by his rebellious barons at Runnymede in 1215. It is seen as one of the seminal documents of English constitutional practice.

> A charter granting fundamental freedoms or political rights

But the Universal Declaration of Human Rights adopted in 1948 stood out as a beacon of hope, if not expectation. Eleanor Roosevelt then expressed the hope that it would become the Magna Carta of all men everywhere.
CNN transcripts: Insight 2001

Magoo, Mr [Cart. & Com.] A US cartoon character whose first appearance was in 1949. Bald-headed, crotchety, and severely myopic, Quincy Magoo blunders around from one mishap to the next, forever mistaking one object for another.

> Someone who is severely myopic, either literally or figuratively; someone who seems bumbling and incompetent

Two economists...found that professional forecasters surveyed by the Federal Reserve Bank of Philadelphia had all the short-term vision of Mr. Magoo when the business cycle turned.
Taipei Times 2004

Honestly, when it comes to shopping, I'm about as clueless as Mr. Magoo.
Fresh Yarn 2005

Magritte, René [Art] (1898–1967) A Belgian Surrealist painter. His paintings have a dreamlike quality, juxtaposing the ordinary, the strange, and the erotic, all depicted with meticulous realism.

> Used when describing a scene which has a surrealistic quality

Men in bowler hats who seem to have stepped directly out of Magritte paintings mysteriously appear and disappear, and a mysterious nude descends a staircase in scenes that tantalize us with the possibility of meaning that is never fully realized.
Context Magazine 2000

Mahalalel [Bible] One of the patriarchs, according to the book of Genesis, who lived to the age of 895 (Gen. 5: 17). He was the great-grandfather of *Methuselah.

➤ Someone who is extremely old

Malaprop, Mrs [Lit.] The aunt and guardian of Lydia Languish in Sheridan's *The Rivals* (1775). She is noted for her aptitude for misusing long words, responsible for such remarks as 'Illiterate him, I say, quite from your memory' and 'She's as headstrong as an allegory on the banks of the Nile'. Solecisms of this kind are now of course known as malapropisms.

➤ Mentioned in the context of a misuse of words

Interspersed throughout the book are George W Bush jokes and then those are followed by Bush quotations, showing that Dubbya is a keen follower of Mrs. Malaprop and the Rev. Spooner, with such gems as, 'Security is the essential roadblock to achieving the road map to peace.'
Pattaya Mail 2005

Malvolio [Shakes.] Olivia's arrogant, pompous, and puritanical steward in *Twelfth Night* (1623). He is described as 'the best persuaded of himself, so cramm'd, as he thinks, with excellencies that it is his grounds of faith that all that look on him love him'.

➤ An arrogant or pompous person

He smiled on me in quite a superior sort of way—such a smile as would have become the face of Malvolio.
BRAM STOKER *Dracula* 1897

Mambrino's helmet [Lit.] The golden helmet of the pagan king Mambrino in Ariosto's poem *Orlando furioso* (1532), which makes its wearer invisible. In Cervantes' *Don Quixote* (1605), Quixote sees a barber riding with his brass basin upon his head and, mistaking this for Mambrino's helmet, gets possession of it.

➤ Something which makes someone appear invisible

Mammon [Bible] A word used to mean wealth when considered as an idol whose worship is in opposition to that of God. The word derives from the Aramaic word for 'riches'. The most familiar reference is probably *Jesus' teaching that 'No man can serve two masters: for either he will hate the one and love the other; or else he will hold to the one, and despise the other. Ye cannot serve God and mammon' (Matt. 6: 24). Mammon was taken by medieval writers as the proper name of the devil of covetousness, and this use was revived by *Milton in *Paradise Lost*.

➤ A personification of wealth, seen as greedy and selfish materialism

These days money is the measure of all things, and on the altar of Mammon we have sacrificed a whole range of values aimed at safeguarding and bolstering respect for human dignity.
Carlow Nationalist 2004

Mandela, Nelson [People] (b. 1918) A former president of South Africa (1994–9). Before coming to power, he spent 27 years in prison as an anti-apartheid activist. After his release from prison, Mandela supported negotiation and reconciliation, and helped lead the transition towards multi-racial democracy in South Africa.

➤ Someone who fights to liberate their people; a velvet revolutionary

The Israeli Government openly bemoaned the growing perception among his followers that Barghouti was the 'Nelson Mandela of the Palestinians'.
Legal Affairs 2004

man for all seasons [Lit.] A phrase taken from the title of the 1954 play *A Man for All Seasons* by Robert Bolt about the life of Sir Thomas More.

> Someone who has many talents and can deal with any situation or adapt to any circumstances

Ronan Keating is fast evolving into a man for all seasons. He is a singer, a songwriter, a father, a husband—and he is still only 24 years old!
Western People (Co. Mayo) 2002

Man Friday [Lit.] The name given by *Crusoe to the man that he meets on his island (on a Friday) in Daniel Defoe's novel *Robinson Crusoe* (1719). Crusoe has spent many years alone on his island following a shipwreck, and when he meets Man Friday the two become close friends and constant companions.

> A constant or loyal companion or helper

The protection professional is the CEO's man Friday, doing all the grunt work ahead of time to ensure his experience is seamless.
CSO Magazine 2005

Manichaean [Philos.] The word used to describe a dualistic religious philosophy founded in Persia in the 3rd century by the prophet Manes (*c*.216–*c*.276). Combining elements of Christian, Gnostic, and Zoroastrian thought, the philosophy was based on a supposed primeval conflict between light and darkness and between the opposing powers of good and evil. It spread widely in the Roman Empire and in Asia, and survived in Chinese Turkestan until the 13th century.

> Used when describing a situation which involves a dualistic conflict between the forces of good and evil

On one side, there are duty, decency, self-sacrifice, and on the other, personal joy. And in that good old Manichaean tradition of ours, never the twain shall meet.
The Observer 1997

Man in the Iron Mask [People] The name given to a mysterious state prisoner during the reign (1643–1715) of *Louis XIV. The 'Man in the Iron Mask' was held for over 40 years in various prisons until he died in the *Bastille in November 1703. Whenever he travelled between different prisons he wore a black mask, made not in fact of iron, but of velvet. Although his identity was never revealed, he was buried under the name of 'M. de Marchiel'. It has been suggested that he was an illegitimate son or an illegitimate elder brother of Louis XIV.

> A prisoner; a mysterious person whose identity remains unknown

At all times the privileged prisoner's cell was in semi-darkness.... The other prisoners nicknamed him 'The Man in the Iron Mask'...No one knew his real name.
ALEXANDER SOLZHENITSYN *The First Circle* trans. M. GUYBON 1968

manna [Bible] The 'bread' provided by God for the *Israelites when they were crossing the desert during their flight from Egypt (Exod. 16). The manna appeared as small white flakes like frost on the desert floor and would not keep overnight except on the sixth day, when enough was provided to keep for the seventh day also, the sabbath, on which the travellers were to rest. It was white like coriander seed and tasted like wafers made with honey, and it sustained the Israelites until they arrived at the border of *Canaan.

> Something that comes your way unexpectedly, bringing relief or benefit

All this exposure is manna from heaven as far as the drug companies are concerned—but only if it is the right sort.
Sunday Business Post 2002

Manson, Charles [Crime] (b. 1934) The US cult leader who in the 1960s founded a hippy commune outside Los Angeles called the Family. The quasi-religious lifestyle of its members was based on free love, experimentation with drugs, and complete subordination to Manson. In 1969 members of the Family carried out a series of brutal murders, including that of the US actress Sharon Tate, for which Charles Manson and some of his followers received the death sentence, later commuted to life imprisonment.

➢ An evil or mad serial killer

Didn't anybody have a clue this would happen when they hired a guy who directed Bicentennial Man? It's like hiring Charles Manson to baby-sit your children.
Australian Screen Education 2003

Marat, Jean-Paul [People] (1743–93) A French revolutionary politician and journalist. Forced into hiding, he hid in the Paris sewers, where he contracted a skin disease which meant he spent much of his later life sitting in his bath. It was here that he was stabbed to death by the Girondist Charlotte Corday. There is a famous painting called *The Death of Marat* by Jacques-Louis David.

➢ Someone sitting in a bath; someone who dies in a bath

On moving my hand above the surface of the water, I experienced the greatest fright I ever received in the whole course of my life; for imagine my horror on discovering my hand, as I thought, full of blood. My first thought was that I had ruptured an artery, and was bleeding to death, and should be discovered, later on, looking like a second Marat, as I remember seeing him in Madame Tussaud's.
GEORGE and WEEDON GROSSMITH *The Diary of a Nobody* 1892

Marceau, Marcel [Theatre] (1923–2007) A French mime artist. He is most closely associated with his white-faced clown character Bip, developed by Marceau from the French Pierrot character.

➢ Someone who does not speak; someone who moves silently

Wednesday's transcript records that Luis Figo scored two goals and never raised his voice. Zinedine Zidane, the Marcel Marceau of public speaking, surprised with one roar when Madrid defended badly at a set-piece.
The Sunday Times 2004

March Hare [Child. Lit.] A character in Lewis Carroll's *Alice's Adventures in Wonderland* (1865), who is present at the *Mad Hatter's tea party: 'The March Hare took the watch and looked at it gloomily: then he dipped it into his cup of tea, and looked at it again.' The term 'as mad as a March hare' comes from the leaping and boxing and other excitable behaviour characteristic of hares in the breeding season in March.

➢ Someone who seems completely mad

Then, mad as a bunch of March hares, yelling and hooting at the top of our voices, we rushed as fast as our legs would carry us, through the wood to home.
WINIFRED FOLEY *Child in the Forest Trilogy* 1974

Marian, Maid [Leg. & Folk.] The lover of *Robin Hood, according to legend, who lived with Robin and his outlaws in Sherwood Forest.

➢ A woman who helps and supports her lover

He is aided in his quest by the beautiful Lady Emilie (a sort of Maid Marian figure to his Robin Hood).
The Press, York (Newsquest) 2003

Marie Antoinette [Hist.] (1755–93) The wife of Louis XVI and queen of France. Her extravagant lifestyle, combined with a much-quoted response 'Qu'ils mangent de la brioche' (traditionally translated as 'Let them eat cake'), supposedly made on being told that the poor people of Paris were unable to afford bread, have led to her being regarded as a figure of arrogance, indifferent to the plight of the poor. She is also said to have had an idealized view of peasant life. At the Petit Trianon, a small country house in the grounds of the Palace of Versailles, she enjoyed living her version of the simple life of a poor country woman.

> ➢ A rich person who shows indifference to or lack of understanding of the suffering of the poor; someone who plays at enjoying an idyllic rural life

> So many hopelessly white and rich federal officials in the US were caught in their Marie Antoinette moments these past weeks, asking why so many New Orleanians hadn't evacuated the city when they had been warned, only to learn the harsh truth that many simply couldn't afford to do so.
> *Sofia Echo* 2005

> The word may summon up images of gutters and dismal shacks, but it appears, from recent interviews with thirtysomethings, that downshifting actually means going a bit further than Marie Antoinette: you sell your London home for a profit, then find a place in the country in which to live a more meaningful, blissfully stress-free life, often featuring rare breeds of chicken.
> *Guardian Unlimited columnists* 2005

Marius, Gaius [Hist.] (157–86 BC) A Roman general who was overcome by his rival Sulla, and fled to Africa, landing at Carthage. When the Roman governor there sent word that he had to leave the country, Marius' reply was: 'Tell the praetor you have seen Gaius Marius a fugitive sitting among the ruins of Carthage.'

> ➢ Someone who is alone with their thoughts

> And here Bartleby makes his home; sole spectator of a solitude which he has seen all populous—a sort of innocent and transformed Marius brooding among the ruins of Carthage!
> HERMAN MELVILLE *Bartleby* 1856

Marlboro Man [Advert.] A tough cowboy character who appeared in advertising campaigns for Marlboro cigarettes.

> ➢ A tough, rugged-looking man who smokes cigarettes

> There's a new Marlboro Man riding-in from Kansas straight for the White House. With his craggy face and a pocketfull of smokes, this mysterious new Marlboro Man is none other than: Bob Dole.
> *AlterNet: Jim Hightower columns* 2000

Marley's ghost [Lit.] The ghost of Jacob Marley, Ebenezer *Scrooge's late business partner in Charles Dickens's *A Christmas Carol* (1843). Marley's chained ghost appears to the miserly Scrooge on the night of Christmas Eve and warns him to change his ways. The long chain Marley has wound round him is made 'of cash-boxes, keys, padlocks, ledgers, deeds, and heavy purses wrought in steel'.

> ➢ Someone or something that comes back to haunt a person; someone who is held by chains, either literal or figurative

Oh great, now that guidance was going to haunt her like Marley's ghost
My Works 87 *Learning to Break Rules* 2003

He says he's been weighted down with worldly possessions all his life, like Marley's Ghost.
Getting rid of some of the stuff makes him feel young again.
A. J. ORDE *A Long Time Dead* 1994

Marlowe, Philip [Lit.; Cin.] The hard-boiled private detective in such novels as *The Big Sleep* (1939) and *Farewell, my Lovely* (1940) by the US writer Raymond *Chandler. Tough, cynical, yet honourable, the Marlowe character is well known from the films of Chandler's novels, notably as embodied by Humphrey Bogart and Robert Mitchum.

➤ A tough, hard-bitten detective

However, Panorama staged its documentary as a thriller with David Healy as hero, a kind of psychiatric Philip Marlowe, walking the mean streets down which a man must go.
British Medical Journal 2002

Marner, Silas [Lit.] The main character in George Eliot's novel *Silas Marner* (1861). Silas is a bitter, antisocial linen-weaver whose only consolation is the growing pile of gold coins he has accumulated. Only after his gold is stolen does he find new meaning to his life when he adopts, and comes to love, an abandoned village girl called Eppie.

➤ A miser

The country blacksmith would not, of course, have a bank account in town. Nor would he have one in the country. Like Silas Marner, Joe would keep his savings under a floorboard.
JOHN SUTHERLAND *The Literary Detective: 100 Puzzles in Classic Fiction* 2000

Marple, Miss [Lit.] The elderly detective created by the crime writer Agatha *Christie. She lives in the village of St Mary Mead, indulging in her hobbies of knitting and gardening. Her disarming appearance as a mildly gossipy old spinster hides a shrewdness and acuteness of observation that she uses to solve murders.

➤ A detective

Detectives had a mystery of Miss Marple proportions on their hands and it remained unsolved for almost 13 years.
Yorkshire Post Today 2001

Mars [Rom. Myth.] The god of war, corresponding to the Greek god Ares.

➤ A way of referring to war

I have already said that I am not much of an actor, but I gave a powerful, if crude impersonation of the hero who is tremendous on the field of Mars but slighted in the courts of Venus.
ROBERTSON DAVIES *Fifth Business* 1970

Martha [Bible] The sister of Mary and *Lazarus and a friend of *Jesus. When Jesus visits their house, Mary sits and listens to Jesus while Martha fusses about with meal preparations and other household chores (Luke 10).

➤ A woman who is constantly busying herself with domestic affairs

Quite frankly, I blame the ladies for the continuation of male arrogance, as there are not too many Marthas prepared to rock boats and claim justice.
Carlow Nationalist 2002

Marvel, Captain [Cart. & Com.] An American comic-book hero from the 1940s, who used his superhuman powers to defeat evil villains. He transformed himself into his costumed form by uttering the magic word 'Shazam!'

> ➢ Someone with superhuman powers

Kasimov has been the 'Captain Marvel' of the Asian Cup, propelling Uzbekistan into the quarter-finals.
The Irish Examiner 2004

Marvin [Lit.] A gloomy and depressed robot in Douglas Adams's book *The Hitch-Hiker's Guide to the Galaxy* (1979, first radio broadcast 1978) and its sequels. Referred to as the Paranoid Android, Marvin takes a universally pessimistic view about everything and is prone to complain that he has a pain down all the diodes on his left side.

> ➢ Someone who sounds exceedingly gloomy

'Hello?' I asked the person on the other end of the line. My voice sounded dull, even to me. I vaguely thought of Marvin the Paranoid Android before turning my attention back to waiting to find out who had been calling me.
PUUUURFECT ANGEL *If You Leave* 2004

Marx, Groucho (Julius Henry Marx) [Cin.] (1890–1977) One of the US comedy team the *Marx Brothers. His urgent, crouching walk was as distinctive as his wisecracking one-liners and his facial appearance, complete with painted black moustache, glasses, and cigar.

> ➢ Someone who walks quickly, with legs bent low to the ground, in a comical way; someone who waggles their eyebrows in an exaggerated way; someone who has a large cigar in their mouth

He rushed out of the car like Groucho Marx to get cigarettes—that furious, ground-hugging walk with the coattails flying.
JACK KEROUAC *On the Road* 1957

'Don't think, baby, it ain't doin' ya no good,' he said, waggling his eyebrows like Groucho Marx.
SUSINA SKYE *Reach for a Star* 2003

Marx, Harpo (Adolph Arthur Marx) [Cin.] (1888–1964) One of the *Marx Brothers, a family of American comedians who made comic films in the 1930s. In the films, Harpo is always mute, communicating by means of an old-fashioned car horn.

> ➢ Someone who does not speak

'How did you know about us?' 'Her mother mentioned it. Talkative woman.' 'Her mother? She's about as talkative as Harpo Marx.'
MAX MARQUIS *Written in Blood* 1995

Marx Brothers [Cin.] A family of American film comedians consisting of the brothers Chico (Leonard, 1886–1961), *Harpo, *Groucho, and Zeppo (Herbert, 1901–79). Their films are characterized by an anarchic humour and madcap zaniness, and include *Duck Soup* (1933) and *A Night at the Opera* (1935).

> ➢ Mentioned in the context of slapstick comedy or zaniness

The daily loading could take an hour and resembled something out of a Marx Brothers' routine.
Sunday Business Post 2001

Mary Celeste [Leg. & Folk.] An American brig (often erroneously referred to as the *Marie Celeste*) that set sail from New York for Genoa and was found drifting in the north Atlantic in December 1872, in perfect condition but abandoned, and with evidence of very recent occupation. The fate of the crew was never discovered, and the abandonment of the ship remains one of the great mysteries of the sea.

> A place that is completely empty, or a place that seems to have been mysteriously abandoned

A quick scoping of the kitchen didn't tell me much. There were no half-eaten meals on the table, no coffee bubbling on the hotplate. This wasn't a Marie Celeste situation, this looked like somebody who'd gone on holiday in a slight rush.
MIKE RIPLEY *Family of Angels* 1996

Mary Magdalene [Bible] One of the followers of *Jesus. She is often identified with the woman, a sinner ashamed of her sins, who came to Jesus in the Pharisee's house, washed his feet with her tears, dried them with her hair, and anointed them with ointment (Luke 7: 38). In art, she is often portrayed weeping repentant tears, and the word 'maudlin' is derived from her name.

> A reformed prostitute

'Trying to help women who've come to grief.' Old Jolyon did not quite understand. 'To grief?' he repeated; then realised with a shock that she meant exactly what he would have meant himself if he had used that expression. Assisting the Magdalenes of London! What a weird and terrifying interest!
JOHN GALSWORTHY *A Man of Property* 1906

Mason, Perry [TV; Lit.] The fictional defence lawyer in a series of novels by Erle Stanley Gardner and in a US television series of the 1960s. The stories frequently end with a dramatic courtroom scene in which Mason proves his client innocent of the crime.

> A talented lawyer

How like Denn to choose a place like this for a rendezvous. He knew perfectly well he should turn himself in to Sheriff Bo Poole and try to hire himself a Perry Mason.
MARGARET MARON *Bootlegger's Daughter* 1992

Mason Dixon Line [Hist.] The boundary between Maryland and Pennsylvania in the USA, which was taken as the northern limit of slave-owning states before the abolition of slavery.

> 'South of the Mason Dixon Line' is used when referring to conservative political opinions or fundamentalist religious opinions in the USA

Suddenly there are morals and cheesy religious lessons zooming around the screen and it's apparent that this is very much a Mason Dixon Line Fundamentalist special.
ABC regional—Tasmania 2004

Massacre of the Innocents [Bible] The killing of all boy children under two years old in Bethlehem, under the order of *Herod after the birth of *Jesus.

> The killing of a large number of civilians, especially children

We should defeat the human evil that showed itself in New York on September 11 2001, in the bombing of Madrid on March 11 2004, and in the massacre of the innocents in Beslan last week.
Guardian Unlimited 2001

Mata Hari [People] (1876–1917) A Dutch dancer (b. Margaretha Geertruida Zelle) who was also a courtesan, and spy. She became a professional 'oriental' dancer in Paris in 1905 and probably worked for both French and German intelligence services during the First World War, obtaining military secrets from high-ranking Allied officers. She was executed by the French for espionage in 1917.

> A beautiful, seductive woman; a woman who uses seduction for her own gain

A junior partner promoted by their lover can be seen as a Mata Hari.
The Observer 1997

Match Girl *See* LITTLE MATCH GIRL.

Matilda [Child. Lit.] A young girl in one of Hilaire Belloc's *Cautionary Tales* (1939). 'Matilda, Who Told Lies and Was Burned to Death' tells the story of Matilda, a young girl who 'told such Dreadful Lies', who had called out the fire brigade as a joke, only to find herself a few weeks later at home when a real fire broke out. Despite her screams for help, no one would believe that there really was a fire:

> For every time She shouted 'Fire!'
> They only answered 'Little Liar!'

Matilda and the house were both burned.

➢ Someone who suffers as a result of telling lies

Mecca [Rel.] A city in western Saudi Arabia (Arabic, Makkah), an oasis town in the Red Sea region of Hejaz, east of Jiddah. It was the birthplace in AD 570 of the prophet *Muhammad. Mecca is held to be the holiest city of the Islamic world and is the destination for Muslims undertaking the haj (pilgrimage).

➢ A place that attracts many visitors or the enthusiasts of a particular activity

'But here we are at the Mecca of English cricket,' said Lord Ickenham, suspending his remarks as the cab drew up at the entrance of Lord's.
P. G. WODEHOUSE *Cocktail Time* 1958

Meddlesome Matty [Child. Lit.] A character in *Original Poems, for Infant Minds by Several Young Persons*, a collection of poems for children by Ann and Jane Taylor and others, published in two volumes in 1804 and 1805. Matilda (or Matty), 'though a pleasant child' in other respects, is a compulsive meddler.

➢ Someone who meddles in others' affairs

His passion for playing the literary Meddlesome Mattie was aroused.
ROBERTSON DAVIES *The Deptford Trilogy* 1975

Medea [Gk Myth.] A princess of Colchis. She was a sorceress who fell in love with *Jason and helped him to obtain the *Golden Fleece. When Jason later abandoned her to marry the daughter of Creon, king of Corinth, she was so enraged that she took revenge by murdering their two children as well as Jason's young bride.

➢ A woman who murders her own children

Few of us wish to disturb the mother of a litter of puppies when mouthing a bone in the midst of her young family. Medea and her children are familiar to us, and so is the grief of Constance.
ANTHONY TROLLOPE *Barchester Towers* 1857

Medes and Persians [Bible] In the book of Daniel, King Darius signed a decree saying that for 30 days no one should pray to any God or man except the king. The king's officials called for him to 'establish the decree, and sign the writing, that it be not changed, according to the law of the Medes and Persians, which altereth not' (Dan. 6: 8). It was as a punishment for ignoring Darius' command that *Daniel was cast into the *lions' den.

➢ Mentioned in the context of a law that cannot be changed

I know what my aim is, and what my motives are; and at this moment I pass a law, unalterable, as that of the Medes and Persians, that both are right.
CHARLOTTE BRONTË *Jane Eyre* 1847

Medusa [Gk Myth.] One of the *Gorgons who, like her sisters, had snakes for hair and the power to turn anyone who looked at her to stone. Medusa, the only mortal one of the sisters, was killed by *Perseus, who cut off her head.

> A woman whose stare inspires great fear; a woman with wild-looking hair

The wind had picked up considerably, invading Anna's hair to create a sort of Medusa effect.
ARMISTEAD MAUPIN *Sure of You* 1990

He was avoiding Crystal's gaze as if she were a Medusa and he feared being turned to stone.
FAERWYN *Heir of Mine* 2003

Mekon [Cart. & Com.] Dan *Dare's arch-enemy in the comic strip by Frank Hampson which appeared in the *Eagle* comic between 1950 and 1967. He originates from the planet Venus, is green-skinned, and has a small body and an enormous bald head.

> A person with a large domelike head

Crash bade farewell to another student, a rich teenage boy with the good build and space-ranger short-back-and-sides and Mekon cranium of the future.
MARTIN AMIS *The Information* 1995

Meldrew, Victor [TV] The prematurely retired curmudgeon played by Richard Wilson in the British television comedy series *One Foot in the Grave* (1990–2000). He continually expresses his irritation with the petty annoyances and indignities of life with the incredulous exclamation 'I don't believe it!'

> Someone who is excessively grumpy or cantankerous

Britain's middle-aged middle classes are, like Victor Meldrew, in a state of constant rage against the world.
Scotland on Sunday 2002

Melpomene [Gk Myth.] The *Muse of tragedy in Greek mythology.

> Mentioned in the context of tragedy or suffering

His face is like the tragic mask of Melpomene.
THOMAS HARDY *Jude the Obscure* 1895

Menjou, Adolph [Cin.] (1890–1963) A dapper French American film actor who was always elegantly dressed and had a curly moustache, turned up at the ends.

> Someone with a small curly moustache

Wags have even posted pictures on the web that show Kerry in a beret, with a little Adolph Menjou moustache.
Lingua Franca (programme transcripts) 2004

Mephistopheles [Leg. & Folk.] The evil spirit to whom *Faust in German legend sold his soul, especially as represented in Marlowe's *Doctor Faustus* (c.1590) and Goethe's *Faust* (1808–32). Mephistopheles entraps Faust with wit, charm, and rationality.

> A fiendish but urbane tempter (adjective *Mephistophelian*)

[The show's] core is the Faustean pact between a young college teacher and the Mephistopheles of NBC television desperate for a hero with whom they believed the viewers could identify.
The Guardian 1995

The opera shows the decline of country boy Tom Rakewell, who inherits a fortune at the outset, courtesy of the Mephistophelian Nick Shadow, his new friend and constant tempter and nemesis throughout the story.
Classical Net Reviews 2005

Mercury [Rom. Myth.] The messenger of the gods, identified with the Greek *Hermes. He is pictured as a herald wearing winged sandals which enable him to travel very swiftly.

➢ A messenger

The affair of the carriage was arranged by Mr Harding, who acted as Mercury between the two ladies.
ANTHONY TROLLOPE *Barchester Towers* 1857

Merlin [Arth. Leg.] The wizard who counselled and guided King *Arthur and his father Uther before him. Late in his life he fell in love with *Nimue. She tricked him into giving her the secrets of his magic and then imprisoned him in the forest of Brocéliande, near Brittany. According to the legend, he never escaped and lies there still.

➢ A magician; a wise counsellor

And you know you were never much of a lover, Magnus. What does that matter? You were a great magician, and has any great magician ever been a great lover? Look at Merlin: his only false step was when he fell in love and ended up imprisoned in a tree for his pains.
ROBERTSON DAVIES *The Deptford Trilogy* 1975

We need a new democratic framework that can engage an active citizenry who can then dispense, for the most part, with the ministrations of modern Merlins.
The Observer 1997

Merry Men [Leg. & Folk.] The name given to the band of outlaws who lived in Sherwood Forest with *Robin Hood, according to legend.

➢ A group of helpers or co-workers who work with someone

Sir Edward George and his band of merry men will sit again in deliberation on UK interest rates.
MotleyFool.co.uk: Comment 2001

Mesmer, Franz Anton [People] (1734–1815) An Austrian physician who had a successful practice in Vienna, where he used a number of novel treatments. He is chiefly remembered for the introduction of hypnotism, known as mesmerism, as a therapeutic technique.

➢ Someone who seems able to control other people's minds and behaviour

Like some magical Mesmer, he has persuaded his people to feel well about themselves.
The Observer 1997

Messiah [Bible] The promised deliverer of the Jewish nation prophesied in the Hebrew Bible. In Christianity, the term is applied to *Jesus Christ.

➢ Someone who is worshipped; someone who saves or delivers others

Santa Claus is the graven image everywhere surrounded by lights, colour displays and the latest versions which are self illuminating, automated and even talking. Here is the Messiah of consumerism, his image everywhere.
Sunday Business Post 2001

mess of pottage [Bible] A stew of lentils cooked by *Jacob in the Old Testament. Jacob's twin brother *Esau, returning from the countryside, found Jacob cooking 'red pottage of lentils'. He was extremely hungry and asked for some of the stew. Jacob would only give

Esau the food if he swore to sell Jacob his birthright as the elder of the twins. Esau sold his birthright to Jacob and ate the stew.

> ➤ Something pleasant and immediately satisfying for which one gives up something more valuable

'The artist who accepts the honors and emoluments of state becomes a "state man",' writes Bill Kauffmann. 'He has sold his birthrights—freedom and independence—for a mess of pottage.'
Ludwig von Mises Institute: Daily Articles 2004

methinks the lady doth protest too much [Shakes.] A popular misquotation from *Hamlet* (1604), the actual quotation being, 'The lady doth protest too much, methinks.' The line is spoken by Gertrude, to say that the promises of love spoken by the Player Queen to her husband seem excessive or insincere.

> ➤ Used when someone denies something very strongly, which suggests that they may in fact be hiding the truth

But one thing is certain: the government's denial was so fierce that it was either a case of 'methinks the lady doth protest too much,' or else the government was trying to reassure the powerful right-wing elite that there was no cause for concern.
The Unofficial British Royal Family Pages 2004

Methuselah [Bible] The oldest of the patriarchs, grandfather of *Noah. He is supposed to have lived 969 years (Gen. 5: 27).

> ➤ An extremely old person

Insurers are increasingly asking for medicals before underwriting an older driver, according to Crowder. The Institute of Advanced Motorists says that our roadhog Methuselahs are themselves aware of the problem, with seven out of 10 saying they would like refresher courses to brush up on busy motorways.
Scotland on Sunday 2005

Micawber, Mr [Lit.] A character in Dickens's novel *David Copperfield* (1850), who dreams up elaborate schemes for making money which never materialize. Ever-impecunious, he famously encapsulates the principle of balancing income and expenditure as follows: 'Annual income twenty pounds, annual expenditure nineteen nineteen six, result happiness. Annual income twenty pounds, annual expenditure twenty pounds nought and six, result misery.' Despite his lack of success, he remains undaunted and optimistic, never losing his belief that something will 'turn up'.

> ➤ Someone who remains optimistic even when circumstances seem bleak; also alluded to in the context of book-balancing and not over-spending (adjective *Micawberesque*)

Who is financially more stable, the City slicker earning £75,000 a year and spending £85,000, or the factory worker earning £10,000 and spending £9,000? Charles Dickens' Mr Micawber had it right: over-spending is a recipe for misery.
MotleyFool.co.uk: Fool's Eye View 2004

As the shadow work and pensions secretary, David Willetts, said yesterday, he takes the Mr Micawber approach to economics: something will turn up.
Guardian Unlimited columnists 2005

Michelangelo (Michelangelo Buonarroti) [Art] (1475–1564) An Italian sculptor, painter, architect, and poet. In his portrayal of the nude, Michelangelo depicted the beauty and strength of the human body. He is probably best known for painting the ceiling of the *Sistine Chapel in Rome (1508–12).

> Used to evoke male beauty

I have seldom seen a more splendid young fellow. He was naked to the waist and of a build that one day might be over-corpulent. But now he could stand as a model to Michelangelo!
WILLIAM GOLDING *Rites of Passage* 1980

Michelin Man [Advert.] A cartoon character used as a symbol of the French Michelin company. The character, a rotund, jolly man made of tyres, was created by the artist O'Galop and first introduced in 1894.

> Someone with thick rolls of fat on their body; someone wearing thick, padded clothes

Mrs Watson had claimed that the operation had left her looking like a Michelin man, complete with 'all the lumps and bumps' around her abdomen and hips that were unsightly and unnatural.
Yorkshire Post Today 2001

Craig Wolstenholme, looking like a 'Michelin Man' in his body padding, can testify to Khan's strength and power as he was pummelled all around the gym by the young boxer in a training exercise.
Bolton Evening News 2005

Mickey Mouse [Cart. & Com.] A Walt *Disney cartoon character in the form of a mouse, who first appeared in 1928 and spoke in a distinctive squeaky, high-pitched voice.

> Used to describe something insignificant or trivial; also used to describe a high-pitched or squeaky-sounding voice

I began to repeat this sentence in a variety of tones, stresses and dialects, ranging from a rapid Mickey Mouse squeak to a bass drawl.
KEITH WATERHOUSE *Billy Liar* 1959

We got a Mickey Mouse educational system that doesn't teach us how things work, how the government works, who runs it.
STUDS TERKEL *American Dreams: Lost and Found* 1980

Midas [Gk Myth.] A legendary king of Phrygia, a country in what is now part of Turkey. In Greek legend, Midas was granted his wish that everything he touched should be turned to gold. However, when the food in his mouth and, according to some versions, even his beloved daughter turned to gold, he begged to be released from his gift.

> Someone who is very rich, or has a gift for making money, seemingly without effort

He has led a charmed life so far—a man with a Midas touch who seems to be able to turn every whim, hobby, and surmise into gold.
Fast Company Magazine 2004

Midian, hosts of [Bible] The Midianites were a tribal group portrayed in the Bible as nomadic shepherds and traders. The book of Judges relates the story of a battle led by Gideon against the Midianites in which he defeated the 'host of Midian'.

> An unfriendly or hostile group

I shouldn't be surprised if Tommy and his little friend weren't still lurking in the shadows somewhere. They're like the hosts of Midian. They prowl and prowl around.
P. G. WODEHOUSE *Laughing Gas* 1936

milk of human kindness [Shakes.] A quotation from *Macbeth* (1606), spoken by Lady *Macbeth as she expressed her concern that her husband lacked the necessary ruthlessness to kill Duncan and seize the throne: 'Yet do I fear thy nature; it is too full o' the milk of human kindness to catch the nearest way.'

> ➤ A way of referring to kindness or compassion

> Well done indeed to all who supported the Lions Club/WLR Christmas Appeal, Charity Swims and all other worthy causes over the Yuletide period as the milk of human kindness flowed abundantly.
> *Waterford News and Star* 2004

Miller, Daisy [Lit.] The heroine of a short novel with the same name by Henry James, published in 1879. She is a naive young American woman who is touring Europe with her mother and brother and finds herself in compromising situations because of her trusting nature and ignorance of social conventions.

> ➤ A naive young woman

Millet, Jean-François [Art] (1814–75) A French painter, etcher, and draughtsman, known especially for his scenes of peasants at work such as *The Gleaners* (1857) and *The Angelus* (1858–9).

> ➤ Used to evoke a scene of simple or idyllic rural life

> I found myself possessed of a surprising interest in the shepherdess, who stood far away in the hill pasture with her great flock, like a figure of Millet's, high against the sky.
> SARAH ORNE JEWETT *A Dunnet Shepherdess* 1899

Mills and Boon [Lit.] The name of a publishing partnership formed by **Gerald Mills** (d. 1927) and **Charles Boon** (1877–1943), which specializes in publishing popular romantic fiction.

> ➤ Mentioned in the context of an over-sentimental love story

> In some respects this is a Mills & Boonish story, with moments of cloying sentimentality and throbbing musical crescendoes.
> *The Independent* 1995

Milquetoast, Caspar [Cart. & Com.] A timid comic-strip character created by the American cartoonist H. T. Webster in 1924.

> ➤ A meek, submissive, or timid person

> And UN Secretary General Kofi Annan, momentarily abandoning his customary Caspar Milquetoast approach, actually has gone to NATO and said a credible threat of force was 'essential' to make diplomacy effective.
> *Chicago Tribune* 1999

Milton, John [Lit.] (1608–74) A major English poet of the 17th century whose works include *Lycidas* (1638), **Paradise Lost* (1667), *Paradise Regained* (1671), and *Samson Agonistes* (1671).

> ➤ A great or poetic writer

Mimir [Norse Myth.] A giant who guarded the well of wisdom near the roots of the great ash tree Yggdrasil.

> ➤ Mentioned in the context of wisdom

> Allfadir did not get a drink of Mimir's spring.
> RALPH WALDO EMERSON *The Conduct of Life* 1860

Mindanao Trench [Places] A submarine trench in the floor of the Philippine Sea bordering the east coast of the island of Mindanao. This abyss is one of the deepest places on earth, its deepest point being 10 850 metres below sea level.

> ➤ A deep, dark, cold place

   'If she had visited my daughter, she would have said so. Frances is incapable of lying. She hasn't the wit,' he said, his voice cold and dark as the Mindanao Trench.
   CYNTHIA HARROD-EAGLES *Shallow Grave* 1998

Minerva [Rom. Myth.] The goddess of handicrafts, wisdom, and also of war, identified with the Greek *Athene. She was also believed to have invented the flute.

> ➤ A woman skilled in handicrafts, a wise woman, a woman playing the flute; a warlike woman

   'Thank you very much,' said Oak, in the modest tone good manners demanded, thinking, however, that he would never let Bathsheba see him playing the flute; in this resolve showing a discretion equal to that related of its sagacious inventress, the divine Minerva herself.
   THOMAS HARDY *Far from the Madding Crowd* 1874

   There was, as I have said, a Minerva fully armed.
   MARILYNNE ROBINSON *Mother Country* 1989

Ministry of Silly Walks [TV] A spoof government department which appeared in a well-known sketch from *Monty Python's Flying Circus*, a popular British television comedy series of the 1970s. The Ministry employs bowler-hatted civil servants, each of whom has an outlandish style of walking.

> ➤ Mentioned when describing a zany or comical style of walking

   He dances with his rifle, a weary bedraggled man on leave, with movements under license from the Ministry of Silly Walks.
   Ballet.co.uk magazine 2004

Minos [Gk Myth.] A legendary king of Crete, son of *Zeus and Europa. His wife *Pasiphae gave birth to the *Minotaur, which was kept in the *Labyrinth constructed by *Daedalus. Minos demanded an annual tribute from Athens of seven youths and seven girls to be fed to the Minotaur. After his death, Minos became the judge of the dead in the underworld.

> ➤ Mentioned in the context of a labyrinth-like arrangement of rooms and passages; also used to denote one stern in judgement

   But it is an ancient, rambling pile, and would require another Minos to trace its regions, with its bedchambers and byrooms and passages and parlours and other rooms severally partitioned.
   PETER ACKROYD *The House of Doctor Dee* 1993

   'Over there!' he bellowed with the authority of Minos sending a damned soul down to the lowest rung of Hell.
   RICHARD DOOLEY *Brainstorm* 1998

Minotaur [Gk Myth.] The creature with a bull's head and a man's body that was confined in the Labyrinth built by *Daedalus, and devoured human flesh. Seven youths and seven girls from Athens were sacrificed to the Minotaur annually, until it was eventually killed by *Theseus, with the aid of *Ariadne.

> ➤ An evil monster; something dangerous lying at the centre of a maze or labyrinth

His mind was a dark labyrinth, intricate and convoluted, with a Minotaur of some
kind crouching at the core. There was something frightening as well as fascinating
about him.
JOHN SPENCER HILL *The Last Castrato* 1995

Miranda [Shakes.] The beautiful and innocent daughter of *Prospero in *The Tempest* (1623).
Brought up on a deserted island with only her father for company, Miranda has never seen
the deceit, wickedness, and corruption of the world, and on becoming acquainted with men
who have been shipwrecked on the island she utters the famous lines:

> How beauteous mankind is! O brave new world,
> That has such people in't!

Ironically, the people she is speaking of are the very ones who deposed and exiled Prospero
many years before.

> ➤ A young innocent unaware of the darker side of human nature and full of wonder and
> joy at the world and human society

She found herself standing, in the character of hostess, face to face with a man she
had never seen before—moreover, looking at him with a Miranda-like curiosity and
interest that she had never yet bestowed on a mortal.
THOMAS HARDY *A Pair of Blue Eyes* 1873

Miriam [Bible] The sister of Aaron, who went with *Moses when he led his people across
the Red Sea and out of Egypt. When they had crossed the Red Sea safely, Miriam 'took up
a timbrel in her hand' and said 'Sing ye to the Lord, for he hath triumphed gloriously'
(Exod. 15: 20–1). This is sometimes referred to as the Song of Miriam.

> ➤ Someone who sings, especially for joy

Mirror, mirror on the wall...[Fairy tales] Part of the rhyme used by the stepmother
in the traditional fairy tale '*Snow White'. The proud and vain stepmother regularly asks
her magic mirror:

> Mirror, mirror on the wall,
> Who is the fairest of them all?

> ➤ Used when asking a question about the biggest, best, etc.

Mirror, Mirror on the Wall, who is the vainest of them all? According to a 30-country
study by trend tracker Roper Starch Worldwide, it is Venezuelan women.
NRIOL news snippets 2004

Mission Impossible [TV; Cin.] The title of a US television drama series about espionage,
originally broadcast 1966–72. The storylines involved a team of secret government agents taking
on and completing seemingly impossible missions. The title was later used for a series of
Hollywood films on the same theme, starring Tom Cruise.

> ➤ An impossible or extremely difficult task

Alexander Downer is taking on mission impossible by trying to secure a breakthrough
with North Korea.
The Australian 2004

Mithras [Myth.] A Persian god of light and truth who was also adopted as a god by the
Romans, especially in the military world. He was usually represented in the act of sacrificing
a bull.

> ➤ A warlike leader

Mitty, Walter [Lit.] The main character in James Thurber's short story 'The Secret Life of Walter Mitty' (1939). The story relates how Mitty, a henpecked husband, escapes his wife's nagging by retreating into his own world of daydreams in which he is the hero of many adventures.

> Someone who lives in a fantasy world, especially someone who has lost touch with reality

During his 1995 court appearance Whiting's mother described her son as a Walter Mitty character, who created plans in his own mind which had no chance of coming to fruition and which bore no resemblance to reality.
Yorkshire Post Today 2001

Mnemosyne [Gk Myth.] The mother of the *Muses and goddess of memory.

> Mentioned in the context of someone's ability to remember

But the sight of old Mr Woodford standing in the entrance archway snapped his line of thought before Mnemosyne could come to his aid.
CHESTER HIMES *Headwaiter* 1937

Moab [Bible] An ancient region east of the Dead Sea, the inhabitants of which, the Moabites, were said to be incestuously descended from Moab, son of *Lot and Lot's daughter. Adultery between *Israelites and 'the daughters of Moab' is fiercely condemned in the Old Testament: 'And Israel abode in Shittim, and the people began to commit whoredom with the daughters of Moab' (Num. 25: 1).

> Mentioned in the context of an interracial union

This resembled, in the divine's opinion, the union of a Moabitish stranger with a daughter of Zion.
WALTER SCOTT *The Bride of Lammermoor* 1819

Möbius strip [Science] A strip of material that is joined in a circle with one 180-degree twist along its length, invented by the German mathematician **August Ferdinand Möbius** (1790–1868). If you start on the outer edge and trace along the length of the strip, you will seamlessly cross to the inner edge and then back again.

> A situation in which you change from one thing to another without being aware of it; a situation that seems to continue in a never-ending loop

It's a trippy well-acted affair, so I can't tell you why it seems so repetitive and awfully boring other than it repeats itself in some endless Mobius strip kind of way so you never know where you are in the story.
DVD Verdict 2005

Moby Dick [Lit.] The name of the great white whale in Herman Melville's *Moby Dick* (1851). The whale is the object of Captain *Ahab's passionate and obsessional quest, driven by revenge for the loss of his leg in a previous encounter with the creature.

> A whale; the object of an obsessional pursuit

Meat was hard to get hold of, but one thing that was available was whale meat. I remember eating whale steak, which was called Moby Dick and chips.
Observer Food Monthly 2004

Despite the film-maker's obsessive pursuit, Maggie is never tracked down. She is Moby Dick to his Ahab.
Screen Online: British television series 2003

Modest Proposal [Lit.] A phrase taken from the title of a 1729 satirical pamphlet by Jonathan Swift: *A Modest Proposal: For Preventing the Children of Poor People from Being a Burden to their Parents or the Country, and for Making them Beneficial to the Public.* The satirical 'proposal' put forward by Swift was for poor Irish peasants to ease their economic difficulties by selling their children as food to their wealthy landlords.

> ➤ An extreme or outrageous suggestion as to how a problem could be solved
>
> In order to achieve this, Melnyk suggests a boycott of things American. Perhaps, this is more a Swiftian 'modest proposal' than a serious and sustainable option.
> *FFWD Weekly (Calgary)* 2004

Modigliani, Amedeo [Art] (1884–1920) An Italian painter and sculptor whose portraits and nudes have boldly simplified features and distinctively elongated forms.

> ➤ Used to evoke a woman's body that seems excessively thin and elongated
>
> She was…waiting like a longbodied emaciated Modigliani surrealist woman in a serious room.
> JACK KEROUAC *On the Road* 1957

Moloch [Bible] A Canaanite deity referred to in several books of the Old Testament to whom worshippers sacrificed their children.

> ➤ Something that has great power and demands a terrible sacrifice
>
> Ginsberg sympathised with the homeless street beggars, victims of industrial capitalism, or 'Moloch' as he called it.
> *Lingua Franca (programme transcripts)* 2000

Mona Lisa [Art] The title of a painting by *Leonardo da Vinci, perhaps the most famous painting in the world. The painting is also known as *La Gioconda* because the sitter was the wife of Francesco di Bartolommeo del Giocondo di Zandi. Her enigmatic smile has become one of the most famous images in Western art.

> ➤ Used to evoke a slight and enigmatic smile
>
> She declined to express an opinion, answering only with a Mona Lisa smile.
> A. S. BYATT *Possession* 1990

Monopoly money Imitation paper money used in the board game Monopoly® in which players engage in buying, selling, and developing property.

> ➤ Money that is or feels like toy money, with no real value; a ridiculously large amount of money
>
> Inflation has turned the Zimbabwean dollar into Monopoly money.
> *Sunday Herald* 2000
>
> A decent house in the Dublin area is about £200,000. That is crazy money for even a couple with both people working—it is Monopoly money because it is not within the average person's reach.
> *Irish Examiner* 2001

Monroe, Marilyn [Cin.] (1926–62) An American film actress, born Norma Jean Mortenson, later Baker. She became the definitive Hollywood sex symbol, a breathy-voiced blonde who combined sex appeal with innocence and vulnerability. She starred in such films as *Gentlemen Prefer Blondes* (1953) and *Some Like It Hot* (1959) before her death from an overdose of sleeping pills in 1962.

> ➤ A beautiful woman, especially one with blonde hair

A small, curvaceous woman with platinum blonde hair sashayed towards us across the newsroom like some latter-day Marilyn Monroe.
ANNIE ROSS *Moving Image* 1995

Montagues and Capulets [Shakes.] The warring Veronese families in *Romeo and Juliet* (1599). Juliet is a Capulet and Romeo a Montague, and their love and secret marriage are doomed when Romeo reluctantly becomes embroiled in the bitter hatred and fighting between the families.

> ➤ Two families or groups engaged in a long-running feud

> There were soon two factions facing off like Montagues and Capulets.
> *BBC Radio 4* 1997

Monte Cristo, Count of [Lit.] The hero of the novel *The Count of Monte Cristo* by Alexandre Dumas published in 1844. The novel relates how Edmond Dantès is betrayed by enemies and incarcerated in the *Chateau d'If. After fourteen years he finally manages to escape, having been told by a fellow prisoner of buried treasure on the island of Monte Cristo. Dantès finds the treasure, assumes the title of Count of Monte Cristo, and sets about taking revenge on those who had brought about his imprisonment.

> ➤ Someone who manages to escape from incarceration; someone who takes revenge on an enemy

> What Wield had said was, 'He's not going back there. He escaped.' Hiding his relief, Digween exclaimed, 'He...it...is a monkey, not the Count of bloody Monte Cristo.'
> REGINALD HILL *On Beulah Height* 1998

Monty Python [TV] The name of a British television comedy series (full title *Monty Python's Flying Circus*) which was first broadcast between 1969 and 1974 and is remembered for its combination of satire, bad taste, and surrealist sense of the absurd.

> ➤ Mentioned when describing zany humour, or a situation that seems bizarre or surreal (adjective *Pythonesque*)

> There before my eyes was this enormous girl staggering under the weight of an enormous tuba. I swear to God, it was pure Monty Python.
> *Irish Examiner* 2002

> There is a gruesome, apocalyptic scene towards the end of the novel, outrageous enough to be almost Monty Pythonesque.
> *Sunday Business Post* 2002

Morgan, John Pierpoint [People] (1837–1913) An American banker whose wealth was sufficient to enable him to stabilize the American economy in 1895.

> ➤ An extremely wealthy man

> I bought a dozen volumes on banking and credit and investment securities and they stood on my shelf in red and gold like new money from the mint, promising to unfold the shining secrets that only Midas and Morgan and Maecenas knew.
> F. SCOTT FITZGERALD *The Great Gatsby* 1925

Morgan le Fay [Arth. Leg.] The half-sister of King *Arthur. A former pupil of *Merlin, she was an enchantress, possessed of magical powers. After Arthur's final battle, Morgan le Fay transported him to *Avalon. In some versions of the legend, she was hostile to Arthur and endeavoured to kill him.

> ➤ An evil enchantress

Moriarty [Lit.] The evil professor in Arthur Conan *Doyle's Sherlock *Holmes stories. The fiendish Professor Moriarty is the detective's greatest enemy, 'the Napoleon of crime'.

> ➤ An evil villain; a hero's arch-enemy

She no longer paled or trembled at the idea of sudden death. The renowned John Goss, with all the cool skill, clever thinking and iron fists of detectives in novels, would get her safely past every Moriarty going.
RICHARD HALEY *Thoroughfare of Stones* 1995

Morpheus [Rom. Myth.] The god of dreams, son of *Somnus, the god of sleep.

> ➤ To be in the arms of Morpheus is to be asleep

Keith, even more irritable than Cooper to be dragged from the arms of Morpheus far away in London, perked up a little to hear that Jack was under arrest.
MINETTE WALTERS *The Scold's Bridle* 1994

Moses [Bible] (c.14th–13th century BC) A Hebrew prophet and lawgiver. According to the Bible, he was born at a time when *Pharaoh had decreed that all male Hebrew children were to be killed at birth. His mother hid him by making a small basket out of bulrushes and placing him in the basket amid the reeds of the Nile. Moses was discovered by Pharaoh's daughter, who took pity on him and decided to raise him as her own child. So Moses was brought up at the court of Pharaoh.

When a grown man, he killed an Egyptian overseer whom he had seen beating a Hebrew, and was forced to flee to the land of Midian. Here Moses lived as a shepherd in the desert, until after 40 years he was called by God to return to Egypt and demand that Pharaoh set his people free. Moses confronted Pharaoh with God's demand 'Let my people go.' Pharaoh finally freed the *Israelites from bondage and Moses led them out of Egypt. Changing his mind, Pharaoh sent his army in pursuit. The Israelites passed through the *Red Sea, which God caused to part for them, but the pursuing Egyptians were drowned when the waters closed on them. God later gave Moses the Ten Commandments on Mount Sinai. Led by Moses, the Israelites wandered through the Sinai desert for 40 years until they finally reached the borders of *Canaan. Moses did not enter the *Promised Land himself, but was allowed a glimpse of it from Mount Pisgah before he died, at the age of 120.

> ➤ Someone who delivers his people or leads them to freedom; a baby who is abandoned or found; someone who clears a way and makes a path through something that seems impossible to cross; a law-maker

Like Moses, he led his followers within sight of the promised land.
London Review of Books 2003

'What's going on here?' she demanded as she parted the crowd like Moses did the Red Sea.
COSETTE DUE *Sora Ni Hoshi Ga Kagayaite Iru* 2001

He's a framer of laws like Moses or Newton.
Chief Executive 2001

Moses, Grandma (Anna Mary Robertson Moses) [Art] (1860–1961) A self-taught US painter who did not begin to paint until she was nearly 70, going on to produce more than a thousand paintings in naïve style, mostly of rural life in New England.

> ➤ A person who produces their best creative work late in life

You might call him 'The Grandma Moses of hockey.' Like a fine wine, Dominik Hasek only improved with age.
Hockey Digest 2002

Mother Hubbard *See* HUBBARD.

mother of all…[Hist.] A phrase used by the Iraqi leader Saddam Hussein, who, in 1991, on the eve of the Gulf War, made a speech to his army in which he said: 'the battle in which you are locked today is the mother of all battles.'

> Used to refer to something which is the biggest or most important of its kind

  Within the next few months, the mother of all financial crises could ruin us.
  In These Times 2005

Mozart, Wolfgang Amadeus [Mus.] (1756–91) An Austrian composer, one of the most gifted and prolific in the history of music. A child prodigy, he was composing by the age of five. His vast output of works includes more than 40 symphonies, nearly 30 piano concertos, over 20 string quartets, and operas including *The Marriage of Figaro* (1786), *Don Giovanni* (1787), and *The Magic Flute* (1791). Mozart came to epitomize classical music in its purity of form and melody.

> A creative genius; a child prodigy

  Each step was like multiplying 235 by 9478 in your head while we walked and slid down a desert mountain in a snowstorm. Mozart would have had no problem with it but we struggled.
  BART KOSKO *Fuzzy Thinking* 1993

Mudville *See* NO JOY IN MUDVILLE.

muggle [Lit.] The name given to humans, in contrast to wizards and other magical beings, in the Harry Potter books by J. K. Rowling.

> An ordinary person or mere mortal

  But who still pays for the magical illusion of exactness of the current auditing system? The silly Muggle shareholders, that's who.
  Scotland on Sunday 2002

Muhammad [Rel.] An Arab prophet and founder of Islam. According to legend, Muhammad summoned Mount Safa to come to him after being challenged to demonstrate his miraculous powers. When it failed to do so, he attributed this to the mercy of Allah, for if it had come it would have crushed him and the bystanders. If the mountain would not come to him, said Muhammad, then he would go to the mountain.

> Mentioned when describing a situation in which a person or thing that you want is unwilling or unable to come to you, as a result of which you must make an effort to go yourself

  The child scrambled up to the top of the wall and called again and again; but finding this of no avail, apparently made up his mind, like Mahomet, to go to the mountain, since the mountain would not come to him.
  ANNE BRONTË *The Tenant of Wildfell Hall* 1848

Munch, Edvard [Art] (1863–1944) A Norwegian painter and engraver. Many of his works portray intense emotional states to express his themes of fear, death, and anxiety. In his most famous painting, *The Scream* (1893), a figure covers his ears, his eyes and mouth wide open, below a swirling red and yellow sky.

> Used to evoke an image of someone screaming silently

The street door opened and a woman's head inserted itself into the space. Her body
didn't follow through. Her mouth was frozen Munch-like, locked in a scream without
sound.
GILLIAN SLOVO *Close Call* 1995

Munchausen, Baron (Münchhausen) [Lit.] The hero of a book by Rudolf Erich Raspe
entitled *Baron Munchausen's Narrative of his Marvellous Travels and Campaigns in Russia*
(1785). The book recounts stories of the Baron's travels and adventures, which always
emphasize the intelligence and prowess of the hero, and are far-fetched in the extreme. The
original Baron Munchausen, believed to have lived in 1720–97, is said to have served in the
Russian army against the Turks and related wildly extravagant tales of his adventures.

 ➤ A teller of tall tales

   From that moment Blenkinthrope was tacitly accepted as the Münchausen of the party.
   No effort was spared to draw him out from day to day in the exercise of testing their
   powers of credulity, and Blenkinthrope, in the false security of an assured and receptive
   audience, waxed industrious and ingenious in supplying the demand for marvels.
   SAKI 'The Seventh Pullet' in *Beasts and Super-Beasts* 1914

Munchkin [Child. Lit.] A member of a small race of people who live in the land of Oz
in L. Frank Baum's children's story *The *Wizard of Oz* (1900).

 ➤ A diminutive person

   'I'm a munchkin compared to those 6'5" athletes,' jokes the 5'6" Arbor.
   Black Enterprise 2003

Munich agreement [Hist.] An agreement between Britain, France, Germany, and Italy,
signed at Munich in September 1938 in an attempt to avert a war. In the agreement, the
Sudetenland was ceded to Germany and Neville *Chamberlain on his return famously waved
the document and declared that he was bringing home 'peace in our time'.

 ➤ A worthless agreement or document; an example of dishonourable appeasement

   'Look what I've got!' he says, waving a piece of paper. 'What—another f—Munich
   agreement?' I ask, humouring him.
   Scotland on Sunday 2003

Munsters [TV] The name of a monster family in a US television series of the 1960s. The
father, Herman Munster, resembled Frankenstein's monster, his wife was a vampire,
and their son a werewolf.

 ➤ A family that is grotesque in appearance or behaviour

   Such themes of alienation return in *What's Eating Gilbert Grape?*, which has at its
   heart the most dysfunctional family since the Munsters.
   Sunday Herald 2000

muppet [TV] One of the puppet characters created by Jim Henson for the television series
The Muppet Show and *Sesame Street*. The characters include Kermit the Frog and Miss *Piggy,
a large pink pig with blonde hair.

 ➤ A foolish person

   I was terrified of making a big Muppet of myself.
   Cotswolds Journal news stories 2004

Muses [Gk Myth.] The nine daughters of *Zeus and *Mnemosyne, the goddess of
memory. They were the patron goddesses of intellectual and creative ability, literature, music,

and dance, providing inspiration to mortals. Later, each individual Muse became associated with one particular art:

Calliope: epic poetry
Clio: history
Erato: the lyre and lyric love poetry
Euterpe: lyric poetry and flute playing
Melpomene: tragedy
Polyhymnia: songs to the gods
Terpsichore: dancing and the singing that accompanies it
Thalia: comedy and bucolic poetry
Urania: astronomy

Poets, writers, and musicians call on the Muses for inspiration, or refer to their inspiration as their Muse.

> A source of poetic inspiration

Creative people are not always languishing about in an ecstasy of creative inspiration. You don't just come down one morning and begin, because the muses don't work that way.
DVD Verdict 2005

Mussolini, Benito [Hist.] (1883–1945) The founder and leader of the Italian Fascist Party, who became known as Il Duce ('the Leader'). He organized a march on Rome by his blackshirts in 1922 and was made prime minister. Mussolini established himself as a dictator and allied Italy with Germany during the Second World War. He was executed by Italian communist partisans shortly before the end of the war.

> A tyrannical leader

Herod wasn't just a tyrant and a unifier of his country, he was also a patron of the arts—perhaps we should think of him as a sort of Mussolini with good taste.
JULIAN BARNES *A History of the World in 10½ Chapters* 1989

Mutiny on the Bounty See BOUNTY.

Mutt and Jeff [Cart. & Com.] Two characters in a US comic strip dating from 1907 and drawn by Bud Fisher. Mutt was tall and lanky, Jeff was short, bald, and wore a top hat.

> A pair of people of greatly disparate heights

They're a real Mutt and Jeff pair and the bigger man hovers protectively behind his companion.
Weblog: Notes from an Eclectic Mind 2005

My Lai [Hist.] A village in Vietnam which was the scene of one of the worst American atrocities of the Vietnam War. On 16 March 1968 a company of US soldiers entered the village and shot dead several hundred unarmed villagers, including women and children. Many of the women were also raped. US army officers conspired to conceal the truth about what had happened, but details of the atrocity eventually emerged.

> A military atrocity against civilians

I knew of aberrant, atrocious behavior of a few soldiers who either lost control or did not understand the discipline required of a soldier in combat, but I did not see anything remotely resembling My Lai.
In These Times 2004

Myrmidon [Gk Myth.] A member of a warlike and brutal Thessalian people who were said to have devotedly followed *Achilles to the siege of Troy. Their name means 'Ant People', and, according to legend, they were originally ants turned into human beings by *Zeus.

> ➤ A loyal follower, especially a subordinate or henchman who carries out orders ruthlessly and without scruple

Hitler and his myrmidons were ensconced in a bunker.
History Today 2002

Myron [Art] (*c.*480–440 BC) A Greek sculptor who produced very lifelike sculptures of people, most famously the *Discobolus*, a figure of a man throwing a discus.

> ➤ A sculptor

Naboth's vineyard [Bible] According to the Old Testament book of Kings (1 Kgs. 21), *Ahab, king of Samaria, coveted the vineyard of Naboth, a Jezreelite, because it was close to his palace. He asked Naboth to give it to him, offering him either another vineyard or money in return. When Naboth refused, saying that the Lord had forbidden him to give away his father's inheritance, Ahab's wife *Jezebel plotted Naboth's death so that her husband could take over the vineyard. Ahab and Jezebel were both punished by God for their greed.

➤ A possession that is coveted and obtained by dishonest means

> Canada, where Biblical references are still understood by quite a few people, sees itself suddenly as Naboth's Vineyard.
> ROBERTSON DAVIES *Merry Heart* 1998

naiad [Class. Myth.] A water-nymph, a beautiful long-haired maiden associated with lakes, rivers, and fountains.

➤ A beautiful young woman wearing flowing clothes

> Fred's tapping causes a sleeping Ginger to awaken 'like a naiad rising from the foam,' as Arlene Croce put it, in a flurry of filmy negligee and satin sheets.
> *Bright Lights Film Journal* 2001

Nanook of the North [Cin.] The title of a silent documentary film made in 1922 by Robert Flaherty. The film chronicles the struggles of an Inuit and his family to survive in Arctic Canada.

➤ Someone wearing multiple layers of clothing to keep warm

> [He] poked his nose out from behind the door of the Piquet Sport motor-home parked at Knockhill, tested the ambient air temperature and then appeared dressed like Nanook of the North.
> *Scotland on Sunday* 2003

Napoleon *See* BONAPARTE.

Narcissus [Gk Myth.] A youth of extraordinary beauty who cruelly spurned many admirers, including the nymph *Echo. On bending down to a pool one day to drink, he fell in love with his own reflection. There are various versions of the fate that subsequently befell Narcissus. According to one version, he fell into the pool as he tried to embrace his own reflection and drowned. Another version relates how, having tried to kiss and embrace his reflection and failed, Narcissus simply pined away and died. After his death, the gods turned his body into the white flower that bears his name.

➤ Someone who is excessively vain; someone who admires his own reflection (adjective *narcissistic*; noun *narcissism*)

> There were gilt cherubs in the bathroom holding white towels through rings in their mouths, and the walls and ceiling were made of looking-glass. Narcissus could lie in his nacreous bath and, gazing upward, see all of himself reflected.
> ALICE THOMAS ELLIS *The 27th Kingdom* 1982

Narnia [Child. Lit.] The imaginary land in which C. S. Lewis set his children's allegorical fantasy *The Lion, the Witch and the Wardrobe* (1950) and six subsequent stories. Narnia's inhabitants include talking beasts (notably the lion Aslan), giants, centaurs, and witches, and it is ruled by the White Witch, who keeps it in a perpetual winter.

> ➤ A place where winter never seems to end; a place inhabited by strange creatures

> It is not only the weather that makes Britain feel like a frozen Narnia at the end of 2005. Our cultural and political landscape also appears to be under the dead hand of the White Witch, who makes it seem 'always winter and never Christmas'.
> *Spiked Online* 2006

nasty, brutish, and short [Lit.] A quotation from Thomas Hobbes's 1651 book *Leviathan*: 'And the life of man, solitary, poor, nasty, brutish, and short.'

> ➤ Used when suggesting that life is a struggle without pleasure, leading only to death

> Life in Britain in the fourteenth century was 'nasty, brutish and short', and it had been that way for the peasantry since long before the Black Death.
> *BBC History—Society and Culture* 2004

naughty but nice [Theatre] A phrase taken from the title of a music hall song 'It's Naughty but It's Nice' (1871). The phrase gained prominence in the late 20th century through an advertisement for cream cakes.

> ➤ Used about things which are pleasurable but may be disapproved of

> Buy tiny boxes of very lavish Belgian chocolates, beautifully wrapped and presented—a little bit naughty but nice.
> *Croydon Guardian* 2004

Nautilus [Lit.] A giant submarine commanded by the mysterious Captain Nemo, in Jules Verne's adventure classic *Twenty Thousand Leagues under the Sea* (1869). The ship contains a library, drawing room, and dining room, all elegantly furnished, and the captain's room, in which hang all manner of instruments for navigating the ship, including thermometers, barometers, hygrometers, chronometers, and manometers.

> ➤ A place with a large number of futuristic controls and gadgets

> Gwyn stepped into his study….Here the two cultures, Gwyn believed, were attractively reconciled: the bright flame of human inquiry, plus lots of gadgets. Give Gwyn a palatinate smoking-jacket, as opposed to a pair of tailored jeans and a lumberjack shirt, and he could be Captain Nemo, taking his seat at the futuristic bridge of the sumptuous Nautilus.
> MARTIN AMIS *The Information* 1995

Nazirite [Bible] An *Israelite specially consecrated to the service of God, whose vows included letting his hair grow. 'All the days of his vow of separation no razor shall come upon his head; until the time is completed for which he separates himself to the Lord, he shall be holy; he shall let the locks of hair of his head grow long' (Num. 6: 1–5). The prophets *Samuel and *Samson were Nazirites. In the quotation below it is almost certainly Nazirite rather than Nazarene (a native of Nazareth) that is meant.

> ➤ Someone whose hair is long and unkempt

> His head was utterly concealed beneath a cascade of matted hair that seemed to have no form or colour. In places it stuck out in twisted corkscrews, and in others it lay in congealed pads like felt; it was the hair of a Nazarene or of a hermit demented by the glory and solitude of God.
> LOUIS DE BERNIÈRES *Captain Corelli's Mandolin* 1994

Nebuchadnezzar [People] (*c.*630–562 BC) A king of *Babylon in 605–562 BC, who built the massive fortification walls of Babylon and the *Hanging Gardens. Daniel interpreted a dream of Nebuchadnezzar's to foretell his insanity, which immediately came to pass. 'The same hour was the thing fulfilled upon Nebuchadnezzar; and he was driven from men, and did eat the grass as oxen, and his body was wet with the dew of heaven, till his hairs were grown like eagles' feathers, and his nails like birds' claws' (Dan. 4: 29–33). There is a famous drawing by William *Blake depicting the king in this condition.

➤ Someone with a wild appearance, with unkempt hair and uncut fingernails

You have a 'faux air' of Nebuchadnezzar in the fields about you, that is certain: your hair reminds me of eagles' feathers; whether your nails are grown like birds' claws or not, I have not yet noticed.
CHARLOTTE BRONTË *Jane Eyre* 1847

nectar [Gk Myth.] The drink of the Greek gods.

➤ A delicious drink

'You and your coffee.' 'The nectar of the gods,' Terese insisted.
S. D. YOUNGREN *Funny Female Fiction* 2003

Nefertiti [People] (14th century BC) An Egyptian queen, the wife of Akhenaten. She is best known from the painted limestone portrait bust of her, now in Berlin, that depicts her as a woman of slender regal beauty.

➤ A beautiful woman, especially one with a long neck

She had a beautiful neck; the throat of a Nefertiti.
JOHN FOWLES *The Magus* 1966

Nelson, Admiral Horatio [Hist.] (1758–1805) A British admiral who commanded the fleet to many victories and lost his right eye at Calvi in Corsica in 1794. According to tradition, at the Battle of Copenhagen in 1801 Nelson put his telescope to his blind eye to look at the approaching Danish fleet, and, with the words 'I see no ships', ignored the order to withdraw the English navy.

➤ Someone who chooses not to see or notice something

'Was there an implication that Slater did a Nelson?' 'Yes. I can just imagine the selfish sod leaving the poor girl to die while he went off to bed.'
MALCOLM HAMMER *Shadows on the Green* 1994

Nemesis [Gk Myth.] The goddess responsible for retribution, either for a person who had transgressed the moral code or for a person who had taken too much pride in their success or luck (*hubris).

➤ A person's doom or terrible but unavoidable fate; a personification of punishment or retribution for wrongdoing or excessive pride

It was six a.m. and Bruce's appointment with nemesis was well under way. His old life was already over. Even if he survived his ordeal, nothing would ever be the same again.
BEN ELTON *Popcorn* 1996

The story finds Jack Sparrow at the mercy of his nemesis, Davy Jones (Bill Nighy), who has emerged from the murky depths of the Caribbean to claim a blood debt.
IndieLondon film reviews 2006

Nepenthe [Leg. & Folk.] An Egyptian drug believed to make people forget their sorrows. In the *Odyssey it is used by *Helen and described as 'a drug that dispelled all grief and anger and banished remembrance of every trouble'.

➤ Anything that causes people to forget grief and anger

Beer is a fine nepenthe. It makes us all jolly and forgetful of our troubles.
LYNETTA RASMUSSEN *A Bay and a Barge* 2003

Neptune [Rom. Myth.] The god of the sea, identified with the Greek god *Poseidon.

➤ A man in water or emerging from water

Breathing hard, he rose out of the pool like Neptune.
C. B. RYKKEN *High Road to Carthage* 2000

Nereid [Gk Myth.] A sea-nymph, a daughter of *Nereus.

➤ A beautiful young woman in water or emerging from water

Mandras was too young to be a Poseidon, too much without malice. Was he a male sea-nymph, then? Was there such a thing as a male Nereid or Potamid?
LOUIS DE BERNIÈRES *Captain Corelli's Mandolin* 1994

Nereus [Gk Myth.] An old god of the sea and a son of Gaia. He and his wife Doris had 50 daughters, the *Nereids.

➤ A man in water or emerging from water

Nero [Hist.] (AD 37–68) A Roman emperor in 54–68, notorious for his tyranny and cruelty. He ordered the murder of his mother Agrippina in 59, and his reign was marked by the persecution of Christians and the executions of leading Romans who had plotted against him. Nero was alleged to have started the fire that destroyed half of Rome in 64. As the city burned, Nero allegedly played his fiddle and simply watched.

➤ A despotic or tyrannical leader; someone who stands by and watches while disaster occurs

Blair has a massive majority in Parliament—a majority which has enabled him to rule like Nero, with contempt for Parliament.
Contemporary Review 2004

Like Nero, fiddling while Rome burned, the Manning Government, in its efforts to portray Port-of-Spain as a suitable site for the capital of the FTAA, has for many months trivialised the crime wave in this country.
Trinidad Guardian 2004

Nessus [Gk Myth.] A centaur killed by *Hercules, who shot him with his bow for trying to rape Hercules' wife, Deianira. As he lay dying, Nessus told Deianira that if ever she suspected that her husband was being unfaithful, she should smear a garment belonging to Hercules with Nessus' blood and this would act as a love potion. Deianira followed this, but the centaur's blood was a corrosive poison that caused Hercules to die in unendurable agony.

➤ A 'shirt of Nessus' is a poisoned garment, or a fate from which escape is impossible

Once, temporarily envious of Boy, I bought a silk shirt and paid nine dollars for it. It burned me like the shirt of Nessus, but I wore it to rags, to get my money out of it, garment of guilty luxury that it was.
ROBERTSON DAVIES *The Deptford Trilogy* 1970

Nestor [Gk Myth.] A king of Pylos. He lived to a great age and was one of the oldest and wisest of the Greek heroes in the *Trojan War, which he survived, returning to Pylos.

➤ A wise old man or mentor

David Starr Jordan (1851–1931), the Nestor of North American ichthyology...captured
the habits and personality of this gaudiest of all freshwater fishes.
Alabama Heritage 2004

Never-Never Land [Child. Lit.] The magical country to which Peter *Pan escorts *Wendy,
John, and Michael Darling in J. M. Barrie's play *Peter Pan* (first performed 1904). The land
is populated by staple characters from children's stories, such as mermaids and pirates,
including the murderous pirate Captain Hook.

> ➤ An ideal place, far from the problems encountered in the real world

> He reserves much spleen for Fianna Fáil and the PDs who, he says, are engaging in
> Never Never Land economics by planning to sell State assets to fund ever-decreasing
> levels of tax, while public services remain in a state of crisis.
> *Irish Examiner* 2002

New Deal [Hist.] A name for the economic measures introduced by Franklin D. Roosevelt
in 1933 to counteract the effects of the Great Depression. It involved, among other things,
a massive public works programme, and succeeded in reducing unemployment to between
7 and 10 million.

> ➤ A government programme designed to tackle a particular problem

> Under a programme called New Deal for Schools, a mix of improving conditions and
> modernising facilities will bring a better environment for learning for thousands of pupils.
> *Rochdale Observer* 2002

Newgate [Places] London's famous historic prison. Originally the gatehouse of one of
the city gates, Newgate was first used as a prison in the early Middle Ages, and the last prison on
the site was closed in 1880 and demolished in 1902. The prison housed many notorious
criminals as well as debtors, and became notorious in the 18th century for the wretched
conditions in which the inmates lived.

> ➤ A prison; a place of wretched living conditions

New Jerusalem [Rel.] The abode of the blessed in Heaven in Christian theology.

> ➤ A paradise

> There was talk of a coming election when the New Jerusalem might again be on offer.
> JOHN MORTIMER *Paradise Postponed* 1985

newspeak [Lit.] The artificial language used by the state as a way of controlling
information in George *Orwell's novel *Nineteen Eighty-Four* (1949).

> ➤ Ambiguous or euphemistic language used by a government or authority to hide an
> unpleasant truth

> Some 40 years ago when my first headteacher told me it was to be my privilege to
> work with a 'challenging' class of youngsters, I soon realised that I'd had my first lesson
> in management newspeak.
> *Bradford and District news stories* 2003

Newton, Isaac [Science] (1642–1727) An English mathematician and physicist
who was the greatest single influence on theoretical physics until *Einstein. In his work *Principia
Mathematica* (1687), Newton gave a mathematical description of the laws and mechanics of
gravitation. According to a famous story, first told by *Voltaire, in 1665 or 1666 Newton
watched an apple fall from a tree in a garden and this inspired his insights into gravity.

> ➤ Mentioned (often together with the apple) in the context of a sudden moment of
> understanding

One answer to my original question dropped out of the blue like Newton's apple.
Daily Gullet 2004

Nibelung [Myth.] The king of a race of Scandinavian dwarfs, also called the Nibelung,
who owned a hoard of treasure and gold. In the 13th-century epic German poem the
Nibelungenlied, the treasure is guarded by the dwarf Alberich and later taken by *Siegfried,
the hero of the poem.

> ➤ A dwarf

> One of his students there, Vera Mukhina, described him as 'A little Nibelung, shorter
> than myself, with an enormous shining high forehead, thick, bushy brows and a black
> wedge-shaped beard.'
> IAN CHILVERS *A Dictionary of Twentieth-Century Art* 2000

Nietzsche, Friedrich Wilhelm [Philos.] (1844–1900) A German philosopher whose works
contain writing on the themes of contempt for Christian ethics and for democracy,
and admiration of the 'will to power', the *Übermensch* (superman), and the 'master class',
the small group of superior people who dominate the mass of inferior people, the 'herd'.
Nietzsche's *Übermensch* was an ideal being whose superior physical and mental qualities
represent the goal of human evolution.

> ➤ Mentioned in the context of someone who strives for power ruthlessly, or believes that
> they are superior to others (adjective *Nietzschean*)

> I am more like the Nietzschean Overman than a loving, altruistic miracle worker.
> JAVE HARRON *Necessary Evil: The Godforge* 2005

Niflheim [Norse Myth.] The underworld, a place of eternal cold, darkness, and mist.
While those who died in battle were believed to go to *Valhalla and feast with *Odin, those who
died of old age or illness were believed to go to Niflheim.

> ➤ A gloomy or depressing place

> But he continued motionless and silent in that gloomy Niflheim or fogland which
> involved him, and she proceeded on her way.
> THOMAS HARDY *The Woodlanders* 1887

Nightingale, Florence [People] (1820–1910) An English nurse and medical reformer who
became famous during the Crimean War for improving sanitation and medical procedures,
achieving a dramatic reduction in the mortality rate. She became known as the Lady of the
Lamp because of her nightly rounds of the wards carrying a lamp.

> ➤ A nurse; a woman who helps or looks after others; a woman carrying a lamp

> She tucks him into bed when his forehead feels hot, taking his temperature like a
> regular Florence Nightingale.
> *DVD Verdict* 2001

Nightmare on Elm Street [Cin.] The title of a gory horror film made in 1984 in which
a killer called Freddy *Krueger, who has knives for fingernails, brutally murders teenagers in
their dreams. The film was followed by several sequels.

> ➤ Used, often humorously, to invoke a gory scene or horrific situation

> If health professionals and writers took the middle line between Never-Never Land
> and Nightmare on Maternity Street perhaps *Life after Babies* wouldn't be quite such a
> rude awakening.
> *The Independent* 1994

night of the long knives [Hist.] The night of 30 June 1934 when, on Hitler's orders, hundreds of his real or suspected opponents were killed.

> ➤ A political purge; a treacherous betrayal

> Then we had Jack McConnell's night of the long knives in which five out of six Labour ministers were axed in an act of numpty municipal factionalism.
> *Sunday Herald* 2002

Nijinsky, Vaslav [Dance] (1890–1950) A Russian dancer, who trained at the Imperial Ballet School in St Petersburg and became one of the leading dancers in Diaghilev's Ballet Russe.

> ➤ An athletic and graceful male dancer

> It is said of the same puppets…that they are *antigrav*, that they can rise and leap, like Nijinsky, as if no such thing as gravity existed for them.
> PAUL DE MAN *Rhetoric of Romanticism* 1983

Nike [Gk Myth.] The Greek goddess of victory, usually represented as a winged figure.

> ➤ A woman wearing flowing robes; also mentioned in the context of victory

> She's a Nike…on the prow of a Greek ship.
> ANNA DOUGLAS SEDGWICK *The Little French Girl* 1924

Nimrod [Bible] The founder of the Babylonian dynasty, according to the Old Testament. He is described as 'a mighty hunter' (Gen. 10: 8–9).

> ➤ A great or skilful hunter or sportsman

> It was not so positively stated, but the consensus seemed to be that Bertha Shanklin had shown poor taste in dying so soon and thus embarrassing the local Nimrod.
> ROBERTSON DAVIES *Fifth Business* 1970

Nimue [Arth. Leg.] The *Lady of the Lake, according to Arthurian legend. Nimue, the wily mistress of the wizard *Merlin, extracted from him the secrets of his craft, which she used against him to imprison him in an oak tree for eternity.

> ➤ A sorceress

nine eleven [Hist.] The eleventh of September (written 9/11) 2001, when hijacked passenger planes were flown into the World Trade Center and the Pentagon in the USA.

> ➤ A terrorist outrage

> The airline pilot's union…has lobbied the government to permit commercial airline pilots to carry firearms in order to protect airline property and avoid another 9/11.
> *Ludwig von Mises Institute: Daily Articles* 2004

Nineteen Eighty-Four [Lit.] The title of a 1949 novel by George *Orwell about a futuristic totalitarian state run by a dictator known as *Big Brother, whose portrait, with the caption 'Big Brother is watching you', is ubiquitous.

> ➤ Mentioned in the context of a totalitarian state

> It is democracy which has been set aside—more than that, it's been severely damaged. It's degenerated into a sort of totalitarian process. It's just like 1984.
> *Yorkshire Post Today* 2002

Nineveh [Places] An ancient city located on the east bank of the Tigris, opposite the modern city of Mosul, Iraq. It was destroyed by the *Medes and the Babylonians in 612 BC, an event forecast by the Old Testament prophet Nahum. Elsewhere in the Bible, the prophet

*Jonah is called by God to preach to the people of Nineveh and warn them of the destruction of their city unless they reform their wicked behaviour. In the opening lines of John Masefield's poem 'Cargoes' (1903), Nineveh and *Ophir are presented as places of far-away exoticism:

> Quinquireme of Nineveh from distant Ophir
> Rowing home to haven in sunny Palestine.

> ➤ A distant and exotic place; a place that is destroyed

> I've been to Europe and the States but never to Nineveh and Distant Ophir.
> JULIAN BARNES *Talking It Over* 1991

ninth plague of Egypt [Bible] One of the plagues of Egypt described in the book of Exodus in the Old Testament. The ninth plague of Egypt was 'a thick darkness in all the land of Egypt three days' (Exod. 10: 22).

> ➤ Used to invoke complete darkness

> By reason of the density of the interwoven foliage overhead, it was gloomy there at cloudless noontide, twilight in the evening, dark as midnight at dusk, and black as the ninth plague of Egypt at midnight.
> THOMAS HARDY *Far from the Madding Crowd* 1874

Niobe [Gk Myth.] The daughter of *Tantalus and the mother of numerous offspring. She boasted that her large family made her superior to the goddess Leto, who only had two children, *Apollo and *Artemis. Angered by this, Apollo slew all Niobe's sons, and Artemis her daughters. Niobe herself was turned into a stone, and her tears into streams that eternally trickled from it.

> ➤ A woman who suffers inconsolable grief

> The Niobe of nations! there she stands,
> Childless and crownless, in her voiceless woe.
> LORD BYRON *Childe Harold* 1818

Nirvana [Rel.] The final goal of Buddhism, a transcendent state in which there is neither suffering, desire, nor sense of self.

> ➤ A place or state of complete happiness

> Like many real-life 1970s professionals, Bernadette Brown (Micheline Lanctot) drops out of city life, expecting to find nirvana down on the farm.
> *Take One Magazine* 2004

Noah [Bible] The book of Genesis (6–9) relates how God, seeing that 'the wickedness of man was great in the earth', decided to send a great flood to destroy the whole of mankind. Only Noah 'found grace in the eyes of the Lord' and so God warned him of the coming flood and instructed him to build an *ark in which to save himself and his family and also two of every species of creature on the earth.

> ➤ Someone who survives a great flood, or is spared when others suffer; also mentioned in the context of people or things in pairs

> I felt like Noah listening to somebody complaining about a small shower.
> *Cybernoon.com (Mumbai)* 2004

> He took us through B&B's wardrobe: 'like Noah's Ark—two of everything.'
> *New Zealand Listener* 2005

Noah's Ark *See* ARK.

noble savage [Lit.] An idealized man living a natural life free from the influences of civilization, in the writings of the French philosopher Jean-Jacques *Rousseau. Rousseau's descriptions of the noble savage reflect his belief in the fundamental goodness of human nature and the corrupting influence of modern society.

➤ Someone living in harmony with nature, who seems uncorrupted by modern vices

In the tradition of the noble savage of literature, Tarzan must confront the hypocrisy, illogic, and brutality of the human world.
DVD Verdict 2004

Nod *See* LAND OF NOD.

Noddy [Child. Lit.] A character in children's stories by Enid *Blyton, a boy whose head nods as he speaks.

➤ Used to describe anything childlike, over-simplistic, or trivial

Medium-sized companies are starting to replace their first phase of 'noddy' security as they become more dependent on the internet.
Sunday Business Post 2003

no joy in Mudville [Lit.] A quotation from the late 19th-century ballad 'Casey at the Bat' by Ernest L. Thayer. Casey was confidently expected to save the day in a baseball game, but struck out: 'There is no joy in Mudville—Mighty Casey has struck out.'

➤ Mentioned in the context of a shared disappointment, especially a sporting one

We normally announce the winner immediately at the Finish Line—over a joyful and raucous celebration from the crowd. But this year, we made no announcement and had no celebration. And there was no joy in Mudville.
LondonSkaters.com 2003

Norns [Norse Myth.] Three goddesses who spun the fate of both people and the gods. They were named Urd (the past), Verdandi (the present), and Skuld (the future), and gathered under the ash tree Yggdrasil.

➤ People who decide another's fate, or look on dispassionately while others suffer

You get a nasty feeling that here indeed are the machinations of eerie Norns who almost manically puppeteer the skein of life.
MV Daily 2002

Nostradamus [People] The Latinized name by which Michel de Nostredame (1503–66) is generally known. He was a French astrologer and physician and the author of *Centuries* (1555), a collection of prophecies written in rhyming quatrains. Although cryptic and obscure, Nostradamus' verses have been interpreted as foretelling prominent global events over a span of more than 400 years.

➤ Someone who foretells the future

I spoke last week to the science fiction writer Arthur C. Clarke, the Nostradamus of space, whose predictions, among other things, have included the development of the communication satellite.
The Observer 1997

not over till the fat lady sings [Opera] A traditional saying about opera.

➤ Used to say that a situation is not finished or decided until it is completely over

The rest is history, and he is world champion. He left us with visual confirmation of the old adage that hopes springs eternal, or for some others, it's never over till the fat lady sings.
Carlow Nationalist 2002

Notre Dame *See* HUNCHBACK OF NOTRE DAME.

not with a bang but a whimper [Lit.] A quotation from T. S. Eliot's poem 'The Hollow Men':

> This is the way the world ends
> Not with a bang but a whimper.

➢ Used in the context of something that ends with an anticlimax

Turner's ironically titled Goodwill Games flop provided a hint that the Soviet Union likely would end with not a bang but a whimper.
Reason Magazine 2003

nul points [TV] A French phrase meaning 'no points', made popular through the televised broadcasts of the annual Eurovision Song Contest in which scores for each country's song were traditionally announced in several languages.

➢ Used to indicate that something achieves or is worth a score of zero

The rice seemed to have got all the saffron and the plate was garnished with a lemon, so the colour presentation was very bland. Taste gets ten out of ten, but nul points for presentation.
Sunday Business Post 2002

Nuremberg defence [Hist.] The defence of 'I was only following orders', which was used unsuccessfully by Nazis put on trial for war crimes at Nuremberg at the end of the Second World War.

➢ A defence in which someone claims they have no personal responsibility for something because they were merely following orders

Howard has always taken the classic Nuremberg defence. He has said he was only following orders—carrying out policy decided on by Fraser and a majority of the other members of the Cabinet he served in.
Crikey.com.au 2004

Nureyev, Rudolph [Dance] (1939-93) A Russian ballet dancer who defected to the West while in Paris in 1961. His partnership with Margot *Fonteyn, dancing for the Royal Ballet, was inspired.

➢ A graceful male dancer

So I Nureyeved the front steps and flowed through the door in a single motion of Yale and Chubb.
JULIAN BARNES *Talking It Over* 1991

nymph [Myth.] A semi-divine spirit represented as a beautiful maiden and associated with aspects of nature, especially with rivers and woods.

➢ A beautiful young woman who seems at one with nature

She let go of Ilse's hand and ran, like a dryad or forest nymph, deeper into the forest.
LORD-OF-FOOLS *Unregarded Truths* 2005

Oakley, Annie [People] (1860–1926) An American markswoman. In 1885 she joined Buffalo Bill's Wild West Show, of which she became a star attraction for the next seventeen years. She was nicknamed Little Sure-Shot by the Sioux Indian chief Sitting Bull.

➤ A woman who is skilled at shooting

'Look'—she stood there, awkwardly, one hand on her waist, the other on her holster. A pint-sized Annie Oakley.
TED WOOD *A Clean Kill* 1995

Oates, Captain Lawrence [People] (1880–1912) An English explorer on *Scott's expedition to the South Pole. Believing that his severe frostbite would jeopardize his companions' survival, he deliberately went out into a blizzard to sacrifice his own life. His famous last words were 'I am just going outside and may be some time.'

➤ Someone who sacrifices their own life for the benefit of others

He didn't believe her. But he said, 'I suppose I'm a bit of a burden on you, Dora, these days. Perhaps I ought to go off and die. Like Oates at the south Pole.'
MURIEL SPARK 'The Father's Daughters' in *The Collected Stories* 1961

odd couple [Lit.; Cin.] A phrase from the title of a 1965 play by Neil Simon, *The Odd Couple*. The play is about two mismatched roommates, one very tidy and uptight, the other more untidy and easygoing. The play has spawned various spin-offs including films and TV series.

➤ A couple who seem mismatched

Amid a flurry of high-flying acrobatics, martial arts action, and quick-witted humour, this comic odd couple have to work together to keep the scroll safe.
This is the Lake District: news stories 2003

Odin [Norse Myth.] The supreme god and creator, worshipped as the god of wisdom, war, poetry, and the dead. Odin obtained his wisdom by drinking from *Mimir's well but had to sacrifice an eye to do so, and is consequently usually represented as one-eyed, often attended by two black ravens, Hugin (thought) and Munin (memory).

➤ Odin's ravens are alluded to for their deep black colour

'You are beautiful,' the girl said, 'though your hair is wrong, black like Odin's ravens.'
The Quantum Muse: Fantasy stories 2004

Odysseus [Gk Myth.] The king of Ithaca, known to the Romans as *Ulysses. When *Helen was abducted by *Paris, Odysseus was part of the expedition that set sail to bring her back from Troy. *Homer's epic poem the *Odyssey* is an account of Odysseus' ten-year journey home to Ithaca after the fall of Troy, in which he faced many dangers and setbacks.

➤ A wanderer who is far from home; someone who experiences a long period of bad luck

It had been demoralising to wander like Odysseus from place to place, far from home, improvising a resistance that never seemed to amount to anything.
LOUIS DE BERNIÈRES *Captain Corelli's Mandolin* 1994

Sometimes I felt like Odysseus in sight of the goal, and not quite getting there.
MV Daily 2000

Odyssey [Gk Myth.] The title of *Homer's epic poem, which recounts the ten-year voyage of *Odysseus during his years of wandering after the fall of Troy, and his eventual return home to Ithaca and his faithful wife Penelope.

> A long series of wanderings, or a long, adventurous journey

This great American terminal was the starting point for his odyssey into homelessness, addiction and back to his new life as a writer.
The Independent 1998

Oedipus [Gk Myth.] The son of Jocasta and of Laius, king of Thebes, who was left to die on a mountainside because of a warning by an oracle that he would grow up to kill his own father. Found by a shepherd, Oedipus was subsequently adopted by the king of Corinth and his wife, whom he believed to be his parents. When an adult, Oedipus heard the oracle's prophecy and fled to Thebes, where he unwittingly killed his real father, Laius, and married his mother Jocasta, by whom he had four children. When they discovered the truth, Oedipus blinded himself in a fit of madness, while Jocasta hanged herself. In psychoanalytical theory, the Oedipus complex is a son's subconscious sexual attraction to his mother and hostility towards his father.

> A man who feels an incestuous love for his mother; someone who is predestined to act in a particular way and is powerless to act otherwise; someone who is blinded

I told him—mockingly, of course—that I was suffering from the Oedipus complex and didn't get any attention from my mom.
COVIN *Eschatology* 2005

Although the traps can be foreseen, the reader can do nothing to change them, just as Oedipus can do nothing to change his fate.
BookRags.com Book Notes 2002

Afterward, the man stands up with the woman wrapped so tightly around his head he's blinded, staggering like Oedipus or Lear with his hands outstretched and helpless.
New York Metro: Dance 2004

off with his/her head [Child. Lit.] A phrase used repeatedly by the Queen of Hearts in Lewis Carroll's children's story *Alice's Adventures in Wonderland* (1865), as a command to execute someone.

> Used to suggest an extremely hostile knee-jerk reaction to a person who has caused offence

While shareholders' portfolios plummeted, many CEOs raked in more cash than some countries' GDP. Cries of 'off with their heads' were voiced in living rooms and office corridors.
Chief Executive 2002

O'Hara, Scarlett [Lit.; Cin.] A beautiful and egotistical Southern belle, the heroine of Margaret Mitchell's novel *Gone with the Wind* (1936), set during the American Civil War. The hugely successful 1939 film starring Vivien Leigh and Clark Gable further popularized the story of Scarlett and her stormy and ultimately unhappy love affair with the handsome Rhett *Butler.

> A romantic heroine

I found myself whistling Mozart under my breath as I got dressed. The Scarlett O'Hara syndrome. Rhett comes and spends the night and suddenly you're singing and happy again.
SARA PARETSKY *Guardian Angel* 1992

OK Corral [Cin.] A place in Tombstone, Arizona, that was the site of a famous gunfight in 1881. The gunfight, along with other similar fictitious ones, has been portrayed many times in western films, including *Gunfight at the O.K. Corral* (1957).

> The site of a showdown or final battle

The United Nations General Assembly isn't exactly the OK Corral, but in the delicate world of international diplomacy, it was a very personal and even pointed duel.
CNN transcripts: Insight 2002

Old Harry [Rel.] Another name for the *Devil or *Satan.

> A devil; an evil tempter

I don't think he realises just how unfair he's being to younger people…to you anyway. He just thinks—quite rightly—that it's his property, and he'll play Old Harry with it if he wants to.
MARY STEWART *The Ivy Tree* 1964

Old Man of the Sea [Lit.] A character in '*Sinbad the Sailor', one of the tales in The *Arabian Nights. He persuades Sinbad to carry him on his shoulders, whereupon he entwines his legs round him, so that Sinbad cannot dislodge him. Sinbad is forced to carry him on his shoulders for many days and nights, until at last he gets the Old Man drunk with wine and manages to shake him off.

> Someone who is tiresome or irritatingly persistent; someone who is a burden

He is the bore of the age, the old man whom we Sinbads cannot shake off.
ANTHONY TROLLOPE *Barchester Towers* 1857

Old Nick [Rel.] Another name for the *Devil or *Satan.

> A devil; an evil tempter

May they not feel inclined to blame 'Old Nick' for every unhappy circumstance of their ship?
Quadrant Magazine 2004

Olive Oyl *See* OYL.

Olympus [Gk Myth.] The mountain in Greece which is traditionally held to be the home of the Greek gods.

> Mentioned in the context of anyone or anything that is superior to or more important than lesser mortals (adjective *Olympian*)

Here's this utterly Olympian figure telling little me that I can do it.
Inc. Magazine 2002

She leaves [Radio 4] next week, ascending to the BBC's own Mount Olympus as its new director of news.
The Sunday Times 2004

Onassis, Aristotle [People] (1906–75) A Greek ship owner who built up an extensive independent shipping empire and founded the Greek national airline, Olympic Airways.

> An extremely wealthy person

Chilcott rubbed his hands together. 'Wickham's something in the City and as rich as Onassis, according to Sir Peter. Could do me a lot of good, business-wise, if I play my cards right.'
SUSAN MOODY *Grand Slam* 1994

Onegin, Eugene (and Tatiana) [Lit.] Characters in Pushkin's novel in verse form *Eugene Onegin* (1823–31). Tatiana, a young country girl, falls in love with Eugene Onegin. Onegin is dismissive when Tatiana pours out her feelings to him in a letter, but some years later he meets her again, when she is married, and falls in love with her. Although admitting that she still loves Onegin, Tatiana holds to her marriage and dismisses him. Pushkin's poem is also the subject of Tchaikovsky's opera of the same name.

➤ Two people who are in love but are prevented by circumstances from being together

one small step...a giant leap [Hist.] A phrase used by the American astronaut Neil *Armstrong, who was the first to descend to the lunar surface in July 1969 as part of the Apollo 11 mission. As he set foot on the surface, he spoke the famous words, 'That's one small step for (a) man, one giant leap for mankind.'

➤ Used when saying that an action or development which seems small is in fact extremely significant

That may be only one small step for Comcast customers, but it's a giant leap toward Roberts's philosophical goal of releasing films simultaneously on cable and at theaters. *Fast Company Magazine* 2005

open sesame [Lit.] The magic words that are used to open the robbers' cave in the story of '*Ali Baba and the Forty Thieves', one of the stories in *The *Arabian Nights*.

➤ A phrase or password which causes something to open, or allows access to something

Think of the right keywords as the Open Sesame! of the Internet.
Article Alley: Search Engines articles 2005

Ophelia [Shakes.] The daughter of *Polonius in *Hamlet* (1604). Ophelia is in love with *Hamlet but rejected by him. Her grief after her father's fatal stabbing at Hamlet's hands sends her into a state of madness. During her famous 'mad scene' in the play, she sings several bawdy and death-obsessed songs. Later it is reported that, while making garlands of flowers by the side of a stream, she fell in and drowned. Ophelia's death scene is the subject of a famous painting (1851–2) by John Everett Millais, which depicts her floating face-upwards in the stream, surrounded by flowers, and about to slip beneath the water.

➤ A woman floating in water; a madwoman

I just hoped there was no way he could trace back to my connection with Tim. Otherwise my lifeless corpse would probably be found floating down the river on Sunday evening after the river cruise, an Ophelia in polluted waters.
LAUREN HENDERSON *The Black Rubber Dress* 1997

Ophir [Bible] An unidentified region in the Bible, perhaps in south-east Arabia, famous as the source of the gold and precious stones brought to King Solomon (1 Kgs. 9: 28, 10: 10).

➤ A distant and exotic place

Oracle *See* DELPHI.

Orestes [Gk Myth.] The son of *Agamemnon and *Clytemnestra, and the brother of *Electra. On reaching manhood in exile, he returned to Argos and killed his mother and her lover Aegisthus in revenge for the murder of Agamemnon. As a punishment for the crime of matricide, he was pursued and driven mad by the avenging *Furies.

➢ Someone pursued or tormented by winged creatures

In some places there were nagging clouds of black flies, so that I climbed through
the trees like a new Orestes, cursing and slapping.
JOHN FOWLES *The Magus* 1966

Orion [Gk Myth.] A giant and hunter who at his death was changed into a constellation by
*Artemis.

➢ A hunter

Orphan Annie [Cart. & Com.] The heroine of a US comic strip *Little Orphan Annie*
created by Harold Gray and first appearing in 1925. Annie is a self-reliant, plucky, 11-year-old
orphan girl with curly red hair. Her life is eased by the intervention of the wealthy Daddy
*Warbucks.

➢ A girl or young woman with red curly hair

Decker shook her hand noticing long, slender fingers. Her face was grave, but childlike—
waifish with big brown eyes. Her hair was auburn and bushy. Little Orphan Annie had
grown up to be a doctor.
FAYE KELLERMAN *Prayers for the Dead* 1996

Orpheus [Gk Myth.] A poet who sang and played his lyre so beautifully that he could charm
wild beasts. He married Eurydice, a dryad, and when she died from a snake bite Orpheus went
down to the underworld to try to recover her. He used his music to persuade the goddess
*Persephone to let Eurydice return with him, to which Persephone agreed on condition that
Orpheus should not look back as he left the underworld. Violating this condition to assure
himself that Eurydice was still following him, Orpheus did look back, whereupon she
vanished for ever.

➢ A musician; someone emerging from a dark place into sunlight; someone who looks
back either literally or figuratively

It was dawn; the almost foreign feeling of sunlight washed warmly over his face. He felt
like Orpheus emerging from the netherworld.
ANORIEL *The Badger Chronicles Book One: Calling* 2005

So, I give up and walk on. But I can't resist looking back. Just like Orpheus at Eurydice.
MARIA BENET *Alembic* 2005 (Weblog)

Orwell, George [Lit.] (1903–50) The pseudonym of the novelist and essayist Eric
Arthur Blair. In Orwell's novel *Nineteen Eighty-Four* (1949), the character referred to as
*Big Brother is a dictator whose portrait with the caption 'Big Brother is watching you' can
be found everywhere.

➢ Mentioned in the context of a dictatorial state that is all-powerful and omnipresent
(adjective *Orwellian*)

The threat of terrorism also opens the door for Orwellian surveillance.
Reason Magazine 2005

Ossa *See* PELION ON OSSA.

Ossian [Leg. & Folk.] The Anglicized form of Oisin, the name of a legendary Irish warrior
and bard, the son of Finn MacCool. He travelled to Tír na nÓg, the land of perpetual youth,
and returned 300 years later. Ossian's name became well known in 1760–3 when the
Scottish poet James Macpherson published what was later discovered to be his own verse as
an alleged translation of 3rd-century Gaelic tales.

➢ Someone who remains perpetually young; someone who returns after a long absence

Othello [Shakes.] The main character in the play of the same name (1622). Othello's ensign *Iago convinces him that his wife *Desdemona is unfaithful to him. Othello, in a state of acute jealousy, smothers Desdemona in her bed. Desdemona is subsequently proved innocent, and Othello, in despair, kills himself, having described himself as 'one that lov'd not wisely, but too well'.

➤ Someone who feels extreme sexual jealousy

SCORPIO:....Jealous as Othello, these dark angels of sexy reputation are formidable lovers—wimps needn't apply.
Northern Rivers Echo News 2003

ours not to reason why A phrase based on a line in the poem 'The *Charge of the Light Brigade' by Alfred, Lord Tennyson (1854), about the soldiers who took part in the ill-fated charge at Balaclava:

Theirs not to reason why
Theirs but to do and die.

➤ Used when expressing resignation at decisions taken or orders given by more senior people

One has to wonder—isn't it worse to surprise viewers with graphic chainsaw-wielding footage than to warn them beforehand about the content? Oh well—ours is not to reason why.
FFWD Weekly (Calgary) 2004

out, damned spot [Shakes.] The cry given by Lady *Macbeth in *Macbeth* (1623). Tortured by her feelings of guilt for inciting her husband to murder the king, she washes her hands repeatedly in an attempt to remove the blood which she continues to see on them.

➤ Used when suggesting that someone is guilty of a political murder or betrayal

When Geoff Hoon lets Kelly meet the select committee he's 'Thrown to Wolves'. Out, out, damned spots.
Guardian Unlimited: The Hutton Report 2004

Outer Mongolia [Places] Mongolia, in eastern Asia, bordered by Russia and China, was known formerly as Outer Mongolia.

➤ A remote, inaccessible place

out of the mouths of babes [Bible] A saying derived from two passages in the Bible, Psalms 8: 2, 'Out of the mouths of babes and sucklings hath thou ordained strength', and Matthew 21: 16, 'Out of the mouths of babes and sucklings thou has perfected praise.'

➤ Used when a child or young person says something that seems disconcertingly wise or honest

Recently, her two-year-old son embarrassed her in front of the grandmother as he dragged a bottle of gin from a press saying: 'This is for mama.' Out of the mouths of babes, eh?
Sunday Business Post 2002

'Over the Rainbow' [Cin.] The title of a song (also known as 'Somewhere over the Rainbow') that was written for the 1939 film *The *Wizard of Oz* and sung by Judy Garland in the film. It begins with the words:

Somewhere over the rainbow
Way up high.

> There's a land that I heard of
> Once in a lullaby.

➤ Used when referring to a faraway or ideal place

McNab's message is implicit: you don't need to visit another country, either over the rainbow or inside the TV. If you want to change your life, just look within yourself.
Scotland on Sunday 2004

Oyl, Olive [Cart. & Com.] A character in Elzie Segar's comic strip *Thimble Theater*, which started in 1919. Olive Oyl is the very skinny girlfriend of *Popeye the Sailor Man.

➤ A woman who is extremely thin

The nice thing about leggings is they fit anybody from Olive Oyl to a lapsed Weightwatcher.
SARAH LACEY *File under: Arson* 1995

Oz [Child. Lit.] The fictional land and city (also called the Emerald City) in L. Frank Baum's children's story *The *Wizard of Oz* (1900).

➤ A fantastic or ideal place

Fundamentalist religion is very big out there, and getting bigger. You have to do things and do them right, and if you don't you're gonna suffer terrible consequences. If you do them right, you're gonna enter Emerald City. You'll be Dorothy and Toto running down the yellow brick road to Oz.
STUDS TERKEL *American Dreams: Lost and Found* 1980

Ozymandias [Lit.] The name of the imaginary ancient king in Shelley's poem of the same name (1819). The poem describes how the shattered remains of parts of a statue of the king are found lying in the empty desert and on the pedestal are carved the ironic words:

> My name is Ozymandias, king of kings:
> Look on my works, ye Mighty, and despair!

➤ Mentioned as an example of hubris and the trap of having too much pride in earthly achievements which will crumble to dust after death

Watching the tearing down of Saddam Hussein's towering statue in Baghdad was a true Ozymandias moment.
OpinionJournal (WSJ): Extra 2003

Ozzie and Harriet [TV] Characters in a long-running US television series *The Adventures of Ozzie and Harriet* (1952–66) about a middle-class American family, in which Ozzie and Harriet Nelson and their sons David and Ricky played fictional versions of themselves.

➤ Used to evoke wholesome, happy, and traditional family life

As a society, we have finally moved away from the Ozzie and Harriet view of family life.
American Demographics 2000

Packer, Kerry [People] (b. 1937) An Australian media tycoon who became famous for creating World Series Cricket in 1977, a series of unofficial one-day matches in Australia for which he paid top cricketers high fees to play.

> ➤ A wealthy business tycoon
>
> 'I wouldn't worry,' Margin told Delaney. 'It's probably only a box number somewhere, and no one can watch a box number twenty-four hours a day. You'd have to be Kerry Packer to afford it.'
> THOMAS KENEALLY *A Family Madness* 1985

Pacolet [Lit.] A dwarf messenger in the early French romance *Valentine and Orson*, whose winged horse, made of wood, carries him instantly wherever he wishes.

> ➤ A messenger
>
> 'And pray how long, Miss Ashton,' said her mother, ironically, 'are we to wait the return of your Pacolet—your fairy messenger—since our humble couriers of flesh and blood could not be trusted in this matter?'
> WALTER SCOTT *The Bride of Lammermoor* 1819

Paddington Bear [Child. Lit.] The hero of a series of children's books by Michael Bond, which first appeared in 1958. He is a bear 'from Darkest Peru' who is found by the Brown family at London's Paddington Station (hence his name) with a label saying 'Please look after this bear'. Paddington wears a duffle coat, wellingtons, and a sou'wester hat with an upturned brim. He is known for giving people a long, hard stare to express disapproval.

> ➤ Someone who gives a disapproving look
>
> Unfortunately, Tube carriage windows are reflective when the train is in a tunnel, so she noticed I was looking, gave me a Paddington Bear hard stare and left to sit opposite.
> *Big Issue* 1994

Pan [Gk Myth.] A god of nature, fecundity, flocks, and herds, usually represented as having a human torso and arms but the legs, ears, and horns of a goat. He lived in Arcadia and was said to be responsible for sudden, irrational fears (the origin of our word 'panic'). On one occasion he pursued the nymph Syrinx, who escaped him by turning into a reed. As he could not distinguish her from all the other reeds, he cut several and made them into the pan pipes which still bear his name.

> ➤ Used to invoke general commotion and disorder, or lechery; also mentioned as a player of sweet music
>
> He could cut cunning little baskets out of cherry-stones, could make grotesque faces on hickory nuts, or odd-jumping figures out of elder-pith, and he was a very Pan in the manufacture of whistles of all sizes and sorts.
> HARRIET BEECHER STOWE *Uncle Tom's Cabin* 1852

There was a general sense of groping and bewilderment. Pan had been amongst them—not the great god Pan, who has been buried these two thousand years, but the little god Pan, who presides over social contretemps and unsuccessful picnics.
E. M. FORSTER *A Room with a View* 1908

Pan, Peter [Child. Lit.] The hero of J. M. Barrie's play of the same name (1904), a boy with magical powers who never grew up. He takes *Wendy Darling and her brothers on an adventure to *Never-Never Land, where they encounter Captain Hook and his pirate gang.

> A man who never seems to grow older or more mature

   More than 20 of the most loyal Cliff Richard fans set up camp outside Sheffield Arena on Monday—six days before tickets go on sale for the Peter Pan of pop.
   Yorkshire Post Today 2002

   The computer games industry never grows up. This does not mean an idyllic Peter Pan-style childhood but rather a perpetual adolescence.
   The Independent 1998

Pandemonium [Lit.] The name, meaning 'All the Demons', which was given by John *Milton to the capital of Hell in his poem *Paradise Lost* (1667).

> A place of utter confusion and uproar, or place of vice and wickedness

   The North Korean leader said on Monday that the U.S. president had turned 'a peaceful world into a pandemonium unprecedented in history'.
   Canoe News 2004

Pandora's box [Gk Myth.] A jar given to Pandora, the first mortal woman, by the gods. Pandora was forbidden to open the box, but, out of curiosity, she disobeyed, and released from it all the evils and illnesses that have afflicted mankind ever since. Only Hope remained at the bottom of the jar.

> A source of many unforeseen and unmanageable problems

   Our leaders have opened a Pandora's Box of problems and risk undermining the stability of the Middle East.
   Croydon Guardian 2003

Pangloss, Dr [Lit.] The tutor in *Voltaire's *Candide* (1759), who imbues *Candide with his guiding philosophy that all is for the best in the best of all possible worlds. No matter what misfortunes they each suffer on their travels—disease, shipwreck, earthquake, flogging, and even attempted hanging and dissection—Pangloss confidently and complacently assures Candide that things could not be otherwise.

> Someone who stubbornly and blindly remains optimistic in the face of obvious problems (adjective *Panglossian*)

   There is a Panglossian tendency to overstate oil reserves by oil-producing countries and oil companies alike.
   Taipei Times 2005

Pantagruel [Lit.] The son of *Gargantua in *Rabelais's satire *Pantagruel* (1532). A giant like his father, Pantagruel has a similarly enormous appetite, especially for wine.

> A bon vivant who enjoys prodigious quantities of food and drink (adjective *Pantagruelian*)

Don Emmanuel, with his rufous beard, his impressive belly, and his flair for ribaldry, made pantagruelian quantities of guarapo, involving hundreds of pineapple skins, which he served with a gourd and his usual good humour.
LOUIS DE BERNIÈRES *Señor Vivo and the Coca Lord* 1991

Pantheon [Gk Myth.] A word meaning 'all the gods' in Greek.

➤ Any group of distinguished people, or people who wield considerable influence

Statistically he is now the greatest Australian Olympian, yet still the debate rages over his position in the pantheon of our sporting gods.
The Australian 2004

Panza, Sancho [Lit.] The short, fat squire who accompanies *Don Quixote on his adventures in the romance *Don Quixote de la Mancha* (1605-15) by Miguel de Cervantes. He repeatedly tries to hold Don Quixote back from his deluded exploits.

➤ A faithful companion; someone who tries to hold a friend back from excess

The real problem is that Gilliam doesn't have a Sancho Panza figure of his own: he has no loyal squire to help him in his hour of trial, still less to urge restraint or compromise.
Guardian Friday Review 2002

Paolo and Francesca [Lit.] Lovers whose story was immortalized in *Dante's *Inferno*. Francesca da Rimini was married to Giovanni Malatesta but fell in love with his brother Paolo. When their affair was discovered, they were both put to death in 1289.

➤ Tragic lovers

But it was no ordinary passion that seized them; it was something so overwhelming that they felt as if the whole long history of the world signified only because it had led to the time and place that had brought them together. They loved as Daphnis and Chloe or as Paolo and Francesca.
SOMERSET MAUGHAM *The Judgment Seat* 1951

Papa Doc (François Duvalier) [Hist.] (1907-71), The president of Haiti (1957-71), whose regime was noted for its brutality and oppressiveness. Many of his opponents were either assassinated or forced into exile by his security force, known as the Tontons Macoutes.

➤ A cruel dictator

At one point his books were banned by the Palestinian Authority because he had, as he put it, 'dared to speak against our own Papa Doc'.
London Review of Books 2003

Paracelsus [People] (*c.*1493-1541) A Swiss physician who introduced a more scientific approach to medicine and saw illness as having an external cause rather than arising as a result of an imbalance in the body's humours.

➤ A doctor; someone who advocates a scientific approach

Paradise [Bible] The Garden of *Eden described in the book of Genesis, the place of perfect happiness enjoyed by *Adam and Eve before their Fall and expulsion. The term is more commonly used, however, to refer not to the biblical Eden but rather to Heaven, 'the second Eden'.

➤ A place or state of complete happiness

Riyadh will soon rival Disney World as a family-friendly vacation paradise.
USA Today News 2002

Paradise Lost [Lit.] The title of an epic poem by John *Milton (1667), which in twelve books relates the story of the *Fall of Man.

> ➤ Used to suggest that a beautiful place has been destroyed, or a good or happy situation has been ruined

> Before suicide bombers ripped through its heart Mombasa's Paradise Hotel was well named. A clutch of heat-seeking missiles and an off-road vehicle packed with three human bombs changed all that. Paradise Hotel had become paradise lost.
> *Sunday Herald* 2002

> But he hopes audiences at his lectures will listen because his message is important: comedy, or at least mainstream television comedy, is in serious decline. Paradise Lost, indeed.
> *Scotland on Sunday* 2006

Parcae Sisters [Rom. Myth.] The Roman name for the *Fates, the three goddesses who presided over the birth, life, and death of humans.

> ➤ People who decide another's fate, or look on dispassionately while others suffer

> Octavian saw his daughter slowly disappearing in the engulfing slush, her smeared face further distorted with the contortions of whimpering wonder, while from their perch on the pigsty roof the three children looked down with the cold unpitying detachment of the Parcae Sisters.
> SAKI 'The Penance' in *The Toys of Peace* 1919

Paris [Gk Myth.] The Trojan prince, son of King Priam, who was appointed to decide which of the three goddesses, *Hera, *Athene, and *Aphrodite should receive the golden apple inscribed with the words 'for the fairest'. Paris chose Aphrodite, who had promised him the most beautiful woman on earth as his wife as a bribe. His reward was to be *Helen of Troy.

> ➤ Someone who has to make a difficult choice, especially a man who has to choose between different women

> In *A Summer's Tale* (1996) Gaston (Melvil Poupard) struggles to choose between three girls. The fact that this makes him rather like Paris before the three Goddesses only adds to the sense that his story needs to be seen as something more than just a teenager's holiday quandary.
> *Senses of Cinema* 2005

Parnassus [Gk Myth.] A mountain a few miles north of Delphi associated with *Apollo and the *Muses. On its slopes was the *Castalian spring, whose waters were believed to give inspiration to those who drank of them.

> ➤ A place or event of cultural or literary greatness

> Edinburgh remains a summit of aspiration, a parnassus among summer festivals.
> NORMAN LEBRECHT *La scena musicale: The Lebrecht Weekly* 2005

Parsifal (Perceval) [Leg. & Folk.] A legendary figure found in French, German, and English poetry from the late 12th century onwards. He is the hero of a number of legends, some of which are associated with the *Holy Grail. Parsifal is often portrayed as a guileless innocent, a 'holy fool'. In some versions of the story, he witnesses a procession of the Grail in the castle of his uncle the Fisher King, who is wounded and will only be healed when the right question about the Grail is asked. Despite his curiosity, Parsifal fails to ask the required question, and his silence prevents his uncle from being restored to health.

> ➤ A hero; someone who fails to speak, or fails to ask questions

As statistic after depressing statistic passed before my eyes, the eccentric crusade to which my uncle had dedicated his life seemed more and more heroic. The White Knight had metamorphosed into Parsifal.
MICHÈLE BAILEY *Haycastle's Cricket* 1996

I, as a dumb Parsifal was the witness of this sickness during the years of my boyhood, and, like Parsifal, speech failed me.
ANTHONY STEVENS *Jung: A Very Short Introduction* 2001

Parthians [Hist.] A group of people who lived and ruled in an area of western Asia in ancient times. They held out against the encroaching Romans until the 2nd century AD and were famous for their cavalry, who had perfected the art of shooting backwards at an enemy from whom they were in retreat, the 'Parthian shot'.

> A 'Parthian shot' is a hostile remark delivered by someone at the moment of departure

The day that Karen had left, angry and shouting as she dragged her bulging suitcase down the hall, her Parthian shot had been, 'You love that bloody truck more than you love me.'
Drifter's Oasis 2004

Pasiphae [Gk Myth.] The wife of *Minos, king of Crete. When Minos refused to sacrifice a bull to Poseidon, *Poseidon punished him by inflicting on Pasiphae a passion for the bull. Helped by *Daedalus to gratify her passion, she became the mother of the *Minotaur, half-man and half-bull.

> Mentioned in the context of an unnatural sexual union

He turned her into Pasiphaë, he bent her over and used her as if she were a young boy.
Senses of Cinema 2005

pass by on the other side [Bible] A phrase taken from the parable of the *Good Samaritan. A victim of thieves is left suffering in the road as both a priest and a Levite 'pass by on the other side' and do not offer help (Luke 10: 30–7). Only the Samaritan stops to help.

> To 'pass by on the other side' is to ignore someone who is suffering

Sadly, the prejudices of Tory MSP Bill Aitken are typical of those who would rather pass by on the other side.
Scotland on Sunday 2002

Passchendaele [Hist.] A village in western Belgium, the site of a battle during the First World War (1917). The battle was in fact a period of prolonged and indecisive trench warfare and involved appalling loss of life in a sea of mud, for no eventual strategic gain.

> A battleground; a place of great suffering

Aldington won: the jury awarded him £1.5 million damages. But in the process the trial churned the business of historical inquiry into a sort of Passchendaele of fear and confusion.
Guardian Unlimited 2005

Patroclus [Gk Myth.] A hero of the *Trojan War and close friend of *Achilles. When Patroclus was killed by *Hector, Achilles avenged his friend's death by slaying Hector.

> A close male friend whose death is greatly mourned and brutally avenged

Patton, General George Smith [Hist.] (1885–1945) An American general who commanded US forces in the Second World War. Known as 'Old Blood and Guts', he pursued an aggressive military strategy, taking the 3rd Army across France and Germany as far as the Czech border.

> Someone who is aggressive, bellicose, or violent

When they say your objective is to 'infiltrate a base,' they mean it in the hardcore General Patton way, where you get in undetected because you shot everyone in the face.
Game-Over Online: PlayStation2 Reviews 2004

Paul [Bible] The name taken by *Saul of Tarsus after his conversion to Christianity. Saul, a committed persecutor of Christians, underwent a dramatic conversion to Christianity on the road to *Damascus. He subsequently saw it as his mission to preach the gospel to the Gentiles and his letters form part of the New Testament.

> Someone who undergoes a sudden and dramatic change of mind; a 'Pauline conversion' is such a change of mind

Like most Italians of his age and background, Vianello had always believed himself immune to statistical probability. Other people died from smoking, other people's cholesterol rose from eating rich food, and it was only they who died of heart attacks because of it....This spring, however five precancerous melanomas had been dug out from his back and shoulders, and he had been warned to stay out of the sun. Like Saul on the road to Damascus, Vianello had experienced conversion, and, like Paul, he had tried to spread his particular gospel.
DONNA LEON *The Anonymous Venetian* 1994

Chisholm was congratulated by the Conservatives for his 'Pauline conversion' to private care.
Sunday Herald 2001

Paul and Virginia [Lit.] Two children in the pastoral romance *Paul et Virginie* (1788) by Jacques Henri Bernardin de Saint-Pierre. The tale relates how the two are brought up by their respective mothers on a tropical island (Mauritius) as if brother and sister, under a regime designed to be in accordance with the laws of nature. They grow to adolescence in happy if frugal circumstances.

> Platonic lovers

Pavlov, Ivan Petrovich [Science] (1849–1936) A Russian scientist who is best known for his work on conditioned reflexes using dogs. He showed that, by linking food with the sound of a bell over a period of time, the salivation response associated with food could become a conditioned response to the sound of the bell alone.

> Used to describe any automatic unthinking response (adjective *Pavlovian*)

The shop-bell rang and, behaving exactly like a Pavlov dog, Stamp got up and began, elaborately, to put on his coat.
KEITH WATERHOUSE *Billy Liar* 1959

There is a suspicion that executives at the company knew there was a dispute coming, wanted it to happen on their terms, and felt they could rely on a Pavlovian response from the trade unions.
Sunday Business Post 2004

Pavlova, Anna [Dance] (1881–1931) A Russian ballerina who became famous for her roles in Fokine's ballets, in particular in his solo dance for her *The *Dying Swan*. She lived in Britain from 1912 and formed her own company, with which she toured Europe and the world.

> A graceful dancer

Johnnyboy draped himself across the workbench like Pavlova in the closing moments of the 'Dying Swan'.
JOYCE HOLMS *Bad Vibes* 1998

Pax [Class. Myth.] The allegorical figure personifying peace in classical times. She was represented by the Athenians as holding *Plutus, the god of wealth, in her lap to demonstrate that peace gives rise to prosperity and opulence. The Romans represented her with the horn of plenty and carrying an olive branch in her hand.

> A way of referring to peace

peace in our time [Hist.] Words used by the British prime minister Neville *Chamberlain when he returned from signing the *Munich agreement in September 1938 in an attempt to avert a war in Europe. In the agreement, the Sudetenland was ceded to Germany and Chamberlain on his return famously waved the document and declared that he was bringing home 'peace in our time'.

> Peace, especially a false peace that will not endure

> More than anyone in Northern Ireland, Trimble knows any 'peace in our time' celebrations will be foolish, premature and especially inside his own party, dangerous.
> *Sunday Herald* 2000

Peale, Norman Vincent [Lit.] (1898–1993) An American clergyman and author, also known humorously as Normal Vincent Peale. He is best known for his 1952 work entitled *The Power of Positive Thinking*, which argues that the only thing necessary for success is a positive attitude: 'Empty pockets never held anyone back. Only empty heads and empty hearts can do that.'

> Someone who is excessively and unrealistically optimistic

> But I believe Seifert when he says his New York experiment was 'great,' simply because he seems to have one of the most sincerely optimistic worldviews of anyone I've met since I served as under-assistant to the secretary of my middle school's Norman Vincent Peale Society.
> *City Pages: The Online News and Arts Weekly of the Twin Cities* 2004

Pearl Harbor [Hist.] A harbour on the island of Oahu, in Hawaii, which was the site of a US naval base. A surprise attack on 7 December 1941 by Japanese aircraft inflicted heavy losses on the Americans and brought the USA into the Second World War.

> A sudden and unexpected attack

> An American attack on Iraq would not be the equivalent of Pearl Harbor, as claimed by a Canadian MP, Bonnie Brown.
> *Guardian Unlimited* 2005

Pecksniff [Lit.] A character in Dickens's *Martin Chuzzlewit* (1844). An architect by profession, Pecksniff is an arch-hypocrite with a 'soft and oily' manner, who uses an outward appearance of virtue and morality to win the affection and respect of old Martin Chuzzlewit, in an attempt to inherit his money. He fails in this attempt and is exposed as the hypocrite that he really is.

> A hypocrite

> Sad for once, as Hayes had struck me as the only exception to the rule that 'decent Tory' is an oxymoron. Accuser looks like a pasty-faced, hard-eyed, sharp-toothed, back-stabbing, nausea-inducing, pocket-lining Pecksniff, who says he is acting in the public interest.
> *The Observer* 1997

Peeping Tom [Leg. & Folk.] A tailor who, according to legend, was said to have peeped at Lady *Godiva when she rode naked through the streets of Coventry, as a result of which he was struck blind. He was thereafter known as Peeping Tom.

> Someone who spies on another person; a voyeur

He lived in a row house and that made surveillance difficult because we couldn't creep
round the entire house and do our Peeping Tom thing.
JANET EVANOVICH *High Five* 1999

Pegasus [Gk Myth.] A winged horse which was ridden by *Perseus in his rescue of
*Andromeda, and by *Bellerophon when he fought the *Chimera. The name Pegasus can
represent a means of escape.

➤ A means of escape

Bertie, in short, was to be the Pegasus on whose wings they were to ride out of their
present dilemma.
ANTHONY TROLLOPE *Barchester Towers* 1857

Pelion on Ossa [Gk Myth.] Mount Pelion in Thessaly was held to be the home of the
centaurs, and the giants were said to have piled Pelion on top of Mount Ossa (or sometimes
Ossa on Pelion) in their attempt to scale Mount *Olympus and destroy the gods.

➤ To 'pile Pelion on Ossa' is to add difficulty to difficulty

Whether one thinks the relevant ministers should have gone or stayed, these have
been abject performances. Their effect has been to make mountains of molehills
(except in the case of the ERM, where it was more a case of piling Pelion on Ossa).
Sunday Telegraph 1994

Pelléas and Mélisande [Lit.; Opera] Two lovers in a story that was initially told in the
poetic drama by Maurice Maeterlinck (1892) and later in Debussy's opera of the same name
(1902). Golaud, the grandson of King Arkel, marries Mélisande, despite the fact that he knows
little about her. They move to his father's gloomy, cold castle, where his younger half-brother
Pelléas is staying, whereupon Pelléas and Mélisande fall in love. Golaud, on discovering
them together, becomes jealous, and stabs and kills Pelléas and wounds himself and Mélisande.
The latter dies giving birth to a child while Golaud is still torturing himself over whether or not
the lovers had slept together or were innocent of anything but embraces.

➤ Mentioned in the context of an illicit love affair

Last night Gillian started quizzing me about one of the girls at the School. Talk about
wide of the mark. Might as well accuse Pelléas of leg-over with Mélisande. (Though
I suppose they must have done it, mustn't they?)
JULIAN BARNES *Talking It Over* 1991

Penelope [Gk Myth.] The wife of *Odysseus who waited patiently and faithfully for her
husband to return home after the end of the *Trojan War. She put off her many suitors by saying
that she would marry only when she had finished the piece of weaving that she had started.
Each night she unravelled the work that she had done during the day.

➤ A faithful wife who waits patiently for her husband's return

She feared in her heart that back home he would dismiss her…that she would be left
forever, faithful and forgotten, waiting like Penelope for a man who never came.
LOUIS DE BERNIÈRES *Captain Corelli's Mandolin* 1994

'Pennies from Heaven' [Mus.] The title of a 1936 song by the American songwriter
Johnny Burke.

➤ An unexpected windfall

In footballing terms, the minnows of Harrogate Railway have just won the National
Lottery—not quite pennies from heaven, more a payday from Sky.
Yorkshire Post Today 2002

Pepys, Samuel [People] (1633–1703) The author of a diary (1660–9) in which he vividly describes life in the early Restoration period and records such contemporary events as the Great Plague, the Fire of London, and the sailing of the Dutch fleet up the Thames.

> ➤ A diarist; a chronicler of events

An American Pepys, Mencken recorded nearly every thought that passed through his mind and practically every major social engagement on his calendar.
Reason Magazine 2003

Perceval *See* PARSIFAL.

perestroika [Hist.] The policy of restructuring the economic system of the Soviet Union proposed by Leonid Brezhnev in 1979 and promoted by Mikhail Gorbachev.

> ➤ Any restructuring of a political or economic system

Ms Alexander could also strike a blow for Scottish council perestroika by introducing proportional representation in local government elections in the coming months.
Sunday Herald 2000

perfidious Albion [Hist.] A phrase (translated from the French *la perfide Albion*) first used by the French in the 18th century to denote English treachery.

> ➤ England or Britain, when considered to be treacherous in international affairs

Only 24 hours earlier, the European parliament had cheered an attack on Britain, denouncing perfidious Albion and its wicked plot to remake the continent in its own image.
Guardian Unlimited 2005

Pericles [People] (*c.*495–429 BC) An influential Athenian statesman who expanded the Athenian Empire and was responsible for the Parthenon and other great buildings. He was noted for his oratory.

> ➤ A great orator (adjective *Periclean*)

Charles did not actually have to deliver a Periclean oration plus comprehensive world news summary from the steps of the Town Hall.
JOHN FOWLES *The French Lieutenant's Woman* 1969

Peripatetic [Philos.] The word (meaning literally 'walking around') which came to be applied to *Aristotle's school at the Lyceum on account of his habit of walking up and down while teaching his students.

> ➤ Used when describing someone who walks around in a thoughtful way

A large group of buyers stood round the auctioneer, or followed him when, between his pauses, he wandered on from one lot of plantation-produce to another, like some philosopher of the Peripatetic school delivering his lectures in the shady groves of the Lyceum.
THOMAS HARDY *The Woodlanders* 1887

Perrin, Reginald [TV] The main character in a British TV series entitled *The Fall and Rise of Reginald Perrin*, which ran from 1976 to 1979. Based on the book *The Death of Reginald Perrin* by David Nobbs (1975), the series follows the life of Reginald Perrin, a middle-aged sales executive combating a mid-life crisis as he attempts to escape his mundane and unfulfilling life by faking his own suicide, leaving a pile of clothes on a beach and walking off into the sunset.

> ➤ Someone who plans their own disappearance

He told everybody he was going to do a Reggie Perrin and vanish but I believe he kept in touch from Scotland with what was happening in Sheffield.
Yorkshire Post Today 2004

Persephone [Gk Myth.] A woman who was abducted by *Hades (also known as Pluto or Dis) to be his queen in the underworld. She was granted the opportunity to return to the earth on condition that no food had passed her lips in the underworld. However, while wandering in the gardens she had eaten some pomegranate seeds from a tree. Persephone was therefore ordered by *Zeus to remain six months with Hades and to spend the rest of the year on the earth with her mother *Demeter.

> ➤ Someone who spends time in a dark place; someone who is punished for eating
>
> She descends to the depths of darkness like Persephone to the underworld.
> *Senses of Cinema* 2004
>
> 'God, I hope I don't end up like Persephone,' she sighed as she took a bite of the food.
> ASHLEY ALQUINE *Forest of Dreams* 2005

Perseus [Gk Myth.] The son of *Zeus and Danae, a hero celebrated for many accomplishments. Helped by the gods, he killed the Gorgon *Medusa by cutting off her head. On his return, flying on *Pegasus, he rescued *Andromeda, who had been chained to a rock and left to be devoured by a monster.

> ➤ A heroic rescuer

Peter Pan *See* PAN, PETER.

Petra [Places] An ancient ruined city in Jordan. It was the capital of the Nabataeans from 312 BC until 63 BC, when they became subject to Rome. The city's extensive ruins include temples and tombs carved in the sandstone cliffs. The poet John Burgon famously described Petra as 'A rose-red city—"half as old as time"'.

> ➤ A deserted place
>
> Think of it. Of a Sunday, Wall Street is deserted as Petra; and every night of every day it is an emptiness.
> HERMAN MELVILLE *Bartleby* 1856

Petrarch and Laura [Lit.] Francesco Petrarch (1304–74) was an Italian Renaissance poet whose father had been expelled from Florence and with whom he moved to Avignon. He met *Laura, the woman who was the inspiration for his love poetry, in Avignon in 1327. Her identity is not known.

> ➤ Mentioned in the context of devoted romantic love
>
> His love was as chaste as that of Petrarch for his Laura.
> THOMAS HARDY *The Return of the Native* 1880

Petruchio [Shakes.] The suitor for Katharina, the ill-tempered shrew in *The Taming of the Shrew* (1623). After marrying Katharina, Petruchio tames her by devising a series of humiliations, including preventing her from eating or sleeping. At the end of the play, he is able to win a bet on who is the most submissive of three wives.

> ➤ A man who 'tames' a woman
>
> In truth, Mrs Proudie was all but invincible; had she married Petruchio, it may be doubted whether that arch wife-tamer would have been able to keep her legs out of those garments which are presumed by men to be peculiarly unfitted for feminine use.
> ANTHONY TROLLOPE *Barchester Towers* 1875

Peyton Place [Lit.] The title of a 1956 novel by Grace Metalious that is set in a small New England town and describes the life of the town as being one of dark secrets and sordid goings-on beneath a veneer of respectability. It was later made into a highly popular US television series (1964–9).

> A seemingly respectable place with dark secrets

Suddenly, the facade of the model city begins to dissolve, replaced by big-city politicking of the most corrupt order. The machinations for power begin to corrode the presumed social harmony as well, and the Garden City suddenly begins looking like Peyton Place. *Sunday Herald* 2000

Phaethon [Gk Myth.] The son of *Helios, the sun-god, who asked to drive his father's sun chariot for a day. However, he did not have the strength to control the horses and the chariot rose so high above the earth that human beings on the ground nearly froze, then plunged so close to the earth that it was scorched. *Zeus intervened to save the world and killed Phaethon with a thunderbolt.

> Someone who is unable to control a vehicle

The sun rose higher on its journey, guided, not by Phaethon, but by Apollo, competent, unswerving, divine.
E. M. FORSTER *A Room with a View* 1908

Phantom of the Opera, The [Cin.; Theatre] A novel by Gaston Leroux, first published in 1911, which tells the story of Erik, a disfigured genius (believed to be a ghost) who lives in the cellars of the Paris Opera. The novel is better known through the 1925 screen version, and the 1986 Broadway musical of the same name.

> Someone who is disfigured; a reclusive madman

The story is centred on 'current' Hollywood heartthrob Todd Pickett who, fearing his looks are going, decides to have plastic surgery. But the operation goes hideously wrong, and he ends up looking like the Phantom of the Opera.
The Press, York (Newsquest) 2001

Pharaoh [Bible] The title of a king of ancient Egypt, most associated with those mentioned in the Old Testament and Hebrew Scriptures in whose time the oppression and *Exodus of Israel took place. During the time when *Joseph was in prison in Egypt, Pharaoh had troubling dreams, including one in which seven fat kine (cows) were followed by seven lean kine which ate the fat ones. Joseph interpreted the dreams as meaning that seven years of plenty would be followed by seven years of famine, advising Pharaoh to store grain for the future famine (Gen. 41: 1–40). At a later period, when *Moses was born, Pharaoh had decreed that all male babies born to the *Israelites should be thrown into the Nile. Moses' mother hid the baby and then placed him in a basket in the reeds of the river. He was discovered by Pharaoh's daughter, who felt sorry for him and decided to raise him as her own son (Exod. 1: 22–2: 10).

> Someone who has prophetic dreams; someone who orders the killing of children

Listen here...I have dreams like a Pharaoh. When I was fourteen and asleep in Fowey, I was here on this exact shore. I saw Will Bryant—it's none of a surprise to me. These days and night, I have dreams I cannot utter...
THOMAS KENEALLY *The Playmaker* 1987

Pharisee [Bible] A member of an ancient Jewish sect who strove to ensure that the state was ruled according to strict Jewish law. According to the Bible, the Pharisees were denounced by *Jesus for their hypocrisy in maintaining an outward appearance of morality and virtue while acting only out of self-interest: 'Woe unto you, scribes and Pharisees, hypocrites! For ye are like unto whited sepulchres, which indeed appear beautiful outward, but are within full of dead men's bones, and of all uncleanness' (Matt. 23: 27).

> ➢ A hypocrite

> You are nothing more than a pharisee with your banning of gay marriages and your use of late term abortion issues to foist your broader paternalistic morals on to us. And like the pharisees, your reliance on laws and judgment make you and your 'morals' a blight on the Christian religion.
> *Brisbane Courier-Mail* 2004

Pheidias (Phidias) [Art] A 5th-century BC Athenian sculptor celebrated for his colossal gold-and-ivory *Athena Parthenos at Athens and for his vast statue of *Zeus at Olympia. He also designed many of the sculptures of the Parthenon and Acropolis.

> ➢ A sculptor

> The Italian sculptor Antonio Canova was known as the modern Praxiteles, and his student John Flaxman as the Pheidias of our times.
> *Daedalus* 2002

Pheidippides [People] (5th century BC) An Athenian messenger who was sent from Athens to Sparta to ask for help after the Persian landing at Marathon in 490 BC. He is said to have covered 150 miles on foot in two days. The long-distance race known as the marathon derives its name from a later story that, after the Greeks had defeated the Persians, a messenger ran the 22 miles from Marathon to Athens with news of the Greek victory, but fell dead on arrival.

> ➢ A marathon runner; someone who dies while running

> Finally, you'll be a marathoner. You and Pheidippides, siblings under the skin.
> *Inc. Magazine* 2002

> The story has it that Kyriakides was advised not to run by some Boston doctors who were afraid that he would do a Pheidippides and pop his sandals en route.
> *Scotland on Sunday* 2004

Philistines [Bible] A group of people who were the traditional enemies of the *Israelites and regarded by them as hostile barbarians.

> ➢ A Philistine is someone who is indifferent to culture and the arts; someone with uncultivated tastes

> This is a philistine agenda, subjecting universities' research and teaching to the narrow interests of the British economy.
> *Spiked Online* 2004

Philoctetes [Gk Myth.] A Greek hero of the *Trojan War. His father was with *Hercules when he died and received from him Hercules' bow and arrows, which Philoctetes inherited. On his way to the war Philoctetes was bitten by a serpent and abandoned by his companions on the island of Lemnos owing to a foul-smelling wound on his foot. When in the tenth year of the war the Greeks were informed by an oracle that only with Hercules' arrows could Troy be taken, *Odysseus and Diomedes came back to fetch Philoctetes to Troy, where he killed Paris.

> ➢ Someone with a wound that will not heal; someone who smells unpleasant; an outcast who returns and achieves great success

> Sometimes, after writing for days without sleep, in dirty pyjamas in a one-room apartment reeking of old hamburger, he began, like Philoctetes in the legend, to stink.
> *Quadrant Magazine* 2004

Mandela walked out of the depths of his long imprisonment and into his destiny as leader and reconciler....The marooned man, the betrayed one...he went on (like Philoctetes) to win the city.
Daily Dispatch Online 2002

Philosopher's Stone [Leg. & Folk.] An imaginary substance, sought after by alchemists, that was supposed to have the power of changing base metals into gold and sometimes of curing all diseases and prolonging life indefinitely.

➤ A universal cure or solution that proves elusive

While Mr. Florida's writings denigrate efforts of cities to power their economies by building sports stadiums and convention centers, the professor thinks that he, by contrast, has found the philosopher's stone that will turn public spending on amenities into economic-development gold.
OpinionJournal (WSJ): Extra 2003

Phlegethon [Gk Myth.] One of the rivers of *Hades.

➤ Used to evoke evil or unpleasantness

Phobos [Gk Myth.] The god of dread and alarm, often represented with a lion's head

➤ A way of referring to fear

Phoebe [Gk Myth.] A daughter of the *Titans Uranus and Gaia, whose name became associated with the moon.

➤ A way of referring to the moon

Like Phoebe breaking through an envious cloud...
PHILIP MASSINGER *Bashful Lover* 1655

Phoebus [Gk Myth.] An epithet of the Greek god *Apollo, used in contexts where the god was identified with the sun.

➤ A way of referring to the sun

He would never have survived the lash of Phoebus.
UMBERTO ECO *The Island of the Day Before* 1994

Phoenix [Myth.] A mythical bird of gorgeous plumage, the only one of its kind. After living for five or six centuries in the Arabian desert, it burnt itself on a funeral pyre ignited by the sun and fanned by its own wings, and rose from the ashes with renewed youth to live through another lifespan.

➤ Anything that has been restored to a new existence after apparent destruction

'I've left Carl,' Lucy said, and my heart lurched. 'This evening, in fact, just before the film started, during that speech when the Chairman of Britmovie was telling us that the phoenix of British film had risen from the ashes.'
BEN ELTON *Inconceivable* 1999

Phryne [People] A celebrated Greek courtesan of the 4th century BC, said to have been the model for such beautiful statues as the Cnidian *Venus of *Praxiteles and the Venus Anadyomene of Apelles. Phryne became so wealthy that she offered to pay for the rebuilding of the walls of Thebes.

➤ A prostitute (adjective *Phrynean*)

Her underclothes are positively Phrynean.
ALDOUS HUXLEY *Point Counter Point* 1928

Piccadilly Circus [Places] A busy road junction in central London, where several major roads meet.

> ➤ A very busy place
>
> Residents in the Bourne Valley and through Old Sarum put up with almost constant traffic throughout Saturday and Sunday, and Amesbury was described as like Piccadilly Circus during the rush hour.
> *This Is Wiltshire news stories* 2004

Picasso, Pablo [Art] (1881–1973) A Spanish painter, sculptor, and graphic artist, one of the most versatile and influential artists of the 20th century. Some of his best-known works show faces and objects disjointed and juxtaposed in strange ways.

> ➤ Used to evoke images that seem strange, incomplete, or disjointed
>
> All of these people fall into place like parts of a Picasso painting—they are pieces that do not really go together but when forced together they form something quite different indeed.
> STELLA PEN *Saturday's Grave* 2003

Pickwick, Mr [Lit.] The central character of Charles Dickens's novel *The Pickwick Papers* (1836–7). Founder of the Pickwick Club, he is jovial, generous, and unworldly in character and short, plump, and bespectacled in appearance.

> ➤ A small, plump man with a round face; a jovial man
>
> Upright, he looked like Mr Pickwick, with a chubby rubicund face and a fringe of long white hair around a gleaming pink scalp.
> ANABEL DONAL *The Glass Ceiling* 1994

Pied Piper [Leg. & Folk.] A legendary figure who is the subject of Robert Browning's narrative poem *The Pied Piper of Hamelin* (1842). The Piper undertakes to rid the town of Hamelin of the rats that have been plaguing its citizens, in return for 1000 guilders. The Piper plays his pipe and the rats follow him to the river and drown. The Mayor then reneges on the payment and, in revenge, the Piper starts to play his pipe again and this time is followed by all the children. He marches to the mountain where a portal opens and he leads the children inside, whereupon it closes. One child, lame and unable to keep up, remains outside.

> ➤ Someone who is pursued by a crowd of children; someone whom others follow blindly; the lame child can be mentioned in the context of someone left behind
>
> Some fall in behind her, and follow her to the lecture theatre, so that she appears to be leading a little procession, a female Pied Piper.
> DAVID LODGE *Nice Work* 1988
>
> A succession of diet experts have become the Pied Pipers of the modern age.
> SARAH MODLOCK *Yahoo.co.uk Money Weekly: Sarah Modlock column* 2005
>
> It is a thought that has occurred to Rio di Angelo, a former member of Heaven's Gate, the suicide cult whose membership checked out en masse in March after announcing their departure on the Internet. Like the last child, too lame to follow the Pied Piper into the mountain, di Angelo was left behind.
> *The Observer* 1997

pie in the sky [Mus.] A phrase from a song by the American labour leader Joe Hill (1879–1915). The song is an attack on religion which, it claims, offers workers no practical help during their life, but only 'pie in the sky when you die'.

> ➤ A dream or promise for the future which is unlikely ever to become reality

It is time we take a step back and come up with a better idea that actually works for farmers, without the pie in the sky promises.
Korea Times: Opinion 2002

Pieria [Gk Myth.] A district on the slopes of Mount *Olympus associated with the *Muses. The Pierian spring was located there, believed to give poetic inspiration to those who drank its waters.

➤ Mentioned in the context of poetic inspiration

A little learning is a dangerous thing;
Drink deep, or taste not the Pierian spring.
ALEXANDER POPE *An Essay on Criticism* 1711

Piggy, Miss [TV] A puppet creation of Jim Henson that has appeared in the television series *The Muppet Show* and *Sesame Street*. She is a large pink pig with long blonde hair.

➤ A fat woman

I just know I've put on at least half a pound. The bus driver's going to notice and give me a pitying look, sort of saying, 'Well, hello, Miss Piggy, how do you expect to get a seat on the bus with that fat arse?'
ARABELLA WEIR *Does My Bum Look Big in This?* 1997

Pilate, Pontius [Bible] The Roman procurator of Judaea (AD 26–36) before whom accusations against *Jesus were brought. After questioning Jesus, Pilate could find no basis for a charge against him, but nonetheless Pilate gave in to the demands of the Jews that Jesus be crucified: 'When Pilate saw that he could prevail nothing, but that rather a tumult was made, he took water and washed his hands before the multitude, saying, I am innocent of the blood of this just person: see ye to it' (Matt. 27: 24).

➤ Someone who colludes in a crime or dishonest act but tries to distance himself from it and assume no responsibility for it. Pilate's gesture proclaiming his innocence has given us the phrase 'to wash one's hands of something', meaning to take no further responsibility for it

The council can't just wash its hands like Pontius Pilate and say it is nothing to do with us.
This is Hampshire news stories 2005

Pilate's wife [Bible] The wife of Pontius *Pilate. In the New Testament, when *Jesus was brought before Pontius Pilate for judgement, Pilate's wife reported to her husband the distress she had suffered in a dream on account of Jesus, and urged him: 'Have thou nothing to do with that just man: for I have suffered many things this day in a dream because of him.'

➤ Someone who has a meaningful or prophetic dream

'All dreams mean something.' 'For Joseph and Pharaoh, or Pilate's wife, perhaps. You will have to work very hard to convince me that they mean anything here and now.'
ROBERTSON DAVIES *The Manticore* 1972

Pilgrim's Progress, The [Lit.] (1678, 1684) A religious allegory by John Bunyan in which *Christian undertakes a pilgrimage to the *Celestial City encountering various allegorical characters on the way.

➤ A difficult spiritual journey

pillar of salt [Bible] A phrase taken from the story of *Lot's wife according to the book of Genesis (19: 24), Lot's wife disobeyed God's order not to look back at the burning city of Sodom, and as a punishment was turned into a pillar of salt.

➤ Mentioned in the context of the dangers of looking back, literally or figuratively

Perhaps then we can look over our shoulders into the past and not be afraid of turning
into pillars of salt.
LA Weekly News 2002

Pillars of Hercules [Gk Myth.] The two promontories at the sides of the Straits of Gibraltar,
one in Europe and one in North Africa, known in ancient times as Calpe and Abyla and now
known as the Rock of Gibraltar and Mount Acho in Ceuta. According to Greek mythology,
they were either erected by *Hercules or pushed apart by him as he travelled to the island
of Erytheia to complete one of his twelve Labours. The Pillars of Hercules were regarded in
ancient times as marking the limit of the known world.

➤ A boundary beyond which lies the unknown

Pillsbury Doughboy [Advert.] A cartoon character that looks like a small person made of
dough, used as an advertising icon by the Pillsbury Company. TV commercials featuring the
character often end with a human finger poking the Doughboy's stomach, to which the
Doughboy responds by rubbing his stomach and giggling.

➤ Someone with a white, flabby body; also used to describe something which bounces
back like dough when it is pressed

Glass took Sullivan's punches like the Pillsbury Dough Boy.
Slate.com: Jack Shafer 2003

General George Casey, the top U.S. commander in Iraq, calls fighting the Iraqi insurgency
the 'Pillsbury Doughboy' idea. You push in one area, and attacks pop out in another.
CNN transcripts: Lou Dobbs Tonight 2005

Pinkerton's [Crime] Pinkerton's National Detective Agency, founded in Chicago in 1850 by
Allan Pinkerton, a Scottish-born US detective. This was the first American private detective
agency, which became famous after solving a series of train robberies. During the American
Civil War, Pinkerton served as chief of the secret service on the Union side, directing espionage
behind the Confederate lines.

➤ Mentioned in the context of detectives or detection skills

I never got caught at school. If my headmistress couldn't catch me, no steward will.
It would take a Pinkerton detective to track me down.
BIJOU1182 *Those in Peril on the Sea: Part 2* 2006

Pinocchio [Child. Lit.] The puppet hero of the story *Le avventure di Pinocchio* (1883) by
G. Lorenzini, who wrote under the name of Carlo Collodi. According to the story, the puppet
Pinocchio is made by the carpenter Geppetto and, after many strange adventures, finally
becomes a real boy. During one of his adventures, his nose magically grows longer every time
he tells a lie.

➤ Someone who tells lies, or is punished for doing so; someone who is free from the
control of others; something that grows ever bigger

We have serious doubts about the U.S. government. I'd like to believe them, but the
U.S. government is like Pinocchio, its nose is longer than the earth's diameter.
Seven Oaks Magazine 2004

I am still unattached. I'm like Pinocchio, I got no strings.
JULLIET05 *Something in the Water* 2005

The pieces averaged about 2500 words for the first few months, then just grew like
Pinocchio's nose .
RICHARD CORLISS *Time Magazine—Richard Corliss column* 2004

Pinter, Harold [Lit.] (1930–2008) A British playwright whose plays include *The Birthday Party* (1957) and *The Caretaker* (1959). Stylistically, his works are characterized by theatrical pauses and silences, irony, and menace.

> ➤ Mentioned in the context of a meaningful silence (adjective *Pinteresque*)

There was the charged Pinteresque pause before the big question: 'What proportion of national income do you think should be taken up with government spending?'
Guardian Unlimited columnists 2005

Piranesi, Giovanni Battista [Art] (1720–78) An Italian engraver and architect famous for his views of the ruins of Rome and fantastic etchings of imaginary prisons (1745–61).

> ➤ Used to evoke a deserted landscape

When it was time for the first train in the morning, he would go back to the mysteriously deserted, Piranesi perspectives of the station, discoloured by dawn.
ANGELA CARTER *Fireworks* 1974

plague on both your houses, a [Shakes.] A quotation from *Romeo and Juliet* (1599), said by the dying Mercutio to express his anger at the long-lasting feud between the Montagues and Capulets: 'I am hurt. A plague o' both your houses!'

> ➤ Used as an expression of anger towards both sides in a quarrel

It would be tempting to stand back and adopt a 'plague on both their houses' attitude to the war between the BBC and the government.
Socialist Worker Online 2003

plagues of Egypt [Bible] Ten plagues sent by God to afflict the Egyptians, according to the book of Exodus, when *Pharaoh refused to allow *Moses to lead the *Israelites out of Egypt. The plagues included plagues of frogs and gnats, the death of cattle, and complete darkness over the land (Exod. 7–12).

> ➤ Mentioned in the context of suffering

Now that I think about it, the day was on par with the plagues of Egypt all occurring simultaneously.
Notes from an Eclectic Mind 2003 weblog

Plato [Philos.] (*c*.429–*c*.347 BC) A Greek philosopher who was a pupil of *Socrates and a teacher of *Aristotle. His *Republic* explores his ideas of a perfect and just society.

> ➤ Used when referring to idealized perfection or love that is spiritual, not sexual (adjective *Platonic*)

The machine is the platonic ideal of rationality. You put something in, and it spits something out, without any digression, moodiness, contemplation: the model of efficiency.
Stylus Magazine album reviews 2003

It's a kind of love, a non-physical, Platonic love.
Scotland on Sunday 2002

Plato's cave [Philos.] A reference to an allegory written by the Greek philosopher *Plato to illustrate that perceptions can be false. In the allegory, men are held in a cave so that they can only see the back wall of the cave, lit by the fire behind them. As they can see only shadows, they assume that the shadows are reality.

> ➤ Mentioned to suggest that something we assume to be reality may in fact be an illusion

We believe we are in control. In reality, we are still prisoners in Plato's cave where our illusions are fed to us by digital technology.
STEVEN KREIS *Lectures on Ancient and Medieval History* 2001

Pluto [Gk Myth.] An alternative name for *Hades, lord of the underworld. It was considered unwise to mention Hades by his true name, so the name Pluto, meaning literally 'the Rich One', was often used instead.

> ➤ Mentioned in the context of an underworld, or a place of perpetual darkness and gloom (adjective *Plutonian*)

> Damien picked his way through the corpse ridden Plutonian landscape.
> SINISTERLY SPEAKING *Battle Scars* 2002

Plutus [Gk Myth.] The son of *Demeter and the god of wealth in Greek mythology. The Greeks represented him as blind because he distributed riches indiscriminately, as lame because riches come slowly, and with wings because riches disappear more quickly than they come.

> ➤ Mentioned in the context of wealth or the worshipping of wealth

> It would be difficult for the most jealous and eager devotee at the shrine of Plutus to devise any securities for property.
> *Harper's Monthly* 1880

Pocahontas [People] (*c.*1595–1617) A beautiful American Indian princess who is alleged to have saved the life of the English colonist John Smith when he was captured by her father Powhatan.

> ➤ A Native American woman

> Then go to America, and drown your sorrows on the bosom of some charming Pocahontas.
> JOHN FOWLES *The French Lieutenant's Woman* 1969

Podsnap, Mr [Lit.] A character in Dickens's *Our Mutual Friend* (1864–5) who is self-satisfied and complacent, and has a high opinion of his own importance: 'Mr Podsnap...stood very high in Mr Podsnap's opinion.'

> ➤ A pompous or self-important person (noun *Podsnappery*)

> Masochists may get their kicks from national self-denigration, but for the rest of us there is neither much fun nor much enlightenment in such bouts of inverted Podsnappery.
> *The Independent* 1992

Poe, Edgar Allen [Lit.] (1809–49) An American short-story writer and poet, best known for his macabre tales of mystery and the supernatural, including 'The Fall of the *House of Usher' (1839), set in an eerie, crumbling mansion.

> ➤ Used to evoke a place or person of an eerie and somewhat sinister character

> He reminded me of a character from one of Edgar Allen Poe's gothic tales, sitting in that great dark room of his, with a restless Dalmatian and a stuffed Siamese cat for company.
> *Sunday Herald* 2001

Poirot, Hercule [Lit.] The Belgian detective in many novels by Agatha *Christie. He has a waxed moustache, drinks tisanes, and uses 'the *little grey cells' to deduce the identity of the murderer.

> ➤ A clever detective

> The emphasis is on police procedure and the logical buildup of evidence rather than on the inspired deductive leaps you might expect from a Sherlock Holmes or a Hercule Poirot.
> RON MILLER *Ron Miller film noir columns* 2004

poisoned chalice [Shakes.] A phrase from *Macbeth* (1606), used by *Macbeth in a speech in which he flinches from the prospective murder of Duncan:

> ...this even-handed justice
> Commends the ingredients of our poisoned chalice
> To our own lips.

> ➤ A role or appointment which is likely to bring problems

> The new IBTS chairman, Donegal county manager, Michael McLoone, said he did not regard his new post as a poisoned chalice.
> *Irish Examiner* 2001

Pollock, Jackson [Art] (1912–56) A US abstract expressionist painter, the foremost exponent of 'action painting'. In 1947 he abandoned the use of brushes, adopting a technique in which he vigorously dribbled or hurled the paint straight onto the canvas. These works, sometimes referred to as his 'drip paintings', are made up of complicated laceworks of swirling coloured lines.

> ➤ Used to evoke an image of splattered colours, or something which seems random and without any logical pattern

> Blood was splashed onto the walls of the ruined and bombed buildings like a Jackson Pollock painting.
> CHRIS CONWAY *After the Pandemic* 2005

> Mintzberg has shown that management itself is as much a Jackson Pollock painting as it is a quantifiable science.
> *Fast Company Magazine* 2000

Pollux *See* CASTOR AND POLLUX.

Pollyanna [Child. Lit.] The heroine of stories for children written by the American author Eleanor H. Porter (1868–1920). Pollyanna is a perpetually cheerful girl who teaches everyone she meets to play the 'just being glad' game: 'the game was to just find something about everything to be glad about—no matter what 'twas'.

> ➤ Someone with an unflagging (and often excessively saccharine) cheerfulness, even in the most unpromising situations

> Those whose cup is half full are the world's optimists, the Pollyannas and the kind of people to be avoided at all costs, particularly at parties.
> *Free India Media* (2004)

Polo, Marco [People] (*c.*1254–*c.*1324) A Venetian traveller and writer. Between 1271 and 1275 he accompanied his father and uncle on a trading expedition east into central Asia, eventually reaching China and the court of *Kublai Khan. His written account of his travels was the West's primary source of knowledge of the Far East until the 19th century, though doubt has subsequently been cast on its veracity.

> ➤ A traveller

> The commonest ailment experienced by modern-day Marco Polos is an intestinal attack known as gyppy tummy.
> *New Scientist* 1970

Polonius [Shakes.] The court chamberlain in *Hamlet* (1604) who hides behind an arras (a tapestry screen) in Gertrude's bedchamber to eavesdrop on *Hamlet's conversation with the queen. Hamlet, believing it is the king, Claudius, he can hear behind the arras, runs his sword through it and mistakenly stabs Polonius to death.

> Someone who eavesdrops on a conversation; someone who suffers as a result of eavesdropping

Polycrates [People] The ruler of Samos, known for being extraordinarily lucky. So much luck put him in danger of retribution from *Nemesis, and in order to appease her he threw away a very valuable ring. The ring was subsequently found in the belly of a fish which a fisherman had presented to Polycrates. He was killed in c.522 BC.

> Someone who is extremely lucky; someone who ultimately suffers when their luck runs out

Polydamas [Leg. & Folk.] A celebrated athlete who imitated *Hercules in whatever he did. He killed a lion with his fist and is said to have stopped a speeding chariot with his hand. He died attempting to catch a falling boulder.

> A great athlete; a strong man

Polyphemus [Gk Myth.] One of the *Cyclopes, huge one-eyed monsters, who fell in love with Galatea, a sea-nymph. She did not love him, but did have a lover by the name of Acis. In a jealous rage, Polyphemus hurled a rock at Acis, crushing him to death.

> A monster

Like so many others who wanted to spend their lives teaching, Richard had been forced to leave the profession. The English profession is a Cyclops, one that like Polyphemus dashes out brains and eats wayfarers.
Bad Subjects Magazine 2002

Pomona [Rom. Myth.] The Roman goddess of fruit, married to Vortumnus, the god of orchards and fruit.

> Mentioned in the context of fruit

Down in the heart of the apple-country nearly every farmer kept a cider-making apparatus and wring-house for his own use, building up the pomace in great straw 'cheeses', as they were called; but here, on the margin of Pomona's plain, was a debatable land neither orchard nor sylvan exclusively, where the apple-produce was hardly sufficient to warrant each proprietor in keeping a mill of his own.
THOMAS HARDY *The Woodlanders* 1887

Pompeii [Places] An ancient city in western Italy, south-east of Naples. Following an eruption of Mount *Vesuvius in AD 79, the city was completely buried beneath volcanic ash. Among the excavated ruins have been found fossilized remains of people trying to flee the destruction.

> A place that is completely destroyed and left in ruins; also used to allude to contorted figures

He was rather glad that they were all out; it was amusing to wander through the house as though one were exploring a dead, deserted Pompeii.
ALDOUS HUXLEY *Crome Yellow* 1921

In such inclemency, folks could perish while cooking, or freeze into statuesque sleeping positions like Pompeii's fossilized figures.
CBC.ca: Books 2005

Pony Express [Hist.] A system of mail delivery in the United States in 1860–1. Relays of horse-riders covered a total distance of 1800 miles between St Joseph in Missouri and Sacramento in California.

➤ An outdated delivery system

Kodak…are now offering a 'printing' service from your emailed photographs which end up as a photo album sent back to you by pony express, or something equally as outdated.
Pattaya Mail 2001

Pooh *See* WINNIE THE POOH.

Pooh-Bah [Opera] The Lord-High-Everything-Else, a character in Gilbert and Sullivan's *The Mikado* (1885).

➤ A self-important person; a person holding many offices at once

He is a kind of grand pooh-bah of marketing, a master brander and hype creator who leverages his reputation as the grandaddy of hip-hop to bring people together and let things combust.
Fast Company Magazine 2003

'Poor Little Rich Girl' [Mus.] The title of a 1925 song by Noel Coward, and also of an earlier film (1917) and play (1913) by Eleanor Gates.

➤ A girl or young woman whose wealth brings her no happiness

Athina inherited £1.56bn from her grandfather on her 18th birthday but it was at the age of just three she was dubbed the 'poor little rich girl' when her mother died aged 37 in Buenos Aires after a history of drug abuse.
Scotland on Sunday 2005

Popeye [Cart. & Com.] A cartoon character, whose full name is Popeye the Sailor Man, created by Elzie Segar for the comic strip *Thimble Theater* in 1929. Eating a can of spinach gave Popeye prodigious strength. He was depicted with hugely bulging forearms, one eye, and a pipe clenched between his teeth. His girlfriend was the skinny Olive *Oyl and his arch-enemy Bluto.

➤ A man with a very muscular physique

They were what you'd expect from a Forces team—they're a big, physical side, all built like Popeye, and they played a simple game.
The Press, York (Newsquest) 2005

Poppins, Mary [Child. Lit.; Cin.] The name of the Edwardian nanny with magical powers who appears in a series of children's books by P. L. Travers and was played by Julie Andrews in the film musical *Mary Poppins* (1964).

➤ A perfect, ever-patient parent or nanny; someone with unfailing cheerfulness and somewhat saccharine wholesomeness

We arrive at nursery—a lovely purpose-built affair with more toys than Hamleys and cheerful staff who could give Mary Poppins a run for her money.
The Press, York (Newsquest) 2002

The thoroughly demure, down-to-earth looks and fresh-faced glee cemented the songstress firmly into her newly allotted position as the Mary Poppins of rock and roll.
Sunday Herald 2002

Porter, Jimmy [Lit.] The main character in John Osborne's 1956 play *Look Back in Anger*. Porter is an amiable but disaffected young man, who criticizes accepted social conventions and typifies the *'angry young man' of the period.

> ➤ Someone ready to criticize accepted social practices or values

> Even his reputation as the critic who saved British theatre from suburban gentility is questionable. He wasn't remotely gritty himself. Indeed, he was a lot more like Noël Coward than Jimmy Porter.
> *The Sunday Times* 2004

Porter KCB, Sir Joseph [Opera] A character in Gilbert and Sullivan's *HMS Pinafore* (1878) who boasts that he has achieved the exalted status of 'ruler of the Queen's Navee' by his industry as an office boy, junior clerk, articled clerk, lawyer, and MP, without any experience in the Navy. His song ends with the instruction that if you want to 'rise to the top of the tree', you should

> Stick close to your desks and never go to sea,
> And you all may be rulers of the Queen's Navee!

> ➤ Someone who rises to a senior position from a humble start

Portia [Shakes.] A rich heiress in *The Merchant of Venice* (1600), who disguises herself as a male lawyer to save Antonio, a friend of her betrothed, Bassanio. Antonio had borrowed money from Shylock to help Bassanio and later, unable to pay it back, is faced with paying the bond of a *pound of his flesh instead. Portia saves Antonio's life by arguing that, although Shylock has the right to take a pound of Antonio's flesh, he has no right to shed any of his blood, making it impossible for Shylock to exact his due.

> ➤ A female lawyer

> Miss Trant, the Portia of our Chambers, once fled in tears from Bullingham's Court, saying that the cause of justice there would be advanced if they brought back trial by ordeal.
> JOHN MORTIMER *Rumpole's Return* 1980

Poseidon [Gk Myth.] The Greek god of the sea, water, earthquakes, and horses, often depicted with a trident in his hand. Poseidon was frequently portrayed as both irritable and vengeful. He corresponds to the Roman god *Neptune.

> ➤ A man in water or emerging from water

> Mandras was too young to be a Poseidon, too much without malice. Was he a male sea-nymph, then? Was there such a thing as a male Nereid or Potamid?
> LOUIS DE BERNIÈRES *Captain Corelli's Mandolin* 1994

Poste, Flora [Lit.] The heroine of the novel *Cold Comfort Farm* by Stella Gibbons (1932) who visits her relatives the Starkadders in Sussex and finds herself in a household full of gloom, seething emotion, dark secrets, and rural intrigue. She cheerfully sets about reforming the characters and sorting out their personal lives.

> ➤ Someone who tries to sort out other people's problems

> 'Oh Ma!' Michael said, when I told him. 'You interfering old busybody!' 'Nonsense,' I said. 'I prefer to think of myself as a sort of Flora Poste, tidying up people's lives and making them happy.'
> HAZEL HOLT *Lilies that Fester* 2000

Potiphar's wife [Bible] The wife of an Egyptian officer mentioned in the book of Genesis. *Joseph, the son of *Jacob, was bought by Potiphar, in whose house he was soon made overseer. Potiphar's wife tried to seduce him but Joseph repeatedly refused her advances because of his loyalty to his master. Finally when Potiphar's wife found herself alone in the house with Joseph, she grabbed hold of him, saying 'Lie with me'. Joseph fled from the house, leaving a piece of his clothing in her hand. She subsequently made a false accusation that he had attempted to rape her (Gen. 39).

> ➤ A woman who harasses a man sexually, or falsely accuses him of rape

So pressing an issue is it [the sexual harassment of men by women]…that the European Union considered it necessary to produce a 93-page booklet on what it described as 'the Potiphar's wife syndrome'.
The Guardian 1994

pottage *See* MESS OF POTTAGE.

pound of flesh [Shakes.] The forfeit demanded by the moneylender *Shylock of the merchant Antonio in *The Merchant of Venice* (1600). Shylock lends 3000 ducats to Antonio on condition that if the sum is not repaid by the agreed date, Antonio will forfeit a pound of his flesh. When Antonio is unable to repay the money, Shylock insists on being paid his pound of flesh. *Portia disguises herself as a lawyer and pleads for mercy for Antonio, outwitting Shylock by insisting that, although he can take his pound of flesh, he must not spill a drop of blood in the process, since the bond allows only for flesh, not blood.

> ➤ Mentioned in the context of someone insisting on an agreed payment or penalty in a way that is excessively harsh

The danger here is that state government employees will now demand their pound of flesh from bankrupt state governments.
Domain B 2004

Prague Spring [Hist.] A brief period of liberalization and political reform which took place in Czechoslovakia in the 1960s, ending in 1968.

> ➤ A period of political, economic, or cultural liberalization

Even analysts who credit the US with instigating some movement in the region find the idea that the Middle East is undergoing a Prague Spring disturbing.
Al-Ahram Weekly (Cairo) 2005

Praxiteles [Art] (4th century BC) An Athenian sculptor. Although only one of his works survives, a sculpture of *Hermes carrying the infant *Dionysus, he is considered to be one of the foremost Greek sculptors. One of his most famous works was a statue of *Aphrodite, which is known through later copies.

> ➤ A sculptor; also used to evoke a beautiful human form

He stood up slowly and went over to close the curtains. His silhouette against the window was like something Praxiteles might have knocked up for personal consumption.
LAUREN HENDERSON *The Black Rubber Dress* 1997

precious [Lit.] The name given to the magic ring by *Gollum in J. R. R. *Tolkien's *The Hobbit* (1937) and *The Lord of the Rings* (1954–5). Gollum, once the holder of the ring, is still held captive by its power and consumed by a desire to regain possession of it.

> ➤ An object of obsessive desire; a ring

It's mine, my precious! A silver ring engraved with a band of stars and a single crescent moon is calling out to me from a dusty shelf in a back-alley jeweller's shop, begging for me to become its new master.
Scotland on Sunday 2006

Pre-Raphaelite [Art] An artist who was a member of the Pre-Raphaelite Brotherhood, a group of English 19th-century artists founded by Dante Gabriel Rossetti, John Everett Millais, and Holman Hunt. The aim of the Pre-Raphaelites was to emulate the vivid use of colour and meticulously detailed fidelity to nature of Italian painting from before the time of Raphael. The female models they chose for their paintings, notably Elizabeth Siddal, Fanny Cornforth, and Jane Morris, all had long, wavy auburn hair.

➤ Used when describing a woman with wavy auburn hair and a pale complexion

She has narrow sloping shoulders, and in those days a soulful pre-Raphaelite look.
FAY WELDON *Life Force* 1992

Prester John [Leg. & Folk.] A legendary Christian priest-king who ruled over a fabulously wealthy empire in Asia. In 14th-century versions of the legend, he was believed to be the king of Ethiopia. Another theory identifies him with a Chinese prince who defeated the sultan of Persia in 1141.

➤ A king in a faraway land

By this good wine, I'll ride to the end of the world—the very gates of Jericho, and the judgment-seat of Prester John, for thee!
WALTER SCOTT *The Bride of Lammermoor* 1818

Priapus [Gk Myth.] A god of fertility and procreation, represented as an ugly human figure with enormous genitals. He was also a god of gardens and vineyards.

➤ A way of referring to a man's penis, or male libido

Then she touched him. King Priapus, he who had been scared to death, now rose up from the dead.
TOM WOLFE *The Bonfire of the Vanities* 1987

The lyrics had always offered tales of priapic men and willing, submissive women.
Guardian Friday Review 2002

primrose path [Shakes.] A quotation from *Hamlet*, spoken by *Ophelia to her brother Laertes, when he has advised her to be wary of the attentions of *Hamlet:

> Do not, as some ungracious pastors do,
> Show me the steep and thorny way to heaven,
> Whiles, like a puffed and reckless libertine,
> Himself the primrose path of dalliance treads...

➤ A path of ease or pleasure, especially when it leads to your future downfall or ruin

But pretending the budget doesn't matter is the primrose path to high taxes and poor services.
This is the Lake District: news stories 2004

Prince Charming [Fairy tales] The hero of the fairy story 'The Blue Bird' ('L'Oiseau bleu') by Mme d'Aulnoy. Having fallen in love with a king's daughter, he falls foul of her wicked stepmother and is condemned to spend seven years in the form of a blue bird. At the end of the seven years, he regains his proper shape and all turns out well. The name has come to be erroneously associated with other fairy stories, particularly with the prince in the '*Cinderella' story.

➤ An idealized young lover or suitor

Madonna, the self-styled queen of pop, finally appeared to have married her Prince Charming, film-maker Guy Ritchie.
Daily Dispatch Online 2000

Prince of Darkness [Rel.] Another name for the *Devil or *Satan.

➤ The epitome of evil

Wanniski describes Perle as 'the genuine article, the Prince of Darkness', who has spent most of his waking hours 'plotting on how to arrange a nice little war with Iraq, with or without coalition partners.'
Sunday Business Post 2002

Princes in the Tower [Hist.] **Edward**, prince of Wales (b. 1470), and **Richard**, duke of York (b. 1472), the two young sons of Edward IV. When Edward IV died in 1483, the young Edward reigned briefly as Edward V, but soon afterwards he and his brother were sent to the Tower of London by their uncle, the future Richard III. It is generally assumed that they were murdered in the tower at the instigation of Richard, although some argue that the culprit was his successor, Henry VII. Two skeletons discovered in the Tower in 1674 are thought to be theirs.

➤ Children who are prisoners

'Princess and the Pea, The' [Fairy tales] Title of a fairy story by Hans Christian *Andersen, about a princess who is so sensitive that she can feel a pea even beneath multiple mattresses.

➤ Mentioned in the context of extreme sensitivity

The Aries psyche is especially sensitive right now—a princess and the pea rating on the Richter sensitivity scale in fact.
Northern Rivers Echo News 2003

Prisoner of Chillon, The [Lit.] A poem (1816) by *Byron which describes the imprisonment of François de Bonnivard (1496–1570) in the castle of Chillon, on Lake Geneva.

➤ A prisoner

Prisoner of Zenda, The [Lit.] A novel by Anthony Hope, published in 1894, which follows the adventures of Rudolf Rassendyll, an Englishman who bears a striking resemblance to the king of *Ruritania. When the king is kidnapped, Rassendyll impersonates him, helps to rescue him from his imprisonment in the castle of Zenda, and thwarts a plot to usurp him.

➤ A prisoner kept in strict isolation

He isn't the prisoner of Zenda. He's allowed to talk to anyone he chooses.
Scotland on Sunday 2003

Procrustes [Gk Myth.] A brigand who forced travellers who fell into his hands to lie on an iron bed. If they were longer than the bed, he cut off the overhanging length of leg; if they were shorter than the bed, he stretched them until they fitted it. He was eventually killed by *Theseus, who attached him to his own bed and then, as he was too long for it, cut off his head.

➤ Someone who attempts to enforce uniformity or conformity by forceful or ruthless methods; also used when describing the process of cutting something down to the correct size

When diversity and originality have been vanquished and every place has become the same, Procrustes will have won.
Shambhala Sun 2003

Because we think in decades, we tend to make decades Procrustean beds, to cut off the bits that do not fit, to imagine that cultural change occurs every ten years.
Composition Studies 2001

Prodigal Son [Bible] A young man who squandered the property his father gave him 'with riotous living', according to a parable told by *Jesus. When, repenting his behaviour, the son returned home, he was received with compassion and forgiveness by his father: 'Bring forth the best robe, and put it on him; and put a ring on his hand, and shoes on his feet: And bring hither the fatted calf, and kill it; and let us eat, and be merry: For this my son was dead, and is alive again; he was lost, and is found' (Luke 15: 11–32).

> A returned wanderer or repentant sinner

He waved to Atwood. 'Hello, Frank. Look who's back! The prodigal returns!'
ROBERT HARRIS *Enigma* 1995

The audience welcomed Rizzi back like the prodigal son.
The Sunday Times 2004

Prometheus [Gk Myth.] A *Titan, the brother of *Atlas, who is seen in many legends as the champion of humankind against the gods. In some stories he actually made the first men by making figures of clay which, with the help of *Athene, he brought to life. When *Zeus withheld fire from men, saying that they could eat their flesh raw, Prometheus responded by going to *Olympus himself and stealing some fire hidden in a stalk of fennel, which he gave to men. As a punishment for his disobedience to the gods, Zeus had Prometheus chained to a rock, where each day an eagle tore out his liver, which grew again each night. He was eventually rescued by *Hercules.

> A courageous rebel who dares to challenge the power of the gods and of fate; someone who suffers an ongoing torment (adjective *Promethean*)

While he lived Beyers Naude, like Prometheus, defied power that seemed omnipotent.
Joburg.org.za news archive 2004

This is more than a monument to Newton's genius; rather, it honors the Promethean scientist who unlocks the mysteries of the cosmos, thereby elevating all humankind to the level of the gods.
Art in America 2001

He groaned slightly and winced, like Prometheus watching his vulture dropping in for lunch.
The Hindu: Sunday Magazine 2002

Promised Land [Bible] The land of *Canaan which, according to the Bible, was promised by God to *Abraham and his descendants as their heritage (Gen. 12: 7). When the *Israelites left Egypt, led by *Moses (Exod. 12: 31–42), they wandered through the Sinai desert for 40 years until they finally reached the borders of Canaan (Num. 34). Moses was not allowed to cross the river Jordan into Canaan but was allowed a glimpse of the Promised Land from Mount Pisgah before he died.

> A desired place of expected happiness, especially heaven

Of course, America seems like the promised land to poor Mexicans.
CNN transcripts: Lou Dobbs Tonight 2005

As captain of the economy, his job is to plan a course and make fine adjustments as necessary along the voyage in order to avoid the icebergs and reach the Promised Land.
BusinessWeek Magazine 2001

Prospero [Shakes.] The usurped duke of Milan in *The Tempest* (1623), who is marooned on a remote enchanted island with his daughter *Miranda. His knowledge of magic enables him to raise the storm at the beginning of the play and gives him power over the airy spirit *Ariel. He finally resolves to renounce his 'rough magic', breaking his staff and burying his books, the sources of his powers.

> Someone who has the ability to control the elements, or control those around them

Director Mark Wing-Davey cannot resist dabbling with the elements, like Prospero in The Tempest.
The Press, York (Newsquest) 2004

Proteus [Gk Myth.] The son of Oceanus and Tethys, who was given by *Poseidon the power to prophesy the future. He also had the power to change his shape, which he would exploit in order to escape those seeking his predictions. In an episode recounted in the *Odyssey*, Proteus changes himself in rapid succession into a lion, a serpent, a panther, a wild boar, a torrent of water, and a tree.

> Someone who is able to change their shape or personality; something that constantly changes, or appears in many forms (adjective *Protean*)

Pushkin had become what he remains today—a poet without intonation, who can't be tied down, who can do anything, like the sea god Proteus who could change his shape at will.
Sign and Sight (German Media in English): In Today s Feuilletons 2005

The Industrial Counterrevolution was protean, and in its many guises captured minds of almost every persuasion.
Reason Magazine 2001

Proust, Marcel [Lit.] (1871–1922) A French novelist, whose masterpiece, *À la recherche du temps perdu* (1913–27), is usually translated into English with the title *Remembrance of Things Past*. In exploring its theme of recovery of the lost past, the novel repeatedly describes how a sensory stimulus in the present, such as the taste of a madeleine cake dipped into tea, can act as the unconscious trigger for a flood of memories from the past, especially from childhood.

> Mentioned in the context of something triggering a vivid memory of the past

Like Proust and his madeleines, I feel myself whisked away to the past.
ADAM ROBERTS *The Amateur Gourmet* 2005

He named the company after a Proustian moment of TV viewing that evoked memories of his grandmother.
Taipei Times 2004

Prynne, Hester [Lit.] The adulteress in Nathaniel Hawthorne's novel *The *Scarlet Letter* (1850) set in 17th-century Boston. Hester is sent by her ageing English husband to Boston, where he joins her two years later. He arrives to find her in the pillory, with her illegitimate baby in her arms. She refuses to name her lover and is sentenced to wear a scarlet 'A', for 'adulteress', on her bosom. Her husband, taking on the assumed name of Roger Chillingworth, sets out to discover the identity of her lover and eventually identifies him as Arthur *Dimmesdale, a young and much-respected church minister. Hester, ostracized by the community, brings up her child on the outskirts of the town, and eventually wins back the respect of the townsfolk by her good works.

> An adulteress

Tristan was finding it difficult to meet Hannah's eyes. He glanced away from her. 'Weren't you and Lucas…I mean, that's what I assumed from what you—' 'That I was sleeping with Lucas, do you mean?' A kind of cold embarrassment dropped over Hannah, as though she were the woman taken in adultery, a latter-day Hester Prynne.
SUSAN MOODY *The Italian Garden* 1994

Psycho [Cin.] The title of an Alfred *Hitchcock thriller, released in 1960. The film centres on Norman *Bates, a murderous psychopath who is the owner of the *Bates motel, and includes a famously shocking murder scene in which a woman is stabbed repeatedly by Bates in her shower.

> Used when describing a feeling of terror, or a gruesome scene in a shower

Nick yourself, and you'll turn your shower into that scene from Psycho.
Girls Life Magazine 2002

Puck [Leg. & Folk.] A mischievous sprite or goblin, also called Robin Goodfellow, believed to roam the English countryside playing pranks. He appears as a character in *Shakespeare's A Midsummer Night's Dream* (1600), where he is described as a 'shrewd and knavish sprite' who delights in frightening village girls, preventing butter from being churned, and leading people off the right path at night.

> A mischievous or impish person (adjective *Puckish*)

She couldn't tell if he was smiling, or if his face always wore that puckish grin.
DOUG BEASON and KEVIN J. ANDERSON *Assemblers of Infinity* 1993

pumpkin [Fairy tales] The item transformed into a coach for *Cinderella by her *fairy godmother in the traditional fairy tale 'Cinderella', so that Cinderella can go to the ball. Cinderella is warned, however, that she must leave the ball by midnight, as at that point the coach will revert to its original form.

> Used in the context of a sudden and negative change, especially one that happens at midnight

Well ladies, we better get home before the car turns into a pumpkin and your beautiful dresses become rags.
SARSTARZS *An Eternal Bond* 2002

Fortunately for procrastinators, mutual fund companies…will go out of their way to help you set up an account before your money turns into a pumpkin.
SANDRA BLOCK *USA Today money: Your Money* 2005

Punch and Judy [Theatre] Characters in a traditional English seaside puppet show presented to children on a stage in a collapsible booth. Punch (also called Punchinello) strangles his baby, is beaten by his wife, whom he then beats to death, and has various violent encounters with other characters including a doctor and a policeman.

> Used to evoke bitter quarrelling

Doctors' leaders yesterday expressed alarm that the National Health Service was becoming the 'Punch and Judy show of British politics'.
Yorkshire Post Today 2002

Purgatory [Rel.] In the Roman Catholic religion, a place of spiritual cleansing after death, for the souls of people who have died in the grace of God but have to expiate venal sins before they may enter Heaven.

> Any place or situation in which a person is waiting to move on

Imagine the distress of two York families who have been waiting for years to conclude the formalities. They are suspended in purgatory until inquests officially identify the causes of death.
The Press, York (Newsquest) 2004

Pygmalion [Leg. & Folk.] **1.** The king of Cyprus who created a statue of a beautiful woman, according to Ovid, and then fell in love with it. He prayed to *Aphrodite for a wife who resembled the statue, and Aphrodite responded by bringing it to life. The woman, whom Pygmalion married, has come to be called *Galatea.

> Someone who brings a person to life, or enables them to express themselves

I was…the Pygmalion who released you, alive and talking, from the marble block.
ROBERTSON DAVIES *The Cunning Man* 1994

2. [Lit.] The phonetician Professor Henry Higgins in Bernard Shaw's play *Pygmalion* (1913). Professor Higgins bets that he can take a cockney flower-seller and train her to speak standard English and fit into an upper-class social life. He succeeds, but she rebels against his relentless coaching and tyrannical behaviour. Eventually, they come to a truce. The play was made into a musical, *My Fair Lady*, which was filmed in 1964.

> Someone who transforms a person to make them socially acceptable

He's to work his Pygmalion's magic to smooth the rough edges off our boyish Gracie and teach her to be a lady.
Tokyo Weekender 2001

Pylades and Orestes [Gk Myth.] Two young men who were constant and close friends.

> Strong, loyal friends

What animal magnetism drew thee and me together I know not; certainly I never experienced anything of the Pylades and Orestes sentiment for you, and I have reason to believe that you, on your part, were equally free from all romantic regard to me.
CHARLOTTE BRONTË *The Professor* 1857

Pynchon, Thomas [Lit.] (b. 1937) A US novelist whose novels include *Gravity's Rainbow* (1973) and *Mason & Dixon* (1997). His novels are noted for being dense and complex.

> Mentioned in the context of a complex plot or story (adjective *Pynchonesque*)

Handled equally as well is his intricate Pynchonesque plot, involving mind-altering biochemicals (for which Alfred holds one of the patents), eastern bloc national fiscal strife, and railroad company business acumen.
Free Williamsburg magazine 2002

Pyramus and Thisbe [Rom. Myth.] Next-door neighbours in Babylon who are in love with each other. Their parents forbid them to marry, but they are able to talk to each other and kiss each other through a hole in the wall that divides their homes. Eventually they arrange to meet outside the city. Thisbe, arriving first, sees a lion fresh from the kill and flees, dropping her cloak. When Pyramus arrives and sees the cloak, now blood-stained having been mauled by the lion, he assumes that Thisbe has been killed by the lion and stabs himself to death. Thisbe returns as he is dying and also kills herself. Their story is told by Ovid and also, comically, by Bottom and his fellow workers in *Shakespeare's *A Midsummer Night's Dream* (1600).

> Young, innocent, or tragic lovers

Jono, too, had kissed her, chastely, as Pyramus had kissed the Wall.
ELIZABETH IRONSIDE *Death in the Garden* 1995

Pyrrhic victory [Hist.] Pyrrhus (*c.*318–272 BC) was king of Epirus *c.*307–272. In defeating the Romans at Asculum in 279, he sustained heavy losses, commenting, 'Such another victory and we are ruined.'

> A victory gained with terrible loss of life or at too great a cost

Venezuela's opposition looks set to blink first in the battle of wills with the government, but with the economy in tatters due to a national strike, it will be Pyrrhic victory for the president.
Scotland on Sunday 2003

Pythias *See* DAMON AND PYTHIAS.

Quasimodo [Lit.] The ugly, deaf, hunchbacked bell-ringer of the Cathedral of Notre Dame in Victor Hugo's novel *Notre-Dame de Paris*, usually translated as *The *Hunchback of Notre Dame* (1831). The popular image of the character has been largely formed by Charles Laughton's 1939 film portrayal in which a hauntingly pitiful Quasimodo finds comfort and solace in the bell tower of the cathedral with his beloved bells. Though grotesque in appearance, Quasimodo is gentle and tender-hearted and becomes devoted to Esmeralda, a gypsy dancer.

➤ A hunchback

I'm going to start walking like Quasimodo if I keep lugging this thing around.
KIRA LERNER ET AL. *About Schuyler Falls* 2001

Quatermain, Allan [Lit.] A principal character in several of Rider *Haggard's adventure stories, including *King Solomon's Mines* (1885) and *Allan Quatermain* (1887). In the former novel, Quatermain sets off with two other men to find George Curtis, who has gone missing while looking for the treasure of King Solomon's mines in the lost land of the Kukuanas. After a perilous journey across deserts and over freezing mountains, they find the missing man and return safely home with enough of the lost treasure to make them wealthy men.

➤ Someone who goes on a long or perilous quest

Queeg, Captain [Lit.] The captain in the 1951 novel *The Caine Mutiny* by Herman Wouk. Queeg is ineffective as a leader, focusing on petty issues, and is given to moments of ranting instability.

➤ A leader who is too concerned with petty rules; someone who shows the strains of leadership by erratic behaviour

Why did that funny little commander-in-chief keep scowling and twitching like Queeg doing his full Caine Mutiny routine?
Guardian Unlimited: 2004 US presidential elections 2004

Quickly, Mistress [Shakes.] The colourful hostess of the Boar's Head tavern frequented by *Falstaff and his companions in *1 Henry IV*, *2 Henry IV*, and *Henry V*.

➤ A perfect hostess

Dame Honeyball was a likely, plump, bustling little woman, and no bad substitute for that paragon of hostesses, Dame Quickly.
WASHINGTON IRVING *The Sketch Book* 1820

quixotic *See* DON QUIXOTE.

Ra [Egypt. Myth.] The sun god and supreme deity, worshipped as the creator of all life and often portrayed with a falcon's head bearing the solar disc. Ra appears travelling in a ship with the other gods, crossing the sky by day and passing through the underworld, the land of the dead, by night.

➢ A way of referring to the sun

rabbit-hole [Child. Lit.] In Lewis Carroll's children's story *Alice's Adventures in Wonderland* (1865), *Alice's adventures begin when she follows a *white rabbit down a rabbit-hole and finds herself tumbling down a very deep well, ending up at the bottom in a strange world where she meets a succession of outlandish characters and experiences some bizarre adventures.

➢ Used to evoke either entry to a strange, surreal, or upside-down world, or the action of falling steeply downwards

'I should think you'd like to see it [Nashville] again.' 'Never—I've kept away for fifteen years. I hope I'll never see it again.' But he would—for the plane was unmistakably going down, down, down, like Alice in the rabbit hole.
F. SCOTT FITZGERALD *The Last Tycoon* 1941

When analyzing Russia, it is easy to get sucked down Alice's rabbit hole, where nothing is ever quite what it seems.
BusinessWeek Magazine 2004

Rabelais, François [Lit.] (*c*.1494–1553) A French writer chiefly known for his two satires *Pantagruel* and *Gargantua*, which, through their larger-than-life characters, express an exuberantly bawdy humour combined with a biting satirical wit and a philosophy of enjoying life to the full.

➢ Used to suggest bawdy or vulgar humour (adjective *Rabelaisian*)

Married or not, I could fancy Paula, were I prepared to wave goodbye to a modestly successful career. Early thirties, unmarried, generous curves and a sense of humour that could have stopped Rabelais in his tracks.
RAYMOND FLYNN *A Public Body* 1996

What disturbs us is ageing *women* having children. There's something ribald, Rabelaisian, about old fathers—'a man is as old as the woman he feels,' as Groucho Marx put it—while old mothers are seen as selfish and unnatural.
The Observer 1997

Rachel [Bible] The second wife of *Jacob, and the mother of *Joseph and Benjamin. In the book of Jeremiah, Rachel is described as weeping for her children who were taken away in captivity to Babylon: 'Thus says the Lord: A voice is heard in Ramah, lamentation and bitter weeping. Rachel is weeping for her children; she refuses to be comforted for her children, because they were not' (Jer. 31: 15).

➢ A woman weeping for her children

She was like Rachel, 'mourning over her children, and would not be comforted.'
WASHINGTON IRVING *The Sketch-Book of Geoffrey Crayton, Gent.* 1820

But by her still halting course and winding, woeful way, you plainly saw that this ship that so wept with spray, still remained without comfort. She was Rachel, weeping for her children, because they were not.
HERMAN MELVILLE *Moby Dick* 1851

Rachman, Peter [People] (1919–62) A Polish-born London landlord whose exploitation and intimidation of his tenants in the early 1960s became legendary.

➤ The archetype of an unscrupulous landlord; such practices are known as Rachmanism

His dream is to banish forever the nightmare of Rachmanism, which still haunts the rented sector over 30 years after the worst excesses of the west London racketeer who gave landlords such a bad name.
The Observer 1996

Rackham, Arthur [Child. Lit.; Art] (1867–1939) A British illustrator best remembered for his illustrations of well-known children's books such as *Peter *Pan* and the *Grimm brothers' *Fairy Tales*. His work often depicts fairies occupying a dreamlike woodland landscape full of gnarled trees and vegetation.

➤ Used to suggest the idea of childhood innocence and simplicity; used to describe a woodland scene reminiscent of Rackham's illustrations

The girls watched mesmerised as Kate wiped the make-up off her face. And Kate watched them in the mirror. Maisie, tall now, with pale translucent skin, narrow limbs, and an aureole of reddish fair hair, an Arthur Rackham girl. Alison, even taller, a Nefertiti head and an easy athletic grace.
MAUREEN O'BRIEN *Dead Innocent* 1999

Drunken yobs disrupt the performance and when one of them comes up on stage he's lured by Valentina through the Imaginarium's ribboned mirror into a set of stage flats. These turn into a frightening Arthur Rackham forest where he gets his comeuppance.
The Observer 2009

Raffles [Lit.] A debonair, cricket-loving gentleman burglar created by the novelist E. W. Hornung (1866–1921). The character of Arthur J. Raffles first appeared in *The Amateur Cracksman* (1899), in which the story is narrated by Raffles's admiring assistant and ex-fag Bunny.

➤ An educated or upper-class man engaged in crime; a gentleman thief

While he was thinking, Signora Pianta told him in no uncertain terms that Argyll and his confederates—she still clearly saw him as some sort of latter-day Raffles, which seemed to Bottando one of the most unlikely comparisons he had ever heard—must have come here in the dead of night, loaded the pictures up and sailed off to hide them.
IAIN PEARS *The Titian Committee* 1991

Raft of the Medusa, The [Art] (1819) The most famous work by the French painter Theodore Géricault. It depicts with harrowing realism the sufferings of survivors of an actual shipwreck who had been cut adrift and left to drown. Some of the figures are based on Géricault's study of corpses and sickness.

➤ Used to evoke a scene involving a group of people in distress or dying, especially at sea

Its central element is a vast, wood-framed pastel on paper whose waterlogged drama recalls Gericault's Raft of the Medusa. The whale surges out of the water on a diagonal, cutting through the picture, tossing men into the sea and capsizing the Pequod.
Art in America 2004

Raggedy Ann [Child. Lit.] A rag doll in books by the American author Johnny Gruelle (1880–1938), the first of which, *Raggedy Ann Stories*, was published in 1918.

> ➤ Used to describe someone that resembles a rag doll

> She turned and raised a sleep-bleared Raggedy Ann face, shoe-button eyes peering, cobweb hair afloat. 'Whumya timezit?' she mumbled.
> J. D. MACDONALD *The Quick Red Fox* 1964

Ragnarok [Norse Myth.] The final battle between the gods and the forces of evil that will result in the destruction of the world. Ragnarok literally means 'Destined End of the Gods' or 'Twilight of the Gods', and is the Scandinavian equivalent of the *Götterdämmerung.

> ➤ A decisive and cataclysmic battle; global destruction

> I've already written that the 'Survivor' and 'Friends' battle is basically the Ragnarok of Old TV vs. New TV—cheap, producer-driven, writerless reality series vs. expensive, star-driven scripted sitcom.
> *Time Magazine* 2004

rainbow *See* END OF THE RAINBOW.

Rambo [Cin.] The hero of David Morrell's novel *First Blood* (1972), a Vietnam War veteran characterized as macho and bent on violent retribution, and popularized in a series of films in which the character is played by Sylvester *Stallone.

> ➤ A man who displays a great deal of physical violence or aggression

> Dressed from head to toe in camouflage gear—the kind that so many fathers and sons wear on hunting expeditions in the surrounding countryside at weekends—they were firing Rambo-style with an array of weapons, including high-velocity rifles and handguns.
> *The Independent* 1998

Raphael (Raffaello Sanzio) [Art] (1483–1520), An Italian painter and architect of the Renaissance known especially for his *Madonnas, usually shown seated with a child on their knee and a beautifully serene expression.

> ➤ Used to describe a woman of serene beauty

> The general effect of Margaret's expression was of rapt devotion like a Raphael Madonna, alternating with disdain for the third form ranged alongside her.
> *Contemporary Review* 2004

Rapunzel [Fairy tales] A beautiful long-haired girl who is locked at the top of a tall tower by a witch. The witch, and subsequently a handsome prince, are able to climb up to her after calling out 'Rapunzel, Rapunzel, let down your long hair'.

> ➤ A girl or woman with unusually long hair, or imprisoned in a tower

> Vicky had the hair for it, yards of beautiful Rapunzel tresses curled and heaped and framing her delicate features like a baroque picture frame carved of chestnut.
> JUSTIN SCOTT *Frostline* 1997

Rashomon [Cin.] The title of a 1950 Japanese film directed by Akira Kurosawa, in which several contradictory accounts are presented of the events surrounding a rape and murder in a forest. The incident is described in a series of flashbacks by a bandit, a samurai (through a medium, after his death), his wife, and a woodcutter (who witnessed the crime), and the four accounts are mutually contradictory.

> ➤ Mentioned in the context of a story or account being told or interpreted from several different points of view or perspectives, especially conflicting ones

It is only when Li is granted an audience with Quin, however, that his true motivations are revealed, via a series of Rashomon-like flashbacks during the course of the conversation between the two.
www.indielondon.co.uk 2004

From this Rashomon perspective, there are many stories within a particular event or time in history.
Bad Subjects Magazine 2004

Rasputin, Grigori [Hist.] (1871–1916) A Russian monk, notorious for his debauchery, who came to exert great influence over the Tsarina Alexandra, wife of Nicholas II, by claiming miraculous powers to heal the heir to the throne, who suffered from haemophilia. Rasputin was eventually assassinated by a group of Russian noblemen loyal to the tsar.

➤ A person who has an insidious or corrupt influence over a ruler; someone who survives repeated attempts to kill them

Members of this devilish clique have insinuated themselves into the higher social circles and, Rasputin-like, have bewitched the governor's wife and high society in general, all the while plotting and scheming behind the scenes.
The American Conservative 2005

Reading jail [Lit.] Oscar Wilde spent time in Reading jail (1895–7) for homosexual offences, and wrote his poem *The Ballad of Reading Gaol* based on his experiences there. The poem highlights the harsh conditions in the prison and the despair of the prisoners.

➤ A harsh prison

And by the end of the evening, Reading Gaol would have felt like the George V.
JULIAN BARNES *Talking It Over* 1991

Reardon, Edwin [Lit.] A character in George Gissing's novel *New Grub Street* (1891), a gifted writer whose literary ambitions are nonetheless thwarted by poverty and by the lack of sympathy of his materialistic wife. Unable to succeed as a writer and deserted by his wife, Reardon is driven to an early grave.

➤ A failed writer

Rebel without a Cause [Cin.] The title of a 1955 film about a moody, confused, rebellious teenager played by James *Dean. He feels betrayed by and rails against the hypocritical adult world in general and his ineffectual parents in particular.

➤ Someone, especially a young person, whose rebellious behaviour stems from general feelings of frustration

Growing up, Des confesses that he was 'a rebel without a cause'; constantly getting into trouble and inevitably getting expelled from school.
Western People 2005

Red Cross Knight [Lit.] In Edmund Spenser's *The Faerie Queene*, the Red Cross Knight, almost certainly meant to be St *George, is sent by the queen to slay a dragon that is ravaging the country of the princess Una. The Red Cross Knight does indeed destroy the dragon and marries Una.

➤ One who comes to the rescue

He himself isn't quite what Simon has been expecting; no heroic delivering Perseus, no Red Cross Knight.
MARGARET ATWOOD *Alias Grace* 1996

red in tooth and claw [Lit.] A phrase originally used in Alfred Lord Tennyson's poem *In Memoriam* (1850) to describe the struggle for survival in nature:

> Who trusted God was love indeed
> And love Creation's final law
> Tho' Nature, red in tooth and claw
> With ravine, shriek'd against his creed.

➤ Used to suggest a ruthless struggle for personal survival

But human nature is just as red in tooth and claw as Mother Nature's is.
Bookslut.com feature articles 2004

The contest between Crowley and Collins is one of the great electoral rivalries of modern Irish politics, as red in tooth and claw as they come.
Sunday Business Post 2004

Red Queen [Child. Lit.] In an episode in Lewis Carroll's *Through the Looking-Glass* (1871), *Alice finds herself running hand in hand with the Red Queen, who repeatedly urges them on with the words 'Faster! Faster!' But 'however fast they went, they never seemed to pass anything'. As the Queen observes to Alice: 'it takes all the running you can do to keep in the same place.'

➤ Mentioned in the context of a situation where it is necessary to expend more and more effort simply to maintain the status quo

Like Alice in Wonderland's Red Queen, many commodity producers face a situation in which they continually struggle just to keep in one place.
Rural Cooperatives 2004

Red Riding Hood [Fairy stories] In the story 'Little Red Riding Hood', first recorded by Perrault in 1697, Little Red Riding Hood, a young girl who earns her name from her red cloak and hood, sets off one day to visit her sick grandmother. Walking through a wood on her way, she meets a wolf, who asks where she is going. On hearing the answer, the wolf runs on ahead, imitates Red Riding Hood's voice to gain entry to the grandmother's cottage, and devours the grandmother. It then puts on the grandmother's clothes and gets into the grandmother's bed to await Red Riding Hood. When she arrives, the wolf talks to her kindly, trying to disguise its voice, but Red Riding Hood is struck by the strange appearance of her grandmother, and comments on the size of her ears, eyes, and finally teeth: 'What big teeth you have, grandmother', at which point the wolf, responding 'All the better to eat you with!', leaps up and devours Red Riding Hood.

➤ A young, unsophisticated innocent in danger of being taken advantage of; the wolf can be alluded to in the context of someone disguising themselves in order to win another's confidence and hide their own dishonest or evil intentions

The animal itself was as peaceful and well-behaved as that father of all picture-wolves, Red Riding Hood's quondam friend, whilst seeking her confidence in masquerade.
BRAM STOKER *Dracula* 1897

Carl May smiled and it seemed to Bethany that his teeth were fangs and growing as long as the wolf's ever were in 'Red Riding Hood'.
FAY WELDON *The Cloning of Joanna May* 1989

Red Sea [Bible] According to the Old Testament book of Exodus, God led *Moses and the *Israelites out of Egypt and through the Red Sea. *Pharaoh, having given them permission to leave Egypt, changed his mind and took his army after them. God parted the waters to let the Israelites cross. 'But the children of Israel walked upon dry land in the midst of the sea; and the waters were a wall unto them on their right hand, and on their left' (Exod. 14: 28). The pursuing Egyptians were drowned when the waters closed on them.

> ➤ Used in the context of someone finding a passage through an obstacle or crowd of people

'I've got eight water bottles shoved down my jersey and I'm looking at the impenetrable wall of international riders thinking, "How am I going to get up to the front of the peloton to hand these off ?" ' she says. 'Over the radio, a seasoned teammate told me the magic word I'm supposed to say: "Aqua". I tried it, sort of expecting a parting of the Red Sea. Apparently I'm no Moses, because not a single butt moved to make way.'
www.olympic-usa.org 2004

Reed, Donna [Cin.] (1921–86) A US film actress (b. Donna Mullenger) closely identified with wholesome girl-next-door roles in such films as Frank *Capra's *It's a Wonderful Life* (1946). In her long-running television series *The Donna Reed Show* (1958–66), she personified the perfect and devoted wife and mother.

> ➤ Archetype of the wholesome girl-next-door and the idealized housewife and mother

Janie, Trish, and Kay had graduated from Dobbs High School together and had then married Cotton Grove boys within two years of each other, which brought them back into the same social orbit where two incomes weren't a necessity quite yet. The 'Donna Reed' syndrome lasted a bit longer in the South than elsewhere, and none of the three had held down real jobs back then.
MARGARET MARON *Bootlegger's Daughter* 1992

The New York Times Magazine has run high-profile stories of six-figure MBAs and lawyers leaving their jobs to be at home with their babies, Time published a recent cover story on the trend toward professional-class stay-at-homes, and Cosmopolitan, of all places, has found a new group of 'housewife wannabes' who would like nothing more than to do a Donna Reed.
City Journal 2004

reign of terror [Hist.] The period of the French Revolution between mid-1793 and July 1794 when the ruling Jacobin faction, dominated by Maximilien Robespierre (1758–94), ruthlessly executed anyone considered a threat to their regime. Also known as the Terror, it ended with the fall and execution of Robespierre.

> ➤ A period in which people live in fear of death or violence; the use of organized intimidation or terrorism

Remember Senator Joseph McCarthy and the reign of terror of his House Un-American Activities Committee? Deja vu. We are there again!
Sunday Business Post 2003

Rembrandt (Rembrandt Harmenszoon van Rijn) [Art] (1606–69) The greatest Dutch painter of the 17th century, particularly celebrated for his portraits and self-portraits and for his subtle use of light and shadow, or chiaroscuro, contrasting highlights and half-lights with deep shadows. He is especially remembered for the obscure lighting and brown-and-black palette of his later paintings.

> ➤ Used to suggest the idea of 'a great painter'; mentioned when describing dimly lit or shadowy interiors

The dim gold lamplight and the restless firelight made Rembrandt shadows in the remoter corners of the kitchen.
STELLA GIBBONS *Cold Comfort Farm* 1932

Revere, Paul [Hist.] (1735–1818) An American patriot, one of the demonstrators involved in the *Boston Tea Party of 1773. In 1775 he rode through the night from Boston to Lexington to warn American revolutionaries of the approach of British troops.

> ➤ Someone making a swift journey on horseback; someone bringing an urgent warning

Mrs Louderer drove, and Tam O'Shanter and Paul Revere were snails compared to us.
ELINORE PRUITT STEWART *Letters of a Woman Homesteader* 1914

In When Smoke Ran Like Water, Devra Lee Davis, a toxicologist who has researched the environmental causes of diseases such as breast cancer and served on scientific advisory boards appointed by the federal government to assess pollution, steps forward as the latest Paul Revere to sound the alarm against toxic chemicals.
Environmental History 2004

Rhadamanthus [Gk Myth.] The son of *Zeus and Europa, and brother of *Minos, who, as a ruler and judge in the underworld, was renowned for his justice.

> ➤ Someone who is stern and incorruptible in judgement (adjective *Rhadamanthine*)

But Tom, you perceive, was rather a Rhadamanthine personage, having more than the usual share of boy's justice in him—the justice that desires to hurt culprits as much as they deserve to be hurt, and is troubled with no doubts concerning the exact amount of their deserts.
GEORGE ELIOT *Mill on the Floss* 1860

Women at forty do not become ancient misanthropes, or stern Rhadamanthine moralists, indifferent to the world's pleasures—no, even though they be widows.
ANTHONY TROLLOPE *The Small House at Allington* 1862

Richard, Cliff [Mus.] (b. Harry Webb, 1940) A British pop singer whose many successful recordings include 'Living Doll' and 'The Young Ones'. He became a born-again Christian in the 1970s and since then has combined his pop career with evangelism.

> ➤ Mentioned with reference to a clean-living image and youthful looks

'And I suppose you got nowhere at Brown's?' 'Squeaky clean.' 'Same here, this pair. They've got Cliff Richard in the front office and Mother Theresa doing the books.'
ALEX KEEGAN *Kingfisher* 1995

Richelieu, Cardinal (Armand Jean du Plessis) [Hist.] (1585–1642) The chief minister of Louis XIII from 1624 to 1642 who dominated the French government. He is remembered as a clever, calculating, and scheming politician.

> ➤ A ruler's chief adviser; a scheming 'power behind the throne'

Now Vaughan has discovered the truth in Atherton's assessment that Fletcher was 'the Cardinal Richelieu to Hussain's Louis XIII, the power behind the throne'.
The Sunday Times 2005

riddle wrapped in a mystery inside an enigma [Hist.] Winston *Churchill's description of *Stalin's Russia in a radio broadcast in 1939: 'I cannot forecast to you the action of Russia. It is a riddle wrapped in a mystery inside an enigma.'

> ➤ Used to describe a person or thing that is puzzling or enigmatic

[Browning's] religion is something of 'a riddle wrapped in a mystery inside an enigma,' like so much of the detail of many of his poems.
Hudson Review 2001

right stuff [Lit.; Cin.] A phrase from the title of Tom Wolfe's 1979 book *The Right Stuff* (later made into a film) about the training of the first American astronauts in the early years of the US space programme. The phrase is a description of the mental and physical qualities required to make the grade as an astronaut.

> ➤ The necessary qualities for a given task or job
>
> Guillen has shown 'the right stuff' in his first two seasons as manager of the Chicago White Sox, the game's surprise team of 2005.
> *Baseball Digest* 2005

Rip Van Winkle [Lit.] The hero of Washington Irving's story of the same name (1820). During a walk in the Catskill Mountains, Rip falls asleep, and wakes some twenty years later to find that the world has changed considerably. His wife has died, his daughter has married, and he has completely missed the War of American Independence.

> ➤ Someone who sleeps for a long time; someone who finds that the world has changed out of all recognition
>
> Having been incarcerated for most of the last forty-five years, he was probably feeling like Rip van Winkle, marveling at all the changes in the world at large.
> SUE GRAFTON *L Is for Lawless* 1995
>
> A political Rip van Winkle who had never watched television and read neither newspapers nor books until the last years of his term, Kim cannot believe, even less comprehend, this changed world. His only reading material until 1990 had been the Bible.
> ANDREW HIGGINS *The Observer* 1997

Ritz [Places] The name of luxury hotels in Paris, London, New York, and elsewhere founded by the Swiss-born hotelier César Ritz (1850–1918).

> ➤ A large and luxurious hotel, or any luxurious place
>
> I enjoyed my dinner at Jessie's Deli, it ain't the Ritz, but then, it's not supposed to be.
> *Pattaya Mail* 2003

Rivera, Diego [Art] (1886–1957) A Mexican painter whose monumental murals for public buildings in the 1920s and 1930s were influenced by Aztec art and deal with political and revolutionary subjects.

> ➤ Used to describe a crowd of Mexican or Latin American people; used to describe a person of Mexican or Latin American appearance
>
> 'Ms Ochoa?' The face that looked up was out of a mural by Rivera. Reddish-brown skin stretched tightly over sharply defined but delicately constructed bones; liquid lips and melting black eyes gabled by full, dark brows. Her hair was long and sleek, parted in the middle, hanging down her back. Part Aztec, part Spanish, part unknown.
> JONATHAN KELLERMAN *When the Bough Breaks* 1992

rivers of Babylon [Bible] Psalm 137, which commemorates the exile of the Jews in *Babylon, opens with the words 'By the rivers of Babylon, there we sat down, yea, we wept, when we remembered Zion.'

> ➤ The phrase 'the rivers of Babylon' has come to be associated with the idea of mourning for the dead
>
> In its beginnings, in the latter half of the fifties, The Movement challenged us to sing the Lord's song in a strange land, a land in which we all sat by the rivers of Babylon and wept, though only a few of us knew we were weeping.
> *Whole Earth* 2000

road less travelled [Lit.] A phrase taken from the poem 'The Road Not Taken' (1916) by Robert Frost. The narrator of the poem pauses on a path in the woods at a point where the path forks:

> Two roads diverged in a wood, and I—
> I took the one less traveled by,
> And that has made all the difference.

> ➤ A course of action that is not the usual or conventional one

> Most of his peers opted for apprenticeships with Dublin firms, but Bradley took the road less travelled.
> *Sunday Business Post* 2001

Roadrunner [Cart. & Com.] An American cartoon character, a bird that can run extremely fast and always manages to outrun its arch-enemy, a coyote called Wile E. Coyote. The characters were created for Warner Brothers by Chuck Jones and date from 1949. The films always take place along the highways of the south-west American desert and are seen from the perspective of the coyote.

> ➤ Mentioned in the context of high-speed chases

> Chow throws in big dance numbers, songs, humour and chase scenes that play like Wiley E Coyote trying to catch Roadrunner.
> *Croydon Guardian* 2005

road to Damascus *See* DAMASCUS.

Robben Island [Places] A small island off the coast of South Africa, Robben Island is the site of a prison in which political prisoners, including Nelson *Mandela, were formerly held.

> ➤ A prison

Robert the Bruce (Robert I) [Hist.] (1274–1329) A Scottish king who led the campaigns against Edward I and Edward II, culminating in the Scottish victory at Bannockburn in 1314. According to tradition, Robert spent some time hiding in a cave after suffering a defeat at the hands of the English. After watching a spider fail many times in its attempt to spin a web but persevere until it finally succeeded, he was inspired to fight on against the English.

> ➤ Mentioned (often in tandem with the spider) in the context of perseverance and refusing to give up

> Berti Vogts has a soft spot for Scotland and its history, so perhaps he has heard of the legend of Robert the Bruce and the spider. Yesterday, in Reykjavik, beleaguered Berti won his first international match at the seventh time of asking, and it was perseverance and industry which provided the German with the much-needed result.
> *Sunday Herald* 2002

Robin Hood [Leg. & Folk.] The legend of Robin Hood probably began in the 12th or 13th century and was well established by the 14th. According to the stories, he was the leader of a band of outlaws living in Sherwood Forest in Nottinghamshire who robbed the rich (most notably the sheriff of Nottingham) and gave the spoils to the poor.

> ➤ Mentioned in the context of taking from the rich and giving to the poor; someone who stands up against tyranny and oppression

> I sit by the River Shannon near the dry docks sipping Mrs. Finucane's sherry. Aunt Aggie's name is in the ledger. She owes nine pounds. It might have been the money she spent on my clothes a long time ago but now she'll never have to pay it because

I heave the ledger into the river. I'm sorry I'll never be able to tell Aunt Aggie I saved her nine pounds....I wish I could tell them, I'm your Robin Hood.
FRANK MCCOURT *Angela's Ashes* 1997

Lula repeated the word. 'Vigilante.' 'Someone who takes the law into his own hands,' I said. 'Hunh. I guess I know what it means. You're telling me Mo is like Zorro and Robin Hood.'
JANET EVANOVICH *Three to Get Deadly* 1997

Rochester, Mr (Edward Fairfax Rochester) [Lit.] The hero of Charlotte Brontë's novel *Jane Eyre* (1847), a handsome man but silent, brooding, and grim of temperament.

➤ A brooding romantic hero

Caroline put on a face of modesty, and then said she thought Mr Ramsay was handsome in a kind of scary way, like Mr Rochester in Jane Eyre.
ROBERTSON DAVIES *Fifth Business* 1970

Talk to me. Don't sit there looking gloomy and enigmatic like Mr Rochester. What's bothering you?
BARBARA MICHAELS *Search the Shadows* 1988

Rochester, Mrs [Lit.] The deranged wife of Edward *Rochester in Charlotte Brontë's *Jane Eyre* (1847) is kept in seclusion at Thornfield Hall. Her existence is only revealed when Jane's marriage to Rochester is about to take place. The early life of Bertha Rochester is imagined by Jean Rhys in her novel *Wide Sargasso Sea* (1966).

➤ A strange or mad person who is kept locked or hidden away, especially in an attic

You saw her once, didn't you?' said Nancy. 'That's right. I just happened to look up and caught her peering at me from an upper window, like the first Mrs Rochester or something, though she kept well back from the window.'
SUSAN MOODY *The Italian Garden* 1994

Dropped at the comfy, modern entrance of St Pat's, the psychiatric hospital where Professor Anthony Clare does his day job, I had no choice but to make my way through the entire building to reach Clare's Georgian lair on the far side. It was oddly quiet—the Mrs. Rochesters of Dublin obviously have good sound-proofing in their attics.
Sunday Telegraph 1999

Rockefeller, John Davison [People] (1839–1937) An American oil magnate who founded the Standard Oil Company, gaining increasing control of all aspects of the oil industry in the 1870s. He later used his money for philanthropic projects, giving money for medical research and educational institutions and establishing the Rockefeller Foundation in 1913 'to promote the well-being of mankind'.

➤ An immensely wealthy person; a philanthropist

No worthy charity ever knocked and found him absent. In his limited way, having only half a million at his disposal instead of the customary millions, he was as much of a philanthropist as Rockefeller. He gave substantially to the Community Fund, aside from which he donated his time and services to many civic enterprises.
CHESTER HIMES *A Modern Fable* 1939

The agent says, There's plenty of work for willing men. You can work overtime till you drop and if you save it up, mate, you'll be Rockefeller at the end of the war.
FRANK MCCOURT *Angela's Ashes* 1997

Rockwell, Norman [Art] (1894–1978) A US illustrator and cartoonist best known for his covers for the magazine the *Saturday Evening Post*. These were typically idealized scenes of everyday small-town American life.

➤ Used to evoke homely small-town American life

The charm was more than visual, however. It was equally compounded of nostalgia for a way of life that had not so much vanished as never really existed. Freckle-faced boys riding bikes and healthy, pink-cheeked nuclear families dressed in their Sunday best, walking hand in hand toward a white, steepled church…A Norman Rockwell cover, flimsy as the paper on which it was printed, with ugly things hidden behind the pretty facade.
ELIZABETH PETERS *Naked Once More* 1989

He reminded me of a Norman Rockwell *Saturday Evening Post* cover, the rural general practitioner about to remove a splinter from a tearful boy's finger. Kindly, gentle, wise, competent.
WILLIAM G. TAPPLY *Tight Lines* 1992

Rogers, Buck [Cart. & Com.] A US cartoon hero who first appeared in the comic strip *Buck Rogers in the 25th Century* in 1929. Originally the hero of the short story *Armageddon 2419* by Philip Nowlan, Buck Rogers is a 20th-century airforce pilot who is trapped down a mine filled with a strange radioactive gas and kept in suspended animation until the 25th century. When he awakes, he has numerous space adventures in which he performs deeds of great daring to save the world from the evil Killer Kane and Ardala, aided by his companion Wilma Deering.

➤ Someone resembling a space-age hero

But he was free, and considered that the roundabout up-and-down-about was going slow enough to make a getaway. No need to wait until it really stops, was his last thought. It was like Buck Rogers landing from a space ship without due care, though a few minutes passed before he was able to think this.
ALAN SILLITOE *The Loneliness of the Long Distance Runner* 1959

Rogers, Ginger [Cin.] (1911–95) An American actress and dancer (b. Virginia Katherine McMath) best known for her dancing partnership with Fred *Astaire. She also won an Oscar for her performance as an actress in *Kitty Foyle* (1940).

➤ A female dancer

I put my hand in his and followed. He was one of those men who can make you feel like Ginger Rogers on the dance floor, conveying an entire set of suggestions in the way he applied pressure to the small of my back.
SUE GRAFTON *H Is for Homicide* 1991

Rogers, Roy [Cin.] (1912–98) A clean-cut American singing cowboy hero, known as the King of the Cowboys, who began his career as a country-and-western singer and went on to appear in several films. He later appeared in his own television series, *The Roy Rogers Show*, first broadcast in 1951. Riding his trusty stallion Trigger, he maintained law and order in the contemporary west with the help of his bumbling sidekick Pat Brady and his wife Dale Evans.

➤ Someone resembling a cowboy

The playwright laughed. He hadn't heard the Yank using bad language until now. It didn't fit with the suit. could it be that Mr Whiz Kid might be human after all? 'Yes. I'll do the other thing myself. Kilmacud, is it?' 'Yes. No Roy Rogers stuff now. Think of it as a part. Imagine yourself as a gangster.'
JOHN BRADY *A Stone of the Heart* 1988

Roland and Oliver [Leg. & Folk.; Lit.] Roland was the legendary nephew of
*Charlemagne and was one of his paladins, the twelve peers of Charlemagne's court. He is the
hero of the *Chanson de Roland*, a 12th-century medieval romance, and of Ariosto's *Orlando
furioso* (1532). Roland is said to have become a close friend of Oliver, another paladin, after
engaging him in a prolonged single combat which was so evenly matched that neither ever won.

> The expression 'a Roland for an Oliver' denotes a well-balanced combat or an
> effective retort or retaliation

  He gave my termagant kinsman a *quid pro quo*—a Rowland for his Oliver, as the
  vulgar say.
  SIR WALTER SCOTT *Antiquary* 1816

Romeo and Juliet [Shakes.] The young lovers in *Romeo and Juliet* (1599) are the
offspring of two warring families, the *Montagues and Capulets. They meet at a feast given by
the Capulets, are instantly attracted, and marry in secret. Juliet's family, unaware of her
marriage, plan to marry her to Count Paris. Juliet takes a potion on the eve of the wedding
which will make her appear dead for 24 hours. A message to Romeo goes astray. Romeo,
hearing of Juliet's death, returns to Verona and to Juliet's body, takes poison, and dies.
Juliet awakes, sees his body, and stabs herself.

> Young lovers, especially star-crossed ones; Romeo's name alone can be used to denote
> a young man in love, though it is now frequently, and somewhat unjustly, applied to
> a womanizer, as in the phrase 'the office Romeo'

  I watched Duncan clipping his hedge this afternoon and could barely remember the
  handsome man he was. If I had been a charitable woman, I would have married him forty
  years ago and saved him from himself and Violet. She has turned my Romeo into a
  sad-eyed Billy Bunter who blinks his passions quietly when no one's looking.
  MINETTE WALTERS *The Scold's Bridle* 1994

  The Jayaram–Parvathy courtship was a Romeo-and-Juliet type affair that started in a
  clandestine fashion on the sets of films in which the stars played lead roles.
  The Hindu 2002

Romulus and Remus [Rom. Myth.] The twin sons of *Mars by the vestal virgin Rhea
Silvia. Abandoned in infancy in a basket on the river Tiber, the twins were found and suckled
by a she-wolf and later raised by a shepherd family. They subsequently undertook to build
a city on the banks of the Tiber; after a quarrel, however, Romulus killed his brother. He went
on to found Rome, naming the city after himself.

> Brothers or twins; mentioned in the context of sibling rivalry or fratricide; also mentioned
> in the context of children being raised by animals

Room with a View, A [Lit.] The title of a 1908 novel by E. M. Forster. The phrase refers
to the opening of the novel in which Lucy Honeychurch and her chaperone Miss Bartlett
complain that the hotel room they have each been given at the Pensione Bertolini is not the
'room with a view' they had been promised.

> A room with an attractive or spectacular view from the window

  I write from the monastery of San Andrea where I inhabit a room that affords me a
  spectacular view of the Spoleto Valley and the Basilica of San Francesco which dates back
  to 1230. When describing my room to friends I have referred to it as the 'Room with a
  View'.
  Contemporary Review 2000

Roscius (Quintus Roscius Gallus) [Theatre] (d. 62 BC) The most celebrated of Roman
comic actors, who later became identified with all that was considered best in acting. Many

great actors, notably David *Garrick, were nicknamed after him. The child actor William Betty (1791–1874) was known as the Young Roscius.

➤ Archetype of the great actor (adjective *Roscian*)

I put my hands in my pocket. A folded piece of paper in one of them attracting my attention, I opened it and found it to be the playbill I had received from Joe relative to the celebrated provincial amateur of Roscian renown.
CHARLES DICKENS *Great Expectations* 1860

Rosebud [Cin.] In the 1941 film *Citizen Kane*, the enigmatic last whispered utterance of the dying tycoon Charles Foster Kane. During the film a reporter tries fruitlessly to discover the meaning of this word. It is only at the very end, as Kane's unwanted possessions are thrown onto a fire, that it is revealed to the audience that 'Rosebud' is the name of the sled that he played with as a small boy.

➤ The key to someone's character, what makes then 'tick'; a person's secret heart's desire; a symbol of the innocence and happiness of childhood

Rodgers was too complex a man to have a 'Rosebud'—a single childhood incident that illuminates all that follows.
City Journal 2003

Rosencrantz and Guildenstern [Lit.] In *Shakespeare's *Hamlet* (1604), Rosencrantz and Guildenstern are two messengers sent with Hamlet to England with sealed orders from the king that Hamlet should be killed on arrival. *Hamlet escapes back to Denmark, where the rest of the action of the play unfolds. The fate of Rosencrantz and Guildenstern is reported right at the end of the play, when an ambassador enters and announces that 'Rosencrantz and Guildenstern are dead.' This line was used as the title of a play by Tom Stoppard (1966), in which he places these two characters at the centre of a drama.

➤ Mentioned in the context of someone who has managed to miss all the action

I was about to learn, apparently, I'd been Rosencrantz or Guildenstern, submerged up to the eyes in the utterly absorbing drama of my own life, and completely out of the loop about the real goings-on with Prince Hamlet at Elsinore.
CAROL BRENNAN *Chill of Summer* 1995

The show's coped remarkably well, but sometimes it's felt like we're only watching the sub-plots, while the real action happens elsewhere. Rosencrantz and Guildenstern as PE and IT teachers.
www.gyford.com/phil/writing 2003

Rosinante (Rozinante) [Lit.] The name of *Don Quixote's scrawny old horse in Cervantes' romance.

➤ A worn-out or emaciated horse

Plump and naked…they [the camels] were a great contrast to our shaggy, Rosinantine beasts.
PETER FLEMING *News from Tartary* 1936

Rothko, Mark [Art] (1903–70) A Russian-born US painter, an abstract expressionist. His most characteristic works are enormous canvases consisting of rectangles or horizontal bands of subtly related colour with blurred edges.

➤ Used when describing large areas of colour, especially red, orange, or purple

The most interesting feature was a veggie terrine, three layers of colour that looked like a Rothko painting: deep burgundy beets followed by a strip of rich carrot orange and topped with a warm beige, possibly potato.
Montreal Mirror 2001

Rothschild, Meyer Amschel [People] (1743–1812) A German Jew who founded a banking house in Frankfurt and a dynasty. His five sons set up banks throughout Europe. His third son **Nathan** (1777–1836), who founded the London bank, made a £1 million profit on the Stock Exchange having staked his fortune on the outcome of the Battle of *Waterloo.

> ➤ An immensely wealthy person or family
>
> If she wanted a new hat, he'd say hadn't he bought her a hat only five or six years ago and get off nasty cracks about women who seemed to think they'd married into the Rothschild family.
> P. G. WODEHOUSE *Cocktail Time* 1958
>
> 'I said I was your housekeeper,' replied that lady…'Oh good,' said Aunt Irene. 'He'll think I'm Rothschild.'
> ALICE THOMAS ELLIS *The 27th Kingdom* 1982

Round Table [Leg. & Folk.] The table at which King *Arthur and his knights sat so that none should have precedence, and which came to represent their chivalric fellowship. It was first mentioned in Wace's *Roman de Brut* (1155).

> ➤ Used (often in the phrase 'Knights of the Round Table') to represent a brotherhood or fellowship, or the idea of chivalry
>
> These beloved colleagues remind me of a multicultural Knights of the Round Table. They launch quests for what is right and what is just.
> *Afterimage* 2000

round up the usual suspects [Cin.] A line from the 1942 film *Casablanca*, starring Humphrey Bogart and Ingrid Bergman. The line is spoken at the end of the film by the French policeman Captain Renault, played by Claude Rains, who instructs his men, 'Major Strasser has been shot. Round up the usual suspects.'

> ➤ Blame the people or circumstances usually suspected of being responsible for something that has happened; 'the usual suspects' can refer to those people, ideas, etc., that would be expected in a particular context
>
> This is one of the few essays in the volume to consider primarily the question of male beauty. Rogers rounds up the usual suspects—Leonardo, Raphael, Parmigianino—in tracing the flowering of the beautiful artist as figure for social advancement and embodiment of divinely designated gifts.
> *Art Bulletin* 2000

Rousseau, Henri [Art] (1844–1910), Known as Le Douanier ('the Customs Officer'), a French naive painter. Self-taught, he is best known for his paintings of exotic jungle landscapes and haunting, dreamlike scenes, including *Tiger in a Tropical Storm* (1891), *The Sleeping Gypsy* (1897), and *The Snake Charmer* (1907). These pictures are bold and colourful, and painted with a painstakingly detailed technique.

> ➤ Used to describe a scene reminiscent of a Rousseau painting
>
> An island with a happy name lay opposite, and on it stood a row of prim, tight buildings, naive as a painting by Rousseau.
> DOROTHY PARKER *The Custard Heart* 1944

Rousseau, Jean-Jacques [Philos.] (1712–78) A philosopher and writer. Born in Switzerland, he left home at the age of 15 to move to Italy and during his life he moved often, living in various parts of France, Italy, Switzerland, and, later, England. He developed the philosophy that 'primitive' man, the 'noble savage', was naturally innocent and that the effect of civilization was to corrupt people. His *Du contrat social* (The Social Contract, 1762) begins with the famous sentence 'Man is born free; and everywhere he is in chains', and he coined the phrase 'Liberty, Equality, Fraternity'.

> An intellectual thinker or writer

To be yearning for the difficult, to be weary of that offered; to care for the remote, to dislike the near; it was Wildeve's nature always. This is the true mark of the man of sentiment. Though Wildeve's fevered feeling had not been elaborated to real poetical compass, it was of the standard sort. He might have been called the Rousseau of Egdon.
THOMAS HARDY *The Return of the Native* 1880

Rubens, Peter Paul [Art] (1577–1640) The foremost Flemish painter of the 17th century, an exuberant master of the baroque. Rubens painted portraits and religious works but is perhaps best known for his mythological paintings featuring voluptuous female nudes, such as *Venus and Adonis* (*c.*1635). These sumptuous paintings display the artist's love of rich colour, sensual feeling for the tactile, and sheer delight in fleshy women.

> Used to describe a woman's attractively plump and rounded figure (adjective *Rubenesque*)

She had none of that dazzling brilliancy, of that voluptuous Rubens beauty.
ANTHONY TROLLOPE *Barchester Towers* 1857

She put down the paper. 'An artist's model?' 'Right.' 'With your figure?' 'My figure is simply crying out to be captured in charcoal, according to my new friend. I have a Rubenesque form and challenging contours.'
PETER LOVESEY *The Summons* 1995

Rubicon [Hist.] In 49 BC Julius Caesar, having defeated the Gauls in the Gallic Wars, brought his troops south to fight a civil war against Pompey and the Roman Senate. When he crossed the Rubicon, a stream marking the boundary between Italy and Gaul, he was committed to war, having violated the law that forbade him to take his troops out of his province.

> To 'cross the Rubicon' is to commit oneself to changing to a new course, leaving no possibility of turning back

He had crossed his Rubicon—not perhaps very heroically or dramatically, but then it is only in dramas that people act dramatically.
SAMUEL BUTLER *The Way of All Flesh* 1903

Another depressing development for Laurence is that his children know about the split now. I think that's a kind of Rubicon as far as he's concerned. As long as they didn't know, there was always the possibility that he and Sally might get back together again with no serious damage done, no embarrassment, no loss of face.
DAVID LODGE *Therapy* 1995

ruby slippers [Cin.] The magic slippers that *Dorothy wears in the 1939 film of L. Frank Baum's children's story *The *Wizard of Oz*. She acquires them when her house, carried to the land of Oz by a tornado, falls on the *Wicked Witch of the East, killing her and leaving only her ruby-slippered feet sticking out. At the end of the film, Dorothy is able to transport herself back home to Kansas by clicking her heels together three times and repeating 'There's no place like home'.

> Something that has the power to instantly take someone to a desired place or away from an unpleasant situation

Here are three women who didn't wait for Prince Charming to bring them financial security. Instead each woman clicked her own ruby slippers together and claimed the power for herself.
Essence Magazine 2002

Rudolph [Mus.] According to the popular song, Rudolph the Red-Nosed Reindeer, despite being ridiculed by the other reindeer because of his shiny red nose, is chosen to pull *Santa Claus's sledge.

> ➤ Someone with a conspicuously red nose

> I am very acclimatized to the sun with nine years of playing golf and visiting beaches in Thailand, but still apply adequate UV factor sun block to exposed and sensitive areas. Never forget the nose and neck. Even some of the experienced golfers here often sport bright red 'Rudolph' noses at the end of the day.
> *Pattaya Mail* 2002

Rumpelstiltskin [Fairy tales] In the *Grimms' story, a miller claims that his daughter can spin straw into gold. The king locks the girl into a room with a pile of straw and a spinning wheel, promising to marry her if she can accomplish the task. Rumpelstiltskin appears and spins the straw into gold, asking for her necklace in payment. He performs this feat for the girl twice more, requiring in payment first her ring and then, when she has no more jewellery, her first child. She becomes queen, and when her first child is born, Rumpelstiltskin says that she may keep the child if she can discover his name within three days. She sends out messengers to find all the strange names they can collect, and one messenger comes across the little man dancing round a fire and chanting a rhyme that ends with the line: 'Rumpelstiltskin is my name!' When the queen confronts him with his name, Rumpelstiltskin becomes so angry that he stamps his foot into the ground and tears himself in two when he tries to pull it out.

> ➤ Someone who flies into a rage; someone who keeps his name a secret

> At such times they fell out over anything which came handy, from the day's work and the morrow's commitments to the points of spaniels or the quality and proof of beer; but never over Claire Falchion. Her name was protected by as exact a taboo as Rumpelstiltskin.
> EDITH PARGETER *By Firelight* 1948

> Sir Ian McKellen, who can't appear on the stage without doing something interesting, is a complicated mixture of rage, precision and desperation. When he performs his impassioned dance he is at first a model of military precision, and later as enraged as Rumpelstiltskin.
> SUSANNAH CLAPP *The Observer* 2003

Ruritania [Lit.] An imaginary central European kingdom used as the setting for Anthony Hope's novels of courtly intrigue and romance, such as *The *Prisoner of Zenda* (1894) and *Rupert of Hentzau* (1898).

> ➤ Mentioned in the context of political scheming

> The singing had gathered strength again, but everyone watched the English party as it went. 'Well,' said Clarence out in the square, 'this may be Ruritania, but it's no longer a joke.'
> OLIVIA MANNING *The Spoilt City* 1962

Rutebeuf [Lit.] (*c*.1230–1286) A French trouvère, the author of *Le Dit de l'herberie*, a comic monologue by a quack doctor.

> ➤ A medical charlatan

> 'Yes,' said the doctor and he was smiling, 'you will be disappointed!…I am no herbalist, I am no Rutebeuf, I have no panacea.'
> DJUNA BARNES *Nightwood* 1936

Ruth [Bible] The book of Ruth in the Old Testament relates the story of Ruth, a widow who refuses to leave her mother-in-law after the death of her husband, saying, 'whither thou goest, I will go; and where thou lodgest, I will lodge: thy people shall be my people, and thy God my God' (Ruth 1: 16).

➤ Used to suggest loyalty and devotion

Then listen to me again, once more, my heart's own darling, my love, my husband, my lord! If I cannot be to you at once like Ruth, and never cease from coming after you, my thoughts to you shall be like those of Ruth—if aught but death part thee and me, may God do so to me and more also.
ANTHONY TROLLOPE *The Small House at Allington* 1862

Ruth, Dr (Dr Ruth Westheimer) [TV] (b. 1928) A popular psychosexual therapist born in Germany but later emigrating to the United States, who has appeared in several US radio and television shows in which she talks about sexuality and tries to resolve people's sexual difficulties.

➤ Mentioned in the context of sexual therapy or counselling

Angela bestowed on Jonathan a look of maternal understanding to rival Dr. Ruth, but he was past consoling.
JANE DENTINGER *Death Mask* 1988

Sabine women [Rom. Myth.] According to (unhistorical) legend, *Romulus, the founder of Rome, secured wives for his citizens by inviting the neighbouring Sabines to witness games in the city. While the games were proceeding Romans carried off and raped the Sabine women.

➢ Mentioned in the context of a group of women being abducted or raped

At the finish of the meal he broke suddenly into a radiant smile, thanked his hostess for a charming repast, and kissed her hand with deferential rapture. Miss Huddle was unable to decide in her mind whether the action savoured of Louis Quatorzian courtliness or the reprehensible Roman attitude towards the Sabine women.
SAKI *Short Stories* 1904

Sadduccees [Bible] A Jewish sect at the time of *Jesus, who accepted only the written law, not oral tradition, denied the existence of angels and demons, and did not believe in the resurrection of the dead.

➢ Someone who refuses to believe things that are readily accepted by others

'Law, mother! I don't doubt he thought so. I suppose he and Cack got drinking toddy together, till he got asleep, and dreamed it. I wouldn't believe such a thing if it did happen right before my face and eyes. I should only think I was crazy, that's all.' 'Come, Lois, if I was you, I wouldn't talk so like a Sadduccee,' said my grandmother.
HARRIET BEECHER STOWE *The Ghost in the Mill* 1872

Sade, Marquis de (Donatien Alphonse François, comte de Sade) [Lit.] (1740–1814) A French writer and soldier. He was frequently imprisoned for sexual offences. While in prison he wrote a number of sexually explicit works, which include *Les 120 Journées de Sodome* (1784), *Justine* (1791), and *La Philosophie dans le boudoir* (1795). Sadism, the deriving of sexual pleasure from inflicting pain or suffering on others, is named after him.

➢ Mentioned in the context of sadistic behaviour or sexual depravity

Well, if your ball lands in poison ivy, the Rules of Golf allow you to take a drop, but not without a penalty stroke. Who wrote this rule, the Marquis de Sade?
Golf Digest 2004

sage *See* SEVEN SAGES OF GREECE.

Saint, the [Lit.; TV] The name used by Simon Templar, the hero of a popular British television series first broadcast in 1963 starring Roger Moore. Based on a series of novels by Leslie Charteris, the Saint is a reformed British gentleman crook, described by Charteris as 'a dashing daredevil, imperturbable, debonair, preposterously handsome, a pirate or a philanthropist as the occasion demands'. In the television shows he battles against crime and international espionage, drives fast cars, and falls for beautiful women.

➢ A dashing British adventurer or crime-fighter

'What, go straight? Me, the local successor to Raffles and the Saint and all those other debonair, gallant British adventurers?'
ELIZABETH PETERS *Street of the Five Moons* 1978

St Agnes, St Augustine, St Bartholomew, etc. *See* AGNES; AUGUSTINE; BARTHOLOMEW, etc.

St Trinian's [Lit.; Cin.] A fictional girls' school invented by the English cartoonist Ronald Searle (b. 1920) in 1941, whose pupils are characterized by unruly behaviour, ungainly appearance, and unattractive school uniform. St Trinian's later also became known through associated books and films.

> ➤ Used to describe a group of schoolgirls behaving badly; a chaotic or undisciplined girls' school
>
> She was quiet and shy and often blushed. I clearly remember on my first day—and hers too—she looked like a frightened rabbit as we all filed past looking like a bunch of St Trinian's drop-outs.
> *The Press (York)* 2004

salad days [Shakes.] A quotation from a speech by Cleopatra in *Antony and Cleopatra*:

> My salad days,
> When I was green in judgement, cold in blood.

> ➤ The period when one is young and inexperienced; the peak or heyday of something
>
> The mid-1960s were, of course, the salad days of Pop art and Minimalism.
> *Art in America* 2003

Saladin (Salah-ad-Din Yusef ibn-Ayyub) [Hist.] (1137–93) A sultan of Egypt and Syria who invaded the Holy Land and reconquered Jerusalem from the Christians in 1187, and fought against the Christians in the Third Crusade. He earned a reputation not only for military skill but also for honesty and chivalry.

> ➤ An Arab military leader
>
> Saddam Hussein, once hailed as a latter-day Saladin who would right Arab wrongs and 'liberate' Palestine from the Israelis, commands little love or admiration in the Arab world these days.
> *The Observer* 1997

Salem [Hist.] A city and port in north-east Massachusetts, north of Boston, which in 1692 was the scene of a notorious series of witchcraft trials. Arthur Miller's play *The Crucible* (1952) uses the story of the mass hysteria which developed as an illustration of the phenomenon of *McCarthyism.

> ➤ Mentioned in the context of witch-hunts
>
> This whole thing is way too much like the Salem witch trials for my taste, where guilt is preordained and nothing a defendant can say will prove otherwise.
> *www.washingtonmonthly.com* 2003
>
> Liberals and their fellow travelers were outed like witches in Salem
> *Columbia Journalism Review* 2005

Salome [Bible] According to the Bible (Matt. 14: 6–9), Salome, the stepdaughter of King *Herod Antipas, danced for the king and 'pleased him'. He then 'promised with an oath to give her whatsoever she would ask' and Salome, instructed by her mother, demanded the head of *John the Baptist.

> ➤ A woman dancing in a provocative way; someone, especially a woman, demanding that a man is beheaded
>
> John Major's head is back on the wish list for a small but determined bunch of Salomes on the back benches.

The World at One, BBC Radio 4 1994

His gradual revelation of the scale of the scandal and the Church's reaction—rather like Salome doing the dance of the seven veils—served only to tantalise and to whet the public's appetite for more.
Sunday Business Post 2003

Samaritan *See* GOOD SAMARITAN.

Samarra [Lit.] The ancient Middle Eastern fable of the 'Appointment in Samarra' relates how a servant, having been sent to market by a merchant, returned home trembling, saying that he had seen Death in the market, and Death had threatened him. The servant asked to borrow the merchant's horse so that he could leave Baghdad and ride to Samarra, where Death would not find him. Later the merchant went to the market and saw Death in the crowd. He asked Death why he had threatened his servant, to which Death replied, 'I did not threaten your servant. It was merely that I was surprised to see him here in Baghdad, for I have an appointment with him tonight in Samarra.' The story is retold by Somerset Maugham in his play *Sheppey* (1933), and is also the title of a novel (1934) by John O'Hara.

➤ Used to evoke the idea that one cannot escape one's destiny or death (especially in the phrase 'an appointment in Samarra')

'I don't know what Val died of. I don't think anyone knows yet.'…'Such a nice lady too,' went on Mrs Kinver. 'She should have got away.' It wasn't clear what she meant by this remark, although Stella could guess. Got away before her fate, whatever it was to be, caught up with her. An appointment in Samarra, she thought. You can't run from what gets there before you.
GWENDOLINE BUTLER *Coffin and the Paper Man* 1990

Samson [Bible] The book of Judges (16: 4–22) relates how Samson, an *Israelite leader (probably 11th century BC) known for his great strength, fell in love with *Delilah. The *Philistines asked her to discover the secret of his great strength, which she did: Samson revealed that the secret of his strength was in his hair, which had never been cut. Delilah arranged to have his hair shaved while he slept. Delilah delivered Samson up to the Philistines, who 'put out his eyes, and brought him down to Gaza, and bound him with fetters of brass' (Judg. 16: 21). During his captivity, his hair grew back and, being brought out to make sport for the Philistines during a religious celebration, he called on God for strength and pulled down the pillars supporting the temple, destroying himself and a large number of Philistines.

➤ Samson's hair can be alluded to when referring to a strong or powerful person rendered weak and vulnerable

Arabella ascended the stairs, softly opened the door of the first bedroom, and peeped in. Finding that her shorn Samson was asleep she entered to the bedside and started regarding him.
THOMAS HARDY *Jude the Obscure* 1895

This is the very dilemma that once confronted a young Hick. Hailed as great before he'd achieved it, he lost the glow of youth with frightening rapidity. With the erosion of innocence went his power, weakened like Samson at the barber's shop.
The Observer 1998

Samuel [Bible] In the book of Samuel, Saul, son of Kish, went looking for some donkeys of his father that had gone missing. After much searching, Saul was about to give up and return home when his servant told him that there was a man of God in the town whose prophecies always came true. Saul was concerned that he would not have enough food with which to reward the holy man, Samuel. When Saul found Samuel, Samuel had meat already set aside to feed Saul (1 Sam. 9: 22–4).

> Someone who has unexpectedly prepared a meal in anticipation of another's arrival

'May be so, Mr Henchard,' said the weather-caster. 'Ah—why do you call me that?' asked the visitor with a start. 'Because it's your name. Feeling you'd come I've waited for 'ee; and thinking you might be leery from your walk I laid two supper plates—look ye here.' He threw open the door and disclosed the supper-table, at which appeared a second chair, knife and fork, plate and mug, as he had declared. Henchard felt like Saul at his reception by Samuel.
THOMAS HARDY *The Mayor of Casterbridge* 1886

Sancho Panza *See* PANZA.

Sandman [Child. Lit.] A man who makes children feel sleepy by sprinkling sand in their eyes.

> A way of referring to sleepiness

Most people find it easy to sleep on trains, but for me it's particularly easy. In fact, I find it almost impossible to stay awake. I grew up in a house that backed on to a train line and night-time was when you'd notice the trains most. My version of the Sandman is the 12:10 from Euston.
ALEX GARLAND *The Beach* 1996

Santa Claus [Leg. & Folk.] In the modern tradition, Santa Claus (or Father Christmas, as he is usually called in Britain) lives at or near the North Pole, where he is aided by elves in making presents for children. He is represented as wearing a red robe and having a long white beard. On the night of Christmas Eve, he sets forth in his sleigh pulled by reindeer to visit all good children, coming down the chimney of each family's house to leave the children their presents. The name Santa Claus derives from St Nicholas, honoured in the Netherlands as the patron saint of children, and the origin of the figure of Father Christmas.

> Someone who gives presents

'Don't be any dafter than you can help. I've a proposition for you. Anyway—' he gave me one of his unexpectedly charming smiles, the hanging judge becoming a Santa Claus who would send absolutely every item on the list—'you might as well have lunch first.'
JOHN BRAINE *Room at the Top* 1957

'When I give, I give to all,' Mrs Tulsi said. 'I am poor, but I give to all. It is clear, however, that I cannot compete with Santa Claus.'
V. S. NAIPAUL *A House for Mr Biswas* 1961

Sappho [Lit.] A celebrated Greek lyric poet of the early 7th century BC, born in *Lesbos. The poetry that survives consists mainly of love poems, many expressing Sappho's passionate friendships with women.

> Mentioned in the context of female homosexuality (adjective *Sapphic*); a female poet

Ralph remembered how Brenham had ranged around the tent, ticking off the rhymes on the fingers of her left hand. Mile, style, file, smile. A lesser Sappho making line endings for a clever poetaster.
THOMAS KENEALLY *The Playmaker* 1987

The leadership of the lesbian advocacy has not commented on the situation, but it's probably safe to assume that there is no joy for the followers of Sappho.
interested-participant.blogspot.com 2004

Sarah [Bible] The wife of *Abraham, who, according to the Old Testament, remained childless for many years. God promised her that she would bear a child to Abraham, which she did at the age of 90. The child was *Isaac.

> Someone whose prayers are finally answered

SAS (Special Air Service) [Hist.] A specialist British army regiment trained in commando techniques of warfare. It was formed during the Second World War and is used in clandestine operations, especially against terrorists and most dramatically in several high-profile rescues of hostages.

> Mentioned in the context of rapid-response military operations, such as storming buildings to rescue hostages

As a group of students in Manchester in the early 80s, we not only had delusions that we were The Young Ones, but we also had a mouse. Just the one. But an annoying little sod, seemingly trained by the SAS, who could abseil into both larder and fridge.
audiolympics.blogspot.com 2002

Satan [Bible; Rel.] According to Christian tradition, Satan (meaning 'the Adversary'), also known as *Lucifer or the *Devil, rebelled against God and as punishment was cast out from heaven. He is characterized as the arch-tempter in the Bible. At the end of *Jesus' 40-day fast in the wilderness he challenged Jesus with a series of temptations: to relieve his hunger by turning stones into loaves of bread; to prove his divine power by throwing himself from the temple-top; to gain absolute earthly power 'if you will fall down and worship me'. Jesus rejected each of these temptations (Matt. 4: 1–11).

> A way of referring to utter evil or wickedness, or temptation

But the deeper the depression of the rest, young Rupert went about Satan's work with a smile on his eye and a song on his lip.
ANTHONY HOPE *The Prisoner of Zenda* 1894

Charles felt himself, under the first impact of this attractive comparison, like Jesus of Nazareth tempted by Satan. He too had had his days in the wilderness to make the proposition more tempting.
JOHN FOWLES *The French Lieutenant's Woman* 1969

Saturn [Rom. Myth.] An ancient god identified with the Greek *Cronus, the father of *Zeus. Because he knew that he would eventually be supplanted by one of his children, he swallowed them all at birth.

> Mentioned to evoke the idea of a father devouring his children

Suddenly, and after all these years, she has no appetite for politics. Vergniaud's dying words keep running through her head: 'The revolution, like Saturn, is devouring its own children.'
HILARY MANTEL *A Place of Greater Safety* 1992

Saturnalian [Hist.] The ancient Roman festival of Saturn in December, called the Saturnalia, was characterized by general unrestrained merrymaking.

> Applied to a scene of wild revelry or an orgy

Satyr [Class. Myth.] A lustful, drunken woodland spirit associated with *Dionysian revelry. In Greek art satyrs were represented with the tail and ears of a horse, whereas Roman sculptors represented them with the ears, horns, tail, and legs of a goat.

> A man with strong sexual desires

The looseness of his lower lip and the droop of his upper eyelids combined with the V's in his face to make his grin lewd as a satyr's.
DASHIELL HAMMETT *The Maltese Falcon* 1930

It was hard to imagine H.E. sniffing after some other country woman, or being discovered mounting one of the milking girls. H.E., even when he was twenty-seven, would not have made a credible farmyard satyr.
THOMAS KENEALLY *The Playmaker* 1987

Saul [Bible] Saul of Tarsus, a persecutor of the Christians, became known as *Paul after his conversion to Christianity on the road to *Damascus.

➤ Someone prior to their conversion to a life of virtue

'You start Saul, and end up Paul,' my grandfather had often said. 'When you're a youngun, you Saul, but let life whup your head a bit and you starts to trying to be Paul—though you still Sauls around on the side.'
RALPH ELLISON *Invisible Man* 1952

Savonarola, Girolamo [Hist.] (1452–98) A Dominican monk and ascetic and a zealous religious and political reformer. A puritanical opponent of the Renaissance, he gained power in Florence, where he preached against immorality, vanity, and corruption in the religious establishment. This led the Pope to excommunicate him, and he was hanged and burnt as a heretic.

➤ Someone considered puritanical in attitude, especially regarding the arts

That evening, as they ate a rather nasty potato salad and some sour canned cherries, he had raged like a Savonarola against the vanities of female dress.
ROBERTSON DAVIES *Tempest-Tost* 1951

Meanwhile, up at the mill, I was slogging away and trying to earn an honest bob or two in conference with the book-seller, who was describing the difficulties which face an honest vendor of adult reading material in the town of Grimble. There was, it seemed, a local Savonarola or Calvin who was a particular thorn in Mr Meacher's flesh.
JOHN MORTIMER *Rumpole's Return* 1980

Sawyer, Tom [Lit.] The hero of Mark Twain's novel *The Adventures of Tom Sawyer* (1876). Tom is a bold, independent, mischievous boy who rejects the conventional values of hard work, honesty, and cleanliness. In a famous episode, Tom is asked by his Aunt Polly to whitewash a fence, a monotonous chore. When one by one his friends come along, Tom pretends to be enjoying the work so much that his friends beg to be allowed to have a go. Tom therefore has 'a nice, good, idle time all the while—plenty of company—and the fence had three coats of whitewash on it!'

➤ A free-spirited or naughty boy; someone persuading others to do a chore or task for them

I was the winner, Miss Illinois. All I could do was laugh. I'm twenty-two, standing up there in a borrowed evening gown, thinking: What am I doing here? This is like Tom Sawyer becomes an altar boy.
STUDS TERKEL *American Dreams: Lost and Found* 1980

Unfortunately, pumpkins also take a lot of room to grow. Back when the competition began, Celeste had a very small suburban yard. So she convinced a few neighbors to plant some seeds in their own gardens. The next thing she knew, the neighbors were arguing over who could grow the biggest and best pumpkin. 'It was like Tom Sawyer conning his friends into painting the fence,' she recalls.
Better Homes and Gardens Magazine 2003

scapegoat [Bible] A goat which was sent into the wilderness after a priest had symbolically laid all the sins of the *Israelites upon it so that the sins would be taken away (Lev. 16: 8–22).

> A person who takes the blame for the wrongdoings or failings of others

Last night I had looked into the heart of darkness, and the sight had terrified me. What part should I play in the great purification? Most likely that of the Biblical scapegoat.
JOHN BUCHAN *Prester John* 1910

Scaramouch [Theatre] A stock character in old Italian farce (literally 'Skirmish'), portrayed as a cowardly braggart. He was usually represented as a Spanish don, wearing a black costume.

> A cowardly boaster

He swore no scaramouch of an Italian robber would dare to meddle with an Englishman.
WASHINGTON IRVING *Tales of a Traveller* 1824

Scarecrow [Child. Lit.] In L. Frank Baum's children's story *The *Wizard of Oz* (1900), the Scarecrow is one of the companions, along with the *Cowardly Lion and the *Tin Woodman, who join *Dorothy on the *Yellow Brick Road on her journey to find *Oz. He does not have, and wants to find, a brain.

> Someone without a brain

scarlet letter [Lit.] In Nathaniel Hawthorne's novel *The Scarlet Letter* (1850), Hester *Prynne is sentenced to wear a scarlet 'A', for 'adulteress', on her bosom when she gives birth to an illegitimate child and refuses to name the child's father.

> A way of referring to adultery

It was the nineties. No one believed dinner—even a late dinner—with a member of the opposite sex doomed a woman to wear the scarlet 'A'.
NEVADA BARR *Mountain of Bones* 1995

Scarlet Pimpernel [Lit.] The name assumed by the English nobleman Sir Percy Blakeney, the hero of a series of novels by Baroness Orczy, including *The Scarlet Pimpernel* (1905). Apparently a lazy fop, Blakeney uses ingenious disguises to outwit his opponents and rescue French aristocrats from the guillotine during the French Revolution. He reveals his true identity to no one, not even to those he rescues, but leaves the sign of a small red flower, the scarlet pimpernel, as his calling-card whenever he has effected a rescue. The Scarlet Pimpernel's exploits inspire the famous rhyme

> We seek him here, we seek him there,
> Those Frenchies seek him everywhere.
> Is he in heaven?—Is he in hell?
> That demmed, elusive Pimpernel?

> Someone who is difficult to find or catch; someone who rescues others in a clandestine way

I'm asking Wilson, but he's gone away—to Lagos for a week or two. The damned elusive Pimpernel. Just when I wanted him.
GRAHAM GREENE *The Heart of the Matter* 1948

One fifteen-year-old was kept isolated for three years in her bedroom. Sometimes all they want is higher education. Legends keep them going. Like the true story of a runaway who is now a graduate and successful businesswoman. Philip Balmforth, Bradford Police's community officer, is the indefatigable local scarlet pimpernel who rescues these girls and who arranges new lives, new identities.
The Independent 1998

Scheherazade [Lit.] The narrator of *The *Arabian Nights*, the bride of King Shahriyar, who, after discovering his first wife's infidelity, has sworn to marry a new wife each day and

execute her the next morning. Scheherazade escapes this fate by telling him stories in
instalments, always breaking off at an interesting point, promising to resume the story the
next night. After 1001 nights of her storytelling, King Shahriyar cancels his threat.

➤ A woman who tells long or numerous stories, especially in instalments

At my next appointment, feeling rather like Scheherazade unfolding one of her
never-ending, telescopic tales to king Schahriar, I took up where I had left off.
ROBERTSON DAVIES *The Manticore* 1972

Her voice fills in the intervals between nurses and consultant's rounds, visitors and
sleep. After days, possibly weeks, maybe years, I realize that she's telling me a story.
She is my own Scheherazade, she knows everything, she must be the storyteller from
the end of the world.
KATE ATKINSON *Human Croquet* 1997

Schindler, Oskar [Hist.] (1908–74) A German industrialist who, during the Second
World War, employed Jewish workers in his factory in Poland and managed to save many of
them from certain death in concentration camps by having them relocated to a new
armaments factory in Czechoslovakia. His life and role in rescuing Polish Jews are celebrated
in Thomas Keneally's novel *Schindler's Ark* (1982) and the film *Schindler's List* (1993),
directed by Steven Spielberg.

➤ Someone responsible for saving a large number of lives

He eventually reached New York in 1940, with the help of a Japanese Schindler figure
called Chiune Sugihara, a vice-consul in Lithuania, who gave him a transit visa and
later helped some 10000 desperate Jews.
The Observer 1997

Schopenhauer, Arthur [Philos.] (1788–1860) A German philosopher whose pessimistic
philosophy, embodied in his chief work *The World as Will and Idea* (1819), argued that
attempts to understand the world rationally are doomed to failure.

➤ Mentioned in the context of pessimism

So we should not go around moping, looking as miserable as Schopenhauer when the
toast has landed marmalade-down in the Wilton.
The Guardian 1998

Schwarzenegger, Arnold [Cin.] (b. 1947) An Austrian-born American actor who
began his career as a bodybuilder, becoming Mr Universe on seven occasions. As a film
actor, he is best known for his role as an impassive killer in *The *Terminator* (1984) and its
sequels. He was elected Governor of California in 2003.

➤ A muscle-bound man

'Nowt better than a bit of exercise,' said Dalziel, patting his gut with all the complacency
of Arnold Schwarzenegger flexing his biceps.
REGINALD HILL *On Beulah Height* 1998

Ranger was waiting under the canopy. He was dressed in a black T-shirt and black
assault pants tucked into black boots. He had a body like Schwarzenegger, dark hair
slicked back off his face and a two-hundred-watt smile.
JANET EVANOVICH *Four to Score* 1998

Schweitzer, Albert [People] (1875–1965) A Franco-German medical missionary,
theologian, and musician, born in Alsace. In 1913 he qualified as a doctor and went as
a missionary to Lambarene in French Equatorial Africa (now Gabon), where he established

a hospital and spent most of his life. Schweitzer was awarded the Nobel Peace Prize in 1952. His philosophy was founded on 'reverence for life'.

> ➢ Alluded to in the context of human goodness

This is the guy who killed my mother, Reverend. And he's going to kill again, that's a fact. He's out there laughing at me, and laughing at the cops, and laughing at you for protecting him, and I would knock down Mother Theresa, run over Albert Schweitzer and shoot the Pope to get at this guy. Do you understand me now?
STEPHEN BOGART *Play It Again* 1994

Was it guilt that had transformed him from a trust-fund kid in dress whites to a would-be Schweitzer?
JONATHAN KELLERMAN *The Web* 1995

Scott, Sir Walter [Lit.] (1771–1832) A Scottish poet and novelist, best known for his historical novels featuring tales of chivalry and romance. During his lifetime and for nearly a century after his death he was a hugely popular writer.

> ➢ Mentioned in connection with gallantry, chivalry, and romance

'Oh, I know all about that old quarrel with this fellow's father. But it was never as bad as you pretended.' 'I think I am the best judge of that. And this young man has offered me insults which I cannot brook.' 'Listen, Wally, stop talking like a novel by Sir Walter Scott. You should have some thought for Liz and Pearlie.'
ROBERTSON DAVIES *Leaven of Malice* 1954

The truth is, he mistook me for a knight out of Walter Scott, because I once fished him out of a scrape in a gaming hell.
KATE ROSS *Cut to the Quick* 1993

Scott of the Antarctic (Robert Falcon Scott) [People] (1868–1912) An English explorer and naval officer who led two expeditions to Antarctica. On the second expedition (1910–12) Scott and four companions reached the South Pole by sled, only to discover that the Norwegian explorer Amundsen had beaten them to their goal by a month. Scott and his companions died on the return journey.

> ➢ Mentioned in the context of very cold weather

'You're making it sound as though I was out for an evening stroll,' Cassie said. 'I don't think you understand what conditions were like out there.' 'Tough, was it?' said Walsh....'It was hell,' said Cassie. 'I mean, we're talking Scott of the Antarctic.'
SUSAN MOODY *Grand Slam* 1994

With low pressure sweeping in from the Bay of Biscay, you'd have to be Scott of the Antarctic to go out collecting conkers.
The Observer 1998

Scrooge [Lit.] The miserly Ebenezer Scrooge is a character in Dickens's *A Christmas Carol* (1843), whose parsimony and lack of charity are most apparent at Christmas. On the night of Christmas Eve he is visited by the ghost of his late partner, *Marley, and sees three spirits, the Ghost of Christmas Past, the Ghost of Christmas Present, and the Ghost of Christmas Yet to Come. These three ghosts allow Scrooge to revisit his childhood, to discover how he is now perceived by other people, and the uncharitable response to his own death that the future holds. The experience shocks him into generous behaviour on Christmas Day.

> ➢ A mean or tight-fisted person; a killjoy; someone who undergoes a transformation in behaviour

Our genetic makeup permits a wide range of behaviours—from Ebenezer Scrooge before to Ebenezer Scrooge after. I do not believe that the miser hoards through

opportunistic genes or that the philanthropist gives because nature endowed him with more than the normal complement of altruist genes.
STEPHEN JAY GOULD *Ever Since Darwin* 1978

When, earlier this year, I decided finally to put my foot down and to ban party bags from my younger son's fifth birthday, there was a certain amount of agonising in the household over whether or not I would go down in local lore as the Scrooge of the reception class.
The Independent 1996

Scylla and Charybdis [Gk Myth.] Scylla was a ferocious sea-monster whose cave was situated in the Straits of Messina opposite Charybdis, a whirlpool. Sailors had to navigate their way between these two dangers. If they steered too hard to avoid one, they would become victims of the other.

> Someone who is 'between Scylla and Charybdis' is in a predicament in which avoiding one of two dangers or pitfalls increases the risk of the other

Between the Scylla of Skullion and the Charybdis of Lady Mary, not to mention the dangers of the open sea in the shape of the Fellows at High Table, the Bursar led a miserable existence.
TOM SHARPE *Porterhouse Blue* 1974

But none of them has soothed us, held our hands, led us past the Scylla and Charybdis of cookery cock-ups, better than Delia.
The Guardian 1995

Sebastian, St [Rel.] A Roman martyr of the 3rd century. According to legend, he was a soldier who was shot with arrows on the orders of Diocletian, and, after surviving this ordeal, was then clubbed to death. The scene of St Sebastian being shot by archers was a popular subject among Renaissance painters.

> Used to evoke the image of a person with arrows sticking out of their body

Here self-defence was impossible, and individual drops stuck into her like the arrows into Saint Sebastian.
THOMAS HARDY *The Return of the Native* 1880

He was so preoccupied with an inner life that he took little notice of the humiliations and slights that pushed and jabbed at him the moment he ventured outside the community. If, like the rest of his kind, he was a Sebastian, the arrows did not penetrate his sense of self.
NADINE GORDIMER *My Son's Story* 1990

see through a glass darkly [Bible] A biblical phrase from *Paul's explanation that our imperfect knowledge resembles the poor reflection seen in a dull mirror, in contrast to the clarity of perception that will come once God's purpose is revealed: 'Now we see through a glass, darkly; but then face to face' (1 Cor. 13: 12).

> Have a limited or imperfect perception of reality

Our ability to remember and recall diminishes as time goes on. What we saw clearly once, we now see as through a glass darkly.
Kildare Nationalist 2002

Selene [Gk Myth.] The moon goddess, the daughter of the *Titans Hyperion and Theia.

> A way of referring to the moon

Sennacherib [Hist.] (d. 681 BC) A king of Assyria in 705–681 BC, devoting much of his reign to suppressing revolts in various parts of his empire. He sacked *Babylon in 689 BC.

According to the account in the Bible, when he invaded Palestine in the reign of Hezekiah, his army was destroyed by a pestilence brought by the *Angel of Death. This episode is the subject of *Byron's poem 'The Destruction of Sennacherib'.

> Used in the context of the sudden destruction or disappearance of an army or crowd

Max felt his suave sophistication return with the rush of elation that an ailing diva must have when she finds her voice again. A touch here, a word there, and the guests disappeared like the hosts of Sennacherib.
SARA PARETSKY *V.I. for Short* 1995

sentence first, verdict afterwards [Child. Lit.] In Lewis Carroll's children's story *Alice's Adventures in Wonderland* (1865), the Queen of Hearts impatiently declares during the trial of the Knave of Hearts, 'Sentence first—verdict afterwards'.

> Mentioned in the context of those flouting due process in matters of law or punishment

One could go on, but the point is that all along, this Administration has followed the Alice in Wonderland logic of the Queen: sentence first, verdict later.
The Nation 2002

Sermon on the Mount [Bible] The long sermon given by *Jesus to his disciples on a mountain, recorded in Matthew 5–7, in which he preached love, humility, and charity. It contains the Beatitudes:

Blessed are the poor in spirit: for theirs is the kingdom of heaven.
Blessed are they that mourn: for they shall be comforted.
Blessed are the meek: for they shall inherit the earth.
Blessed are they which do hunger and thirst after righteousness: for they shall be filled.
Blessed are the merciful: for they shall obtain mercy.
Blessed are the pure in heart: for they shall see God.
Blessed are the peacemakers: for they shall be called the children of God.
Blessed are they which are persecuted for righteousness' sake: for theirs is the kingdom of heaven. (Matt. 5: 3–10)

It also includes the Lord's Prayer.

> Used to describe a long or tedious discourse or harangue

They listened to the words of the man in their midst, who was preaching, while they abstractedly pulled heather, stripped ferns, or tossed pebbles down the slope. This was the first of a series of moral lectures or Sermons on the Mount, which were to be delivered from the same place every Sunday afternoon as long as the fine weather lasted.
THOMAS HARDY *The Return of the Native* 1880

Serpent [Bible] In the book of Genesis, the Serpent, which was 'more subtil than any beast of the field which the Lord God had made', persuaded Eve to eat the forbidden fruit from the Tree of Knowledge of good and evil in the Garden of *Eden, saying that 'in the day ye eat thereof, then your eyes shall be opened, and ye shall be as gods, knowing good and evil' (Gen. 3). She in turn tempted *Adam to eat and as a result of this disobedience they were banished from the Garden of Eden.

> A source of problems in an otherwise happy situation; someone showing cunning or offering temptation

The fresh hill air had exhilarated my mind, and the aromatic scent of the evening gave the last touch of intoxication. Whatever serpent might lurk in it, it was a veritable Eden I had come to.
JOHN BUCHAN *Prester John* 1910

It is necessary…to be innocent as the dove with Monsieur de Toiras, but also sly as the serpent in the event that his king wishes them to sell Casale.
UMBERTO ECO *The Island of the Day Before* 1994

Seven against Thebes, The [Theatre] In this tragedy by the Greek dramatist
Aeschylus, seven heroes lead the attack by the Argive army on the town of Thebes, one at
each of the seven gates of Thebes.

> ➤ Mentioned in the context of heroic courage

seven ages of man [Shakes.] According to Jaques in *As You Like It*,

> All the world's a stage,
> And all the men and women merely players.
> They have their exits and their entrances,
> And one man in his time plays many parts,
> His acts being seven ages.

These he proceeds to enumerate: the infant 'mewling and puking in the nurse's arms',
the whining schoolboy 'creeping like a snail...Unwillingly to school', the lover, the soldier,
the justice, the 'lean and slippered Pantaloon', and finally 'second childishness
and mere oblivion'.

> ➤ Mentioned when considering the various stages of a person's life

> In the seven ages of man, we've done the mewling, puking and backpacking, been
> through yuppiedom and done the TWINKY bits, and now we have excess baggage of the
> noisy variety—but that doesn't mean our holidays need to be condemned to a rental
> cottage in Suffolk, England.
> *www.travelintelligence.net* 2005

Seven Sages of Greece [Hist.] The name given in ancient times to the following
wise men: Solon of Athens, Thales of Miletus, Bias of Priene, Chilo of Sparta,
Cleobulus of Lindus, Pittacus of Mitylene, and Periander of Corinth. They lived in the
7th and 6th centuries BC and were, variously, philosophers, scientists, lawmakers, and
statesmen.

> ➤ Mentioned in the context of wisdom

Seven Sleepers [Leg. & Folk.] In early Christian legend, seven Christian youths of
Ephesus who, while fleeing persecution, entered a cave and fell asleep. They slept for almost
200 years. The legend is also told in the Koran.

> ➤ Someone asleep for a long time or difficult to wake up

> I wonder by my troth, what thou and I
> Did, till we loved? Were we not weaned till then,
> But sucked on country pleasures, childishly?
> Or snorted we in the seven sleepers' den?
> JOHN DONNE 'The Good Morrow' in *Songs and Sonnets* 1633

> We shouted back loud enough to wake the seven sleepers.
> JEROME K. JEROME *Three Men in a Boat* 1889

Seventh Cavalry (US Cavalry) [Cin.] In many old American western films, the US Cavalry
arrives just in time to save the heroes from certain death.

> ➤ Someone who arrives to help out in the nick of time

> By the time the US cavalry of Woods and Davis Love had arrived at the 18th, the
> European flag had already been hoisted.
> *Observer Sport Monthly* 2004

> I...had just moved on to considering what I would do in the event of an O-ring blow-out
> or first-stage failure when my buddy appeared, like the 7th Cavalry, over the gunwale.
> *DiverNet.com: Travel* 2004

Shadrach, Meshach, and Abednego [Bible] The Old Testament relates a famous episode during *Nebuchadnezzar's reign, in which the king set up a golden idol and commanded all to worship it. When three Jews, Shadrach, Meshach, and Abednego, refused to do so, the king ordered some of his soldiers to throw them into a 'fiery furnace'. Although the soldiers were consumed by the flames, Shadrach, Meshach, and Abednego miraculously came out unharmed: 'these men, upon whose bodies the fire had no power, nor was an hair of their head singed, neither were their coats changed, nor the smell of fire had passed on them.'

➤ Someone standing very close to a source of heat

Left to its own devices, the class tied Eunice Ann Simpson to a chair and placed her in the furnace room. We forgot her, trooped upstairs to church, and were listening quietly to the sermon when a dreadful banging issued from the radiator pipes, persisting until someone investigated and brought forth Eunice Ann saying she didn't want to play Shadrach any more—Jem Finch said she wouldn't get burnt if she had enough faith, but it was hot down there.
HARPER LEE *To Kill a Mockingbird* 1960

It's a tandoor oven, basically a large clay pot with a hole in the top and a wood fire inside. Nasrullah squats as close to the lip of the oven as he can without becoming a long-lost brother of Shadrach, Meshach, and Abednego.
www.rebeccablood.net 2004

Shakespeare, William [Lit.] (1564–1616) A great English dramatist and poet, born in Stratford upon Avon in Warwickshire. As an adult, he moved to London, where he made his career as a writer and actor in the theatre company the Lord Chamberlain's Men, later to become the King's Men. The company built the Globe theatre in south London. Shakespeare lived in London during the theatrical seasons while his wife and family remained in Stratford. He retired back to Stratford in his late forties.

➤ Mentioned as the epitome of the literary or theatrical genius (adjective *Shakespearean*)

The appointed day came....Rampion presented himself....Mrs Felpham tried to rise to the occasion. The village Shakespeare, it was obvious, must be interested in the drama.
ALDOUS HUXLEY *Point Counter Point* 1928

'What did you want to write it out again for?' 'There were some mistakes in it. I just thought it would stand a better chance if it was better written, that's all.' I was beginning to feel annoyed with her for picking at trivialities at a time like this. 'Yes, well we can't all be Shakespeares, can we,' she said, in a way that was supposed to shame me.
KEITH WATERHOUSE *Billy Liar* 1959

Shangri-La [Lit.] A Tibetan utopia depicted in James Hilton's novel *Lost Horizon* (1933), frequently used as a type of an earthly paradise, a place of retreat from the worries of modern civilization.

➤ An idyllic place or retreat

He gave a quick, nervous cough. 'Jesus. You can run but you can't hide. I figured that place was Shangri-la. But it's getting as bad up there as it is in the city.'
TED WOOD *A Clean Kill* 1995

Sharp, Becky [Lit.] Along with **Amelia Sedley**, one of the main characters in Thackeray's satirical novel *Vanity Fair* (1847–8). Becky starts out penniless and orphaned, unlike the comfortably off Amelia. However, she harnesses her charm and wits in her relentless pursuit of her own comfort and wealth.

➤ A socially ambitious, wilful, or resourceful woman

But there was a minute tilt at the corner of her eyelids, and a corresponding tilt at the corner of her lips...that denied, very subtly but quite unmistakably, her apparent total obeisance to the great god Man. An orthodox Victorian would perhaps have mistrusted that imperceptible hint of a Becky Sharp; but to a man like Charles she proved irresistible.
JOHN FOWLES *The French Lieutenant's Woman* 1969

She [Lit.] A novel, full title *She: A History of Adventure* (1887), by Sir Henry Rider *Haggard. The underground tombs of Kor are ruled over by a mysterious queen known as Ayesha, or She-Who-Must-Be-Obeyed. She possesses the secret of eternal life, but when she tries to demonstrate to the novel's narrator how to gain immortal life by passing through the fire of Life, she herself becomes instantly old and dies.

➢ Used to suggest absolute power over others, mysterious youthful beauty, or a rapid descent into old age and death

He could feel his face wrinkling and his hair greying as they spoke, like She after the ill-advised second bath.
CYNTHIA HARROD-EAGLES *Shallow Grave* 1998

Sheba, queen of [Bible] In the Old Testament, the queen of Sheba, having heard about the famous *Solomon, went to visit him, taking with her a magnificent caravan 'with camels that bare spices, and very much gold, and precious stones' (1 Kgs. 10: 2).

➢ A woman or girl who is conscious of her own superiority; also used to suggest privilege and wealth

The very first night he insisted on having Lind and his gang join us for what he called a snack on our drawing-room. Snack! Solomon and the Queen of Sheba would have been happy with such a snack.
ROBERTSON DAVIES *The Deptford Trilogy* 1975

Marge, six feet tall, jet-black hair, big skirt, nipped-in waist, immense hat, once walked through the garden gate at Old Mill Lane looking like the Queen of Sheba and her sisters were madly jealous.
serenawombat.blogspot.com 2004

Sheppard, Jack [Hist.] (1702–24) A notorious thief who was famous for his prison escapes, including one in which he escaped from *Newgate prison through a chimney. He was later captured and hanged.

➢ Someone who is able to escape from imprisonment or confinement

He is safe now at any rate. Jack Sheppard himself couldn't get free from the strait-waistcoat that keeps him restrained.
BRAM STOKER *Dracula* 1897

Sherlock Holmes *See* HOLMES.

Shermanesque [People] **William Tecumseh Sherman** (1820–91) was an American general who commanded the Union army in the west during the American Civil War. He set out with 60000 men on a march through Georgia, during which he crushed Confederate forces and broke civilian morale by his policy of deliberate destruction of the territory he passed through. In 1884 he unequivocally declined an invitation to be the Republican candidate in the presidential election, with the famous statement: 'I will not accept if nominated and will not serve if elected.'

➢ A 'Shermanesque statement' is one made by a potential candidate to say that they will not be running for a particular political position; also used in the context of an army destroying a region's infrastructure as it marches through it

Meanwhile, Howell Raines has apparently decided on a Shermanesque approach in departing from the Times—burning every bridge possible.
www.danieldrezner.com 2003

She Stoops to Conquer [Lit.] The title of a comic play by Oliver Goldsmith (1773). It refers to the upper-class Kate Hardcastle's posing as a common servant girl to make it possible for Charles Marlow, a young man who is nervous and inhibited in the presence of upper-class ladies but completely at ease with lower-class women, to fall in love with her.

> Used in the context of someone taking an apparently inferior position or role in order to achieve their goal

It's dangerously easy to underestimate a modest Finn. He stoops to conquer. Finnish modesty does not mean that Finns are not ambitious, not determined and not confident.
www.crikey.com.au 2005

shirt of Nessus *See* NESSUS.

shot heard round the world [Hist.; Sport] A phrase coined by Ralph Waldo Emerson and originally referring to the Battle of Lexington and Concord, the first clash of the American Revolutionary War. In US baseball history, it also refers to the winning home run hit by Bobby Thomson for the New York Giants in the deciding game of the National League pennant play-off series against the Brooklyn Dodgers in 1951.

> An event that draws global attention and has momentous consequences

The explosions of 9/11 were indeed a 'shot heard round the world'.
Al-Ahram Weekly 2005

Shylock [Shakes.] The Jewish moneylender in *The Merchant of Venice* (1600). Shylock lends the sum of 3000 ducats to the merchant Antonio on condition that if the sum is not repaid by the agreed date, Antonio will forfeit a pound of his flesh. When the time to pay falls due, Antonio is unable to refund Shylock, who insists on being paid his pound of flesh. Portia, the betrothed of Bassanio for whom Antonio has borrowed the money, disguises herself as a lawyer and conducts Bassanio's defence. When a plea for mercy fails, she outwits Shylock by insisting that, although he can take his pound of flesh, he must not spill a drop of blood in the process, since the bond allows only for flesh, not blood.

> Someone demanding or extorting repayment

'You want paying, that's what you want,' she said quietly, 'I know.' She produced her purse from somewhere and opened it. 'How much do you want, you little Shylock?'
L. P. HARTLEY *The Go-Between* 1953

Siberia [Places] The vast region of northern Russia noted for its severe winters, traditionally used as a place of banishment and exile.

> An inhospitable place of exile (adjective *Siberian*)

She and her family are still living in the projects—exiled to an urban Siberia where shops, banks, and other amenities of city living are few and far between.
Washington City Paper 1992

In the grim Siberian wastes of the Brighton Conference Centre…not one pro-Mandelson joke was to be heard.
The Observer 1997

Sibyl [Hist.; Lit.] The Sibyls were prophetesses in ancient Greece. They included the Cumaean Sibyl, who guided *Aeneas through the underworld. Sibyls gave their prophecies in an ecstatic state, when they were believed to be possessed by a god, and their utterances were often ambiguous and riddle-like.

➤ Someone, especially a woman, who predicts the future, especially when their pronouncements are mysterious, enigmatic, and hard to interpret

She would lie with far-seeing eyes like a sibyl, stroking my face and repeating over and over again: 'If you knew how I have lived you would leave me. I am not the woman for you, for any man. I am exhausted.'
LAWRENCE DURRELL *Justine* 1957

When Ken Cracknell asked me about our strategy, I would utter such Sibylline phrases as 'I propose to play it largely by ear', or 'Sufficient unto the day, my dear fellow', or 'Let's just deny everything and then see where we go from there.'
JOHN MORTIMER *Rumpole's Return* 1980

Siegfried [Germanic legend] A prince of the Netherlands (equivalent to the Sigurd of Norse legend) and the hero of the first part of the *Nibelungenlied*. Having obtained a hoard of treasure by killing the dragon Fafner, Siegfried helped Gunther to win Brunhild. He was treacherously slain by Hagen, who discovered that Siegfried was vulnerable in only one spot on his back. Siegfried had become invulnerable after being bathed in the hot blood of a dragon he had slain, but a linden leaf had fallen between his shoulder-blades, preventing that part from being covered in the blood. Siegfried's story is also told in the opera of the same name in *Wagner's *Ring Cycle*.

➤ Alluded to in the context of a person's vulnerable spot, their 'Achilles' heel'

Silas Marner See MARNER.

Silent Spring [Lit.] The title of a 1962 book by Rachel Carson which drew attention to the danger to the natural environment inherent in the use of toxic chemicals. It refers to a spring with no bird song, because the widespread use of pesticides has had such a devastating effect on the bird population. The book is credited with helping to launch the environmental movement.

➤ An ecological disaster; a work which radically changes public opinion on a particular issue

And I think one of the writers who saw this book recently described it as kind of like the Silent Spring of the criminal justice system.
CNN transcripts: Larry King Live 2000

Silenus [Gk Myth.] An old woodland spirit who was a teacher of *Dionysus. Silenus is generally represented as a fat and jolly old man, riding an ass, intoxicated, and crowned with flowers.

➤ Used to describe a man who is fat or drunk

She wriggled away and stared with cold judgment at his white Silenus-paunch and rosy appendages on the sheets.
A. S. BYATT *The Virgin in the Garden* 1978

But now, of all inappropriate beings, who should appear but Silenus? Brocklebank, perhaps a little recovered or perhaps in some extraordinary trance of drunkenness, reeled out of his cabin and shook off the two women who were trying to restrain him.
WILLIAM GOLDING *Rites of Passage* 1980

silly walks See MINISTRY OF SILLY WALKS.

Silver, Long John [Lit.] The one-legged ship's cook who is the leader of the mutinous pirates among the crew of the *Hispaniola* in R. L. Stevenson's *Treasure Island* (1883).

➤ A pirate; also used humorously when describing someone with only one good leg

But I do play a bit of tennis still, wearing a kind of brace on the knee which keeps it more or less rigid. I have to sort of drag the right leg like Long John Silver when I hop around the court, but it's better than nothing.
DAVID LODGE *Therapy* 1995

Simeon Stylites, St *See* STYLITES.

Simple Simon [Nurs. Rhym.] A character in a children's nursery rhyme, which begins:

> Simple Simon met a pieman
> Going to the fair;
> Says Simple Simon to the pieman,
> Let me taste your ware.

➤ Someone lacking intelligence or common sense; a foolish or gullible person

He looks like he was taught to pass—both short and long—at the same school as David Beckham. And he's a clever player. Definitely no Simple Simon and as cool as a cucumber.
Manchester Evening News 2001

Simpson, Homer [TV] The beer-loving, incompetent patriarch of the dysfunctional Simpson family in the American cartoon series *The Simpsons* (1989–), created by Matt Groening. When frustrated about things not going well, Homer exclaims the annoyed grunt 'D'oh!'

➤ A stupid or incompetent man

Significantly, the King is almost never shown in traditional Court costume. He goes about clad only in shirt and breeks. And he's expressive. He grunts, he groans. He's clownish. He's Homer Simpson.
www.etoile.co.uk 2004

Sinai, Voice from [Bible] According to the Old Testament, God spoke to *Moses on Mount Sinai and gave him the Ten Commandments (Exod. 19–34). The Voice from Sinai is thus the voice of God, giving moral instruction.

➤ A way of referring to the voice of God

To all who have been born in the old faith there comes a time of danger, when the old slips from us, and we have not yet planted our feet on the new. We hear the voice from Sinai thundering no more, and the still small voice of reason is not yet heard.
OLIVE SCHREINER *The Story of an African Farm* 1883

Sinbad (Sinbad the Sailor) [Lit.] The hero of one of the tales in the *Arabian Nights*. He is a rich young man of Baghdad who undertakes seven extraordinary sea voyages during which he meets with various fantastic adventures, including encounters with the *Old Man of the Sea and the Roc, a giant bird.

➤ Someone who has many exciting adventures, especially at sea

He delighted the rustics with his songs, and, like Sinbad, astonished them with his stories of strange lands, and shipwrecks, and sea-fights.
WASHINGTON IRVING *The Sketch-Book* 1819–20

Sirens [Gk Myth.] One of the sea-creatures, usually portrayed as bird-women, whose singing had the power to lure sailors to their deaths on dangerous rocks. In the *Odyssey*, when *Odysseus had to sail past the island of the Sirens, he ordered his crew to plug their ears with wax so that they would not hear the singing of the Sirens. He had himself lashed to the mast of his ship so that he would not be able to respond to their call.

> Someone or something that lures a person away from a safe course to danger or uncertainty; a seductive woman who lures men to their doom

Charles and his father sometimes disagreed. But they always parted with an increased regard for one another, and each desired no doughtier comrade when it was necessary to voyage for a little past the emotions. So the sailors of Ulysses voyaged past the Sirens, having first stopped one another's ears with wool.
E. M. FORSTER *Howards End* 1910

Of course such a marriage was only what Newland was entitled to; but young men are so foolish and incalculable—and some women so ensnaring and unscrupulous—that it was nothing short of a miracle to see one's only son safe past the Siren Isle and in the haven of a blameless domesticity.
EDITH WHARTON *The Age of Innocence* 1920

Sistine Chapel [Art] A chapel in the Vatican, built in the late 15th century by Pope Sixtus IV, after whom it is named. It contains a painted ceiling and fresco of the *Last Judgement by *Michelangelo.

> An artistic masterpiece; a painted ceiling

Fleet Logistics Squadron (VR) 55's ladderwell may not be the Sistine Chapel, but Airman Brian Bose is honing his artistic skills to give Michelangelo a run for his money. Mounted on a ladder, secured by ropes and pulleys for safety, Bose is hand-painting an intricate six-by-seven foot mural in the commanding officer's ladderwell.
All Hands 2001

Sisyphus [Gk Myth.] A king of Corinth, punished in *Hades for his misdeeds in life by being condemned to the eternal task of rolling a huge stone to the top of a hill. Every time Sisyphus approached the summit, the stone slipped and rolled down to the bottom again.

> Used in the context of efforts to achieve or finish something that constantly fail or to a seemingly endless ordeal (adjective *Sisyphean*)

Is that the only future humanity has, to push the boulder, like Sisyphus, up to the top of a hill, only to see it roll to the bottom again?
ISAAC ASIMOV *Forward the Foundation* 1994

The team gets hot, threatens to win the Championship, blows it. The players move on, the side rebuilds, then it happens all over again. The club's official historians compared its existence to that of Sisyphus. Now yet again the boulder has gone all the way uphill and rolled straight back over all our toes.
The Guardian 1994

Skid Row [Places] Believed to be derived from 'skid road', originally a track for hauling logs and later used to refer to a part of town frequented by loggers. The term is now used to refer to a part of town where the poorest people live, the haunt of drunks and vagrants.

> Mentioned in the context of a desperately unfortunate or difficult situation

Harry's father had died when Harry was five, leaving his family not exactly on Skid Row, but certainly much less well-provided for than might have been expected.
SUSAN MOODY *Dummy Hand* 1998

Skywalker, Luke [Cin.] The young hero of the initial trilogy of *Star Wars* films, the first of which, *Star Wars*, was released in 1977. The films portray a classic struggle between good and evil, in which Luke Skywalker fights against the evil Empire and its general, Darth *Vader.

> Someone thought of as battling against evil forces

Labour's chief whip versus an amiable rebel—it sounds like a battle between
Torquemada and Luke Skywalker.
The Observer 1997

'Sleeping Beauty' [Fairy tales] A tale told in its most famous version by Perrault (1696).
A princess is born to a childless king and queen who invite fairies to her christening. One fairy,
who is mistakenly not invited, takes offence and curses the princess, prophesying that she
will pierce her hand with a spindle and die. Another fairy ameliorates the curse, saying that
rather than die she will sleep. As a result of this spell, Sleeping Beauty and all those in her
palace fall asleep for 100 years. A forest grows up around the sleeping palace. The instant
Sleeping Beauty is finally wakened from her slumber by a prince's kiss, all life and bustle
return to the palace.

➤ Someone who sleeps for a long time

Edith came in from the back drawing-room, winking and blinking her eyes at the
stronger light, shaking back her slightly-ruffled curls, and altogether looking like the
Sleeping Beauty startled from her dreams.
ELIZABETH GASKELL *North and South* 1854–5

The front door was opened. They entered. In the silent, empty hall three and a half
centuries of life had gone to sleep…'Like the Sleeping Beauty,' she said. but even as she
spoke the words, the spell was broken. Suddenly, as though the ringing glass had
called the house back to life, there was sound and movement.
ALDOUS HUXLEY *Point Counter Point* 1928

Sleepy Hollow [Lit.] An isolated valley in Washington Irving's short story 'The Legend
of Sleepy Hollow', described as 'one of the quietest places in the whole world'.

➤ A rural backwater

'This place is what I call Sleepy Hollow.' 'Oh yes.' 'Most of the people are so old
they've retired from their retirement.'
FRANK PARRISH *Voices from the Dark* 1993

slings and arrows [Shakes.] A phrase from *Hamlet*:

Whether 'tis nobler in the mind to suffer
The slings and arrows of outrageous fortune.

➤ Mentioned when referring to adverse factors or circumstances

Just as a man might insure his house against fire, he should also take steps to protect
his business, rather than leave it exposed to the slings and arrows of commodity price
fluctuations.
Dairy Field 2005

Slough of Despond [Lit.] A bog into which *Christian and his fellow traveller Pliable
fall because they were not paying attention to the path, in John Bunyan's religious allegory
*The *Pilgrim's Progress* (1678, 1684). Christian sinks deeply into the mire because he carries
a burden on his back but manages to struggle through to the other side, where he is helped
out. Pliable is quickly discouraged, manages to struggle out of the bog on the side he
entered, and gives up the journey.

➤ A state of utter hopelessness and despondency

Burdens fell, darkness gave place to light, Marjorie apocalyptically understood all the
symbols of religious literature. For she herself had struggled in the Slough of Despond
and had emerged; she too had climbed laboriously and without hope and had
suddenly been consoled by the sight of the promised land.
ALDOUS HUXLEY *Point Counter Point* 1928

Brussels he sees as 'utterly complacent, and a negative force of great influence', but not quite the Slough of Despond.
The Observer 1996

slow and steady wins the race [Lit.] The moral of *Aesop's fable about the *hare and the tortoise, in which a hare is so confident of winning a race with a tortoise that he takes a nap. When he awakes, he finds that the tortoise has plodded slowly but surely to the finishing line and the hare is unable to sprint fast enough to beat him.

➤ Used when saying that slow, steady progress is the best way to achieve success

Balance in all areas of life is recommended. Slow and steady wins the race today.
Cybernoon.com (Mumbai) 2004

Smiles, Samuel [People] (1812–1904) A Scottish doctor who wrote several works of advice. His books include *Self Help* (1859) and *Thrift* (1875).

➤ Used to suggest financial prudence and hard work

British banks and finance houses, their fingers so badly burnt by colossal debt write-offs, have behaved with the caution of Samuel Smiles in their lending policies.
WILL HUTTON *The Observer* 1997

Snark [Child. Lit.] A fabulous animal, the quarry of the expedition undertaken by the Bellman and his crew, in Lewis Carroll's nonsense poem *The Hunting of the Snark* (1876).

➤ An elusive goal

If Truth is the Snark of Westminster, it is most effectively pursued by those ambitious journalists who will seek to scoop each other and make their names by peddling the spin, delivered to favoured trusties by spokespeople, spin-doctors, sources and 'friends'.
SHEENA MCDONALD *The Guardian* 1998

Snow Queen [Fairy tales] In Hans Christian *Andersen's 'The Snow Queen', Kai, a young boy, is carried off by the cold and cruel Snow Queen after two splinters of glass become lodged in his eyes and heart, making him unable to feel any human emotions. He is rescued by his sister Gerda, who melts his frozen heart with her tears.

➤ A person, especially a woman, who seems incapable of human emotions

I was so young I thought it didn't matter. Infatuated! His unhappiness had to be loaded on to me; that was what it was. He denied life, made me deny it too. He turned me into some sort of snow queen and when I made just one small attempt to thaw myself out he used it as an excuse to throw me out of his life.
FAY WELDON *The Cloning of Joanna May* 1989

Snow White [Fairy tales] The heroine of the traditional tale 'Snow White and the Seven Dwarfs', who is 'as white as snow, as red as blood and had hair as black as ebony'. Her stepmother is proud and vain, and regularly demands of her magic mirror:

*Mirror, mirror on the wall,
Who is the fairest of them all?

When Snow White grows to be more beautiful than her, the stepmother orders that her stepdaughter be taken into the forest and killed so that she will once again be 'the fairest of them all'. The men charged with Snow White's murder take pity on her and simply abandon her in the forest, where she lives for a while in the house of the Seven Dwarfs and eventually marries a handsome prince.

➤ A pure and virtuous young woman

'She didn't look very dangerous,' I said, bristling. 'She just seemed like a silly young girl.'
'Yeah, a regular Snow White. Who just happened to be packing a gun.'
LINDSAY MARACOTTA *Playing Dead* 1999

Socrates [Philos.] (469–399 BC) A Greek philosopher concerned with the search for truth and reason in questions of morality and ethics. His method of enquiry (the Socratic method) was based on debating moral issues with those around him: he systematically questioned his pupils and then cross-examined them to expose inconsistencies and errors. Through this discourse and careful questioning, he challenged accepted beliefs and attempted to expose foolishness, irrationality, and error. He wrote nothing himself, but is known through the works of one of his pupils, *Plato, who recorded his dialogues and teachings. Socrates was charged with impiety and corrupting the young, and was condemned to die by taking hemlock.

➤ Someone who engages in moral enquiry, especially by using questions and answers

'I do, as it happens,' said Philip and, still skirmishing...in the realm of dialectic, went on like a little Socrates, with his cross-examination.
ALDOUS HUXLEY *Point Counter Point* 1928

I hope that you will be glad to know that I have decided to make my own dowry. I think that my father has no sense of shame, and sometimes I feel very angry with him for refusing the very thing that is normal for every other girl. He is not fair because he is too rational. He thinks that he is a Socrates who can fly in the face of custom.
LOUIS DE BERNIÈRES *Captain Corelli's Mandolin* 1994

Sodom and Gomorrah [Bible] Towns in ancient Palestine, probably south of the Dead Sea, which, according to Genesis 19: 24, were destroyed by fire and brimstone from heaven as a punishment for the depravity and wickedness of their inhabitants. In particular 'the sin of Sodom' is traditionally taken to refer to buggery. *Lot, the nephew of *Abraham, was allowed to escape from the destruction of Sodom with his family. His wife disobeyed God's order not to look back at the burning city and was turned into a *pillar of salt.

➤ Used when describing an extremely wicked or corrupt place

The landslip had swept away a whole Sodom and Gomorrah of private fantasies and unacted desires. He felt a new man in the calm, initially sexless atmosphere of Desiree Zapp's luxurious eyrie high up on the peak of Socrates Avenue.
DAVID LODGE *Changing Places* 1975

Solomon [Bible] The son of *David and *Bathsheba, and the king of ancient Israel c.970–c.930 BC. Solomon was famed for his wisdom and justice. The phrase 'the Judgement of Solomon' refers to his arbitration in a dispute about a baby claimed by each of two women (1 Kgs. 3: 16–28). Solomon proposed dividing the baby in half with his sword, and then gave it to the woman who showed concern for its life: 'And all Israel heard of the judgement which the king had rendered; and they stood in awe of the king, because they perceived that the wisdom of God was in him, to render justice.'

➤ An extremely wise person, especially in matters of justice

I, who am all-powerful, I, whose loveliness is more than the loveliness of that Grecian Helen, of whom they used to sing, and whose wisdom is wider, ay, far more wide and deep than the wisdom of Solomon the Wise.
H. RIDER HAGGARD *She* 1887

It was beginning to dawn on me that I am the member of the public to whom the public interest requirement refers. In effect, the police are saying, 'You were there. Was it bad? Do you think that person deserves to be punished?' But this requires the judgement of Solomon.
The Independent 1995

Solomon's temple [Bible] In 957 BC King *Solomon built the *Israelites' first temple on Mount Zion, Jerusalem (1 Kgs. 5–7 and 2 Chr. 3–4). The magnificence of this temple became legendary. Each room had walls panelled with cedar wood, carved with palm trees and cherubim, and overlaid with gold.

➤ A fabulously ornate building

In this process the chamber and its furniture grew more and more dignified and luxurious; the shawl hanging at the window took upon itself the richness of tapestry; the brass handles of the chest of drawers were as golden knockers; and the carved bed-posts seemed to have some kinship with the magnificent pillars of Solomon's temple.
THOMAS HARDY *Tess of the D'Urbervilles* 1891

Solon [Hist.] (*c*.630–*c*.560 BC) An Athenian statesman and lawgiver noted for his economic, constitutional, and legal reforms. He was one of the supposed *Seven Sages of Greece.

➤ A sage, especially a wise statesman

Are you Socrates or Solon, always right?
BARBARA MICHAELS *The Wizard's Daughter* 1980

some are more equal than others [Lit.] A phrase from the fable *Animal Farm* by George *Orwell (1945) which satirizes Russian Communism as it developed under *Stalin. The animals on the farm, led by the pigs, revolt against the farmer and achieve a life of apparent freedom and equality. However, power gradually corrupts their rulers until the ideal of all animals being equal is replaced by the slogan 'all animals are equal but some animals are more equal than others.'

➤ Used to suggest that people or groups who are supposedly equal do not in fact enjoy complete equality

We don't want a Europe where all countries are equal but some are more equal than others.
Guardian Unlimited columnists 2005

something nasty in the woodshed [Lit.] A phrase taken from Stella Gibbons's comic novel *Cold Comfort Farm* (1932), in which Ada Doom's dominance over her family is maintained by constant references to her having 'seen something nasty in the woodshed' in her youth. The details of the experience remain unexplained.

➤ Something extremely unpleasant or traumatic in a person's past that has been kept secret

They each remember their father, but in quite different ways. Ella's memories of a loving, benign parent are contradicted by the memories of uptight Beth and bitter, spiky Liz. It turns out there is something rather nasty in the woodshed.
Guardian 2004

The opening story is the most imaginative, featuring a young divorcee whose anxieties over tap water lead to the sense of something nasty in the water tank.
Scotland on Sunday 2005

something rotten [Shakes.] A phrase taken from *Hamlet*. It is spoken by Marcellus, an officer of the guard, just after he has seen the ghost of the dead king, *Hamlet's father, on the castle battlements: 'Something is rotten in the state of Denmark.'

➤ Used to express a suspicion of moral, social, or political corruption; used to say that something is wrong

If a vendor tries to sell you a $5000 watch for $250, or a $1000 suit for $100, you know something is rotten in the state of Denmark.
AskMen.com 2004

Somme [Hist.] The Battle of the Somme was one of the major battles of the First World War, fought in northern France from July to November 1916. The British soldiers were ordered up out of their trenches to face, on foot, the German machine guns opposite. Over a million men on both sides were killed or wounded. Going 'over the top' at the Somme was seen as going to certain death.

➤ A battle with massive casualties; a situation in which a large number of people are sent charging forward to face an enemy or opponent; an extremely muddy place

Lippi's side are doing their level best, storming forward, throwing all sorts of defenders into attack. What a melee! Such Somme-like tactics barely have time to work though before the referee's whistle blows.
Guardian Unlimited 2002

Somnus [Rom. Myth.] The Roman god of sleep, father of *Morpheus.

➤ A way of referring to sleep

Sorcerer's Apprentice, The [Mus.] The title of an orchestral composition by Paul Dukas (1897), after a ballad by Goethe (1797). It was one of the pieces used in the 1940 *Disney animated film *Fantasia*. According to the story on which Dukas's work is based, the sorcerer's apprentice finds a spell to make objects do work for him but is then unable to cancel it. In the Disney version, *Mickey Mouse is the apprentice and the spell causes a broom to keep fetching buckets of water from a well.

➤ Used to describe a person who instigates but is unable to control a process

The giant deer had evolved from small forms with even smaller antlers. Although the antlers were useful at first, their growth could not be contained and, like the sorceror's apprentice, the giant deer discovered only too late that even good things have their limits.
STEPHEN JAY GOULD *Ever Since Darwin* 1978

sound and fury [Shakes.] A phrase from *Macbeth*. Life, according to *Macbeth, is

> a tale
> Told by an idiot, full of sound and fury,
> Signifying nothing.

➤ Used to describe a commotion or angry debate

There have been resignations, allegations, tears and harsh words. Mostly though it is sound and fury signifying nothing.
Sunday Herald 2000

Sound of Music, The [Cin.] The title of a 1965 film musical, with a score by Richard Rodgers and Oscar Hammerstein. Set in 1930s Austria, the film tells the story of Maria, a postulant nun, who is sent by her convent to work as a governess to the seven children of a retired Austrian naval officer, Captain Von Trapp. She brings joy and music into the lives of the Von Trapp children and falls in love with their father.

➤ Mentioned to describe a scene involving a large family of children, especially when they are singing

As the two couples on the Democratic ticket strolled hand-in-hand onto a grassy meadow at the Heinz baronial farm in Pittsburgh, followed by their children, it almost seemed like a scene from The Sound of Music.
USA Today 2004

South Sea Bubble [Hist.] The name given to a fever of speculation in 1720 in shares of the South Sea Company, a company formed in 1711 to trade with South America. The boom was followed by the company's failure and a general financial collapse.

➤ Alluded to in the context of something that appears to be successful and stable, but could fail suddenly; a large-scale investment disaster

Later on, when the dotcom boom bursts like the South Sea Bubble, Lizzie has to play by business rules and there is no room for individuals like Paul.
BBC Press Release 2005

sow dragon's teeth [Gk Myth.] The legendary hero Cadmus killed a dragon which guarded a spring, and when (on *Athene's advice) he sowed its teeth in the ground, a harvest of armed men sprouted up. He disposed of the majority by setting them to fight one another, and the survivors formed the ancestors of the Theban nobility.

➤ To take action that (perhaps unintentionally) brings about trouble or conflict

The Treaty of Versailles sowed dragon's teeth, generations of enmity.
Whole Earth 2001

Spade, Sam [Cin.; Lit.] An American private investigator in *The Maltese Falcon* (1930) and in other stories written by Dashiell Hammet in the 1930s. Spade was the first in a long line of tough, hard-boiled American private detectives. Essentially an honourable man, he is willing to break the law on occasion to see justice done.

➤ Someone resembling a tough private investigator

The downtown office buildings were just sparkling on their lights; it made you think of Sam Spade.
JACK KEROUAC *On the Road* 1957

In fact, computer searching of data protects privacy more than a Sam Spade-style hand search through title deeds, say, or hotel registries, which does in fact sentiently peruse records of the innocent as well as the guilty.
City Journal 2004

Spartans [Hist.] The inhabitants of an ancient Greek city state in the southern Peloponnese. They were known for their austerity and self-discipline and their toughness in enduring pain and hardship.

➤ Used to describe someone displaying frugality and simplicity of lifestyle, or endurance and bravery

A Spartan matron, iron-hearted, bearing warrior-sons for the nation.
J. M. COETZEE *Age of Iron* 1990

The water temperature would have struck even a Spartan as low and the soap was as carbolic as Hamilton's temper, but I felt better afterwards.
PAUL JOHNSTON *Body Politic* 1997

Spartan boy [Lit.] The story of the Spartan Boy and the Fox, told by the Roman writer Plutarch (*c.*46–*c.*120), relates how a Spartan boy, having stolen a young fox and hidden it under his cloak, let it tear out his guts with its teeth and claws and died, rather than let it be seen.

➤ Someone who hides a secret and suffers as a result

Willow did not say aloud the thought in her mind: 'And so you did not completely trust him. Did you feel that there was something wrong with him after all?' But she

could tell that Caroline had thought the same thing. No wonder she looked just as the Spartan boy with the fox gnawing at his vitals must have looked.
NATASHA COOPER *Poison Flowers* 1990

Speedy Gonzalez [Cart. & Com.] A Mexican mouse in a series of Warner Brothers cartoons, noted for his ability to run very fast. The first cartoon appeared in 1953 and the second, *Speedy Gonzalez* (1955), won an Oscar.

➤ Used to suggest great speed

Gardner's name spread across the nation faster than Speedy Gonzalez on steroids.
Men's Fitness Magazine 2002

Spencer, Frank [TV] A character played by Michael Crawford in the BBC television comedy series *Some Mothers Do 'Ave 'Em*, first broadcast in 1973. The well-intentioned Frank is hopelessly incompetent and accident-prone, and causes chaos and mayhem all around him.

➤ Someone who is extremely clumsy or accident-prone

December started with a flood of suitably biblical proportions, thanks to my other half and his questionable skills as a plumber. Though talented in many other respects, he is the Frank Spencer of DIY. He only has to drag his tool box out of the shed for the electricity to spontaneously short out and the pictures to leap suicidally from the walls.
The Press, York 2004

Sphinx [Gk Myth.] A winged monster with a woman's head and a lion's body. It lay outside Thebes and asked travellers a riddle, killing anyone who failed to solve it. When *Oedipus gave the right answer, the Sphinx killed itself. The Sphinx asked what animal walked on four legs in the morning, two legs at noon, and three in the evening. Oedipus correctly answered that man crawls on all fours as a child, walks on two legs as an adult, and is supported by a stick in old age. In ancient Egypt, a sphinx was a stone figure with a lion's body and the head of a man, ram, or hawk.

➤ An enigmatic or mysterious person

This human mind wrote history, and this must read it. The Sphynx must solve her own riddle.
RALPH WALDO EMERSON 'History' in *Essays* 1841

At times he tries too hard (such as filming a map with dominoes falling across it), but the idiosyncratic director certainly deserves credit for taking on the Sphinx-like enigma that is Robert Strange McNamara and achieving as personal an insight into the man's psyche as we're ever likely to get.
www.shakingthrough.net 2004

Spock [TV; Cin.] In the original series of the television science fiction series *Star Trek* (1966–9), Mr Spock, played by Leonard Nimoy, is the ultra-logical science officer on the USS *Enterprise*. He has a human mother and a Vulcan father, and it is the Vulcan side of his nature that causes his actions to be governed by logical reasoning rather than by intuition or emotion. Mr Spock has large, sharply pointed ears.

➤ A person with a logical and unemotional demeanour; someone with pointed ears

We would like to believe we reasoned with Aristotle's logic. That's why Sherlock Holmes and Star Trek's Mr. Spock are heroes and not fictional commoners.
BART KOSKO *Fuzzy Thinking* 1993

If you were doing OK, you'd be sitting in the posh downstairs office in that place of yours, dumping the unpromising cases on someone else and clipping off part of their fee, 'stead of that pint-sized smart aleck with the Mr. Spock ears.
LIZ EVANS *Who Killed Marilyn Monroe?* 1997

Sprat, Jack [Nurs. Rhym.] According to the traditional rhyme,

> Jack Sprat could eat no fat,
> His wife could eat no lean:
> And so betwixt them both, you see,
> They lick'd the platter clean.

Jack Sprat is usually pictured as extremely thin, and his wife as very plump.

> ➤ A couple where the husband is thin and the wife is fat; two people with very different (often complementary) tastes

The Galls, thought Solly, might have posed for a picture of Mr. and Mrs. Jack Sprat. Alfred Gall was thin to the point of being cadaverous, stooped, pale and insignificant. His wife was covered with that loose, liquid fat which seems to sway and slither beneath the skin.
ROBERTSON DAVIES *A Mixture of Frailties* 1951

Like some dark, fairy-tale hero, he is as hot as she is cold, smells of sulphur and raises burn marks on her skin with every touch. When they kiss, she has to fill her mouth with ice. They are like a sexed-up Mr and Mrs Jack Sprat.
The Sunday Times 2005

Springer, Jerry [TV] (b. 1944) A London-born US talk show host. His show, *The Jerry Springer Show*, was first broadcast in the United States in 1991 and became known for guests expressing extreme views, fighting on stage, and shouting foul language.

> ➤ Used to describe a discussion or debate that becomes violent

But argument is crucial. It should be encouraged not hidden or denied or even quashed. It's such an elementary point that it should not, here of all places, need to be made. But any deviation from consensus is depicted now—and by people who should know better, and indeed who do know better but cynically pretend otherwise—as some sort of Jerry Springer free-for-all.
NIGELLA LAWSON *The Observer* 1998

Squeers, Wackford [Lit.] The ignorant headmaster of the Yorkshire school *Dotheboys Hall in Dickens's *Nicholas Nickleby* (1839). Squeers presides over a cruel regime, starving and bullying his miserable pupils under pretence of education.

> ➤ A cruel and sadistic schoolmaster

Jon Voight, as the camp commandant, or second in command under the mean spirited Warden, overacts to a point of absurdity. He's called Mr Sir and goes around tormenting the children like a Texas equivalent of Wackford Squeers.
www.iofilm.co.uk 2003

Stakhanov, Aleksei Grigorievich [Hist.] (1906–77) A Russian coalminer who started an incentive scheme in 1935 for exceptional output and efficiency by individual steelworkers, coalminers, etc. Prize workers became known as Stakhanovites.

> ➤ An exceptionally hard-working and productive person (adjective *Stakhanovite*)

Now, as the only female among the four partners in a small City law firm specialising in patents and intellectual property, her Stakhanovite capacity for work could only be applauded.
ELIZABETH IRONSIDE *Death in the Garden* 1995

Leicester's work-rate makes Comrade Stakhanov look like a clock-watcher and nowhere more so than in midfield.
The Guardian 1998

Stalin, Joseph [Hist.] (1879–1953) Born Iosif Vissarioniovich Dzhugashvili, he changed his name to Stalin ('Man of Steel') in 1912. He became a Bolshevik in 1903 and general secretary of the Communist Party in 1924. After Lenin's death in 1924, he became increasingly powerful and was leader of the party by 1926. Stalin's attempts to collectivize agriculture led to the death of up to 10 million peasants, and his purges against anyone thought to oppose him were ruthless. After the Second World War he gained power over eastern Europe and imposed the iron curtain which divided Europe until 1989.

➤ Used to describe an authoritarian leader or organization (adjective *Stalinist*, noun *Stalinism*)

At the same time Clemmow was addressing the massed ranks of the BBC *Newsnight* operation facing, ashen-faced, allegations of 'editorial Stalinism' and 'centralised control'.
The Observer 1997

Stallone, Sylvester [Cin.] (b. 1946) An American actor best known for his lead roles in the *Rambo films, the first of which, *First Blood*, was released in 1982. He also played the title role in the Rocky series, the first of which appeared in 1976. In these and other films he plays tough, muscle-bound, monosyllabic heroes.

➤ A macho, muscular man

I pulled on jogging pants and a sweatshirt without showering and drove over to the Thai boxing gym in South Manchester where I punish my body on as regular a basis as my career in crime prevention allows. It might not be the Hilton, but it meets my needs. It's clean, it's cheap, the equipment is well maintained and it's mercifully free of muscle-bound macho men who think they've got the body and charm of Sylvester Stallone when in reality they don't even have the punch-drunk brains of Rocky.
VAL MCDERMID *Crack Down* 1994

Stanislavsky [Theatre] (1863–1938) A great Russian actor, director, and teacher, born Konstantin Sergeevich Alekseev. He founded the Moscow Art Theatre in 1898 and was known for his productions of Chekhov and Gorky. His theories about technique, in particular in paying attention to the characters' backgrounds and psychology, eventually formed the basis for the US movement known as 'method acting'.

➤ A way of referring to method acting

'What? I didn't! That's absurd!' he protested, emoting surprise and shock in a sub-Stanislavskian style.
REGINALD HILL *Child's Play* 1987

Stanley, Sir Henry Morton [People] (1841–1904) The Welsh explorer and journalist who, sent by the *New York Herald*, 'found' Dr *Livingstone at Ujiji in 1871, and, according to the popular account, greeted him with the words 'Doctor Livingstone, I presume?'

➤ Someone who eventually finds another after much searching

It would take a Stanley to find Dr. Livingstone on board. I presume. Even with the aid of one of Grandma Belle's hand-drawn maps, I could never do this on my own.
SUSAN SUSSMAN with SARAJANE AVIDON *Cruising for Murder* 2000

Starship Enterprise [TV; Cin.] In the television science fiction series *Star Trek*, and the subsequent films, the Starship USS *Enterprise* is the spaceship captained by Captain Kirk and, later, Captains Picard and Janeway. The bridge is dominated by computer monitors and other futuristic technology.

> ➤ Mentioned to suggest high-tech or futuristic technology

Christ, the office will look like the Starship Enterprise by the time you've finished with it. Didn't we leave Maher and Malcolm to escape the tyranny of computers?
MARTIN EDWARDS *Yesterday's Papers* 1994

She patted the whale-sized flank of the Buick. 'This car is absurd. I feel as if I'm driving the Starship *Enterprise*.'
NORA KELLY *Old Wounds* 1998

Star Trek [TV; Cin.] The American television science fiction series *Star Trek*, first broadcast in 1966, depicts the adventures of the *Starship USS *Enterprise* as it explores space, the 'final frontier', and overcomes evil aliens under the direction of Captain James T. Kirk and his first officer, Mr *Spock. One of the most memorable features of the series is the ship's transporter system, by which crew members can be made to dematerialize from one place and then rematerialize elsewhere (*See* BEAM ME UP, SCOTTY). The mission of the *Enterprise*, with its famously split infinitive, 'to *boldly go where no man has gone before', has also become a catchphrase.

> ➤ Mentioned in the context of: high-tech or futuristic gadgetry; instantaneously transporting someone from one place to another, especially out of an undesirable or dangerous situation; people who resemble aliens

One became aware of [Knebworth] manifesting rather than entering. Bone compared it to *Star Trek*. He and Grizel had become hilarious over the idea of Mrs Knebworth beaming Knebworth up from a console in the kitchen, his molecules assembling where he was wanted.
STAYNES AND STOREY *Bone Idle* 1993

Elegant Swan chairs dominate a sleekly modern lobby, where staff check you in through pods that could have come out of Star Trek.
Scotland on Sunday 2004

Star Wars [Cin.] The title of the first (1977) of a series of science-fiction films portraying a classic struggle between good and evil set in space, with the hero, Luke *Skywalker, battling against the evil Empire and its general, Darth *Vader. The name Star Wars was later given informally to the Strategic Defense Initiative, a proposed US defence system based partly in space and intended to protect the United States from nuclear attack by intercepting intercontinental ballistic missiles before they reached their targets.

> ➤ Used to evoke any battle on a huge scale; high-tech or futuristic gadgetry

Drivers in Scandinavia may do a double take when a vehicle that looks like something straight out of Star Wars hits the road on a tour of Norway and Sweden this week.
Electric New Paper 2004

Steen, Jan [Art] (1626–79) A Dutch painter of humorous subjects, especially crowded tavern scenes and social gatherings in middle-class households. His prolific output includes such works as *The World Upside-Down* (c.1663), *Interior of a Tavern with Cardplayers and a Violin Player* (1665–8), and *The Wedding Party* (1667). The term 'Jan Steen household' is still used today by the Dutch to describe a boisterous and chaotic family.

> ➤ Used to describe a crowded household scene

As I went past, a drunk stumbled out, and for a second, before the door swung shut again, I had a glimpse inside. I walked on without pausing, carrying the scene in my head. It was like something by Jan Steen: the smoky light, the crush of red-faced

drinkers, the old boys propping up the bar, the fat woman singing, displaying a mouthful of broken teeth.
JOHN BANVILLE *The Book of Evidence* 1989

Stentor [Gk Myth.] A Greek herald in the *Trojan War, supposed to have the voice of 50 men combined. He was unwise enough to challenge *Hermes to a shouting match and when he lost paid the penalty for his presumption by being put to death.

➤ Used to describe a person with a powerful voice (adjective *Stentorian*)

And his voice rang out into the night like that of Stentor as he bawled.
RICHARD BUTLER *Against Wind* 1979

Stepford Wives, The [Cin.] The title of a film made in 1975 (and remade in 2004), based on a book by Ira Levin, which tells the story of a young couple who move into the commuter village of Stepford, near New York. The wife is shocked that the other wives she meets are interested only in trivial domestic issues and in serving their husbands' needs, to the point that they seem incapable of even thinking about anything else. It gradually emerges that the men of the village, in their chauvinistic search for ideal wives, have in fact killed their real wives and replaced them with androids programmed to behave in this way.

➤ A 'Stepford Wife' is a dutiful wife who is mindlessly devoted to the minutiae of domestic life and blindly obeys her husband, seeming to have no mind or wishes of her own; more generally, anyone who unthinkingly supports another person or behaves according to a set pattern

She went off without a word, as obedient and unquestioning as a Stepford wife.
RICHARD HALEY *Thoroughfare of Stones* 1995

He leaned over and kissed me. 'Mmmmmm, you smell nice,' then offered me a cigarette. 'No thank you, I have found inner poise and given up smoking,' I said, in a pre-programmed, Stepford Wife sort of way, wishing Daniel wasn't quite so attractive when you found yourself alone with him.
HELEN FIELDING *Bridget Jones's Diary* 1996

Stephen, St [Rel.] The first Christian martyr (d. *c*.35), charged with blasphemy and stoned to death in Jerusalem.

➤ A person having stones thrown at them

Illidge sat down and recounted his adventure, boastfully and with embellishments. He had been, according to his own account, a mixture of Horatius defending the bridge and St Stephen under the shower of stones.
ALDOUS HUXLEY *Point Counter Point* 1928

Stockholm syndrome [Hist.] Feelings of trust or affection felt in many cases of kidnapping or hostage-taking by a victim towards a captor. The term derives from the aftermath of a bank robbery in 1973 in Stockholm, Sweden, when four employees of the Sveriges Kreditbank were taken hostage and came to form strong bonds with their captors.

➤ Used to say that someone has become sympathetic to or formed a bond with someone holding them captive or after contact with someone they would normally be opposed to

It takes on average about eight months for the bureaucracy to capture the heart and minds of high-level newcomers. Then a kind of Stockholm syndrome comes into play, a survival mechanism that leads presidential appointees to defend and sympathize with their bureaucratic captors.
writ.news.findlaw.com 2001

Stover, Dink (John Humperdink Stover) [Child. Lit.] The hero of a series of boys' novels by the American novelist Owen Johnson (1878–1952). The best known, *Stover at Yale* (1911), follows the adventures of the young Dink as he goes through Yale University, working hard and becoming a successful athlete and respected student.

> ➤ The archetype of the all-American boy, admired by his peers

> The client can always take a walk in estate planning, my lawyer had said, so estate lawyers, especially estate lawyers for the very rich, tend to be a cross between Dink Stover and Uriah Heep, unless of course they're very rich themselves.
> MAX BYRD *Finders Weepers* 1983

Struldbrug [Lit.] In Jonathan Swift's *Gulliver's Travels* (1726), the Struldbrugs are inhabitants of Luggnagg, a race endowed with immortality but who become increasingly infirm and decrepit. After the age of 80 they are regarded as legally dead.

> ➤ Used to describe a person who is incapacitated by age or infirmity

> Yet which of us in his heart likes any of the Elizabethan dramatists except Shakespeare? Are they in reality anything else than literary Struldbrugs?
> SAMUEL BUTLER *The Way of All Flesh* 1903

Sturm und Drang [Lit.; Art] A literary and artistic movement in Germany in the late 18th century, influenced by Jean-Jacques *Rousseau and characterized by the expression of emotional unrest and a rejection of neoclassical literary norms. The phrase is German, and means literally 'Storm and Stress'.

> ➤ Emotional turmoil; high emotion

> Never mind the slump—home sales are near historic levels. For all the Sturm und Drang in the broader economy, a surprising number of Americans are still rushing to get their piece of the American Dream.
> *BusinessWeek Magazine* 2001

Stygian *See* STYX.

Stylites, St Simeon [Rel.] (*c*.390–459) A Syrian monk who is said to have become the first to practise an extreme form of asceticism which involved living for 30 years on top of a tall pillar.

> ➤ Someone who spends time on top of a pillar or other tall structure

> At Boulogne, Patrick was usually to be found, like Simeon Stylites, on the top of a purpose-built pillar.
> JEANETTE WINTERSON *The Passion* 1987

Styx [Gk Myth.] The main river of *Hades, the underworld, across which the souls of the dead were said to be ferried by *Charon.

> ➤ A way of referring to death or to describe deep, gloomy, or foggy darkness (adjective *Stygian*)

> The report Dr. Fraker had dictated effectively reduced Rick's death to observations about the craniocerebral trauma he'd sustained, with a catalogue of abrasions, contusions, small-intestine avulsions, mesenteric lacerations, and sufficient skeletal damage to certify Rick's crossing of the River Styx.
> SUE GRAFTON *C is for Corpse* 1990

> It was a Stygian night. Outside the rain drifted in drapes and an east wind was gusting.
> LOUIS DE BERNIÈRES *Captain Corelli's Mandolin* 1994

sulk in one's tent [Gk Myth.] A reference to *Achilles' withdrawal from fighting during the *Trojan War following a bitter quarrel with *Agamemnon over a slave girl called Briseis.

➤ Withdraw from an activity because of a perceived insult or grievance

Labour, it was said, did not need Brown to mastermind the election campaign; now the spin is that the chancellor is not doing enough for the cause and is sulking in his Treasury tent. *Guardian* 2005

Sun King [Hist.] The sobriquet of *Louis XIV, whose palace Versailles was richly furnished and who surrounded himself with wealth. The title *Le Roi Soleil* derived from a heraldic device he used and was intended to convey his pre-eminence as a ruler.

➤ Used to evoke a life of rich, lavish, and sumptuous splendour

These two small tables were surrounded and bedecked by a buildup of objects, fabrics, and bibelots so lush it would have made the Sun King blink.
TOM WOLFE *The Bonfire of the Vanities* 1987

Superman [Cart. & Com.; Cin.] A US comic-book superhero who possesses prodigious strength, the ability to fly, X-ray vision, and other powers which help him to battle against crime and evil. His alter ego is Clark *Kent, a shy, bespectacled reporter for the *Daily Planet* newspaper. He is invulnerable except when exposed to pieces of the green rock *Kryptonite, fragments of the planet of his birth, Krypton. Superman was created by the writer Jerry Siegel and the artist Joe Shuster, both aged 17, in 1938.

➤ A man of extraordinary power or ability; a man who performs brave deeds or comes to someone's rescue

'You haven't met Zach Ralston. He's one man in a million, Jacob.' 'Well, he damn well better be Superman, to drag me all the way out here to the doggamned *tundra*.'
DEANNIE FRANCIS MILLS *The Trap Door* 1995

You're mixing me up with Superman. I just do what I can to hold the tide back a bit. I leave saving planets to the Met.
LIZ EVANS *Who Killed Marilyn Monroe?* 1997

Superwoman [Cart. & Com.] **1.** A US comic-book heroine, a female version of *Superman who uses her superhuman powers to fight against evil. Like Superman, she wears a cloak and can fly.

➤ A woman of extraordinary power or ability

I looked over at Amanda, looked for a Superwoman cape. No. No hero statement—just ironed blah beige and pearls. Maybe she'd left her cape at home.
KAREN KIJEWSKI *Wild Kat* 1994

2. [Lit.] *Superwoman* is the title of a book by Shirley Conran (1975), which gives tips to women on how to pursue a successful career and be a good mother at the same time. The book has been criticized for establishing an unrealistic role model for working women.

➤ A woman who successfully combines the roles of career-woman, wife, and mother

She's a sort of grim Superwoman type: runs a home and x children plus dog, makes them cakes for their birthdays and incidentally manages a business as well.
LINDA MATHER *Gemini Doublecross* 1995

Susanna [Bible] The central character in the book of Susanna, one of the books of the Apocrypha. She was a beautiful young woman who aroused the lust of two of the elders, who secretly spied on her when she was bathing naked in a garden. The two elders threatened her that unless she slept with them they would accuse her of adultery with a young man, which would mean her certain death. Susanna chose the latter, saying that she preferred to suffer death than to 'sin in the sight of the Lord'. Susanna was tried and condemned to death, but, in answer to her prayer, God 'raised up the spirit of a young youth, whose name was *Daniel'. Daniel cross-examined the two elders and showed that they were lying, upon which they were condemned to death and Susanna was released.

> ➤ A woman who is falsely accused; also, a naked or bathing woman being spied on by men
>
> Well, we are playing rough, aren't we? And the virtuous Val presenting herself like Susannah, she who suffered from the horny-pawed Elders.
> JULIAN BARNES *Talking It Over* 1991
>
> 'I went for a walk. It was warm and I was aching to be outside.' 'Did you leave the island?' 'No. I hiked to the pond and wound up skinny-dipping.' 'Anybody see you?' 'You mean paddling around in my birthday suit like Susanna and the Elders?'
> MICHAEL MEWSHAW *True Crime* 1991

Svengali [Lit.] A musician in George du Maurier's novel *Trilby* (1894), who trains Trilby's voice and makes her a famous singer. His control over her is so great that when he dies, she loses her ability to sing.

> ➤ Someone who establishes considerable or near-total influence over someone else
>
> Just over two years of marriage to a man twice her age, and she seemed to have wholeheartedly embraced the philosophy along with the man himself. Svengali and Trilby? Or a slavish acceptance of the good old fashioned motto, money talks?
> RAYMOND FLYNN *Busy Body* 1998
>
> Karl Rove, Bush's political Svengali, has told the party that security will be a Republican issue in this year's mid-term elections.
> *Guardian Unlimited* 2005

Swaffham tinker [Leg. & Folk.] According to a traditional story, John Chapman, a tinker from Swaffham in Norfolk, dreamt that if he went to London Bridge he would hear news greatly to his advantage. Having gone there, he was accosted by a man who asked him what he wanted, to which he explained his errand based on his dream. The man replied, 'Alas, good friend, if I had heeded dreams I might have proved myself as very a fool as thou hast, for 'tis not long since I dreamt that at a place called Swaffham, in Norfolk, dwells John Chapman, a pedlar, who hath a tree at the back of his house, under which is buried a pot of money.' The tinker hurried home, found the pot of money, and lived the rest of his life a wealthy man.

> ➤ Mentioned in the context of dreams that bring good fortune
>
> That night was an eventful one to Eustacia's brain, and one which she hardly ever forgot. She dreamt a dream; and few human beings, from Nebuchadnezzar to the Swaffham tinker, ever dreamt a more remarkable one.
> THOMAS HARDY *The Return of the Native* 1880

Swallows and Amazons [Child. Lit.] The title of the first of a series of adventure stories for children written by Arthur Ransome. Set in the Lake District, *Swallows and Amazons* (1930) recounts the adventures on holiday of two families of children, the Walkers and the Blacketts, who sail dinghies called *Swallow* and *Amazon* respectively.

> ➤ Mentioned in the context of children enjoying outdoor activities, especially sailing, or of idyllic childhood holidays

We look very serious but that is of course normal for children having their picture taken while pretending to be soldiers or explorers. This is beginning to sound very 'Swallows and Amazons'.
robertab.blogspot.com 2002

swineherd [Fairy tales] In Hans *Andersen's story 'The Swineherd', a prince, having failed to win an emperor's daughter by presenting her with a beautiful rose and a nightingale, disguises himself and obtains a job at her father's palace as a swineherd in order to try to win her attention. Although there is no equivalent traditional story of a princess disguising herself as a swine-girl, D. H. Lawrence uses this idea in the quotation below.

➤ A person who pretends to be from a lower social class

She herself was something of a princess turned into a swine-girl in her own imagination. And she was afraid lest this boy, who, nevertheless, looked something like a Walter Scott hero, who could paint and speak French, and knew what algebra meant, and who went by train to Nottingham every day, might consider her simply as the swine-girl, unable to perceive the princess beneath; so she held aloof.
D. H. LAWRENCE *Sons and Lovers* 1913

sword of Damocles [Leg. & Folk.] Damocles was a legendary courtier of Dionysius I of Syracuse, who had talked openly of how happy Dionysius was. To show him how precarious this happiness was, Dionysius invited Damocles to a sumptuous banquet, and seated him under a sword which was suspended by a single thread.

➤ The 'sword of Damocles' refers to a danger that is always present and might strike at any moment

True, in old age we live under the shadow of Death, which, like a sword of Damocles, may descend at any moment.
SAMUEL BUTLER *The Way of All Flesh* 1903

Daphne took another call. I knew even before I had registered her hushed and respectful tone that the sword of Damocles was suspended above me.
BEN ELTON *Inconceivable* 1999

Sybaris [Places] A Greek colony in southern Italy, founded in around 720 BC. It was an important trading centre, and its wealth and luxury became proverbial.

➤ Suggesting sensuous luxury and self-indulgence (adjective *Sybaritic*)

'It's very nice,' said Jennifer. 'We certainly didn't have vast open fires at St Hilda's.' She sniffed. 'Mmm. Smells like apple logs. And look at those rugs. For a women's college this is a veritable Sybaris.'
RUTH DUDLEY EDWARDS *Ten Lords A-Leaping* 1995

Sycorax [Shakes.] In *The Tempest* (1623), a witch, the mother of *Caliban, who enchanted the island and imprisoned the spirit *Ariel for disobedience.

➤ A woman resembling an old witch

Dame Gourlay's tales were at first of a mild and interesting character...Gradually, however, they assumed a darker and more mysterious character, and became such as, told by the midnight lamp, and enforced by the tremulous tone, the quivering and livid lip, the uplifted skinny forefinger, and the shaking head of the blue-eyed hag, might have appalled a less credulous imagination, in an age more hard of belief. The old Sycorax saw her advantage, and gradually narrowed her magic circle around the devoted victim on whose spirit she practised.
SIR WALTER SCOTT *The Bride of Lammermoor* 1819

Symplegades [Gk Myth.] Rocks (literally 'Clashing Ones') at the north end of the Bosporus which were believed to clash together, crushing ships that passed between them. When *Jason and the Argonauts had to pass between them, a bird was released to fly ahead of the ship. The rocks came together and nipped off the bird's tail feathers, and as they recoiled again the Argonauts rowed through with all speed and lost only the ornament on the stern of the ship. After this, in accordance with a prophecy, the rocks remained still.

> ➢ A dangerous situation, especially one involving being crushed between two massive objects

Taliesin [Lit.] A 6th-century Welsh bard, to whom a considerable quantity of poetry has been ascribed. He is the supposed author of *The Book of Taliesin* (14th century), a collection of heroic poems.

> A storyteller

> It was quite impossible—recounting tales in the presence of people who knew them already. She wondered how Taliesin, Demodocus and all the other storytellers had coped.
> ALICE THOMAS ELLIS *The 27th Kingdom* 1982

Tamburlaine (Tamerlane) [Hist.; Lit.] (1336–1405) The Mongol ruler of Samarkand, born Timur Lenk, from 1369 to 1405. With his force of Mongols and Turks he conquered a large area of Persia, northern India, and Syria and established his capital at Samarkand. Christopher Marlowe's play about him (1590) is entitled *Tamburlaine the Great*.

> A mighty ruler or conqueror

> With Pinsent, Redgrave entered an era of certainty: gold medals taken as of right, and by crushing margins, in Barcelona and Atlanta. This was his Tamburlaine period: Redgrave became Jack the Giant Killer.
> *The Times* 2004

Tammany Hall [Places] The headquarters of a US Democratic Party organization that was very influential in New York City during the 19th and early 20th centuries. The organization was notorious for corruption and for maintaining power by the use of bribes.

> Used to describe a place of political or municipal corruption

> Talk to the right 'community leader' and they will get out the vote in the best Tammany Hall fashion.
> *yorkshire-ranter.blogspot.com* 2005

Tannhäuser [Leg. & Folk.] (*c.*1200–*c.*1270) A German lyric poet who became a legendary figure as a knight enamoured of a beautiful woman. She takes Tannhäuser into the grotto of *Venus, where he spends seven years in revelry and debauchery. He then repents and goes to the Pope to ask for forgiveness. The Pope answers that it is as impossible for Tannhäuser to be forgiven as it is for his dry staff to burgeon. Tannhäuser leaves in despair, but after three days the Pope's staff does in fact blossom. The Pope sends for Tannhäuser, but he has returned to the grotto of Venus. The story is the subject of an opera by *Wagner.

> Someone who repents their misdeeds but is refused forgiveness

> Her Tannhäuser still moved on, his plodding steed rendering him distinctly visible yet.
> THOMAS HARDY *The Woodlanders* 1887

Tantalus [Gk Myth.] The king of Phrygia who was punished for his misdeeds (including killing his son Pelops and offering his cooked flesh to the gods) by being condemned in *Hades to stand up to his chin in water which receded whenever he tried to drink it and under branches of fruit which drew back when he tried to reach them.

> Used in the context of something desirable that is offered or promised but withheld or kept out of reach

That must be it, it was all planned from the beginning, I was never to have her, always to be tormented, mocked like Tantalus.
JOHN FOWLES *The Magus* 1977

This is not the first time ill luck has befallen one of her projects: in fact her career has been punctuated by similar misfortunes. It's an architectural version of the torments of Tantalus: a competition is held; against all the odds Hadid wins; the photographers, the 15 minutes of fame ensue; then before one spade of earth can be turned, fate intervenes and kills the thing off.
Independent on Sunday 1996

Tara's halls [Places] The Hill of Tara, to the north of Dublin, was the seat of the Irish god-kings in Irish mythology, and later associated with the historical high kings of Ireland until the 6th century AD. In the buildings there, 'Tara's halls', were held a national assembly and also gatherings for music and games. The idea of Tara's halls being empty and abandoned comes from Thomas Moore's poem 'The harp that once through Tara's halls' (1807):

> The harp that once through Tara's halls
> The soul of music shed,
> Now hangs as mute on Tara's walls
> As if that soul were fled.

> A silent, empty place

Now the vast press rooms were empty; as silent as Tara's halls.
MICHAEL MOLLOY *Dogsbody* 1995

tar baby [Lit.] In one of Joe Chandler Harris's stories of Uncle Remus (pub. 1881–1910), Brer Fox, in one of his many attempts to catch *Brer Rabbit, makes a baby out of tar and places it by the side of the road. When Brer Rabbit comes along, he tries to talk to the tar baby and, receiving no reply, becomes angry and hits out at it, whereupon he sticks fast.

> Something that is to be avoided, because it will cause problems for anyone who touches it

The trouble is that both men are tar babies, contaminating anyone who deals with them.
The Observer 1996

We might get some marginal assistance from other countries, but they look at this and think it's a tar baby. They're not likely to rush in.
CNN transcripts: Late Edition 2003

Tardis [TV] An acronym of Time and Relative Dimensions in Space, the time machine in which *Dr Who travels around the galaxy in the BBC's long-running children's television series. From the outside it looks like an old-fashioned police box, and its most surprising feature is the fact that it is significantly larger on the inside than it is on the outside.

> A place that has more room inside than it appears to from the outside

The club at Hawaiian Gardens is like Dr Who's Tardis: from the outside it looks like a windowless brick box dumped between a liquor store, a discount petrol station, a health centre and an empty plot of land. Inside it is a hive of concentrating humanity, a sea of numbers.
The Observer 1997

The Peugeot…may not feel quite as roomy as the Tardis-like Fiat, but there is not too much to separate the British-built French-designed car from its Italian rival.
Sunday Business Post 2001

Tarentine [Places] Tarentum was an ancient city and seaport in southern Italy, now named Taranto. Lying in very fertile country, it became renowned for its wealth and luxury. Its honey, olives, and other products were praised by Horace.

➤ Used to describe a luxurious place

That Royal port and watering-place, if truly mirrored in the minds of the health-folk, must have combined, in a charming and indescribable manner, a Carthaginian bustle of building with Tarentine luxuriousness and a Baian health and beauty.
THOMAS HARDY *The Return of the Native* 1880

Tarquin [Leg. & Folk.] Tarquinius was the name of two semi-legendary kings of ancient Rome. According to legend, Sextus, the son of Tarquinius Superbus, raped *Lucretia (or Lucrece), which led to the expulsion of the Tarquins from Rome by a rebellion under Brutus, and the introduction of republican government. The story is told in *Shakespeare's poem *The Rape of Lucrece* (1594).

➤ A man who forces himself upon a woman

There was but little of the Roman about Mr Harding. He could not sacrifice his Lucretia even though she should be polluted by the accepted addresses of the clerical Tarquin at the palace.
ANTHONY TROLLOPE *Barchester Towers* 1857

Tartarus [Gk Myth.] The lowest region of *Hades, which was reserved for the punishment of the wicked for their misdeeds, especially those such as *Ixion and *Tantalus, who had committed some outrage against the gods.

➤ The lowest part of a place, in 'the depths'; Hell; also mentioned in the context of punishment

Your soul gets judged, then it's punishment or reward. Tartarus or the Elysian fields.
CHARLES HIGSON *Getting Rid of Mr Kitchen* 1996

His imagination is as black as the pits of Tartarus, and his artwork is just insanely expressive.
www.collisiondetection.net 2005

Tartuffe [Lit.] The main character of Molière's play *Le Tartuffe; ou, L'Imposteur*, first performed in 1664. Tartuffe is a religious hypocrite who uses the sly pretence of virtue and religious devotion to win the admiration and friendship of an honest but foolish man, Orgon. Tartuffe cleverly persuades the wealthy Orgon to sign over all his property to him, while behind Orgon's back he makes advances to his wife and mocks his gullibility.

➤ A hypocrite; someone who pretends to be virtuous; a dissembling confidence trickster

The football World Cup is gradually overtaking the Olympic Games as the leading sporting festival because it has never had much pretension to virtue. But the Olympic Games has always played the Tartuffe: right from the very beginning, in 1896, on in an unbroken line of hypocrisy up to Sydney on September 15.
The Times 2004

Tarzan [Lit.; Cin.] A character in novels by Edgar Rice Burroughs and subsequent films and television series. *Tarzan of the Apes* (1914) is the first of Burroughs's tales. Tarzan is an English aristocrat, Lord Greystoke, who is abandoned as a small child in the African jungle and reared by apes. He is a very strong and fearless hero, often depicted as wrestling with wild animals or using liana vines to swing through the trees of the jungle.

> ➤ A man of great physical strength and agility; a person or animal swinging from one tree to another

'The other side now, viejo,' he shouted up to Anselmo and climbed across through the trestling, like a bloody Tarzan in a rolled steel forest.
ERNEST HEMINGWAY *For Whom the Bell Tolls* 1941

Taylor, Jeremy [Rel.] (1613–67) An Anglican clergyman and theologian. On the royalist side during the Civil War as chaplain to Charles I, he stayed true to his faith despite three periods of imprisonment.

> ➤ Someone who resolutely sticks to their beliefs

Well, if I were so placed, I should preach Church dogma, pure and simple. I would have nothing to do with these reconciliations. I would stand firm as Jeremy Taylor; and in consequence should have an immense and enthusiastic congregation.
GEORGE GISSING *Born in Exile* 1892

Teflon° A material used as a non-stick coating for pans and kitchen utensils.

> ➤ Used to describe someone whose reputation remains undamaged despite scandals or blunders; also used to describe a mind in which nothing seems to stick

I've tried to learn other languages, can 'pretend talk' authentic-sounding Spanish, French, Italian, Russian, German and Swedish. But my Teflon mind won't hold real words and grammar.
SUSAN SUSSMAN with SARAJANE AVIDON *Cruising for Murder* 2000

But up close, Chicagoans can see that the continuing scandals have scraped away the Mayor's Teflon coating.
In These Times 2005

Teletubbies [TV] Characters created for a British children's television programme aimed at pre-school children and first broadcast in 1997. The four characters, Tinky Winky, Laa-Laa, Dipsy, and Po, look like lifesize dolls and speak in simplified babylike language.

> ➤ Used to suggest something babyish, childish, or unsophisticated

Turok is a lucid champion of his discipline and is thoughtful enough to give me what I suspect is the Teletubbies' version of events.
The Observer 1997

Tempe [Places] A narrow valley between Mount *Olympus and Mount Ossa in north-eastern Thessaly, Greece. The ancient Greeks dedicated Tempe to the cult of *Apollo, so it became associated with music and beauty. Because of its proximity to Mount Olympus, the home of the gods, Tempe also came to represent earthly life rather than divine.

> ➤ A beautiful rural spot; earthly as opposed to divine life

Marty said no more, but occasionally turned her head to see if she could get a glimpse of the Olympian creature who, as the coachman had truly observed, hardly ever descended from her clouds into the Tempe-vale of the parishioners.
THOMAS HARDY *The Woodlanders* 1887

Temple, Shirley [Cin.] (b. 1928) An American child star who appeared in a succession of films in the 1930s, including *Curly Top* (1935) and *Dimples* (1936), in which she sang and danced. She is remembered for her sweet, innocent good looks, especially her mop of golden curls.

> ➤ A sweetly attractive young girl, especially one with curly blonde hair

Beside McConnachie's massive bulk, Fizz looked like a kitten smiling up at a Rottweiler.
Sun-bleached tendrils of hair framed a face that made Shirley Temple look depraved and
her denim-blue eyes rested on Duncan with absolute faith and affection.
JOYCE HELM *Foreign Body* 1997

Teresa, Mother [Rel.] (1910–97) A Roman Catholic missionary, born Agnes Gonxha
Bojaxhiu of Albanian parents in what is now Macedonia. She became a nun in 1928 and went
to India, where she devoted herself to helping the destitute. She founded the order of
Missionaries of Charity, which became noted for its work among the poor and dying in Calcutta.
Mother Teresa was awarded the Nobel Peace Prize in 1979.

> ➢ Someone demonstrating great compassion or engaged in charitable work

> Or maybe she could go in for superhuman goodness, instead. Hair shirts, stigmata,
> succouring the poor, a kind of outsized Mother Teresa.
> MARGARET ATWOOD *The Robber Bride* 1993

termagant [Lit.] Termagant was the name given in medieval morality plays to an imaginary
deity of violent and turbulent character.

> ➢ An overbearing, quarrelsome, or shrewish woman

Terminator [Cin.] In the film *The Terminator* (1984) and its sequels, Arnold
*Schwarzenegger plays an almost indestructible android sent from the future. The films are
extremely violent, and the Terminator destructively deploys an arsenal of massive weaponry.

> ➢ A relentless or seemingly indestructible enemy

> 'I need you to help me take down a skip.' This meant Ranger either needed a good laugh
> or else he needed a white female to use as a decoy. If Ranger needed serious muscle
> he wouldn't call me. Ranger knew people who would take on the Terminator for a pack
> of Camels and the promise of a fun time.
> JANET EVANOVICH *Four to Score* 1998

Terpsichore [Gk Myth.] One of the nine *Muses, associated with dancing (the name means
literally 'Delighting in Dance'), particularly choral dancing and its accompanying song.

> ➢ A way of referring to dancing (adjective *Terpsichorean*)

> The old-fashioned fronts of these houses…rose sheer from the pavement, into which the
> bow-windows protruded like bastions, necessitating a pleasing *chassez-déchassez*
> movement to the time-pressed pedestrian at every few yards. He was bound also to
> evolve other Terpsichorean figures in respect of door-steps, scrapers, cellar-hatches,
> church buttresses.
> THOMAS HARDY *The Mayor of Casterbridge* 1886

> He offended her by refusing to go into a dance-hall on the grounds that the music was
> so bad that it was a sacrilege against St Cecilia and Euterpe and Terpsichore, when
> she just wanted to go in and lose her unhappiness in dancing.
> LOUIS DE BERNIÈRES *Señor Vivo and the Coca Lord* 1991

Thais [People] An Athenian courtesan, mistress of *Alexander the Great, who accompanied
Alexander on his Asiatic expedition. She was the subject of the novel *Thais* (1890) by
Anatole France, which was made into an opera by Massenet (1894).

> ➢ A prostitute

> A thousand taxis would yawn at a thousand corners, and only to him was that kiss
> forever lost and done. In a thousand guises Thais would hail a cab and turn up her face for
> loving. And her pallor would be virginal and lovely, and her kiss chaste as the moon.
> F. SCOTT FITZGERALD *The Beautiful and the Damned* 1922

Thalia [Gk Myth.] One of the nine *Muses, associated especially with comedy and bucolic poetry.

> A way of referring to comedy

Call me the Great Escapologist. Call me Harry Houdini. Hail Thalia, Muse of Comedy. Oh boy I need a round of applause.
JULIAN BARNES *Talking It Over* 1991

Thermopylae [Places] A narrow pass in ancient Greece which was along the main route into southern Greece taken by armies invading from the north and consequently an important site for defence. The most famous battle fought at the pass was between invading Persians, commanded by *Xerxes, and an army of approximately 6000 Greeks, including 300 *Spartans, under the leadership of Leonidas, king of Sparta. The Persians found an alternative mountain pass and were able to come upon the Greeks from behind. Many of the Greek allies departed before the battle, but Leonidas, his Spartans, and many Thespians and Thebans died in defence of the pass. Simonides' epitaph on the battle read:

> Go, tell the Spartans, thou who passest by,
> That here obedient to their laws we lie.

> Mentioned in the context of heroic resistance when heavily outnumbered against strong opposition

He shivered and then stood erect. He had made a decision; it would be another Thermopylae. If three hundred Spartans could hold out against five million of the bravest Persians, what could he not achieve with twenty divisions against the Italians?
LOUIS DE BERNIÈRES *Captain Corelli's Mandolin* 1994

Theseus [Gk Myth.] The son of Aegeus, king of Athens, who volunteered to be one of the seven youths sacrificed annually to the *Minotaur, a creature with a man's body and a bull's head, in the *Labyrinth at Knossus. Theseus managed to kill the Minotaur and escaped from the Labyrinth using a ball of thread given to him by *Ariadne, which he unravelled as he went in and followed back to find his way out again.

> Mentioned in the context of someone facing a monster or entering (or finding their way out of) a labyrinth

I often feel like Theseus entering the labyrinth and meeting the minotaur. In my case, the monster is environmental damage. And like Theseus, I wonder will we make it out of the labyrinth?
Whole Earth 2002

Under water, divers can hook the end of their bottom winder lines to the chain and head off on the dive, secure in the knowledge that they will, like Theseus in Greek mythology, find their way back out of the underwater labyrinth and safely to the surface.
DiverNet.com 2004

Thespis [Theatre] (6th century BC) A Greek dramatic poet generally regarded as the founder of Greek tragedy, having introduced the role of the actor in addition to the traditional chorus.

> Used to refer to drama or acting (adjective *Thespian*)

But once you enter the theatre, this vibrant bazaar of Thespis, and take your seat to Dreamland, you will soon wish you were back on the street taking your chances with the druggies and thugees.
Guardian 2005

they seek him here...[Lit.] A phrase based on a quotation from the novel *The Scarlet Pimpernel* by Baroness Orczy (1905). In the novel, the '*Scarlet Pimpernel' is the name assumed by the English nobleman Sir Percy Blakeney, who rescues French aristocrats from the guillotine during the French Revolution. Despite many attempts to catch him, the Pimpernel remains ever elusive, inspiring the rhyme:

> We seek him here, we seek him there.
> Those Frenchies seek him everywhere.
> Is he in heaven?—Is he in hell?
> That demmed, elusive Pimpernel?

➤ Used to suggest that someone is difficult to find or catch

They seek him here, they seek him there, but Roy Keane just ain't anywhere.
Irish Examiner 2002

Thinker, The [Art] The title of a famous sculpture (1902) by the French sculptor Auguste Rodin (1840–1917) which depicts a seated male nude leaning forward and resting his chin on his fist, apparently absorbed in intense contemplation.

➤ Used to describe someone deep in thought or sitting with their head resting on their fist

While his teammates dressed and left the room, O'Neal stayed in full uniform, adopting a pose not unlike Rodin's Thinker, trying to explain his disappointment and mute his growing anger.
Sporting News 2004

thirty pieces of silver [Bible] The payment made to *Judas Iscariot for betraying *Jesus.

➤ Mentioned in the context of betrayal

This has led to the perception that, if a sports book is to be a bestseller, it must be controversial. In many cases it means the author will betray the trust of those he has worked with for thirty pieces of silver.
The Kingdom 2003

Thor [Norse Myth.] The son of *Odin and Frigga, and the god of thunder and war. Thor was also the god of the weather, agriculture, and the home. He was usually represented as a man of enormous strength armed with a hammer called Mjollnir, which returned to his hand after he had thrown it. Thor also wore a pair of iron gloves to help him grasp his hammer and a belt which doubled his strength.

➤ Someone wielding a hammer or other weapon

But Arthur never faltered. He looked like a figure of Thor as his untrembling arm rose and fell, driving deeper and deeper the mercy-bearing stake, whilst the blood from the pierced heart welled and spurted up around it.
BRAM STOKER *Dracula* 1897

Thoth [Egypt. Myth.] The god of the moon, wisdom, writing, and the sciences. Thoth is usually represented in human form with the head of an ibis.

➤ Mentioned in the context of learning and knowledge

He was an important man. He wielded power: power of appointment, power of disappointment, power of the cheque book, power of Thoth and the Mercurial access to the Arcana of the Stant Collection.
A. S. BYATT *Possession* 1990

Thought Police [Lit.] In George *Orwell's novel *Nineteen Eighty-Four* (1949), the Thought Police are the secret police whose job is to control and change the thoughts of anyone who dares to think independently, using brainwashing and torture.

> A group intent on stifling thought, often in the context of political correctness

The law as proposed also raises the extremely worrying precedent of finding someone guilty of a crime even when that crime hasn't taken place or even been attempted. This is truly Thought Police material.
The Register 2001

thou shouldst be living at this hour [Lit.] A phrase from William Wordsworth's sonnet 'London, 1802' (1807), which begins:

> Milton! Thou shouldst be living at this hour:
> England hath need of thee.

> Used (usually with another name substituted for that of Milton) to suggest that a particular person from the past is much needed in the current situation

In a Blairite age, one feels like exclaiming: Gillray, thou shouldst be living at this hour. England hath need of thee.
City Journal 2002

Thraso [Lit.] A boastful soldier in the Roman writer Terence's comedy *Eunuchus* (first performed in 161 BC).

> Someone who is vain and boastful (adjective *Thrasonical*)

Mr O'Rourke, surely you are not so Thrasonical as to declare yourself a genius?
TIMOTHY MO *An Insular Possession* 1986

Three Musketeers [Lit.] Athos, Porthos, and Aramis are the three friends whose adventures with D'Artagnan are celebrated in Alexandre Dumas's novel *The Three Musketeers* (1844). They declare their comradeship with the famous rallying-cry '*All for one, and one for all!*'

> Three close friends or associates

And then Weary tied in with two scouts, and they became close friends immediately, and they decided to fight their way back to their own lines. They were going to travel fast. They were damned if they'd surrender. They shook hands all around. They called themselves 'The Three Musketeers'.
KURT VONNEGUT *Slaughterhouse-Five* 1969

Three Stooges [Cin.] An American comedy act of the 20th century known for their physical and sometimes cruel brand of slapstick comedy. The original three stooges were **Larry Fine** (Louis Feinberg), **Moe Howard** (Harry Moses Horwitz), and **Curly Howard** (Jerome Lester Horwitz). They starred in over 200 short films from the 1930s to 1960s, and several feature-length films, including *Snow White and the Three Stooges* (1961) and *The Three Stooges Meet Hercules* (1962).

> Mentioned in the context of slapstick humour; three clumsy or inept people

In a rare slapstick moment that would have turned The Three Stooges green with envy, Voss tried to get back into the play after hitting the carpet. He got to his feet and took off after the ball. Once again his face hit the turf with his legs still pumping…
AustralianRules.com 2002

three wise monkeys [Art] A conventional sculptured group of three monkeys. One monkey is depicted with its paws over its mouth (taken as representing 'speak no evil'), one with its paws over its eyes ('see no evil'), and one with its paws over its ears ('hear no evil').

> Used to refer to a person, or group of people, who choose to ignore or keep silent about wrongdoing

[O]ther European leaders did not utter a word of criticism. They resembled the three wise monkeys—seeing nothing, hearing nothing and saying nothing.
World Socialist Website 2003

three witches [Shakes.] In *Macbeth* (1623), three weird sisters, or witches, are encountered by *Macbeth and Banquo on the blasted heath. Their first words at the beginning of the play are

> When shall we three meet again
> In thunder, lightning, or in rain?

Later, the witches gather round a cauldron, chanting

> Double, double toil and trouble;
> Fire burn and cauldron bubble

and throwing into their potion such ingredients as

> Eye of newt, and toe of frog,
> Wool of bat, and tongue of dog.

➤ Three women meeting together; mentioned in the context of a bizarre collection of ingredients

His specimen bottles are not for the faint-hearted. Macbeth's witches would have had a field day with the contents: dried geckos and caterpillars, antler velvet, pickled snakes and seahorses, ox tendons and duck's webs, and an array of deer penises or 'pizzles' that would makes Santa Claus's eyes water.
Travel Intelligence 2005

throw someone to the lions [Hist.] A phrase alluding to the practice in imperial Rome of throwing religious and political dissidents, especially Christians, to lions and other wild animals as a means of execution.

➤ To put someone in a dangerous position, or a position in which they are likely to fail

Everyone there reckoned the BBC were throwing him to the lions, but he waltzed through it and has gone from strength to strength ever since.
Sunday Herald 2002

Thule *See* ULTIMA THULE.

Thumbelina [Fairy tales] A tiny girl in a tale by Hans Christian *Andersen who, after being rescued by a swallow, marries the equally tiny king of the Angels of the Flowers.

➤ A diminutive girl or woman

Thyestes [Gk Myth.] The brother of *Atreus, with whose wife he committed adultery. In revenge, Atreus invited him to a banquet and served him the flesh of Thyestes' own children to eat. Thyestes fled in horror, laying a curse on the house of Atreus.

➤ Used in the context of unwitting cannibalism

Her heroine, Hilary, announces straight off that 'I first decided to cook my husband on the day he left me'. To that end she arranges a Thyestean feast for ex-hubby Kenneth and his new wife Laura.
Guardian 2004

Tiananmen Square [Places] A large square in the centre of Beijing, scene of a pro-democracy protest in spring 1989, which became a massacre when government troops opened fire on the unarmed protestors. The most iconic image is the photograph or piece of news footage of a lone protester standing in front of an advancing tank.

> A ruthless massacre; brutal political oppression; also evoking a scene in which a person defiantly stands in front of a large vehicle

Mr. Game Theory doesn't rush off to the ammo bunker or pull a Tiananmen Square, lay-in-front of the bulldozer shtik.
Bahamas Blog 2005

Tiffany's [Places] A fashionable New York jewellery store founded by Charles L. Tiffany (1812–1902).

> Used to describe a company or organization known for its high-quality craftsmanship or exclusiveness

That was the scene on Christmas Eve at Lobel's, a pricey Upper East Side butcher shop that is to meat what Tiffany's is to jewelry.
USA Today 2003

Tigger [Child. Lit.] The cheerful bouncy tiger in A. A. Milne's children's book *The House at Pooh Corner* (1928).

> Someone who is irrepressibly cheerful, enthusiastic, or hyperactive; someone who bounces along

In through the door bursts Marlon Devonish—bouncing along like Tigger and leaping onto the leather sofa with a disarming little 'wheeee'.
The Sunday Times 2004

tilt at windmills [Lit.] In a famous episode in *Don Quixote de la Mancha* (1605–15) by Miguel de Cervantes, *Don Quixote mistakes a group of windmills in the distance for giants and proceeds to charge at them on horseback armed with a lance.

> Attack imaginary or unimportant obstacles or enemies

Every crank believes passionately that they are Don Quixote tilting at the windmills of orthodoxy, oppressed by the High Priesthood of Science, so jealous to protect their domain against revolutionary ideas.
www.pandasthumb.org 2004

Timbuctoo (Timbuktu) [Places] A town in northern Mali. It became a Muslim centre of learning and a major trading centre for gold and salt on the trans-Saharan trade routes.

> A distant or remote place

And he yelled at us to get out of the station before he kicked our arses to Timbuctoo.
CHRISTOPHER HOPE *Darkest England* 1996

Tinker Bell (Tinkerbell) [Child. Lit.] In J. M. Barrie's play *Peter Pan (first performed in 1904), a fairy and a friend of Peter's. It is said in the play that every time someone says that they do not believe in fairies, a fairy dies. When Tinker Bell herself is close to death, members of the audience are invited to clap their hands to show that they do believe in fairies, and thus save Tinker Bell's life.

> Someone of diminutive size; mentioned in the context of people's belief in something being necessary for its survival

She wondered about it. But only for a second. The lorries from W Crisp were due in an hour to take away one hundred thousand. She looked at herself backed by all this moving product. A small, a fragile, young thing achieving, magnifying. Tinkerbell with a mobile phone.
MICHAEL CARSON *Dying in Style* 1998

'I call it the Tinkerbell phenomenon,' says Liroff. 'If everyone believes Tinkerbell can fly, this whole media economy will work. But if there are too many doubters, and Tinkerbell has a hard time getting off the ground, the question becomes: what drives the media economy?'
Columbia Journalism Review 2005

Tin Man (Tin Woodman) [Child. Lit.; Cin.] In L. Frank Baum's children's story *The *Wizard of Oz* (1900), the Tin Woodman is one of *Dorothy's companions on her journey to find Oz. When Dorothy and the *Scarecrow first meet the Tin Woodman, he is frozen in position, having been caught in the rain while chopping wood. He is freed by Dorothy, who locates his oil can and oils his joints. The Tin Woodman is now more popularly known as the Tin Man, as the character was called in the 1939 film of the book starring Judy Garland.

➤ Someone who is unable to move or does so with great difficulty

He stood from a crouched position, his knees cracking as he rose. He and the Tin Man—they needed oil.
FAYE KELLERMAN *Sanctuary* 1994

I froze. I understand now why rape victims say that they didn't do anything—you know, scream or try to fight the man off—because I seized up like the Tin Man in *The Wizard of Oz*.
LAURA WILSON *Dying Voices* 2000

Tin Pan Alley [Places] The name given to a district in New York (28th Street, between 5th Avenue and Broadway) where many songwriters, arrangers, and publishers of popular music were based. The district gave its name to the American popular music industry between the late 1880s and the mid 20th century.

➤ Mentioned in the context of songwriters or composers of popular music

Tiresias [Gk Myth.] A blind soothsayer from Thebes who was renowned for his wisdom. According to some legends, he spent seven years as a woman. When asked by *Zeus and *Hera to settle an argument as to who derives more pleasure from love-making, the man or the woman, he answered that a man gives more pleasure than he receives. Hera punished him for this answer with blindness, but Zeus gave him the gift of prophecy in compensation.

➤ A blind person, especially someone who is wise or can foretell the future; someone who has changed sex

The eyes of Lucian Freud's sitters as they stare out from his pictures suggest that, like the blind Tiresias, they 'have foresuffered all'.
New York Review of Books 1993

Titans [Gk Myth.] The older gods who preceded the Olympians and were the children of Uranus (Heaven) and Gaia (Earth). They rebelled against and overthrew Uranus and were in turn defeated by their own children, the Olympians, led by *Zeus.

➤ Someone of very great strength and size

However thin and bedraggled he had become since he had gone to the front, Velisarios was still the biggest man that anyone had ever seen, and Carlo, despite his equivalent experiences on the other side of the line, was also the biggest man that anyone had ever seen. Both of these Titans had become accustomed to the saddening suspicion within themselves that they were freaks.
LOUIS DE BERNIÈRES *Captain Corelli's Mandolin* 1994

Titania [Shakes.] In *A Midsummer Night's Dream* (1600), the queen of the fairies, and wife of Oberon. While she sleeps in her 'flow'ry bed', Oberon drops on her eyelids the juice from a magic flower which will make her fall in love with the first creature she sees when she wakes. This turns out to be Bottom the weaver, who has been given an ass's head by the mischievous sprite *Puck.

> A sleeping woman

She lay curled up on the sofa in the back drawing-room in Harley Street, looking very lovely in her white muslin and blue ribbons. If Titania had ever been dressed in white muslin and blue ribbons, and had fallen asleep on a crimson damask sofa in a back drawing-room, Edith might have been taken for her.
ELIZABETH GASKELL *North and South* 1854–5

Titanic [Hist.] A British passenger liner which was claimed to be unsinkable. On her maiden voyage in 1912, the ship struck an iceberg in the North Atlantic and sank with the loss of 1490 lives. The scale of the loss of life, mainly men, was a consequence of the over-confidence of the owners of the liner, the White Star Line. The company was so sure of the ship's design and engineering they provided only a few lifeboats, believing that they would never be needed.

> Mentioned in the context of an unavoidable disaster, especially one befalling something supposedly indestructible

Jane Collingswood looked at Rachel for a second, then said, 'I think you're being very brave. I don't know how I'd hold up if I were in your shoes.' I did. Jane Collingswood could survive the sinking of the *Titanic*.
STEVEN WOMACK *Dead Folks' Blues* 1992

My guest tonight says the American economy is like the Titanic headed toward an iceberg.
CNN transcripts: Lou Dobbs Tonight 2005

Tithonus [Gk Myth.] A Trojan prince who was so beautiful that the goddess *Aurora fell in love with him. She asked *Zeus to grant him immortality but forgot to ask for eternal youth, and he became very old and decrepit although he talked perpetually. Tithonus pleaded with Aurora to remove him from this world and she changed him into a grasshopper.

> A once-beautiful man who becomes incapacitated by age or infirmity

Titian (Tiziano Vecellio) [Art] (1477–1576) A Venetian painter and one of the greatest artists of the high Renaissance. Titian is known particularly for his sumptuous mythological works, such as *Bacchus and *Ariadne* (1522–3) and *Diana Surprised by *Actaeon* (1556–9), noted for their brilliant colours, especially glowing reds and deep blues.

> Used to describe a woman with bright auburn hair

It was all getting a bit Mills & Boon. Titian-haired, finely-chiselled English widow lady meets craggily handsome (in the dark) Scots journalist in romantic Ligurian location.
Sunday Herald 2002

Tityus [Gk Myth.] A giant who was punished with eternal torture in the underworld for attempting to rape Leto, the mother of *Apollo and *Artemis. Vultures continually devoured his liver.

> Someone who suffers an ongoing torment

Toad, Mr [Child. Lit.] In Kenneth Grahame's story for children *The Wind in the Willows* (1908), Mr Toad of Toad Hall is passionately devoted in turn to boats, gypsy caravans, and then the motorcar. He buys 'a shiny new motor-car, of great size, painted a bright red (Toad's favourite colour)'. Because of his inability to resist the lure of fast driving, Badger and Rat take his car and try to keep him off the road, deeming him unsafe, but he steals a car and sets off again.

> Someone susceptible to fads; someone who enjoys driving fast

Crouching over the wheel, a cross between Jehu and Mr Toad of Toad Hall, Crosby bent his mind to covering the distance, while Detective Inspector Sloan addressed himself over the car radio to every police officer in 'F' division.
CATHERINE AIRD *After Effects* 1996

A few months ago he would have been hunched forward on one of the straight-backed dining chairs, glued to the screen of his computer. But Norman, like Mr Toad, flits in and out of hobbies, changing corresponding identities with a fickleness that belies his constancy when it comes to the two things that matter to him: money and friends.
PAUL BENNETT *False Profits* 1998

Todd, Sweeney [Lit.] A fictional barber who murdered his customers with a razor and then had his lover serve up the remains in a meat pie. He was the central character in several plays by George Dibdin Pitt (1799–1855), including *Sweeney Todd: The Demon Barber of Fleet Street.*

> A barber, especially a disreputable one

Men and women now walk through the doors for everything from a crew-cut to dreadlocks—all in surroundings more akin to Sweeney Todd than Nicky Clarke.
Yorkshire Post Today 2001

Tolkien, J. R. R. [Lit.] (1892–1973) The author of fantasy novels such as *The *Hobbit* (1937) and the *Lord of the Rings* trilogy (1954–5). The climax of the latter takes place in the hostile, mountainous land of Mordor.

> Mentioned in the context of fantasy literature or forbidding mountain landscapes (adjective *Tolkienesque*)

Next day I leave the interminable flatness of the Patagonian plain behind, for the mountains of Tierra del Fuego, which, as the plane drops out from thick cloud, looks like something out of a Tolkien novel.
Sunday Herald 2000

Tom Brown's Schooldays [Lit.] The title of a novel (1857) by Thomas Hughes, which recounts the adventures of a boy at Rugby School in the 1830s. Tom is bullied during his first year there by an older boy called Flashman.

> Used to evoke life at a traditional English public school in former times, especially with reference to corporal punishment

We all knew the punishment for being a 16-year-old caught in possession of strong drink—a severe caning by the Captain of the House, in front of all the senior prefects, or possibly, for a second offence, 'a flogging from the head man'—six strokes of a birch rod wielded with some ferocity by the headmaster. If this all sounds like something out of Tom Brown's Schooldays, then I dare say life was a bit like that at an independent school in those distant days.
Scotland on Sunday 2002

Tom Thumb [Leg. & Folk.] The hero of an English folk tale, the son of a ploughman and his wife who was only as tall as his father's thumb. After many adventures he was knighted by King *Arthur. General Tom Thumb was the name given to Charles Stratton (1838–83), an American midget exhibited in the *Barnum and Bailey shows.

> Someone of diminutive stature

The arenas are a good size, which is not bad, but when your character is Tom Thumb proportions you spend 80% of your time trying to figure out where you are (unless you want to sit really close to your TV).
www.armchairempire.com 2004

Tonto [Radio; TV] The trusty Native American companion and friend of the masked law-enforcer the *Lone Ranger in the radio and television series *The Lone Ranger* (1956–62).

> A close companion or sidekick

Come on Mark. The days of the Lone Ranger are far behind. Everybody needs their Tonto.
MEL STEIN *White Lines* 1997

Tophet [Bible] The name of a place in the Valley of *Hinnom to the south of Jerusalem. Hinnom was known as the Valley of Slaughter (Jer. 7: 31–2), and was used for idolatrous worship, with children being burnt alive as sacrifices to the idol *Moloch. Later Tophet was used for burning refuse, and bonfires were kept burning there for this purpose. Hence there is a strong association between the name and the fires of Hell.

> A way of referring to the fires of Hell

It seemed the great Black Parliament sitting in Tophet. A hundred black faces turned round in their rows to peer; and beyond, a black Angel of Doom was beating a book in a pulpit.
HERMAN MELVILLE *Moby Dick* 1851

Topsy [Lit.] The mischievous little black slave girl in Harriet Beecher Stowe's novel *Uncle Tom's Cabin* (1852), whose 'woolly hair was braided in sundry little tails, which stuck out in every direction'. She has been kept in complete ignorance by her owners, and knows nothing about her family. When asked who she is and who were her parents, Topsy replies, 'Never was born, never had no father, nor mother, nor nothin'. I 'spect I grow'd. Don't think nobody never made me.'

> Something that seems to have grown of its own accord, without being planned or directed

Up to that time the drilling industry had grown a little like Topsy. There were no standards for any of the equipment.
The Chronicle of the Early American Industries Association, Inc. 2000

Torquemada, Tomás de [Hist.] (1420–98) A Dominican monk and the first inquisitor-general of Spain, remembered for his pitiless cruelty.

> Someone who questions a person or investigates a matter persistently and rigorously

He brought up Rosemary's loss of faith almost at once, and at every subsequent opportunity thereafter. He was very dissatisfied with Rosemary's explanation that 'it just went', but he failed to get much more out of her. He clearly had ambitions to be a Torquemada, without any of the necessary skills.
ROBERT BARNARD *The Bad Samaritan* 1995

Practically every invoice led to an inquiry worthy of Torquemada.
Sunday Business Post 2003

tortoise [Lit.] *Aesop's fable 'The *Hare and the Tortoise' relates how a hare, jeering at the slow pace of a tortoise, challenged the latter to a race. On the day of the race the hare, confident of his greater speed, lay down to rest and fell asleep. The tortoise plodded on and won the race, leading to the moral that *'Slow but steady wins the race'.

> Someone who makes slow progress but shows patient perseverance

So long, India has been the proverbial tortoise to China's hare when it came to economic growth. Maybe, now the tortoise is all set to overtake the hare.
India First Foundation 2004

Toulouse-Lautrec, Henri Marie Raymonde de [Art] (1864–1901) A French painter and lithographer. His reputation largely rests on his colour lithographs from the 1890s depicting scenes of Parisian low life, actors, music hall singers, circus artists, prostitutes, and waitresses in Montmartre. The Moulin Rouge series of posters (1894) is particularly well known. Toulouse-Lautrec's work is characterized by strong silhouettes, large areas of flat garish colour, and theatrical lighting. The artist broke both his legs in childhood, as a result of which he was stunted in growth.

> Someone of diminutive stature; used to evoke a scene of bohemian Parisian night life

There's an unmarked route between the front bar and the back bar which is like a seaside promenade. Women sit along it. Men stroll up and down strutting their stuff and surveying the scene. It's a bit like whores in a Toulouse Lautrec brothel.
intheaquarium.blogspot.com 2005

Tower Hill [Places] The scaffold on Tower Hill was the place where traitors imprisoned in the *Tower of London, often high-ranking state prisoners, were executed by beheading. The first such execution there was in 1388 and the last in 1747, though the site was also used for public hangings until 1783.

> A place of execution

His execution was a hole-and-corner affair. There was no high scaffolding, no scarlet cloth (did they have scarlet cloth on Tower Hill? They should have had), no awe-stricken multitude to be horrified at his guilt and be moved to tears at his fate—no air of sombre retribution.
JOSEPH CONRAD *Lord Jim* 1900

Tower of Babel [Bible] According to the book of Genesis, the descendants of *Noah decided to build a city and a tower, the Tower of Babel, 'whose top may reach unto heaven'. On seeing the tower, God was concerned that man was becoming too powerful and so decided to thwart him by introducing different languages. Having caused the people to be mutually incomprehensible, God then dispersed and scattered them.

> Mentioned in the context of linguistic diversity, particularly when this severely hampers communication; a confused noise of many voices; a lofty structure

'This is the original Tower of Babel,' Harris said. 'West Indians, Africans, real Indians, Syrians, Englishmen, Scotsmen in the office of Works, Irish priests, French priests, Alsatian priests.'
GRAHAM GREENE *The Heart of the Matter* 1948

Tower of London [Places] A fortress in central London, built by William the Conqueror, used as a royal residence and later as a state prison. Famous prisoners include Thomas More, Anne Boleyn, Sir Walter Raleigh, Guy *Fawkes, and Rudolf Hess. *See also* PRINCES IN THE TOWER.

> Mentioned (especially in the phrase 'sent to the Tower (of London)') in the context of treasonable acts, especially committing an offence against the Royal family

He continued by explaining how, in the first round of this event, he had run the risk of being sent to the Tower of London for lèse-majesté when he went over to Prince Andrew, stuck out his hand and said: 'Hi, I'm Skip Kendall.'
The Times 2004

Tower of Siloam [Bible] In the Gospel of St Luke, *Jesus tells the story of the collapse of the Tower of Siloam, which killed eighteen people, saying that we should not assume that because these eighteen suffered this fate they were more wicked than others. 'Or those eighteen, upon whom the tower in Siloam fell, and slew them, think ye that they were sinners above all men that dwelt in Jerusalem? I tell you, Nay: but, except ye repent, ye shall all likewise perish' (Luke 13: 14-15).

> ➤ Mentioned in the context of the randomness of human suffering or tragedy, which can befall the virtuous and sinful alike
>
> How did their household differ from that of any other clergyman of the better sort from one end of England to the other? Why then should it have been upon them, of all people in the world, that this tower of Siloam had fallen?
> SAMUEL BUTLER *The Way of All Flesh* 1903

town mouse and country mouse [Lit.] In *Aesop's fable 'The Town Mouse and the Country Mouse', the town mouse visits the country mouse and is unimpressed by the food that he has to offer. He invites the country mouse to visit him in town and the country mouse is amazed at the quality and variety of the food available. But they are interrupted by people and have to flee, terrified. Eventually the country mouse retires back to the country where the food might be plain but at least he can eat it in safety.

> ➤ Referring to a town-dweller unfamiliar with country life and a country-dweller unfamiliar with urban life
>
> But now those old feelings were rising to the surface again, the feelings of inadequacy, of being the country mouse, the poor relation, the social misfit, the butt of someone's joke.
> LISA JEWELL *Ralph's Party* 1999
>
> In fact this year I've been to theatre more than in the whole of last year. It's been a conscious decision, mind you, to act like a town mouse a bit more.
> *www.overyourhead.co.uk* (weblog) 2002

Tracy, Dick [Cart. & Com.] One of the first American comic-strip detectives, drawn by Chester Gould and first appearing in 1931. Tracy joins forces with the police to find the criminals who have kidnapped his girlfriend and murdered her father, and goes on to become a tireless fighter for justice, pursuing criminals at great risk to himself.

> ➤ A detective
>
> The work I do for nonprofits is limited to writing the occasional check. Anyway, I never wanted to be Dick Tracy, running around town with a gun.
> SARA PARETSKY *Tunnel Vision* 1994

Trafalgar [Hist.] The Battle of Trafalgar, one of the decisive naval battles of the Napoleonic Wars, was fought on 21 October 1805 off the Cape of Trafalgar on the south coast of Spain. The British fleet under *Nelson won a victory over the combined fleets of France and Spain, and *Napoleon was never again able to mount a serious threat to British naval supremacy. Nelson was killed during the battle.

> ➤ A sea battle

Trail of Tears [Hist.] The forced removal, in 1838-9, of the Cherokee people from their homeland. They were forced to march from Georgia to new homes in Oklahoma, and about 4000 died on the journey.

> ➤ The forced relocation of a people; an ordeal endured by a people or group

Maybe the day will come when some folks won't wince when a story makes light of concentration camps or plays around with the phrase 'Trail of Tears'.
www.poynter.org 2005

Tree of Knowledge [Bible] According to the book of Genesis, the Tree of Knowledge of good and evil grew in the Garden of *Eden and bore the forbidden fruit which *Eve was tempted by the *Serpent to eat. She then persuaded *Adam to do the same. 'Then the eyes of both were opened, and they knew that they were naked' (Gen. 3: 6-7).

> ➤ To 'eat from the Tree of Knowledge' is to obtain knowledge at the cost of a loss of innocence

I do not actually remember the curtains of my room being touched by the summer wind although I am sure they were; whenever I try to bring to mind this detail of the afternoon sensations it disappears, and I have knowledge of the image only as one who has swallowed some fruit of the Tree of Knowledge—its memory is usurped by the window of Mrs Van der Merwe's house and by the curtains disturbed, in the rainy season, by a trifling wind, unreasonably meaning a storm.
MURIEL SPARK 'The Curtain Blows by the Breeze' in *The Collected Stories* 1961

triffids [Lit.] In the science fiction novel *The Day of the Triffids* (1951) by John Wyndham, the triffids are a race of predatory plants which are capable of growing to a gigantic size and possess locomotive ability and a poisonous sting.

> ➤ Plants showing vigorous growth; anything showing invasive and rapid development

A hoarder by nature, he let piles of papers grow unfettered like Triffids, until there was no way in or out of his house.
Scotland on Sunday 2002

Tripps, Captain [Lit.] The name given to a deadly flu virus which is accidentally released from a laboratory in Stephen King's science fiction novel *The Stand* (1978), killing over 90 per cent of the population. The book was made into a successful film in 1994.

> ➤ A devastating plague or epidemic

A plague: the American version of the Black Death, an antiquated form of Captain Tripps, killing two out of every three people. The survivors abandoning a desolated community, carting thousands and thousands of dead bodies with them? Not bloody likely.
NEVADA BARR *Mountain of Bones* 1995

Tristram (Tristan, Tristrem) and Iseult (Isolde) [Leg. & Folk.] In the medieval legend, Tristram is sent to seek the hand of Iseult on behalf of his uncle King Mark of Cornwall. During the voyage in which Tristram escorts Iseult to Cornwall, the couple mistakenly drink a love potion which had been intended for Iseult and Mark on their wedding night. Tristram and Iseult fall hopelessly in love, although Iseult is contracted to marry Mark. In one version of the story, King Mark finds the pair lying in the forest with a sword between them. In another version, Tristram marries another woman but, when dying, sends for Iseult. He arranges a signal from the boat in which she would be travelling to let him know whether she is on board. If she is, a white flag will be flown; a black flag will be flown if she is not. When the boat arrives, the white flag is flying, but his wife tells him it is black and he dies in despair, believing that Iseult has not come. The relationship is the subject of *Wagner's opera *Tristan and Isolde*, which ends after Tristan has died in Isolde's arms.

> ➤ Tragic lovers

I longed to sleep with her, I longed to be joined to her. But always my dreadful secret lay between us, like the sword between Tristan and Isolde.
JOHN FOWLES *The Magus* 1966

Passion is destructive. It destroyed Antony and Cleopatra, Tristan and Isolde.
W. SOMERSET MAUGHAM *The Razor's Edge* 1944

Triton [Gk Myth.] The son of *Poseidon and Amphitrite. He was half-man and half-fish, having a fish's tail and usually holding a trident and a shell-trumpet.

➤ A person connected with or at home in the sea

Sometimes diving under her and emerging the other side, spouting water like a Triton.
PATRICK O'BRIAN *Treason's Harbour* 1983

Troilus and Cressida [Gk Myth.; Lit.] Lovers whose story is set against the background of the *Trojan War, the main characters in *Chaucer's *Troilus and Criseyde* (c.1385) and *Shakespeare's play *Troilus and Cressida* (1609). Troilus, a son of the Trojan king Priam, falls in love with Cressida, and she is persuaded to start a love affair with him by Pandarus, her uncle. Cressida is then required to move to the Greek camp, either because her father has defected to the Greeks or as part of the war negotiations. Once in the Greek camp, she betrays Troilus by falling in love with the Greek commander, Diomedes.

➤ Tragic lovers; mentioned in the context of a man forsaken by his lover

'Troilus loved and was fooled,' said the more manly chaplain. 'A man may love and yet not be a Troilus. All women are not Cressids.'
ANTHONY TROLLOPE *Barchester Towers* 1857

Trojan Horse [Gk Myth.] A device (also known as the Wooden Horse of Troy) used by the Greeks after the death of Achilles to capture the city of Troy. The Greek craftsman Epeius constructed a large wooden horse and left it outside the walls of the city. The Greeks then sailed out of sight, leaving behind just one man, Sinon, who pretended to be a Greek deserter. Sinon reported to the Trojans that the horse was an offering to *Athene, which, if brought within the city walls, would render Troy impregnable. The horse was in fact full of Greek soldiers, and once it had been brought into Troy and night had fallen, these soldiers came out and took the city.

➤ A person or thing that is insinuated into a place to secretly overthrow an enemy or to undermine something from within

New Urbanists often say that nostalgia is the Trojan Horse in which they deliver their radical planning ideas: small lots, mixed use, limited parking.
Design Observer 2005

Trojans [Hist.] The inhabitants of ancient Troy, who had a reputation for working hard without complaining.

➤ Someone working with great energy or endurance

And before long he was weeding away by moonlight like a Trojan—just as though the garden were his own and no danger threatened him within a thousand miles.
HUGH LOFTING *Dr Dolittle's Circus* 1924

Trojan War [Gk Myth.] The legendary Trojan War is described in *Homer's *Iliad*. It took place when Agamemnon put together a fighting force of Greeks to travel to Troy and recover Menelaus' wife *Helen, who had been abducted by *Paris. The first nine years of the war were taken up by a siege of the city of Troy. After the Trojans drove the Greeks back to the shore, there was a period of fighting; then the Greeks devised the ruse of the *Trojan Horse, which enabled them to enter and take the city. Troy was sacked and razed by fire. Many of the incidents and characters who are associated with the Trojan War are covered in more detail in other entries in this book.

> A lengthy conflict

Max had got into conversation with a Welshman about some detail of trade union politics that sounded as complicated as the Trojan war and would probably go on as long. GILLIAN LINSCOTT *Blood on the Wood* 2003

Tuck, Friar [Leg. & Folk.] The jolly, rotund friar who forms part of *Robin Hood's band of outlaws in the legend of Robin Hood.

> A large, plump person; someone with a tonsure-like bare patch on the top of their head

Rosie is about eighteen inches long, she has got a big head with fuzzy black hair in a Friar Tuck style. SUE TOWNSEND *The Growing Pains of Adrian Mole Aged 13³/4* 1984

tumbril [Hist.] An open cart that tilted backwards to empty out its load, in particular one used to convey condemned prisoners to the guillotine during the French Revolution.

> Mentioned to suggest the idea of someone being carried to a place of execution

Flush with Lieberman's defeat, Michael Moore, the left-wing film-maker, warned that the tumbrils would keep rolling. *Sunday Times* 2006

Turner, Joseph Mallord William [Art] (1775–1851) An English landscape painter who became interested in capturing the effects of atmospheric light in his pictures. His best-known paintings, such as *The Fighting Téméraire* (1838), depict dramatic skies using yellows, oranges, and reds in an impressionistic style.

> Used to evoke a scene of swirling light and colours, especially a sunset or sunrise (adjective *Turneresque*)

As we skim through the mangroves, a Turneresque dawn breaks, and fat pink clouds pummel the tepui like boxing gloves. *The Sunday Times* 2006

Turpin, Dick [Crime] (1705–35) A famous English highwayman who started his career as a smuggler and cattle- and horse-thief. He was hanged at York for horse-stealing and murder. According to legend, his escapades included a dramatic ride from London to York on his horse Black Bess.

> Used to suggest the idea of 'daylight robbery'

Keighley returned from their short trip to Brighouse convinced they had been refereed by Dick Turpin. The official's leanings towards the home side prevented the Cats from claiming a deserved victory. *www.thisisbradford.co.uk* 2003

Tussaud, Madame [People] (1761–1850) The French founder of Madame Tussaud's waxworks, resident in Britain from 1802. She took death masks in wax of prominent victims of the French Revolution and later toured Britain with her wax models. In 1835 she founded a permanent waxworks exhibition in Baker Street, London.

> Mentioned in the context of waxworks, or people who have the appearance of waxworks

With his leathery skin and botoxic features, he appears to have been the victim of a terrible mix-up at Madame Tussaud's, as if they accidentally re-sculpted the actor to look more like his waxwork. *Eye Weekly* 2004

Tutankhamun [Hist.] The tomb of Tutankhamun, in the Valley of the Kings in Egypt, was discovered by Howard Carter (1874–1939) and the earl of Carnarvon (1866–1923) in

November 1922. Carnarvon died in Luxor shortly after the discovery from a mosquito bite which led to a blood infection and pneumonia. Carter died seventeen years later but before he was able to provide a final report on the find, having spent the intervening years conserving the contents of the tomb and sending them to the Cairo Museum. The association of the two deaths gave rise to a popular tradition that the tomb was cursed.

> ➤ A place discovered to be full of treasures; also mentioned in the context of a curse
>
> When Darger died soon after, the landlord braced himself for the job of cleaning out Darger's apartment. Lerner was, of course, entirely unaware that he was about to enter the Tutankhamun's Tomb of modern art.
> *toffeewomble.blogspot.com* 2005

Tutu, Desmond [Rel.; Hist.] (b. 1931) A South African clergyman. He served as general secretary of the South African Council of Churches in 1979–84, and during this time he became a leading figure in the struggle against the country's apartheid policies, advocating non-violent opposition. He was awarded the Nobel Peace Prize in 1984. Tutu became Johannesburg's first black Anglican bishop in 1985 and was archbishop of Cape Town from 1986 to 1996, when he retired. He was made head of the Truth and Reconciliation Commission in 1995.

> ➤ A peacemaker; someone who facilitates reconciliation between opposing sides
>
> And I'm telling you, when Bacon gets hold of something, things happen. He's not Martin Luther King or Bishop Tutu. Okay? He's not gonna win any Nobel Prize. He's got his own way of doing things, and sometimes it might not stand close scrutiny.
> TOM WOLFE *The Bonfire of the Vanities* 1987

Tweedledum and Tweedledee [Child. Lit.] Originally names applied to the rival composers Handel and Bononcini in a 1725 satirical poem by John Byrom, making the point that the differences between them were so small as to be negligible. The names were later popularized when Lewis Carroll used them for two identical characters in *Through the Looking-Glass* (1872). They are fat, quarrelsome twin brothers who fight a ridiculous battle with one another.

> ➤ Two people or things that are so alike that they are practically indistinguishable
>
> Economically, the two main parties in Britain are Tweedledum and Tweedledee.
> *The Ecologist* 2001

Twiggy [People] (b. Lesley Hornby 1949) An English fashion model of the 1960s. She began her modelling career in 1966, becoming famous for her short-haired, thin-bodied boyish look. Twiggy later appeared in films such as *The Boyfriend* (1971) and *The Blues Brothers* (1980).

> ➤ A skinny woman or girl
>
> He looked over at waiflike Louise, a Twiggy lookalike with her cropped hair and miniskirt.
> EILEEN GOUDGE *Such Devoted Sisters* 1992

Twilight Zone, The [TV] An American television series (1959–65) that told a different supernatural or science fiction story every week.

> ➤ Mentioned (sometimes with reference to the series' theme music) in the context of a seemingly supernatural occurrence or a highly improbable coincidence
>
> And in a moment, I am left standing alone on the street. As I am prone to doing with or without an audience, I put on the expression of one who has been totally weirded-out by one too many light, if entertaining, encounters with the terminally demented, music from the Twilight Zone playing through my head.
> *stairs.happenchance.com (blog)* 2003

Twist, Oliver [Lit.] In Charles Dickens's novel *Oliver Twist* (1837–8), Oliver is born a pauper in a workhouse and suffers the cruel and restrictive conditions of the regime under the parish beadle, Mr *Bumble. Inadequately fed, he infuriates the authorities by asking for more food. He later runs away to London, where he falls into the hands of a gang of pickpockets led by *Fagin.

➤ A poor, hungry boy; someone asking for more

Poor Davey! How you have starved! A real little work-house boy, an Oliver Twist of the spirit!
ROBERTSON DAVIES *The Manticore* 1972

The parliament will fuel high expectations that cannot be met under the Government's current spending plans. Scots would pretty soon come to see London as a hindrance and would act like little Oliver Twists, asking for more and more.
The Observer 1997

Tyburn [Places] A place in London, near Marble Arch, where public hangings were held from 1388 to 1783. The triangular gallows there were often referred to as Tyburn Tree.

➤ Used to refer to public execution, especially hanging

She didn't deserve to die. Perhaps none of us do, not like that. We don't even hang the Whistler now. We've learned something since Tyburn, since Agnes Poley's burning.
P. D. JAMES *Devices and Desires* 1989

Typhoid Mary [People] The name given to **Mary Mallon** (d. 1938), an Irish-born American cook who transmitted typhoid fever in the United States.

➤ Someone whose presence can instantly empty a place of people, or whom nobody wants to know or be near

Archie Young looked round the canteen which was almost empty, all the tables near them had cleared with speed. It was like being Typhoid Mary, he thought.
GWENDOLINE BUTLER *The Coffin Tree* 1994

Tyr [Norse Myth.] The god of battle, corresponding to the Roman *Mars.

➤ A way of referring to war

Udolpho [Lit.] Ann Radcliffe's *The Mysteries of Udolpho* (1794) is a Gothic novel set at the end of the 16th century. Most of the action takes place in the sinister castle of Udolpho in which the sliding panels, secret passages, and apparently supernatural occurrences are all typical of the genre.

➢ Suggesting a place in which mysterious, supernatural, and sinister activities occur

Was there a 'secret' at Bly—a mystery of Udolpho or an insane, an unmentionable relative kept in unsuspected confinement?
HENRY JAMES *The Turn of the Screw* 1898

'Ugly Duckling, The' [Fairy tales] In Hans Christian *Andersen's story (1846), a cygnet in a brood of ducklings is mocked by the other ducks and hens for his drab appearance. He runs away, struggles through the winter, and in the spring meets three swans. Looking at his reflection in the water, he discovers that he too has turned into a beautiful swan.

➢ An ugly person, or a person initially thought ugly who turns out to be extremely beautiful

She was a fairy princess who had taken a fancy to a little boy, clothed him, petted him, turned him from a laughing stock into an accepted member of her society, from an ugly duckling into a swan.
L. P. HARTLEY *The Go-Between* 1953

Ugly Sisters [Fairy tales] In the children's story, Cinderella has two ugly stepsisters who despise and ill-treat her. The stepsisters are invited to the prince's ball and spend days fussing over what they are going to wear to the ball and how beautiful they are going to look. In pantomime versions of the tale, the stepsisters are presented as the Ugly Sisters, played by men, and made grotesquely ugly so that their vanity becomes ridiculous and comical.

➢ A person or thing thought of as unattractive, unpleasant, or inferior compared to others of the same group; an unpleasant or undesirable counterpart

Between 1886 and 1895 some 300 photographs were taken of its inpatients. At that time, evolution and its ugly sister, eugenics, were on the rise, and one can only speculate on the purpose of these images (though they were probably used for teaching).
British Medical Journal 2003

Ultima Thule [Places] Thule was a land first described by the ancient Greek explorer Pytheas as being six days' sail north of Britain, thought to be Iceland, Norway, or the Shetland Islands. To the Romans it was the northernmost extremity of the world, described by Virgil as Ultima Thule, literally 'Furthest Thule'.

➢ A distant unknown region; the limit of what is attainable

After a brief crawl he reached the end, striking his head against hard larch, the Ultima Thule of the *Daphne*, beyond which he could hear the water slapping against the hull.
UMBERTO ECO *The Island of the Day Before* 1994

Ulysses [Gk Myth.] The Roman name for *Odysseus.

➢ A wanderer who is far from home; a man who resists the temptations of a seductive woman

Many older and wiser heads have been enmeshed in her toils, and you would do well
to stop your ears with wax, as Ulysses made his sailors do, to escape the Sirens.
MARGARET ATWOOD *Alias Grace* 1996

Uncle Tom [Lit.] A loyal and ever-patient black slave, the main character of Harriet
Beecher Stowe's anti-slavery novel *Uncle Tom's Cabin* (1852).

> ➢ A black man whose behaviour to white people is regarded as submissively servile;
> anyone regarded as betraying his or her cultural or social allegiance

> 'Mary Lou's being modest. She had them rolling in the aisles with her tour de force
> called "Black Studies as a Floating Signifier".' Amiss seized the claret. 'What's the female
> equivalent of an Uncle Tom?'
> RUTH DUDLEY EDWARDS *Matricide at St Martha's* 1994

> I guess I'd worried it'd be full of stereotypes, the gay Uncle Toms we're used to seeing:
> sexless, neutered camp bits of fluff.
> *barbelith.com* 2004

Undine [Leg. & Folk.] A supernatural female being, the spirit of water created by Paracelsus.
She had no soul, but if she married a mortal and bore him a child, she could obtain a soul
along with all the pains of the human race.

> ➢ A woman thought of as resembling a water spirit or nymph

> 'You looked like Undine.' And so she had, with all the brilliant colour of her eyes,
> fern-green and pebble-brown, caught into the sudden light, and the quivering reflections
> of rain upon the window staining the whiteness of her face with greenish gleams.
> EDITH PARGETER *By Firelight* 1948

unkindest cut [Shakes.] A phrase from *Julius Caesar*. It occurs in Mark *Antony's speech
over Caesar's corpse: 'Through this the well-beloved Brutus stabb'd...This was the most
unkindest cut of all.'

> ➢ The most hurtful thing that could be done or said

> Only three episodes left to go and, the unkindest cut of all, HBO has announced that
> there will be no more until 2006.
> *New Zealand Listener* 2004

Uriah (Uriah the Hittite) [Bible] An officer in *David's army, the husband of *Bathsheba.
David slept with Bathsheba, whom he had seen bathing, and when she became pregnant, sent
Uriah to his death in the front line of battle so that he could marry her. Uriah was given a letter
to carry to his commanding officer, Joab, which was in fact Uriah's own death warrant: 'Set
Uriah in the forefront of the hardest fighting, and then draw back from him, that he may
be struck, and die' (2 Sam. 11: 15).

> ➢ Someone whose death is treacherously engineered by a rival

Usher *See* HOUSE OF USHER.

usual suspects *See* ROUND UP THE USUAL SUSPECTS.

Utopia [Lit.] The name (literally 'No-Place') of an imaginary island, governed on a
perfect political and social system, in the book *Utopia* (1516) by Sir Thomas More.

> ➢ An imaginary place or condition of ideal perfection (adjective *Utopian*)

> We got talking about the permissive sexual mores of the ancient Polynesians, which
> Yolande described as 'the kind of sexual Utopia we were all pursuing in the sixties—free
> love and nudity and communal child-rearing'.
> DAVID LODGE *Paradise News* 1992

Vader, Darth [Cin.] The ruthlessly aggressive villain in the film *Star Wars* (1977) and its sequels. Formerly Anakin Skywalker, a Jedi knight who has been corrupted to 'the dark side', Darth Vader is always dressed in black cloak and armour and wears a concealing vizor, through which his deep, heavy-breathing voice can be heard.

> ➤ An evil, ruthless, or menacing character, especially someone whose face is concealed by a mask or helmet; someone who speaks with a deep voice accompanied by heavy breathing
>
> Graham, spray-painting the sidings on the back of the house, clad in protective gear, looking and sounding like Darth Vader taking a day off in the country.
> JOHN BAILEY *Journal of a Writing Man* 2001, weblog

Valhalla [Norse Myth.] The great banqueting hall in Asgard in which heroes who had been slain in battle feasted with *Odin eternally.

> ➤ A place assigned to people worthy of special honour; an earthly paradise
>
> Her pale eyes glittered and her face was deathly pale. With her colourless eyelashes and blonde hair she presented a strange sight, almost like a carved marble head. He thought she looked terrifying, like a Valkyrie come to escort him to some icy-halled Valhalla, whether he wanted to go or not.
> ANN GRANGER *Candle for a Corpse* 1995
>
> Those factors, coupled with MacArthur's penchant for public relations by which he created an image of a lonely hero defending America on a distant shore, permitted MacArthur to occupy a position in the Valhalla of American military figures.
> *Naval War College Review* 2002

Valkyrie [Norse Myth.] One of *Odin's twelve handmaidens (literally 'Choosers of the Slain') who hovered over battlefields, selected the most valiant warriors to die in battle, and escorted them to *Valhalla, the hall of heroes. The Valkyries appear in *Wagner's opera *Die Walküre* (1854–6).

> ➤ A woman who decides someone's fate; a woman present at a battle; sometimes used to refer to a female warrior
>
> Dorothy Thompson seemed to me an overpowering figure in a Wagnerian opera, a Valkyrie, deciding with careless pointing of her spear who should die on the battlefield.
> JOHN HERSEY 'Sinclair Lewis' in *Life Sketches* 1987
>
> Martya ducked the tub aimed at her; the second exploded at Kareen's feet. Muno's attempt to lay down a covering fire for his party's retreat backfired when Enrique dropped to his knees and scrambled away down the hall toward his screaming Valkyriesque protectors.
> LOIS MCMASTER BUJOLD *A Civil Campaign* 1999

Valley of (the Shadow of) Death [Bible; Lit.] The phrases 'the Valley of the Shadow of Death' and 'the Valley of Death' have various literary sources. Psalm 23 contains the lines 'Yea, though I walk through the valley of the shadow of death, I will fear no evil.' In John Bunyan's allegory *The *Pilgrim's Progress*, *Christian passes through the Valley of the

Shadow of Death, with a dangerous bog on one side and a deep ditch on the other, and the mouth of Hell close by. Alfred, Lord Tennyson's poem 'The *Charge of the Light Brigade' (1854) contains the famous refrain

> Into the valley of Death
> Rode the six hundred.

> ➢ Used in the context of approaching death

> I thought I might jump down from the wagon, and run off into the woods; but knew I would not get far, and even if I did, I would then be eaten by the bears and wolves. And I thought, I am riding through the Valley of the Shadow of Death, as it says in the Psalm; and I attempted to fear no evil, but it was very hard, for there was evil in the wagon with me, like a sort of mist.
> MARGARET ATWOOD *Alias Grace* 1996

Valley of Humiliation [Lit.] One of the places that *Christian and Christiana pass through in John Bunyan's allegory *The *Pilgrim's Progress*.

> ➢ To 'enter the Valley of Humiliation' is to be humbled or humiliated

> Melbury had entered the Valley of Humiliation even further than Grace. His spirit seemed broken.
> THOMAS HARDY *The Woodlanders* 1887

Vandals [Hist.] A Germanic people that overran part of Roman Europe in the 4th and 5th centuries AD. Of the various invading peoples of this period (*Goths, Visigoths, *Huns, etc.), it is the Vandals whose name is most closely associated with the idea of mass invasion and wanton destruction.

> ➢ People who wilfully or maliciously destroy something beautiful or worthy of preservation; barbarians

> For too long, Scotland has measured itself against England and contented itself that things aren't so bad. Exiles, ironically, return with their gold with tales of a society and civilisation inhabited by Vandals and Goths.
> *The Observer* 1997

Vanderbilt, Cornelius [People] (1794–1877) A US businessman and philanthropist who amassed a fortune from shipping and railroads. Subsequent generations of his family increased the family wealth and continued his philanthropy.

> ➢ An exceptionally rich person; a member of a wealthy family

> The word 'mural' suggests to most people either the wall spaces of Rockefeller Center or the wealth of a Vanderbilt.
> *American Home* 1936

Van Dyck (Vandyke), Sir Anthony [Art] (1599–1641) A Flemish painter chiefly famous for his portraits of the English aristocracy and royalty, including a number of Charles I. Van Dyck's refined and languidly elegant portrait style determined the course of English portraiture for at least 200 years.

> ➢ Used to suggest a 17th-century portrait of a member of the English aristocracy or royal family

> Well, I see this rather like a portrait by Van Dyck, with a good deal of atmosphere, you know, and a certain gravity, and with a sort of aristocratic distinction.
> W. SOMERSET MAUGHAM *Cakes and Ale* 1930

Van Gogh, Vincent [Art] (1853–90) A Dutch Post-Impressionist painter. The bright colours (especially the vivid yellows) and thick, frenzied, swirling brushwork give his paintings a passionate intensity. Among his best-known works are several studies of sunflowers and landscapes such as *A Starry Night* (1889). Van Gogh suffered from depression, and after a violent quarrel with Gauguin he cut off part of his own ear. He eventually committed suicide. Among his portraits is *Self-Portrait with Bandaged Ear* (1889).

> A great artist; someone who cuts off their own ear; mentioned to suggest a vivid landscape or sky

I went in search of Randolph. He wore a large lint pad pressed to the left side of his head, held in place by a rakishly angled and none-too-clean bandage....he bore a striking resemblance to poor, mad Vincent in that self-portrait made after he had disfigured himself for love.
JOHN BANVILLE *The Book of Evidence* 1989

As a child I would go with my friends to the little woods at Montjean, across fields of wheat as evocative as a Van Gogh.
Boston Review 2003

Varden, Dolly [Lit.] The daughter of Gabriel Varden, who marries Joe Willet, in *Barnaby Rudge* (1841) by Charles Dickens. She is a pretty, lively girl, but somewhat proud and wilful, qualities which she comes to regret.

> A proud or flirtatious young woman

What I needed was not one of those stuck-up Dolly Vardens but a good sensible girl with her head screwed on straight who would do what she was told.
ROBERTSON DAVIES *Fifth Business* 1970

Vashti [Bible] The Old Testament book of *Esther relates how King *Ahasuerus ordered that his wife, Queen Vashti, should come before him, 'But the queen Vashti refused to come at the king's commandment by his chamberlains: therefore was the king very wroth, and his anger burned in him' (Esther 1: 12). As a result of this disobedience, Vashti was banished and the king married Esther in her place.

> A woman who refuses to obey her husband

Rumour, for a wonder, exaggerated little. There threatened in fact, in Grace's case as in thousands, the domestic disaster, old as the hills, which, with more or less variation, made a mourner of Ariadne, a by-word of Vashti, and a corpse of Amy Dudley.
THOMAS HARDY *The Woodlanders* 1887

veil of Isis [Myth.] Isis was an ancient Egyptian nature and fertility goddess, wife and sister of Osiris and mother of Horus. She is usually depicted as a woman with cow's horns, between which was the disc of the sun. Statues of her often carried the inscription 'I am all that is, has been, and shall be, and none among mortals has lifted my veil'.

> The phrase 'to lift the veil of Isis' means to penetrate a great mystery

That Fitzpiers would allow himself to look for a moment on any other creature than Grace filled Melbury with grief and astonishment. In the simple life he had led it had scarcely occurred to him that after marriage a man might be faithless. That he could sweep to the heights of Mrs. Charmond's position, lift the veil of Isis, so to speak, would have amazed Melbury by its audacity if he had not suspected encouragement from that quarter.
THOMAS HARDY *The Woodlanders* 1887

Velázquez, Diego Rodríguez de Silva y [Art] (1599–1660) The foremost Spanish artist of the 17th century. In 1623 he was appointed court painter to Philip IV in Madrid, where he painted many notable portraits of the royal family. He produced several portraits of the king's daughter, the doll-like Infanta Margareta Teresa, including *Las Meninas* (1656), which portrays her with her retinue of maidservants and dwarfs, and *The Infanta Margareta in Blue* (1659).

> Used to suggest a scene reminiscent of Velázquez's court paintings

Style? Why, she had the style of a little princess; if you couldn't see it you had no eye. It was not modern, it was not conscious, it would produce no impression in Broadway; the small, serious damsel, in her stiff little dress, only looked like an Infanta of Velazquez.
HENRY JAMES *Portrait of a Lady* 1881

Venus [Rom. Myth.] The Roman goddess identified with the Greek *Aphrodite, the goddess of beauty, fertility, and sexual love. She was supposed to have been born from the sea-foam, though she is sometimes depicted (as in Botticelli's painting *The Birth of Venus*) emerging from a large seashell. She was the mother of *Eros.

> A beautiful woman; a person emerging from the sea or a shell

She ducked gracefully to slip into the lacy fabric which her mother held above her head. As she rose Venus-like above its folds there was a tap on the door, immediately followed by its tentative opening.
EDITH WHARTON *The Custom of the Country* 1913

Here was beauty. It silenced all comment except that of eager praise. A generation that had admired piquante women, boyish women, ugly, smart, and fascinating women was now confronted by simple beauty, pure and undeniable as that of the young Venus whom the Greeks loved to carve.
STELLA GIBBONS *Cold Comfort Farm* 1932

Venus de Milo [Art] A classical marble statue of the goddess *Aphrodite (*c.*100 BC), now in the Louvre in Paris. The statue, missing its arms, was discovered on the Greek island of Melos in 1820.

> A figure, especially that of a woman, with no arms

T.K. hates LeCroy's defense, but if you can get a .280/.360/.500 season from a catcher making major-league minimum, I don't care if he throws like the Venus de Milo, you put him in pads.
www.strikethree.com 2001

Veronese, Paolo [Art] (*c.*1528–1588) An Italian painter, born in Verona as Paolo Caliari and later named after his birthplace. He specialized in biblical, allegorical, and historical subjects, and is particularly known for his richly coloured feast and banquet scenes such as *The Marriage at Cana* (1562) and *The Feast in the House of Levi* (1573). The latter, originally entitled *The *Last Supper*, was the subject of a trial by the Inquisition, which objected to Veronese's habit of inserting profane details (dogs, soldiers, drunkards, etc.) into his sacred pictures.

> Used to evoke a crowded colourful scene, especially a banquet

Let me set the scene. There were ten of us...at the back of the restaurant, at a long table in a slight alcove—a touch Last Supper after Veronese.
JULIAN BARNES *Talking It Over* 1991

Vespucci, Amerigo [People] (1451–1512) An Italian-born navigator in whose honour the Americas were named. He made two voyages to the New World, in which he discovered the mouth of the Amazon and explored the north-east coast of South America. His distorted and embroidered account of his travels, *Four Voyages*, was published in 1507, and, based on this, the Latin version of his name, 'Americus', was given to the two American continents.

> An explorer

She first reached Wildeve's Patch, as it was called, a plot of land redeemed from the heath, and after long and laborious years brought into cultivation. The man who had discovered that it could be tilled died of the labour: the man who succeeded him in possession ruined himself in fertilizing it. Wildeve came like Amerigo Vespucci and received the honours due to those who had gone before.
THOMAS HARDY *The Return of the Native* 1878

Vesuvius [Places] An active volcano near Naples, in southern Italy. It erupted violently in AD 79, burying the towns of *Pompeii and Herculaneum.

> An eruption of emotion; a person or thing liable to sudden outbursts

A Vesuvius of violence has erupted from the dead center of American life, the executive branch of the government.
The Nation 2003

Via Dolorosa [Places] Latin for 'Sorrowful Way', this is another name for *Jesus Christ's route to *Calvary to be crucified.

> A difficult or distressing experience that has to be borne with fortitude

A national referendum in a country of 60 million is not cost-free. And most importantly, letting the treaty stagger on along a Via Dolorosa of months of rejection is dangerous.
yorkshire-ranter.blogspot.com 2005

Vicar of Bray [Lit.] The subject of an anonymous 18th-century song in which he boasts that he has been able to adapt to the differing religious regimes of, successively, Charles II, James II, William III, Anne, and George I.

> Someone who readily changes their opinions or principles to suit the circumstances

Inevitably, his success had encouraged sniping and his detractors claimed that, amongst political turncoats, he made the Vicar of Bray look like a model of constancy.
MARTIN EDWARDS *Yesterday's Papers* 1994

Victoria, Queen [People] (1819–1901), Queen of the United Kingdom (reigned 1837–1901). The famous line 'We are not amused' is attributed to Queen Victoria in Caroline Holland's *Notebooks of a Spinster Lady* (1919), though whether she actually uttered these words is not at all certain.

> Alluded to in the context of a lack of a sense of humour or an inability to see the funny side of a situation

His smile was wide, about three-quarters of an inch. 'I don't amuse easy,' he said. 'Just like Queen Victoria,' I said.
RAYMOND CHANDLER *The High Window* 1943

Vietnam [Hist.] The Vietnam War was a lengthy conflict between South Vietnam and the communist North Vietnam. The United States became militarily involved on the side of the South in the 1960s, but the war became unpopular and the United States withdrew its troops in 1973 under the presidency of Richard Nixon, ceding victory to the North.

> Used in the context of a worsening disaster from which it is difficult to extricate oneself

Anderson Country is Forgan's Vietnam: she's committed to it and can't get out.
The Independent 1994

Vitus, St [Rel.] (d. *c*.300) A Christian martyr said to have died during the reign of Diocletian. He was the patron of those who suffered from epilepsy and certain nervous disorders, including St Vitus' dance (Sydenham chorea).

> Alluded to in the context of violent physical movement

Not a limb, not a fibre about him was idle; and to have seen his loosely hung frame in full motion, and clattering about the room, you would have thought Saint Vitus himself, that blessed patron of the dance, was figuring before you in person.
WASHINGTON IRVING *The Legend of Sleepy Hollow* 1819–20

Vivien *See* NIMUE.

Vlad the Impaler [Hist.] (*c*.1431–1476) A Romanian prince, remembered as a cruel tyrant, whose punishments included impaling victims on stakes. Because of his legendary cruelty, including rumours that he drank the blood of his victims, he is believed by some to be the inspiration behind the *Dracula legend and Bram Stoker's novel *Dracula* (1879).

> ➤ Someone behaving in a cruel or ruthless manner

> Thousands of words—and calories in Downing Street dinners—have been expended in a vain attempt to work out whether Tony Blair is really the Vlad the Impaler of the public sector or a last-ditch defender of public provision.
> *Sunday Herald* 2001

voice crying in the wilderness (voice in the wilderness) [Bible] A reference to a passage in the Bible in which *John the Baptist, proclaiming the coming of Christ, says, 'I am the voice of one crying in the wilderness'.

> ➤ An individual advocating a course of action or proclaiming a message, who is unheeded; an individual whose opinion is proved to be right despite being ignored or contradicted by others

> Regular readers will know I do not believe the ombudsman made the right decision, because I don't have a problem with borrowers being kept to the deal they signed up for. But I am a lone voice in the wilderness here, because most other commentators are fully behind the ombudsman.
> *Sunday Herald* 2002

Volpone [Lit.] The main character in Ben Jonson's comedy of the same name (printed 1607). Volpone, a childless man, lures potential heirs to his bedside, where he pretends he is about to die imminently. His sidekick, Mosca, persuades each of these suitors that a suitable expensive present will confirm that he is the heir, and Volpone gloats gleefully over the gifts. Eventually Mosca engineers a position in which he can blackmail Volpone. Rather than lose his wealth to him, Volpone confesses to the authorities and the two are punished for their scheme.

> ➤ A cunning schemer or miser

Voltaire [Lit.] (1694–1778) The pseudonym of François-Marie Arouet. A French writer, dramatist, and poet, Voltaire was a leading figure of the Enlightenment. He condemned intolerance and superstition and was an outspoken critic of religious and social institutions, his radical views earning him several periods of imprisonment and banishment.

> ➤ Mentioned in the context of mocking scepticism

> 'Sue, you are terribly cutting when you like to be—a perfect Voltaire!'
> THOMAS HARDY *Jude the Obscure* 1895

Vulcan [Rom. Myth.] The Roman god of fire and metalworking, corresponding to the Greek Hephaestus. He was lame as a result of having interfered in a quarrel between his parents (*Juno and Jupiter). Ugly in appearance, he was married to the most beautiful of the goddesses, *Venus (who had many affairs). He is said to have made Pandora (the first woman on earth), the thunderbolts of *Zeus, and the armour of *Achilles. Vulcan is often depicted at the forge.

> A blacksmith; also mentioned in the context of infidelity or lameness

A Vulcan guarding the flames, he gives us instructions about which doors to keep closed or opened for proper distribution of heat, lays kindling by, discusses qualities of coal, and teaches us how to rake, feed, and bank the fire.

TONI MORRISON *The Bluest Eye* 1970

Wagner, Richard [Mus.] (1813–83) A German composer who developed an operatic genre which he called music drama, combining music, drama, verse, legend, and spectacle. His cycle of four operas known as the *Ring Cycle* (*Das Rheingold, Die Walküre, Siegfried,* and *Götterdämmerung*) are based loosely on ancient German sagas.

> Used to evoke the dramatic music, storms, and strong emotions depicted in Wagner's operas (adjective *Wagnerian*)

The vroom and whoosh of the storm created an atmosphere of Wagnerian drama in a city now almost deserted, the usual late-night ravers keeping their heads down until the tempest blew itself out.
VIVIEN ARMSTRONG *Fly in Amber* 2000

Investors have lost enthusiasm and direction, listless and forlorn actors in a Wagnerian twilight of seemingly endless gloom.
Scotland on Sunday 2002

Waiting for Godot See GODOT.

Waltons, The [TV] A popular US television series (1972–81) based on the life of its creator, Earl Hamner, Jr. Set in a poor area of Virginia during the Depression and the Second World War, the stories, often fairly sentimental, concerned the struggles and trials of a good-natured, honest family. The usual closing sequence, in which each member of the family called goodnight to the others, is much parodied.

> Alluded to in the context of a family that seems just too good to be true

Stewart's early life, I learnt, was rather sweet and Waltons-like. He loved his father and mother. He went to church.
WILLIAM LEITH *The Observer* 1997

Drew Barrymore has pursued all of these paths and yet somehow survived the journey, and a family life that makes the Mansons look like the Waltons.
Scotland on Sunday 2003

Wandering Jew [Leg. & Folk.] In medieval legend, a man condemned to roam the earth until the Day of *Judgement, as a punishment for having taunted Christ on the way to the *Crucifixion, urging him to go faster. In some versions of the legend he is given the name Ahasuerus.

> Someone wandering or travelling restlessly from place to place

He would slouch out, like Cain or the Wandering Jew, as if he had no idea where he was going and no intention of ever coming back.
CHARLES DICKENS *Great Expectations* 1861

But her thoughts soon strayed far from her own personality; and, full of a passionate and indescribable solicitude for one to whom she was not even a name, she went forth into the amplitude of tanned wild around her, restless as Ahasuerus the Jew.
THOMAS HARDY *The Return of the Native* 1880

War and Peace [Lit.] The title of an epic novel (1865–8) by Leo Tolstoy, vast in scope and widely regarded as one of the greatest novels of all time. It deals with the *Napoleonic invasion of Russia and its impact on several aristocratic families.

> ➤ A very long book; a literary masterpiece

> I understand the reasons for the bill. I also understand why its review through the Law and Order Committee needs to be truncated, but why has the bill taken so long to get to the House and deny other parties the ability to look at it as it was presented? In itself, it is hardly a rival for War and Peace; at 7 pages, it would not break one's foot if it were dropped on it.
> *New Zealand Parliamentary Debates* 2004

Warbucks, Daddy [Cart. & Com.] A rich businessman in the American comic strip *Little *Orphan Annie*, who takes care of Annie. As his name suggests, he was originally a munitions manufacturer.

> ➤ A wealthy benefactor

> The law of averages says there is, in your part of the country, a woman of appropriate age who shares your values and isn't looking for a Daddy Warbucks to put a roof over her head, stave off the repo man, or support her children.
> MARGO HOWARD *Slate.com: Dear Prudence* 2001

> The Daddy Warbucks of the sports world got richer on Monday.
> *Crikey.com.au* November 2004

Warshawski, V. I. [Lit.] The Chicago-based private investigator heroine of a series of novels by Sara Paretsky. Feisty, tough, and feminist, she is, in the American tradition, not above breaking the law herself when necessary.

> ➤ A female detective or private investigator

> She knew as well as I that a million people pass through Heathrow every week. That London's a big place. That without a point of contact, not even V. I. Warshawski would have a hope in hell of locating Claire.
> MICHELLE SPRING *Running for Shelter* 1994

Washington, George [Hist.] (1732–99) The first president of the United States, serving from 1789 to 1797. An early biographer of Washington, Mason Weems, recounted a fanciful story of how as a boy, on receiving a new hatchet, he chopped down his father's prized cherry tree. When his father asked how the tree had fallen, Washington was tempted to tell a lie, but then, 'looking at his father with the sweet face of youth brightened with the inexpressible charm of all-conquering truth, he bravely cried out, "I can't tell a lie. I did cut it with my hatchet."'

> ➤ Someone who tells the truth and admits to wrongdoing

> 'You must have looked like George Washington or something.' 'If that was the old darling who never told a lie,' I had to admit, 'well really, not much.'
> JOHN MORTIMER *Rumpole's Return* 1980

wash one's hands [Bible] According to the New Testament, Pontius *Pilate, after questioning *Jesus, could find no basis for a charge against him, but nonetheless gave in to the demands of the Jews that Jesus be crucified: 'When Pilate saw that he could prevail nothing, but that rather a tumult was made, he took water and washed his hands before the multitude, saying, I am innocent of the blood of this just person: see ye to it' (Matt. 27: 24).

> ➤ To 'wash one's hands of something' is to take no further responsibility for it

Members of the local community feel let down by Dempsey. They claim he has washed his hands of the recent decision.
Sunday Business Post 2001

Waterloo [Hist.] The battle between the French on one side and the British under *Wellington, the Dutch, and the Prussians on the other near the village of Waterloo (now in Belgium) in 1815 was the final battle in the Napoleonic Wars and marked the end of *Napoleon's rule in Europe.

> A decisive defeat from which recovery is impossible

As Stephen Fay meticulously details in his volume, *The Collapse of Barings*, the failure of the bank which manages the Queen's personal assets was in effect a Waterloo for British banking.
The Guardian 1996

Wayne, John [Cin.] (1907–79) A US film actor (b. Marion Michael Morrison) nicknamed the Duke and chiefly associated with his roles in such classic westerns as *Stagecoach* (1939), *Red River* (1948), *The Searchers* (1956), and *True Grit* (1969). He was known for his portrayals of tough but honest gunfighters or lawmen.

> A tough, rugged man; someone advocating the use of military force; a cowboy

'Don't threaten me, McGraw,' Thayer growled. John Wayne impersonation.
SARA PARETSKY *Indemnity Only* 1982

A mythical John Wayne America, a land of free, rugged individualists that has been progressively undermined by federal laws and regulations.
The Independent 1996

we are not amused [People] A phrase attributed to Queen *Victoria in Caroline Holland's *Notebooks of a Spinster Lady* (1919). It is not at all certain whether Victoria actually uttered the words.

> Used to express displeasure about a situation; also used when suggesting that someone lacks a sense of humour

We are everywhere advised that suddenly there has been ordained a Big Four in golf, and these designees will lead the field in the Masters this week. We are not amused.
Sports Illustrated: Frank Deford columns 2005

wedding guest *See* ANCIENT MARINER.

Wee Willie Winkie [Nurs. Rhym.] A character who makes sure that all children are in bed and asleep:

> Wee Willie Winkie runs through the town
> Upstairs and downstairs in his night gown,
> Rapping at the window, crying through the lock,
> Are the children all in bed, for it's past eight o'clock?

> Someone wearing a nightgown or nightshirt, a nightcap, and carrying a candle

Candle holders with finger handles—'Wee Willie Winkie' style—are made from clay. These will hold hand-dipped candles the kids make themselves.
Arts and Activities 2000

we few, we happy few [Shakes.] A phrase from *Henry V*. It appears in King Harry's stirring St Crispin's Day address to his men before the Battle of Agincourt:

> And Crispin Crispian shall ne'er go by
> From this day to the ending of the world,

But we in it shall be remembered;
We few, we happy few, we band of brothers;
For he today that sheds his blood with me
Shall be my brother.

➤ Used to refer to a small group of colleagues or a minority

And this 80 per cent represents an even more thumping majority [in favour of ID cards] than is immediately apparent. 50 per cent are strongly in favour, 30 per cent moderately so, with only 5 per cent moderately opposed, and a lonely 6 per cent ('We few, we happy few, we band of brothers') strongly opposed.
The Register 2004

Wellington, duke of [Hist.] (1769–1852) A British soldier and statesman, born Arthur Wellesley, created first duke of Wellington in 1809. His military victories included those against the French during the Peninsular War (1808–14) and in particular the defeat of *Napoleon at the Battle of *Waterloo (1815).

➤ A brilliant military strategist or commander

Well, I don't want to be a soldier, he thought. I know that. So that's out. I just want us to win this war. I guess really good soldiers are really good at very little else, he thought. That's obviously untrue. Look at Napoleon and Wellington. You're very stupid this evening, he thought.
ERNEST HEMINGWAY *For Whom the Bell Tolls* 1941

Wells, H. G. [Lit.] (1866–1946) An English novelist best remembered for his science fiction novels, including *The Time Machine* (1895) and *The War of the Worlds* (1898).

➤ Mentioned in the context of imagining the future or time travel

He'd already established a business in Tehran. Cables, satellites, mobile phones, they were all a dream of the future when he started out, but he anticipated them all. When they were still close Yasmin had described him proudly as 'my own H. G. Wells'.
MEL STEIN *White Lines* 1997

Wendy [Child. Lit.] In J. M. Barrie's *Peter Pan* (1904), Wendy Darling is the girl who is taken with her brothers to the magical *Never-Never Land and offers to become a mother to the Lost Boys there. When the Darling children finally return home, Wendy is allowed to go back once a year to Never-Never Land to do Peter's spring cleaning for him.

➤ An idealized vision of motherhood

Oh, you know, she makes everything seem so snug and homey; she wants to be a dear little Wendy-mother to us all. Not being a Peter Pan myself, I don't like it.
ROBERTSON DAVIES *Tempest-Tost* 1951

we're not in Kansas anymore [Cin.] A line from the 1939 film of L. Frank Baum's children's story *The *Wizard of Oz*. These are *Dorothy's words to her dog when they are transported by a tornado from monochrome Kansas to the Technicolor splendour of *Oz: 'Toto, I have a feeling we're not in Kansas anymore.'

➤ Used when someone realizes that circumstances have radically changed and that things are no longer familiar

Sometimes you read or hear something, and realize that things have changed. You get that 'we're not in Kansas anymore' feeling.
Language Log 2004

Werther [Lit.] In Goethe's romance *The Sorrows of Young Werther* (1774), Werther falls in love with Charlotte, who is betrothed to Albert, and gives himself up to a few weeks' happiness in Albert's absence. Then he tears himself away. Albert and Charlotte are married, and despair gradually comes over Werther, who finally takes his own life.

> Used to describe morbidly sentimental, emotional distress, or suicide (adjective *Wertherian*)

And he went away to dress for dinner, with the air of young Werther on his way to his suicide chamber.
KATE ROSE *Cut to the Quick* 1993

Looking into this doubly reflected film, I am disappointed, though not ashamed, that my cinematic suicide is Wertherian, and when I finally muster the courage to squeeze the trigger, the squib on my temples doesn't even detonate properly, only sparking bloodlessly.
Bright Lights Film Journal 2002

West Side Story [Film] A film musical by Bernstein and Sondheim (1961) which relocates the story of *Romeo and Juliet to 20th-century New York. *Shakespeare's feuding families the Montagues and the Capulets are represented as rival gangs, the Jets and the Sharks. Among several memorable dance sequences featuring fast, aggressive, athletic movements in the film is the 'rumble', danced as a stylized gang fight.

> Mentioned in the context of gang warfare or dancing that mimics a fight

The sweating, red-faced cops in their blue uniforms and white helmets slashed the hot night air with their long white billies as though dancing a cop's version of West Side Story.
CHESTER HIMES *Blind Man with a Pistol* 1969

'Oh I know, princess. But a little word to the wise, you're on my turf now.' 'What is this, "West Side Story"? I can't believe you just said turf!'
www.fictionpress.com 2005

whiff of grapeshot [Hist.] In October 1795, during the later stages of the French Revolution, the young Napoleon *Bonaparte dispersed a mob of royalist insurrectionists on the streets of Paris with what the 19th-century historian Thomas Carlyle later described as 'a whiff of grapeshot', that is, by firing cannons at them.

> A show of force

The revolutionaries who were to transform the Labour Party surrendered at the first whiff of grapeshot.
Socialist Review 2005

white cliffs of Dover [Places] The chalk cliffs on the Kent coast near Dover, taken as a national and patriotic symbol, and popularized as such in the patriotic wartime song 'The White Cliffs of Dover' (1941), written by Nat Burton and sung by Vera Lynn.

> A symbol of Great Britain or England, especially for those returning from abroad

The team had a single focused aim, the staff at the club all knew what they were doing within the new system, everything was explained to the press, who for 'football experts' showed they knew next to nothing about the game beyond the white cliffs of Dover.
SquareFootball.net 2004

Whitehouse, Mary [People] (1910–2001) A British schoolteacher who founded the National Viewers and Listeners Association (now Mediawatch-UK) to campaign against bad language and immorality on television and radio.

> Mentioned in the context of censorship or a puritanical attitude to sex

It is an absorption, as Foucault has noted, which links prudes and libertines. The Mary Whitehouses of this world are as preoccupied with sexuality as those they oppose.
The Observer 1996

In response to all this, Sir Digby Jones, the director general of the CBI, has recently transformed himself into the business equivalent of Mary Whitehouse and launched a series of attacks on television bosses for demonising business people.
Scotland on Sunday 2005

White Rabbit [Child. Lit.] In Lewis Carroll's *Alice's Adventures in Wonderland* (1865), *Alice follows the White Rabbit down a *rabbit-hole and into Wonderland as he hurries along, constantly muttering to himself 'Oh dear! Oh dear! I shall be so late!' and 'Oh my ears and whiskers, how late it's getting!'

> Someone who is always hurrying or anxious about being late; someone who repeatedly looks at their watch

'Look, a student!' my friend cried, and we watched as he rolled by, wearing khaki shorts, a Stanford logo T-shirt and baseball hat, muttering like the white rabbit about being late for class.
The Independent 1997

Everything in William Hague's life points to an obsession with the passage of time. Like Lewis Carroll's ever-anxious White Rabbit, he seems to have lived his 43 years in a mighty hurry.
Yorkshire Post Today 2004

white smoke [Rel.] A reference to the white smoke that signals that a new pope has been elected by cardinals of the Roman Catholic Church. After each round of voting, the ballots are burned. If the vote is inconclusive, black smoke emerges from a chimney on the roof of the Vatican. White smoke means that a new pope has been chosen.

> A sign that someone has been chosen for or elected to a position

After a weekend waiting for the puff of white smoke, he was appointed last week as controller of BBC Scotland, in succession to John McCormick.
Scotland on Sunday 2004

Whore of Babylon [Bible] A figure referred to in the book of Revelation and described as a woman sitting on a scarlet beast with seven heads and ten horns: 'The woman was arrayed in purple and scarlet colour, and decked with gold and precious stones and pearls, having a golden cup in her hand full of abominations and filthiness of her fornication.' On her forehead was written, '*Babylon the great, mother of harlots and abominations of the earth' (Rev. 17: 3–5). The term was applied to the Roman Catholic Church by the early Puritans.

> Used to represent sexual immorality

Now there was Valentine—toute belle—and Mrs O'Connor, who at her best mightily resembled the Whore of Babylon.
ALICE THOMAS ELLIS *The 27th Kingdom* 1982

Wicked Witch of the East [Child. Lit.] In L. Frank Baum's story for children *The *Wizard of Oz* (1900), the heroine, *Dorothy, destroys the Wicked Witch of the East inadvertently when her house, carried to the land of *Oz by a cyclone, falls on the witch, killing her and leaving only her feet sticking out.

> Someone crushed or flattened by a large object, with only their feet sticking out from under it

Wicked Witch of the West [Child. Lit.] In L. Frank Baum's story for children *The *Wizard of Oz* (1900), the heroine, *Dorothy, destroys the Wicked Witch of the West, who has imprisoned her, by throwing a bucket of water over her, causing the witch to 'melt away to nothing'.

➢ A disliked or unpleasant woman; a person or thing that appears suddenly to 'melt' or 'dissolve' away

But this Methuselah angle which we scribes somehow still regard as a fresh theme is played out. The way Jerry Sloan's players use it as some contrived motivation each and every season is a joke on the rest of us who somehow think they'll melt away like a water-soaked Wicked Witch of the West.
Sporting News 2000

A lot has been said about Camilla Parker Bowles, perhaps deservedly so but on Saturday there was no Wicked Witch of the West in attendance. Instead, a nervous, very elegant woman took her place.
www.etoile.co.uk 2005

Wife of Bath [Lit.] In Geoffrey *Chaucer's *The Canterbury Tales* (*c*.1343–1400), one of the characters who tells a tale to the other travellers. She is a domineering, licentious, pleasure-seeking woman who has had five husbands and is on the lookout for her sixth. Her tale, the Wife of Bath's Tale, develops the theme of women's mastery over men.

➢ A woman who is earthy, outspoken, and has a large sexual appetite

The lyrics of the 'ballads' that our young women are exposed to on a daily basis would make the Wife of Bath blush.
www.evangelicaloutpost.com 2004

Wild Boy of Aveyron [People] An 11-year-old boy who was found running wild and naked in a wood near Aveyron in the south of France in the early part of the 19th century. The French physician Jean Itard tried to train and educate him, and published an account of his experiences in *Rapports sur le sauvage d'Aveyron* (1807).

➢ Used to describe someone who has absolutely no experience of the ways of the world, society, or people

'People divide writers into two categories,' she went on, deeply embarrassed by his silence. 'Those who are preternaturally wise, and those who are preternaturally naïve, as if they had no real experience to go on. I belong in the latter category,' she added, flushing at the truth of what she said. 'Like the Wild Boy of the Aveyron.'
ANITA BROOKNER *Hotel du Lac* 1984

Wilde, Oscar [Lit.] An Irish dramatist, novelist, and poet (1854–1900), famous for the numerous witty lines with which he filled his plays and conversation. He was imprisoned for two years in *Reading jail (1895–7) for homosexual offences.

➢ Mentioned in the context of homosexuality or someone making a witticism

'Your brother Roderick, I think,' Colefax continued, 'had a fiancée and was engaged to be married?' 'Oh yes. They'd both dined with me that night at my club. There was absolutely none of the Oscar Wildes about Rory.'
JOHN MORTIMER *Rumpole's Return* 1980

The object of the attention was a giant of a young man clad in slacks and a casual jacket making his way through the hall. 'Blimey!' cooed Johnny Boy. 'He's a big bastard. You don't get many of them to a pound.' Not exactly Oscar Wilde, but it hit the spot.
Flex Magazine 2005

wilderness, in the [Bible] A phrase that occurs many times in the Bible, as in 'your children shall be shepherds in the wilderness forty years' (Num. 14: 33).

> Out of office, out of favour, or removed from influence

Seedorf has been recalled after five months in the wilderness. He could make the starting line-up.
Irish Examiner 2001

Wimsey, Lord Peter [Lit.] The eccentric amateur sleuth created by Dorothy L. Sayers in a series of detective novels beginning with *Whose Body?* (1923). A perfect gentleman with a degree from Oxford, he solves crimes with the aid of his loyal retainer Bunter.

> Someone resembling a genteel or aristocratic detective

Detective Inspector Tom Thorne...is involved in extracting information from a witness through the somewhat unconventional use of a steam iron. We have indeed come a long way since the days of Sherlock Holmes and Lord Peter Wimsey, for whom such behaviour would have been anathema.
The Independent 2004

windmill *See* TILT AT WINDMILLS.

Winnie the Pooh [Child. Lit.] Christopher Robin's teddy bear in A. A. Milne's books *Winnie the Pooh* (1926) and *The House at Pooh Corner* (1928). He is a rather plump bear who is not particularly intelligent (he describes himself as 'a Bear of Very Little Brain') and has a constant craving for honey, often suggesting that it is 'time for a little something'. In one episode, he enters a rabbit's burrow, eats a considerable amount of honey, and then becomes stuck when trying to get out of the hole again.

> Someone who is not very intelligent; someone who likes honey; mentioned in the context of someone getting stuck in a hole or opening

Charlie as crime preventer was like Winnie the Pooh as honey warden.
SARAH LACEY *File under: Deceased* 1992

It had been a long day. First, there had been the inspection of the roof-space at the Chavanacs' villa: an undignified episode, in which he had almost got stuck in a very small trapdoor (like Pooh Bear wedged in a window, Hugo said later).
HILARY WHELAN *Frightening Strikes* 1995

winter of (our) discontent [Shakes.] A phrase from the opening lines of *Richard III*:
Now is the winter of our discontent
Made glorious summer by this son of York.

The term Winter of Discontent was applied to the British winter of 1978–9 when there were widespread strikes by public service trade unions in protest against the Labour government's attempts to freeze pay.

> A period (especially in the winter) of unrest or unhappiness

Europe is bracing itself for a winter of public discontent as governments across the continent prepare to deal with a rash of union-led strikes.
Sunday Business Post 2002

Wise Men *See* MAGI.

Wise Men of Gotham [Leg. & Folk.] Gotham is a village in Nottinghamshire which is associated with the English folk tale 'The Wise Men of Gotham', in which the inhabitants of the village demonstrated cunning by feigning stupidity. Gotham was proverbial in the Middle Ages for folly, and the phrase 'wise man of Gotham' used to mean a fool.

> Mentioned to suggest stupidity or folly

Witch of Endor *See* ENDOR.

Wizard of Oz [Child. Lit.] In L. Frank Baum's *The Wizard of Oz* (1900) *Dorothy journeys with her companions to see the Wizard of Oz in the hope that he will help her return home. Though he initially appears intimidatingly powerful, he turns out to be a fraud, not a wizard at all, but an old man who was blown to *Oz from Omaha in a balloon.

> ➤ A charlatan; used to refer to an illusion or deception
>
>> Suddenly, as if by magic, like something from the *Wizard of Oz*, the huge doors behind Gayfryd start to open by themselves, very slowly.
>> IRENE DARIA *Fashion Cycle* 1990
>
>> 'You could say he was three parts mighty tycoon to one part Wizard of Oz.' 'What do you mean?' 'Just that. I think he was a bit of a charlatan in some ways.'
>> LAURA WILSON *Dying Voices* 2000

Wodehouse, P. G. [Lit.] (1881–1975) An English writer whose best-known works are humorous stories of the upper-class world of Bertie *Wooster and his valet *Jeeves, the first of which appeared in 1917.

> ➤ Used to describe eccentric upper-class gentlemen or good-natured buffoons
>
>> With a name like Michael Lindsay-Hogg, you expect the theatre and film director to be a character out of P.G. Wodehouse—'What ho, old chap,' 'Ripping, positively ripping' and all of that.
>> *www.cbc.ca* 2005

wolf *See* BIG BAD WOLF; RED RIDING HOOD.

wolf in sheep's clothing [Lit.] The story of the wolf in sheep's clothing is one of the fables of *Aesop, a Greek storyteller who lived in the 6th century BC. The fable relates how a wolf decides to disguise himself as a sheep in an attempt to obtain an easy meal. He spends the day with a flock of sheep, fooling sheep and shepherd alike, and in the evening is shut into the fold with the other sheep. However, when the shepherd gets hungry later in the evening he comes to the fold to choose a sheep to eat and chooses the wolf, which he proceeds to eat on the spot.

> ➤ Someone who uses an outward appearance of friendship or kindness to conceal underlying hostility or cruelty
>
>> I'm ordinarily the sweet soul, too good for this world, too kind for my own good, too gentle, a little lamb. To discover the wolf cub in lamb's skin doesn't suit my mother's preconceptions.
>> EDMUND WHITE *A Boy's Own Story* 1982

Woman in White [Lit.] The mysterious Anne Catherick in Wilkie Collins's novel *The Woman in White* (1860), who escapes from a mental asylum having been locked up there because she knows a discreditable secret about the past of the book's villain, Sir Percival Glyde.

> ➤ A woman dressed all in white

Wonderland *See* ALICE IN WONDERLAND.

Wonder Woman [Cart. & Com.; TV] A US comic-book heroine created in the 1940s by Charles Moulton and later developed into a television series. She was a member of a race of Amazon women with superhuman powers. Having travelled to the United States, Wonder Woman led an ordinary life as Diana Prince, but, when trouble threatened, could transform herself into

Wonder Woman, clad in a red-and blue costume reminiscent of the American flag. She could repel bullets with her indestructible bracelets and corral wrongdoers with her golden lasso.

➤ A woman of extraordinary power or ability

Jones, the 24-year-old Wonder Woman, was the ultimate competitor at these Olympics.
Sporting News 2000

Wooden Horse [Gk Myth.] Another name for the *Trojan Horse.

➤ Something that seems harmless but is in fact extremely dangerous

Two years ago, Huang converted a household noodle-making machine into a killing tool which he called the 'intelligent wooden horse'.
Shanghai Star 2003

woodshed *See* SOMETHING NASTY IN THE WOODSHED.

Woodstock [Places] A small town in New York State, situated in the south-east near Albany. It gave its name in the summer of 1969 to a huge rock festival held some 96 km (60 miles) to the south-west.

➤ A large open-air gathering or festival

AirVenture, organized by the Experimental Aircraft Association, attracts more than 750,000 attendees each summer. [It] feels like a flier's version of Woodstock, with pilots in tents beneath the wings of their aircraft.
Fast Company Magazine 2003

Woody Woodpecker [Cart. & Com.] A cartoon character with a tall comb of red hair. He was created in 1940 by Ben Hardaway and has a raucous, staccato laugh.

➤ Used to refer to a high-pitched, staccato laughing or clicking sound, or to a hairstyle that sticks up in a comb

He has red hair that stands up at the top like Woody Woodpecker's.
MARGARET ATWOOD *Cat's Eye* 1988

At present, however, I work in an office that seems to harbour disease like nobody's business—if there was a Geiger counter for cold germs, you could wave it around the air conditioning and it'd sound like Woody Woodpecker on acid.
www.casino-avenue.co.uk 2004

Wooster, Bertie [Lit.] The amiable but vacuous young man about town in *The Inimitable Jeeves* (1924) and the subsequent series of novels by P. G. *Wodehouse. He relies on his resourceful valet, *Jeeves, to rescue him from the predicaments his dim-wittedness lands him in.

➤ Someone who behaves like an amiable upper-class buffoon

At the time the Tory press was portraying Tony Blair as a sort of upper-class twit, a Bertie Wooster figure with an idiotic grin.
The Observer 1997

Would-Be, Lady [Lit.] Along with her husband, Sir Politic Would-Be, a character in Ben Jonson's comedy *Volpone* (1606). Both are pompous, foolish, and, as their name suggests, socially ambitious.

➤ A pompous, talkative, or social-climbing woman

And whomsoever you are to go to, will excuse you, when they are told 'tis *I* that command you not to go; and *you* may excuse it too, young Lady *Would-be*, if you

recollect, that 'tis the unexpected arrival of your late lady's daughter, and your master's sister, that requires your attendance on her.
SAMUEL RICHARDSON *Pamela* 1740

'Wreck of the *Hesperus*, The' [Lit.] A poem by H. W. Longfellow (1840) which tells of the destruction of a schooner, the *Hesperus*, which was caught in a storm and wrecked on the reef of Norman's Woe, off the coast of Massachusetts, in 1839.

➤ Used to describe a state of disorder or disrepair

When he went back to the room it was filled with the slight but offensive smell of face powder and there were clothes everywhere. Miserably, he dressed. 'The wreck of the blasted Hesperus,' he said.
V. S. NAIPAUL *A House for Mr Biswas* 1961

Wright, Frank Lloyd [People] (1869–1959) An American architect whose early work, with its use of new building materials and cubic forms, was particularly significant for the development of modernist architecture.

➤ Mentioned in the context of modern architecture

The house I'd been directed to looked more Frankenstein than Frank Lloyd Wright. It had more turrets and crenellations than Windsor Castle, all in bright red Accrington brick.
VAL MCDERMID *Clean Break* 1995

Our guest is Calvin Klein, one of the world's most successful designers. 'Time' magazine called him fashion's Frank Lloyd Wright.
CNN transcripts: Larry King Live 2000

writing on the wall [Bible] A phrase from the story in the book of Daniel of writing that appeared on the palace wall at a feast given by *Belshazzar, last king of *Babylon, foretelling that he would be killed and the city sacked.

➤ A warning of impending disaster; a herald of doom

It's too bad the tech industry refuses to read the writing on the wall, because its efforts are almost certainly doomed.
BusinessWeek Magazine 2004

Xanadu [Places; Lit.] The name of the ancient city in south-east Mongolia where *Kublai Khan, the Mongol emperor of China, had his residence. Coleridge's poem 'Kubla Khan' (1816) begins with the famous words

> In Xanadu did Kubla Khan
> A stately pleasure-dome decree.

➢ Used to describe a place of dreamlike magnificence, beauty, and luxury

Levy's Lodge—that was what the sign at the coast road said—was a Xanadu of the senses; within its insulated walls there was something that could gratify anything.
JOHN KENNEDY TOOLE *A Confederacy of Dunces* 1980

[The film] is *Hoop Dreams*, a three-hour documentary about two black inner city kids who dream of playing in the NBA, the professional basketball league and Xanadu to every deprived teenager who can dribble 20 yards.
The Guardian 1995

Xerxes [Hist.] (*c.*519–465 BC) The king of Persia, son of Darius I. Xerxes led the invasion of Greece, building a bridge from boats to allow his army to cross the Hellespont (now the Dardanelles) and winning the battles of Artemisium and Thermopylae. He was later defeated at the Battle of Salamis and had to withdraw from Greece.

➢ A mighty ruler or conqueror

Gina made it clear that Anstice had consistently portrayed Richard as a Lionheart, a Tamburlaine, a veritable Xerxes in the sack.
MARTIN AMIS *The Information* 1995

X-Files, The [TV] A successful television series (1993–2002) that relates the adventures of the FBI special agents Dana Scully and Fox Mulder as they encounter various preternatural and extra-terrestrial phenomena.

➢ Alluded to in the context of strange or surprising incidents or coincidences

In fact, his medical analysis indicates he had been simultaneously exposed to as many as five unlikely viruses. The change in his appearance is mighty bizarre. Like something out of the X-files.
medpundit.blogspot.com 2004

Yahoos [Lit.] An imaginary race of brutish creatures, resembling human beings, in Jonathan Swift's *Gulliver's Travels* (1726). They embody all the baser vices and instincts of the human race.

➢ A rude, noisy, or violent person, or one who engages in wanton vandalism

An unprecedented number of Americans now daydream, at least, about the possibility of living somewhere else, somewhere where Yahoos don't abound.
Spiked Online 2004

Yates, Dornford [Lit.] (1885-1960) The pseudonym of the English novelist Cecil William Mercer. His novels featuring the hero Richard Chandos are adventure thrillers and include the titles *Blind Corner* (1927) and *Perishable Goods* (1928).

➢ Mentioned in the context of an exciting adventure story

At other times, Mary would have enjoyed the circumstances of their departure: they had elements of romantic adventure, as if lifted from a novel by John Buchan or Dornford Yates.
ANDREW TAYLOR *Mortal Sickness* 1995

Yellow Brick Road [Child. Lit.] In L. Frank Baum's children's story *The Wizard of Oz* (1900) *Dorothy follows the Yellow Brick Road to *Oz in the hope that the *Wizard will help her to get home. She is joined on her journey by three companions she meets on the way: the *Scarecrow, who wants a brain; the *Cowardly Lion, who wants courage; and the *Tin Woodman, who wants a heart.

➢ A road to happiness or quest to find what one most desires

Every political party has supported the expansion of student numbers, but no one has adequately explained why that expansion is necessary. We have skipped gaily down the yellow brick road towards 50% participation, without ever asking whether it is a good thing for half the population to possess a university degree.
Scotland on Sunday 2003

Yoda [Cin.] In the *Star Wars* films, a small, scrawny-looking, sage-like creature with pointed ears who instructs Luke *Skywalker on how to become a Jedi knight and battle against the evil Empire.

➢ Someone who displays great wisdom or insight; a short person, especially someone with big ears

Because we all secretly entertain the idea that a vast reservoir of greatness lurks untapped somewhere inside us, and that someone with Yoda-like insight will come along and unleash that special ability, we find ourselves fascinated by the spectacle of makeovers.
City Pages 2004

Yogi Bear [Cart. & Com.] An American animated-cartoon character who appeared on television in the 1950s and 1960s. Living in Jellystone Park, Yogi Bear considers himself 'smarter than the average bear' and with his companion Boo Boo spends his time trying to outwit the park ranger and steal picnic baskets from visitors to the park.

➤ Someone who shows quick-witted intelligence

It also supports other Nokia enhancements, such as the foldable Nokia Wireless Keyboard, which provides easy means when replying to e-mails or messages. Definitely smarter than your average Yogi bear, isn't it?
Electric New Paper 2004

You shall go to the ball! [Fairy tales] A phrase used by the *fairy godmother in the story *'Cinderella'. Cinderella is unhappy because her stepsisters have gone to the royal ball, but she must stay at home and do chores. The fairy godmother transforms Cinderella's rags into beautiful clothes and turns a pumpkin into a coach to take her to the ball.

➤ Used when telling someone that they will be able to attend an important or prestigious event

Dig out your best dress or don your tux—this weekend you shall go to the ball.
This is Hampshire news stories 2004

Ypres [Places] The Battle of Ypres is the name given to each of three battles of the First World War that took place near the town of Ypres in north-west Belgium. As with the Battle of the *Somme, going 'over the top' at Ypres was seen as going to certain death.

➤ A battle with massive casualties; a place of great suffering

The realization that one day he himself was going to have to rent or buy a house of some sort would fill him with dismay and despair, like the thought of going over the top at Ypres or the Somme without any prospect of a medal.
KINGSLEY AMIS *The Riverside Villas Murder* 1973

Zapata, Emiliano [People] (1879–1919) A Mexican revolutionary leader who fought successive federal governments to repossess expropriated village lands. Probably because of the appearance of Marlon Brando in the film *Viva Zapata* (1952), the term 'Zapata' can be used to describe a type of moustache in which the two ends extend downwards to the chin.

➢ Used to describe a moustache in which the two ends extend downwards to the chin

He knew—he even hoped—this was probably false (and felt the formation, across his upper lip, of a Zapata moustache of sweat).
MARTIN AMIS *London Fields* 1989

Zeboiim *See* ADMAH AND ZEBOIIM.

Zelig [Cin.] The title of a 1983 Woody Allen film. Its main character Leonard Zelig is able to change his appearance and persona to suit his surroundings, and participates in important historical events.

➢ Someone who is able to change their appearance, behaviour, or attitudes in order to be comfortable in any situation; someone who is unexpectedly seen at important or historic events or in the presence of famous people

In her book, Fonda obsessively insists that her whole life has been spent in trying to please various men. She does have a Zelig-like ability to morph into what is most acceptable to those around her; most actors do.
Bright Lights Film Journal 2005

Zenobia [People] (3rd century AD) A queen of Palmyra who succeeded her murdered husband as ruler and then conquered Egypt and much of Asia Minor.

➢ A powerful and aloof woman

She has been very farouche with me for a long time; and is only just beginning to thaw a little from her Zenobia ways.
MRS GASKELL *North and South* 1854–5

Zeus [Gk Myth.] The supreme ruler of the Olympian gods in Greek mythology, identified by the Romans with Jupiter. Zeus was the protector and ruler of mankind, the dispenser of justice, and the god of weather (whose most famous weapon was the thunderbolt). Although he was the husband of *Hera, he had many amorous liaisons with goddesses, nymphs, and mortal women. He often disguised himself to accomplish seductions, encountering Danae in the form of a shower of gold, Leda as a swan, and Europa as a bull.

➢ A seemingly all-powerful or all-knowing figure; a man who seduces many women

'You never slept with Oupa?' I repeat, inanely. 'Yet you had six children.' 'Nine. Three died.' 'So the Holy Ghost got going on you too?' I say sarcastically. 'Like Zeus, the Holy Ghost has been known to assume many shapes.'
ANDRÉ BRINK *Imaginings of Sand* 1996

Pinsent knows well the legacy he carries into his fourth—and, very probably, last—Games, not just in his hopes for a fourth gold but in his much harder quest to step out of the shadow of the Zeus-like figure of Redgrave, with whom he won his three golds. *The Times* 2004

Zeuxis [Art] (5th century BC) A Greek painter known for creating extremely lifelike paintings. One anecdote relates how birds flew to his painting of a bunch of grapes, taking them to be real.

➤ Mentioned as an example of one skilled in producing extremely lifelike art

Is she pretty? More—beautiful. A subject for the pen of Nonnus, or the pencil of Zeuxis. THOMAS LOVE PEACOCK *Crotchet Castle* 1831

Zorba [Cin.] In the 1964 film of Nikos Kazantzakis's novel *Zorba the Greek* (1946), Anthony Quinn plays Zorba, a larger-than-life Cretan much given to exuberant solo dancing.

➤ Mentioned in the context of Greek dancing

Michael was already imagining the scenario. Ol' frizzy-haired Mona, sullen and horny in some smoky taverna. Mrs Madrigal holding court in her oatmeal linen caftan, doing that Zorba dance as the spirit moved her. ARMISTEAD MAUPIN *Sure of You* 1990

Zorro [Cin.] The masked swordsman hero of Hollywood films of the 1930s to 1960s who first appeared in a comic strip in 1919. In reality he is Don Diego de la Vega, a member of a wealthy Spanish family, but his true identity remains a secret, and in his disguise as Zorro (the Fox) he rights wrongs and protects the weak, leaving as his calling card a letter 'Z' (the 'mark of Zorro') slashed into the clothing or body of his enemies.

➤ A swashbuckling hero; a mysterious rescuer or avenger; someone leaving a distinctive 'calling card'

These ideas were swimming around in my mind, not quite as coherently as I have expressed them, as I went loping across the roofs of Trastevere like Zorro or the Scarlet Pimpernel or somebody of that ilk. ELIZABETH PETERS *Street of the Five Moons* 1978

'Dammit, Sarah, who else knew she called you her scold's bridle? Surely it's occurred to you that the message is directed at you.' 'What message?' 'I don't know. A threat, perhaps. You next, Dr Blakeney.' She gave a hollow laugh. 'I see it more in terms of a signature.' She traced a line on the desk with her fingertip. 'Like the mark of Zorro on his victims.' MINETTE WALTERS *The Scold's Bridle* 1994

Thematic Index

Dionysus
Flora

Fierce Women
Amazon
Norma Desmond
harpy
termagant

Food and Drink
Amalthea
ambrosia
Bacchanalia
Bacchante
Bacchus
Belshazzar
Cornucopia
Betty Crocker
fatted calf
Feeding of the five
thousand
Horn of Plenty
Jacob's pottage
Last Supper
Lucullus
manna
nectar
Prodigal Son
Samuel
Saturnalian
Silenus

Forgiveness
Jesus
Prodigal Son
Tannhäuser

Freedom
John Brown
Patrick Henry
Jim
Abraham Lincoln
Nelson Mandela
Messiah
Moses
Prague Spring

Friendship
Achates
Achilles and
Patroclus
Androcles
Damon and Pythias
David and Jonathan
Don Quixote and
Sancho Panza
Lassie
Man Friday
Merry Men
Pylades and Orestes
Round Table

Three Musketeers
Tonto

Generosity
Lady Bountiful
Father Christmas
Robin Hood
Mistress Quickly
Rockefeller
Santa Claus

Gesture
Aeneas
Elisha
Uriah Heep
Ithuriel
Lady Macbeth
Pontius Pilate
Thinker

Gluttony
Sir Toby Belch
Billy Bunter
Cookie Monster
Gargantua
Pantagruel
Winnie the Pooh
Yogi Bear

Goodness
Admirable Crichton
Christ
Christian
Princess Diana
Mrs Doasyouwoul-
dbedoneby
Dudley Do-Right
St Francis of Assisi
Gabriel
Sir Galahad
Good Samaritan
Goody Two-Shoes
Gunga Din
Jesus
Joseph
Martin Luther King
Madonna
Florence Nightingale
Flora Poste
Oskar Schindler
Albert Schweitzer
Dink Stover
Mother Teresa
Archbishop Tutu

Grief and Sorrow
Constance
Deirdre
Hecuba
Mary Magdalene
Niobe

Rachel
rivers of Babylon

Guarding
Argus
Cerberus

Guilt
Cain
Judas
Lady Macbeth
Macbeth
Mary Magdalene
Pontius Pilate
scapegoat

Hair
Alice
Betty Boop
Byron
Chewbacca
Esau
Greta Garbo
Lady Godiva
Goldilocks
Betty Grable
Heathcliff
Judas
Veronica Lake
Little Orphan Annie
Medusa
naiad
Nazirite
Nebuchadnezzar
Peter Pan
Pre-Raphaelite
Rapunzel
Samson
Satan
Shirley Temple
Topsy
Venus de Milo
Woody Woodpecker

Happiness
Adam and Eve
Cheeryble brothers
Correggio
Dionysus
Epicurus
halcyon days
Hyperboreans
Lotus-eaters
Nirvana
Tigger

Hatred
Captain Ahab
basilisk
Esau
Dr Fell

Heat and Fire
Hell
Phoebus
Shadrach, Meshach,
and Abednego

Height
Alice
Tower of Babel
Jack and the
beanstalk
St Simeon Stylites

Heroes and Heroines
Batman and Robin
Biggles
Modesty Blaise
James Bond
Boy Wonder
Bulldog Drummond
Rhett Butler
Byron
Davy Crockett
Dan Dare
Mr Darcy
Doctor Who
Flash Gordon
Errol Flynn
Hector
Jack the Giant-Killer
Indiana Jones
Lochinvar
Lancelot
Lawrence of Arabia
Captain Marvel
Buck Rogers
Roy Rogers
The Saint
Arnold
Schwarzenegger
Siegfried
Luke Skywalker
Superman
Superwoman
Theseus
John Wayne
Wonder Woman

Honesty and Truth
Cordelia
Diogenes
Galileo
Iago
George Washington

Horror
Hieronymus Bosch
Dante
Goya
Grünewald

Horses
Pegasus
Rosinante

Humility
Uriah Heep
Jesus
Job
Man of Uz
She Stoops to
  Conquer

Hunters
Actaeon
Artemis
Atalanta
Calydonian boar
  hunt
Diana
Elmer Fudd
Nimrod
Orion
Tristram

Hypocrisy
Archimago
Uriah Heep
Pecksniff
Pharisee
Tartuffe

Idealism
Marie Antoinette
Arcadia
Don Quixote
Plato
Utopia

Idyllic and Pleasant Places
Albion
Arcadia
Arden
Avalon
Baiae
Beulah
Big Rock Candy
  Mountain
Brave New World
Camelot
Canaan
Celestial City
Cloud Cuckoo Land
Cockaigne
Delectable
  Mountains
Eden
El Dorado
Elysium
Fortunate Isles
Goshen

Happy Islands
Islands of the Blest
Kublai Khan
Land of Promise
Never-Never Land
New Jerusalem
Oz
Paradise
Promised Land
Shangri-la
Utopia
Valhalla
Xanadu

Illusion
Apples of Sodom
Barmecide's Feast
Dead Sea Fruit
Don Quixote
Emperor's New
  Clothes
Magic beans
Walter Mitty
Pie in the sky
Plato's Cave

Immobility
Daphne
Gulliver
Joshua
Tin Man

Importance
Ark of the Covenant
Book of Kells
Holy of Holies
Lilliputian
Olympus
Titan

Indifference
Marie Antoinette
Ariel
Belle Dame Sans
  Merci
Fates
Jolly Miller
Laodicean
Levite
Nero
Parcae Sisters
Snow Queen

Innocence
Adam and Eve
Bambi
Caesar's wife
Desdemona
Dreyfus
Gretchen
Lamb of God

Pontius Pilate
Rosebud
Susanna

Insanity
Captain Ahab
Bedlam
Lon Chaney
Don Quixote
George III
Ben Gunn
King Lear
Mad Hatter
March Hare
Nebuchadnezzar
Ophelia
Mrs Rochester

Inspiration
Aganippe
Apollo
Castalia
Dulcinea
Erato
Helicon
Hippocrene
Laura
Melpomene
Muses
Parnassus
Pieria
Polyhymnia
Terpsichore
Thalia

Intelligence
Aristotle
St Augustine
Professor Challenger
Darwin
Einstein
Stephen Hawking
Sherlock Holmes
Houyhnhnms
Hypatia
Jesuit
Mozart
Isaac Newton
Plato
Socrates
Spock
Thinker

Invisibility
Alberich's cloak
Bilbo Baggins
Gyges
Harvey
Invisible Man
Mambrino's helmet

Jealousy
Cephalus
Leontes
Medea
Oedipus
Othello
Polyphemus

Judgement and Decision
Aristeides the Just
Judge Jeffreys
Last Judgement
Minos
Paris
Rhadamanthus
Solomon

Knowledge
Argus
Charlie Chan
Chingachgook
GCHQ
Janus
Sibyl
Topsy
Tree of Knowledge

Large Size
Anak
Brobdingnagian
Buckingham Palace
Colossus
Gargantua
Goliath
Gulliver
Jotun
King Kong
Leviathan
Mutt and Jeff
Procrustes
Tardis
Titan
War and Peace

Leaders
Abraham
Alfred the Great
Napoleon Bonaparte
Boudicca
Caesar
Charlemagne
Cleopatra
Oliver Cromwell
Fagin
Garibaldi
Hippolyta
Joan of Arc
Pantheon
Saladin
Tamerlane